Contents

2 BASIC ENCRYPTION AND DECRYPTION

Preface

When the first edition of this book was published in 1989, viruses and other forms of malicious code were fairly uncommon, the Internet was used largely by just computing professionals, a Clipper was a sailing ship, and computer crime was seldom a headline topic in daily newspapers. In that era most people were unconcerned about—even unaware of—how serious is the threat to security in the use of computers.

The use of computers has spread at a rate completely unexpected back then. Now you can bank by computer, order and pay for merchandise, and even commit to contracts by computer. And the uses of computers in business have similarly increased both in volume and in richness. Alas, the security threats to computing have also increased significantly.

Why Read This Book?

Are your data and programs at risk? If you answer "yes" to any of the following questions, you have a potential security risk.

- Have you acquired any new programs within the last year?
- Do you use your computer to communicate electronically with other computers?
- Do you ever receive programs or data from other people?
- Is there any significant program or data item of which you do not have a second copy?

Relax; you are not alone. Most computer users have a security risk. Being at risk does not mean you should stop using computers. It does mean you should learn more about the risk you face, and how to control that risk.

Users and managers of large mainframe computing systems of the 1960s and 1970s developed computer security techniques that were reasonably effective against the threats of that era. However, two factors have made those security procedures outdated:

- *Personal computer use.* Vast numbers of people have become dedicated users of personal computing systems, both for business and pleasure. We try to make applications "user friendly" so that computers can be used by people who know nothing of hardware or programming, just as people who can drive a car do not need to know how to design an engine. Users may not be especially conscious of the security threats involved in computer use; even users who are aware may not know what to do to reduce their risk.

- *Networked remote-access systems.* Machines are being linked in large numbers. The Internet and its cousin, the World-Wide Web, seem to double every year in number of users. A user of a mainframe computer may not realize that access to the same machine is allowed to people throughout the world from an almost uncountable number of computing systems.

Every computing professional must understand the threats and the countermeasures currently available in computing. This book addresses that need.

This book is designed for the student or professional in computing. Beginning at a level appropriate for an experienced computer user, this book describes the security pitfalls inherent in many important computing tasks today. Then, the book explores the controls that can check these weaknesses. The book also points out where existing controls are inadequate and serious consideration must be given to the risk present in the computing situation

Uses of This Book

The chapters of this book progress in an orderly manner. After an introduction, the topic of encryption—the process of disguising something written to conceal its meaning—is presented as the first tool in computer security. The book continues through the different kinds of computing applications, their weaknesses, and their controls. The applications areas include

- general programs
- operating systems
- data base management systems
- remote access computing
- multicomputer networks

These sections begin with a definition of the topic, continue with a description of the relationship of security to the topic, and conclude with a statement of the current state of the art of computer security research related to the topic. The book concludes with an examination of risk analysis and planning for computer security, and a study of the relationship of law and ethics to computer security.

Background required to appreciate the book is an understanding of programming and computer systems. Someone who is a senior or graduate student in computer science or a professional who has been in the field for a few years would have the appropriate level of understanding. Although some facility with mathematics is useful, all necessary mathematical background is developed in the book. Similarly, the necessary material on design of software systems, operating systems, data bases, or networks is given in the relevant chapters. One need not have a detailed knowledge of these areas before reading this book.

The book is designed to be a textbook for a one- or two-semester course in computer security. The book functions equally well as a reference for a computer professional. The introduction and the chapters on encryption are fundamental to the understanding of the rest of the book. After studying those pieces, however, the reader can study any of the later chapters in any order. Furthermore, many chapters follow the format of introduction, then security aspects of the topic, then current work in the area. Someone who is interested more in background than in current work can stop in the middle of one chapter and go on to the next.

This book has been used in classes throughout the world. Roughly half of the book can be covered in a semester. Therefore, an instructor can design a one-semester course that considers some of the topics of greater interest.

What Does This Book Contain?

This is the revised edition of *Security in Computing*. It is based largely on the previous version, with many updates to cover newer topics in computer security. Among the salient additions to the new edition are these items:

- *Viruses, worms, Trojan horses, and other malicious code.* Complete new section (first half of Chapter 5) including sources of these kinds of code, how they are written, how they can be detected and/or prevented, and several actual examples.
- *Firewalls.* Complete new section (end of Chapter 9) describing what they do, how they work, how they are constructed, and what degree of protection they provide.
- *Private e-mail.* Complete new section (middle of Chapter 9) explaining exposures in e-mail, kind of protection available, PEM and PGP, key management, and certificates.
- *Clipper, Capstone, Tessera, Mosaic, and key escrow.* Several sections, in Chapter 3 as an encryption technology, and Chapter 4 as a key management protocol, and in Chapter 11 as a privacy and ethics issue.
- *Trusted system evaluation.* Extensive addition (in Chapter 7) including criteria from the United States, Europe, Canada, and the soon-to-be-released *Common Criteria*.
- *Program development processes,* including ISO 9000 and the SEI CMM. A major section in Chapter 5 gives comparisons between these methodologies.
- *Guidance for administering PC, Unix, and networked environments.*

In addition to these major changes, there are numerous small changes, ranging from wording changes to subtle notational changes for pedagogic reasons, to replacement, deletion, rearrangement, and expansion of sections.

The focus of the book remains the same, however. This is still a book covering the complete subject of computer security. The target audience is college students (advanced undergraduates or graduate students) and professionals. A reader is expected to bring a background in general computing technology; some knowledge of programming, operating systems, and networking is expected, although advanced knowledge in those areas is not necessary. Mathematics is used as appropriate, although a student can ignore most of the mathematical foundation if he or she chooses.

Acknowledgments

Many people have contributed to the content and structure of this book. The following friends and colleagues have supplied thoughts, advice, challenges, criticism, and suggestions that have influenced my writing of this book: Lance Hoffman, Marv Schaefer, Dave

Balenson, Terry Benzel, Curt Barker, Debbie Cooper, and Staffan Persson. Two people from outside the computer security community were very encouraging: Gene Davenport and Bruce Barnes. I apologize if I have forgotten to mention someone else; the oversight is accidental.

Lance Hoffman deserves special mention. He used a preliminary copy of the book in a course at George Washington University. Not only did he provide me with suggestions of his own, but his students also supplied invaluable comments from the student perspective on sections that did and did not communicate effectively. I want to thank them for their constructive criticisms.

Finally, if someone alleges to have written a book alone, distrust the person immediately. While an author is working 16-hour days on the writing of the book, someone else needs to see to all the other aspects of life, from simple things like food, clothing, and shelter, to complex things like social and family responsibilities. My wife, Shari Lawrence Pfleeger, took the time from her professional schedule so that I could devote my full energies to writing. Furthermore, she soothed me when the schedule inexplicably slipped, when the computer went down, when I had writer's block, or when some other crisis beset this project. On top of that, she reviewed the entire manuscript, giving the most thorough and constructive review this book has had. Her suggestions have improved the content, organization, readability, and overall quality of this book immeasurably. Therefore, it is with great pleasure that I dedicate this book to Shari, the other half of the team that caused this book to be written.

Charles P. Pfleeger
Washington DC

1

Is There a Security Problem
in Computing?

In this chapter:

- *Risks of computing*
- *Goals of secure computing: confidentiality, integrity, availability*
- *Threats to security in computing: interception, interruption, modification, fabrication*
- *Controls: encryption, programming controls, operating systems, network controls, administrative controls, law, and ethics*

You seldom hear of bank robberies these days. In the wild west, banks kept large amounts of cash as well as gold and silver, which could not be traced. Cash was much more commonly used than checks. Communications and transportation facilities were such that it might be hours before the legal authorities were informed of a robbery and days before they could actually arrive at the scene of the crime, by which time the robbers were long gone. A single guard for the night was only marginally effective. Robbery might require a little common sense and perhaps several days spent analyzing the situation, but it did not require much sophisticated training; one usually learned on the job in a form of apprenticeship. All of these factors led to a balance tipped very much in the favor of the criminal, so that bank robbery used to be fairly profitable.

Today, however, many factors work against the potential criminal. Very sophisticated alarm systems protect the bank silently, whether people are around or not. The techniques of criminal investigation have become very effective, so that a person can be identified by fingerprint, voice recognition, composite sketch, ballistics evidence, or other hard-to-mask characteristics. Many bank branches carry less cash than some large retail stores because much of a bank's business is conducted with checks. Places that do store large amounts of cash or currency are protected with many levels of security: several layers of physical systems, complex locks, two-party systems requiring agreement of two people to allow access, and many more schemes. Transportation and communication mean that police can be at the scene of a crime in minutes and can alert other officers to suspects to watch for in seconds. The risk and required sophistication are so high that the average criminal usually turns to an easier target than a bank.

This book is about security for computing systems, not banks. Consider the security differences between how people protect computing systems and how banks protect money

- *Size and portability.* The physical devices in computing are so small that a thousand dollars' worth of computing gear fits comfortably in a briefcase; ten thousand dollars' worth can be carried comfortably in two arms.
- *Ability to avoid physical contact.* Electronic funds transfers account for most transfers of money between banks. For example, many private companies pay employees by direct computer transfer instead of check. Utilities, insurance companies, and mortgage companies can automatically process deductions against their clients' bank accounts. Customers can even bank at home, moving funds between accounts and arranging withdrawals via a personal computer.
- *Value of assets.* The value of the information stored in a computer is also high. Some computers contain confidential information about a person's taxes, investments, medical history, or education. Other computers contain very sensitive information about new product lines, sales figures, marketing strategy, or military targets, troop movements, weapons capabilities, and so forth.

In terms of security, computing is very close to the wild west days. Some installations recognize computers and their data as a valuable and vulnerable resource and have applied appropriate protection. Other installations are dangerously deficient in their security measures. But unlike the "wild west" bankers, some computing professionals and managers do not even recognize the value of the resources they use or control. This failure to protect is complicated by the fact that we are not always conscious when computers are being used (as in the telephone network or the extensive banking–financial services complex).

Worse yet, in the event of a crime, some companies do not investigate or prosecute, for fear that it will damage their public image. For example, would you feel safe depositing your money in a bank that had just suffered a five million dollar loss through computer embezzlement? In fact, that bank has just been made painfully aware of its security weaknesses. That bank will probably enhance its security substantially, quickly becoming safer than a bank that had not been recently victimized. Criminal investigation and prosecution are hindered by statutes that do not recognize electromagnetic signals as property. The news media sometimes portray computer intrusion by teenagers as a prank no more serious than tipping over an outhouse.

Obviously, security in computing is a very important issue. It is an area that deserves study by computer professionals, managers, and even many computer users. This book is written for all of those people. By studying this book, you will learn what are the security problems in computing and what methods are available to deal with those problems.

The purpose of this book is to

- examine the *risks* of security in computing
- consider available *countermeasures* or *controls*
- stimulate thought about *uncovered vulnerabilities*
- identify areas where *more work* is needed.

In this chapter, we start by examining the *what:* the kinds of vulnerabilities to which computing systems are prone. We then consider *how* these vulnerabilities are exploited: different kinds of attacks that are possible. The third area we look at in this chapter is *who:* the kinds of people who contribute to the security problem in computing. Finally, we introduce *controls:* ways to prevent the attacks on systems.

1.1   Characteristics of Computer Intrusion

The target of a crime involving computers may be any piece of the computing system. A **computing system**[1] is a collection of hardware, software, storage media, data, and people that an organization uses to do computing tasks. Whereas the obvious target of a bank robbery is cash, a list of names and addresses of depositors might be valuable to a competing bank. The list might be on paper, recorded on a magnetic medium, stored in internal computer memory, or transmitted electronically across a medium such as a telephone line. The variety of targets makes computer security difficult.

In any security system, the *weakest point* is the most serious vulnerability. A robber intent on stealing something from your house will not attempt to penetrate a two-inch thick metal door if a window gives easier access. A sophisticated perimeter physical security system does not compensate for unguarded access by means of a simple telephone line and a modem. The "weakest point" philosophy can be restated as the following principle.

> **Principle of Easiest Penetration:** An intruder must be expected to use any available means of penetration. This is not necessarily the most obvious means, nor is it necessarily the one against which the most solid defense has been installed.

This principle implies that computer security specialists must consider all possible means of penetration, because strengthening one may just make another means more appealing to intruders. We now consider what these means of penetration are.

1.2   Kinds of Security Breaches

In security, an **exposure** is a form of possible loss or harm in a computing system; examples of exposures are unauthorized disclosure of data, modification of data, or denial of legitimate access to computing. A **vulnerability** is a weakness in the security system that might be exploited to cause loss or harm. A person who exploits a vulnerability perpetrates an **attack** on the system. **Threats** to computing systems are circumstances that have the potential to cause loss or harm; human attacks are examples of threats, as are natural disasters, inadvertent human errors, and internal hardware or software flaws. Finally, a **control** is a protective measure—an action, device, procedure, or technique—that reduces a vulnerability.

The major assets of computing systems are **hardware**, **software**, and **data**. There are four kinds of threats to the security of a computing system: interruption, interception, modification, and fabrication. The four threats all exploit vulnerabilities of the assets in computing systems, and are shown in Figure 1-1.

---

[1] In this book, **boldface** is used to identify new terms being introduced.

Figure 1-1   System Security Threats

- In an **interruption**, an asset of the system becomes lost, unavailable, or unusable. An example is malicious destruction of a hardware device, erasure of a program or data file, or malfunction of an operating system file manager so that it cannot find a particular disk file.

- An **interception** means that some unauthorized party has gained access to an asset. The outside party can be a person, a program, or a computing system. Examples of this type of failure are illicit copying of program or data files, or wiretapping to obtain data in a network. Although a loss may be discovered fairly quickly, a silent interceptor may leave no traces by which the interception can be readily detected.

- If an unauthorized party not only accesses but tampers with an asset, the threat is a **modification**. For example, someone might change the values in a data base, alter a program so that it performs an additional computation, or modify data being transmitted electronically. It is even possible to modify hardware. Some cases of modification can be detected with simple measures, but other, more subtle changes may be almost impossible to detect.

- Finally, an unauthorized party might **fabricate** counterfeit objects on a computing system. The intruder may insert spurious transactions to a network communication system, or add records to an existing data base. Sometimes these additions can be detected as forgeries, but if skillfully done, they are virtually indistinguishable from the real thing.

These four classes of threats—interruption, interception, modification, and fabrication—describe the kinds of exposures possible. The problems are described in the next section.

1.3   Security Goals and Vulnerabilities

In this section we study the goals of secure computing and examine the vulnerabilities that computer professionals must counter in order to reach these goals.

Security Goals

Computer security consists of maintaining three characteristics: **confidentiality**, **integrity**, and **availability**.

- **Confidentiality** means that the assets of a computing system are accessible only by authorized parties. The type of access is read-type access: reading, viewing, printing, or even just knowing the existence of an object. Confidentiality is sometimes called **secrecy** or **privacy**.
- **Integrity** means that assets can be modified only by authorized parties or only in authorized ways. In this context, modification includes writing, changing, changing status, deleting, and creating.
- **Availability** means that assets are accessible to authorized parties. An authorized party should not be prevented from accessing objects to which he, she, or it has legitimate access. For example, a security system could preserve perfect confidentiality by preventing everyone from reading a particular object. However, this system does not meet the requirement of availability for proper access. Availability is sometimes known by its opposite, denial of service.

These three goals make up security in computing.

These three qualities can overlap, and they can even be mutually exclusive. (For example, strong protection of confidentiality can severely restrict availability.) Computer security is often depicted as in Figure 1-2, which shows how these three properties are largely independent but sometimes overlapping.

Confidentiality

Confidentiality sounds pretty straightforward: only authorized people can see protected data. However, as you will see later in this book, there are some problems: who determines who is "authorized"? What constitutes "seeing"—a single bit? Pieces out of context?

Confidentiality is the best understood security property because its meaning is narrower than the other two and because there are good examples for preserving confidentiality in the real world.

Integrity

Integrity is much harder to pin down. As Welke and Mayfield [WEL90, MAY91, NCS91b] point out, *integrity* means different things in different contexts. Some meanings of *integrity* are

- precise
- accurate

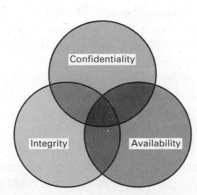

Figure 1-2   Relationship Between Confidentiality, Integrity, and Availability

- unmodified
- modified only in acceptable ways
- modified only by authorized people
- modified only by authorized processes
- consistent
- internally consistent
- meaningful and correct results

In fact, people mean all of these in common use of the word *integrity*.

Welke and Mayfield recognize three aspects to integrity: authorized actions, separation and protection of resources, and error detection and correction. Integrity can be enforced in much the same way as can confidentiality: by rigorous control of who can access which resources in what ways. Some forms of integrity are well-represented in the real world, and those precise representations can be implemented in a computerized environment. But not all interpretations of integrity are well-reflected by computer implementations.

Availability

Availability is similarly complex. Availability applies both to data and to service (access to computing resources). Differents expectations of *availability* include

- presence of object or service in usable form
- capacity to meet service needs
- progress: bounded waiting time
- adequate time/timeliness of service

Goals of availability are

- timely response
- fair allocation
- fault tolerance
- utility or usability (can be used as intended)
- controlled concurrency: support for simultaneous access, deadlock management, and exclusive access, as required

The security community is just beginning to understand what availability implies and how to ensure it. A small, centralized control of access is fundamental to preservation of confidentiality and integrity, but it is not clear that a single access control point is able to enforce availability. Much of the success in computer security has been in the areas of confidentiality and integrity; protection of availability will not be possible until some time in the future.

Vulnerabilities

We reverse these three security objectives when we consider vulnerabilities. It is sometimes easier to consider vulnerabilities as they apply to the three broad categories of system resources (hardware, software, and data). Figure 1-3 shows these vulnerabilities as

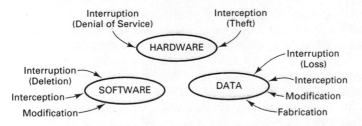

Figure 1-3   **Computing System Vulnerabilities**

they apply to the assets of hardware, software, and data. These three assets, and the connections between them, are all potential security weak points.

The following sections address the vulnerabilities of each specific asset of a computing system.

Threats to Hardware

Because a physical device is so visible, it is a rather simple point to attack; fortunately, however, reasonable safeguards are usually in place. Computers have been drenched with water, burned, gassed, and electrocuted with lightning or power surges from other sources. People have spilled soft drinks, corn chips, ketchup, beer, and many other kinds of food on computing devices. Mice have chewed through cables. Particles of dust, especially particles of ash from cigarette smoke, have threatened precisely engineered moving parts. Computers have been kicked, slapped, bumped, jarred, and punched. All of this abuse might come under the category of involuntary machine-slaughter: accidental acts not intended to do serious damage to the hardware involved.

A more serious attack could be called voluntary machine-slaughter or machinicide, in which someone actually wishes to do harm to the computer. Machines have been shot with guns and stabbed with knives. Bombs, fires, and collisions have destroyed computer rooms. Ordinary keys, pens, and screwdrivers have been used to short out circuit boards and other components. Machines have been carried off by thieves. The list of human attacks on computers goes on almost without end.

Of all the ways people have deliberately attacked computer equipment in order to limit availability, theft and destruction are the primary techniques. Managers of major computing centers long ago recognized the vulnerability of their machines and installed physical security systems to protect them. However, the proliferation of microcomputers in offices has left people with several thousands of dollars' worth of equipment sitting unattended on desks. (Curiously, the supply cabinet, containing only a couple hundred dollars' worth of pens, stationery, and paper clips, is often locked.) Sometimes the security of hardware components can be enhanced greatly by simple physical measures such as locks and guards.

Threats to Software

Computing equipment is worthless without the *software* (the operating system, utility programs, and application programs) that users expect. Software can be destroyed maliciously, or it can be modified, deleted, or misplaced accidentally. The result is the same, however, regardless of the motive: a loss of software becomes apparent when one tries to run it. These attacks are all problems of availability of software.

More subtle is software that runs but has been altered. Physical equipment usually shows some mark of inflicted injury, but the loss of one crucial line of source or object code may not leave an obvious mark in a program. Furthermore, it is possible to change a program so that it does all it did before, and then some. In this case, it is very hard to detect that the software has been changed, let alone to determine the extent of the change.

Software Deletion   Software is surprisingly easy to delete. Probably every programmer has accidentally erased a file, or saved a bad copy of a program, destroying a good previous copy. Because of software's high value to a commercial computing center, access to software is usually carefully controlled through a process called **configuration management** so that software is not deleted, destroyed, or replaced accidentally.

Software Modification   In this attack, a working program is modified, either to cause it to fail during execution or to cause it to do some unintended task. Software is relatively easy to modify: changing a bit or two can convert a working program into one that fails. Depending on which bit was changed, the program may crash when it begins, or it may execute for some time before it falters.

With a little work, the change can be much more subtle, so that the program works well most times but fails in specialized circumstances. One such change produces a program effect known as a **logic bomb**. For example, a disgruntled employee may modify a crucial program so that it accesses the system date and halts abruptly after July 1. The employee might quit on May 1 and plan to be at a new job miles away by July.

Another type of change can extend the functioning of a program so that an innocuous program has a hidden side effect. For example, a program that ostensibly structures a listing of files belonging to a user may also modify the protection of all those files to permit access by another user.

The category of software modification includes

- a **Trojan horse**, a program that overtly does one thing while covertly doing another
- a **virus**, a specific type of Trojan horse, that can be used to spread infection from one computer to another
- a **trapdoor**, a program that has a secret entry point
- **information leaks** in a program, which make information accessible to unintended people or programs

Of course, it is possible to invent a new program and install it on a computing system. Inadequate control over the programs that are installed and run on a computing system permit this kind of software security breach.

Software Theft   This attack includes unauthorized copying of software. Software authors and distributors are entitled to fair compensation for use of their product, as are musicians and book authors. Unauthorized copying of software has not been stopped satisfactorily.

Threats to Data

Hardware security is usually the concern of a relatively small staff of computing center professionals. Software security is a larger problem, extending to all programmers and analysts who create or modify programs. Computer programs are written in a dialect intelligible primarily to computer professionals, so that a "leaked" source listing of a program would be meaningless to the general public.

Printed data, however, can be readily interpreted by the general public. Because of its visible nature, data attack is a more widespread and serious problem than either hardware or software attack. Thus, data items have a greater public value than hardware and software, because more people know how to use or interpret data.

Data has essentially no intrinsic value. For this reason, it is hard to measure the value of data. However, data does have a cost, perhaps measurable by the cost to reconstruct or redevelop lost data. Confidential data leaked to a competitor may narrow a competitive edge. Data incorrectly modified can cost human lives. (For example, think of flight coordinate data on an airplane that is guided partly or fully by computer, as many now are.) Finally, inadequate security may lead to a financial liability if certain personal data is made public. Thus, data has a definite value, although that value is often difficult to measure.

Both hardware and software have a relatively long life, with a gradual decline in value over that time. The value of data may be high, but some data items are of interest for only a short period of time. Consider the following example.

Government analysts periodically generate data on the national economy; the results are released to the public at a predetermined time and date. Before that time, access to the data could allow someone to profit from advance knowledge of the probable effect of the data on the stock market. Suppose the analysts develop the data 24 hours before its release, and they wish to communicate their results to other analysts for independent verification before release. A protection scheme expected to take an outsider more than 24 hours to break is adequate for this data because after 24 hours there is no further need for confidentiality.

Study of the security of data raises the second principle of computer security.

> **Principle of Adequate Protection:** Computer items must be protected only until they lose their value. They must be protected to a degree consistent with their value.

This principle says that things that have a short life can be protected with security measures that are effective only for that short lifetime. This principle applies primarily to data because it is the element in computer security that usually has the shortest life.

Figure 1-4 illustrates the three qualities of data security: **confidentiality** (preventing unauthorized disclosure), **integrity** (preventing unauthorized modification), and **availability** (preventing denial of authorized access).

Data Confidentiality   Data can be gathered by many means, such as tapping wires, planting bugs in output devices, sifting through trash receptacles, monitoring electromagnetic radiation, bribing key employees, inferring one data point from other values, or simply requesting it. Because data is often available in a form people can read, the confidentiality of data is a major concern in computer security.

Data Integrity   Stealing, buying, finding, or hearing data requires no computer sophistication, whereas modifying or making new data requires an understanding of the technology by which the data is transmitted or stored, as well as the format in which the data is maintained. Thus, a higher level of sophistication is needed to modify existing data or to fabricate new data than to intercept existing data. The most common sources of this kind of problem are malicious programs, errant file system utilities, and flawed communication facilities.

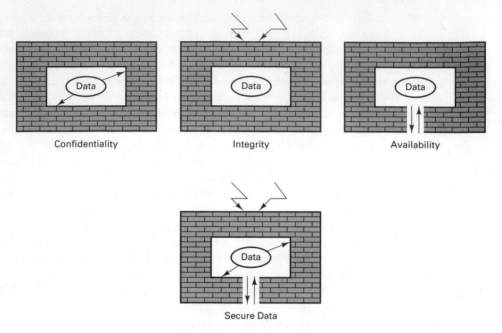

Figure 1-4   Security of Data

Data is especially vulnerable to modification. Small and skillfully done modifications may not be detected in ordinary ways. For example, a criminal could write a program to reduce the value of interest paid on a bank's savings accounts by a small amount per customer, and then credit the collected amount to one particular account. It is unlikely that a customer would calculate interest independently, and even more unlikely that a customer would alert the bank to a suspected small error. This attack is called a **salami attack** because the crook shaves a little from many accounts and puts these shavings together to form a valuable result, like the meat scraps joined together in a salami.

A more complicated process is trying to reprocess used data items. With telecommunications between banks, a fabricator might intercept a message ordering one bank to credit a certain amount to a certain person's account. The fabricator might try to **replay** that message, causing the receiving bank to think it should credit the same account again. The fabricator might also try to modify the message slightly, changing the account to be credited or the amount, and then transmit this revised message.

Other Exposed Assets

The major points of exposure in a computing system are hardware, software, and data. However, other components of the system are also possible targets. In this section we identify some of these other points of attack.

Storage Media   The storage media holding data are also potential loss points, although they are more often considered hardware because they are physical objects. Effective security plans consider adequate backups of data and physical protection for the media containing these backups.

Networks   Networks are really collections of hardware, software, and data, the three fundamental assets of computing systems. Each node of the network is a computing system with all the normal security problems. To these, a network adds the problems of communication, which may be via a very exposed medium, and access from distant, and potentially untrustworthy, computing systems.

Networks simply multiply the problems of computer security. Lack of physical proximity, use of insecure, shared media, and inability to identify remote users positively are all security problems that are made more difficult in computer networks.

Access   Another exposure is access to computing equipment. First, the intruder may steal computer time just to do computing. Theft of computer services is analogous to theft of electricity or any other utility; the value of the services stolen may be substantially higher than electricity, however. This unpaid access spreads the true costs of maintaining the computing system to the other legitimate users. Second, malicious access to a computing system can destroy software or data. Finally, unauthorized access may deny service to a legitimate user. For example, a user who has a time-critical task to perform may depend on the availability of the computing system. For all three of these reasons, unauthorized access to a computing system must be prevented.

Key People   Finally, people can be crucial weak points in security. If only one person knows how to use or maintain a particular program, trouble can arise if that person gets sick, has an accident, or leaves. A disgruntled employee can cause serious damage because employees are insiders. Trusted individuals, such as operators and systems programmers, are usually selected carefully because of their potential ability to affect all computer users.

Summary of Exposures

In this section, the three basic security goals of computing systems—confidentiality, integrity, and availability—have been applied to the assets of a computing system. Problems such as loss of data, leakage of data, theft of services, failure of hardware, and modification of software fit the framework of these three goals.

The rest of this book is an analysis of how these factors operate and how they can be controlled. Most controls work on the people who exploit vulnerabilities. The next section describes people who pose threats to computer security.

1.4   The People Involved

In TV westerns, the "bad guys" always wore shabby clothes, had mean and sinister looks, and lived in gangs somewhere out of town. By contrast, the sheriff dressed well, stood proud and tall, was known and respected by everyone in town, and struck fear into the hearts of most criminals.

Some computer criminals, to be sure, are mean and sinister types. Many more wear business suits, have college degrees, and appear to be the pillars of their community. Some are teenagers or college students. Others are middle-aged business executives. Some are mentally deranged, or overtly hostile, or extremely committed to a cause, and they attack computers as a symbol. Others are ordinary people presented with temptation for personal profit, revenge, challenge, advancement, or job security.

Whatever their motivations, computer criminals have access to enormous amounts of hardware, software, and data; they have the potential to cripple much of effective business and government throughout the world.

Let us define *computer crime* as any crime involving or aided by the use of a computer (admittedly a pretty broad definition).

FBI uniform crime statistics do not separate computer crime from crime of other sorts. Furthermore, many companies do not report computer crime because they fear damage to reputation, they are ashamed, or they have agreed not to prosecute if the criminal will "go away." Therefore, dollar estimates of computer crime losses are only vague suspicions. Estimates range from $300 million to $500 billion per year.

Most experts acknowledge that computer security is a major problem, however. Studies have been made to determine characteristics of people who commit computer crime. These studies are intended to help spot likely criminals and prevent crime. Here are some of the kinds of people who commit computer crimes.

Amateurs

Amateurs have committed most of the computer crimes reported to date. Most embezzlers are not career criminals but are normal people who observe a flaw in a security system that allows them access to cash or other valuables. In the same sense, most computer criminals are ordinary computer professionals or users, doing their jobs, when they discover they have access to something valuable.

When nobody objects, the amateur may start using the computer at work to write letters, maintain soccer league team standings, or do accounting. The situation may expand until the employee is carrying on a business in accounting, stock portfolio management, or desktop publishing on the side, using the employer's computing facilities. Alternatively, amateurs may become disgruntled over a negative work situation (such as a reprimand or denial of a promotion) and vow to "get even" with management by wreaking havoc on a computing installation.

Crackers

System crackers may be university or high school students who attempt to access computing facilities for which they have not been authorized. Cracking a computer's defenses is seen as the ultimate victimless crime. Nobody is hurt, or even endangered, by stealing a little machine time, or even trying to log on, just to see if it can be done. Most cracking can be done without confronting anybody, not even a human voice. In the absence of explicit warnings not to trespass in a system, crackers infer that access is permitted. An underground network of crackers helps to pass along secrets of success; as with a jigsaw puzzle, a few isolated pieces joined together may produce a large effect. Others attack for personal gain or self-satisfaction. And still others enjoy causing chaos, loss, or harm. There is no common profile or motivation to attackers.

Cracking is a serious offense that has caused millions of dollars in damage. Crackers are prosecuted seriously with harsh penalties, but cracking continues to be an appealing crime, especially to juveniles.

Career Criminals

By contrast, the career computer criminal understands the targets of computer crime. Criminals seldom change fields from arson, murder, or auto theft to computing; more often, career computer criminals start as computer professionals who engage in computer crime and find the prospects and the payoff good. There is some evidence that organized crime and international groups are engaging in computer crime. Recently, electronic spies and information brokers have begun to recognize that trading in companies' or individuals' secrets can be lucrative.

As mentioned earlier, some companies are reticent to prosecute computer criminals; in fact, after having discovered a computer crime, the companies are often thankful if the criminal quietly resigns. In other cases, the company is (understandably) more concerned about protecting its assets and so it closes down an attacked system rather than gathering evidence that could lead to identification and conviction of the criminal. The criminal is then free to continue the same illegal pattern with another company.

1.5   Methods of Defense

Computer crime is certain to continue. The goal of computer security is to institute controls that preserve confidentiality, integrity, and availability. Sometimes these controls are able to prevent attacks; other less powerful methods can only detect a breach as or after it occurs.

Controls

In this section we survey the controls or countermeasures that attempt to prevent exploitation of the vulnerabilities of computing systems.

Encryption

The most powerful tool in providing computer security is coding. By transforming data so that it is unintelligible to the outside observer, security professionals can virtually nullify the value of an interception and the possibility of a modification or a fabrication.

Encryption provides confidentiality for data. Additionally, encryption can be used to achieve integrity because data that cannot be read generally also cannot be changed in a meaningful manner. Furthermore, encryption is the basis of some **protocols**, which are agreed-upon sequences of actions to accomplish some task. Some protocols ensure availability of resources. Thus, encryption is at the heart of methods for ensuring all three goals of computer security.

Encryption is an important tool in computer security, but one should not overrate its importance. Users must understand that encryption does not solve all computer security problems. Furthermore, if encryption is not used properly, it may have no effect on security or could, in fact, degrade the performance of the entire system. Weak encryption can actually be worse than no encryption because it gives an unwarranted sense of security. Thus, it is important to know the situations in which encryption is useful and to use it effectively.

Software Controls

Programs themselves are the second link in computer security. Programs must be secure enough to exclude outside attack. They must also be developed and maintained so that one can be confident of the dependability of the programs.

Program controls include the following:

- *Internal program controls:* parts of the program that enforce security restrictions, such as access limitations in a data base management program
- *Operating system controls:* limitations enforced by the operating system to protect each user from all other users
- *Development controls:* quality standards under which a program is designed, coded, tested, and maintained

Software controls may use tools such as hardware components, encryption, or information gathering. Because software controls generally affect users directly, they are often the first aspects of computer security that come to mind. Because they influence the way users interact with a computing system, software controls must be carefully designed. Ease of use and potency are often competing goals in the design of software controls.

Hardware Controls

Numerous hardware devices have been invented to assist in computer security. These devices range from hardware or smartcard implementations of encryption to locks limiting access, to theft protection, to devices to verify users' identities, to circuit boards that control access to disk drives in PCs.

Policies

Some controls on computing systems are achieved through added hardware or software features, as already described. Other controls are matters of policy. In fact, some of the simplest controls, such as frequent changes of passwords, can be achieved at essentially no cost but with tremendous effect. Training and administration follow immediately after establishment of policies.

Legal and ethical controls are an important part of computer security. The law is slow to evolve, and the technology involving computers has emerged suddenly. Although legal protection is necessary and desirable, it is not as dependable in this area as it would be in more well-understood and long-standing crimes.

The area of computer ethics is likewise unclear. It is not that computer people are unethical, but rather that society in general and the computing community in particular have not adopted formal standards of ethical behavior. Some organizations are attempting to devise codes of ethics for computer professionals. Although these are important, before codes of ethics become widely accepted and therefore effective, the computing community and the general public need to understand what kinds of behavior are inappropriate and why.

Physical Controls

Some of the easiest, most effective, and least expensive controls are physical controls. Physical controls include locks on doors, guards at entry points, backup copies of important software and data, and physical site planning that reduces the risk of natural disasters. Often the simple physical controls are overlooked while more sophisticated approaches are sought.

Effectiveness of Controls

Merely having controls does no good unless they are used properly. The next section contains a survey of some factors that affect the effectiveness of controls.

Awareness of Problem

People using controls must be convinced of the need for security; people will willingly cooperate with security requirements only if they understand why security is appropriate in each specific situation. Many users, however, are unaware of the need for security, especially in situations in which a group has recently undertaken a computing task that was previously performed by a central computing department.

Likelihood of Use

Of course, no control is effective unless it is used. The lock on a computer room door does no good if people block the door open. During World War II, code clerks used outdated codes because they had already learned them and could encode messages rapidly. Unfortunately, the opposite side had already broken some of those codes and could decode those messages easily.

> **Principle of Effectiveness:** Controls must be used to be effective. They must be efficient, easy to use, and appropriate.

This principle implies that computer security controls must be efficient enough, in terms of time, memory space, human activity, or other resources used, so that using the control does not seriously affect the task being protected. Controls should be selective so that they do not exclude legitimate accesses.

Overlapping Controls

Several different controls may apply to one exposure. For example, security for a microcomputer application may be provided by a combination of controls on program access to the data, on physical access to the microcomputer and storage media, and even by file locking to control access to the processing programs. Combinations of controls are shown in Figure 1-5.

Periodic Review

Few controls are permanently effective. Just when the security specialist finds a way to secure assets against certain kinds of attacks, the opposition doubles its efforts in an effort to defeat the security mechanism. Thus, judging the effectiveness of a control is an ongoing task.

1.6   Plan of Attack

This book is a study of all aspects of security in computing. By studying it, you will become acquainted with the major problem areas of computer security, the controls that are effective against those problems, and the directions of current work in computer security.

This book has three parts that span the field of computer security. The first part of the book is an analysis of encryption. Encryption is defined, several different methods of

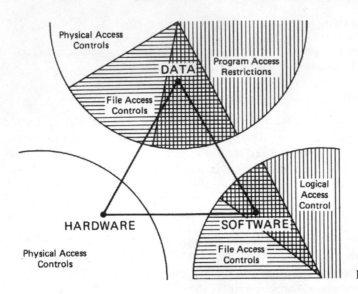

Figure 1-5   Overlapping Controls

encryption are explained, and the uses, strengths, and weaknesses of those methods are presented. The second part contains material on the hardware and software components of computing systems, the types of problems to which each is subject, and the kinds of protection that can be implemented for each component. Finally, the third part of the book is about the factors outside the hardware, software, and data of the system. It contains a study of physical factors in security and characteristics of the people who use the system.

Following is a brief description of the contents of each of these parts.

Encryption

In the next two chapters you will study the techniques of data encryption, beginning with simple encryption methods and progressing to the current standard practices in the field. Then in Chapter 4 you will study different protocols, which are algorithms or procedures, often using encryption, to accomplish certain higher-level security goals.

Hardware and Software Security

In the second part of this book, you will consider general programs, operating systems, data base management systems, and networks. The security problems and features of programs are introduced in Chapter 5.

Operating systems play a major role in security because they are fundamental to the use of computers. Operating systems both provide security features to protect one user from another and introduce security vulnerabilities themselves. Chapter 6 addresses the security facilities for users, and Chapter 7 presents security considerations for designers of operating systems.

Data base management systems are really applications programs that also permit many users to share access to one common set of data. These systems are partially responsible for the confidentiality, integrity, and availability of the shared data. In this way, they have characteristics of both user programs and operating systems. These issues are described in Chapter 8.

Chapter 9 contains material on security problems and solutions particular to computer networks and the communications media by which networked computers are connected. Network security has become very significant because of the rapid growth in use of networks, especially the Internet.

Human Controls in Security

The first two parts of this book form a progression from security tools to security in complex multiuser, multicomputer systems. The security methods described are rather sophisticated. However, most security problems of computing systems are caused by either human or environmental factors. Thus, another approach to computer security is to treat the causes (humans and the environment) rather than the symptoms (attacks and vulnerabilities). The third part of this book describes procedures that can be implemented in spite of, or in addition to, any controls built into hardware and software.

Chapter 10 is about administration of security. It begins with personal computers and then covers Unix workstations and networks. The chapter also explains physical security mechanisms that can be used to protect computing systems against human attacks or natural disasters. It concludes with planning in computer security: designing security policies, performing risk analysis, and establishing a security plan. It also raises the issue of disaster recovery: how to deal with a failure of other controls.

Finally, Chapter 11 considers the human controls of law and ethics. Although computer law is a relatively new field, its use is evolving rapidly, and it is an important tool in the defense of computing systems. Ethics covers some situations where the law is ineffective or inappropriate.

Thus, the organization of this book is from basic tools; through single-user computers, multiuser systems, and multisystem systems; and finally to human and environmental factors that apply to the gamut of computer configurations. The book raises the important problems of computer security, shows some known solutions, and tries to identify work in progress.

Computer security is a relatively new field. The pace of development in computing far outpaces capabilities in computer security. It sometimes seems as if each advance in computing brings new security problems. In a sense, this is true. However, a more optimistic view of the field is appropriate. The fundamental work in security provides tools (such as encryption and operating system features) that form the basis of controls for these new problems as the problems arise. Part of the challenge and excitement of computer security is that new problems arise continually.

1.7   Summary

Computer security is ensuring the confidentiality, integrity, and availability of components of computing systems. The three principal pieces of a computing system subject to attacks are hardware, software, and data. These three pieces, and the communications between them, constitute the basis of computer security vulnerabilities. This chapter has identified four kinds of attacks on computing systems: interruption, interception, modification, and fabrication.

Three principles affect the direction of work in computer security. By the principle of easiest penetration, a computing system penetrator will use whatever means of attack is the easiest; therefore, all aspects of computing system security must be considered at once. By the principle of timeliness, a system must be protected against penetration only long enough so that penetration is of no value to the penetrator. The principle of effectiveness states that controls must be usable and used in order to serve their purpose.

Controls can be applied at the levels of data, programs, the system, physical devices, communications links, the environment, and personnel. Sometimes several controls are needed to cover a single vulnerability, and sometimes one control addresses several problems at once.

1.8   Bibliographic Notes

Two key works that have laid the foundation for much of the work in computer security (and are still relevant even though they were written in the 1970s) are the exploration of vulnerabilities and control by Ware [WAR79] and the security technology planning study by Anderson [AND72].

Confidentiality is explored nicely by the Dennings [DEN79a]. Integrity is studied carefully by Mayfield and Welke [WEL90, MAY91, NCS91b]. Availability considerations are documented by Pfleeger and Mayfield [PFL92] and by Millen [MIL92].

1.9   Terms and Concepts

Virus, Trojan horse, worm, rabbit, salami, firewall, spray paint, mental poker, orange book, war dialer—the vocabulary of computer security is rich with terms that capture your attention. Also, the field is filled with acronyms: DES, RSA, TCSEC, CTCPEC, ITSEC, PEM, PGP, and SSE CMM, to list a few. All of these are explained in this book. The chapters end with a list of terms and concepts, and the page numbers on which they are introduced, as a way to review and see whether you have learned the important points of the chapter.

The list for this chapter includes some terms that may be new, as well as the major concepts introduced in this chapter. Although these terms are expanded upon in future chapters, it is good to begin now to learn the terms and the underlying concepts.

computing system, 3	integrity, 5
principle of easiest penetration, 3	availability, 5
exposure, 3	secrecy, 5
vulnerability, 3	privacy, 5
attack, 3	configuration management, 8
threat, 3	logic bomb, 8
control, 3	Trojan horse, 8
hardware, 3	virus, 8
software, 3	trapdoor, 8
data, 3	information leak, 8
interruption, 4	principle of adequate protection, 9
interception, 4	salami attack, 10
modification, 4	replay, 10
fabrication, 4	protocol, 13
confidentiality, 5	principle of effectiveness, 15

1.10   **Exercises**

1. Distinguish between a vulnerability, a threat, and a control.

2. If someone steals your car, the kinds of harm you probably feel include financial loss, inconvenience (loss of transportation), and emotional upset (invasion of your personal space). List at least three kinds of harm a company could experience from theft of computer equipment.

3. List at least three kinds of harm a company could experience from electronic espionage or unauthorized viewing of confidential company materials.

4. List at least three kinds of damage a company could experience from damage to the integrity of a program or company data.

5. Describe two examples of vulnerabilities of automobiles for which auto manufacturers have instituted controls. Tell whether you think these controls are effective, somewhat effective, or ineffective.

6. One control against accidental software deletion is to save all old versions of a program. Of course, this control is prohibitively expensive in terms of cost of storage. Suggest a less costly control against accidental software deletion. Is your control effective against all possible causes of software deletion? If not, what threats does it not cover?

7. On a typical multiuser computing system (such as a shared Unix system at a university or an industry), who can modify the code (software) of the operating system? Of a major application program such as a payroll program or a statistical analysis package? Of a program developed and run by a single user? Who should be able to modify each of these examples of code?

8. Suppose a program to print paychecks secretly leaks a list of names of employees earning more than a certain amount each month. What controls could be instituted to limit the vulnerability of this leakage?

9. Some terms have been introduced intentionally without definition in this chapter. You should be able to deduce their meanings. What is an electronic spy? What is an information broker?

10. Preserving confidentiality, integrity, and availability of data is a restatement of the concern over interruption, interception, modification, and fabrication. How do the first three concepts relate to the last four? That is, is any of the four equivalent to one or more of the three? Is one of the three concerns encompassed by one or more of the four?

11. Do you think attempting to break into (obtain access to or use of) a computing system without authorization should be illegal? Why or why not?

12. Describe an example (other than the one mentioned in this chapter) of data whose confidentiality has a short timeliness, say a day or less. Describe an example of data whose confidentiality has a timeliness of more than a year.

13. Do you currently use any computer security control measures? If so, what? What attacks are you trying to protect against?

14. Describe an example where absolute denial of service to a user (that is, the user gets no response from the computer) is a serious problem to that user. Describe another example where 10 percent denial of service to a user (that is, the user's computation progresses, but at a rate 10 percent slower than normal) is a serious problem to that user. Could access by unauthorized people to a computing system result in a 10 percent denial of service to the legitimate users? How?

2

Basic Encryption and Decryption

In this chapter:

- *Concepts of encryption*
- *Cryptanalysis: how encryption systems are "broken"*

Suppose we have a message to communicate, but our message might fall into the wrong hands. By using encryption we disguise the message so that even if the transmission is diverted, the message will not be revealed. Encryption is a means of maintaining secure data in an insecure environment. Encryption is probably the most fundamental building block of secure computing. (It is not the *only* building block, however.) You will study encryption used in the protection of programs, data bases, networks, and electronic communications. For these purposes, you need to develop a good understanding of what encryption does and how it works. But weak or flawed encryption provides only the illusion of protection; therefore, you also need to know how encryption can fail.

In this chapter you will learn the basic principles of encryption. Two basic methods of encryption—substitution and transposition—are introduced. Along with these, you will study the analysis techniques used to reveal encrypted data, that is, to break through an encryption.

This chapter contains a discussion of many aspects of encryption, including several examples of encryption systems and the theoretical foundations of encryption. To keep things easy to understand, sometimes we will study simple approaches that extend easily to more sophisticated ones.

2.1 Terminology and Background

Suppose *S* wants to send a message to *R*; we will call *S* the **sender** and *R* the **receiver**. *S* entrusts the message to *T*, who will deliver it to *R*; *T* then becomes the **transmission medium**. If an outsider, *O,* wants the message and tries to access it, we will call *O* an **interceptor** or **intruder**. Any time after *S* transmits it via *T*, the message is exposed, so *O* might try to access the message in any of the following ways:

- *block* it, by preventing its reaching R, thereby affecting the availability of the message
- *intercept* it, by reading or listening to the message, thereby affecting the secrecy of the message
- *modify* it, by seizing the message and changing it in some way or adding to it, affecting the message's integrity
- *fabricate* an authentic-looking message, arranging for it to be delivered as if it came from S, thereby also affecting the integrity of the message

Notice that this list is just a restatement of the four possible failures of security listed in Chapter 1. Encryption is a technique that can address all of these problems.

Terminology

Encryption is a process of encoding a message so that its meaning is not obvious; **decryption** is the reverse process: transforming an encrypted message back into its normal form. Alternatively, the terms *encode* and *decode* or *encipher* and *decipher* are used instead of the verbs *encrypt* and *decrypt*.[1] A system for encryption and decryption is called a **cryptosystem**.

The original form of a message is known as **plaintext**, and the encrypted form is called **ciphertext**. This situation is shown in Figure 2-1. For convenience in explanations, we may denote a plaintext message P as a sequence of individual characters $P = (p_1, p_2, \ldots, p_n)$; similarly ciphertext can be written as $C = (c_1, c_2, \ldots, c_m)$. Formally, the transformations between plaintext and ciphertext are denoted $C = E(P)$ and $P = D(C)$, where C represents the ciphertext, E is the encryption algorithm, P is the plaintext, and D is the decryption algorithm. Obviously, we want a cryptosystem for which $P = D(E(P))$.

Encryption Algorithms

Some encryption algorithms use a **key** K, so that the ciphertext message depends on both the original plaintext message and the key value, denoted $C = E(K, P)$. Essentially, E is a *set* of encryption algorithms, and the key K selects one specific algorithm.

Sometimes the encryption and decryption keys are the same, so that $P = D(K, E(K,P))$. This style of encryption is call **symmetric** encryption because D and E are mirror-image processes. Other times encryption and decryption keys come in pairs. Then a decryption key, K_D, inverts the encryption of key K_E, so that $P = D(K_D, E(K_E,P))$. Encryption algorithms of this form are called **asymmetric**, because converting C back to P is not just reversing the steps of E. These two cases are shown in Figure 2-2.

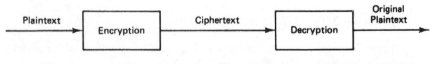

Figure 2-1   Encryption

---

[1] There are slight differences in the meanings of these three pairs of words, although they are not significant in this context. Strictly speaking, **encoding** is the process of translating entire words or phrases to other words or phrases, whereas **enciphering** is translating letters or symbols individually; **encryption** is the group term that covers both encoding and enciphering.

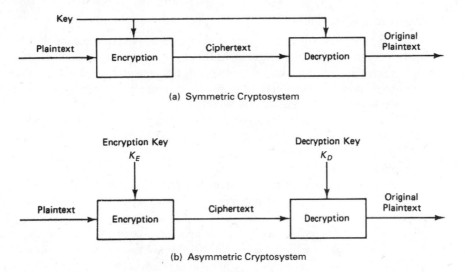

(a) Symmetric Cryptosystem

(b) Asymmetric Cryptosystem

Figure 2-2   Encryption with Keys

A key allows different encryptions of one plaintext message just by changing the key. Use of a key provides additional security. If the encryption algorithm should fall into the interceptor's hands, future messages can still be kept secret because the interceptor will not know the key value. A cipher that does not require the use of a key is called a **keyless cipher**.

Cryptography means hidden writing, the practice of using encryption to conceal text. A **cryptanalyst** studies encryption and encrypted messages, with the goal of finding the hidden meanings of the messages. Both a cryptographer and a cryptanalyst attempt to translate coded material to its original form; normally a cryptographer works on behalf of a legitimate sender or receiver, whereas a cryptanalyst works on behalf of an unauthorized interceptor. Finally, **cryptology** is the research into and study of encryption and decryption; it includes both cryptography and cryptanalysis.

Cryptanalysis

A cryptanalyst's chore is to **break** an encryption; this means that the cryptanalyst attempts to deduce the meaning of a ciphertext message, or to determine a decrypting algorithm that matches an encrypting algorithm. The analyst can do any or all of three different things:

- attempt to break a single message
- attempt to recognize patterns in encrypted messages, in order to be able to break subsequent ones by applying a straightforward decryption algorithm
- attempt to find general weaknesses in an encryption algorithm, without necessarily having intercepted any messages

An analyst works with encrypted messages, known encryption algorithms, intercepted plaintext, data items known or suspected to be in a ciphertext message, mathematical or statistical tools and techniques, properties of languages, computers, and plenty of ingenuity and luck.

Breakable Encryption

An encryption algorithm may be **breakable**, meaning that given enough time and data, an analyst could determine the algorithm. However, practicality is also an issue. For a given cipher scheme, there may be 10^{30} possible decipherments, so the task is to select the right one out of the 10^{30}. On a current-technology computer performing on the order of 10^{10} operations per second, finding this decipherment would require 10^{20} seconds, or roughly 10^{12} years. In this case, although we know that theoretically a deciphering algorithm exists, determining the deciphering algorithm by examining all possibilities can be ignored as infeasible using current technology.

Note two things about the breakability of encryption algorithms. First, the cryptanalyst cannot be expected to try just the hard, long way. In the example just presented, the obvious decryption might require 10^{30} machine operations, but a more ingenious approach might require only 10^{15} operations. At the speed of 10^{10} operations per second, 10^{15} operations take slightly more than one day. The ingenious approach is certainly feasible. Some of the algorithms we will study are based on known "hard" problems. But the cryptanalyst does not necessarily have to solve the underlying problem to break the encryption of a single message.

Second, estimates of breakability are based on current technology. An enormous advance in the technology of computers has occurred since 1950. Things that were infeasible in 1940 became possible by the 1950s, and every succeeding decade has brought greater improvements. Operating characteristics of computers, such as numbers of operations per second and numbers of bits stored, have regularly increased by an order of magnitude every few years. It is risky to pronounce an algorithm secure just because it cannot be broken with *current* technology.

Representation of Characters

Ultimately we want to study ways of encrypting any computer material, whether it is ASCII or EBCDIC characters, binary data, object code, or a control stream. However, to simplify the explanations, we begin with the encryption of messages written in the standard 26-letter English[2] alphabet, A–Z.

Most encryption algorithms are mathematical in nature, or can be explained or studied easily in mathematical form. Therefore, we will switch back and forth between letters and the numeric encoding of each letter as shown here. (In this chapter plaintext is usually written in uppercase letters, and ciphertext is in lowercase.)

Letter	A	B	C	D	E	F	G	H	I	J	K	L	M
Code	0	1	2	3	4	5	6	7	8	9	10	11	12

Letter	N	O	P	Q	R	S	T	U	V	W	X	Y	Z
Code	13	14	15	16	17	18	19	20	21	22	23	24	25

This representation allows arithmetic to be performed on letters. Addition and subtraction on letters are performed on the corresponding code number. Expressions such as A + 3 = D or K − 1 = J have their natural interpretation. Arithmetic is performed as if the alphabetic table were circular. That is, addition wraps around from one end of the table to the other, so that Y + 3 = B. Thus, every result is between 0 and 25.

---

[2] Because this book is written in English, the explanations refer to English. However, with slight variations, the techniques are applicable to most other written languages as well.

This form of arithmetic is called **modular arithmetic**, written mod n, which means that any result greater than n is reduced by n as many times as necessary to bring it back into the range $0 \leq result < n$. Another way to obtain this result is to use the remainder after dividing the number by n. The value of 95 mod 26 is the remainder of 95/26, which is 17, while $95 - 26 - 26 - 26 = 17$; alternatively, starting at position 0 (A) and counting ahead 95 positions (and returning to position 0 each time after passing position 25) also arrives at position 17.

The remainder of this chapter concentrates on two forms of encryption: **substitutions**, where one letter is exchanged for another, and **transpositions**, where the order of the letters is rearranged. The goal of studying those two forms of encryption is to become familiar with the concept of encryption and decryption, to learn some of the terminology and methods of cryptanalysis, and to study some of the weaknesses to which encryption is prone. The chapter concludes with a discussion of characteristics of good encryption algorithms.

2.2   Monoalphabetic Ciphers (Substitutions)

Children sometimes devise "secret codes" that use a correspondence table with which to substitute each character by another character or symbol. Such a technique is called a **monoalphabetic cipher** or a **simple substitution.** A substitution is an acceptable way of encrypting text. In this section we study several kinds of monoalphabetic ciphers.

The Caesar Cipher

The **Caesar cipher** is named for Julius Caesar, said to be the first to use it. In the Caesar cipher, each letter is translated to the letter a fixed number of letters after it in the alphabet. Caesar used a shift of 3, so that plaintext letter p_i was enciphered as ciphertext letter c_i by the rule

$$c_i = E(p_i) = p_i + 3$$

A full translation chart of the Caesar cipher is shown here.

Plaintext   A B C D E F G H I J K L M N O P Q R S T U V W X Y Z
Ciphertext d e f g h i j k l m n o p q r s t u v w x y z a b c

Using this encryption, the message

        TREATY IMPOSSIBLE

would be encoded as

        T R E A T Y   I M P O S S I B L E
        w u h d w b   l p s r v v l e o h

Advantages and Disadvantages of the Caesar Cipher

Early ciphers had to be easy to perform in the field. Any cipher that was so complicated that its algorithm had to be written out was at risk of being revealed if the interceptor caught a sender with the written instructions. Then the interceptor could readily decode any ciphertext messages intercepted (until the encryption algorithm could be changed).

The Caesar cipher is quite a simple cipher. (Remember that in the era of Julius Caesar, anything written, even in plaintext, was rather well-protected because few people could read.) The pattern $p_i + 3$ was easy to memorize; a sender in the field could write out a plaintext and a ciphertext alphabet, encode a message to be sent, and then destroy the paper containing the alphabets.

That obvious pattern is also the major weakness of the Caesar cipher. A secure encryption should not allow an interceptor to use a little piece to predict the entire pattern of the encryption.

Cryptanalysis of the Caesar Cipher

Look at the result of the encryption. Clues from the plaintext shine through, like the break between the two words, the SS, which is translated to vv, and the repeated letters T, I, and E, which always translate to w, l, and h. These clues make this cipher easy to break.

Suppose you were trying to break the following ciphertext message.

> wklv phvvdjh lv qrw wrr kdug wr euhdn

The message has actually been enciphered with a 27-symbol alphabet: A through Z and the "blank" character or separator between words. Worst of all, the blank has been translated to itself! This is an exceptional piece of information, because it shows which are the small words. (In encryption, spaces between words often are deleted, under the assumption that a legitimate receiver can breakmostmessagesintowordsfairlyeasily. For ease of writing and decoding, messages are often then arbitrarily broken into blocks of a uniform size, such as every five characters, so that it is clear to an interceptor that there is no significance to the places where the message is broken.)

English has relatively few small words, such as *am, is, to, be, he, we, and, are, you, she,* and so on. Therefore, one attack is to substitute known short words at appropriate places in the ciphertext and to try substituting for matching characters other places in the ciphertext.

A stronger clue is the repeated R in the word wrr. Two very common three-letter words having the pattern *xyy* are *see* and *too*; other less common possibilities are *add, odd,* and *off*. (Of course, there are also obscure possibilities like *woo* or *gee*, but it makes more sense to try the common cases first.)

If wrr is SEE, wr would have to be SE, which is unlikely, but if wrr is TOO, wr would be TO, which is quite reasonable. Substituting T for w and O for r, the message becomes

```
wklv phvvdjh lv qrw wrr kdug wr euhdn
T--- ------- -- -OT TOO ---- TO -----
```

The -OT could be *cot, dot, got, hot, lot, not, pot, rot,* or *tot*; a likely choice is *not*. Unfortunately, q = N does not give any more clues, because q appears only once in this sample.

The word lv is also the end of the word wklv, which probably starts with T. Likely two-letter words that can also end a longer word include *so, is, in,* etc. However, *so* is unlikely because the form T-SO is not recognizable; IN is ruled out because of the previous assumption that q is N. A more promising alternative is to substitute IS for lv throughout, and continue to analyze the message in that way.

The ciphertext letters uncovered are just three positions away from their plaintext counterparts. A cryptanalyst might try that same pattern on all the unmatched ciphertext. The completion of this decryption is left as an exercise.

The cryptanalysis described here is ad hoc, using deduction based on guesses instead of solid principles. Another approach is to consider which letters commonly start words, which letters commonly end words, and which prefixes and suffixes are common. Cryptanalysts have compiled lists of common prefixes, common suffixes, and words having particular patterns (such as *sleeps* is a word that follows the pattern *abccda*). A different analysis technique will be introduced in the next section.

Other Monoalphabetic Substitutions

In monoalphabetic substitutions, the alphabet is scrambled, and each plaintext letter maps to a unique ciphertext letter. Formally, a **permutation** is a reordering of the elements of a series. Two examples of permutations of the numbers 1 to 10 are $\pi_1 = 1, 3, 5, 7, 9, 10, 8, 6, 4, 2$; and $\pi_2 = 10, 9, 8, 7, 6, 5, 4, 3, 2, 1$. A permutation is a function, so we can write $\pi_1(3) = 5$ or $\pi_2(7) = 4$. If $a_1, a_2, \ldots, a_k$ are the letters of the plaintext alphabet, and π is a permutation of the numbers $1, 2, \ldots, k$, in a monoalphabetic substitution each c_i is $a_{\pi(p_i)}$.

For example, $\pi(\lambda)$ might be the function $\pi(\lambda) = 25 - \lambda$, so that A would be encoded as z, B as y, and Z would be encoded as a. This permutation is easy to write out from memory, so it could be used in the field. However, each plaintext–ciphertext pair maps both ways: $E(F) = $ u and $E(U) = $ f. This double correspondence gives unnecessary aid to the interceptor.

An alternative is to use a **key**, a word that controls the enciphering. If the keyword is *key*, the sender or receiver first writes the alphabet and then writes the key under the first few letters of the alphabet.

```
ABCDEFGHIJKLMNOPQRSTUVWXYZ
key
```

The sender or receiver then fills in the remaining letters of the alphabet, in some easy-to-remember order, after the keyword.

```
ABCDEFGHIJKLMNOPQRSTUVWXYZ
keyabcdfghijlmnopqrstuvwxz
```

In this example, because the key was short, most plaintext letters were only one or two positions off from their ciphertext equivalents. With a longer keyword, the distance is greater and less predictable, as shown below. Because π must map one plaintext letter to exactly one ciphertext letter, duplicate letters in a keyword such as spectacular are dropped.

```
ABCDEFGHIJKLMNOPQRSTUVWXYZ
spectaulrbdfghijknnoqvwxyz
```

Near the end of the alphabet replacements are rather close, and the last five characters map to themselves. Conveniently, the last characters of the alphabet are among the least frequently used, so that this exposure would give little help to the interceptor.

A less regular rearrangement of the letters is desirable. One possibility is to count by 3s (or 5s or 7s or 9s) and rearrange the letters in that order. For example, one encryption uses a table that starts with

```
ABCDEFGHIJKLMNOPQRSTUVWXYZ
adgj
```

using every third letter. At the end of the alphabet, the pattern continues mod 26, as shown below.

```
ABCDEFGHIJKLMNOPQRSTUVWXYZ
adgjmpsvybehknqtwzcfilorux
```

This permutation is $\pi(\lambda) = (3 * \lambda) \bmod 26$. For example, $\pi(K) = (3 * 10) \bmod 26 = 30 - 26 = 4 = e$.

Complexity of Monoalphabetic Encryption and Decryption

Encryption and decryption with this algorithm can be performed by direct lookup in a table like the ones shown. Transforming a single character can be done in a constant amount of time, so the time to encrypt a message of n characters is proportional to n.

Cryptanalysis of Monoalphabetic Ciphers

The techniques just described for breaking the Caesar cipher can also be used on other monoalphabetic ciphers. Short words, words with repeated patterns, and common initial and final letters all give clues for guessing the permutation.

Of course, this is a lot like working a crossword puzzle: you try a guess, and continue to work to substantiate that guess until you have all the words in place, or until you reach a contradiction. For a long message this process can be extremely tedious. Fortunately there are other approaches.

Frequency Distributions

In English, some letters are used more often than others. The letters *E, T,* and *A* occur far more often than *J, Q,* and *Z,* for example. The text being analyzed also affects the distribution. (For example, a medical article in which the term *x-ray* was used often would have an uncommonly high frequency of the letter *x.*)

Table 2-1 shows the counts and relative frequencies of letters in a chapter of a book on computing. These frequencies are quite close to published counts from other sources. The table also shows the counts and relative frequencies of letters from a Pascal source program. Notice that the Pascal frequencies are similar, as one might expect, because Pascal uses English keywords and variables often resemble English words. The English letter frequencies are shown in Figure 2-3, which shows relative frequencies including and excluding the "space" character.

This table can be used to analyze the following passage of ciphertext.

```
hqfubswlrq lv d phdqv ri dwwdlqlqj vhfxuh
frpsxwdwlrq ryhu lqvhfxuh fkdqqhov
eb xvlqj hqfubswlrq zh glvjxlvh wkh phvvdjh vr wkdw
hyhq li wkh wudqvplvvlrq lv glyhuwhg wkh phvvdjh zloo
qrw eh uhyhdohg
```

Table 2-1   Letter Frequency Distributions in English and Pascal

| Letter | English | | Pascal | |
	Count	Percent	Count	Percent
a	3312	7.49	664	4.70
b	573	1.29	197	1.39
c	1568	3.54	878	6.22
d	1602	3.62	511	3.61
e	6192	14.00	1921	13.60
f	966	2.18	504	3.57
g	769	1.74	294	2.08
h	1869	4.22	478	3.39
i	2943	6.65	1215	8.60
j	119	0.27	6	0.04
k	206	0.47	87	0.61
l	1579	3.57	722	5.11
m	1500	3.39	270	1.91
n	2982	6.74	1157	8.19
o	3261	7.37	835	5.91
p	1074	2.43	340	2.41
q	116	0.26	12	0.08
r	2716	6.14	1147	8.12
s	3072	6.95	594	4.21
t	4358	9.85	1311	9.28
u	1329	3.00	377	2.66
v	512	1.16	127	0.89
w	748	1.69	193	1.36
x	123	0.28	139	0.98
y	727	1.64	137	0.96
z	16	0.04	5	0.03
All	44232		14121	

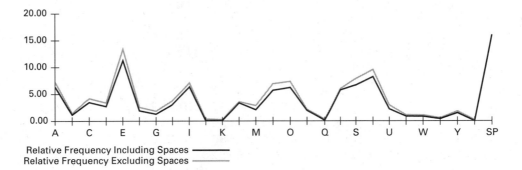

Relative Frequency Including Spaces ——————
Relative Frequency Excluding Spaces ——————

Figure 2-3   Relative Frequencies of Characters in English Text

The counts shown in Table 2-2 are obtained by counting the frequencies of the letters of the text.

The relative frequencies of these counts are shown in Figure 2-4, where they have been plotted against the relative frequencies from English text in the previous tables. Notice that this plot matches the first closely, except that the second is shifted right by three positions. This encryption used the Caesar cipher.

Table 2-2 Frequencies in Example Cipher

Letter	Count	Percent	Letter	Count	Percent
a	0	0.00	n	0	0.00
b	3	1.80	o	4	2.41
c	0	0.00	p	5	2.99
d	11	6.59	q	16	9.58
e	2	1.20	r	9	5.39
f	6	3.61	s	3	1.80
g	4	2.40	t	0	0.00
h	26	15.56	u	8	4.79
i	2	1.20	v	17	10.18
j	5	2.99	w	14	8.38
k	5	2.99	x	5	2.99
l	16	9.58	y	4	2.40
m	0	0.00	z	2	1.20

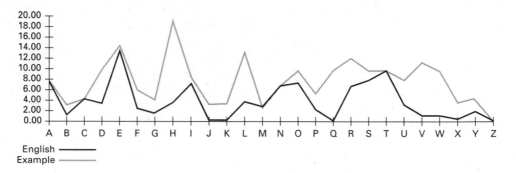

English ———
Example ———

Figure 2-4 Frequencies of Sample Cipher Against Normal Text

```
hqfubswlrq lv d phdqv ri dwwdlqlqj vhfxuh
frpsxwdwlrq ryhu lqvhfxuh fkdqqhov
eb xvlqj hqfubswlrq zh glvjxlvh wkh phvvdjh vr wkdw
hyhq li wkh wudqvplvvlrq lv glyhuwhg wkh phvvdjh zloo
qrw eh uhyhdohg
```

```
ENCRYPTION IS A MEANS OF ATTAINING SECURE
COMMUNICATION OVER INSECURE CHANNELS
BY USING ENCRYPTION WE DISGUISE THE MESSAGE SO
THAT EVEN IF THE TRANSMISSION IS DIVERTED THE
MESSAGE WILL NOT BE REVEALED
```

Table 2-3 shows the counts and relative frequencies of letters in the cipher examined in the previous section.

```
wklv phvvdjh lv qrw wrr kdug wr euhdn
```

The message was only 30 letters long, and there were only 14 distinct letters, so there cannot be a great frequency variation. Thus, we cannot conclude that v, the most frequent ciphertext letter, is E, the most frequently occurring English letter. Counts do help to narrow the possibilities, however. The frequently occurring letters in the ciphertext are likely to be among the more frequently occurring letters in English.

Table 2-3   Frequencies of Letters in `wklv...` Cipher

Letter	Count	Percent	Letter	Count	Percent
w	4	13.33	k	2	6.66
l	2	6.66	v	4	13.33
p	1	3.33	h	3	10.00
d	3	10.00	j	1	3.33
q	1	3.33	r	4	13.33
e	1	3.33	u	2	6.66
g	1	3.33	n	1	3.33

Recall the earlier statement that cryptanalysts are going to try every tool at their disposal and are not necessarily going to attack hard problems to solve encryptions. At face value, monoalphabetic ciphers seem secure because there are 26! possible different encipherments. By a brute force attack, the cryptanalyst could try all 26! decipherments of a particular ciphertext message. Working at one decipherment per microsecond (assuming the cryptanalyst had the patience to review the probable-looking plaintexts produced by some of the decipherments), it would still take over 10^3 years to test all 26! decipherments.

However, for messages that are long enough, the frequency distribution analysis betrays quickly many of the letters of the plaintext. In this and other ways, a good cryptanalyst finds easier approaches to bypass hard problems. An encryption based on a hard problem is not secure just because of the difficulty of the problem.

The Cryptographer's Dilemma

As with many analysis techniques, having very little ciphertext inhibits the usefulness of the technique. A cryptanalyst works by finding patterns. Short messages give the cryptanalyst little to work with, and so they are fairly secure with even simple encryption.

Monoalphabetic encryption displays the cryptographer's dilemma: an encryption algorithm has to be regular in order for it to be algorithmic and in order for cryptographers to be able to remember it. Unfortunately, the regularity gives clues to the cryptanalyst.

There is no solution to this dilemma. In fact, cryptography/cryptanalysis at times seems like a dog chasing its tail. The cryptographer invents a new encryption algorithm. The cryptanalyst studies the algorithm and finds its patterns and its weaknesses, which the cryptographer then sets out to try to secure by inventing a new algorithm. The principle of timeliness from Chapter 1 applies throughout cryptography: a security measure must be strong enough to keep out the attacker for the life of the data. Data with a short time value can be protected with simple measures.

2.3   Polyalphabetic Substitution Ciphers

The weakness of monoalphabetic ciphers is that their frequency distribution reflects the distribution of the underlying alphabet. A cipher that is more cryptographically secure would display a rather flat distribution, which gives no information to a cryptanalyst.

One way to flatten the distribution is to combine distributions that are high with ones that are low. If T is sometimes enciphered as a and sometimes as b, and if X is also sometimes enciphered as a and sometimes as b, the high frequency of T mixes with the low frequency of X to produce a more moderate distribution for a and b. In Figure 2-5,

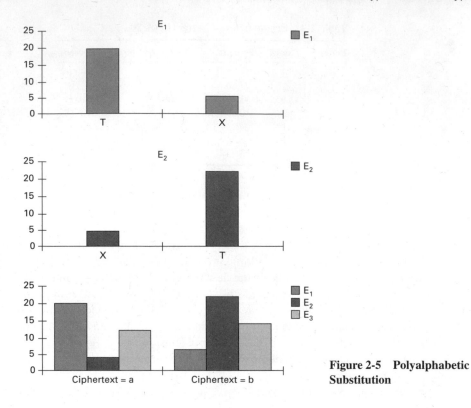

Figure 2-5   Polyalphabetic Substitution

$E_1(\text{T}) = \text{a}$ and $E_2(\text{T}) = \text{b}$ while $E_1(\text{X}) = \text{b}$ and $E_2(\text{X}) = \text{a}$. Thus, E_3 is shown as the average of E_1 and E_2.

We can combine two distributions by using two separate encryption alphabets, the first for all the characters in odd positions of the plaintext message, the second for all the characters in even positions. This just requires alternating between two translation tables. An example of this technique follows.

Suppose the two encryption algorithms are as shown below.

Table for Odd Positions

```
A B C D E F G H I J K L M N O P Q R S T U V W X Y Z
a d g j n o s v y b e h k n q t w z c f i l o r u x
```

Table for Even Positions

```
A B C D E F G H I J K L M N O P Q R S T U V W X Y Z
n s x c h m r w b g l q v a f k p u z e j o t y d i
```

(The first table uses the permutation $\pi_1(\lambda) = (3 * \lambda) \bmod 26$; the second uses the permutation $\pi_2(\lambda) = ((5 * \lambda) + 13) \bmod 26$.)

Encryption with these tables would proceed as follows. For the message *TREATY IMPOSSIBLE,*

```
TREAT YIMPO SSIBL E
```

the encryption would be

`fumnf dyvtv czysh h`

Notice that the double S becomes `cz`, and that the two Es are enciphered as m and h, respectively. The two Ts of TREATY happen to encipher to `f`, and similarly the two Is encipher to `ys`. On the other hand, the final two hs come from two different letters, L and E. Because of alternating tables, half of the time repeated ciphertext letters are the result of identical plaintext letters, but half of the time not.

Polyalphabetic encryption flattens the frequency distribution of the plaintext considerably. Table 2.4 is the frequency analysis of Dickens' opening paragraph of *A Tale of Two Cities* ("It was the best of times, it was the worst of times . . ."). This example uses two very easy monoalphabetic substitutions. The first substitution is $\pi_1(\lambda) = \lambda$, where each letter goes to itself, and the second is $\pi_2(\lambda) = 25 - \lambda$, where each letter goes to the letter the same distance from the opposite end of the alphabet. The use of a second alphabet smooths the distribution. Notice that e loses some of its strength to v, whereas g and h help to dissipate the frequency of s and t.

Vigenère Tableaux

The distribution of Table 2-4 shows how some of the peaks and valleys of normal frequency distribution can be smoothed by allowing plaintext letters to "share" ciphertext equivalents. Of course, this has to be done in a systematic way so that the receiver can know how to decrypt a message.

The table also shows the effect of the accidental collision of two low-frequency letters, such as J and Q, which both mapped to j and q. The remaining variance in the frequency table is attributed to the accidental collision of letters of similar high or low frequency.

One approach to this situation is to select any permutation as π_1, and then carefully choose π_2 to complement π_1; if π_1 maps a high-frequency letter such as E to x, then π_2 should map a low-frequency letter to x. This technique requires a little planning, but it is not too difficult.

Table 2-4   Two-Alphabet Encryption Letter Frequencies

Letter	Count	Percent	Letter	Count	Percent
a	14	2.95	n	20	4.22
b	4	0.84	o	25	5.27
c	3	0.63	p	7	1.27
d	17	3.59	q	0	0.00
e	35	7.38	r	39	8.23
f	14	2.95	s	27	5.70
g	31	6.54	t	30	6.33
h	43	9.07	u	10	2.11
i	33	6.96	v	39	8.23
j	0	0.00	w	18	3.80
k	5	1.05	x	3	0.63
l	31	6.54	y	5	1.05
m	7	1.48	z	14	2.95

Another approach is to extend the number of permutations. With three permutations, used in rotation, the chances of a flat distribution increase. But if three permutations are good, four should be better, and five should be great. The ultimate extension is 26 permutations, so that a plaintext letter can be enciphered as any ciphertext letter. Keeping track of which column to use is the principal disadvantage of rotating through all 26 permutations. A useful modification is to use a keyword, and let the letters of the keyword select the columns for encipherment.

For example, suppose you want to encipher the message "but soft, what light through yonder window breaks," using the keyword *juliet*. You would write the message and write one character of the keyword above each message character, repeating the keyword as often as necessary.

```
julie tjuli etjul ietju lietj uliet julie tjuli
BUTSO FTWHA TLIGH TTHRO UGHYO NDERW INDOW BREAK
```

A **Vigenère tableau** is a collection of 26 permutations. Usually these permutations are written as a 26×26 matrix, with all 26 letters in each row and each column. Such an arrangement is shown in Table 2-5.

For reference, assume that the characters in the line of keys have been numbered k_1, $k_2, \ldots, k_n$, to correspond to the letters of the plaintext. Each plaintext letter p_i is then converted to the ciphertext letter in row p_i, column k_i of the tableau. For example, the first let-

Table 2-5   Vigenère Tableau

	0					5					10					15					20					25	
	a	*b*	*c*	*d*	*e*	*f*	*g*	*h*	*i*	*j*	*k*	*l*	*m*	*n*	*o*	*p*	*q*	*r*	*s*	*t*	*u*	*v*	*w*	*x*	*y*	*z*	*π*
A	a	b	c	d	e	f	g	h	i	j	k	l	m	n	o	p	q	r	s	t	u	v	w	x	y	z	0
B	b	c	d	e	f	g	h	i	j	k	l	m	n	o	p	q	r	s	t	u	v	w	x	y	z	a	1
C	c	d	e	f	g	h	i	j	k	l	m	n	o	p	q	r	s	t	u	v	w	x	y	z	a	b	2
D	d	e	f	g	h	i	j	k	l	m	n	o	p	q	r	s	t	u	v	w	x	y	z	a	b	c	3
E	e	f	g	h	i	j	k	l	m	n	o	p	q	r	s	t	u	v	w	x	y	z	a	b	c	d	4
F	f	g	h	i	j	k	l	m	n	o	p	q	r	s	t	u	v	w	x	y	z	a	b	c	d	e	5
G	g	h	i	j	k	l	m	n	o	p	q	r	s	t	u	v	w	x	y	z	a	b	c	d	e	f	6
H	h	i	j	k	l	m	n	o	p	q	r	s	t	u	v	w	x	y	z	a	b	c	d	e	f	g	7
I	i	j	k	l	m	n	o	p	q	r	s	t	u	v	w	x	y	z	a	b	c	d	e	f	g	h	8
J	j	k	l	m	n	o	p	q	r	s	t	u	v	w	x	y	z	a	b	c	d	e	f	g	h	i	9
K	k	l	m	n	o	p	q	r	s	t	u	v	w	x	y	z	a	b	c	d	e	f	g	h	i	j	10
L	l	m	n	o	p	q	r	s	t	u	v	w	x	y	z	a	b	c	d	e	f	g	h	i	j	k	11
M	m	n	o	p	q	r	s	t	u	v	w	x	y	z	a	b	c	d	e	f	g	h	i	j	k	l	12
N	n	o	p	q	r	s	t	u	v	w	x	y	z	a	b	c	d	e	f	g	h	i	j	k	l	m	13
O	o	p	q	r	s	t	u	v	w	x	y	z	a	b	c	d	e	f	g	h	i	j	k	l	m	n	14
P	p	q	r	s	t	u	v	w	x	y	z	a	b	c	d	e	f	g	h	i	j	k	l	m	n	o	15
Q	q	r	s	t	u	v	w	x	y	z	a	b	c	d	e	f	g	h	i	j	k	l	m	n	o	p	16
R	r	s	t	u	v	w	x	y	z	a	b	c	d	e	f	g	h	i	j	k	l	m	n	o	p	q	17
S	s	t	u	v	w	x	y	z	a	b	c	d	e	f	g	h	i	j	k	l	m	n	o	p	q	r	18
T	t	u	v	w	x	y	z	a	b	c	d	e	f	g	h	i	j	k	l	m	n	o	p	q	r	s	19
U	u	v	w	x	y	z	a	b	c	d	e	f	g	h	i	j	k	l	m	n	o	p	q	r	s	t	20
V	v	w	x	y	z	a	b	c	d	e	f	g	h	i	j	k	l	m	n	o	p	q	r	s	t	u	21
W	w	x	y	z	a	b	c	d	e	f	g	h	i	j	k	l	m	n	o	p	q	r	s	t	u	v	22
X	x	y	z	a	b	c	d	e	f	g	h	i	j	k	l	m	n	o	p	q	r	s	t	u	v	w	23
Y	y	z	a	b	c	d	e	f	g	h	i	j	k	l	m	n	o	p	q	r	s	t	u	v	w	x	24
Z	z	a	b	c	d	e	f	g	h	i	j	k	l	m	n	o	p	q	r	s	t	u	v	w	x	y	25

ter (B) is converted to the ciphertext letter in row 1 (B), column 9 (j), in this tableau. The letter in that position is k. The encryption of this message starts as shown below.

```
julie tjuli etjul ietju lietj uliet julie tjuli
BUTSO ETWHA TLIGH TTHRO UGHYO NDERW INDOW BREAK
koeas ycqsi ...
```

With a six-letter keyword such as *juliet* this algorithm effectively spreads the effect of the frequency of each letter onto six others, which flattens the distribution substantially. Long keywords can be used, but a keyword of length three usually suffices to smooth out the distribution.

Cryptanalysis of Polyalphabetic Substitutions

With a little help from frequency distributions and letter patterns, you can break a monoalphabetic substitution by hand. Therefore, with the aid of computer programs, and with an adequate amount of ciphertext, a good cryptanalyst can break such a cipher in an hour. Even an untrained but diligent interceptor could probably determine the plaintext in a day or so. Nevertheless, in some applications, the prospect of one day's effort, or even the appearance of a sheet full of text that makes no sense, may be enough to protect the message. Encryption, even in a simple form, will deter the casual observer.

As we have seen, polyalphabetic substitutions are apparently more secure than monoalphabetic substitutions. The casual observer has little hope of breaking one without some knowledge of cryptanalysis, and the cryptanalytic tools are tedious enough that use of a computer is necessary for all but the most patient people.

Unfortunately, polyalphabetic substitutions are not immune to breaking. The method to break such an encryption is to determine the number of alphabets used, break the ciphertext into pieces that were enciphered with the same alphabet, and solve each piece as a monoalphabetic substitution. In fact, there are two powerful tools that can decrypt messages written even with a large number of alphabets. The two tools we will study are the Kasiski method, to determine when a pattern of encrypting permutations has repeated, and the index of coincidence, to predict the number of alphabets used for substitutions.

The Kasiski Method for Repeated Patterns

The **method of Kasiski**, named for its developer, a Prussian military officer, is a way of finding the number of alphabets that were used for encryption.

The method relies again on the regularity of English. Not only letters but also letter groupings and full words are repeated. For example, English uses endings *-th, -ing, -ed, -ion, -tion, -ation,* beginnings *im-, in-, un-, re-,* and patterns *-eek-, -oot-, -our-,* and so forth, disproportionately often. Furthermore, words such as *of, and, to, with, are, is,* and *that* also appear with high frequency.

The Kasiski method follows this rule: if a message is encoded with n alphabets in cyclic rotation, and if a particular word or letter group appears k times in a plaintext message, it should be encoded approximately k/n times from the same alphabet. As an example, if a keyword is six characters long, there are only six different ways to position the keyword over the plaintext word. A plaintext word or letter group that appears more than six times must be encrypted at least twice by the same position of the keyword, and those occurrences will all be enciphered identically.

The Dickens *It was the best of times* . . . example has much repetition so it demonstrates this argument quickly. Suppose the keyword is *dickens*.

```
dicke nsdic kensd icken sdick ensdi ckens dicke
ITWAS THEBE STOFT IMESI TWAST HEWOR STOFT IMESI

nsdic kensd icken sdick ensdi ckens dicke nsdic
TWAST HEAGE OFWIS DOMIT WASTH EAGEO FFOOL ISHNE

kensd icken sdick ensdi ckens dicke nsdic kensd
SSITW ASTHE EPOCH OFBEL IEFIT WASTH EEPOC HOFIN
```

The phrase IT WAS THE is enciphered with keyword *nsdicken* once in the first line and twice in the third line. These three cases all appear as identical 8-character patterns in the ciphertext.

The Kasiski approach works on duplicate fragments in the ciphertext. In order for a plaintext phrase to be enciphered the same way twice, the key must have gone through a whole number of rotations and be back at the same point. Therefore, the distance between the repeated patterns must be a multiple of the keyword length.

To use the Kasiski approach, you identify all repeated patterns in the ciphertext. Short repeated patterns, such as two letters, are often accidental, so it is more trouble to consider them than to ignore them. Any pattern over three characters is almost certainly not accidental. (The likelihood of two four-letter sequences *not* being from the same plaintext segment is $1/26^4$, which is approximately 0.0000021).

For each instance of a pattern, you write down its starting position and then compute the distance between successive starting positions. The distance between repeats must be a multiple of the key length, so you then determine all the factors of each distance.

The three repeated sequences in the example have the following characteristics.

Starting Position	Distance from Previous	Factors
20		
83	63 (83 – 20)	3, 7, 9, 21, 63
104	21 (104 – 83)	3, 7, 21

From this short example, we may guess that a keyword of 21 is improbable. Thus the key length is probably either 3 or 7. With more repeats you could reduce the number of possibilities for key length. Let us continue with the key length possibilities of 3 and 7.

For the Kasiski method, the steps are

1. Identify repeated patterns of three or more characters.
2. For each pattern write down the position at which each instance of the pattern begins.
3. Compute the difference between the starting points of successive instances.
4. Determine all factors of each difference.
5. If a polyalphabetic substitution cipher was used, the key length will be one of the factors that appears often in step 4.

With key length possibilities of 3 and 7, the next step is to try to divide the message into pieces enciphered with the same alphabet. If you want to try the assumption that the key length is 3, for example, you would form sets of the letters 3 positions apart in the ciphertext, $S_1 = \{c_1, c_4, c_7, c_{10}, \ldots\}$, $S_2 = \{c_2, c_5, c_8, c_{11}, \ldots\}$, and $S_3 = \{c_3, c_6, c_9, c_{12}, \ldots\}$. If all characters in one of these sets have been enciphered with the same alphabet, they should have a frequency distribution similar to English, and they should have a distribution similar to the other sets (although with high values at different letters, of course).

Index of Coincidence

The other cryptanalytic tool we will study is a way to rate how well a particular distribution matches the distribution of letters in English. Suppose we have a body of text that we suspect was encrypted with a monoalphabetic substitution. If our suspicion is correct, the frequencies of ciphertext letters should be the same as the frequencies of the corresponding English letters. The **index of coincidence** is a measure of the variation between frequencies in a distribution. (This description follows the lines of Sinkov [SIN66].)

As we have seen, English plaintext has a predictable nonuniform distribution. With a monoalphabetic substitution, this same distribution appears in the ciphertext. With two alphabets, however, high- and low-frequency letters blend, so that high-frequency letters are not as high and low-frequency letters are not as low. With more alphabets, the highs are even less high and the lows are even lower. Ultimately, if the distributions all blended perfectly, every letter would appear just as often as every other letter.

We can derive a measure that describes how high are the highs and how low are the lows in any distribution. With this measure we can tell whether a sample is encrypted with just one substitution (monoalphabetic) or with two or more alphabets. This measure is the index of coincidence. Notice that the index just measures distribution; we do not need to know *which* ciphertext letter matches plaintext *a* or *b*.

Let us try to measure the nonuniformity of a distribution. Suppose we pick a letter λ at random from an English text. From the distribution in Table 2.1, there is a probability of 0.0985 that λ is a *t*, or a probability of 0.0028 that λ is an *x*. In general, let Prob_a be the probability of an *a*, Prob_b of a *b*, and Prob_z of a *z*. The random letter is certain to be either an *a*, or a *b* . . . or a *z*, and so

$$\text{Prob}_a + \text{Prob}_b + \cdots + \text{Prob}_z = \sum_{\lambda=a}^{\lambda-z} \text{Prob}_\lambda = 1$$

Imagine the graph of a distribution with the letters along the horizontal axis and their relative frequency of occurrence along the vertical axis. For a perfectly flat distribution,

$$\text{Prob}_a = \text{Prob}_b = \cdots = \text{Prob}_z = \frac{1}{26} \cong 0.0384$$

The graph of such a distribution would be a horizontal straight line. If a distribution is not flat, the difference between Prob_a and $1/26$ is its variance from the flat distribution. The graph of such a distribution would have peaks and valleys at the letters that occur with high and low frequencies, respectively.

Sinkov defines a **measure of roughness**, which is a measure of the size of the peaks and valleys. If $1/26 \cong 0.0384$ is a baseline, a peak is a relative frequency above 0.0384, whereas a valley is a relative frequency below 0.0384. Figure 2-6 shows the roughness of the distribution of English text against a baseline of 0.0384.

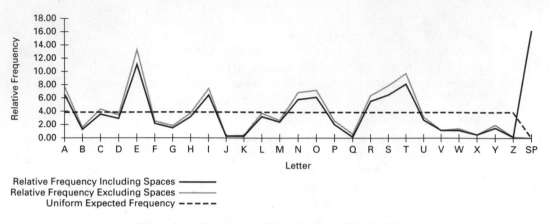

Figure 2-6   Roughness of Distribution of English Text

The roughness or nonuniformity of a distribution is how much it varies from flat. If $RFreq_\lambda$ is the relative frequency of λ, $RFreq_\lambda - (1/26)$ is the size of an observed peak or valley for λ, and $Prob_\lambda - (1/26)$ is its expected size.

We want to compute a measure that shows the nonuniformity of a whole distribution, not individual letters. Because a peak is positive and a valley is negative, simply summing these values would cause peaks to cancel valleys. Using $(Prob_\lambda - (1/26))^2$ prevents these cancellations.

The measure of roughness or variance is then

$$var = \sum_{\lambda=a}^{\lambda=z} \left(Prob_\lambda - \frac{1}{26} \right)^2$$

$$= \sum_{\lambda=a}^{\lambda=z} \left(Prob_\lambda^2 - \frac{2}{26} Prob_\lambda + \left(\frac{1}{26} \right)^2 \right)$$

$$= \sum_{\lambda=a}^{\lambda=z} Prob_\lambda^2 - \frac{2}{26} * \sum_{\lambda=a}^{\lambda=z} Prob_\lambda + \sum_{\lambda=a}^{\lambda=z} \left(\frac{1}{26} \right)^2$$

$$= \sum_{\lambda=a}^{\lambda=z} Prob_\lambda^2 - \frac{2}{26} * 1 + 26 * \left(\frac{1}{26} \right)^2$$

$$= \sum_{\lambda=a}^{\lambda=z} Prob_\lambda^2 - \frac{1}{26}$$

If a distribution were perfectly flat, each of the probabilities would be $1/26$, and *var* would be $26 * (1/26^2) - 0.0384 = 0.0384 - 0.0384 = 0$. Using the frequencies of Table 2-1 as probabilities gives $var = 0.0680 - 0.0384 = 0.0296$.

Each term in the sum of $Prob_\lambda^2$ is the probability of two events occurring at once: $Prob_\lambda^2$ is the probability that any two given characters from the text will both be λ. The vari-

ance can be estimated from a sample by counting the number of pairs of identical letters
and dividing by the total number of pairs possible.

But we do not know how often a particular letter *ought* to occur without knowing the
algorithm from which the letters were generated. We will approximate the probability from
observed frequencies.

In an observed sample of n ciphertext letters, suppose there are Freq_λ instances of
the character λ. We want to know the likelihood of picking λ twice at random. There are
Freq_λ ways to choose the first λ and $(\text{Freq}_\lambda - 1)$ remaining occurrences of λ from which to
choose the second λ. There are thus $\text{Freq}_\lambda * (\text{Freq}_\lambda - 1)$ ways of choosing the letter λ
twice. Because the pair (α,β) is the same as the pair (β,α), this product counts each pair
twice. Thus, there are $\text{Freq}_\lambda * (\text{Freq}_\lambda - 1)/2$ ways to select a pair of λs. In total, there are
$n * (n - 1)/2$ pairs of letters in a ciphertext of n characters.

Therefore,

$$\frac{\text{Freq}_\lambda * \left(\text{Freq}_\lambda - 1\right)}{n * (n-1)}$$

represents the likelihood that any two letters picked randomly would both be λ. But the
likelihood of picking the letter λ twice is approximately Prob_λ^2.

The **index of coincidence**, written *IC*, is a way to approximate variance from
observed data.

$$IC = \sum_{\lambda=a}^{\lambda=z} \frac{\text{Freq}_\lambda * \left(\text{Freq}_\lambda - 1\right)}{n * (n-1)}$$

The index of coincidence ranges from 0.0384, for a polyalphabetic substitution with a perfectly flat distribution, to 0.068, for a monoalphabetic substitution from common English.

If the amount of ciphertext is large and the underlying plaintext has a fairly normal
distribution of letters, the index of coincidence can be used to predict the number of alphabets. Table 2-6 shows *IC* values for several numbers of alphabets used in a polyalphabetic
substitution. Notice that the *IC* drops rapidly from one to three alphabets, but that its
change tapers off for many alphabets. The index of coincidence is a good predictor of how
many alphabets were used when the number is small, but cannot discriminate well for a
large number of alphabets.

Return to the previous example in which the Kasiski method was used to predict possible key lengths. In that example, the suspected key length was 3 or 7, which represents
the number of alphabets used. The index of coincidence might not differentiate successfully between three or seven alphabets.

Remember, however, that to test 3 as a possible key length, we formed the three sets
$S_1 = \{c_1,c_4, \ldots\}$, $S_2 = \{c_2,c_5, \ldots\}$, $S_3 = \{c_3,c_6, \ldots\}$. If the key length is 3, each of these
sets represents one enciphering alphabet, so $IC(S_1)$, $IC(S_2)$, and $IC(S_3)$ should all be

Table 2-6   Number of Enciphering Alphabets Versus Index of Coincidence

Alphabets	1	2	3	4	5	10	Large
IC	.068	.052	.047	.044	.044	.041	.038

close to 0.068. If that were not so, you would test a key length of 7 by forming sets $S_1 = \{c_1, c_8, \ldots\}, \ldots S_7 = \{c_7, c_{14}, \ldots\}$ and computing $IC(S_1), \ldots IC(S_7)$. When you use the correct key length, you will find all IC values close to 0.068.

Concluding Remarks on Polyalphabetic Ciphers

The steps in analyzing a polyalphabetic cipher are

1. Use the Kasiski method to predict likely numbers of enciphering alphabets. If no numbers emerge fairly regularly, the encryption is probably not simply a polyalphabetic substitution.
2. Compute the index of coincidence to validate the predictions from step 1.
3. Where steps 1 and 2 indicate a promising value, separate the ciphertext into appropriate subsets and independently compute the index of coincidence of each subset.

The Kasiski method of analysis of a polyalphabetic cipher assumes that there is some regular period to the use of alphabets. It attempts to find this period through analysis of repeated plaintext that happens to fall at the same point with respect to the key.

The index of coincidence can be used in two ways. First, it can help to confirm a suspicion that a given body of ciphertext has been enciphered with a polyalphabetic cipher. Second, given a guess as to the number of alphabets used and the frequency counts for the pieces supposedly enciphered using those alphabets, the index can confirm that the frequency distribution resembles a standard English distribution.

Both the Kasiski method and the index of coincidence depend on having available a large quantity of ciphertext. They work well when the enciphering alphabets are applied repeatedly at periodic intervals.

The "Perfect" Substitution Cipher

The ideal substitution would use many alphabets for an unrecognizable distribution and no apparent pattern for the choice of an alphabet at a particular point. What would happen if a text were enciphered with an unlimited number of alphabets? In this section we will consider ways to extend the number of alphabets.

The Vigenère tableau is fairly rigid in form, allowing the use of only 26 different permutations. However, suppose there were a way to generate an unlimited sequence of numbers between 0 and 25. Then each member of that sequence could select an alphabet (column) to be used to encipher the next plaintext character.

An infinite *nonrepeating* sequence of alphabets would confound the Kasiski method. First, a repeated plaintext phrase would not be encrypted the same way twice because there is no repeating pattern to the choice of alphabets. Second, suppose some piece of ciphertext was a duplicate of a previous piece. That duplicate would almost certainly be accidental. The distance between two duplicate passages of plaintext would not denote a period in the encryption pattern, because there is no pattern and hence no period. The index of coincidence for such a body of ciphertext would be close to 0.038, indicating a large number of enciphering alphabets. But counting the frequencies for characters k positions apart in the ciphertext, for $k = 1, 2, \ldots$ would yield nothing because the characters k positions apart would not necessarily have been enciphered with the same alphabet.

Thus, a nonrepeating selection of encryption alphabets would confound the cryptanalyst using tools we have seen so far. In the following sections we explore some ways of obtaining an unlimited, nonrepeating series of numbers.

One-Time Pads

This is the idea behind the "perfect" cipher, also called a **one-time pad**. The name comes from an encryption method in which a large nonrepeating set of keys is written on sheets of paper, glued together into a pad. If the keys are, for example, 20 characters long and a sender needs to transmit a message 300 characters in length, the sender would tear off the next 15 pages of keys. The sender would write them one at a time above the letters of the plaintext and encipher the plaintext with a chart like a Vigenère tableau. The sender would then destroy the used keys.

The receiver needs a pad identical to that of the sender. Upon receiving a message, the receiver takes the appropriate number of keys and deciphers the message as if it were a plain polyalphabetic substitution with a long key. Essentially this algorithm gives the effect of a key as long as the number of characters in the pad.

There are two problems with this method: the need for absolute synchronization between sender and receiver, and the need for an unlimited number of keys. Although generating a large number of random keys is no problem, there is a problem printing, distributing, storing, and accounting for such keys.

Long Random Number Sequences

A close approximation of a one-time pad for use on computers is a random number generator. In fact, computer random numbers are not random; they really form a sequence with a very long period. In practice, a generator with a long period can be acceptable for a limited amount of time or plaintext.

The sender with a 300-character message would interrogate the computer for the next 300 random numbers, scale them to lie between 0 and 25, and use one number to encipher each character of the plaintext message.

The Vernam Cipher

The **Vernam cipher** is a type of one-time pad devised by Gilbert Vernam for AT&T. The Vernam cipher is immune to most cryptanalytic attacks. The basic encryption involves an arbitrarily long nonrepeating sequence of numbers that are combined with the plaintext. Vernam's invention used an arbitrarily long punched paper tape that fed into a teletype machine. The tape contained random numbers that were combined with characters typed into the teletype. The sequence of random numbers was nonrepeating, and each tape was used only once. As long as the key tape does not repeat or is not reused, this type of cipher is immune to cryptanalytic attack because the available ciphertext does not display the pattern of the key. A model of this process is shown in Figure 2-7.

As an example, we will perform a Vernam encryption in decimal notation. Assume that the alphabetic letters are combined by sum mod 26 with a stream of random two-digit numbers. If the message is

VERNAM CIPHER

the letters would first be converted to their numeric equivalents, as shown here.

```
V    E    R    N    A    M    C    I    P    H    E    R
21   4    17   13   0    12   2    8    15   7    4    17
```

Next we need some random numbers to combine with the letter codes. Suppose the following series of random two-digit numbers is generated.

```
76  48  16  82  44  03  58  11  60  05  48  88
```

The encoded form of the message is the sum mod 26 of each coded letter with the corresponding random number. The result is then encoded in the usual base-26 alphabet representation.

Plaintext	V	E	R	N	A	M	C	I	P	H	E	R
Numeric Equivalent	21	4	17	13	0	12	2	8	15	7	4	17
+ Random Number	76	48	16	82	44	3	58	11	60	5	48	88
= Sum	97	52	33	95	44	15	60	19	75	12	52	105
= mod 26	19	0	7	17	18	15	8	19	23	12	0	1
Ciphertext	t	a	h	r	s	p	i	t	x	m	a	b

Thus, the message

VERNAM CIPHER

is encoded as

tahrsp itxmab

In this example, the repeated random number 48 happened to fall at the places of repeated letters, accounting for the repeated ciphertext letter a; such a repetition is highly unlikely. The repeated letter t comes from different plaintext letters, a much more likely occurrence. Duplicate ciphertext letters are generally unrelated with this encryption algorithm.

The Binary Vernam Cipher

This scheme works just as well with an "alphabet" of any other base. In order to encrypt a binary string (perhaps a series of words of binary data), random binary digits can be combined mod 2 with bits from the binary string. The result is another binary string.

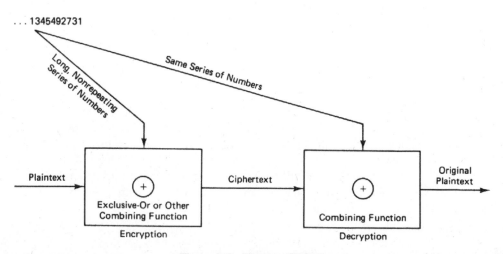

Figure 2-7   Vernam Cipher

For example, the binary number

1011011001010111001011010111100101

can be encoded with the random binary stream

1011110111101101011001001001110001

to produce the following ciphertext.

0000101110111010010010011111010100

Binary addition mod 2 can be calculated by the "exclusive-or" function, which is addition without carry. Exclusive or is often supplied as a basic machine instruction on computers, making it easier to implement this algorithm. Adding 0 produces no change, whereas adding 1 "complements" or reverses a bit.

Cracking Random Number Generators

Notice that many encryption algorithms, like the Vernam cipher, incorporate random numbers. The safety of the encryption depends on the randomness of the numbers used. A random sequence for a Vernam cipher has to be truly random, meaning without any discernible pattern. For example, the binary string 01010101 has the obvious pattern of alternating 0s and 1s. Such a string would make a very bad choice for a random stream because of the discernible pattern.

Where can we get truly random numbers, especially in a form easy to use with computers? The two-digit decimal numbers used in the Vernam cipher example are middle digits from a list of phone numbers in a residential directory. As such, they would be expected to be free from patterns. (There may still be some nonuniformity because many easy-to-remember sequences, such as *ddd-d000, ddd-1234,* or *ddd-1212,* are assigned to businesses. Exploiting that nonuniformity would require the interceptor to acquire and analyze great amounts of ciphertext.) A telephone directory is rather limited as a source of random numbers, and the numbers may not be available in a machine-readable format.

A more common source of random numbers is a pseudo-random number generator computer program. Contrary to their name, these programs generate numbers from a predictable, repeating sequence. In this section we will examine typical random number generators.

The most common type, the **linear congruential random number generator**, begins with an initial value or "seed," r_0. Each successive random number r_{i+1} is generated by

$$r_{i+1} = (a * r_i + b) \bmod n$$

where $a, b,$ and n are constants.[3] Often, n is chosen as 1 more than the maximum number that can be stored in a computer word, so that this computation can be performed by discarding any portion of the intermediate result that exceeds storage. This generator produces random integers between 0 and $n - 1$. (See [KNU81] for a thorough study of random number generators.)

---

[3] In formulas that follow, we will drop the parentheses, so that mod will apply to the entire formula unless indicated otherwise.

If r_0 and a are relatively prime to n, each number between 0 and $n - 1$ will be generated before the sequence repeats. But once the repetition begins, the entire sequence repeats in order.

The problem with this form of random number generator is its dependability. Because each number depends only on the previous number, you can determine constants by solving a series of equations.

$$r_1 = a * r_0 + b \bmod n$$
$$r_2 = a * r_1 + b \bmod n$$
$$r_3 = a * r_2 + b \bmod n$$

An interceptor who has r_0, r_1, r_2, and r_3 can solve for a, b, and n.

An interceptor can get r_0, r_1, r_2, and r_3 by a **probable word attack.** With a Vernam cipher, each ciphertext letter comes from the formula

$$c_i = r_i + p_i \bmod n$$

If an interceptor of the ciphertext guesses that the message starts with *MEMO* ($M = 12, E = 4, O = 14$), the interceptor can try to substitute probable values of p_i and solve for values of r_i.

$$r_0 = c_0 - 12 \bmod n$$
$$r_1 = c_1 -\ \ 4 \bmod n$$
$$r_2 = c_2 - 12 \bmod n$$
$$r_3 = c_3 - 14 \bmod n$$

With these values of r_0 to r_3, the interceptor may be able to solve the three equations for a, b, and n. Given those, the interceptor can generate the full sequence of random numbers and obtain plaintext directly.

Long Sequences from Books

Another source of supposedly "random" numbers is any book, piece of music, or other object of which the structure can be analyzed. A possible one-time pad is a telephone book. The sender and the receiver both need access to identical telephone books. They might agree, for example, to start at page 35, and use two middle digits (ddd-DDdd) of each phone number, mod 26 as a key letter for a polyalphabetic substitution cipher using a pre-agreed form of Vigenère tableau. This approach would not provide an unlimited number of key digits, but it might last for a year until a new telephone book became available.

A similar idea is the use of any book of prose as a key. Then, the key is the letters of the text, in order. For example, one might select a passage from Descarte's meditation: "What of thinking? I am, I exist, that is certain." The meditation goes on for a great length, certainly long enough to encipher many very long messages. If you wanted to encipher the message *MACHINES CANNOT THINK* you would write the message under enough of the key, and encode the message, again as with a conventional polyalphabetic cipher.

```
iamie xistt hatis cert
MACHI NESCA NNOTT HINK
```

It would seem as if this cipher, too, would be impossible to break. Unfortunately, that is not true. The flaw lies in the fact that neither the message nor the key text is evenly distributed and, in fact, the distributions of both cluster around high-frequency letters. For example, the four letters *A, E, O,* and *T* account for approximately 40 percent of all letters used in standard English text. Each ciphertext letter is really the intersection of a plaintext letter and a key letter. But if the probability of the plaintext or the key letter's being *A, E, O,* or *T* is 0.4, the probability of *both* being one of the four is 0.4 * 0.4 = 0.16, nearly 1/6. The top six letters, adding *N* and *I,* increases the sum of the frequencies to 50 percent and increases the probability for a pair to 0.25.

Assuming a standard Vigenère tableau has been used, given a piece of ciphertext, we look for frequent letter pairs that could have generated each ciphertext letter. The encrypted version of the message *MACHINES CANNOT THINK* is

```
uaopm kmkvt unhbl jmed
```

To break the cipher, assume that each letter of the ciphertext comes from a situation in which the plaintext letter (row selector) and the key letter (column selector) are both one of the six most frequent letters. (This guess will be correct approximately 25 percent of the time.) The trick is to work the cipher inside out. For a ciphertext letter, look in the body of the table for the letter to appear at the intersection of one of the six rows with one of the six columns. Find combinations in the Vigenère tableau that could yield each ciphertext letter as the result of two high-frequency letters.

The ciphertext u in this message could be in row **A**, column *u,* but that is not a pair of frequent letters, or it could be row **B**, column *t,* but that is not a common pair, nor is **C***s,* **D***r,* **E***q,* **F***p,* or any other pair. Thus, we cannot say much about the plaintext letter that produced u. The second letter, a, could come from row **A**, column *a*, but that is the only plaintext–keytext combination of the letters *A, E, O, T, N, I* that can produce an a. The likelihood is 0.25 that a represents *A*.

It will help to build a reduced table of the six frequent letter rows and columns.

	a	*e*	*i*	*n*	*o*	*t*
A	a	e	i	n	o	t
E	e	l	m	r	s	x
I	i	m	r	w	x	c
N	n	r	w	b	c	h
O	o	s	x	c	d	l
T	t	x	b	g	h	m

This table is more useful "inside out": a could represent A, b could stand for N or T, and so on.

Searching through this table for possibilities, we transform the cryptogram.

Ciphertext	u	a	o	p	m	k	m	k	v	t	u	n	h	b	l	j	m	e	d
Possible plaintexts	?	**A**	A	?	E	?	**E**	?	?	**A**	?	A	N	N	?	?	E	A	?
		O		**I**		I				T		**N**	T	**T**			**I**	E	
		T				T		T									T		

This technique does not reveal the entire message, or even enough of it to make the message MACHI NESCA NNOTT HINK easy to identify. The technique did, however, make predictions in 10 letter positions, and there was a correct prediction in 7 of those 10 positions. (The correct predictions are shown in **bold** type.) The algorithm made 20 assertions about probable letters, and 7 of those 20 were correct. (A score of 7 out of 20 is 35 percent, even better than the 25 percent expected.) The algorithm does not come close to solving the cryptogram, but it reduces the 26^{19} possibilities for the analyst to consider. Giving this much help to the cryptanalyst is significant. A similar technique can be used even if the order of the rows is permuted.

Dual-Message Entrapment

We can encipher two messages at once so that an interceptor cannot distinguish between the messages. One message is the real message, and another is a realistic-looking spurious message, called the dummy. Assume that the sender and receiver both know the dummy message. The dummy is then used as a key.

The cryptanalyst may deduce both key (dummy) and plaintext messages, but nobody can tell from the messages which is which. This occurs because the encryption of letter x with key y is the same as the encryption of letter y with key letter x. For instance, the message and key

Key (dummy)	`disregardthismessage`
Message	`THISMESSAGEISCRUCIAL`

can be interchanged. The encryption of either the key or message with the other as the key is

```
wpajqejvdzlqkovvmulgp
```

Thus, the key cannot be distinguished from the message.

Summary of Substitutions

Substitutions are effective cryptographic devices. In fact, they were the basis of many cryptographic algorithms used for diplomatic communication through the first half of this century. They show up in mysteries by Arthur Conan Doyle, Edgar Allan Poe, Agatha Christie, Ken Follett, and others.

The presentation of substitution ciphers has also introduced several cryptanalytic tools:

- frequency distribution
- index of coincidence
- consideration of highly likely letters and probable words
- repeated pattern analysis and the Kasiski approach
- persistence, organization, ingenuity, and luck

The next section introduces the other basic cryptographic invention: the transposition (permutation). Substitutions and permutations together form a basis for the most widely used encryption algorithms (the Data Encryption Standard) as well as numerous other algorithms, which are described and analyzed in Chapter 3.

2.4 Transpositions (Permutations)

The goal of a substitution is confusion, an attempt to make it difficult to determine how a message and key were transformed into ciphertext. A **transposition** is an encryption in which the letters of the message are rearranged. With a transposition the goal is diffusion, spreading the information from the message or the key out widely across the ciphertext. Transpositions try to break established patterns. Because a transposition is a rearrangement of the symbols of a message, it is also known as a **permutation**.

Columnar Transpositions

As with substitutions, we begin this study of transpositions with an easy one. The **columnar transposition** is a rearrangement of the characters of the plaintext into columns. The following example is a five-column transposition. The plaintext characters are separated into blocks of five and arranged one block after another, as shown here.

$$
\begin{array}{ccccc}
c_1 & c_2 & c_3 & c_4 & c_5 \\
c_6 & c_7 & c_8 & c_9 & c_{10} \\
c_{11} & c_{12} & \text{etc.} & &
\end{array}
$$

The resulting ciphertext is formed by traversing the columns.

$$
\begin{array}{ccccc}
c_1 & c_2 & c_3 & c_4 & c_5 \\
c_6 & c_7 & c_8 & c_9 & c_{10} \\
c_{11} & c_{12} & \text{etc.} & &
\end{array}
$$

As an example, you would write the plaintext message as

```
T   H   I   S   I
S   A   M   E   S
S   A   G   E   T
O   S   H   O   W
H   O   W   A   C
O   L   U   M   N
A   R   T   R   A
N   S   P   O   S
I   T   I   O   N
W   O   R   K   S
```

The resulting ciphertext would then be read as

```
tssoh oaniw haaso lrsto imghw
utpir seeoa mrook istwc nasns
```

The length of this message happened to be a multiple of five, so all columns came out the same length. If the message length is not a multiple of the length of a row, the last columns will be a letter short. An infrequent letter such as X is sometimes used to fill in any short columns.

Encipherment/Decipherment Complexity

This cipher involves no additional work beyond arranging the letters and reading them off again. Therefore, the algorithm is constant in the amount of work per character, and the time for the algorithm is proportional to the length of the message.

However, the other ciphers we have seen so far require only a constant amount of space (admittedly up to 26^2 locations). This algorithm requires storage for all characters of the message, so the space required is not constant but depends directly on the length of the message.

Furthermore, output characters cannot be produced until all characters of the message have been read. This restriction occurs because all characters must be entered in the first column before output of the second column can begin, but the first column is not complete until all characters have been read. Thus, the delay associated with this algorithm also depends on the length of the message, as opposed to the constant delay we have seen in previous algorithms.

Because of the storage space and the delay involved, this algorithm is not especially appropriate for long messages.

Digrams, Trigrams, and Other Patterns

Just as there are characteristic letter frequencies, there are also characteristic patterns of pairs of adjacent letters, called **digrams**. Letter pairs such as -*re*-, -*th*-, -*en*-, and -*ed*- appear very frequently. Table 2-7 lists the 10 most common digrams and **trigrams** (groups of three letters) in English. (They are shown with the most frequent ones first.)

Digram combinations such as -*vk*- and -*qp*- occur very infrequently. (The infrequent combinations can occur in acronyms, in foreign words or names, or across word boundaries.) The frequency of appearance of letter groups can be used to match up plaintext letters that have been separated in a ciphertext. Table 2-8 shows the frequency per 10,000 characters of all letter pairs. These counts and relative frequencies were obtained from a representative sample of over 250,000 characters of English text, not counting digrams that consist of the last letter of one word and the first letter of the next word. The table shows adjacent letter pairs, with the first letter of the pair along the column to the left and the second letter across the row on the top (so that, for example, the combination -*ca*- occurs 42.5 times per 10,000 characters). The space character (denoted by *SP*) is used to show the beginnings and endings of words. For example, the entry for (*SP,T*) shows the relative occurrence of *T* as the first letter of a word.

Table 2-7 Most Common Digrams and Trigrams

Digrams	Trigrams
EN	ENT
RE	ION
ER	AND
NT	ING
TH	IVE
ON	TIO
IN	FOR
TF	OUR
AN	THI
OR	ONE

Table 2-8   Frequencies per 10,000 Characters of Digrams in English Example

	A	B	C	D	E	F	G	H	I	J	K	L	M	N	O	P	Q	R	S	T	U	V	W	X	Y	Z	SP
A	0.0	19.2	41.3	11.4	0.1	3.7	10.2	0.6	13.9	0.6	4.7	70.7	19.0	119.1	0.00	10.9	0.0	65.9	49.8	118.8	6.6	9.8	1.8	0.9	9.6	0.0	55.8
B	5.6	0.0	0.0	0.1	35.7	0.0	0.0	0.0	7.0	13.1	0.0	19.8	0.4	0.0	4.5	0.0	0.0	1.9	1.8	0.6	7.5	0.3	0.0	0.0	8.2	0.0	7.4
C	42.5	1.6	15.1	0.1	56.1	0.1	0.0	37.1	14.5	0.0	5.9	10.3	0.0	0.0	57.4	0.0	0.1	11.7	2.4	63.2	28.5	0.0	0.0	0.0	3.0	0.0	126.6
D	11.7	0.1	0.0	3.4	73.6	0.0	0.8	0.0	26.7	0.0	0.0	0.8	0.6	0.1	11.0	0.0	0.0	2.0	5.8	0.1	12.5	1.1	1.6	0.0	3.0	0.0	126.6
E	39.3	0.5	80.9	70.4	16.1	12.9	8.6	0.6	5.9	0.1	0.3	41.2	37.8	99.2	2.0	13.3	8.0	143.0	132.0	26.4	1.8	27.0	3.1	28.9	4.4	0.0	310.9
F	8.6	0.0	0.0	0.0	17.7	14.2	0.0	0.0	25.5	0.0	0.0	3.8	0.0	0.0	37.2	0.0	0.0	8.2	0.2	5.3	7.7	0.0	0.0	0.0	1.9	0.0	70.2
G	6.6	0.0	0.0	0.0	19.2	0.1	0.4	11.4	7.6	0.0	0.0	1.6	0.8	16.6	3.5	0.0	0.0	12.8	1.0	0.5	8.5	0.0	0.0	0.0	0.5	0.0	50.4
H	50.4	0.0	0.0	0.0	146.4	0.1	0.0	0.1	24.7	0.0	0.0	0.4	0.5	3.2	23.4	0.0	0.0	7.3	0.4	5.8	2.3	0.0	0.0	0.0	3.4	0.0	36.3
I	16.9	8.4	43.4	17.4	18.6	21.7	32.7	0.0	0.0	0.0	1.3	22.5	27.8	142.3	70.6	4.9	2.6	15.9	64.4	80.6	0.3	15.9	0.0	1.9	0.0	6.9	1.4
J	0.0	0.0	0.0	0.0	16.1	0.0	0.0	0.0	0.0	0.0	0.0	0.0	0.0	0.0	1.3	0.0	0.0	0.0	0.0	0.0	1.2	0.0	0.0	0.0	0.0	0.0	0.6
K	0.5	0.0	0.0	0.0	10.5	0.0	0.0	0.0	2.8	0.0	0.0	0.1	0.0	3.1	0.1	0.0	0.0	0.0	2.4	0.0	0.2	0.1	0.1	0.0	0.0	0.0	6.8
L	32.1	0.1	0.2	7.9	65.7	0.6	0.5	0.0	30.6	0.0	0.1	30.6	0.3	0.4	18.1	1.0	0.0	0.2	11.1	9.2	9.2	2.3	0.5	0.0	24.6	0.0	67.9
M	33.9	4.8	0.1	0.3	62.3	0.0	0.0	0.0	15.9	0.0	0.0	0.4	7.3	0.3	20.3	25.2	0.0	0.0	12.9	0.0	8.9	0.6	0.0	0.0	0.5	0.0	32.3
N	20.2	0.2	28.5	67.8	41.4	9.7	58.5	0.5	21.1	0.1	0.9	3.5	2.2	4.0	21.2	0.1	0.1	0.7	37.5	83.0	3.6	6.5	0.0	0.0	6.1	0.0	151.5
O	1.8	10.3	11.6	21.3	2.0	67.7	8.5	0.1	2.4	2.9	2.3	20.4	35.5	12.1	9.1	23.1	0.0	88.7	14.6	28.3	45.1	8.3	17.6	0.3	0.5	0.0	64.3
P	19.4	0.1	0.2	0.1	48.4	0.2	0.0	2.7	2.7	0.0	0.0	24.6	1.6	0.0	20.3	9.7	0.0	46.9	2.2	6.3	4.9	0.0	0.0	0.0	0.3	0.0	6.4
Q	0.0	0.0	0.0	0.0	0.0	0.0	0.0	0.0	0.0	0.0	0.0	0.0	0.0	0.0	0.0	0.0	0.0	0.0	0.0	0.0	14.8	0.0	0.0	0.0	0.0	0.0	1.0
R	52.0	0.1	12.4	7.8	132.3	3.0	5.1	0.3	75.2	0.0	2.7	2.4	18.6	5.7	62.1	2.1	0.0	5.9	21.5	20.3	11.9	5.6	0.3	0.0	10.7	0.0	94.0
S	8.1	0.0	7.8	0.2	97.2	1.8	0.0	10.2	52.5	0.0	1.7	1.4	4.2	0.5	23.6	7.4	0.1	0.1	43.7	77.9	30.7	0.0	2.6	0.0	21.1	0.0	257.8
T	37.5	0.0	3.8	0.2	101.5	0.3	0.0	196.8	121.0	0.0	0.0	2.7	4.4	0.7	60.4	0.5	0.0	31.9	38.3	4.4	14.3	0.0	10.9	0.0	34.2	0.2	137.7
U	16.8	8.3	13.5	7.7	9.9	0.5	3.6	0.0	6.9	0.0	0.0	24.4	6.1	18.6	0.5	6.0	0.0	53.7	43.9	16.9	0.0	0.0	0.0	0.1	0.1	0.1	13.3
V	17.0	0.0	0.0	0.0	51.5	0.0	0.0	0.0	20.3	0.0	0.0	0.0	0.5	0.0	2.8	0.0	0.0	0.0	0.5	0.0	0.4	0.0	0.0	0.0	0.0	0.0	0.1
W	12.6	0.0	0.1	0.0	19.2	0.0	0.0	16.2	16.7	0.0	0.0	0.2	0.0	3.4	10.4	0.0	0.0	1.6	2.8	0.0	0.0	0.0	0.0	0.0	0.0	0.0	10.2
X	6.4	0.0	0.3	0.0	1.9	0.0	0.0	0.1	1.8	0.0	0.0	0.0	0.0	0.0	0.1	16.5	0.0	0.0	0.0	2.1	0.0	0.0	0.0	0.0	0.0	0.0	3.6
Y	0.2	0.1	0.1	0.2	2.6	0.0	0.0	0.0	1.7	0.0	0.0	0.0	0.2	0.6	15.5	5.0	0.0	0.2	25.2	0.3	0.1	0.0	0.1	0.0	0.0	0.9	96.1
Z	3.2	0.0	0.0	0.0	4.6	0.0	0.0	0.0	0.3	0.0	0.0	0.0	0.0	0.0	0.2	0.0	0.0	0.0	0.0	0.0	0.0	0.0	0.0	0.0	0.0	0.1	0.0
SP	201.1	60.0	98.4	65.4	63.9	64.0	12.4	27.8	120.7	2.2	7.1	31.4	58.2	27.4	135.2	71.6	4.8	53.2	136.3	251.9	30.0	15.7	54.7	0.5	16.6	0.1	0.0

t s s o h o a n i w h a a s o l r s t o i m g h w · · ·

Figure 2-8   Positions of Adjacent Letters in Ciphertext

Cryptanalysis by Digram Analysis

The basic attack on columnar transpositions is not as precise as the attack on substitution ciphers. Even though transpositions look less secure than substitutions, because transpositions leave the plaintext letters intact, the work for the cryptanalyst is more exhausting, because more relies on a human judgment of what "looks right."

The first step in analysis of the transposition is to compute the letter frequencies. The fact that all letters appear with their normal frequencies implies that a transposition has been performed. Given a string of text, the trick is to break it into columns.

Two different strings of letters from a transposition ciphertext can represent pairs of adjacent letters from the plaintext. See Figure 2-8, which shows where adjacent plaintext characters end up in a ciphertext string. The problem is to find where in the ciphertext a pair of adjacent columns lies, and where the ends of the columns are.

The process involves exhaustive comparison of strings of ciphertext. The process compares a block of ciphertext characters against characters successively farther away in the ciphertext. Imagine a moving window that locates a block of characters for checking. Assume the block being compared is seven characters. The first comparison is c_1 to c_8, c_2 to $c_9, \ldots, c_7$ to c_{14}. Then the window of comparison shifts, and c_1 is compared to c_9, c_2 to c_{10}, and so forth. The window shifts again to c_1 against c_{10} and so forth. This process is shown in Figure 2-9.

Two questions must be asked for each window position. First, do common digrams appear, and second, do most of the digrams look reasonable? The first question addresses whether this is a promising position for the start of a transposition; the second question tries to eliminate chance occurrences of common digrams. The first question is answered by recording, for each of the seven pairs of letters, the frequency of that digram in normal English. The second question is answered by computing the variance between the seven recorded digram frequencies. (To be manageable, this example demonstrates the technique using only eight characters in the block being compared. In practice, however, this technique would be implemented by computer, using a much longer block length.)

t	n		n		n		n		n		n
s	i	t	i		i		i		i		i
s	w	s	w	t	w		w		w		w
o	h	s	h	s	h	t	h		h		h
h	a	o	a	s	a	s	a	t	a		a
o	a	h	a	o	a	s	a	s	a	t	a
a	s	o	s	h	s	o	s	s	s	s	s
	o	a	o	o	o	h	o	o	o	s	o
	l		l	a	l	o	l	h	l	o	l
	r		r		r	a	r	o	r	h	r
	s		s		s		s	a	s	o	s
	t		t		t		t		t	a	t
	o		o		o		o		o		o

Figure 2-9   Moving Comparisons

As another example, consider again the cryptogram from the beginning of this section.

```
tssoh oaniw haaso lrsto imghw
utpir seeoa mrook istwc nasns
```

The first comparison is of the first seven characters against the next seven: TSSOHOA to NIWHAAS. Some of the digrams produced that way are likely, such as: -SI- and -SW-, but -TN- and -OH- are unlikely.

The next window places TSSOHOA against IWHAASO. Again, there are some likely digrams, but -AO- is very suspicious. The third window's comparison also has some suspicious points.

We know the next window is the correct one because the column length was 10. The comparison there is TSSOHOA against HAASOLR. We observe that all the digrams are reasonable. In Table 2-9, we have listed the relative frequency of all of the digrams for a given window position. That table also shows the mean and standard deviation of each list of frequencies. A high mean implies that the digrams are likely; a low standard deviation implies that all of the digrams are likely, so that the mean is not being raised artificially by a few popular digrams.

When digrams indicate a possible match for a fragment of ciphertext, the next step is to try to extend the match. The distance between c_1 and c_{k+1} implies that another column might begin k positions later (the distance is k). If c_i and c_{i+k} match, so also should c_{i+k} and c_{i+2k}, and so forth. To test that theory, c_k is checked against c_{2k}, and so on.

Double Transposition Algorithm

The **double transposition** cipher involves two columnar transpositions, with different numbers of columns, applied one after the other. The first transposition displaces adjacent letters, and the second breaks up the adjacency of short series of letters that happened to appear in adjacent columns of the first transposition. Table 2-10 is a duplicate of the columnar transposition from the earlier section. Letters from the third column have been preceded with a "(", and letters from the fourth column have been followed by a ")" to make them easy to locate in the resulting ciphertext. The transposed text becomes

```
tssoh oaniw haaso lrsto (i(m(g(h(w
(u(t(p(i(r s)e)e)o)a) m)r)o)o)k) istwc nasns
```

Because there were 50 characters, they fit perfectly into a 10 by 5 matrix. For the second transposition the ciphertext is written in an 8 by 7 matrix, as shown in Table 2-11. The

Table 2-9   Matching Possible Column Positions

First Letter		Second Letter, Digram, Relative Frequency										
c_1	t	n	tn	60	i	ti	121	w	tw	11	h	th	197
c_2	s	i	si	53	w	sw	3	h	sh	10	a	sa	8
c_3	s	w	sw	3	h	sh	10	a	sa	8	a	sa	8
c_4	o	h	oh	37	a	oa	2	a	oa	2	s	os	15
c_5	h	a	ha	50	a	ha	50	s	hs	0	o	ho	23
c_6	o	a	oa	2	s	os	15	o	oo	9	l	ol	20
c_7	a	s	as	50	o	ao	0	l	al	71	r	ar	66
	Mean			36			29			16			48
	Std. Dev.			24			44			25			69

Table 2-10   Single Columnar Transposition

T	H	(I	S)	I
S	A	(M	E)	S
S	A	(G	E)	T
O	S	(H	O)	W
H	O	(W	A)	C
O	L	(U	M)	N
A	R	(T	R)	A
N	S	(P	O)	S
I	T	(I	O)	N
W	O	(R	K)	S

Table 2-11   Second Columnar Pattern

T	S	S	O	H	O	A
N	I	W	H	A	A	S
O	L	R	S	T	O	(I
(M	(G	(H	(W	(U	(T	(P
(I	(R	S)	E)	E)	O)	A)
M)	R)	O)	O)	K)	I	S
T	W	C	N	A	S	N
S	X	X	X	X	X	X

symbols (and) have been retained to show the original locations of these characters. Because 50 characters do not fill an 8 by 7 matrix, the extra positions must be filled with a padding character, such as *X*.

The result from the second columnar transposition is shown here.

```
tno(m(i m)tssi l(g(rr)w xswr(h s)o)cxo
hs(we)o) nxhat (ue)k)ax oao(to) isxas (i(pa)sn x
```

Even letters from adjacent columns of the first transposition, such as the (im) pair at the beginning, come from widely separated letters. The i is the last *i* of *transposition*, the m is from the earlier word *columnar*.

The six extra xs filling the last row stand out. A better way of padding is to use letters that would occur frequently anyway, such as *a, e, i, n, o,* or *s,* so that the padding characters are not so obvious.

Cryptanalysis

There is a functional relationship between plaintext and ciphertext character positions. With single transposition, the plaintext character in position *i* moves to position

$$E(i) = 10 * \left(\left[(i-1) \bmod 5 \right] + (i-1)/5 + 1 \right)$$

so that

$$c_{10*\left(\left[(i-1) \bmod 5 \right] + (i-1)/5+1 \right)} = p_i$$

With the second transposition, the relationship uses 8s and 7s instead of 10s and 5s, with a similar formula.

Double transpositions are an example of **product ciphers**, in which one encryption is applied to the result of another. Product ciphers resemble the product or composition of two functions in mathematics. If E_1 and E_2 are two transposition ciphers following a regular pattern, their product is also a regular pattern, $E_2(E_1(p))$. The product cipher formed by using the output of E_1 as the input to E_2 is a complicated function, but it is still regular.

This encryption algorithm can be broken with a chosen plaintext attack or a probable plaintext attack. It may even be broken by analysis of letters that appear together very often (such as *Q* followed by *U*, or *X* preceded by *E*). In all three cases, the cryptanalyst

remainder of the message will be uninte
umn for a polyalphabetic substitution a
unaffected.

5. The size of the enciphered text
message.

The idea behind principle 5 is tha
not possibly carry more information th
data from which to infer a pattern. Furt
storage and more time to communicate
These principles were developed
although Shannon was aware of comp
Some of the concerns of hand impleme
ple, a cipher's implementation need n
implementation is tolerable.

Confusion and Diffusion

Two additional concepts relate to the
encrypting algorithm should take the
that the interceptor cannot readily rec
able to predict what changing one char
characteristic is called **confusion**. An
complex functional relationship betwe
way, it will take an interceptor a long
key, and ciphertext; therefore, the code
As an example, the Caesar cipher
lyst who deduces the transformation of
the remaining letters, with no additiona
tution with a key longer than the mes
plaintext letter can be transformed to a
There is no apparent pattern to the way
The cipher should also spread th
ciphertext. Changes in the plaintext sho
ple is called **diffusion**, the characterist
text letters over the entire output. Goo
to much ciphertext to infer the algorith
The fractionating scheme present
the substitution and permutation ciphe
text character affects only one cipherte

Information Theoretic Tests

A **secure cryptographic system** is o
message from its ciphertext, regardle
transformation, the one-time pad, is
assumes access to the pad through thef
ceptor and a sender or receiver.

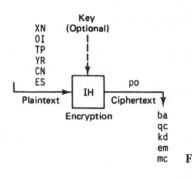

Figure 2-11   Block Cipher Systems

transposition, the entire message is translated as one block. The block size need not have any particular relationship to the size of a character. Block ciphers work on blocks of plaintext and produce blocks of ciphertext, as shown in Figure 2-11.

In fractionated Morse, parts of characters are enciphered separately as a block. In this case, a block could consist of part of a four-symbol letter, one complete three-symbol letter, a two-symbol letter plus a space (before or after), a one-symbol letter surrounded by spaces, part of a letter plus a space, two one-symbol letters and a space, a one-symbol letter plus a space and part of another letter, or parts of two letters and a space. For example, the letter T (–) could be represented in four different ways, depending whether the T falls at the start, middle, or end of a block and what comes before and after the T.

Block ciphers have advantages that stream ciphers lack, but the disadvantages of block ciphers are the strengths of stream ciphers. First we list the advantages:

+ *Diffusion.* Information from the plaintext is diffused into several ciphertext symbols. One ciphertext block may depend on several plaintext letters.

+ *Immunity to insertions.* Because blocks of symbols are enciphered, it is impossible to insert a single symbol into one block. The length of the block would then be incorrect, and the decipherment would quickly reveal the insertion. Furthermore, one character from the plaintext does not produce just one ciphertext character. Therefore, an active interceptor cannot simply cut one ciphertext letter out of a message and paste a new one in to change an amount, a time, a date, or a name in a message.

On the other hand, block ciphers are subject to

– *Slowness of encryption.* Block ciphers must wait until an entire block of plaintext symbols has been received before starting the encryption process. The columnar transposition is the extreme case; there this delay must be for the entire message. In shorter cases, as with fractionated Morse, the delay is only until the next one or two characters fill the block. Clearly, block encryption schemes where the delay is limited to a small, fixed number of characters are preferable to unbounded delay.

– *Error propagation.* An error will affect the transformation of all other characters in the same block. In a stream cipher message it may be possible to interpret the message correctly with one character irretrievably garbled. With a block cipher, one error will cause loss or misinterpretation of an entire block, which may be part of one character, parts of two characters, or all or parts of many characters.

2.7 Characteristics of "Good" (

At this point we can reconsider what we
have looked at two broad classes of algo
tions "hide" the letters of the plaintext.
frequencies. Transpositions scramble t
have also noted drawbacks to each type

How do we choose an encryption a
mean for a cipher to be "good"? The me
cipher. A cipher to be used by military
from one that will be used in a secure in
section contains some discussion of diff

Shannon Characteristics

In 1949, Claude Shannon [SHA49] pro
ria are listed here.

1. The amount of secrecy needed sho
   the encryption and decryption.

Principle 1 is a reiteration of the p
earlier observation that even a simple
interceptor or to hold off any interceptor

2. The set of keys and the enciphering

This principle implies that we sho
plaintext on which the algorithm can wo
ing an equal number of As and Es is use
keys such that the sum of the values of t
tions such as these make the use of the e
is too complex it will not be used. Furt
remembered, so it must be short.

3. The implementation of the process

Principle 3 was formulated with h
rithm is prone to error or likely to be fo
digital computers, algorithms far too cc
Still, the issue of complexity is importa
severely hinders message transmission,

4. Errors in ciphering should not prop
   in the message.

Principle 4 acknowledges that hur
algorithms. One error early in the proces
text. For example, dropping one letter
remaining encipherment. Unless the rec

Perfect security defined this way is hard to achieve. A more reasonable interpretation of security is "secure enough," defined as follows. The cryptanalyst will try to find a transformation h that converts ciphertext into plaintext. The cryptographer hopes that the transformation h is not exact; that is, it can produce many possible plaintexts. For example, recall the frequent-letters analysis of the cipher that gets its key from a prose passage. The analysis predicted several possibilities for some character positions of the message, and no possibilities for other positions. Therefore, the cryptanalyst has a transformation that maps one ciphertext to none, one, or several possible plaintexts.

Suppose $C = E(P)$ is the encipherment, and h is the cryptanalyst's suspected decipherment. Then, let $h(C)$ be a set of possible plaintexts, $h(C) = \{\text{Poss}_1, \text{Poss}_2, \ldots\}$. The actual plaintext, P, may or may not be one of the possibilities Poss_i.

An encryption is **effectively secure** if the probability that $h(C)$ is P is arbitrarily small; that is,

$$\text{Prob}\big(h(C) = P\big) < \varepsilon$$

for some arbitrarily small value ε. For example, the dual-message entrapment scheme described previously produces a probability no larger than 1/2. The analyst deducing the one message will also find the other, but the analyst cannot determine which is authentic.

As another example, consider the encryption system shown in Figure 2-12. The figure shows a situation where five plaintext messages, P_1 through P_5, are encrypted with the five keys, k_1 through k_5. Suppose it happened that those five encryptions produced only five different ciphertexts, C_1 through C_5. (Normally five plaintexts under five keys would produce about 25 distinct ciphertexts, with equal likelihood.) An interceptor might obtain one of the ciphertexts, say C_1, and might even have access to the keys $k_1 \ldots k_5$ and the matching plaintexts $P_1 \ldots P_5$. Having C_1 gives the interceptor no additional information about which plaintext was sent because any of the five plaintexts could have produced ciphertext C_1. In this case,

$$\text{Prob}_{C_1}\big(h(C_1) = P\big) = \text{Prob}\big(h(C_1) = P\big) = \text{Prob}(P)$$

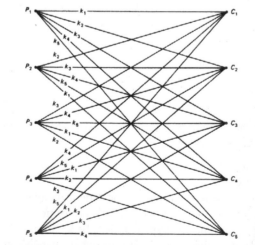

Figure 2-12   Example of Perfect Secrecy[4]

---

[4] Adapted from [SHA49].

That is, the probability that any particular plaintext P was sent is not influenced by the fact that ciphertext C_1 was sent.

By contrast, consider the more common case in which a single ciphertext is the encipherment of very few plaintext-key combinations. Here, knowing all the ks, all the Ps, and which C was sent instantly reveals the corresponding plaintext. This situation is shown in Figure 2-13. For example, knowing that C_1 was sent reveals that the plaintext could only have been P_2 or P_3. Thus, we can deduce more information about the cipher, such as

$$\text{Prob}_{C_1}\left(h(C_1) = P_1\right) = 0$$

because there is no key k for which $E(k,P_1) = C_1$.

Redundancy

Languages are inherently redundant. The minimum number of bits of information needed to represent the unique letters of an alphabet is $A = \lceil \log_2(k) \rceil$ where k is the number of letters in the alphabet and $\lceil \ \rceil$ denotes rounding up to the nearest integer. This measure is called the **absolute rate** of the language. For example, English has a 26-letter alphabet. Therefore, $\lceil \log_2(26) \rceil$ or 5 bits are needed to represent all letters uniquely.

The number of possible n-letter messages in the language is 2^{An}. Some of these are meaningful, but most are not. Let 2^{Rn} be the number of meaningful messages. The **rate** of the language is R. The **redundancy** of the language is $D = A - R$; in other words, D is the number of excess bits available that are not needed to represent meaningful messages.

As an example, imagine writing out all strings that are 20 characters long. (There are $26^{20} \cong 2 * 10^{28}$ such strings.) Most of them, like $AAA\ldots AA$, $AAA\ldots AB$, $AAA\ldots AC$, and $ZZZ\ldots ZZ$ are meaningless, but all meaningful messages 20 letters long will be there (see Figure 2-14). If you had a list of only the meaningful messages, a more economical way of referring to one would be to number them and use just the number of the one you want. If there were 1,000 meaningful messages, $\lceil \log_2(1000) \rceil \cong 10$ bits would suffice to

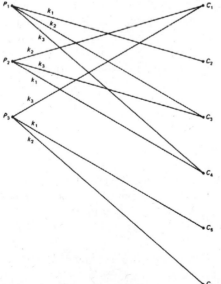

Figure 2-13   Example of Imperfect Secrecy

```
        A A A ...                               A A
        A A A ...                               A B
        A A A ...                               A C
        A                                       A D
                               .
                               .
                               .
        A                                       A Z
        A                                       B A
        A                                       B B
                               .
                               .
                               .
        A                                       B Z
        A                                       C A
                               .
                               .
                               .
        A                                       Z Z
        A                                     B A A
                               .
                               .
                               .
        B A                                     A A
                               .
                               .
                               .
    S E N D M E C H O C O L A T E C A K E
                               .
                               .
                               .
        Z A                                     A A
        Z Z                                     Z Z
```

Figure 2-14   All Messages of Length 20

refer to a single message, instead of the 20 ∗ 5 = 100 bits to write it in letters. This difference between the conventional representation and the most economical representation in a language is the redundancy of the language.

If an encryption algorithm encrypts two or more different messages to the same ciphertext, an interceptor cannot determine which of two or more possible meaningful plaintext messages is the authentic one. When the number of such multiple-message encodings is high, the encryption system is also secure. If a language is highly redundant, the number of possible multiple-message encodings can be high.

For example, if you could identify meaningless plaintext, you could devise an encryption algorithm to encrypt nine meaningless plaintext messages and one meaningful one to each ciphertext. An interceptor, presumably unable to distinguish meaningful from meaningless messages, would have a probability of only 1/10 of selecting the right decipherment. Note that the phrasing here is *can be* high; the number is not necessarily high.

Unicity Distance

Define Prob(P) as the probability of plaintext message P having been sent. Given that C was received, let Prob$_C$(P) be the probability that P was the message sent. (That is, Prob$_C$(P) is the probability that $C = E(P)$.) Perfect secrecy occurs only if Prob$_C$(P) = Prob(P). In other words, knowing that C was received gives the analyst no additional information about what message was sent.

Shannon defined a concept, called the **unicity distance**, that describes the amount of ciphertext needed in order to break a cipher. Define

$$H_C(P) = \sum_P \text{Prob}_C(P) * \log_2\left(\frac{1}{\text{Prob}_C(P)}\right)$$

The **unicity distance** is the smallest message length n for which $H_C(P)$ is close to 0. That is, the unicity distance measures the amount of uncertainty in an encryption system. For some systems, like the one-time pad systems, $H_C(P)$ is never close to 0.

If an encryption has $2^{H(P)}$ keys, the unicity distance is

$$N = \frac{H(P)}{D}$$

where D is the redundancy of the language, as described earlier. If there are as many keys as messages, the cipher is theoretically unbreakable. This situation occurs with the dual message entrapment and the Vernam cipher, as well as the other infinite-length key systems. It also explains why you can break standard substitutions given enough ciphertext.

The probability of getting a spurious decryption of a ciphertext is $p = (1 - q)$, where

$$q = \frac{2^{Rn}}{2^{An}} = 2^{(R-A)n} = 2^{-Dn}$$

and D is the redundancy of the language, described earlier. This is so because there are 2^{An} possible ways of encoding n characters, but there are only 2^{Rn} meaningful messages; therefore, the leftover $(2^{An} - 2^{Rn})$ encodings represent nothing. Therefore, q is the likelihood of getting a string that represents nothing.

2.8   What the Cryptanalyst Has to Work With

Four possible situations confront the cryptanalyst, depending on what information is available. These four cases suggest five different approaches the analyst can take. (In all of these cases, also keep in mind that the cryptanalyst will also use any other collateral information that can be obtained.)

Ciphertext Only

In most of the discussions so far, it was assumed that the analyst had only the ciphertext with which to work. The decryption had to be done based on probabilities, distributions, and characteristics of the available ciphertext, plus publicly available knowledge. This method of attack is called a **ciphertext-only attack**.

Full or Partial Plaintext

The analyst may be fortunate enough to have a sample message and its decipherment. For example, a diplomatic service may have intercepted an encrypted message, suspected to be the text of an official statement. If the official statement (in plaintext) is subsequently released, the interceptor has both C and P and only needs to deduce the E for which $C = E(P)$ to find D. In this case the analyst is attempting to find E (or D) using a **known plaintext attack**.

The analyst may have additional information, too. For example, the analyst may know that the message was intercepted from a diplomatic exchange between Germany and

Austria. From that information, the analyst may guess that the words Bonn, Vienna, and Chancellor appear in the message. Alternatively, the message may be a memorandum to the sales force from a corporate president, and the memo would have a particular form (To: Sales Force, From: The President, Date: ---, Subject: New Product Pricing Schedule).

In these cases, the analyst can use what is called a **probable plaintext analysis**. After doing part of the decryption, the analyst may find places where the known message fits with the deciphered parts, thereby giving more clues about the total translation.

After cryptanalysis has provided possible partial decipherments, a probable plaintext attack may permit a cryptanalyst to fill in some blanks. For example, letter frequencies may suggest a substitution for the most popular letters, but leave gaps such as *SA_ES _OR_E*. With a probable plaintext, the cryptanalyst can expect *SALES FORCE* to appear somewhere in the memo and could easily fill in these blanks.

Ciphertext of Any Plaintext

The analyst may have infiltrated the sender's process so as to be able to cause messages to be encrypted and sent at will. This attack is called a **chosen plaintext attack**. For instance, the analyst may be able to insert and delete records into a data base and observe the change in statistics after the insertions. Linear programming will sometimes enable such an analyst to infer data that should be kept confidential in the data base. Alternatively, an analyst may tap wires in a network and be able to notice the effect of sending a particular message to a particular user on the network. A chosen plaintext attack is very favorable to the analyst.

Algorithm and Ciphertext

Finally, the analyst may have available the encryption algorithm and the ciphertext. In a **chosen ciphertext attack**, the analyst can run the algorithm on massive amounts of plaintext in order to find one plaintext message that encrypts as the ciphertext. The purpose of a chosen ciphertext attack is to deduce the sender's encryption key in order to decrypt future messages by simply applying the sender's decryption key to intercepted ciphertext. This approach fails if two or more distinct keys can produce the same ciphertext as the result of encrypting (different) meaningful plaintext.

2.9   Summary of Basic Encryption

This chapter has examined the basic processes of encryption and cryptanalysis. The two basic methods of encipherment—substitution and transposition or permutation—have been introduced in this chapter. These methods will be used again in Chapter 3 in the study of other encryption methods.

Several cryptanalytic tools have also been introduced in this chapter. These tools include frequency distribution, digram (and trigram) study, index of coincidence, searching for repeated patterns, and study of probable letters. Five classic cryptanalytic attacks have been presented; these are the ciphertext-only, known plaintext, probable plaintext, chosen plaintext, and chosen ciphertext methods. Finally, the chapter has presented some of the formal material on cryptanalysis and cryptography, including notions of redundancy in a language and the unicity distance.

2.10 **Bibliographic Notes**

This chapter does not present much of the history of encryption. Because encryption has been used for military and diplomatic communications, many of the stories are fascinating. David Kahn's thorough study of encryption [KAH67] still stands as the masterpiece. Other interesting sources are the works by Friedman [FRI76a], [FRI76b], and [FRI76c]; [DEA85]; [BAM82]; and [YAR31].

The highly readable presentation of elementary cryptography by Sinkov [SIN66] is well worth study. A more precise and mathematical analysis is done by Konheim [KON80] and Meyer and Matyas [MEY82]. A description of the unicity distance can be found in [DEA77]. Many more simple encryption algorithms are presented in [FOS82]. Schneier's book [SCH96] gives a very up-to-date description of encryption systems.

2.11 **Terms and Concepts**

sender, 21
receiver, 21
transmission medium, 21
interceptor, 21
intruder, 21
encryption, 22
decryption, 22
encode, 22
decode, 22
encipher, 22
decipher, 22
cryptosyste, 22
plaintext, 22
ciphertext, 22
key, 22
symmetric encryption, 22
asymmetric encryption, 22
keyless cipher, 23
cryptography, 23
cryptanalyst, 23
cryptology, 23
break an encryption, 23
breakable encryption, 23
modular arithmetic, 25
substitution, 25
transposition, 25
monoalphabetic cipher, 25
simple substitution, 25
Caesar cipher, 25
permutation, 27
Vigenère tableau, 33

method of Kasiski, 35
index of coincidence, 37
measure of roughness, 37
one-time pad, 41
Vernam cipher, 41
linear congruential random
    number generator, 43
probable word attack, 44
transposition, 47
columnar transposition, 47
digram, 48
trigram, 48
double transposition, 51
product cipher, 52
fractionated Morse, 53
stream cipher, 55
block cipher, 55
confusion, 59
diffusion, 59
secure cryptographic system, 59
effectively secure encryption, 60
absolute rate, 61
rate, 61
redundancy, 61
unicity distance, 62
ciphertext-only attack, 63
known plaintext attack, 63
probable plaintext analysis, 64
chosen plaintext attack, 64
chosen ciphertext attack, 64

2.12 Exercises

The first several exercises ask you to decrypt a piece of ciphertext. Each of these is an English prose quotation. More important than the precise quotation is the *process* you use to analyze the encryption. Justify your answer by describing the various tests you performed and the results you obtained for those tests.

1. Decrypt the following encrypted quotation.

   ```
   fqjcb rwjwj vnjax bnkhj whxcq nawjv nfxdu
   mbvnu ujbbf nnc
   ```

2. Decrypt the following encrypted quotation.

   ```
   oczmz vmzor jocdi bnojv dhvod igdaz admno
   ojbzo rcvot jprvi oviyv aozmo cvooj ziejt
   dojig toczr dnzno jahvi fdiyv xcdzq zoczn
   zxjiy
   ```

3. Decrypt the following encrypted quotation.

   ```
   pbegu uymiq icuuf guuyi qguuy qcuiv fiqgu
   uyqcu qbeme vp
   ```

4. Decrypt the following encrypted quotation.

   ```
   jrgdg idxgq anngz gtgtt sitgj ranmn oeddi
   omnwj rajvk sexjm dxkmn wjrgm ttgdt gognj
   ajmzg ovgki nlaqg tjamn xmsmj jrgko jtgnw
   jrgnj rgvat tmgta wamno jjrgw izgtn sgnji
   babgu
   ```

5. Decrypt the following encrypted quotation.

   ```
   ejitp spawa qleji taiul rtwll rflrl laoat
   wsqqj atgac kthls iraoa twlpl qjatw jufrh
   lhuts qataq itats aittk stqfj cae
   ```

6. Decrypt the following encrypted quotation.

   ```
   auqrq rkrzd dmhxk ageho kfalu hkmog rlagm
   hznhf fhglm hkrlh mvzmr znvir klhgl vhodw
   krnra przgr jozdl vzkra gmvrw almka xomah
   gmvrf zbhka mtqho dwxre dzwmh mzcro imvra
   khqgz gwwri zkm
   ```

7. Decrypt the following encrypted quotation.

   ```
   jmjmj gsmsg lrjgu csqyj quflr mfajq erdmc
   cmqlv lqyhg gawgq arpgq sblce jrlrj lnemc
   cyjqu flrmf ajqer d
   ```

8. Decrypt the following encrypted quotation.

   ```
   vcwpc kwblm smljy glbgu gbtwj jyats lwsgm
   lwjjy vcrfc rikwl qjwte fscpw lbgqm jwscb
   ktpbc pqats vfwsm dvwpw lbsfc ktrfu wtlsc
   brpgk cmdqj wtefs cpgle vfmjc ncmnj cq
   ```

9. Decrypt the following encrypted quotation.

```
ptgpz ggprf bdkrg pequt tngtf ggpzf zfqgp
tukrw wkzfg kquyd qxwzu ltuet zfrfl ptgpz
ggprf bdkrg pequt dhmgw tgokr wwdtt bxqug
tuedq xequt fraty rdaur erfzg rqfot gjzfr
gorfa wrftd hdgqx rfyxz hwgdz fokpt utuzg
ptugp zfrfq hudtw jtdpt gpzgu tzydz fyluq
kdfqk rdtud hdcta gdfqg prdqk fytxr artfa
omhga qecwz rfdqx pzuyk quydz fyqmd ahutd
tfgtf atdzf yzdbd kpomq qbdzu tkurg gtfkp
rapaz ffqgm thfyt udgqq y
```

10. Decrypt the following encrypted quotation.

```
mszkx ijddj nzatm lrkdj mlwmc qrktj tnwir
zatnj bxdrj amlrs zxrzd dbjbk wsrir mlrxc .
icnic qrkza tmlrb cbriz mlkco mnizx r
```

11. Decrypt the following encrypted quotation.

```
gahzh zgaff irfcc fqgmx eefsp xmgab bxscy
gadgb afqbf dsfzh rvhqm xsgnq fxmgf qgafz
nsmfh gxmxn sxbqk faduh xnsbf jdvft nhcgp
xmxns yhzdz gfszg afznq gafjx xqdqy gafzg
dszdz hmbfb fsfuh ccdhq zkpqf rfzzh gpmxx
czkpa fdufq cprxj enczh xq
```

12. Decrypt the following encrypted quotation.

```
gasaz afxfk hqbzp zbqnq hfkqf zdfgr gsaaf
afdfz fzujz fhhxh irxxg rvnqp fhsdm cqbqx
cmfyx fxjgc qsdaz ggvfk mnfzp xqtga efndf
exhsd fmczu sggdf pfpzq xqxhc mgmmp gaxbr
afnfx bzsbj bnyfe xshsn smzfc cfduz yhzhh
gggcx axfcq dmsdi
```

13. What characteristics would make an encryption absolutely unbreakable? What characteristics would make an encryption impractical to break?

14. Does a substitution need to be a permutation of the plaintext symbols? Why or why not?

15. Why is it better to use a permutation that is not regular instead of a permutation that follows a pattern, such as $\pi(i) = i + 3$ or $\pi(i) = 5 * i \bmod 26$?

16. Suppose the rows of a Vigenère tableau have been scrambled. For example, row A might be *jklmno* . . . How could you determine the table of the six frequent letters (AEINOT)?

17. Explain why the index of coincidence decreases as the number of enciphering alphabets increases.

18. Explain why the index of coincidence for five alphabets is close to that for ten alphabets, which is close to that for many alphabets.

19. Suppose a six-symbol alphabet is used for encryption, and the relative frequencies of the six ciphertext symbols (denoted a, b, c, d, e, f) are 1/4, 1/4, 3/16, 1/8, 1/8, and 1/16, respectively. Compute the variance of this system. Compute the index of coincidence for this system.

20. Suppose a Kasiski analysis identifies the following pairs of repeated sequences: (10,34), (21,62), (37,109), (49,105), (58,162), (72,132). What can you conclude about the number of alphabets used to encrypt this message? Explain your answer.

21. Explain why $\text{Freq}_i * (\text{Freq}_i - 1)/n * (n - 1)$ is approximately Prob_i.

22. What is the plaintext message of Table 2-2? What encryption algorithm was used?

23. Explain why two substitution ciphers, applied one after another, may provide no more security than one substitution. (Such a cipher is called the product of the two underlying ciphers.)

24. Explain why the product of two relatively simple ciphers, such as a substitution and a transposition, can achieve a high degree of security.

25. What will be the value of the index of coincidence of the ciphertext of a transposition cipher applied to some English text?

26. In a particular language there are 12 letters. Two of these are used with relative frequency 3, four are used with relative frequency 2, and the remaining six are used with relative frequency 1. Compute the index of coincidence for monoalphabetic substitutions in this language.

3

Secure Encryption Systems

Chapter 2 introduced the concepts of encryption and cryptanalysis. The encryption methods described there were relatively simple because they were designed many years ago for use before the invention of computers. They are reasonably secure for short messages, for short periods of time, or for messages where the interceptor is not expected to want to work too hard to break the code. However, you should already have concluded that these methods are inappropriate for situations affecting national security, bank transfer operations involving large amounts of money, or other times when a high degree of security is important.

Cryptanalysts now have new tools for analyzing codes. Even such simple tasks as frequency counts are very tedious and error-prone by hand, but they are fast, simple, and reliable by computer. The computer has made a host of cryptanalytic approaches feasible that were effectively impossible in the past.

Fortunately, the same can be said of encryption. Previous algorithms had to be carried out exclusively by hand, which was both tedious and error-prone. Some algorithms were just too difficult to implement by hand. The next step was slow, awkward encryption machines, used in the first half of the twentieth century for military and diplomatic purposes. Now the computer has revolutionized the process of encryption within a relatively few years.

This chapter surveys three important encryption algorithms, which represent the state of the art of public encryption algorithms. All three of these algorithms require extensive computation. Interestingly, all three algorithms were presented about the same time: in the mid-1970s. Then we explore some very recent developments in cryptography.

The first algorithm, the Merkle–Hellman knapsack, is an example of a good method based on a solid foundation. Unfortunately, within a few years of its presentation, a way was found to break the algorithm. It still stands, however, as illustrative of a class of algorithms based on very difficult problems. The second algorithm, the Rivest–Shamir–Adelman (RSA) algorithm, appeared about the same time as the Merkle–Hellman algorithm, but to date it has withstood much cryptanalytic attack from the research community. RSA can be rather slow if implemented in software, although it has been implemented in hardware. The third algorithm, the Data Encryption Standard (DES), was designed with support from the U.S. National Institute of Standards and Technology (formerly National Bureau of Standards) in order to provide the public with a secure encryption method for use in commercial applications. Questions about the soundness of this algorithm have been raised since its introduction. Nevertheless, it is still appropriate for some applications.

In 1993 the U.S. government announced the Clipper program, which used a cryptographic algorithm suite known as Skipjack. The algorithm is kept secret, although it is expected to be widely used. The Skipjack algorithms feed into a new encryption concept called key escrow.

This chapter begins with a study of hard problems that can form the basis of secure encryption schemes. Following that discussion are a few mathematical concepts needed for the encryption schemes that follow. Three sophisticated schemes are presented and analyzed next. Then there are sections on three recent U.S. government–sponsored cryptographic developments. Finally, this chapter concludes with a survey of encryption algorithms in general and a discussion of where the field of encryption/cryptanalysis is likely to lead.[1]

3.1 "Hard" Problems: Complexity

The encryption algorithms described so far have been based on very simple problems: substituting characters, permuting their order, and performing relatively minor changes at the bit level. A disadvantage with these kinds of algorithms is that not very much work is involved with a "brute force" attack. (A **brute force attack** is one that tries all possible solutions.) For example, if the interceptor knows a single transposition was used, the interceptor might print all $n!$ permutations of an n-character message if the message is short enough. By scanning these, the interceptor can locate the one that looks right. Of course, this attack is feasible by hand only up to about five or six characters. The use of a computer increases the value of n for which a brute force attack is feasible.

We would like the interceptor to have to solve a hard problem, such as figuring out the *algorithm* that selected one of $n!$ permutations. In fact, however, the interceptor may simply generate all possible permutations and scan them visually (or with some computer

---

[1] *Note to the reader:* It is possible to study this chapter at two levels. For each of the three major encryption schemes presented—Merkle–Hellman, RSA, and DES—there is an introductory section describing the method in understandable terms but without all the detail of how the algorithm actually works. Some people who read this chapter need to know only the rudiments of each algorithm. These people may want to have background knowledge of current encryption practices, but they do not need a working ability. For these people the introduction to each algorithm may be adequate. Other people want a more detailed understanding of how these three schemes work. For example, these people may want to judge the suitability of the algorithm for a particular situation or to do further work in cryptanalysis of these or similar algorithms. These people should read the introductory sections and then study the detailed sections following. In this way, practitioners and researchers can both use this important material in whatever way suits their needs.

assistance), looking for probable text. Thus, the interceptor need not solve our hard problem (determine how one permutation of the $n!$ was chosen); the interceptor can solve the easier problem of determining which permutation was used *in this instance.*

> **Principle of Easiest Work:** We cannot expect the interceptor to choose the hard way to do something.

A recent trend in encryption has been to consider problems that are known to be hard to solve, and for which the number of possible solutions is large. Then, even with computer support, an exhaustive brute force solution is expected to be infeasible. Concurrent with this effort, there has been an analysis of the inherent complexity of problems. The goal is to say that not only is a *particular* solution (or algorithm) time-consuming, there simply isn't *any* easy solution. Substantial progress occurred in this area, not coincidentally, in the early 1970s. We begin our study of secure encryption systems by developing a foundation in problem complexity and some mathematical concepts we will need.

NP-Complete Problems

An important investigation of the complexity of problems explored what are called **NP-complete problems**, based on work by Cook [COO71] and Karp [KAR72]. We try to approach the notion of NP-complete problems intuitively, by studying three problems. Each of the problems is easy to state, not hard to understand, and straightforward to solve. Each also happens to be NP-complete. After the problems are displayed, we can develop the precise meaning of NP-completeness.

Satisfiability

The problem is to determine whether any given logical formula is satisfiable, that is, whether there is a way of assigning the values *TRUE* and *FALSE* to the variables so that the result of the formula is *TRUE*. Formally, the problem is presented as follows:

Given a formula

- composed of the variables $v_1, v_2, \ldots, v_n$ and their logical complements $\neg v_1, \neg v_2, \ldots, \neg v_n$
- represented as a series of clauses in which each clause is the logical *OR* ($\vee$) of variables and their logical complements
- expressed as the logical *AND* ($\wedge$) of the clauses

is there a way to assign values to the variables so that the value of the formula is *TRUE*? If there is such an assignment, the formula is said to be **satisfiable**.

For example, the formula

$$(v_1) \wedge (v_2 \vee v_3) \wedge (\neg v_3 \vee \neg v_1)$$

is satisfiable, whereas

$$(v_1) \wedge (v_2 \vee v_3) \wedge (\neg v_3 \vee \neg v_1) \wedge (\neg v_2)$$

is not. Both of these formulas are in the form prescribed.

Knapsack

The name of the problem relates to packing items into a knapsack. Is there a way to select some of the items to be packed such that their "sum" (the amount of space they take up) exactly equals the knapsack capacity (the target)? We can express the problem as a case of adding integers. Given a set of nonnegative integers and a target, is there a subset of the integers whose sum equals the target?

Formally, given a set $S = \{a_1, a_2, \ldots, a_n\}$ and a target sum T, where each $a_i \geq 0$, is there a selection vector, $V = [v_1, v_2, \ldots, v_n]$, each of whose elements is 0 or 1, such that

$$\sum_{i=1}^{n}(a_i * v_i) = T$$

(The selection vector records a 1 for each element chosen for the sum and a 0 for each not chosen.)

For example, the set S might be $\{4, 7, 1, 12, 10\}$. A solution exists for target sum $T = 17$, because $17 = 4 + 1 + 12$. The selection vector is $V = [1,0,1,1,0]$. No solution is possible for $T = 25$.

Clique

Given a graph G and an integer n, is there a subset of n vertices such that every vertex in the subset shares an edge with every other vertex in the subset? (A graph in which each vertex is connected to every other vertex is called a **clique**.)

Formally, we are given a graph $G = (V, E)$ where V is a set of vertices and $E \subseteq V \times V$ is the set of edges, and given a number $n > 0$. The problem is to determine whether there is a subset of n vertices, $V_S \subseteq V$, such that for each pair of vertices v_i, v_j in V_S, the edge (v_i, v_j) is in E.

As an example, consider Figure 3-1. Vertices (v_1, v_2, v_7, v_8) form a clique of size 4, but there are no cliques of 5 vertices.

Characteristics of NP-Complete Problems

The problems just listed are reasonable representatives of the class of NP-complete problems. Notice the following characteristics of these problems.

- Each problem *is* solvable, and a relatively *simple* approach solves it (although the approach may be time-consuming). For each of them, we can simply enumerate all the possibilities: all ways of assigning the logical values of n variables, all subsets of

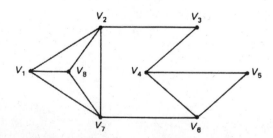

Figure 3-1   Clique Subgraphs in a Graph

the set S, all subsets of n vertices in G. If there is a solution, it will appear in the enumeration of all possibilities; if there is no solution, testing all possibilities will demonstrate that.

- There are 2^n cases to consider if we use the approach of enumerating all possibilities (where n depends on the problem). Each possibility can be tested in a relatively small amount of time, so the time to test all possibilities and answer *yes* or *no* is proportional to 2^n.

- The problems are apparently unrelated, having come from logic, number theory, and graph theory, respectively.

- If it were possible to guess perfectly, we could solve each problem in relatively little time. For example, if someone could guess the correct assignment or the correct subset, we could simply verify that the formula had been satisfied or a correct sum had been determined, or a clique had been identified. The verification process could be done in time bounded by a polynomial function of the size of the problem.

The Classes P and NP

Let **P** be the collection of all problems for which there is a solution that runs in time bounded by a polynomial function of the size of the problem. For example, you can determine whether an item is in a list in time proportional to the size of the list (simply by examining each element in the list to determine whether it is the correct one), and you can sort all items in a list into ascending order in time bounded by the square of the number of elements in the list (using, for example, the well-known bubble sort algorithm.) There may also be faster solutions; that is not important here. Both the searching problem and the sorting problem are in **P** because they can be solved in time n and n^2, respectively.

For most problems, **polynomial time algorithms** are about the limit of feasible complexity. Any problem that could be solved in time $n^{1,000,000,000}$ would be in **P**, even though for large values of n, the time to perform such an algorithm might be prohibitive. Notice also that we do not have to know an explicit algorithm, we just have to be able to say that such an algorithm exists.

By contrast, let **NP** be the set of all problems that can be solved in time bounded by a polynomial function of the size of the problem, *assuming the ability to guess perfectly*. (In the literature, this "guess function" is called an **oracle machine** or a **nondeterministic Turing machine**). This guessing is called **nondeterminism**.

Of course, no one can guess perfectly. Guessing is simulated by cloning an algorithm and applying one version of it to each possible outcome of the guess, as shown in Figure 3-2. Essentially, the idea is equivalent to a computer programming language in which IF statements could be replaced by GUESS statements: instead of testing a known condition and branching depending on the outcome of the test, the GUESS statements would cause the program to fork, following two or more paths concurrently.

The ability to guess can be useful. For example, instead of deciding whether to assign the value *TRUE* or *FALSE* to variable v_1, the nondeterministic algorithm can proceed in two directions: one assuming *TRUE* had been assigned to v_1, and the other assuming *FALSE*. As the number of variables increases so does the number of possible paths to be pursued concurrently.

Certainly every problem in **P** is also in **NP** because the guess function does not have to be invoked. There is also a class **EXP**, which consists of problems for which a deterministic

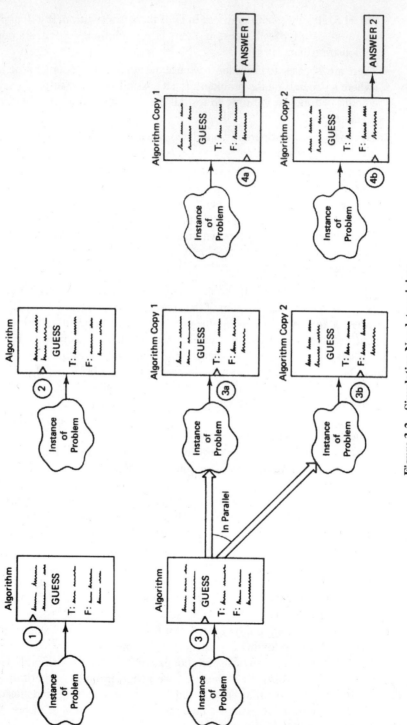

Figure 3-2   Simulating Nondeterminism

solution exists in exponential time, c^n for some constant c. As noted earlier, every NP-complete problem has such a solution. Every problem in **NP** is also in **EXP** so $\mathbf{P} \subseteq \mathbf{NP} \subseteq \mathbf{EXP}$.

The Meaning of NP-Completeness

Cook [COO71] showed that the satisfiability problem is **NP-complete**, meaning that it can represent the entire class **NP**. His important conclusion was that *if* there is a *deterministic*, polynomial time algorithm (one without guesses) for the satisfiability problem, then there is a deterministic, polynomial time algorithm for *every* problem in **NP**; that is, $\mathbf{P} = \mathbf{NP}$.

Karp [KAR72] extended Cook's result by identifying several other problems, all of which shared the property that if any *one* of them could be solved in a deterministic manner in polynomial time, then *all* of them could. The knapsack and clique problems were identified by Karp. The results of Cook and Karp included the converse: if for even *one* of these problems (or any NP-complete problem) it could be shown that there was *no* deterministic algorithm that ran in polynomial time, then no deterministic algorithm could exist for *any* of them.

Be careful to distinguish between a problem and an instance of a problem. An **instance** is a specific case: one formula, one specific graph, or one particular set S. Certain simple graphs or simple formulas may have solutions that are very easy and fast to identify. A **problem** is more general; it is the description of all instances of a given type. For example, the formal statements of the satisfiability, knapsack, and clique sections are statements of problems because they tell what each specific instance of that problem must look like. Solving a problem requires finding *one* general algorithm that will solve *every* instance of that problem.

Essentially the problem space (that is, the classification of all problems) looks like Figure 3-3. There are problems known to be solvable deterministically in polynomial time

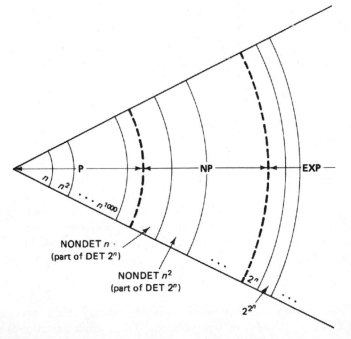

Figure 3-3 Hierarchies of Complexity Classes

(**P**), and there are problems known *not* to have a polynomial time solution (**EXP** and beyond), so that $\mathbf{P} \subseteq \mathbf{EXP}$ and $\mathbf{P} \neq \mathbf{EXP}$, meaning $\mathbf{P} \subset \mathbf{EXP}$. The class **NP** fits somewhere between **P** and **EXP**: $\mathbf{P} \subseteq \mathbf{NP} \subset \mathbf{EXP}$. It may be that $\mathbf{P} = \mathbf{NP}$, or that $\mathbf{P} \neq \mathbf{NP}$.

The significance of Cook's result is that NP-complete problems have been studied for a long time by many different groups of people: logicians, operations research specialists, electrical engineers, number theorists, operating systems specialists, and communications engineers. If there were a practical (polynomial time) solution to any one of these problems, you would hope that someone would have found it by now. Currently, several hundred problems have been identified as NP-complete. (Garey and Johnson [GAR79] catalog many NP-complete problems.) The more problems in the list, the stronger the reason to believe that there is no simple (polynomial time) solution to any (all) of them.

NP-Completeness and Cryptography

Hard-to-solve problems are fundamental to cryptography. Basing an encryption algorithm on one of these hard problems would seem to be a way to require the interceptor to do a prodigious amount of work to break the encryption. This line of reasoning has four fallacies.

- An NP-complete problem does not *guarantee* that there is *no* solution easier than exponential; it merely indicates that we are unlikely to find an easier solution. This distinction means that the basis of the difficulty to crack the encryption algorithm might deteriorate if someone should later show that $\mathbf{P} = \mathbf{NP}$. This is the least serious of the fallacies.
- Every NP-complete problem has a deterministic exponential time solution, that is, one that runs in time proportional to 2^n. For small values of n, 2^n is not large, and so the work of the interceptor using a brute force attack may not be prohibitive. You can get around this difficulty by selecting the algorithm so that the instance of the problem is very large, that is, if n is large, 2^n will be appropriately deterring.
- Continuing advances in hardware make problems of larger and larger size tractable. For example, parallel processing machines are now being designed with a finite but large number of processors running together. With a GUESS program, two processors could follow the paths from a GUESS point simultaneously. A large number of processors could complete certain nondeterministic programs in deterministic mode in polynomial time. However, we can select the problem's setting so that the value of n is large enough to require an unreasonable number of parallel processors. (What seems unreasonable now may become reasonable in the future, so we need to select n with plenty of room for growth.)
- Even if an encryption algorithm is based on a hard problem, the interceptor does not always have to solve the hard problem in order to crack the encryption. To be useful for encryption, these problems must have a secret, easy solution. An interceptor may look for the easy way instead of trying to solve a hard underlying problem. We will study an example of this type of exposure later with respect to the Merkle–Hellman knapsack algorithm.

Other Inherently Hard Problems

Another source of inherently difficult problems is number theory. These problems are appealing because they relate to numeric computation, so their implementation is natural on computers. Number theory problems appear as important tasks. Because these problems have been the subject of much research recently, the lack of easy solutions inspires confidence in their basic complexity. Although most of these number theory problems are not NP-complete, the known algorithms are very time-consuming.

Two such problems that form the basis for secure encryption systems are computation in Galois fields and factoring large numbers. In the next section we review some topics in algebra and number theory that will allow us to understand and use these problems.

3.2 Properties of Arithmetic

We begin with a study of properties of multiplication and division on integers. In particular, we investigate prime numbers, divisors, and factoring because these topics have major implications in the secure encryption algorithms. We also study a restricted arithmetic system, called a field. The fields we consider are finite and have convenient properties that make them very useful for representing cryptosystems.

Unless we explicitly state otherwise, in this section we consider only arithmetic on integers. Also, unless explicitly stated otherwise, we use conventional, not mod n arithmetic in this section.

Inverses

Let $\bullet$ be an operation on numbers. For example, $\bullet$ might be + or *. A number i is called an **identity** for $\bullet$ if $x \bullet i = x$ and $i \bullet x = x$ for every number x. For example, 0 is an identity for + because $x + 0 = x$ and $0 + x = x$. Similarly, 1 is an identity for *.

Let i be an identity for $\bullet$. The number b is called the **inverse** of a under $\bullet$ if $a \bullet b = i$. An identity holds for an entire operation; an inverse is specific to a single number. The identity element is always its own inverse because $i \bullet i = i$. The inverse of an element a is sometimes denoted a^{-1}.

Using the example of addition again, we observe that the inverse of any element a is $(-a)$ because $a + (-a) = 0$. When we consider the operation of multiplication on the rational numbers, the inverse of any element a (except 0) is $1/a$ because $a * (1/a) = 1$. However, under the operation of multiplication on the *integers*, there are no inverses (except 1). Consider, for example, the integer 2. There is no other integer b such that $2 * b = 1$. The positive integers under the operation + have no inverses, either.

Primes

To say that one number **divides** another, or that the second is **divisible by** the first, means that the remainder of dividing the second by the first is 0. Thus, we say that 2 divides 10 because $10/2 = 5$ with remainder 0. However, 3 does not divide 10 because $10/3 = 3$ with remainder 1. Also, the fact that 2 divides 10 does not necessarily mean that 10 divides 2; $2/10 = 0$ with remainder 2.

A **prime number** is any positive number that is divisible (with remainder 0) only by itself and 1.[2] For example, 2, 3, 5, 7, 11, and 13 are primes; 4 (2 * 2), 6 (2 * 3), 8 (2 * 2 * 2), and 9 (3 * 3) are not. A number that is not a prime is a **composite**.

---

[2] We disregard –1 as a factor because $(-1) * (-1) = 1$.

Greatest Common Divisor

The **greatest common divisor** of two numbers, a and b, is the largest integer that divides both a and b. The greatest common divisor is often written $gcd(a, b)$. For example, $gcd(15, 10) = 5$ because 5 divides both 10 and 15, and nothing larger than 5 does. If p is a prime, for any number $q < p$, $gcd(p, q) = 1$. Clearly, $gcd(a, b) = gcd(b, a)$.

Euclidean Algorithm

The **Euclidean algorithm** is a procedure for computing the gcd of two numbers. This algorithm exploits the fact that if x divides a and b, x also divides $a - (k * b)$ for every k. To understand why, suppose x divides both a and b; then $a = x * a_1$ and $b = x * b_1$. But

$$a - (k * b) = x * a_1 - (x * k * b_1)$$
$$= x * (a_1 - k * b_1)$$
$$= x * d$$

so that x divides (is a factor of) $a - (k * b)$.

This result leads to a simple algorithm for computing gcd. Suppose we want to find x, the gcd of a and b, where $a > b$. Rewrite a as

$$a = m * b + r$$

where $0 \leq r < b$. (In other words, compute $m = a/b$ with remainder r.) If $x = gcd(a,b)$, x divides a, x divides b, and x divides r. But $gcd(a, b) = gcd(b, r)$ and $a > b > r \geq 0$. Therefore, we can simplify the search for gcd, by working with b and r instead of a and b:

$$b = m' * r + r'$$

where $m' = b/r$ with remainder r'. This leads to a simple iterative algorithm, which terminates when a remainder 0 is found.

Example

For example, we will compute $gcd(3615807, 2763323)$.

$$3,615,807 = (1) * 2,763,323 + 852,484$$
$$2,763,323 = (3) * 852,484 + 205,871$$
$$852,484 = (4) * 205,871 + 29,000$$
$$205,871 = (7) * 29,000 + 2,871$$
$$29,000 = (10) * 2,871 + 290$$
$$2,871 = (9) * 290 + 261$$
$$290 = (1) * 261 + 29$$
$$261 = (9) * 29 + 0$$

Thus $gcd(3615807, 2763323) = 29$.

Modular Arithmetic

In Chapter 2, modular arithmetic was introduced as a way of confining results to a particular range; in that instance we wanted to perform some arithmetic operations on a plaintext character[3] and guarantee that the result would be another character. Modular arithmetic has the required property: results stay in the underlying range of numbers. An even more useful property is that the operations $+$, $-$, and $*$ can be applied before or after the modulus is taken, with similar results.

Recall that a modulus applied to a nonnegative integer means *remainder after division*, so that 11 mod 3 = 2 since 11/3 = 3 with remainder 2. If a mod $n = b$ then

$$a = c * n + b$$

for some integer c. Two different integers can have the same modulus: 11 mod 3 = 2 and 5 mod 3 = 2. Any two integers are **equivalent** under modulus n if their results mod n are equal. This is denoted

$$x \equiv_n y \quad \text{if and only if } (x \text{ mod } n) = (y \text{ mod } n)$$

Equivalently

$$x \equiv_n y \text{ if and only if } (x - y) = k * n \text{ for some } k$$

In the following sections, unless we use parentheses to indicate otherwise, a modulus applies to a complete expression. Thus you should interpret $a + b$ mod n as $(a + b)$ mod n, not $a + (b$ mod $n)$.

Properties of Modular Arithmetic

Modular arithmetic on the nonnegative integers forms a construct called a **commutative ring** with operations $+$ and $*$ (addition and multiplication). Furthermore, if every number other than 0 has an inverse under $*$, the group is called a **Galois field**. All rings have the properties of associativity and distributivity; commutative rings, as their name implies, also have commutativity. Inverses under multiplication produce a Galois field. The integers mod n are a Galois field. The properties of this arithmetic system are listed here.

Property	Example
Associativity	$a + (b + c)$ mod $n = (a + b) + c$ mod n
	$a * (b * c)$ mod $n = (a * b) * c$ mod n
Commutativity	$a + b$ mod $n = b + a$ mod n
	$a * b$ mod $n = b * a$ mod n
Distributivity	$a * (b + c)$ mod $n = ((a * b) + (a * c))$ mod n
Existence of identities	$a + 0$ mod $n = 0 + a$ mod $n = a$
	$a * 1$ mod $n = 1 * a$ mod $n = a$
Existence of inverses	$a + (-a)$ mod $n = 0$
	$a * (a^{-1})$ mod $n = 1$ if $a \neq 0$
Reducibility	$(a + b)$ mod $n = ((a \text{ mod } n) + (b \text{ mod } n))$ mod n
	$(a * b)$ mod $n = ((a \text{ mod } n) * (b \text{ mod } n))$ mod n

---

[3] Strictly speaking, these operations were on a numeric value associated with the character.

Example

As an example, consider the field of integers mod 5 shown here. These tables show one way of computing the sum or product of any two integers mod 5. However, the reducibility rule gives a method that you may find easier to use. To compute the sum or product of two integers mod 5, we compute the regular sum or product and then reduce this result by subtracting 5 until the result is between 0 and 4. Alternatively, we divide by 5 and keep only the remainder after division.

+	0	1	2	3	4
0	0	1	2	3	4
1	1	2	3	4	0
2	2	3	4	0	1
3	3	4	0	1	2
4	4	0	1	2	3

*	0	1	2	3	4
0	0	0	0	0	0
1	0	1	2	3	4
2	0	2	4	1	3
3	0	3	1	4	2
4	0	4	3	2	1

For example, let us compute 3 + 4 mod 5. Because 3 + 4 = 7 and 7 − 5 = 2, we can conclude that 3 + 4 mod 5 = 2. This fact is confirmed by the table. Similarly, to compute 4 * 4 mod 5, we compute 4 * 4 = 16. We can compute 16 − 5 = 11 − 5 = 6 − 5 = 1, or we can compute 16/5 = 3 with remainder 1. Either of these two approaches shows that 4 * 4 mod 5 = 1, as proven by the table. Because constructing the tables shown is difficult for large values of the modulus, the remainder technique is especially helpful.

Computing Inverses

In the ordinary system of multiplication on rational numbers, the inverse of any number a ($a \neq 0$) is $1/a$ because $a * (1/a) = 1$. Finding inverses is not quite so easy in the finite fields just described. In this section we find how to determine the multiplicative inverse of any element.

The inverse of any element a is the element b such that $a * b = 1$. The multiplicative inverse of a may be written a^{-1}. Looking at the table for multiplication mod 5, we find that the inverse of 1 is 1, the inverse of 2 is 3 and, because multiplication is commutative, the inverse of 3 is also 2; finally, the inverse of 4 is 4. These values came from inspection, not from any systematic algorithm.

To perform one of the secure encryptions, we need a procedure for finding the inverse mod n of any element, even for very large values of n. An algorithm to determine a^{-1} directly is likely to be faster than searching a table, especially for large values of n. Also, although there is a pattern to the elements in the table, it is not easy to generate the elements of a particular row, looking for a 1, each time we need an inverse. Fortunately there is an algorithm that is reasonably simple to compute.

Fermat's Theorem

In number theory, Fermat's theorem states that for any prime p and any element $a < p$,

$$a^p \bmod p = a$$

or

$$a^{p-1} \bmod p = 1$$

This result leads to the inverses we want. For a prime p and an element $a < p$, the inverse of a is the element x such that

$$ax \bmod p = 1$$

Combining the last two equations, we obtain

$$ax \bmod p = 1 = a^{p-1} \bmod p$$

so that

$$x = a^{p-2} \bmod p$$

This method is not a complete method for computing inverses in that it works only for a prime p and an element $a < p$.

Example

We can use this formula to determine the inverse of 3 mod 5:

$$
\begin{aligned}
3^{-1} \bmod 5 &= 3^{5-2} \bmod 5 \\
&= 3^3 \bmod 5 \\
&= 27 \bmod 5 \\
&= 2
\end{aligned}
$$

as we determined earlier from the multiplication table.

Algorithm for Computing Inverses

Another method to compute inverses is shown in the following algorithm. This algorithm, adapted from [KNU73], is a fast approach that uses Euclid's algorithm for finding the greatest common divisor.

$\{ ** \text{Compute } x = a^{-1} \bmod n \text{ given } a \text{ and } n ** \}$

$c_0 := n$

$c_1 := a$

$b_0 := 0$

$b_1 := 1$

$i := 1$

repeat

  $c_{i+1} := c_{i-1} \bmod c_i$

  $t := c_{i-1} \textbf{ div } c_i$

  $b_{i+1} := b_{i-1} - t * b_i$

  $i := i + 1$

until $c_i = 0$

if $(b_{i-1} \geq 0)$ **then** $a := b_{i-1}$ **else** $a := n + b_{i-1}$

We use these mathematical results in the next sections as we examine two encryption systems based on arithmetic in finite fields.

3.3 Public Key Encryption Systems

In 1976, Diffie and Hellman [DIF76] proposed a new kind of encryption system: with a public key encryption system, each user would have a key that did not have to be kept secret. The public nature of the key would not compromise the secrecy of the system. The public key transformation is essentially a one-way encryption with a secret (private) way to decrypt.

Motivation

Public key systems have an enormous advantage over the conventional key systems: anyone can send a secret message to a user, while the message remains adequately protected from being read by an interceptor. With a conventional key system, a separate key is needed for each pair of users.

A **channel** is a pathway for information flow; in a private environment, a channel is a pathway for information flow with protection against access by anyone outside the channel. Assume that three users, A, B, and C, want to set up communication channels in pairs: A and B want to be able to exchange information that C cannot interpret, A and C want to be able to exchange information concealed from B, and B and C want to be able to exchange information without its being available to A. To handle this situation, three keys are necessary; call these keys k_{AB}, k_{AC} and k_{BC}.

If we want to add a fourth user, D, and establish channels with the other three users, another three keys are needed: one to connect D to each of the existing users. Each time we add a new user to a system of n users, n additional keys are needed. Adding a sixth user is shown in Figure 3-4.

In general, an n-user system requires $n * (n - 1)/2$ keys. As the number of users grows, the number of keys increases very rapidly. Determining and distributing these keys is a problem; more serious is maintaining security for the keys already distributed, because we cannot expect users to memorize so many keys.

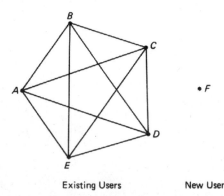
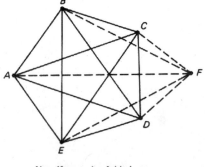

Existing Users   New User   New Keys to be Added — — — —

Figure 3-4   Creating New Private Channels

Characteristics

With a **public key** or **asymmetric encryption system**, each user has two keys: a public key and a private key. The user may publish the public key freely. The keys operate as inverses. Let k_{PRIV} be a user's private key, and let k_{PUB} be the corresponding public key. Then,

$$P = D(k_{PRIV}, E(k_{PUB}, P))$$

That is, a user can decode with a private key what someone else has encrypted with the corresponding public key. Furthermore, with the second public key encryption algorithm,

$$P = D(k_{PUB}, E(k_{PRIV}, P))$$

so that a user can encrypt a message with a private key, and the message can be revealed only with the corresponding public key. (We will study an application of this second case in the next chapter on digital signature protocols.)

These two properties imply that public and private keys can be applied in either order. Ideally, the decryption function D can be applied to any argument, so that we can decrypt first and then encrypt. With conventional encryption, one seldom thinks of decrypting *before* encrypting. With public keys, it simply means to apply the private transformation first, and then the public one.

With public keys, only two keys are needed per user: one public and one private. B, C, and D can all encrypt messages for A using A's public key. If B has encrypted a message using A's public key, C *cannot* decrypt it, even if C knew it was encrypted with A's public key. Applying A's public key twice, for example, would not decrypt the message. (We assume, of course, that A's private key remains secret.)

3.4 Merkle–Hellman Knapsacks

Merkle and Hellman [MER78b] developed an encryption algorithm based on the knapsack problem described earlier. The knapsack problem posed a set of positive integers and a target sum, with the goal of finding a subset of the integers that summed to the target. The knapsack problem is NP-complete, implying that to solve it probably requires time exponential to the size of the problem: in this case, the number of integers.

Introduction to Merkle–Hellman Knapsacks

This section contains an outline of the operation of the Merkle–Hellman knapsack encryption method.

The idea behind the Merkle–Hellman knapsack scheme is to encode a binary message as a solution to a knapsack problem, reducing the ciphertext to the target sum obtained by adding terms corresponding to 1s in the plaintext. That is, we convert blocks of plaintext to a knapsack sum by adding into the sum the terms that match with 1 bits in the plaintext, as shown in Figure 3-5.

A knapsack is represented as a vector of integer terms in which the order of the terms is very important. There are actually two knapsacks: an easy one, to which a fast (linear time) algorithm exists, and a hard one, derived by modifying the elements of the easy knapsack. The modification is such that a solution with the elements of either knapsack is a

Plaintext	1	0	1	0	0	1	
Knapsack	1	2	5	9	20	43	
Ciphertext	1		5			43	
Target Sum							49

Plaintext	0	1	1	0	1	0	
Knapsack	1	2	5	9	20	43	
Ciphertext		2	5		20		
Target Sum							27

Figure 3-5   Knapsack for Encryption

solution with the other one as well. This modification is a trapdoor, permitting legitimate users to solve the problem simply. Thus the general problem is NP-complete, but a restricted version of it has a very fast solution.

The algorithm begins with a knapsack set each of whose elements is larger than the sum of all previous elements. Suppose we have a sequence where each element a_k is larger than $a_1 + a_2 + \cdots + a_{k-1}$. If a sum is between a_k and a_{k+1}, it must contain a_k as a term, because no combination of the values $a_1, a_2, \ldots, a_{k-1}$ could produce a total as large as a_k. Similarly, if a sum is less than a_k, clearly it cannot contain a_k as a term.

The modification of the algorithm disguises the elements of the easy knapsack set by changing this increasing size property in a way that preserves the underlying solution. The modification is accomplished using multiplication by a constant mod n.

Detailed Explanation of the Merkle–Hellman Technique

In this section we explain the Merkle–Hellman technique in full detail. This section is intended for people who want a detailed understanding of the algorithm.

General Knapsacks

The knapsack problem examines a sequence $a_1, a_2, \ldots, a_n$ of integers and a target sum, T. The problem is to find a vector of 0s and 1s such that the sum of the integers associated with 1s equals T. That is, given $S = [a_1, a_2, \ldots, a_n]$, and T, find a vector V of 0s and 1s such that

$$\sum_{i=1}^{n} a_i * v_i = T$$

For example, consider the list of integers (17, 38, 73, 4, 11, 1) and the target number 53. The problem is to find which of the integers to select for the sum, that is, which should correspond with 1s in V. Clearly 73 cannot be a term, so we can ignore it. Trying 17, the problem reduces to finding a sum for $(53 - 17 = 36)$. With a second target of 36, 38 cannot contribute, and $4 + 11 + 1$ are not enough to make 36. We then conclude that 17 is not a term in the solution.

If 38 is in the solution, then the problem reduces to the new target $(53 - 38 = 15)$. With this target, a quick glance at the remaining values shows that 4 and 11 complete the solution because $4 + 11 = 15$. A solution is thus $38 + 4 + 11$.

This solution proceeded in an orderly manner. We considered each possible integer as contributing to the sum and reduced the problem correspondingly. When one solution did not produce the desired sum, we backed up, discarding recent guesses and trying alternatives. This backtracking seriously impaired the speed of solution.

With only six integers, it did not take long to determine the solution. Fortunately, we discarded one of the integers (73) immediately as too large, and in a subproblem we could dismiss another integer (38) immediately. With many integers, it would have been much more difficult to find a solution, especially if they were all of similar magnitude so that we could not dismiss any immediately.

Superincreasing Knapsacks

Suppose this problem has an additional restriction: the integers of S must form a **superincreasing sequence**, that is, one where each integer is greater than the sum of all preceding integers. Then, every integer a_k would be of the form

$$a_k > \sum_{j=1}^{k-1} a_j$$

In the previous example, [1,4,11,17,38,73] is a superincreasing sequence. If we restrict the knapsack problem to superincreasing sequences, we can easily tell whether a term is included in the sum. No combination of terms less than a particular term can yield a sum as large as the term. For instance, 17 is greater than $1 + 4 + 11$ (= 16). If a target sum is greater than or equal to 17, 17 or some larger term must be a term.

The solution of a **superincreasing knapsack** (also called a **simple knapsack**) is easy to find. Start with T. Compare the largest integer in S to it. If this integer is larger than T, it is not in the sum, so let the corresponding position in V be 0. If the largest integer is less than or equal to T, that integer is in the sum, so let the corresponding position in V be 1 and reduce T by the integer. Repeat for all remaining integers in S. An example solving a simple knapsack for targets 96 and 95 is shown in Figure 3-6.

The Encryption Technique

The Merkle–Hellman encryption technique is a public key cryptosystem. That is, each user has a public key, which can be distributed to anyone, and a private key, which is kept secret. The public key is the set of integers of a knapsack problem (*not* a superincreasing knapsack); the private key is a corresponding superincreasing knapsack. The contribution of Merkle and Hellman was the design of a technique for converting a superincreasing knapsack into a regular one. The trick is to change the numbers in a nonobvious but reversible way.

96:	73?	Yes		95:	73?	Yes	←
96 − 73 = 23:	38?	No		95 − 73 = 22:	38?	No	
23:	17?	Yes		22:	17?	Yes	←
23 − 17 = 6:	11?	No		22 − 17 = 5:	11?	No	
6:	4?	Yes		5:	4?	Yes	←
6 − 4 = 2:	1?	Yes		5 − 4 = 1:	1?	Yes	←
2 − 1 = 1:	No solution			1 − 1 = 0	Solution		

Figure 3-6   Example of Solving a Simple Knapsack

Principles of Modular Arithmetic

In normal arithmetic, adding to or multiplying a superincreasing sequence preserves its superincreasing nature, so that the result is still a superincreasing sequence. That is, if $a > b$ then $k * a > k * b$ for any positive integer k.

However, in arithmetic mod n the product of two large numbers may in fact be smaller than the product of two small numbers because results larger than n are reduced to between 0 and $n - 1$. Thus, the superincreasing property of a sequence may be destroyed by multiplication by a constant mod n.

Consider a system mod 11. The product $3 * 7$ mod $11 = 21$ mod $11 = 10$, whereas $3 * 8$ mod $11 = 24$ mod $11 = 2$. Even though $7 < 8$, $3 * 7$ mod $11 > 3 * 8$ mod 11. Multiplying a sequence of integers mod some base may destroy the superincreasing nature of the sequence.

Modular arithmetic is sensitive to common factors. If all products of all integers are mapped into the space of the integers mod n, clearly there will be some duplicates; that is, two different products can produce the same result mod n. If $w * x$ mod $n = r$ then $w * x + n$ mod $n = r$, $w * x + 2n$ mod $n = r$, and so on. Furthermore, if w and n have a factor in common, then not every integer between 0 and $n - 1$ will be a result of $w * x$ mod n for some x.

Look at the integers mod 5. If $w = 3$ and $x = 1, 2, 3, \ldots$, the multiplication of $x * w$ mod 5 produces all the results from 0 to 4, as shown in Table 3-1. Notice that after $x = 5$, the modular results repeat.

However, if we choose $w = 3$ and $n = 6$, not every integer between 0 and 5 is used. This occurs because w and n share the common factor 3. Table 3-2 shows the results of $3 * x$ mod 6. Thus, there may be some values that cannot be written as the product of two integers mod n for certain values of n. To produce all values between 0 and $n - 1$, n must be relatively prime to w.

If w and n are **relatively prime**, w has a multiplicative inverse mod n. That means that for every integer w, there is another integer w^{-1} such that $w * w^{-1} = 1$ mod n. A multiplicative inverse is a way of undoing the effect of multiplication: $(w * q) * w^{-1} = q$. (Remember that multiplication is commutative and associative in the group mod n so that $w * q * w^{-1} = (w * w^{-1}) * q = q$ mod n.)

With these results from modular arithmetic, Diffie and Hellman found a way to break the superincreasing nature of a sequence of integers. We can break the pattern by multiplying all integers by a constant w, and taking the result mod n where w and n are relatively prime.

Table 3-1	$3 * x$ mod 5	
x	$3 * x$	$3 * x$ mod 5
1	3	3
2	6	1
3	9	4
4	12	2
5	15	0
6	18	3
7	21	1

Table 3-2	$3 * x$ mod 6	
x	$3 * x$	$3 * x$ mod 6
1	3	3
2	6	0
3	9	3
4	12	0
5	15	3
6	18	0
7	21	3

Transforming a Superincreasing Knapsack

In order to perform an encryption using the Merkle–Hellman algorithm, we need a super-increasing knapsack that we can transform into a hard knapsack. In this section we learn just how to do that.

We begin by picking a superincreasing sequence S of m integers. Such a sequence is easy to find. Select an initial integer (probably a relatively small one). Choose the next integer to be larger than the first. Then select an integer larger than the sum of the first two. Continue this process by choosing new integers larger than the sum of all integers already selected.

For example,

Sequence	Sum so far	Next term
[1,		
[1,	1	2
[1,2,	$1 + 2 = 3$	4
[1, 2, 4,	$1 + 2 + 4 = 7$	9
[1, 2, 4, 9,	$1 + 2 + 4 + 9 = 16$	19

is such a sequence.

The superincreasing sequence just selected is called a **simple knapsack**. Any instance of the knapsack problem formed from that knapsack has a solution that is easy to find.

After selecting a simple knapsack $S = [s_1, s_2, \ldots, s_m]$, we choose a multiplier w and a modulus n. The modulus should be a number greater than the largest integer, s_m. The multiplier should have no common factors with the modulus. One easy way to guarantee this is to choose a modulus that is a prime number because no number smaller than it will have any common factors with it.

Finally, we replace every integer s_i in the simple knapsack with the term

$$h_i = w * s_i \bmod n$$

Then $H = [h_1, h_2, \ldots, h_m]$ is a hard knapsack. We will use both the hard and simple knapsacks in the encryption.

For example, start with the superincreasing knapsack $S = [1, 2, 4, 9]$ and transform it by multiplying by w and reducing mod n where $w = 15$ and $n = 17$.

$$1 * 15 = 15 \bmod 17 = 15$$
$$2 * 15 = 30 \bmod 17 = 13$$
$$4 * 15 = 60 \bmod 17 = 9$$
$$9 * 15 = 135 \bmod 17 = 16$$

The hard knapsack derived in this example is $H = [15, 13, 9, 16]$.

Example Using Merkle–Hellman Knapsacks

Now we show how to use Merkle–Hellman encryption on a plaintext message P. The encryption algorithm using Merkle–Hellman knapsacks starts with a binary message. The message is envisioned as a binary sequence $P = [p_1, p_2, \ldots, p_k]$. Divide the message into blocks of m bits, $P_0 = [p_1, p_2, \ldots, p_m]$, $P_1 = [p_{m+1}, \ldots, p_{2m}]$, and so forth. The value of m is the number of terms in the simple or hard knapsack.

The encipherment of message P is a sequence of targets, where each target is the sum of some of the terms of the hard knapsack H. The terms selected are those corresponding to 1 bits in P_i, so that P_i serves as a selection vector for the elements of H. Each term of the ciphertext is $P_i * H$, the target derived using block P_i as the selection vector.

Encrypting a Message

For this example, we use the knapsacks $S = [1, 2, 4, 9]$ and $H = [15, 13, 9, 16]$ obtained in the previous section. With those knapsacks, $w = 15$, $n = 17$, and $m = 4$. The public key (knapsack) is H, while S is kept secret.

The message

$$P = 0100101110100101$$

is encoded with the knapsack $H = [15, 13, 9, 16]$ as follows.

$$P = 0100 \ 1011 \ 1010 \ 0101$$

$$[0,1,0,0] * [15, 13, 9, 16] = 13$$
$$[1,0,1,1] * [15, 13, 9, 16] = 40$$
$$[1,0,1,0] * [15, 13, 9, 16] = 24$$
$$[0,1,0,1] * [15, 13, 9, 16] = 29$$

The message is encrypted as the integers 13, 40, 24, 29, using the public knapsack $H = [15, 13, 9, 16]$.

Decryption Algorithm

The legitimate recipient knows the simple knapsack and the values of w and n that transformed it to a hard public knapsack. The legitimate recipient determines the value w^{-1} so that $w * w^{-1} = 1 \bmod n$. In our example, $15^{-1} \bmod 17$ is 8 because $15 * 8 \bmod 17 = 120 \bmod 17 = (17 * 7) + 1 \bmod 17 = 1$.

Remember that H is the hard knapsack derived from the simple knapsack S. H is obtained from S by

$$H = w * S \bmod n$$

(This notation, in which a constant is multiplied by a sequence, should be interpreted as $h_i = w * s_i \bmod n$ for all i, $1 \le i \le m$.)

The ciphertext message produced by the encryption algorithm is

$$C = H * P = w * S * P \bmod n$$

To decipher, multiply C by w^{-1} because

$$w^{-1} * C = w^{-1} * H * P = w^{-1} * w * S * P = S * P \bmod n$$

To recover the plaintext message P, the legitimate recipient would solve the simple knapsack problem with knapsack S and target $w^{-1} * C_i$ for each ciphertext integer C_i. Because $w^{-1} * C_i = S * P \bmod n$, the solution for target $w^{-1} * C_i$ is plaintext block P_i, which is the message originally encrypted.

Example of Decryption

Let us continue our example, in which the underlying simple knapsack was $S = [1, 2, 4, 9]$, $w = 15$, and $n = 17$. The transmitted messages were 13, 40, 24, and 29.

To decipher, these messages are multiplied by 8 mod 17 because 8 is $15^{-1} \bmod 17$. Then we can easily solve the simple knapsacks, as shown here:

$$13 * 8 = 104 \bmod 17 = 2 = [0100]$$
$$40 * 8 = 320 \bmod 17 = 14 = [1011]$$
$$24 * 8 = 192 \bmod 17 = 5 = [1010]$$
$$29 * 8 = 232 \bmod 17 = 11 = [0101]$$

The recovered message is thus `0100101110100101`.

Cryptanalysis

In this example, because m is 4, we can readily determine the solution to the knapsack problem for 13, 40, 24, and 29. Longer knapsacks (larger values of m), which also imply larger values of the modulus n, are not so simple to solve.

Practical Implementation

Typically, you want to choose the value of n to be 100 to 200 binary digits long. If n is 200 bits long, the s_i are usually chosen to be about 2^{200} apart. That is, there are about 200 terms in the knapsacks, and each term of the simple knapsack is between 200 and 400 binary digits long. More precisely, s_0 is chosen so that

$$1 \quad \le s_0 < 2^{200}$$
$$2^{200} \le s_1 < 2^{201}$$
$$2^{201} \le s_2 < 2^{202}$$

and so on, so that there are approximately 2^{200} choices for each s_i.

You can use a sequence of random numbers to generate the simple knapsack just described. A sequence of m random numbers, $r_1, r_2, r_3, \ldots, r_m$ is generated. Each r_i must be between 0 and 2^{200}. Then each value s_i of the simple knapsack is determined as

$$s_i = 2^{200 + i - 1} + r_i$$

for $i = 1, 2, \ldots, m$.

With such large terms for S (and H), it is infeasible to try all possible values of s_i in order to infer S given H and C. Even assuming a machine could do one operation every microsecond, it would still take 10^{47} years to try every one of the 2^{200} choices for each s_i. A massively parallel machine with 1000 or even 1,000,000 parallel elements would not reduce this work factor enough to weaken the encryption.

Weaknesses of the Merkle–Hellman Encryption Algorithm

The Merkle–Hellman knapsack method seems secure. With appropriately large values for n and m, the chances of someone's being able to crack the method by brute force attack are slim.

However, an interceptor does not have to solve the basic knapsack problem in order to break the encryption because the encryption depends on specially selected instances of the problem. In 1980, Shamir found that if the value of the modulus n is known, it may be possible to determine the simple knapsack. The exact method is beyond the scope of this book, but the method of attack will be outlined. For more information, see the article of Shamir and Zippel [SHA80].

First, notice that because all elements of the hard knapsack are known, you can readily determine which elements correspond with which elements of the simple knapsack. Consider h_0 and h_1, the first two elements of a hard knapsack, corresponding to simple knapsack elements s_0 and s_1.

Let

$$\rho = h_0/h_1 \bmod n$$

Since $h_0 = w * s_0 \bmod n$ and $h_1 = w * s_1 \bmod n$, it is also true that

$$\rho = (w * s_0)/(w * s_1) = s_0/s_1 \bmod n$$

Given the ratio ρ, determine the sequence

$$\Delta = \rho \bmod n, 2 * \rho \bmod n, 3 * \rho \bmod n, \dots, k * \rho \bmod n, \dots, 2m * \rho \bmod n$$

For some k, k and s_1 cancel each other mod n; that is, $k * (1/s_1) = 1 \bmod n$. Then

$$k * \rho \bmod n = k * s_0 * 1/s_1 \bmod n = s_0 \bmod n = s_0$$

It is reasonable to expect that s_0 will be the smallest element of Δ. Once s_0 is known, determining w, then w^{-1} and each of the s_i, is not hard.

A more serious flaw was identified later by Shamir [SHA82]. The actual argument is also beyond the scope of this book, but again it can be sketched fairly briefly. The approach tries to deduce w and n from the h_i alone.

The approximate size of n can be deduced from the fact that it will be longer than any of the h_i because they have been reduced mod n; however, n will not be substantially longer than the longest h_i, because it is likely that the results after taking the modulus will be fairly evenly distributed between 1 and n.

Assume you are trying to guess w. You might iteratively try different candidate values $\omega = 1, 2, 3, \dots$ for w. The graph of $\omega * h_i \bmod n$ as a function of ω would increase steadily until a value of $\omega * h_i$ was greater than n. At that point, the graph of $\omega * h_i$ would be discontinuous and have a small value. The values of $\omega * h_i$ would then resume their steady increase as ω increased until $\omega * h_i$ exceeded n again. The graph would form a progression of jagged peaks, resembling the teeth of a saw. The slope of each "tooth" of the graph is h_i. (See Figure 3-7 for a graphical representation of this process.)

The correct value of $\omega = w$ occurs at one of the points of discontinuity of the graph of $\omega * h_i \bmod n$. This same pattern occurs for all values h_i: h_1, h_2, and so forth. Because ω is a discontinuity point of $\omega * h_i \bmod n$, it is also a discontinuity of $\omega * h_2 \bmod n$, of $\omega * h_3 \bmod n$,

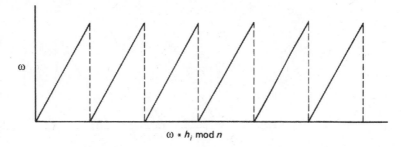

$\omega * h_i \bmod n$

Figure 3-7   Graph of Change of Merkle–Hellman Knapsack Function

and so forth. To determine ω, superimpose the graph of $\omega * h_1 \bmod n$ on $\omega * h_2 \bmod n$ and superimpose those graphs on $\omega * h_3 \bmod n$, and so on. Then w will be at one of the places where all of the curves are discontinuous and fall from a high value to a low one. Two such graphs are shown in Figure 3-8. The problem of determining w is thus reduced to finding the point where all of these discontinuities coincide.

The actual process is a little more difficult. The value of n has been replaced by real number N. Because n and N are unknown, the graphs are scaled by dividing by N, and then approximating by successive values of the real number ω/N in the function $(\omega/N) * h_i \bmod 1.0$. Fortunately, this reduces to the solution of a system of simultaneous linear inequalities. That problem can be solved in polynomial time. Therefore, the Merkle–Hellman knapsack problem can be broken in reasonable time.

Notice that this solution does not apply to the general knapsack problem; it applies only to the special class of knapsack problems derived from superincreasing sequences by multiplication by a constant modulo another constant. Thus, the basic knapsack problem is intact; only this restricted form has been solved. This result underscores the point that a cryptosystem based on a hard problem is not necessarily as hard to break as the underlying problem.

Since it has become known that the Merkle–Hellman knapsack can be broken, other workers have analyzed variations of Merkle–Hellman knapsacks. (See, for example, [BRI83] and [LAG83].) To date, transformed knapsacks do not seem secure enough for an application where a concerted attack can be expected. The Merkle–Hellman algorithm or a variation would suffice for certain low-risk applications. However, because the Merkle–Hellman method is fairly complicated to use, it is not often recommended.

3.5   Rivest–Shamir–Adelman (RSA) Encryption

Another cryptosystem based on an underlying hard problem is the RSA algorithm, named after its three inventors, Rivest, Shamir, and Adelman. This algorithm was introduced in 1978 and, to date, it remains secure. Like the Merkle–Hellman algorithm, RSA has been the subject of extensive cryptanalysis. No serious flaws have yet been found. Although the amount of analysis is no guarantee of the security of a method, it does suggest a confidence level.

Introduction to the RSA Algorithm

This section contains an overview of the RSA encryption scheme. On the surface the RSA algorithm is similar to the Merkle–Hellman method, in that solving the encryption amounts to finding terms that add to a particular sum or multiply to a particular product.

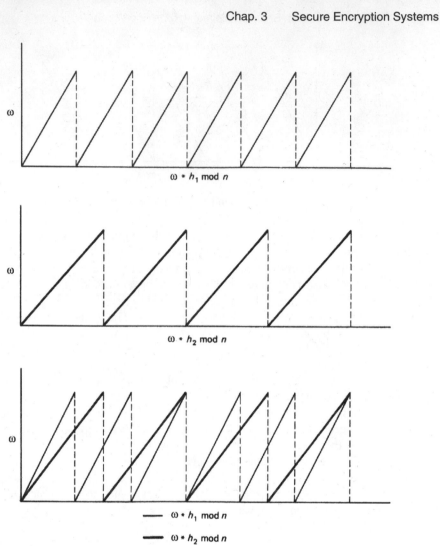

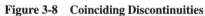

Figure 3-8   Coinciding Discontinuities

The RSA encryption algorithm incorporates results from number theory, combined with the difficulty of determining the prime factors of a target. The RSA algorithm also operates with arithmetic mod n.

Two keys, d and e, are used for decryption and encryption. They are actually interchangeable. (The keys for Merkle–Hellman were not interchangeable.) The plaintext block P is encrypted as P^e mod n. Because the exponentiation is performed mod n, factoring P^e to uncover the encrypted plaintext is difficult. However, the decrypting key d is carefully chosen so that $(P^e)^d$ mod $n = P$. Thus, the legitimate receiver who knows d simply computes $(P^e)^d$ mod $n = P$ and recovers P without having to factor P^e.

The encryption algorithm is based on the underlying problem of factoring large numbers. The factorization problem is not even known to be NP-complete; the fastest known algorithm is exponential in time.

Detailed Description of the Encryption Algorithm

In this section we present in detail the background and implementation of the RSA algorithm.

The RSA algorithm uses two keys, d and e, which work in pairs for decryption and encryption, respectively. A plaintext message P is encrypted to ciphertext C by

$$C = P^e \bmod n$$

The plaintext is recovered by

$$P = C^d \bmod n$$

Because of symmetry in modular arithmetic, encryption and decryption are mutual inverses and commutative. Therefore,

$$P = C^d \bmod n = (P^e)^d \bmod n = (P^d)^e \bmod n$$

This means that one can apply the encrypting transformation and then the decrypting one, or the decrypting one followed by the encrypting one.

Choosing Keys

The encryption key consists of the pair of integers (e, n), and the decryption key is (d, n). The starting point in finding keys for this algorithm is to select a value for n. The value of n should be quite large, a product of two primes p and q. Both p and q should be large themselves. Typically p and q are nearly 100 digits each, so that n is approximately 200 decimal digits (about 512 bits) long; depending on the application, 768, 1024, or more bits may be more appropriate. A large value of n effectively inhibits factoring n to infer p and q.

Next, a relatively large integer e is chosen so that e is relatively prime to $(p-1) * (q-1)$. (Recall that relatively prime means that e has no factors in common with $(p-1) * (q-1)$.) An easy way to guarantee that e is relatively prime to $(p-1) * (q-1)$ is to choose e as a prime that is larger than both $(p-1)$ and $(q-1)$.

Finally, select d such that

$$e * d \equiv 1 \bmod (p-1) * (q-1)$$

Mathematical Foundations of the RSA Algorithm

The Euler totient function $\varphi(n)$ is the number of positive integers less than n that are relatively prime to n. If p is prime, then

$$\varphi(p) = (p-1) \ .$$

Furthermore, if $n = p * q$, where p and q are both prime,

$$\varphi(n) = \varphi(p) * \varphi(q) = (p-1) * (q-1)$$

Euler and Fermat proved that

$$x^{\varphi(n)} \equiv 1 \bmod n$$

for any integer x if n and x are relatively prime.

Suppose we encrypt a plaintext message P by the RSA algorithm, so that $E(P) = P^e$. We need to be sure we can recover the message. The value e is selected so that we can easily find its inverse d. Because e and d are inverses mod $\varphi(n)$,

$$e * d \equiv 1 \bmod \varphi(n)$$

or

$$e * d = k * \varphi(n) + 1 \qquad\qquad (*)$$

for some integer k.

Because of the Euler/Fermat result,

$$P^{p-1} \equiv 1 \bmod p$$

and because $(p - 1)$ is a factor of $\varphi(n)$,

$$P^{k*\varphi(n)} \equiv 1 \bmod p$$

Multiplying by P produces

$$P^{k*\varphi(n)+1} \equiv P \bmod p$$

The same argument holds for q, so

$$P^{k*\varphi(n)+1} \equiv P \bmod q$$

Combining these last two results with $(*)$ produces

$$
\begin{aligned}
(P^e)^d = P^{e*d} \\
= P^{k*\varphi(n)+1} \\
= P \bmod p \\
= P \bmod q
\end{aligned}
$$

so that

$$(P^e)^d = P \bmod n$$

and e and d are inverse operations.

Example

Let $p = 11$ and $q = 13$, so that $n = p * q = 143$ and $\varphi(n) = (p - 1) * (q - 1) = 10 * 12 = 120$. Next, an integer e is needed, and e must be relatively prime to $(p - 1) * (q - 1)$. Choose $e = 11$.

The inverse of 11 mod 120 is also 11 because $11 * 11 = 121 = 1 \bmod 120$. Thus, both encryption and decryption keys are the same: $e = d = 11$. (For the example, $e = d$ is not a problem, but in a real application you would want to choose other values.)

Let P be a "message" to be encrypted. For this example we use $P = 7$. The message is encrypted as follows: $7^{11} \bmod 143 = 106$, so that $E(7) = 106$. (Note: This result can be computed fairly easily with the use of a common pocket calculator. $7^{11} = 7^9 * 7^2$. Then $7^9 =$ 40,353,607, but we do not have to work with figures that large. Because of the reducibility rule, $a * b \bmod n = (a \bmod n) * (b \bmod n) \bmod n$. Because we will reduce our final result mod 143, we can reduce any term, such as 7^9, which is 8 mod 143. Then, $8 * 7^2 \bmod 143 = 392 \bmod 143 = 106$.)

This answer is correct because $D(106) = 106^{11} \bmod 143 = 7$.

Practical Implementation of the Algorithm

The user of the RSA algorithm chooses primes p and q, from which the value $n = p * q$ is obtained. Next e is chosen to be relatively prime to $(p - 1) * (q - 1)$; e is usually a prime larger than $(p - 1)$ or $(q - 1)$. Finally, d is computed as the inverse of $e \bmod n$.

The user distributes e and n, and keeps d secret; p, q, and $\varphi(n)$ may be discarded (but not revealed) at this point. Notice that even though n is known to be the product of two primes, if they are relatively large (such as 100 digits long), it will not be feasible to determine the primes p and q or the private key d from e. Therefore, this scheme provides adequate security for d.

It is not even practical to verify that p and q themselves are primes because that would require considering on the order of 10^{50} possible factors. A heuristic algorithm from Solovay and Strassen [SOL77] can determine the probability of primality to any desired degree of confidence.

Every prime number passes two tests. If p is prime and r is any number less than p,

$$\gcd(p,r) = 1$$

(where gcd is the greatest common divisor function) and

$$J(r,p) \equiv r^{(p-1)/2} \bmod p$$

where $J(r,p)$ is the Jacobi function defined as follows.

$$J(r,p) = \begin{cases} 1 & \text{if } r = 1 \\ J(r/2) * (-1)^{(p^2-1)/8} & \text{if } r \text{ is even} \\ J(p \bmod r, r) * (-1)^{(r-1)*(p-1)/4} & \text{if } r \text{ is odd and } r \neq 1 \end{cases}$$

If a number is suspected to be prime but fails either of these tests, it is definitely *not* a prime. If a number is suspected to be a prime and passes both of these tests, the likelihood that it is prime is at least 1/2.

The problem relative to the RSA algorithm is to find two large primes p and q. With the Solovay and Strassen approach, you first guess a large candidate prime p. You then generate a random number r and compute $\gcd(p,r)$ and $J(r, p)$. If either of these tests fails, p was not a prime, and you stop the procedure. If both pass, the likelihood that p was not prime is at most 1/2. The process repeats with a new value for r chosen at random. If this second r passes, the likelihood that a nonprime p could pass both tests is at most 1/4. In general, after repeating the process k times without either test failing, the likelihood that p is not a prime is at most $1/2^k$.

Zimmerman [ZIM86] gives a method for computing RSA encryptions efficiently.

Cryptanalysis of the RSA Method

Like the Merkle–Hellman knapsack algorithm, the RSA method has been scrutinized intensely by professionals in computer security and cryptanalysis. Several minor problems have been identified with it, but there have been no flaws as serious as those for the Merkle–Hellman method.

3.6   El Gamal and Digital Signature Algorithms

Another public key algorithm was devised in 1984 by El Gamal [ELG84, ELG85]. Although this algorithm is not widely used directly, it is of considerable importance in the U.S. Digital Signature Standard (DSS) [NIS91a, NIS92b, NIS94] of the National Institute of Standards and Technology (NIST). This algorithm relies on the difficulty of computing discrete logarithms over finite fields. Because it is based on arithmetic in finite fields, as is RSA, it bears some similarity to RSA.

Digital signatures are discussed more fully in the following chapter. For now, it suffices to know that a digital signature is, like a handwritten signature, a means of associating a mark unique to an individual with a body of text. The mark should be unforgeable, meaning that only the originator should be able to compute the signature value. But the mark should be verifiable, meaning that others should be able to check that the signature does come from the originator. The general way of computing digital signatures is with public key encryption, such that the signer computes a signature value using a private key, and others can use the public key to verify that the signature came from the corresponding private key.

El Gamal Algorithm

In the El Gamal algorithm, to generate a key pair, first choose a prime p and two integers, a and x, such that $a < p$ and $x < p$ and calculate $y = a^x \bmod p$. The prime p should be chosen so that $(p - 1)$ has a large prime factor, q. The private key is x and the public key is y, along with parameters p and a.

To sign a message m, choose a random integer k, $0 < k < p - 1$, which has not been used before, and which is relatively prime to $(p - 1)$ and compute

$$r = a^k \bmod p$$

and

$$s = k^{-1} (m - xr) \bmod (p - 1)$$

where k^{-1} is the multiplicative inverse of $k \bmod (p - 1)$, so that $k * k^{-1} = 1 \bmod (p - 1)$. The message signature is then r and s. A recipient can use the public key y to compute $y^r r^s \bmod p$ and determine that it is equivalent to $a^m \bmod p$. To defeat this encryption and infer the values of x and k given r, s, and m, the intruder could find a means of computing a discrete logarithm to solve $y = a^x$ and $r = a^k$.

Digital Signature Algorithm

The U.S. Digital Signature Algorithm (DSA) [NIS94] is the El Gamal algorithm with a few restrictions. First, the size of p is specifically fixed at $2^{511} < p < 2^{512}$ (so that p is roughly 170 decimal digits long). Second, q, the large prime factor of $(p - 1)$ is chosen so that $2^{159} < p <$

2^{160}. The algorithm explicitly uses $H(m)$ a hash value (as described in the next section), instead of the full message text m. Finally, the computations of r and s are taken mod q. Largely, one can argue that these changes make the algorithm easy to use for those who do not want or need to understand the underlying mathematics. However, they also limit the potential strength of the encryption by reducing the uncertainty for the attacker.

3.7   Hash Algorithms

A **hash algorithm** is a check that protects data against most modification. If you want to protect data against undetected modification, you compute the hash algorithm result of the data. Later, you or someone else can compute the hash algorithm result again and compare the two results. If the two results are different, a change has certainly occurred to the underlying data; if the results are the same, it is likely (although not certain) that no change has occurred.

Hash functions produce a reduced form of a body of data such that most changes to the data will also change the reduced form. This result is sometimes called a **digest** or **check value**. Hash functions are covered more completely in the next chapter. However, one important one is based on a cryptographic algorithm, and also relates to the Digital Signature Standard, so it will be presented here.

Description of Hash Algorithms

A simple example of a hash function is the exclusive or of all bits in the body of data. This function reduces the data to a single bit. But with only one bit of result, you would expect that half of all data sets produce a hash value of 0 and half of 1. Therefore, any change to the data would have only a likelihood of 0.5 of changing the hash value.

By contrast, if the data consists of 8-bit bytes, and the hash function is to compute the exclusive or of all bytes, there are 2^8 or 256 possible different hash values. Therefore, any change to the data would have a likelihood of $1/256 \cong 0.003906$ of *not* causing a change to the hash value. A hash function reduces a large amount of data to a smaller result, called a **digest**. In general, the smaller the digest, the more data values have to map to each digest value, and the greater the likelihood that changes to data will *not* produce a change to the digest. For this reason, digests tend to be small, but not extremely small, often between 100 and 1000 bits.

Both of these hash algorithms are easy to invert; that is, an attacker could easily determine what would be the result of a change. If these algorithms were used as hash algorithms, an attacker could easily determine how to modify the underlying data without affecting the hash value.

A **cryptographic hash function** uses a cryptographic function as part of the hash function. With a cryptographic hash function, the sender can compute the hash value of a block of data to be communicated and send both the data and the hash value in the communication. A legitimate recipient would also have access to the cryptographic function and would compute the hash value of the received data. An intruder would presumably not have access to the cryptographic function. The intruder could modify data or the hash value or both but, without knowing the (cryptographic) relationship between the data and the hash value, the intruder would be unlikely to be able to modify both in such a way that they matched. Thus, modifications could be detected at the recipient's end, with a probability depending on the strength of the cryptographic algorithm and on the degree to which the data was reduced.

Secure Hash Algorithm

In addition to providing a standard for digital signatures, NIST produced a standard hash algorithm. This algorithm, called the **Secure Hash Algorithm** (SHA) [NIS92a, NIS93, NIS95], was designed by the U.S. National Security Agency (NSA) to work with the Digital Signature Algorithm. The algorithm takes as input data of length less than 2^{64} bits, which it reduces to a 160-bit digest.

The symbol $\oplus$ means logical exclusive or, $\vee$ means logical or, $\wedge$ means logical and, and $\neg$ means logical not. The function $S(n,v)$ means v shifted left n positions circular (meaning that each bit is moved n positions to the left, toward the most significant bit, and each bit cycled out of the most significant bit position circles around to the least significant bit position). All addition is performed mod 2^{32}.

First the message is padded with a 1, 0s to fill, and a 64-bit value for the number of bits in the original message, so that the combined length of the message, the 1, any 0s, and the 64-bit length is a multiple of 512 bits.

The message is processed in blocks of 16 32-bit words, denoted W(0), W(1), W(2), ... W(15), where W(0) is the leftmost word. Each block is expanded from 16 words to 80 words by $W(t) := W(t-3) \oplus W(t-8) \oplus W(t-14) \oplus W(t-16)$ for $t := 16$ to 79. Five constants are initialized: H0 := 67452301, H1 := EFCDAB89, H2 := 98BADCFE, H3 := 10325476, and H4 := C3D2E1F0 (expressed in hexadecimal notation). The algorithm is shown in Figure 3-9.

After completion of processing the last 16-word block, the 160-bit digest is the five words H0 H1 H2 H3 H4.

This algorithm shows diffusion, the process of spreading the effect of a single plaintext bit throughout the ciphertext. For example, in the initial expansion of 16 words to 80, a change in word 14 directly affects words 17, 22, 28, and 30, but a change in word 17 affects words 20, 25, 31, and 33, a change in word 22 affects words 25, 30, 36, and 41, and so forth; the single-bit change in word 14 affects words 17, 20, 22, 25, 28, 30, 31, 33, 34, 36, 37, 39, 41, 42, 44, 45, 47, 48, 49, and so forth. Then in the 80 steps of the algorithm, each W(I) affects TEMP, which affects A, B, C, D, and E, which affect each of H0 through H4, which becomes the final result. (This compounding effect of a bit change is known as the avalanche effect.)

The secure hash algorithm is a variant of the **MD4** (Message Digest algorithm number 4) designed by Rivest [RIV91, RIV92a], of which **MD5**, also designed by Rivest [RIV92b], is also a variant. MD4 is, in the author's words, "designed to be exceptionally fast [and] 'at the edge' in terms of risking successful cryptanalytic attack." MD5 is described as "back[ing] off a bit, giving up a little in speed for a much greater likelihood of ultimate security." Both MD4 and MD5 operate on a 16-word block. Neither has an expansion of 16 words to 80, as does SHA. MD4 uses 48 steps divided into three rounds (where a round is 16 similar operations like the 20 operations of I := 0 to 19, I := 20 to 39, and so forth of SHA); MD5 uses 64 steps in four rounds and SHA uses 80 steps in four rounds. MD4 uses four pattern constants, like constants H0 to H4 of SHA, where there is a pattern to the hex digits of each constant; MD5 uses the same pattern constants, but also adds a pseudo-random constant derived from the trigonometric sine of the number of the step. MD4 and MD5 both produce a 128-bit digest; the digest for SHA is 160 bits.

```
for each 16-word block begin
    A := H0; B := H1; C := H2; D := H3; E := H4
    for I := 0 to 19 begin
        TEMP := S(5,A) + ((B ∧ C) ∨ (¬ B ∧ D)) + E + W(I) + 5A827999;
        E := D; D := C; C := S(30,B); B := A; A := TEMP
    end
    for I := 20 to 39 begin
        TEMP := S(5,A) + (B ⊕ C ⊕ D) + E + W(I) + 6ED9EBA1;
        E := D; D := C; C := S(30,B); B := A; A := TEMP
    end
    for I := 40 to 59 begin
        TEMP := S(5,A) + ((B ∧ C) ∨ (B ∧ D) ∨ (C ∧ D)) + E + W(I) + 8F1BBCDC;
        E := D; D := C; C := S(30,B); B := A; A := TEMP
    end
    for I := 60 to 79 begin
        TEMP := S(5,A) + (B ⊕ C ⊕ D) + E + W(I) + CA62C1D6;
        E := D; D := C; C := S(30,B); B := A; A := TEMP
    end
    H0 := H0+A; H1 := H1+B; H2 := H2+C; H3 := H3+D; H4 := H4+E
end
```

Figure 3-9   Secure Hash Algorithm

All three of these algorithms are based on nonlinear functions that interweave bits in complex ways, which have traditionally been difficult to invert. Unfortunately, these kinds of transformations do not lend themselves to proofs of security, only to demonstrations of insecurity. MD4 seems, as its author says, to be a careful balance between high security and computational efficiency. Cryptanalysts were able to attack some, but not all, rounds of MD4. In response to these attacks, Rivest introduced MD5. A collision attack has been shown for MD5 [BOE93], but so far that attack does not significantly weaken the algorithm for general use. The longer digest size of SHA over MD4 and MD5 reduces the number of collisions.

3.8   Secure Secret Key (Symmetric) Systems

The Merkle–Hellman and RSA algorithms are both public key or asymmetric algorithms. They provide users with two keys, one for encryption and another for decryption, so that one key can be made available to anyone wishing to send encrypted information, and the other key—which is kept secret—is the only key that can decrypt that information.

The algorithms presented in the last chapter were all **single key** or conventional encryption algorithms, in which both the encryptor and the decryptor use the same key, which must be kept secret. Single key systems are called **secret key** or **symmetric encryption systems**, or sometimes **private key** systems. Because of the possibility of confusing that term with the private key of a public key system, we will use **secret key** or **symmetric** throughout this book.

Advantages and Disadvantages

The symmetric systems provide a two-way channel to their users: A and B share a secret key, and they can both encrypt information to send to the other as well as decrypt information from the other. The symmetry of this situation is a major advantage.

As long as the key remains secret, the system also provides **authentication**, proof that a message received was not fabricated by someone other than the declared sender. Authenticity is ensured because only the legitimate sender can produce a message that will decrypt properly with the shared key.

Problems of Symmetric Key Systems

Symmetric key systems have several difficulties.

- With all key systems, if the key is revealed (stolen, guessed, bought, or otherwise compromised), the interceptors can immediately decrypt all encrypted information they have available. Furthermore, an impostor using an intercepted key can produce bogus messages under the guise of a legitimate sender. For this reason, in secure encryption systems, the keys are changed fairly frequently so that a compromised key will reveal only a limited amount of information.

- Distribution of keys becomes a problem. Keys must be transmitted with utmost security because they allow access to all information encrypted under them. For applications that extend throughout the world, this can be a complex task. Often couriers are used to distribute the keys securely by hand. Another approach is to distribute the keys in pieces under separate channels, so that any one discovery will not produce a full key. (The Clipper program uses a 2-piece key distribution.) This approach is shown in Figure 3-10.

- As described earlier, the number of keys increases with the square of the number of people exchanging secret information. This problem is usually contained by having only a few people exchange secrets directly so that the network of interchanges is relatively small. If people in separate networks need to exchange secrets, they may do so through a central clearinghouse or forwarding office, which accepts secrets from one person, decrypts them, reencrypts them using another person's secret key, and transmits them. This technique is shown in Figure 3-11.

- The symmetric key encryption systems described in Chapter 2 have been relatively weak, vulnerable to various cryptanalytic attacks. Both the Merkle–Hellman and the RSA algorithms are based on much more complex problems, problems that have interested mathematicians for years. A secure symmetric key system must be based on an equally solid approach.

3.9   The Data Encryption Standard (DES)

The **Data Encryption Standard** (DES) [NBS77] is a system developed for the U.S. government for use by the general public. It has been officially accepted as a cryptographic standard both in the United States and abroad. Many hardware and software systems have been designed using the DES. However, recently its adequacy has been questioned.

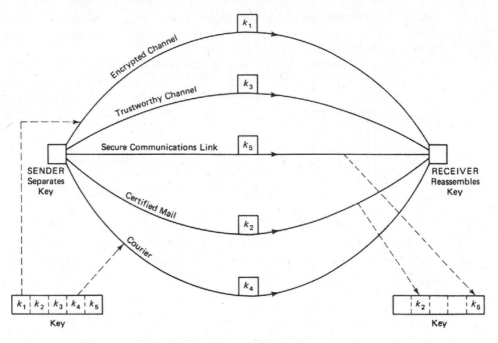

Figure 3-10 Key Distribution in Pieces

Background and History

In the early 1970s, the U.S. National Bureau of Standards (NBS) recognized the need for a secure encryption technique that the public could use for sensitive information. The U.S. Department of Defense and Department of State had continuing interest in encryption systems and had perhaps the greatest expertise in cryptology. However, precisely because of the nature of the information they were encrypting, they could not release any of their work.

Several private vendors had developed encryption devices, using either mechanical means or programs that individuals or firms could buy to protect their sensitive communi-

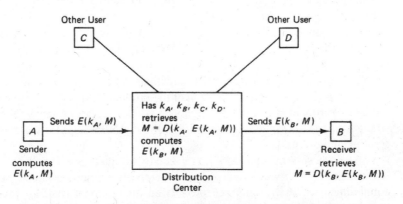

Figure 3-11   Distribution Center for Encrypted Information

cations. The difficulty with this proliferation was one of exchange: two users with different devices could not exchange encrypted information. Furthermore, there was no independent body capable of extensive testing of these devices.

Standardization of encryption was needed to promote the ability of unrelated parties to exchange encrypted information and to provide a single encryption system that could be rigorously tested and publicly certified. In 1972 the NBS issued a call for proposals for a public encryption algorithm. The call specified desirable criteria for such an algorithm.

- It must provide a high level of security.
- It must be completely specified and easy to understand.
- The algorithm itself must provide the security; the security should not depend on the secrecy of the algorithm.
- It must be available to all users.
- It must be adaptable for use in diverse applications.
- It must be economical to implement in electronic devices.
- It must be efficient to use.
- It must be able to be validated.
- It must be exportable.

Clearly, the NBS envisioned providing the encryption as a separate hardware device. The NBS also wanted to be able to reveal the algorithm itself, basing the security of the system on the keys (which would be under the control of the users).

Response to the call was not promising, so the NBS issued a second call in August 1974. The idea judged the most promising was the **Lucifer** algorithm on which IBM had been working for several years. This idea had been published earlier, so the basic algorithm was public and open to scrutiny and validation. Although lengthy, the algorithm was straightforward, a natural candidate for iterative implementation in a computer program. Furthermore, unlike the Merkle–Hellman and RSA algorithms, which use arithmetic on 100-or 200-digit binary numbers (far larger than most machine instructions would handle as a single quantity), Lucifer used only simple logical operations on relatively small quantities. Thus, the algorithm could be implemented fairly efficiently in either hardware or software on conventional computers.

A data encryption algorithm based on Lucifer was developed by IBM for the NBS; this algorithm became known as the DES (Data Encryption Standard), although its proper name is DEA (Data Encryption Algorithm) in the U.S. and DEA1 (Data Encryption Algorithm-1) in other countries. The NBS negotiated with IBM to determine a fair compensation for public release and distribution of the product IBM had developed. The NBS called on the Department of Defense through its National Security Agency (NSA) to analyze the strength of the encryption algorithm. Finally, the NBS released the algorithm for public scrutiny and discussion.

After these steps, the DES was officially adopted as a U.S. federal standard on 23 November 1976. It was authorized for use on all public and private sector unclassified communication. It was later accepted as an international standard by the International Standards Organization.

Overview of the DES Algorithm

The DES algorithm is a careful and complex combination of two of the fundamental building blocks of encryption: substitution and permutation (transposition). The algorithm derives its strength from repeated application of these two techniques, one on top of the other, for a total of 16 cycles. The sheer complexity of tracing a single bit through 16 iterations of substitutions and permutations has so far stopped researchers in the public from identifying more than a handful of general properties of the algorithm.

Plaintext is encrypted as blocks of 64 bits. Although the key is 64 bits long, in effect the key can be any 56-bit number. The user can change the key at will any time security of the old key may be uncertain.

The algorithm is derived from two concepts of Shannon's theory of information secrecy, published in 1949 ([SHA49]). Shannon identified two techniques to conceal information: confusion and diffusion. Recall from Chapter 2 that in **confusion** a piece of information is changed, so that the output bits have no obvious relationship to the input bits. **Diffusion** attempts to spread the effect of one plaintext bit to other bits in the ciphertext.

The two ciphers of the DES are substitutions and permutations. The substitutions, just like the substitutions of Chapter 2, provide confusion by systematically substituting some bit patterns for others. The transpositions, called **permutations** in the DES, provide diffusion, as did the transposition ciphers of Chapter 2, by reordering the bits. Plaintext is affected by a series of cycles of a substitution then a permutation. The iterative substitutions and permutations are performed as outlined in Figure 3-12.

The algorithm uses only standard arithmetic and logical operations on up to 64-bit numbers, so it is suitable for implementation in software on most current computers. Although complex, the algorithm is repetitive, making it suitable for implementation on a single-purpose chip. In fact, several such chips are available on the market for use as basic components in devices that use DES encryption in an application.

Details of the Encryption Algorithm

The basis of Lucifer and of the DES is two different ciphers, applied alternately. Shannon noted that two weak but complementary ciphers can be made more secure by applying them together, called the "product" of the two ciphers, alternately, in a structure called a **product cipher**. The product of two ciphers is depicted in Figure 3-13.

After initialization the DES algorithm operates on blocks of data. It splits a data block in half, scrambles each half independently, combines the key with one half, and swaps the two halves. This process is repeated 16 times. It is an iterative algorithm using just table lookups and simple bit operations. Although the bit-level manipulations of the algorithm are quite complex, the algorithm itself can be implemented quite efficiently. The rest of this section identifies the individual steps of the algorithm. In the next section each step is described in full detail.

Input to the DES is divided into blocks of 64 bits. The 64 data bits are permuted by a so-called initial permutation. The data bits are transformed using a 64-bit key (of which only 56 bits are used.) The key is reduced from 64 bits to 56 bits by dropping bits 8, 16, 24, . . . 64 (where the most significant bit is named bit 1). These bits are assumed to be parity bits that carry no information in the key.

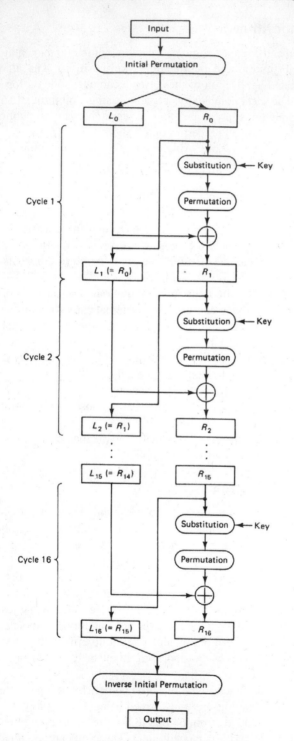

Figure 3-12   Cycles of Substitution and Permutation

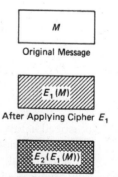

Figure 3-13   Product Ciphers

Next begins the sequence of operations known as a **cycle**. The 64 permuted data bits are broken into a **left half** and a **right half** of 32 bits each. The key is shifted left by a number of bits and permuted. The key is combined with the right half, which is then combined with the left half. The result of these combinations becomes the new right half; the old right half becomes the new left half. This sequence of activities, which constitutes a cycle, is shown in Figure 3-14. The cycles are repeated 16 times. After the last cycle there is a final permutation, which is the inverse of the initial permutation.

In order to combine a 32-bit right half with a 56-bit key, two changes are needed. First, the 32-bit half is expanded to 48 bits by repeating certain bits, while the 56-bit key is reduced to 48 bits by choosing only certain bits. These last two operations, called **expansion permutations** and **permuted choices**, are shown in the diagram of Figure 3-15.

Details of Each Cycle of the Algorithm

Each cycle of the algorithm is really four separate operations. First a right half is expanded from 32 bits to 48. Then it is combined with a form of the key. The result of this operation is then substituted for another result and condensed to 32 bits at the same time. The 32 bits are permuted, and then combined with the left half to yield a new right half. This whole process is shown in Figure 3-16.

Expansion Permutation

Each right half is expanded from 32 to 48 bits by means of the expansion permutation. The expansion permutes the order of the bits and also repeats certain bits. The expansion has two purposes: to make the intermediate halves of the ciphertext comparable in size to the key, and to provide a longer result that can later be compressed.

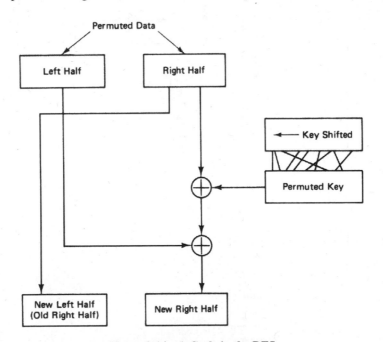

Figure 3-14   A Cycle in the DES

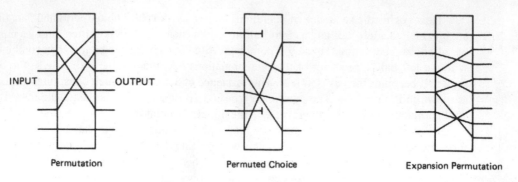

Permutation   Permuted Choice   Expansion Permutation

Figure 3-15   Types of Permutations

The expansion permutation is defined by Table 3-3. For each 4-bit block, the first and fourth bits are duplicated, whereas the second and third are used only once. This table shows *to which* output positions the input bits move. Because this is an expansion permutation, some bits move to more than one position. Each row of the table shows the movement of eight bits. The interpretation of this table is that bit 1 moves to positions 2 and 48 of the output, and bit 10 moves to position 15. A portion of the pattern is also shown in Figure 3-17.

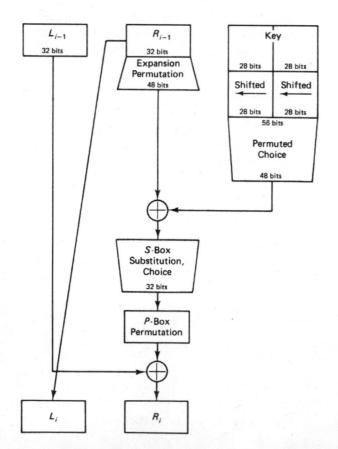

Figure 3-16   Detail of a Cycle

Table 3-3   Expansion Permutation

Bit	1	2	3	4	5	6	7	8
Moves to Position	2,48	3	4	5,7	6,8	9	10	11,13
Bit	9	10	11	12	13	14	15	16
Moves to Position	12,14	15	16	17,19	18,20	21	22	23,25
Bit	17	18	19	20	21	22	23	24
Moves to Position	24,26	27	28	29,31	30,32	33	34	35,37
Bit	25	26	27	28	29	30	31	32
Moves to Position	36,38	39	40	41,43	42,44	45	46	47,1

Key Transformation

As just described, the 64-bit key immediately becomes a 56-bit key by deletion of every eighth bit. At each step in the cycle, the key is split into two 28-bit halves, the halves are shifted left by a specified number of digits, the halves are pasted together again, and 48 of these 56 bits are permuted to use as a key during this cycle.

The key for the cycle is combined by an exclusive-or function with the expanded right half just described. That result moves into the S-boxes described in the next step.

At each cycle, the halves of the key are independently shifted left circularly by a specified number of bit positions. The number of bits shifted is given in Table 3-4.

After being shifted, 48 of the 56 bits are extracted for the exclusive-or combination with the expanded right half. The choice permutation that selects these 48 bits is shown in Table 3-5. From this table, for example, bit 1 of the shifted key goes to output position 5, whereas bit 9 is ignored in this cycle.

S-Boxes

Substitutions are performed by eight **S-boxes**. An S-box is a table in which six bits of data are replaced by four bits. The 48-bit input is divided into eight 6-bit blocks, identified as $B_1 B_2 \ldots B_8$; block B_j is operated on by S-box S_j, as shown in Figure 3-18.

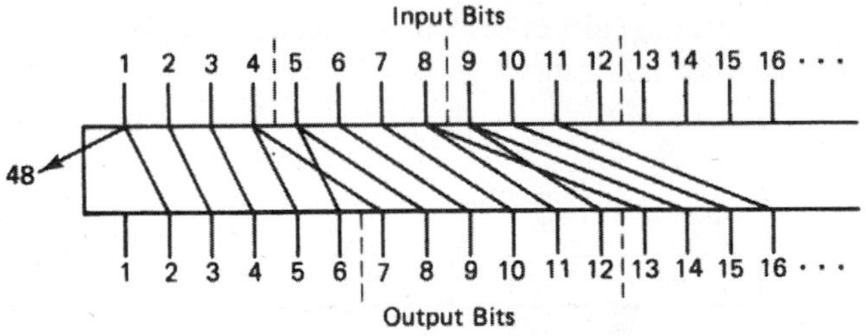

Figure 3-17   Pattern of Expansion Permutation

Table 3-4   Bits Shifted by Cycle Number

Cycle Number	Bits Shifted
1	1
2	1
3	2
4	2
5	2
6	2
7	2
8	2
9	2
10	2
11	2
12	2
13	2
14	2
15	2
16	1

Table 3-5   Choice Permutation to Select 48 Key Bits

Key Bit	1	2	3	4	5	6	7	8	9	10	11	12	13	14
Selected for Position	5	24	7	16	6	10	20	18	—	12	3	15	23	1
Key Bit	15	16	17	18	19	20	21	22	23	24	25	26	27	28
Selected for Position	9	19	2	—	14	22	11	—	13	4	—	17	21	8
Key Bit	29	30	31	32	33	34	35	36	37	38	39	40	41	42
Selected for Position	47	31	27	48	35	41	—	46	28	—	39	32	25	44
Key Bit	43	44	45	46	47	48	49	50	51	52	53	54	55	56
Selected for Position	—	37	34	43	29	36	38	45	33	26	42	—	30	40

The S-boxes are substitutions based on a table of 4 rows and 16 columns. Suppose that block B_j is the six bits $b_1b_2b_3b_4b_5b_6$. Bits b_1 and b_6, taken together, form a two-bit binary number b_1b_6, having a decimal value from 0 to 3. Call this value r. Bits b_2, b_3, b_4, and b_5 taken together form a four-bit binary number $b_2b_3b_4b_5$, having a decimal value from 0 to 15. Call this value c. The substitutions from the S-boxes transform each 6-bit block B_j into the 4-bit result shown in row r, column c of section S_j of Table 3-6. For example, assume that block B_7 in binary is 010011. Then $r = 01 = 1$ and $c = 1001 = 9$. The transformation of block B_7 is found in row 1, column 9 of section 7 of Table 3-6. The value $3 = 0011$ is substituted for the value 010011.

P-Boxes

After an S-box substitution, all 32 bits of a result are permuted by a straight permutation, P. Table 3-7 shows the position to which bits are moved. Eight bits are shown on each row. For example, bit 1 of the output of the substitution moves to bit 9, and bit 10 moves to position 16.

Initial and Final Permutations

The DES algorithm begins with an **initial permutation** that reorders the 64 bits of each input block. The initial permutation is shown in Table 3-8.

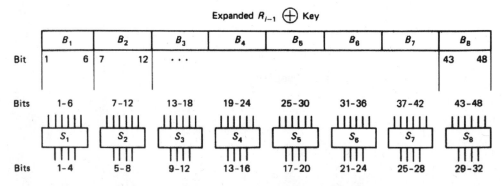

Figure 3-18   S-Boxes Operating on Eight 6-bit Blocks

Table 3-6   S-Boxes of DES

Box	Row	0	1	2	3	4	5	6	7	8	9	10	11	12	13	14	15
									Column								
S_1																	
	0	14	4	13	1	2	15	11	8	3	10	6	12	5	9	0	7
	1	0	15	7	4	14	2	13	1	10	6	12	11	9	5	3	8
	2	4	1	14	8	13	6	2	11	15	12	9	7	3	10	5	0
	3	15	12	8	2	4	9	1	7	5	11	3	14	10	0	6	13
S_2																	
	0	15	1	8	14	6	11	3	4	9	7	2	13	12	0	5	10
	1	3	13	4	7	15	2	8	14	12	0	1	10	6	9	11	5
	2	0	14	7	11	10	4	13	1	5	8	12	6	9	3	2	15
	3	13	8	10	1	3	15	4	2	11	6	7	12	0	5	14	9
S_3																	
	0	10	0	9	14	6	3	15	5	1	13	12	7	11	4	2	8
	1	13	7	0	9	3	4	6	10	2	8	5	14	12	11	15	1
	2	13	6	4	9	8	15	3	0	11	1	2	12	5	10	14	7
	3	1	10	13	0	6	9	8	7	4	15	14	3	11	5	2	12
S_4																	
	0	7	13	14	3	0	6	9	10	1	2	8	5	11	12	4	15
	1	13	8	11	5	6	15	0	3	4	7	2	12	1	10	14	9
	2	10	6	9	0	12	11	7	13	15	1	3	14	5	2	8	4
	3	3	15	0	6	10	1	13	8	9	4	5	11	12	7	2	14
S_5																	
	0	2	12	4	1	7	10	11	6	8	5	3	15	13	0	14	9
	1	14	11	2	12	4	7	13	1	5	0	15	10	3	9	8	6
	2	4	2	1	11	10	13	7	8	15	9	12	5	6	3	0	14
	3	11	8	12	7	1	14	2	13	6	15	0	9	10	4	5	3
S_6																	
	0	12	1	10	15	9	2	6	8	0	13	3	4	14	7	5	11
	1	10	15	4	2	7	12	9	5	6	1	13	14	0	11	3	8
	2	9	14	15	5	2	8	12	3	7	0	4	10	1	13	11	6
	3	4	3	2	12	9	5	15	10	11	14	1	7	6	0	8	13
S_7																	
	0	4	11	2	14	15	0	8	13	3	12	9	7	5	10	6	1
	1	13	0	11	7	4	9	1	10	14	3	5	12	2	15	8	6
	2	1	4	11	13	12	3	7	14	10	15	6	8	0	5	9	2
	3	6	11	13	8	1	4	10	7	9	5	0	15	14	2	3	12
S_8																	
	0	13	2	8	4	6	15	11	1	10	9	3	14	5	0	12	7
	1	1	15	13	8	10	3	7	4	12	5	6	11	0	14	9	2
	2	7	11	4	1	9	12	14	2	0	6	10	13	15	3	5	8
	3	2	1	14	7	4	10	8	13	15	12	9	0	3	5	6	11

Table 3-7   Permutation Box P

Bit	Goes to Position							
1–8	9	17	23	31	13	28	2	18
9–16	24	16	30	6	26	20	10	1
17–24	8	14	25	3	4	29	11	19
25–32	32	12	22	7	5	27	15	21

Table 3-8   Initial Permutation

Bit	Goes to Position							
1–8	40	8	48	16	56	24	64	32
9–16	39	7	47	15	55	23	63	31
17–24	38	6	46	14	54	22	62	30
25–32	37	5	45	13	53	21	61	29
33–40	36	4	44	12	52	20	60	28
41–48	35	3	43	11	51	19	59	27
49–56	34	2	42	10	50	18	58	26
57–64	33	1	41	9	49	17	57	25

At the conclusion of the 16 substitution–permutation rounds, the DES algorithm finishes with a **final permutation** (or **inverse initial permutation**), which is shown in Table 3-9.

Complete DES

Now we can put all the pieces back together. First the key is reduced to 56 bits. Then a block of 64 data bits is permuted by the initial permutation. Following are 16 cycles in which the key is shifted and permuted, half of the data block is transformed using the substitution and permutation functions, and the result is combined with the remaining half of the data block. After the last cycle, the data block is permuted using the final permutation. The full operation of the DES is shown in Figure 3-19.

Decryption of the DES

The same DES algorithm is used for both encryption and decryption. This result is true because cycle j derives from cycle $(j-1)$ in the following manner:

$$L_j = R_{j-1} \tag{1}$$
$$R_j = L_{j-1} \oplus f(R_{j-1}, k_j) \tag{2}$$

where $\oplus$ is the exclusive-or operation and f is the function computed in an expand–shift–substitute–permute cycle. These two equations show that the result of each cycle depends only on the previous cycle.

Table 3-9   Final Permutation (Inverse Initial Permutation)

Bit	Goes to Position							
1–8	58	50	42	34	26	18	10	2
9–16	60	52	44	36	28	20	12	4
17–24	62	54	46	38	30	22	14	6
25–32	64	56	48	40	32	24	16	8
33–40	57	49	41	33	25	17	9	1
41–48	59	51	43	35	27	19	11	3
49–56	61	53	45	37	29	21	13	5
57–64	63	55	47	39	31	23	15	7

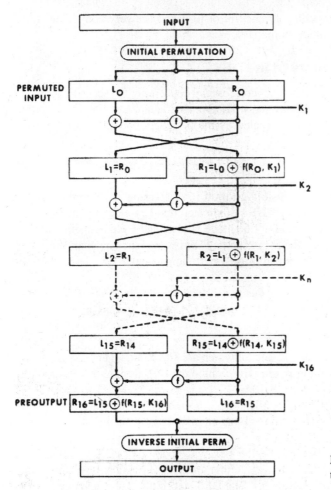

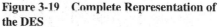

Figure 3-19   Complete Representation of the DES

By rewriting these equations in terms of R_{j-1} and L_{j-1}, we get

$$R_{j-1} = L_j \qquad (3)$$

and

$$L_{j-1} = R_j \oplus f(R_{j-1}, k_j) \qquad (4)$$

Substituting (3) into (4) gives

$$L_{j-1} = R_j \oplus f(L_j, k_j) \qquad (5)$$

Equations (3) and (5) show that these same values could be obtained from the results of *later* cycles. This property makes the DES a reversible procedure; we can encrypt a string and also decrypt the result to derive the plaintext again.

With the DES the same function f is used forward to encrypt or backwards to decrypt. The only change is that the keys must be taken in reverse order ($k_{16}, k_{15}, \ldots, k_1$) for decryption. Using one algorithm either to encrypt or to decrypt is very convenient for a hardware or software implementation of the DES.

Questions About the Security of the DES

Since its first announcement, there has been controversy concerning the security provided by the DES. Although much of this controversy has appeared in the open literature, certain features of the DES have neither been revealed by the designers nor inferred by outside analysts.

Design of the Algorithm

Initially, there was concern with the basic algorithm itself. During development of the algorithm, the National Security Agency (NSA) indicated that key elements of the algorithm design were "sensitive" and would not be made public. These elements include the rationale behind transformations by the S-boxes, the P-boxes, and the key changes. There are many possibilities for the S-box substitutions, but one particular set was chosen for the DES.

Two issues arose about the secrecy of the design. The first involved a fear that certain **trapdoors** have been imbedded in the DES algorithm, so that a covert, easy means is available to decrypt any DES-encrypted message. Such trapdoors would give NSA the ability to inspect private communications.

After a congressional inquiry, the results of which are classified, an unclassified summary exonerates NSA from any improper involvement in the DES design. (For a good discussion on the design of DES, see [SMI88a].)

The second issue addresses the possibility that a design flaw will be (or perhaps has been) discovered by a cryptanalyst, this time giving an interceptor the ability to access private communications.

Both Bell Laboratories [MOR77] and the Lexan Corporation [LEX76] scrutinized the operation (not the design) of the S-boxes. Neither analysis revealed any weakness that impairs the proper functioning of the S-boxes. The DES algorithm has been studied extensively and, to date, no serious flaws have been publicized.[4]

In response to criticism, the NSA released certain information on the selection of the S-boxes ([KON81], [BRA77]).

- No S-box is a linear or affine function of its input; that is, the four output bits cannot be expressed as a system of linear equations of the six input bits.
- Changing one bit in the input of an S-box results in changing at least two output bits; that is, the S-boxes diffuse their information well throughout their outputs.
- The S-boxes were chosen to minimize the difference between the number of 1s and 0s when any single input bit is held constant; that is, holding a single bit constant as a 0 or 1 and changing the bits around it should not lead to disproportionately many 0s or 1s in the output.

---

[4] Not too curiously, the NSA has withdrawn further support of the DES. See the subsequent section.

Number of Iterations

Many analysts wonder whether 16 iterations are sufficient. Because each iteration diffuses the information of the plaintext throughout the ciphertext, it is not clear that 16 cycles diffuse the information sufficiently. For example, with only one cycle, a single ciphertext bit is affected only by a few bits of plaintext. With more cycles, the diffusion becomes greater, so that ideally there is no dependence of any one ciphertext bit on any subset of plaintext bits.

Experimentation with both the DES and its IBM predecessor Lucifer was performed by the NBS and by IBM as part of the certification process of the DES algorithm. These experiments have shown [KON81] that 8 iterations are sufficient to eliminate any observed dependence. Thus, the 16 iterations of the DES should surely be adequate.

Key Length

The length of the key is the most serious objection raised. The key in the original IBM implementation of Lucifer was 128 bits, whereas the DES key is effectively only 56 bits long. The argument for a longer key centers around the feasibility of an exhaustive search for a key.

Given a piece of plaintext known to be enciphered as a particular piece of ciphertext, the goal for the interceptor is to find the key under which the encipherment was done. This attack assumes that the same key will be used to encipher other (unknown) plaintext. Knowing the key will allow the interceptor to decipher intercepted ciphertext easily.

The attack strategy is the brute force attack: encipher the known plaintext with an orderly series of keys, repeating with a new key until the enciphered plaintext matches the known ciphertext. There are 2^{56} 56-bit keys. If someone could test one every 100 ms, the time to test all keys would be 7.2×10^{15} seconds, or about 228 million years. If the test took only 1 ms, then the total time for the search is (only!) about 2,280 years. Even supposing the test time to be 1 ns, infeasible on current technology machines, the search time still exceeds two years, working full time with no hardware or software failures!

Diffie and Hellman [DIF77] suggest a **parallel attack**. With a parallel design, multiple processors can be assigned the same problem simultaneously. If one chip, working at a rate of one key per microsecond, can check about 8.6×10^{10} keys in one day, it would take 10^6 days to try all $2^{56} \approx 7 \times 10^{16}$ keys. However, 10^6 chips working in parallel at that rate could check all keys in one day.

One estimate of the cost of such a machine is $50 million. Assuming a "key shop" existed where people would bring their plaintext/ciphertext pairs to obtain keys, and assuming that there was enough business to keep this machine busy 24 hours a day for five years, the proportionate cost would be only about $20,000 per solution. As hardware costs continue to fall, the cost of such a machine becomes lower. The stumbling block in the economics of this argument is prorating the cost over five years: if such a device became available at affordable prices, use of the DES would cease for important data.

An alternative criticism is the table lookup argument [HEL80]. For this attack, assume a **chosen plaintext attack**, that is, the ability to insert a given plaintext block into the encryption stream and obtain the resulting ciphertext under a still-secret key. Hellman argues that with enough advance time and enough storage space, it would be possible to compute all of the 2^{56} results of encrypting the chosen block under every possible key. Then determining which key was used is a matter of looking up the output obtained.

By a heuristic algorithm, Hellman suggests an approach that will limit the amount of computation and data stored to 2^{37}, or about 6.4×10^{11}. Again assuming many DES devices working in parallel, it would be possible to precompute and store all results. As the cost of hardware decreases and the speed of hardware increases, Hellman argues that implementing such a machine may become feasible.

Weaknesses of the DES

The DES has known weaknesses, but these weaknesses are not believed to limit the effectiveness of the algorithm seriously.

Complements

The first known weakness concerns complements. (Throughout this discussion, *complement* means ones complement, the result obtained by replacing all 1s by 0s and 0s by 1s.) If a message is encrypted with a particular key, the complement of that encryption will be the encryption of the complement message under the complement key. Stated formally, let p represent a plaintext message and k a key, and let the symbol $\neg x$ mean the complement of the binary string x. If $c = \text{DES}(p, k)$ (meaning c is the DES encryption of p using key k), then $\neg c = \text{DES}(\neg p, \neg k)$. Because most applications of encryption do not deal with complement messages, and because users can be warned not to use complement keys, this is not a serious problem.

Weak Keys

A second known weakness concerns choice of keys. Because the initial key is split into two halves, and the two halves are independently shifted circularly, if the value being shifted is all 0s or all 1s, the key used for encryption in each cycle is the same as for all other cycles. Remember that the difference between encryption and decryption is that the key shifts are applied in reverse. Key shifts are right shifts and the number of positions shifted is taken from the bottom of the table up, instead of top down. But if the keys are all 0s or all 1s anyway, right or left shifts by 0, 1, or 2 positions are all the same. For these keys, encryption is the same as decryption: $c = \text{DES}(p, k)$, and $p = \text{DES}(c, k)$. These keys are called weak keys. The same thing happens if one half of the key is all 0s and the other half is all 1s. Because these keys are known, they can simply be avoided, so this is not a serious problem.

The four weak keys are shown in hexadecimal notation in Table 3-10. (The initial key permutation extracts every eighth bit as a parity bit and scrambles the key order slightly. Therefore, the "half zeros, half ones" keys are not just split in the middle.)

Table 3-10   Weak DES Keys

Left Half	Right Half	Weak Key Value			
zeros	zeros	0101	0101	0101	0101
ones	ones	FEFE	FEFE	FEFE	FEFE
zeros	ones	1F1F	1F1F	0E0E	0E0E
ones	zeros	E0E0	E0E0	F1F1	F1F1

Semi-Weak Keys

A third difficulty is similar: specific pairs of keys have identical decryption. That is, there are two different keys k_1 and k_2 for which $c = \text{DES}(p, k_1)$ and $c = \text{DES}(p, k_2)$. This implies that k_1 can decrypt a message encrypted under k_2. These "semi-weak" keys are shown in Table 3-11. Other key patterns have been investigated with no additional weaknesses found to date. However, you should avoid any key having an obvious pattern such as these.

Design Weaknesses

In another analysis of the DES, [DAV83a] shows that the expansion permutation repeats the first and fourth bits of every 4-bit series, crossing bits from neighboring 4-bit series. This paper further indicates that in S-box S_4 the last three output bits can be derived the same way as the first by complementing some of the input bits. This small weakness, of course, raises the question whether there are similar weaknesses in other S-boxes or in pairs of S-boxes.

It has also been shown that two different, but carefully chosen, inputs to S-boxes can produce the same output (see [DAV83a]). Desmedt [DES84] makes the point that in a single cycle, by changing bits only in three neighboring S-boxes, it is possible to obtain the same output; that is, two slightly different inputs, encrypted under the same key, will produce identical results at the end of just one of the 16 cycles.

Key Clustering

Finally, the researchers in [DES84] investigate a phenomenon called **key clustering**. They seek to determine whether there are two different keys that can generate the same ciphertext from the same plaintext, that is, two keys that produce the same encryption. The semi-weak keys are key clusters, but the researchers seek others. Their analysis is very involved, looking at ciphertexts that produce identical plaintext with different keys in one cycle of the DES, then looking at two cycles, then three, and so forth. Up through three cycles, they found key clusters. Because of the complexity involved, they had to stop the analysis after three cycles.

Differential Cryptanalysis

In 1990 Biham and Shamir [BIH90] (see also [BIH91], [BIH92], and [BIH93]) announced a technique they named **differential cryptanalysis**. The technique applied to cryptographic algorithms that use substitution and permutation. This very powerful technique was the first to have impressive effect against a broad range of algorithms of this type.

Table 3-11   Semi-Weak DES Key Pairs

01FE	01FE	01FE	01FE	FE01	FE01	FE01	FE01
1FE0	1FE0	0EF1	0EF1	E01F	E01F	F10E	F10E
01E0	01E0	01F1	01F1	E001	E001	F101	F101
1FFE	1FFE	0EFE	0EFE	FE1F	FE1F	FE0E	FE0E
011F	011F	010E	010E	1F01	1F01	0E01	0E01
E0FE	E0FE	F1FE	F1FE	FEE0	FEE0	FEF1	FEF1

The technique uses carefully selected pairs of plaintext with subtle differences and studies the effects of these differences on resulting ciphertexts. If particular combinations of input bits are modified simultaneously, particular intermediate bits are also likely with a high probability to change in a particular way. The technique looks at the exclusive or of a pair of inputs; the XOR will have a 0 in any bit in which the inputs are identical and a 1 where they differ.

The full analysis is rather complicated, but a sketch is presented here. The S-boxes transform six bits into four. If the S-boxes were perfectly uniform, one would expect all 4-bit outputs to be equally likely. However, as Biham and Shamir show, certain similar texts are more likely to produce similar outputs than others. For example, examining all bit strings with an XOR pattern 35 in hexadecimal notation (that is, strings of the form *ddsdsd* where *d* means the bit value is different between the two strings and *s* means the bit value is the same) for S-box S_1, the pairs have an output pattern of *dsss* 14 times, *ddds* 14 times, and all other patterns a frequency ranging between 0 and 8. That is, an input of the form *ddsdsd* has an output of the form *dsss* 14 times out of 64, and *ddds* another 14 times out of 64; each of these results is almost 1/4, which continues to the next round. Biham and Shamir call each of these recognizable effects a characteristic; they then extend their result by concatenating characteristics. The attack lets them infer values in specific positions of the key. If m bits of a k-bit key can be found, the remaining $(k - m)$ bits can be found in an exhaustive search of all $2^{(k-m)}$ possible keys; if m is large enough, the $2^{(k-m)}$ exhaustive search is feasible.

In [BIH90] the authors give the conclusions of many results they have produced using differential cryptanalysis; they proceed to present the details of these results in the succeeding papers. The attack on Lucifer, the IBM-designed predecessor to DES, succeeds with only 30 ciphertext pairs, Feal-8 can be broken with 1000 pairs, and Feal-N for N ≤ 31 can be broken faster using differential cryptanalysis than using full exhaustive search.

The results concerning DES are very impressive. Shortening DES to fewer than its normal 16 rounds allows a key to be determined from chosen ciphertexts in *fewer* than the 2^{56} (actually, expected value of 2^{55}) searches: with 15 rounds, only 2^{52} tests are needed (which is still a large number of tests), with 10 rounds, the number of tests falls to 2^{35}, and with 6 rounds, only 2^8 tests are needed. *However,* with the full 16 rounds, this technique requires 2^{58} tests, or $2^2 = 4$ times *more* than exhaustive search would require.

Finally, the authors show that with randomly selected S-box values DES is easier to break, and even with a change of only one entry in one S-box DES becomes easier to break. One might conclude that the design of the S-boxes and the number of rounds were chosen to be optimal.

In fact, that is true. Don Coppersmith of IBM, one of the original team working on Lucifer and DES, acknowledged [COP92] that the technique of differential cryptanalysis was known to the design team in 1974 when they were designing DES. The S-boxes and permutations were chosen in such as way as to defeat that line of attack.

Security of the DES

There are two arguments on a collision course: Hellman argues that because of increasing hardware speed and decreasing hardware cost, it may be feasible to perform an exhaustive key search in a known plaintext attack. Other researchers show that some keys may not work differently from others, thus reducing the proportion of keys to consider in an exhaustive key search. When hardware power surpasses the number of keys to search, the exhaustive key search becomes a real threat.

Does this mean the DES is insecure? No, not yet. Nobody has yet shown serious flaws in the DES, nor do people really believe that hardware power has reached the point of feasibility.

NSDD-145 and Support of the DES

DES was accepted by the NBS in 1978 and was approved later by the American National Standards Institute (ANSI) as a standard in the private sector. The NBS/NIST has reviewed DES several times since 1978.

However, the National Security Agency (NSA) has veto power over the NIST in matters of cryptography. This power comes under a controversial executive directive called **NSDD-145** that gave NSA the authority to develop a national policy on computer and communications security. The directive extends the authority of the NSA beyond government agencies to the private sector. "In cases where the implementation of security measures to nongovernmental systems would be in the national security interest, the private sector shall be encouraged, advised, and where appropriate, assisted in undertaking the application of such measures."

NSA has already announced that it will not recertify the standard. The problem with DES is not that it is known, or even suspected, to *have been* broken; it is just becoming more likely that it *could be* broken. The extensive debate about the feasibility of an exhaustive key search machine, coupled with the exhaustive analysis of the DES algorithm, has made DES too risky.

In the same way that users should change passwords, encryption keys, and procedures periodically—even without suspecting a security lapse—the NSA seems to think the DES has become too obvious a target.

The NSA has already indicated that future generations of encryption will be in the form of "black boxes," **sealed encryption devices** to which NSA will not disclose the algorithms. NSA will distribute devices and keys to users. Without access to the algorithm, it will be substantially more complex to analyze the devices in an attempt to uncover weaknesses. DES equipment can still be sold to and used by government and private agencies. New sealed encryption devices have been developed for the NSA Clipper program (described in the next section).

Public reaction to NSDD-145 has identified several problems.

- Export of the new devices to foreign countries will be prohibited because of national security concerns. This raises serious problems for U.S. companies doing business abroad or having foreign affiliates.
- Security of communications and data currently protected by DES is in question.
- Some companies have invested substantial sums in hardware that uses DES. Replacing this machinery will be expensive. Other companies that manufacture DES-based devices may have produced merchandise that they will be unable to sell.
- Perhaps even more significant is the investment in the *use* of the DES: many organizations have much data that has already been encrypted under DES, and they will

continue to need DES products and services to be able to retrieve the plaintext of that data. There is no apparent transition plan for phase-out of existing uses of DES.

- NSA's plan to distribute the devices *and the keys* constitutes government control of who can use encryption. In addition, if the government retains records of who has received what keys, the government then has the capability to decrypt any intercepted encrypted data, within the private or public sector.

Computer Security Act of 1987

In a piece of legislation passed late in 1987, the National Institute of Standards and Technology, or NIST (formerly National Bureau of Standards) has been given responsibility for improving computer security in civilian government agencies. This responsibility is taken from the NSA, which had been given that authority under NSDD-l45. Under the new law, NIST must create security standards, design security measures, and develop training programs for computer security.

Each federal agency will identify computing systems that process or maintain sensitive information. Information that is sensitive is "any information, the loss, misuse or unauthorized access to or modification of which could adversely affect the national interest or the conduct of federal programs or an individual's rights under the Privacy Act." Previously *national interest* was taken to mean just defense activities or affairs of state; this new legislation indicates that the national interest could include commerce, such as banking and securities trading, as well as areas such as energy and health care. These documents will be reviewed by NIST, working with the technical support of NSA.

An important point of the new law is that it places an entirely new emphasis on computer security. This confirmation from Congress of the importance of unclassified information advises upper level management of civilian agencies to develop stronger computer security programs.

3.10 Key Escrow and Clipper

In this, the final encryption technique presented, the algorithm will not be given, because the algorithm itself is classified by the U.S. government. However, both the design parameters and possible alternative implementations are interesting. Furthermore, the program including the technique has generated more public attention and debate in the computer security community than probably any other single aspect of computer security.

The Clipper Program

The program is known by at least seven names: Clipper, Capstone, Skipjack, MOSAIC, Tessera, Fortezza, and Escrowed Encryption Standard (EES). Originally there was an announcement of a **Clipper chip** and a **Capstone chip**, both of which implemented the **Skipjack algorithm**. Unfortunately, Clipper™ was already the name of a successful computer software program and so confusion resulted. The program was renamed **MOSAIC**, the chip became **Fortezza**, and Capstone became a **Tessera** cryptographic device. So, duplicate names abound. Furthermore, because the original program had no name, it was called the Clipper program, from the Clipper chip that was its basis; that name has stuck with many in the public.

History and Politics

The initial goal of the program was both reasonable and technically interesting. On the basis of compelling evidence, in the U.S. a court can order a wiretap of a telephone line, permitting law enforcement authorities to intercept conversations (or any other communications) on that line. However, if the communication is in ciphertext, the authorities must break the encryption to access the conversation to which a court has authorized them access.

In 1993 the U.S. telecommunications provider AT&T had just begun to market a telephone device that would convert a conversation to digital form, encrypt the conversation, reconvert the ciphertext to analog form for transmission across a sound-based network, and be able to reverse this process at the receiving end. These devices would handle their own key management by generating a new encryption key for each conversation, encrypting that key, and transmitting it to the receiving device ahead of the encrypted conversation. Law enforcement wanted a means to break this encryption without weakening the encryption enough that other interceptors could break the encryption as well. Because of public concerns about government abuse of power, the government knew the public would not accept a scheme in which all encryption keys were available at one point. The idea developed by NSA was a concept called **key escrow**. Escrowed encryption is contrasted to conventional encryption in Figure 3-20. Encryption keys can be escrowed to any trustworthy agencies. To protect (at least partially) the security of the encryption, the key can be separated into pieces, with each piece stored with a different escrow agency.

In the Clipper proposal, the encryption key was to be split into two halves, so that both halves were necessary to decrypt. Each half of the key would be held by a different government agency. Only when authorized by a court order would these two agencies bring together their key halves and deliver both halves to the law enforcement authorities.

To provide greater security, the NSA classified the encryption algorithm and would release only hardware embodiments of the algorithm, either as a computer chip or as a separate encryption device. In so doing the NSA hoped to limit the successes of cryptanalysts by denying them the ability to analyze the algorithm's structure.

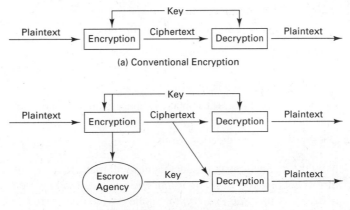

(a) Conventional Encryption

(b) Escrowed Encryption

Figure 3-20   Escrowed Encryption

Public relations for the announcement of the program were handled very badly.

- The announcement was rushed, so that in the first briefings several key elements were undecided, such as which agencies would hold the key halves or whether the encryption devices would be exportable from the United States.
- The program was not released first to key members of the computer security community, either inside or outside the government.
- The need for the program was not clearly justified at the outset.
- No provision was made initially for review and comment by Congress, by government agencies, or by the general public.

Thus, public reaction was strongly negative due to a general fear of government's intrusion into private communication, and the fear that the government might have something to hide because it was not releasing the design of the algorithm, as well as a sense that the government was rushing to put the program in place and therefore must have something to hide. Political considerations aside, the technical properties of Clipper are interesting.

Technical Aspects

The Skipjack encryption process is a repetitive scrambling process like DES; Skipjack uses 32 rounds (whereas DES uses 16 rounds). The Skipjack algorithm uses an 80-bit key (whereas DES uses a 56-bit key) to encrypt 64-bit blocks of plaintext.

Data transmission is accompanied by a law enforcement agents' field (LEAF) as shown in Figure 3-21. A message M and key k operate in the usual way: $D(E(M,k), k) = M$. The law enforcement agents' field contains $E((E(k,u)\&n\&a), f)$, where u is an 80-bit encryption key specific to this encryption unit, n is a 30-bit number identifying the unit, a is an escrow authenticator and f is an 80-bit encryption key for the entire family of Clipper chips. Each chip contains the value of f and its own value of u. These are also known outside the chip: f by law enforcement authorities, and the u value corresponding to each unit n by the two escrow agencies (half by each). A law enforcement authority with right to tap a line will

1. Intercept the communication.
2. Determine that it is encrypted using Clipper.
3. Decrypt $E((E(k,u)\&n), f)$ to obtain n.
4. Deliver n and a copy of the court order to each of the two escrow agencies.
5. Receive back the two halves of the key u.
6. Use u to decrypt $E(k,u)$ to obtain k, the session key under which this communication was encrypted.
7. Decrypt the communication using k.

Now the distinctions in product names will make more sense. **Clipper** is a basic chip that implements the Skipjack algorithm and appends the key escrow block (LEAF) to the output stream. **Capstone** is a cryptographic device that performs the Skipjack algorithm and appends the key escrow block (LEAF) to the output stream and provides a key exchange algorithm (KEA) for transmission of a session key to the remote unit, the Secure

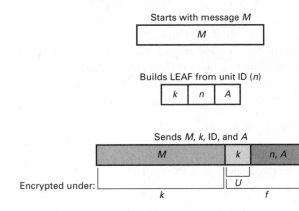

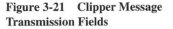

Figure 3-21   **Clipper Message Transmission Fields**

Hash Algorithm (SHA), and the Digital Signature Algorithm (DSA). A Capstone chip is the equivalent of a Clipper chip embedded in a context that makes it usable in electronic messaging. The Capstone chip is now known as **Tessera** (also sometimes **Fortezza**), which is most commonly implemented as a PCMCIA computer "smart card." The so-called Clipper program has been named the **MOSAIC** program.

Security of Skipjack

The primary question to be answered is how secure Skipjack is, both from external crypt-analysts and from the U.S. government. The Skipjack algorithm was developed by the NSA during the 1980s and was released for testing (internal to NSA) in 1990. Skipjack is one of a class of algorithms developed by the NSA; the other algorithms are used for protection of classified data. Although the NSA had originally intended to not allow any public review of the algorithm, in light of significant public controversy surrounding the entire Clipper program, NSA allowed a panel of experts in cryptography to review the design and definition of the Skipjack algorithm. The panel members had impeccable reputations for sound and fair analysis. The conclusions of the review panel [BRI93] were as follows:

- Under an assumption that the cost of processing power is halved every eighteen months, it will be 36 years before the cost of breaking Skipjack by exhaustive search will be equal to the cost of breaking DES today. Thus, there is no significant risk that Skipjack will be broken by exhaustive search in the next 30 to 40 years.
- There is no significant risk that Skipjack can be broken through a shortcut method of attack.
- Although the internal structure of Skipjack must be classified in order to protect law enforcement and national security objectives, the strength of Skipjack against cryptanalytic attack does not depend on the secrecy of the algorithm.

Conclusions

At this point we have seen the basis of the Clipper technology: an encryption unit that associates with its ciphertext an encrypted field containing the product number of the encrypting (sending) unit and an encrypted version of the encryption key for the current communication. The more sophisticated Capstone/Fortezza/Tessera model adds key exchange, digital signature, and secure hash algorithms. We will return to the Clipper technology again in the rest of this book: in Chapter 4 as a protocol, we will study the strengths and weaknesses of the original Clipper escrow design, and at the end, in Chapter 11, we will consider the legal and ethical ramifications of key escrow.

3.11   Summary of Secure Encryption

In this chapter we have studied several encryption algorithms. The Merkle–Hellman algorithm is based on the NP-complete knapsack problem of finding a set of numbers that add to a specific sum. The underlying problem is known to be at least of polynomial difficulty to solve, and it is likely to require exponential work. Unfortunately, there is a technique to solve the restricted version of the knapsack problem (without solving the underlying knapsack problem) in reasonable time.

The RSA algorithm is based on the underlying hard problem of factoring large numbers. The factoring problem is not even NP-complete. The algorithm is conceptually simple: to encrypt and to decrypt you treat a plaintext as a number and raise it to a particular power. Encryption and decryption can be performed in either order, and multiple encryptions and decryptions commute with one another. These properties make this a very desirable algorithm. The principal difficulty with this algorithm is its implementation: raising 200-digit numbers to a 200-digit power is not easy to implement on popular computers. Hardware devices have been produced to implement this algorithm efficiently.

The DES algorithm was designed for the U.S. government and has been officially certified as a standard for encryption. It uses a series of 16 iterations of a loop involving simple arithmetic and logical operations. It can be implemented reasonably easily on any popular computer. Certain minor design faults have been uncovered, but there has been nothing conclusive published regarding a major vulnerability. Still, controversy has raged about its security since its introduction.

Clipper is still very new and, because it is classified, its design is not subject to public scrutiny and challenge. The panel that examined the design did agree it seemed to be safe. However, from past experience, it can take years for cryptanalysts to discover an effective attack. The political aspects of Clipper are more likely to affect its acceptance than its inherent cryptographic strength.

3.12   Bibliographic Notes

Konheim [KON81] and Denning [DEN82] both present the secure encryption systems described in this chapter. Lempel [LEM79] and Schneier [SCH96] also cover this material. Cryptanalysis of the Merkle–Hellman method is given in [SHA80], [SHA82], [ADL82], and [SIM92]. An attack on the RSA method is given in [WAG83]. Discussion of the security of the DES appears in [HEL79], [MOR77], [LEX76], [DAV82], and [DAV83a]. Other public key cryptosystems are given in [GOO84], [SAL90], [SIM92] and [LAG83]. Salomaa [SAL90] gives a good presentation of public key cryptography. Simmons [SIM92] has edited an excellent collection of papers on cryptanalysis.

The technical details on Clipper are summarized in [BRI93]. Other key escrow technologies are reviewed in [DEN96].

3.13   **Terms and Concepts**

3.14 Exercises

1. Show that formula $F = (v_1) \land (v_2 \lor v_3) \land (\neg v_3 \lor \neg v_1)$ is satisfiable, and justify that formula $G = (v_1) \land (v_2 \lor v_3) \land (\neg v_3 \lor \neg v_1) \land (\neg v_2)$ is not.

2. Are there any other cliques in the graph of Figure 3-1?

3. Give a procedure for locating a clique of size n in any given graph. What is the time complexity of your algorithm?

4. An algorithm with a GUESS statement can be replaced by two clones of procedures executing the algorithm, one clone executing as if TRUE were the correct guess, and the other executing as if FALSE were correct. If one of these clones later encounters another guess, it clones itself again, so that two clones become three. Suppose an algorithm executes in n steps. What is a limit to the number of cloned processes needed to simulate that algorithm?

5. Differentiate between a problem and an instance of a problem. Cite an example of each.

6. Suppose an encryption algorithm is based on the satisfiability problem. Estimate the number of machine instructions necessary to solve the satisfiability problem by testing all cases. Using current-technology hardware, how many variables are needed in the formula so that the time to solve this problem exceeds one year? What is the corresponding figure for hardware of five years ago? Ten years ago? Assuming similar speed improvements in the next five years, how long will it take then to solve today's one-year-sized problem?

7. Compute gcd(1875, 405).

8. Justify that $(a * b) \bmod n = ((a \bmod n) * (b \bmod n)) \bmod n$.

9. Write the addition and multiplication tables for the integers mod 4 and for the integers mod 7.

10. By Fermat's theorem, what is the multiplicative inverse of 2 in the field of integers mod 11?

11. With a public key encryption, suppose A wants to send a message to B. Let A_{PUB} and A_{PRIV} be A's public key and private key, respectively; similarly for B. Suppose C knows both public keys, but neither private key. If A sends a message to B, what encryption should A use so that only B can decrypt the message? (This property is called secrecy.) Can A encrypt a message so that anyone receiving the message will be assured the message came only from A? (This property is called authenticity.) Can A achieve both secrecy and authenticity for one message? How or why not?

12. Given the knapsack [17, 38, 23, 14, 11, 21] is there a solution for the target 42? Is there a solution for the target 43? Is there a solution for the target 44?

13. Convert the superincreasing knapsack [1, 3, 5, 11, 23, 47, 97] to a hard knapsack by multiplying by 7 mod 11; by 7 mod 29.

14. Encrypt the message 10110110100101 by each of the two hard knapsacks of Exercise 13.

15. Encrypt the message 10110110100101 by each of the two simple knapsacks of Exercise 13.

16. Is the Merkle–Hellman algorithm an "onto" algorithm? That is, is every number k, $0 \le k < n$, the result of encrypting some number using a fixed knapsack?

17. Explain why the graph of $\omega * h_i$ is discontinuous when $\omega * h_i > n$.

18. Find keys d and e for the RSA cryptosystem where $p = 7$ and $q = 11$.

19. Find primes p and q so that 12-bit plaintext blocks could be encrypted with RSA.

20. Is the DES an onto function; that is, is every 64-bit binary string the result of encrypting some string?

21. Prove the complement property for the DES.

22. Suppose you are designing a processor that would compute with encrypted data. For example, given two encrypted data values $E(x)$ and $E(y)$, the processor would compute $E(x) \oplus E(y)$, where $\oplus$ is an encrypted addition operator that performs addition on encrypted numbers. $D(E(x) \oplus E(y))$ must be the same as $x + y$. None of the encryption algorithms of this chapter has the property that $E(x) + E(y) = E(x + y)$, although the encrypted addition operator does not necessarily have to be $+$. For the algorithms of this chapter, is there a relationship between $E(x)$, $E(y)$, and $E(x + y)$?

4

Using Encryption:
Protocols and Practices

In this chapter:
- *Characteristics of protocols*
- *Tasks suited to protocols: cryptographic key exchange, digital signatures, anonymous communication*
- *Modes of cryptography: block chaining, feedback*

In Chapter 3 we considered examples of encryption systems believed to be secure. There are hundreds of other encryption methods, but the DES and the RSA are the two most widely acclaimed secure single key and public key systems in general distribution today.

But simply having or using a strong encryption system does not mean that all transactions using the system *will* be secure. There are right and wrong ways to use these methods of encryption. Furthermore, these algorithms can be used to solve problems for which secrecy or authenticity is only a part of the solution. In this chapter we study and evaluate techniques that use encryption to establish secure communication between two users. We also explore appropriate ways to use encryption.

4.1 Protocols: Orderly Behavior

Encryption systems are an important tool in computer security: they let you transmit information in a concealed form. Their obvious use is in transmitting documents and data over a channel that may be intercepted. By use of established conventions between two parties, cryptosystems can be used for purposes other than just secret communication. These conventions, called protocols, are the topic of the next section.

Definition of Protocols

A **protocol** is an orderly sequence of steps two or more parties take to accomplish some task. Everyone using a protocol must agree to the protocol before using it. The order of the steps is important, as is the activity of each step. People use protocols to regulate behavior for mutual benefit.

Using a telephone is a simple example of a protocol. The person dialing hears both the ringing sound and the click when the connection is established. Protocol, standard practice, is that the receiver speaks first, saying "hello," or "j'écoute," or "pronto," or something similar. The originator answers this with a greeting that identifies himself or herself. The two parties then alternate pieces of the conversation. Without this standard practice, both people might speak at once when the connection was established, and neither would hear the other.

This sequence of steps is an example of a protocol. Like this example, a good protocol has the following characteristics:

- *Established in advance.* The protocol is completely designed before it is used.
- *Mutually subscribed.* All parties to the protocol agree to follow its steps, in order.
- *Unambiguous.* No party can fail to follow a step properly because the party has misunderstood the step.
- *Complete.* For every situation that can occur there is a prescribed action to be taken.

Protocols are also used in computer-to-computer communication. A computer needs to know when to "speak," when to "listen," with whom it is communicating, whether it has received all of a particular communication, and so forth. In a two-computer communication, both computers must follow the same protocol in order for either to participate.

Kinds of Protocols

Certain tasks, such as negotiating contracts, voting, distributing information, and even playing poker, are simple human activities. However, many of these tasks depend on a witness to ensure fairness. Would you trust someone who said he was going to shuffle cards, not look at them, and mail you your hand? Would you trust the person if you did not know him, or if the stakes were high?

Modern society requires the use of computers and communications as tools of commerce. Many users of computers are not personally acquainted with the managers or other users of a system. In many cases the computer communication is over a long distance. Because of anonymity and distance, one user will not, and often should not, trust the managers or other users of a system. In order to use computers effectively, we must develop protocols by which two suspicious parties can interact with each other and be convinced of fairness.

In addition to regulating behavior, protocols serve another very important purpose: protocols separate the *process* of accomplishing a task from the *mechanism* by which it is done. A protocol specifies only the rules of behavior. In this way, we can examine a protocol to convince ourselves that it achieves the desired result. We verify the correctness of the process at a high level.

After becoming convinced of the correctness of the design, we can implement the protocol using some mechanism, that is, using some particular language or encryption system. The implementation is separate from the design. Therefore, we need only verify that the mechanism correctly reflects the design; we do not need to reverify that the implementation solves the problem for which the protocol was originally designed. Furthermore, we can later change the implementation without affecting the design. Separating design from implementation is an important advantage of using protocols.

Arbitrated Protocols

An **arbiter** is a disinterested third party trusted to complete a transaction between two distrusting parties. If you sell a car to a stranger and the stranger gives you a check, you have no way to know that the check is good. You would like to deposit the check and hold the car for a few days until you are sure the check has cleared. A suspicious buyer would not tolerate this because you have both the car and the check and could leave town with both.

A solution is to use a trusted third party, such as a banker or a lawyer, as an arbiter. You give the car's title and keys to the arbiter, and the buyer gives the arbiter a check. You three agree on a time for the check to clear. The arbiter deposits the check to your account. If the check clears within the specified time, the arbiter turns the car over to the buyer. If the check doesn't clear, you show evidence of that to the arbiter, who returns your car to you. In a computer protocol, an arbiter is a trustworthy third party who ensures fairness. The arbiter might be a person, a program, or a machine. For example, in a network an arbiter might be a program running on one machine of the network. The program receives and forwards messages between users. The users trust that when the arbiter forwards a message saying it came from A, the message really did come from user A.

The notion of an arbiter is the basis for a type of secure protocol called an **arbitrated protocol**.

Arbitrated computer protocols have several disadvantages.

- The two sides may not be able to find a neutral third party that both sides trust. Suspicious users are rightfully suspicious of an unknown arbiter in a network.
- Maintaining the availability of an arbiter represents a cost to the users or the network; that cost may be high.
- Arbitration causes a time delay in communication because a third party must receive, act on, and then forward every transaction.
- If the arbitration service is heavily used, it may become a bottleneck in the network as many users try to access a single arbiter.
- Secrecy becomes vulnerable, because the arbiter has access to much sensitive information.

For these reasons, an arbitrated protocol is avoided if possible.

Adjudicated Protocols

Similar to the arbiter is the idea of an **adjudicator**: a third party who can judge whether a transaction was performed fairly. For example, a **notary public** is a trusted, disinterested third party who attests that a document was signed voluntarily and that the notary has taken reasonable care to ascertain that the signer is authentic. A notary's signature is often required for legal documents whose authenticity might later be challenged. The notary adds nothing to the transaction other than as a witness who could testify later, in the event of a challenge.

Some computer protocols use the equivalent of a notary to build evidence of fairness. With an **adjudicable protocol** enough data is available for a disinterested third party to judge fairness based on the evidence. Not only can a third party determine whether two disputing parties acted fairly, that is, within the rules of the protocol, but the third party can also determine who cheated.

Adjudicated protocols involve the services of a third party only in case of a dispute. Therefore, they are usually less costly, in terms of machine time or access to a trusted third-party software judge, than arbitrated protocols. However, adjudicated protocols detect a failure to cooperate only after the failure has occurred.

Self-Enforcing Protocols

A **self-enforcing protocol** is one that guarantees fairness. If either party tries to cheat, that fact becomes evident to the other party. No outsider is needed to ensure fairness. Obviously, self-enforcing protocols are preferable to the other types. However, there is not a self-enforcing protocol for every situation.

Thus, there are three levels of protocols:

- *Arbitrated protocols,* in which a trusted third party participates in each transaction to ensure that both sides act fairly
- *Adjudicated protocols,* in which a third party could judge after the fact whether both parties had acted fairly and if not, which party had not
- *Self-enforcing protocols,* in which either party's attempt to cheat becomes immediately obvious to the other party

These three types of protocols are shown in Figure 4-1.

Next we turn our attention to the use of protocols to solve problems in computer security.

4.2   Protocols to Solve Problems

Now we investigate uses of protocols on real problems. Clearly, when two humans interact directly, they do so differently than if there is a computer between them. Although there may be differences in the approach, we want to devise protocols for the automated environment by which people can carry out everyday tasks, such as signing contracts, paying bills, or casting votes with as much security as in human-to-human interactions. We will study several problems for which there are secure protocols.

Key Distribution

Changing encryption keys is important but nontrivial. As Chapter 2 points out, the more ciphertext the cryptanalyst has to work with, the greater the likelihood of a success. Ciphertext from different keys can help to determine the structure of an unpublished algorithm or the keys, but ciphertext from the same key can help to reveal the value of the key. Thus, good cryptographic practice is to change keys regularly enough that the amount of ciphertext available from any one key is not a significant aid to an outsider.

However, consider the use of encryption for digital signatures on contracts. If you issue or receive a digitally signed contract, you want to keep the contract as evidence until

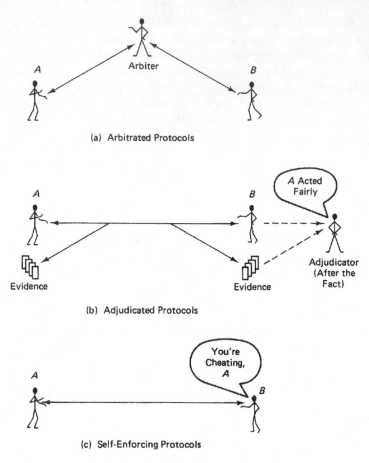

(a) Arbitrated Protocols

(b) Adjudicated Protocols

(c) Self-Enforcing Protocols

Figure 4-1   Types of Protocols

after any possible disputes have been resolved, which might be many years after the contract is performed. The sender and receiver need to keep any encryption keys necessary to
validate the contract's signatures. If the sender changes encryption keys daily, or even
monthly, hundreds or thousands of keys could need to be retained. And these keys must be
retained securely, thus creating pressure not to change keys more often than is necessary.
On the other hand, if a key is lost or exposed, the fewer items for which it is used the less
the risk. Therefore, the appropriate frequency of key exchange is not simple to decide.

Several protocols have been developed for key distribution. The protocols depend on
how much information the sender and receiver already share.

Symmetric Key Exchange Without Server

Assume that two users already each have a copy of a symmetric (secret) encryption key K
known only to them. For relatively small numbers of messages, or if there is not a significant risk of intrusion, they may use K for exchange of messages.

However, if the two want greater security, they can agree to change keys on a frequent
basis, even as often as a different key for each message. To do this, either one can generate
a fresh key, called K_{NEW}, encrypt it under K, and send $E(K_{NEW},K)$ to the other. In some

cryptosystems K is called a **key encrypting** or **master key** and K_{NEW} is called a **traffic** or **session** key.

The disadvantage of this approach is that the two users must both share one key that is unique to them. Other pairs of users need unique keys and, in general, n users need $n(n + 1)/2$ keys.

Symmetric Key Exchange with Server

An alternative is for the two users to appeal to a central key distribution service. In this protocol the number of keys is reduced but the flexibility of the solution is also reduced somewhat.

Suppose Pablo and Renee want a secret encryption key by which they can exchange messages, but they have no key in common. Suppose, however, that a central key repository exists such that Pablo and the repository share one key, K_P, and Renee and the repository share another, K_R. As presented in [NEE78], first Pablo sends to the repository (P,R,I_P), that is, his identity, P, the identity of his intended recipient, R, and a unique identifier, I_P, to mark the result the repository sends back for Pablo's reference (assuming that Pablo might send many requests to the repository and need the identifier to keep them separate) and to prevent replay attacks that might force Pablo and Renee to reuse a previous key. This information does not need to be encrypted because

- If the message is read by an outsider, Octavia, there is no harm in knowing that Pablo and Renee want to exchange a private message
- If the message is intercepted and modified by outsider the worst that could happen is that the request would be changed from a Pablo/Renee request to a Pablo/Octavia request, because the change will become apparent in the next step
- If the message is intercepted by Octavia and never delivered, Pablo will notice the lack of a response and take some corrective action
- If the message is intercepted by Octavia and she fakes a response, Pablo will notice that the response is not encrypted properly in the next step

The key distribution center generates a fresh encryption key for Pablo and Renee to use; call it K_{PR}. The distribution center sends Pablo $E((I_P,R,K_{PR}, E((K_{PR},P), K_R)), K_P)$. In that transaction, Pablo receives the following four pieces encrypted under K_P:

- the message identifier, I_P
- Renee's identification, R
- a key for the communication, K_{PR}
- a string containing his identification and the same key, encrypted under the distribution center's key shared with Renee, $E((K_{PR},P), K_R)$

Pablo cannot decrypt this last item, but he can send it to Renee. Again attacks from Octavia fail because

- If Octavia replaces R with O in Pablo's original message to insert her identifier in place of Renee's, in the response from the distribution center Pablo will notice that Renee's identifier has changed to Octavia's

- If Octavia replaces P with O in Pablo's original message to insert her identifier in place of Pablo's, Octavia will receive the response, not Pablo, and the part for Renee (encrypted under the key known only to the distribution center and Renee) will identify Octavia, not Pablo, as the other party to Renee
- If Octavia intercepts the message from the distribution center, the entire thing is encrypted under K_P so Octavia can neither see nor modify it meaningfully

Finally, Pablo sends to Renee $E((K_{PR}, P), K_R)$, the key sealed and implicitly signed by the distribution center as appropriate for communication with Pablo. The protocol is shown in Figure 4-2.

The protocol suggested here requires a constantly available key distribution center. In addition to the distribution center's being a potential bottleneck (as many people request keys), it is also a very appealing target for overtaking: why should Octavia waste her time trying to intercept and change individual messages if she can overtake, impersonate, or disable the distribution center?

However, this scheme extends well, because adding a new user requires only one key shared with the key distribution center. Also, a user can change keys as often as desired, only needing to lodge that new key with the distribution center. This protocol also handles the situation in which Pablo and Renee have never needed to exchange private communication before, as long as each is registered with the distribution center.

Asymmetric Key Exchange Without Server

Using asymmetric (public) encryption reduces the need for individual keys, and also reduces the vulnerability of the central repository. Suppose Pablo and Renee want to exchange a message, each has a public/private key pair, and each has access to the other's public key. Denote Pablo's public and private keys as E_P and D_P, respectively, with Renee's E_R and D_R.

Pablo can send $E_R(M)$ directly to Renee. However, typically public key encryption algorithms are *significantly* slower than symmetric ones, often by several orders of magnitude. Thus, while encryption itself burdens communication speed, public key encryption burdens it to a degree that is often unacceptable. For this reason, Pablo and Renee may not want to use a public key algorithm to protect their entire communication.

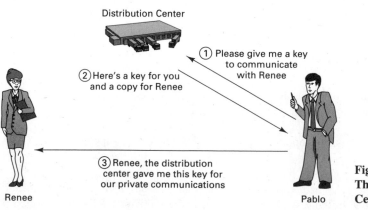

Figure 4-2   Key Distribution Through Key Distribution Center

Pablo can select an encryption key K_{PR} for a symmetric algorithm S to use with Renee. If Pablo sends $E_R(K_{PR})$ to Renee, only Renee can read it, because only she has the private key D_R to decrypt the key. Furthermore, use of public key encryption for this one relatively short exchange does not strain computing resources. However, Renee has no assurance that this key actually came from Pablo, even if he sends $E_R(P, K_{PR})$. These messages could have been forged by Octavia.

Pablo could send $E_R(D_P(K_{PR}))$ to Renee. Only Renee can unwrap the outer layer, so she is assured of the secrecy of the message. Similarly, only Pablo could have applied the inner wrapping $(D_P(\ ))$, so Renee is assured of its authenticity. Thus, this one message passes an authenticated, confidential key.

Typically, however, with asymmetric key exchange, the two sides also exchange a test message to prove that each has properly received a live key (that is, not a replay). After receiving Pablo's key, Renee would send an encrypted random number, n; Pablo would decrypt that number and, to prove he had done so, he would return an encryption of the number $(n + 1)$. Such a concealment is shown in Figure 4-3.

This protocol begs the question of how Pablo and Renee got each other's public keys securely. An answer to this is again a key distribution center.

Asymmetric Key Exchange with Server

This protocol is a straightforward extension of the symmetric key distribution center protocol. Pablo sends a message to the distribution center saying he would like to communicate with Renee (P,R). As before, this message can be in the clear. The distribution center responds with $D_D(E_R, R)$, Renee's public key and her identifier, encrypted under the distribution center's private key. There is no confidentiality issue with this information, only integrity, so anyone with the public key of the distribution center can read it, but only the distribution center could have created it.

Pablo now has Renee's public key and could start communicating directly with Renee, but the protocol is not over. If Pablo sends a message under Renee's public key, he is sure that only she can read it. However, Renee has no key with which to respond. Even if Pablo sent his public key with his message, Renee would have no reason to believe it was from Pablo and not Octavia.

Pablo sends $E_R(P, I_P)$ to Renee: his identity and a reference for her return message. Renee now communicates with the distribution center in the same way as Pablo did, to

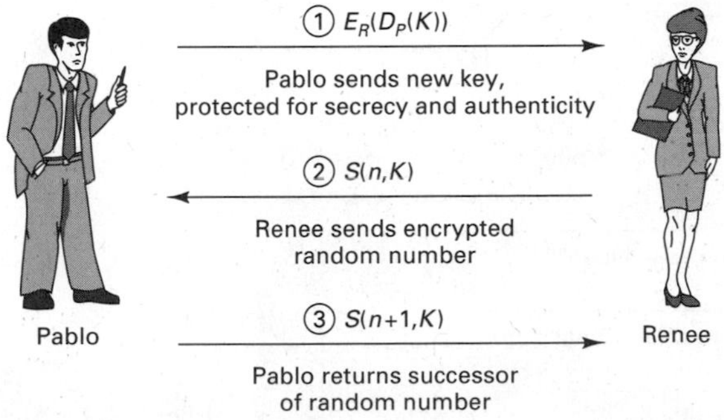

① $E_R(D_P(K))$

Pablo sends new key,
protected for secrecy and authenticity

② $S(n,K)$

Renee sends encrypted
random number

③ $S(n+1,K)$

Pablo returns successor
of random number

Pablo   Renee

Figure 4-3   Symmetric Key Exchange Protocol

obtain his key. She sends (R,P) and receives back $D_D(E_P, P)$. She sends Pablo $E_P(I_P, I_R)$ so that Pablo will know she has received his message, retrieved his public key, and is ready to communicate. The I_P tells Pablo this message comes from Renee (because he sent it to her encrypted under her public key). Pablo completes the protocol by sending Renee his message M and I_R to show that the message is really from Pablo; that is, it follows from her having gotten his public key from the center. He sends $E_R(M,I_R)$ to Renee. (Typically M is a symmetric encryption key for them to use for their actual communication. Otherwise, they can continue sending I identifiers to ensure continuous authenticity.) This protocol has seven steps, as shown in Figure 4-4.

How does the distribution center get keys? A distribution center can publish its own public key widely, and anybody who wishes to register with that center simply delivers the key and the personal identity under the center's key. There can also be multiple distribution centers, because of performance, reliability, or size. In steps 2 and 5, if the distribution center contacted does not have the requested keys, it can negotiate with other centers to obtain and redistribute keys. This negotiation does not need to be apparent to the users. Two or more centers could serve as each other's backup, so that if one is overloaded or down, another center can supply the same key values. Also, once Pablo and Renee have the other's public key, they can store that key locally, needing to inquire of the distribution center only if one changes public key.

The key distribution center is the crucial link in this protocol: it must be available any time anyone needs a public key. Notice, however, that the distribution center sends Renee $D_D(E_P, P)$, which is both Pablo's key and its assurance that this key really came from the distribution center (because the result is encrypted under D_D, the private key of the distribution center). Pablo could request his own key at any convenient time and receive this same result from the distribution center. Then he could pass copies of this authenticated version of his key to anyone with whom he wanted to establish communication. In this way, the continuous availability of the distribution center is no longer crucial.

The remaining question is what gives us confidence that the keys are authentic; that is, that they belong to the people whose identities are associated. That is, Octavia could register a public key of her own, claiming that it was Renee's. The issue here is how can we securely bind an identity and a public key in a trustworthy manner? The answer is called a certificate.

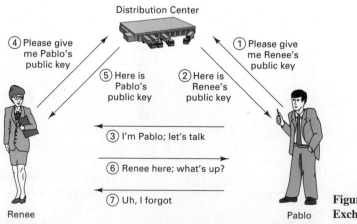

Figure 4-4   Asymmetric Key Exchange Protocol

Certificates

As humans we establish trust all the time. People we know, whose voices or faces or handwriting we recognize, we identify from these characteristics. Sometimes, however, we answer the telephone and hear "I represent the local government . . ." or "I am calling on behalf of this charity . . ." or "I am calling from the school/hospital/police about your mother/father/son/daughter/brother/sister . . ." Depending on the content of the call, we decide whether to believe the caller or to seek independent verification, for example, by telephoning the police back at the number published in the telephone directory. We may seek additional information from the caller ("What color jacket was she wearing?"). We may act so as to exclude an outsider ("I will mail a check directly to your charity."). But for all of these kinds of interactions, we have what we might call a trust threshold, a degree to which we are willing to believe an unidentified individual. For electronic communication to succeed we have to develop ways for two people to establish trust without having met.

There is great use of trust in the commercial world. Acorn Manufacturing Company sends Big Steel Company an order for 10,000 sheets of steel, to be shipped within a week and paid for within ten days. The order is printed on an Acorn form, signed by someone identified as Helene Smudge, Purchasing Agent. Big may begin preparation of the steel. Big may check Acorn's credit rating to decide whether to ship the order without payment first. If suspicious, Big might telephone Acorn and ask to speak to Ms Smudge in the purchasing department. But more likely Big will actually ship the goods without knowing who Ms Smudge is, whether she is actually the purchasing agent, whether she is authorized to commit to an order of that size, or even whether the signature is actually hers. Sometimes a transaction like this occurs by fax, so that Big does not even have on file an original signature. These kinds of transactions occur all the time. Trust here is based on appearance of authenticity (printed, signed form), outside information (credit report), and urgency (Acorn requested the steel quickly).

We all lend things to friends. You meet someone at a party who says she is a friend of a friend, and she asks you to lend her money. You exchange details and become satisfied that she at least knows this friend. Based on that relationship, you may decide to lend her money. Trust is based on her appearance of credibility and her knowing your friend. The pattern could continue with a friend of a friend of a friend ("I live next to Anand, and he speaks often of Clara, who lives in your neighborhood; do you know her?"). You might lend money to a friend of a friend of a friend if you feel comfortable enough with this chain of friendship. The relationship "friend of" does not transfer readily.

But in fact, we have seen a concept we might call "vouch for" several times in these examples. The police vouch for the authenticity of the previous caller, Acorn vouches for the fact that Ms Smudge is its purchasing agent (indirectly by transferring the call to her in the purchasing department), and in a sense the telephone company vouches for the authenticity of the police department or Acorn by listing them in the directory. This concept of "vouching for" can be used as a basis for trust in commercial settings where two parties do not know each other. The concept can be stated as "someone I trust trusts this other person" (or similar words for organizations).

A large company may have several divisions, each division may have several departments, each department may have several projects, and each project may have several task groups (with variations in the names, the number of levels, and the degree of completeness of the structure). The top executive may not know by name or sight every employee in the company, but a task group leader does know all the members of the task group, and the project leader knows all the task group leaders, and so on.

Let us use the organization of a company to show how trust can be developed. Two people meet; call them Ann and Bob. Bob says he works for the same company as Ann. Ann wants to be convinced by independent authorities that he does.

In our company, Andrew and Betty are two task group leaders for the same project (led by Camilla), and Ann works for Andrew and Bob for Betty. These facts can give Ann and Bob a basis for trusting each other's identity. (The organizational relationships are shown in Figure 4-5.) Ann asks Andrew who Bob is; Andrew either asks Betty, if he knows her directly, or Camilla, if not; (Camilla asks Betty); Betty replies he works for her, and the reply follows the return path of this chain. But if Bob is in a different task group, it may be necessary to go higher in the tree before finding a common point.

We can use a similar process for cryptographic key exchange. If Bob and Ann want to communicate, Bob can give his public key to Betty, who passes it to Camilla or directly to Andrew, who gives it to Ann. Well, this is not exactly the way it would work in real life. The key would probably be accompanied by a note saying it is from Bob, ranging from a bit of yellow paper to a form 947 Statement of Identity. And if a form 947 is used, then Betty would have to attach a form 632a Transmittal of Identity, Camilla would attach another 632a, and Andrew would attach a final one, as shown in Figure 4-6. This chain of forms 632a would say, in essence, "I am Betty and I received this key and the attached statement of identity personally from a person I know to be Bob," "I am Camilla and I received this key and the attached statement of identity and the attached transmittal of identity personally from a person I know to be Betty," and so forth. When Ann receives the key, she can review the chain of evidence and conclude with reasonable assurance that the key really did come from Bob. This protocol is a way of obtaining an authenticated public key, a binding of a key and a reliable identity.

This model works well within a company because there is always someone common to any two employees, even if the two employees are in different divisions so that the common person is the president. The process bogs down, however, if Ann, Andrew, Camilla, Betty, and Bob all have to be available whenever Ann and Bob want to communicate. If Betty is away on a business trip or Andrew is off sick, the protocol falters. It also does not work well if the president cannot get any meaningful work done because every day is occupied with handling forms 632a.

To handle the first of these problems, Bob can ask to obtain his complete chain of forms 632a from the president down to him. Bob can then give a copy of this full set to anyone in the company who wants his key. Instead of working from the bottom up to a common point, Bob starts at the top and derives his full chain. He gets these signatures any time his superiors are available, so they do not need to be available when he wants to give away his authenticated public key.

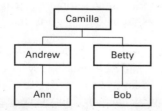

Figure 4-5   Organization in Hypothetical Company

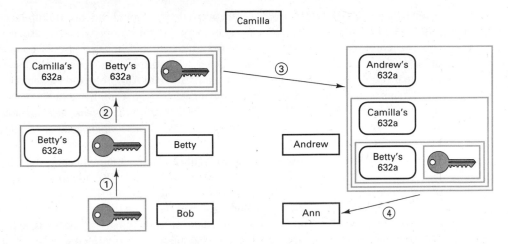

Figure 4-6   Bob Passes a Key to Ann

The second problem is resolved by reversing the process. Instead of starting at the bottom (task members) and working to the top of the tree (the president), we start at the top. Bob thus has a pre-authenticated public key for unlimited use in the future. We will expand the structure of our hypothetical company to show the president and other levels, as shown in Figure 4-7.

The president creates a letter for each division manager saying "I am Edward, the president, I attest to the identity of division manager Diana, whom I know personally, and I trust Diana to attest to the identities of her subordinates." Each division manager does similarly, copying the president's letter with each letter the manager creates, and so on. Bob

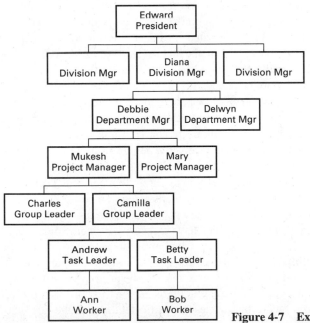

Figure 4-7   Expanded Corporate Structure

receives a packet of letters, from the president down through his task group leader, each letter linked by name to the next. If every employee in the company receives such a packet, any two employees who want to exchange authenticated keys need only compare each other's packets; both packets will have at least Edward in common, perhaps some other high managers, and at some point will deviate. Bob and Ann, for example, could compare their chains, determine that they were the same through Camilla, and trace the bottom parts. Bob knows Alice's chain is authentic through Camilla because it is identical to his chain, and Ann knows the same. Each knows the rest of the chain is accurate because it follows an unbroken line of names and signatures.

This protocol is represented more easily electronically than on paper. With paper, it is necessary to guard against forgeries, to prevent part of one chain being replaced, and to ensure that the public key at the bottom is bound to the chain. Electronically the whole thing can be done using digital signatures and hash functions. Kohnfelder [KOH78] seems to be the originator of the concept of a chain of authenticators, which is expanded in Merkle's paper [MER80], and more recently adopted in international standard X.509.

A public key and user's identity are bound together in a **certificate**, which is then signed by someone certifying the accuracy of the binding. First Edward selects a public key pair, posts the public part where everyone in the company can retrieve it, and retains the private part. Then a division manager, Diana, creates her public key pair, puts the public key in a message together with her identity, and passes the message securely to Edward. Edward signs it by creating a hash value of the message and then encrypting the message and the hash with his private key. By signing the message Edward affirms that the public key (Diana's) and the identity (also Diana's) in the message are for the same person. This message is called Diana's certificate.

Diana's department managers all create messages with their public keys, Diana signs and hashes each, and returns them. She also appends to each a copy of the certificate she received from Edward. In this way, anyone can verify a manager's certificate by starting with Edward's well-known public key, decrypting Diana's certificate to retrieve her public key (and identity), and using Diana's public key to decrypt the manager's certificate. Figure 4-8 shows how certificates are created for Diana and one of her managers, Delwyn. This process continues all the way down the hierarchy to Ann and Bob. As shown in Figure 4-9, Bob's certificate is really his individual certificate combined with all certificates for those above him in the line to the president.

In this example, the certificates were issued on managerial lines. It is not necessary to have or follow a management structure to use certificate signing for authentication. Anybody who would be accepted as an authority can sign a certificate. For example, if you wanted to determine whether a person received a degree from a university, you would not contact the president or chancellor but would instead go to the office of records or the registrar. To verify someone's employment you might go to a personnel office or a director of human resources. And to check whether someone lived at a particular address, you might consult the office of public records. A notary public attests to the validity of a (written) signature on a document. Some companies have a security officer. Some companies have a separate personnel office for each site or each plant location. Any of these officers or heads of offices could credibly sign certificates for people under their purview. Natural hierarchies exist in society, and these same hierarchies can be used to validate certificates.

The only problem with a hierarchy is the need for trust of the top level. The entire chain of authenticity is secure because each certificate contains the key that decrypts the

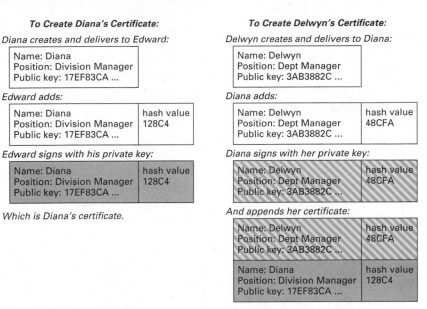

Figure 4-8   Signed Certificates

next certificate, except for the top. Within a company, it is reasonable to trust the person at the top. But if certificates are to become widely used in electronic commerce, people must be able to exchange certificates securely across companies, organizations, and countries.

The Internet is a large federation of networks for intercompany, interorganizational, and international (as well as intracompany, intraorganizational, and intranational) communication. The Internet is run (*coordinated* is probably a better term) by a small group called the Internet Society. The Internet Society has proposed that it be the top signer for certificates with public keys for Internet communications. The Internet Society will sign certificates for Policy Certifying Authorities who, in turn, certify certificates for government

Key to encryptions

- Encrypted under Betty's private key
- Encrypted under Camilla's private key
- Encrypted under Mukesh's private key
- Encrypted under Delwyn's private key
- Encrypted under Diana's private key
- Encrypted under Edward's private key

Name: Bob Position: Worker Public key: 7013F82A ...	hash value 60206
Name: Betty Position: Task Leader Public key: 2468ACCD ...	hash value 00002
Name: Camilla Position: Group Leader Public key: 44082CCA ...	hash value 12346
Name: Mukesh Position: Project Manager Public key: 47F0F008 ...	hash value 16802
Name: Delwyn Position: Dept Manager Public key: 3AB3882C ...	hash value 48CFA
Name: Diana Position: Division Manager Public key: 17EF83CA ...	hash value 128C4

Figure 4-9   Chain of Certificates

agencies, businesses, schools, other organizations, and private individuals. This approach is probably the most likely to succeed.

We have now gone through several approaches to key distribution, ranging from direct exchange to distribution through a central distribution facility to certified advance distribution. There are advantages and distadvantages to each. Points to keep in mind about these protocols, as well as others we will study, are these:

- What *operational restrictions* are there? For example, does the protocol require a continuously available facility such as a key distribution center?
- What *trust* requirements are there? Who and what entities must be trusted to act properly?
- What is the protection against *failure?* Can an outsider impersonate any of the entities in the protocol and subvert security? Can any party of the protocol cheat without detection?
- How *efficient* is the protocol? A protocol requiring several steps to establish an encryption key that will be used many times is one thing; it is quite another to go through several time-consuming steps for a one-time use.
- How easy is the protocol to *implement?* Note that complexity in computer implementation may be different from manual use.

The descriptions of the protocols have raised some of these issues, and some others are brought out in the exercises at the end of this chapter. You should keep these points in mind as you study the remaining protocols in this chapter.

Digital Signatures

Let us examine another typical computer situation that parallels a common human need: an order to transfer funds from one person to another. This is, in essence, a computerized check. We understand how this transaction is handled in the conventional, paper mode:

- A check is a *tangible object* authorizing a financial transaction.
- The signature on the check *confirms authenticity,* because (presumably) only the legitimate signer can produce that signature.
- In the case of an alleged forgery, a third party can be called in to *judge authenticity.*
- A check is canceled, so that it *cannot be reused.*
- The paper check is *not alterable,* or most forms of alteration are easily detected.

Transacting business by check depends on *tangible objects* in a *prescribed form.*

Tangible objects do not exist for transactions on computers. Therefore, authorizing payments by computer requires a different model. Let us consider the requirements of such a situation, both from the standpoint of a bank and from the standpoint of a user.

Sandy sends her bank a message authorizing it to transfer $100 to Tim. Sandy's bank must be able to verify and prove that the message really came from Sandy, if she should later disavow sending the message. The bank also wants to know that the message is entirely Sandy's, that it has not been altered along the way. On her part, Sandy wants to be certain that her bank cannot forge such messages. Both parties want to be sure that the message is new, not a reuse of a previous message, and that it has not been altered during transmission. Using electronic signals instead of paper complicates this transaction.

A **digital signature** is a protocol that produces the same effect as a real signature: it is a mark that only the sender can make, but others people can easily recognize as belonging to the sender. Just like a real signature, a digital signature is used to confirm agreement to a message.

Digital signatures must meet two primary conditions:

- *Unforgeable.* If person *P* signs message *M* with signature *S(P,M)*, it is impossible for anyone else to produce the pair [*M, S(P,M)*].
- *Authentic.* If a person *R* receives the pair [*M, S(P,M)*] purportedly from *P*, *R* can check that the signature is really from *P*. Only *P* could have created this signature, and the signature is firmly attached to *M*.

The first two requirements, shown in Figure 4-10, are the major hurdles in computer transactions. Two additional properties are desirable for transactions completed through the aid of digital signatures:

- *Not alterable.* After being transmitted, *M* cannot be changed by *S, R,* or an interceptor.
- *Not reusable.* A previous message presented will be instantly detected by *R*.

Initially, we present a mechanism that meets the first two requirements. Then we add to that solution to satisfy the other requirements.

Symmetric Key Digital Signatures

With a private key encryption system, the secrecy of the key guarantees the authenticity of the message, as well as its secrecy. If Sandy and the bank have an encryption key in common, she can encrypt her request to transfer money. The bank can be sure of the authenticity of this message because nobody else has Sandy's key.

Conventional symmetric key encryption does not prevent forgery, however: the bank can create an identical message because it also has access to the key. Thus, the bank is sure of the authenticity of the message, but it has no protection against **repudiation** (denial of sending a message). Because both Sandy and the bank have the same key, either Sandy or

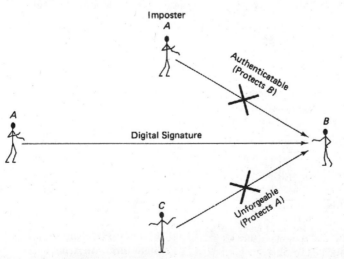

Figure 4-10   Requirements for a Digital Signature

the bank could create any message. When Sandy receives a message from the bank, she is sure of its authenticity, but she could not convince anyone else. Authenticity but not non-repudiation is a characteristic of symmetric encryption. With symmetric encryption such as Data Encryption Standard (DES), an arbiter is needed to prevent forgery.

Here is an outline of the digital signature protocol. Let S be the sender (Sandy), A be the arbiter, and R be the recipient (the bank). The sender has key K_S in common with the arbiter, and the recipient has key K_R in common with the arbiter. Assume that S and R have previously agreed to a format for a digital signature. S wants to send a message M to R, with the added requirements that the message is unforgeable and that its authenticity can be verified.

As shown in Figure 4-11, S first sends $E(M, K_S)$ to the arbiter, A. The arbiter decrypts M using K_S. After verifying that the message is actually from S (because the arbiter can decrypt it with Sandy's key K_S), the arbiter sends $E((M, S, E(M, K_S)), K_R)$ to R. In this way, R receives all of M encrypted under K_R so that R can decrypt the message and act on it. R receives the arbiter's message S, showing that the arbiter will attest that the message came from S. R also receives $E(M, K_S)$, which R cannot decipher because it is encrypted with K_S. However, R files a copy of M and $E(M, K_S)$ in case there is a future dispute.

The authentication condition is met because the receiver trusts the arbiter who says the message came from the sender. The no-forgery property is satisfied, because if S later claims that there was a forgery, R produces M and $E(M,K_S)$. The arbiter can reencrypt M using K_S and certify that only S (or the arbiter, who we presume is honest) could have produced $E(M, K_S)$ because it is encrypted with K_S. Therefore, the arbiter can attest that S (or someone with K_S) sent M.

This protocol produces a system that is actually stronger than required: the message is transmitted in encrypted form, even though secrecy is not needed in every situation. As we have seen, some encryption algorithms are time-consuming, and their use could degrade the speed of message transmission. Therefore, we would like another protocol that did not require encryption of the entire message.

Digital Signatures Without Encryption

If S and R are not concerned with secrecy, they can agree on a **cryptographic sealing function** to use as a signature. A seal is a stamp, mark, or imprint permanently bound to a document to prove its authenticity. A sealing function is a mathematical function affected

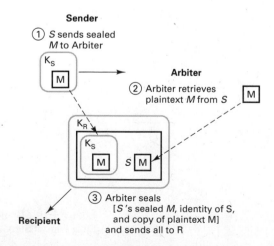

Figure 4-11   Symmetric Key Digital Signature with Arbiter

by every bit of its input. For example, the bytes of a message can be used as numbers, and the sum of all bytes of a message can be computed. This sum is unique to the message because a change to the message will produce a change to the sum as well. The sealing function can be a hash or one-way encryption function, as defined in Chapter 3, or it can be any other function that depends on the entire input and is easy to compute.

Suppose S and R have each registered a personal sealing function with the arbiter; let f_S and f_R be these two functions. Then S sends M and $f_S(M)$ to A. A also computes $f_S(M)$ from the copy of M received from S. If the two values of $f_S(M)$ match, the message is presumed to be authentic, from S. Then, A sends M, S, $f_S(M)$, and $f_R((M,S))$ to R. Again, R cannot interpret $f_S(M)$, but R retains this as evidence that S sent the original message. R does verify the correctness of $f_R((M, S))$ in order to know the authenticity of the message.

Preventing Reuse or Alteration

Both of these solutions meet the requirements for authenticity and preventing forgeries; therefore, they are acceptable digital signature protocols. However, we also want to prevent reuse or alteration of an old message. Although R cannot create *new* messages under K_S or f_S, the receiver can reuse old ones. For example, the receiver can save an old order to pay Tim $100 and process it every month. Furthermore, knowing the encryption technique but not the encryption key, the receiver may be able to cut pieces from old messages and paste them together to form a new message. Paper checks solve this problem: the bank cancels the check and returns it to the sender, so that the sender knows it cannot be reused. We need a way to create a similarly self-destructing computer signature, one that cannot be reused.

To document the use of a message, we make part of the signature into a **time stamp**. For example, if Sandy's message shows the date and time sent, the bank cannot reprocess that same message a week later without Sandy or anyone else detecting the forgery. The time stamp need not be literally the time or date; any nonrepeating code, such as an increasing series of numbers, will do. This solves the reprocessing difficulty.

To prevent cutting the message into pieces and reusing a single piece, Sandy can make each piece depend on the time stamp. For example, with DES, which encrypts 64-bit text blocks into a 64-bit output, Sandy could encrypt the date and time in the first 8 bits of each block, leaving 56 bits of each block for the message. Because all 64 bits of a DES output block depend on all 64 input bits, the bank cannot combine the 56 message bits with a different 8-bit time stamp. This process is shown in Figure 4-12. As we will discover at the end of this chapter, the cipher block chaining mode of DES is another way to prevent reuse of a block of one message in another message.

These solutions are somewhat complicated. They require an active arbiter on each transaction, and ensuring secrecy requires the message to be encrypted twice. Fortunately, the public key protocol is simpler.

Public Key Protocol

Public key encryption systems are ideally suited to digital signatures. For simple notation, let us assume that the public key encryption for user U is accessed through $E(M, K_U)$, and that the private key transformation for U is written as $D(M,K_U)$. We can think of E as the *privacy* transformation (because only U can decrypt it) and D as the *authenticity*

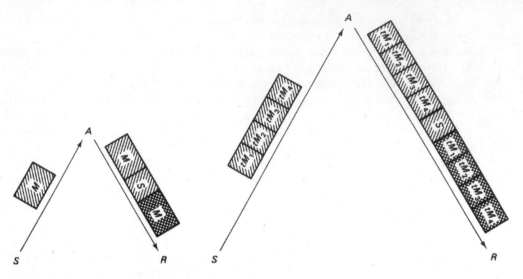

Figure 4-12   Symmetric Key Digital Signature with Time Stamp

transformation (because only U can produce it). Remember, however, that under some asymmetric algorithms such as RSA, D and E are commutative, and either one can be applied to any message. Thus,

$$D(\ E(M,-),\ -) = M = E(\ D(M,-),\ -)$$

If S wishes to send M to R, S uses the authenticity transformation to produce $D(M, K_S)$. S then sends $D(M, K_S)$ to R. R decodes the message with the public key transformation of S, computing $E(\ D(M,K_S),\ K_S) = M$, as shown in Figure 4-13. Because only S can create a message that makes sense under $E(-,K_S)$, the message must genuinely have come from S. This test satisfies the authenticity requirement.

R will save $D(M,K_S)$. If S should later allege that the message is a forgery (not really from S), R can simply show M and $E(M,K_S)$. Anyone can verify that because $D(M,K_S)$ is transformed to M using the public key transformation of S—but only S could have produced $D(M,K_S)$—$D(M,K_S)$ must be from S. This test satisfies the unforgeability requirement.

The public key solution is obviously much less cumbersome than the private key solution. One disadvantage of this approach is that the message is authentic but not private; that is, anyone who knows the public key of S can translate the message. We can overcome this disadvantage by using two encryptions.

Because S is sending M to R, authenticity can be achieved through the private key of S, and secrecy can be achieved through the public key of R. For example, S could send

$$E(D(M, K_S), K_R)$$

```
   D:K_S
    ┌─┐  For authenticity,           ┌ Decrypts M
    │M│  unforgeability              │
    └─┘                         ┌    │              D:K_S
 S ─────────────────────────► R ┤    Saves a copy to    ┌─┐     Figure 4-13    Asymmetric Digital
                                │    answer future      │M│     Signature
                                └    disputes            └─┘
```

Figure 4-13   Asymmetric Digital Signature

to R, as shown in Figure 4-14. Because only S can produce $D(-, K_S)$, the message must be from S. But because only R can decrypt $E(-, K_R)$, the message content remains private until R transforms it. With two encryptions, then, we have a protocol that provides both privacy and authenticity.

Time stamps as we have just described can be used to guard against replays. A sealing function can also prevent substitution of pieces of ciphertext.

Key Escrow

Suppose you lose a house key. With some inconvenience you can call a locksmith, who will open your lock and even make you another key. You need to convince the locksmith to let you in, but either some identification or neighbors can vouch for your authorization. If you lose the combination to a safe, the process may be a little more complicated, and it will take the locksmith longer, but in relatively short time you can get back in. That is because house locks and safes are designed to withstand only relatively short attacks: a day or two at most. Physical security plays an important part in the safety of houses and offices: we would expect to be able to block a prolonged attack—one that went on for several hours.

Ciphertext does not enjoy physical security. In fact, it is intended for communication over insecure channels, where you expect the attacker to be able to retrieve the ciphertext and analyze it at will for hours, days, weeks, even years. Thus, encryption algorithms have to be strong, to withstand this potential long-term attack. Therefore, there are no crypto locksmiths who can retrieve lost or forgotten keys. If you work for a company and have encrypted your files, someone else may legitimately need access to them if you are away from the office, on a business trip or holiday, ill, or no longer with the company, for example. Or you may simply have forgotten your key This is one of the advantages of key escrow and why it makes sense in these situations: key escrow provides a means for data to be adequately secure, but to also allow other legitimate users access on an emergency basis.

Clipper Key Escrow

The Clipper approach (as described in Chapter 3) is an example of a **key escrow** protocol. The essence of the algorithm is dividing a key into n pieces, presumably given to n individuals, so that any k of these n can decrypt, but no $(k - 1)$ of them can. This is called a **k of n protocol**. For Clipper $k = n = 2$. (The more general problem of n > 2 was studied by Shamir [SHA79], who presented a solution based on finding roots of an nth degree polynomial, while Blakley [BLA79b] solved the problem independently in a different way; Chapter 9 of Simmons [SIM92] includes an excellent overview of other schemes.)

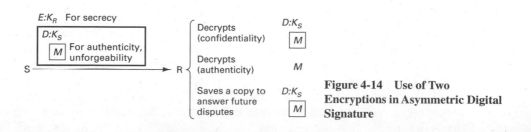

Figure 4-14   Use of Two Encryptions in Asymmetric Digital Signature

The requirements for a key escrowing protocol are as follows:

- Communication must identify its encrypting source.
- Identification must reveal only the encrypting unit, not the specific encryption key.
- Key must be retrievable under a k of n protocol.

The Clipper encryption protocol satisfies these requirements. With the Clipper protocol, the originating encryption unit randomly generates an 80-bit session key. It encrypts this 80-bit key under a key unique to the physical unit, appends a serial number for the physical unit, and encrypts both of these under a key shared by all such units; this encrypted group is called the Law Enforcement Access Field (LEAF).

It also uses its own key exchange protocol to pass this key to the recipient. All Clipper units are preprogrammed from the factory with a shared symmetric encryption key, called a **family key**. Clipper uses a three-stage protocol for key exchange. This problem has the following requirements:

- Encryption keys may be transmitted only in encrypted form.
- An exchange between Clipper units must protect against replay.
- The two Clipper units in the exchange must authenticate each other.

The algorithm requires three steps for key exchange, plus four more for mutual authentication. This algorithm comes from Bellovin and Merritt [BEL92b].

The sender S and receiver R share a common password, P, plus they have a common symmetric Y and an asymmetric E encryption algorithm.

1. S generates a random public key E_S. S encrypts E_S with Y_P and sends $Y_P(E_S)$ to R.
2. R knows P and uses that to decrypt and obtain E_S. R generates a random session key X. R returns X to S, doubly encrypted under both Y_P and E_S: R sends $E_S(Y_P(X))$.
3. S uses E_S and P to obtain X. At this point the key exchange is complete. Now S and R must ensure that the other has obtained functional use of the new key X.
4. S generates a random string M and sends $E_X(M)$ to R.
5. R decrypts this to obtain M. R chooses another random string N and returns the concatenation of these two strings, encrypted under X to S: $E_X((M,N))$
6. S decrypts this message to obtain (M,N). If the first part, M, is what S sent, then R has been authenticated to S. S returns $E_X(N)$ alone to R.
7. If R receives the N sent in step 4, S has now been authenticated to R.

After Clipper has completed a key interchange, it begins the message traffic with the recipient, each message being accompanied by the LEAF. As shown in Figure 4-15, a message is accompanied by the LEAF, which will permit authorized parties to obtain the key used to encrypt a communication.

With this protocol, law enforcement authorities intercepting the message can use the common family key F to decrypt the last piece of $E((E(K,U) + \text{ID}), F)$ and obtain ID, the unit number that generated the message encryption key. They can appeal to a court to obtain the corresponding U that will let them obtain K from $E(K,U)$.

There are some undesirable characteristics of this protocol, however. First, once law enforcement authorities have obtained U from a court, that value gives them access to all

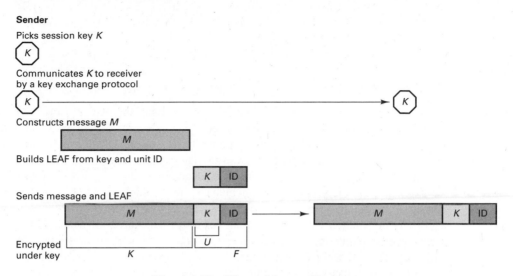

Figure 4-15   Clipper Message Exchange

messages ever sent by that unit, in the past or in the future, even if the unit was legally obtained from or sold to someone else. Also, once law enforcement authorities have obtained U, they can generate messages purported to be from the sender, because E is a symmetric algorithm. However, the users can circumvent law enforcement by superencrypting: law enforcement authorities might decrypt $E(M,K)$ only to find out that the sender had encrypted M before passing it to Clipper for encryption; that is, M might be $E'(M,K')$ for some other encryption E' or some other key K'. Note that distributing Skipjack encryption only in hardware effectively prevents tampering with the cryptographic implementation.

Software Key Escrow

Software implementations of cryptography have both advantages and disadvantages over hardware. They are easier to change or to customize for demands of particular applications. They can be embedded in or integrated with applications so that they can be installed or run on any computer. Errors in them can easily be repaired. And their cost to reproduce can be insignificant. However, their changability is also their biggest drawback: they can be changed by accident or by a malicious program on their storage medium, in memory, or during execution. As we have seen, even a small change, as small as one bit, can have a serious effect on the strength of cryptography. Still, the flexibility of software makes them a reasonable candidate for some environments.

Software-based key escrowed encryption would operate very much like the Clipper escrow. An escrow agency would preprogram a software cryptographic implementation with a family key and a unit identifier. This implementation would be sold to a software manufacturer, who would embed it in a software product. Each copy of the software (similar to an individual physical unit) would have its own identifier. The product would accept plaintext and an encryption key and generate a LEAF and ciphertext. The receiving software would check for the existence of a LEAF and decrypt. Key escrow is more appropriately done using public key encryption, so that a different algorithm is used for key management from that for messages and so that neither the manufacturer nor law enforcement can circumvent the other without its being evident. Denning and Branstad [DEN96] present a good study of numerous software key escrow protocols.

Mental Poker

In this section we consider a similar situation involving the need for both secrecy and authenticity. Consider a poker game played by people who cannot see each other, for example, by mail. Even though playing poker by mail is not an important task, the underlying protocol has some very important uses. The most difficult part of playing poker by mail is ensuring that cards are dealt and distributed fairly. In a later section we use this protocol to distribute encryption keys, in which case the "cards" become keys. The card-playing setting makes the protocol easy to explain.

Suppose Ann and Bill decide to play poker by mail. Ann is the dealer and shuffles the cards. (For simplicity the deck is assumed to contain only 10 cards, of which each player will get 5. The protocol can be extended easily to conventional 52-card decks by replacing 10 by 52, or any other number, in the following explanation.)

Distribution Protocol

To shuffle the cards, Ann puts them in an arbitrary order, places each card in an unmarked box, and puts a lock on each box. Ann then sends all 10 boxes to Bill. Because the boxes appear indistinguishable, Bill selects any 5 boxes, and puts a second lock on these boxes. These 5 boxes constitute Bill's hand. Bill leaves the other 5 boxes untouched, so they have only Ann's locks on them. Bill then sends all 10 boxes back to Ann.

Upon receiving the boxes, Ann can determine that Bill has so far acted fairly: he has selected only 5 boxes and has not peeked at the cards (because Ann's locks are intact). Ann removes all 10 of her locks. Now Ann has access to the 5 cards Bill left alone; these constitute Ann's hand.

Ann returns the remaining 5 boxes, still bearing Bill's lock. Bill removes his 5 locks from the 5 boxes containing the cards of his hand. Ann does not know these cards because Bill's locks have not been tampered with. Bill, satisfied by the fairness of the deal, continues to play. This sequence of events is shown in Figure 4-16.

Symmetric Key Implementation

This protocol works easily with conventional encryption systems. For generality we will use the term *message* instead of *card* in the protocol. The protocol is depicted in Figure 4-17.

Ann "shuffles" the messages and encrypts each under K_A, Ann's key. Ann then sends all 10 encrypted messages to Bill. As the messages arrive Bill chooses 5 at random. Bill cannot identify these messages because they are encrypted under Ann's key. Bill sends these back to Ann untouched.

Bill takes the remaining 5; call them B_1 to B_5. Bill sends $E(B_1, K_B)$ through $E(B_5, K_B)$ back to Ann. Remember that Ann sent encrypted messages to Bill, so that each B_i is really $E(c_j, K_A)$, message c_j encrypted with Ann's key. Therefore, Bill really sends $E(E(c_j, K_A), K_B)$ back to Ann. The encryption with Bill's key forms a double lock on these messages, in order to guarantee that Bill will get just these back and that Ann cannot know the content of the messages.

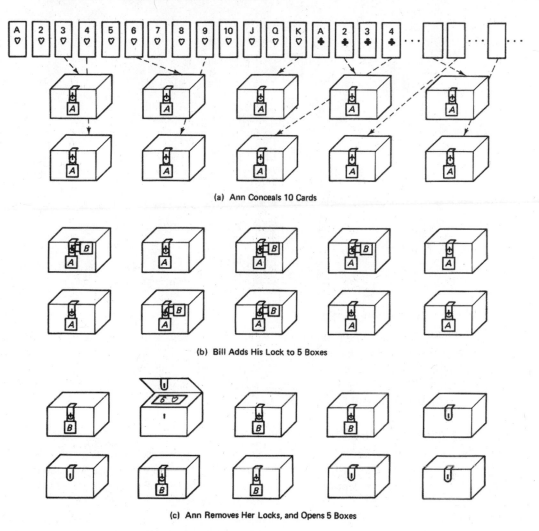

(a) Ann Conceals 10 Cards

(b) Bill Adds His Lock to 5 Boxes

(c) Ann Removes Her Locks, and Opens 5 Boxes

Figure 4-16   Poker Protocol

Ann has now received 5 messages encrypted once, $E(c_i,K_A)$, and 5 more messages encrypted under two keys, $E(\,E(c_j,K_A),\,K_B)$. Ann now unlocks the 5 messages she is to keep; Ann does this by decrypting the 5 $E(c_j,K_A)$ messages. She also decrypts each of the 5 messages that Bill chose, producing $D(\,E(\,E(c_j,K_A),\,K_B),\,K_A)$. If encryption and decryption are commutative,

$$D(\,E(\,E(c_j\,K_A),\,K_B),\,K_A) = E(\,D(\,E(c_j,K_A),K_A),\,K_B) = E(c_j,K_B)$$

Thus, these messages are now concealed only under Bill's key. Ann then returns these messages to Bill, who decrypts them and continues the game. In Figure 4-17, the messages are shown as cards with different shadings to indicate encryption by Ann and by Bill. (In fact, this protocol has a flaw if Ann provides Bill only 10 messages from which to choose. See the exercises at the end of the chapter for a description of the flaw.)

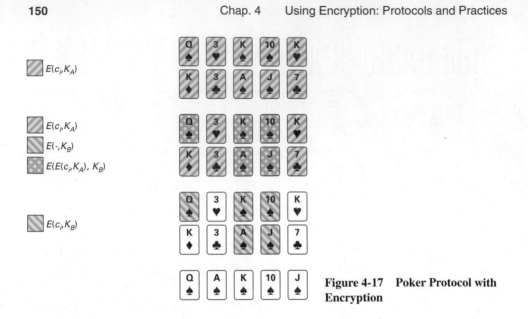

$E(c_i, K_A)$

$E(c_i, K_A)$
$E(-, K_B)$
$E(E(c_i, K_A), K_B)$

$E(c_i, K_B)$

Figure 4-17   Poker Protocol with Encryption

Public Key Implementation

The public key implementation is the natural substitution, using the notation $D(\ )$ for the private transformation and $E(\ )$ for the public transformation. Ann first locks the messages with a public transformation; Bill then locks his selected hand again with his public transformation. Ann removes her public lock, so that now they are concealed only under Bill's public lock. Finally Bill removes his lock, obtaining his messages.

Key Distribution: An Application of the Protocol

The protocol is not limited to the rather unrealistic situation of distributing playing cards by computer. Consider instead an encryption system that requires special keys, so that not every number is an acceptable key. (Some implementations of the DES require that every eighth bit of the key be a parity bit for the previous seven bits of the key. This is easily done with any 56-bit key. Other than that, any 56-bit binary number can be a key. However, as described in Chapter 3, the RSA, Merkle–Hellman, and El Gamal algorithms require a special pair of keys, which can be determined only by the implementer of the algorithm.)

General users either cannot or will not want to generate keys themselves. Thus, providing keys for users is a problem. One solution is to have a central key server that generates and distributes keys. There is legitimate concern about maintaining secrecy for a central repository that holds and assigns keys.

A protocol is needed to enable a user to obtain a new key, while nobody—not even the central repository—knows what key the user has received. There are two possible exposures here:

- *No one should be able to determine a user's private key given the public key.* We cannot publish a "key directory" and let everyone choose a key at random. If there were such a directory someone could look up the private key matching a public key as soon as a user chose a pair of keys and revealed the public key. Thus the privacy of a private key must be maintained while a user is selecting a new key.

- *The key distributor should not know what key a user has selected.* Thus, the facility cannot distribute one key to a user and expect the user to ask for the mate to the key selected. Nor can the facility distribute only one pair to a user; the user should have some choice so that the key distributor cannot be sure which key the user has chosen. Essentially we want the key distributor to put the keys in sealed envelopes in a barrel, and let a user pick one envelope.

A possible key distributor is a central source that generates and encrypts keys (like Ann in the previous example). Ann sends out a continuous stream of *encrypted* encryption keys. Because the keys are encrypted, no one can determine the keys themselves by monitoring the encrypted keys.

A particular user wanting a new key (like Bill) allows a few of Ann's encrypted keys to pass by and then chooses one, $E(k_i, K_A)$, at random. Some time later (after enough additional keys have been sent so that Ann cannot know which one Bill has chosen), Bill encrypts the selected key, forming $E(E(k_i, K_A), K_B)$. Bill sends this twice-encrypted key back to Ann. Ann decrypts the key, so that it is now concealed only under Bill's key, and sends it back to Bill. Finally, Bill decrypts the key to use it. This process, which is exactly like the poker protocol described earlier, is shown in Figure 4-18, where shading again shows how the messages are encrypted. Notice that if used for a public key system, each key, or message, from Ann is really a pair of keys, $E((k_{PUB}, k_{PRIV}), K_A)$.

Voting by Computer

A similar problem involves transmitting an untraceable yet authentic message. Such communication could, for example, allow human participants in an experiment to answer a confidential questionnaire anonymously. In another case, votes might be submitted electronically for tabulation by a computer. A third example involves automating private

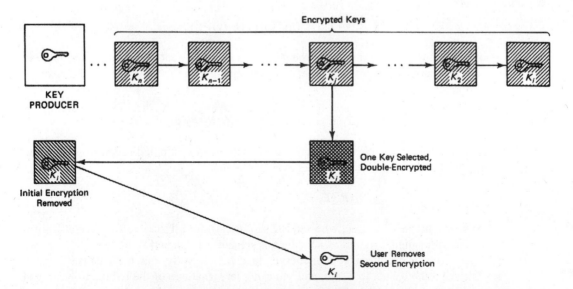

Figure 4-18   Secure Key Distribution Protocol

transactions (such as Swiss bank accounts), where financial transfers are authentic but cannot be traced back to their originators.

In all three cases, we need a protocol to ensure secrecy and legitimacy. Every message in the system must have come from some legitimate user, but no user can be associated with a particular message once the message is transmitted. The security requirements of this protocol are as follows:

- Only authorized users can transmit messages.
- Each user can transmit only one message at a time.
- Nobody can determine who sent a particular message.

Demillo and Merritt [DEM82, DEM83] designed such a protocol. To show how the protocol works we consider a voting example. Suppose three voters, Jan, Keith, and Lee, are voting "yes" or "no" on one issue. Let each voter have two public key encryption functions. The first function, E, is a regular public key encryption function, but the second, R, embeds the message in a random string and then encrypts the result. D is the decrypting function for E and Q for R. Because there are several layers of functions, we change notation to E_U as the transformation for individual U.

Two people could have identical votes. The protocol must permit each user to recognize his or her vote without being able to know which other votes, if any, are identical. The R encryption with a random string provides the desired secrecy and identifiability. Outwardly, the votes are concealed, because two identical votes have different random strings attached. However, each voter can uniquely identify his or her vote. Because each person's R decryption is known only to that person, only the sender can affirm that his or her ballot is among those to be counted.

Voting Protocol

Each voter chooses a vote, v, and computes

$$R_J(R_K(R_L(E_J(E_K(E_L(v))))))$$

using the public encryptions. All of the encrypted votes are sent to the first voter, Jan. Jan verifies that her ballot is among the set received. Jan then removes the first level of encryption from all ballots with

$$Q_J(R_J(R_K(R_L(E_J(E_K(E_L(v))))))) = R_K(R_L(E_J(E_K(E_L(v)))))$$

because $Q_J(R_J(x)) = x$. Now Jan forwards the ballots, in scrambled order, to Keith, who checks for his ballot and decrypts one level, producing

$$Q_K(R_K(R_L(E_J(E_K(E_L(v)))))) = R_L(E_J(E_K(E_L(v))))$$

Keith sends this result to Lee, who sends $E_J(E_K(E_L(v)))$ for all the v to Jan. Lee also signs the votes with a digital signature, sending this signature to Jan and Keith.

Jan removes one more level of encryption, checks to verify that her vote is still in the set, forwards the ballots to Keith, and sends digital signatures of the ballots to Keith and

Lee. Keith receives $E_K(E_L(v))$ from Jan, which he decrypts to produce $E_L(v)$ for Lee. Lee removes E_L and publishes the results.

This protocol works because the analysis process is a six-link chain: $J \rightarrow K \rightarrow L \rightarrow J \rightarrow K \rightarrow L$. Results at each link of the chain can be made public without destroying the anonymity of any ballot. Furthermore, for the last three links of the chain, anyone can go "backward," but only one person can go "forward." That is, suppose Jan transforms the votes and passes them to Keith. Only Jan can perform this transformation. But Keith or anyone else can perform the reverse transformation, $J \leftarrow K$, to see whether what Jan passed to Keith matches what Jan started with. This ability to check each other's work inhibits anyone from cheating.

Analysis of the Protocol

Let us analyze each step of this protocol. First, there is nothing that associates a vote with a single person, so the votes remain secret. Second, each person could have voted only once because there are only three votes and everyone attests in the first round that his or her vote is among the three. Finally, nobody other than the three could have voted because one of the three voters would find his or her vote missing.

Suppose during the second round someone decides to tamper with a vote. Once the results have been announced, the three voters can encrypt the result votes with R to verify that these match the set originally sent around. Because each of the three signs the set of votes being passed forward, it is possible to detect who falsified the results.

Figure 4-19 depicts an example of this protocol. For simplicity, the E-type encryptions are shown with directed shadings, and the R-type encryptions are shown by Jan adding one random bit on the left, Keith adding two random bits on the right, and Lee adding three random bits on the left.

Oblivious Transfer

The next protocol is a tool that will be used in later, more complicated protocols. The problem involves sending one of two messages, with the restriction that neither the sender nor the receiver will know until later which message was sent. An example of this problem is flipping a coin at some distance. One person (the sender) flips a coin and writes down the result (heads or tails). The other (the receiver) writes down a guess of how the coin landed. The two people meet later and exchange pieces of paper. In this case, if the words on the papers match, the receiver has won; otherwise the sender has won.

Suppose the two people cannot meet to exchange pieces of paper. Imagine this scenario. Pete and Nancy agree to go out one evening. On the telephone Pete suggests flipping a coin; if it turns out heads, Pete will pay for dinner and a movie, but if it is tails, Nancy will pay. Nancy replies that this is fine with her. Pete knows that if Nancy flips the coin, she will call it "heads" regardless of what it turns out; Pete knows this because he would do the same thing himself. Nevertheless, they have to decide over the phone so that the other can go to the bank to get money for the evening.

This problem is called the **oblivious transfer**; Pete wants to send one of two messages to Nancy with a probability of 0.5 that each message is received. Pete's first message could be "I will pay. Pete." If Nancy shows him this message he is obligated to pay; the other message Nancy might receive is a meaningless garble, in which case she will be

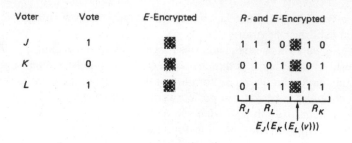

Voter	Vote	E-Encrypted	R- and E-Encrypted
J	1	▓	1 1 1 0 ▓ 1 0
K	0	▓	0 1 0 1 ▓ 0 1
L	1	▓	0 1 1 1 ▓ 1 1

$$R_J \quad R_L \quad R_K$$

$$E_J(E_K(E_L(v)))$$

J, K, and L compute their encrypted votes; K and L send theirs to J

J Receives   1 1 1 0 ▓ 1 0   0 1 0 1 ▓ 0 1   0 1 1 1 ▓ 1 1

J removes R, scrambles the votes, and sends them to K

K Receives   1 0 1 ▓ 0 1   1 1 0 ▓ 1 0   1 1 1 ▓ 1 1

K removes R, scrambles the votes, and sends them to L

L Receives   1 0 1 ▓   1 1 1 ▓   1 1 0 ▓

L removes R, scrambles the votes, and sends them to J

J Receives   ▓   ▓   ▓

J removes E, signs all votes, and sends them to K and L

   to K and L   ▓ Signed J   ▓ Signed J   ▓ Signed J

K removes E, signs all votes, and sends them to J and L

   to J and L   ▓ Signed K   ▓ Signed K   ▓ Signed K

L removes E, signs all votes, and sends them to J and K

   Public   0   1   1
   to J and K   0 Signed L   1 Signed L   1 Signed L

Figure 4-19   Voting Protocol

obligated. If the probability of each of Pete's messages being received is 0.5, it is equivalent to flipping a coin fairly.

Transfer Protocol

The original protocol was devised by Blum [BLU81]. A solution by Even [EVE85] is easy to understand, even though it requires several encryption keys. Here are the steps of the protocol.

1. Pete chooses two pairs of public encryption keys (four keys in all). For reference sometimes we denote these keys as functions, E_i, D_i, E_j, and D_j. E_i is the public transformation with key i, and D_i is its corresponding private transformation. (That is, $D_i(E_i(M)) = M$ for any message M.) The same notation is used for E_j and D_j.

2. Nancy chooses a key, K_N, to a symmetric encryption algorithm, S.

3. Pete sends both public keys (E_i, E_j) to Nancy, retaining the private ones himself.

4. Nancy picks one at random, call it h, and sends $E_h(K_N)$ to Pete; that is, she encrypts her symmetric key K_N with one of the public keys E_h.

5. Pete picks either i or j at random; suppose it is j. Pete computes $P = D_j(E_h(K_N))$. This is just a binary string to Pete, so he cannot tell whether j is the h Nancy chose. If $h = j$, the P is Nancy's key K_N; otherwise P is a meaningless binary string.[1]

6. Pete computes $S($"I will pay. Pete."$, P)$, which he sends to Nancy, along with the value of j.

7. Nancy decrypts Pete's message with K_N. She picked h and Pete picked j. If $h = j$ she wins, for she properly decrypts Pete's message; she sends M and h to Pete as evidence that she picked right. If $h \neq j$, she loses, getting only a meaningless tangle of bits.

8. After the winner is known, Pete gives the private keys D_i and D_j to Nancy. From these keys, she can verify whether her h was i or j, and that the j Pete used was one of these two. If $h = j$ and she gets no message, she can conclude that Pete cheated.

The steps of this protocol are shown in Figure 4-20.

Analysis of the Protocol

How does this protocol work? Nancy first picks one of Pete's keys, which she disguises and returns to Pete. Pete cannot tell which Nancy has picked because he does not have access to K_N with which to decrypt it. Therefore, when he picks j, the chance that he picks the one Nancy picked is 1 in 2. He encrypts a message that Nancy must reproduce exactly in order to convince him that he picked her key. If they picked the same key, Nancy's K_N decrypts the message; if not, K_N produces a meaningless string. When they get together later, they can exchange keys and verify that each party lived up to the rules of the protocol.

Of course, flipping coins over a telephone is not a very important task. However, this protocol is the basis for the two protocols we consider next.

Contract Signing

Suppose that Charles and Diane agree to something and wish to sign a contract to show their agreement. Both of them are committed to performing some act by the contract, but each wants to commit only if the other does also. For example, Charles might commit to selling his car to Diane if Diane agrees to give him a part interest in her pizza franchise.

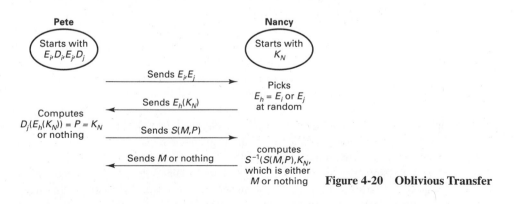

Figure 4-20   Oblivious Transfer

---

[1]If length is significant, for example, 64 bits for a DES key, the two can agree to send any length string and use, for example, only the first 64 bits.

Charles is in California and Diane is in New York. Charles will not sign the contract first and mail it to Diane, because that leaves him at Diane's mercy: he has agreed to sell the car, so he must take it off the market. But Diane could tear up the contract, leaving Charles with the car; on the other hand, Diane could sign the contract, forcing Charles to produce the car. Charles is bound by the contract as soon as he signs. However, he does not know whether Diane will sign or not, so she is not bound by it. The situation is the same if Diane signs first: she is bound but not Charles.

In practice, this would be handled by both people signing together. We want to establish a protocol for signing contracts by computer. Physical proximity and written signatures are what we want to avoid with our solution.

A solution would be to appeal to a trustworthy third party: Charles and Diane each sign a copy of the contract, which they forward to a trusted third party, who holds these two copies with one signature each. These constitute evidence of their willingness to enter into the contract. When the third party announces that a signed copy has been received from each, Charles signs another copy, which he sends to Diane, and she signs a copy, which she sends to him. Charles and Diane inform the third party that the contracts are in order, and the third party destroys the ones with only one signature each. We want to avoid appeal to a third party, too, if possible.

Thus, a contract protocol requires two things:

- *Commitment.* After a certain point both parties are bound by the contract; until then neither is.
- *Unforgeability.* The signatures on the contract must be demonstrably authentic; that is, it must be possible for either party to prove that the signature of the other is authentic.

The protocol must be able to achieve these two things *indirectly*, without face-to-face participation. An indirect protocol is suitable for use in a computerized situation.

With Pen and Paper

A protocol without face-to-face cooperation might operate in the following manner. This protocol would probably not actually be used, but it is similar to a computer protocol that is described in the next section. Charles and Diane pass at least three copies of the contract back and forth. Each holds one copy as proof of what has happened up until then; a copy can also be in transit. It is fairly clear who sends which copy to whom in order to hold onto a piece of evidence, so we will not describe the different copies that move back and forth.

Charles writes the first part of his name on the contract, "C," and sends it to Diane. She writes her first initial, "D," and sends it back. Charles writes the next part of his name, "h," and they continue trading the contract, each affixing a piece of the signature. With only the letter "C" on the contract, Charles knows that nobody could require him to fulfill the contract. However, the letter is an act of good faith that he shows to Diane. Diane responds with a similar act of good faith.

After several letters are in each signature, Diane knows that she could convince a judge that Charles should really be bound by the terms of the contract. She would explain the circumstances and hope the judge would agree. There is a measure of uncertainty in this: Charles is not bound by just the letter "C," but he is bound by his full signature. However, the point at which he becomes bound is not obvious: is it 1/2 of the letters? 2/3? 3/4?

Because they are uncertain at exactly what point they become bound, both Charles and Diane must fear they are bound at each point, so there is no reason not to continue the protocol. They also know that the longer they continue, the greater probability of proving the other is also bound, so again it is in their best interest to continue. Besides, both wanted to sign the contract anyway; they just wanted to be bound at the same time. This issue of uncertainty of point of commitment is the basis of the computer solution.

Overview of the Indirect Protocol

The computer solution works much the same way. The parties exchange a message of commitment in pieces, using the oblivious transfer protocol from the previous section. Remember that the oblivious transfer is a way of transmitting one of two messages, so that neither the sender nor the receiver is sure which message has been transmitted. Therefore, neither party knows when half of this message has been transmitted, because with oblivious transfer neither knows exactly what the other has received.

Suppose each person's signature is divided into four blocks, and that it is impossible to recognize the signature just by looking at it. Charles and Diane execute the oblivious transfer eight times each. Charles sends each block once under an i and once under the corresponding j; Diane does likewise.

For the first three times, Charles feels safe because Diane cannot have all four blocks of his signature. Charles sends the fourth piece. With this, Diane may have a full signature, but she cannot tell that. In fact, the probability is low, less than 0.02, that she has received all four signature blocks. If she stops, Charles might have received 3/4 of her signature and be able to convince a judge that Diane had reneged on the contract. Diane has no choice but to continue. As Charles and Diane continue, they come closer and closer to assurance.

At any point after four rounds, neither can stop, because he or she might already have transmitted a full signature, thereby being bound by the contract anyway. Therefore, it is in the best interest of both to continue until the end, when the full signatures are definitely exchanged.

Indirect Contract-Signing Protocol

The following protocol, designed by Even et al. [EVE85], follows this outline.

1. Charles randomly selects $2n$ keys for a symmetric-key cryptosystem, such as DES. Let these keys be $c_1, c_2, \ldots, c_{2n}$. The keys are treated as pairs, (c_1, c_{n+1}), (c_2, c_{n+2}), and so forth. There is nothing distinctive about c_i and c_{n+i} that marks them as a pair, however.

2. For each key, Charles computes $C_i = E(S, c_i)$ for some standard message S whose content is irrelevant. Charles sends C_1 through C_{2n} to Diane. That is, Diane has the encrypted version of the standard message under each key.

3. Charles agrees that he is committed to the contract if Diane can present *both* keys c_i and c_{n+i} for any i. (Note: in the description by Even et al. each C_i is called an S-puzzle, and the key (c_i, c_{n+i}) is called its solution.)

4. Diane repeats these three steps similarly, with keys d_i and encrypted messages D_i.

5. Charles sends each pair c_i and c_{n+i}, $1 \le i \le n$, to Diane via the oblivious transfer. That is, Charles sends either c_i or c_{n+i} to Diane, but neither he nor she is sure which has been received. Diane does the same with all d_i and d_{n+i} for $1 \le i \le n$. At this point, Charles and Diane each have half of the other's secrets.

6. Let l be the length of each c_i or d_i.
   For $1 \le j \le l$ **begin**
   > Charles transmits the jth bit of all c_i, $1 \le i \le n$ to Diane.
   > Diane transmits the jth bit of all d_i, $1 \le i \le n$ to Charles.

   end

7. Assuming neither stops early, at the end both have all l bits of all of the other's secrets, and the contract is signed.

When step 6 begins, both Diane and Charles have half of the other's secrets; however, it is infeasible to determine the key c_i from its encrypted message C_i, assuming Diane received c_{n+i}. As this step progresses, Diane receives one bit of c_i, then the next bit, then the next bit, etc. If Diane uses a brute force attack to determine c_i, each bit she receives cuts her workload in half.

At some point, she may think the work still to be done is easy enough that she will attempt to determine c_i for some i. Thus she may stop sending bits to Charles. At this same point, Charles has an equivalent amount of information about each d_i. If it is feasible for Diane to determine c_i, it is just as feasible for Charles to determine d_k for some k. Thus, the time Diane needs to cheat gives Charles time to match her solution, so that they are both bound to the contract.

Certified Mail

Sending certified mail is the last problem for which we will develop a protocol solution. Suppose Gina wants to send a message to Hal, but she wants proof that Hal received the message. She does not want to release the message to Hal without getting a receipt. Of course, he is not going to sign the receipt until he actually has the message. Postal employees and arbiters can solve this problem. However, as usual, we would like a solution that works without an arbiter. The solution is very much like the contract signing protocol just studied; in fact, this solution also comes from Even et al. in [EVE85].

Let Gina's message to Hal be M. She will transmit M to Hal in encrypted form and will give Hal the encryption key only when she has received an adequate acknowledgment from Hal of his having received M. Hal will acknowledge receiving M only when he receives a key that lets him obtain the plaintext M.

1. Gina randomly selects $n + 1$ keys for a symmetric cryptosystem (such as DES), naming them $g_0, g_1, g_2, \ldots, g_n$. She also computes $g_{n+i} = g_0 \oplus g_i$ for $1 \le i \le n$. (The symbol $\oplus$ denotes exclusive or.)

2. Gina computes $G = E(M,g_0)$, the encryption of her message M with key g_0. She sends G to Hal. Because for each i, $g_{n+i} = g_0 \oplus g_i$, $g_{n+i} \oplus g_i = g_0 \oplus g_i \oplus g_i = g_0 \oplus 0 = g_0$. Thus Hal can determine M given any pair (g_i, g_{n+i}).

3. Gina computes and sends to Hal $G_i = E(S,g_i)$ for $1 \le i \le 2n$, where S is some standard message whose content is irrelevant. At this point Hal has the encrypted message G and a standard message S encrypted with each of Gina's $2n$ different keys.

4. Hal chooses $2n$ keys $h_1, h_2, \ldots, h_{2n}$. Hal computes $H_i = E(S,h_i)$ for $1 \le i \le 2n$. Hal sends all the H_i to Gina.

5. Hal sends a statement to Gina that he acknowledges receipt of the plaintext of message G if Gina can produce *both* one of Hal's pairs (h_i and h_{n+i}) *and* all g_j for $1 \le j \le 2n$.

Saying this, Hal acknowledges that if Gina has the time to determine one of his pairs, h_i and h_{n+i}, he would also have time to determine one of her pairs, g_m and g_{n+m}. Any time Hal gets a pair, Hal can compute the encryption key g_0 and obtain the message $M = D(G, g_0)$. The second condition on Hal's statement ensures that Gina acted fairly—that each pair does yield g_0.

6. As in the contract signing protocol, Gina and Hal exchange pairs (g_1, g_{n+1}), (g_2, g_{n+2}), and so forth, and (h_1, h_{n+1}), (h_2, h_{n+2}), and so forth, by oblivious transfer. That is, Hal receives either g_1 or g_{n+1}, but neither he nor Gina knows which; Gina receives half of each (h_i, h_{n+i}) pair, without knowing which

7. As in the contract signing protocol, let l be the length of each key g_i.

   For $j = 1$ to l **begin**
      Gina sends Hal the jth bit of each g_i for $1 \leq i \leq 2n$.
      Hal sends Gina the jth bit of each h_j for $1 \leq i \leq 2n$.
   end

The amount of work to be done to break the other's code is the same as for contract signing, so the same rationale for continuing applies. Although both the contract signing and the certified mail protocol are too complicated for easy implementation by humans, they are easily suited for computer communication.

4.3 How to Use Encryption

In the previous sections we have studied several examples of protocols for computer use. We have examined protocols as orderly sequences of steps for interaction between two parties. The methods presented clever ways of exchanging information while preserving secrecy, anonymity, or privacy. The protocols used encryption as a tool to achieve secrecy, authenticity, or integrity, although the focus was on the protocol and the security properties to be achieved, not on the encryption itself. Protocols, which are independent of any specific encryption algorithm, assume only the existence of a particular type of encryption (symmetric or asymmetric), perhaps having a fairly general property (such as commutativity).

In this section we study the practices of using encryption. Although these practices are not as formal as protocols, they do guide us in our use of encryption to perform tasks with computers. Some situations in computing involve only one user. No sequence of steps is needed because there can be no disagreement about fairness or adherence to a rule. In these cases, secrecy and authenticity are of prime importance. These situations, called **encryption practices** or **encryption techniques**, are the subject of the remainder of this chapter.

We must be familiar with the characteristics, the advantages, and the disadvantages of encryption algorithms. In this way, we can select algorithms correctly and use appropriate methods of encryption. In this section we consider criteria by which to judge specific encryption systems. We study limitations of these systems and ways to avoid the limitations. The two major schemes to be considered are the RSA and the DES. We also study general limitations of symmetric and asymmetric key systems.

Recall from Chapter 2 that Shannon suggested overall criteria for encryption systems. Although these criteria were developed before the popularity of modem computers, they are still remarkably applicable to the problems encountered today. Shannon's criteria are repeated here.

- The degree of secrecy needed should determine the amount of labor appropriate for encryption and decryption.
- The set of keys should be free from complexity.
- The implementation of the process should be as simple as possible.
- Errors in ciphering should not propagate and cause corruption of further information in the message.
- The size of the enciphered text should be no larger than the text of the original message.

The first criterion is a basis of cryptosystems. The second criterion was more important when keys—and the entire encryption system—had to be applied by hand. With computers to perform the tedious or complicated work, complexity of key choice is not a concern. In fact, with mathematical algorithms such as RSA and El Gamal, keys are very complex in that only certain integers or pairs of integers can be keys. Distributing keys to users is difficult when a key change is due or desired, however. The implementation of an encryption scheme should still be as simple as possible. However, with the use of computers, previously infeasible algorithms can now be implemented. The propagation of errors described in the fourth criterion is still a concern. Finally, size may or may not be a concern. We address each criterion in greater detail in the sections following.

Amount of Secrecy

The controversy concerning recertification of DES is a good example of the relevance of secrecy today. It has not been argued, or even suggested, that the DES *is* flawed, only that it *could be* compromised, given enough time and computing resources.

Hellman [HEL79b] argues that a dedicated attacker could break the secrecy of a message encrypted using DES. The argument centers around speed of computation on a dedicated, special-purpose, multiprocessor machine designed solely to discover DES keys. The number of processors needed for such a machine—several hundred thousand to a million—would certainly attract attention if bought on the open market, unless the purchase were done over a very long time. However, current hardware prices are lower than in the late 1970s, when this argument was first raised. The cost to build such a machine would be very high, though, even at current prices. It is doubtful that any private company in the United States could amass the hardware resources or cash necessary to acquire such a machine. This reservation is also true for any underworld group or for any government agency that wants the ability to break DES encryptions.

Some uses of encryption are like padlocks: to keep out casual intruders, not to keep out someone really determined to break in. For example, a company might encrypt memoranda dealing with a new line of products in order to maintain an edge over the competition. Banks encrypt messages to transfer funds to prevent unauthorized modification and to detect spurious transmission errors more than to preserve privacy. A user may encrypt the file of a source program to prevent unauthorized modifications.

In these and other cases, the value of the encrypted information must be weighed against the value to others who might be able to break in. DES is still adequately safe to keep out most casual interceptors. The same may be said of RSA. Since its invention in 1978, no serious challenge has been raised to the security of RSA.

In summary, then, the security of the encryption system should be appropriate to the degree of confidentiality of the data being preserved. Users of encryption systems should consider the value of the data being encrypted when selecting an encryption system.

Key Management

Keys for the more complex encryption systems cannot simply be chosen at random. The public key systems, for example, require two keys in carefully determined pairs. And even for symmetric algorithms, pathological "weak" keys preclude completely random key generation. For these reasons, keys are often generated centrally.

With this consideration, key distribution can be a major issue. When it is time to change keys, each possessor of a key must be informed of the key change, and all users must start to use the new key at the same time (in order to avoid having some messages encrypted with the old instead of the new key, and being unable to distinguish between them).

Key replacement or **key supercession** is also an issue, because old keys must be kept in order to allow stored messages encrypted under old keys to be retrieved.

Lost (Revealed) Keys

Both symmetric and asymmetric key systems are sensitive to lost, revealed, or stolen keys. The only known approach is time checking. A user must know when a key may have been compromised. If this is so, the user notifies a central repository, or all correspondents who might receive messages from the user, that the key is believed to have been revealed. All receivers of messages from the user are thereby notified that they should suspect any message received after the date of the loss; they are also notified that they should not send any further messages under the user's public key.

This procedure, which is not really optimal, is about the best available. A user who wishes to back out of a signed contract simply claims disclosure of the private key at some time before the date of the contract. Because the private key was allegedly not private at the time of the contract, anyone could have acted as the user whose key was supposedly lost.

Complexity to Encrypt

Consider next the complexity to perform an encryption. Two major complexity issues are the delay before the encryption algorithm can begin to produce ciphertext and the slowness of the encryption algorithm itself.

Delay to Encrypt

The delay before encryption commences depends on the type of encryption—block or stream—and the size of a block. As described in Chapter 2, stream ciphers are desirable, so that the encryption algorithm can encrypt each new character as it appears. Slightly less desirable, although usually adequate, are stream ciphers that work on blocks. Each character cannot be enciphered as it appears, but new characters are held until a block (for example eight 8-bit characters or 64 bits, with DES) has been received. The least desirable encryption functions are those for which the whole plaintext message, or an unbounded amount of the message, must be received before encryption can begin.

Many common cryptographic algorithms (including RSA, Merkle–Hellman, El Gamal, DES, and Skipjack) are block ciphers. With the DES, a block is 64 bits. With the RSA there is no required block length (although there is limited security with a short block). The maximum block length is also a matter of choice for the implementer.

The developers of RSA propose a block of 100 to 200 bits. The lengths of both DES and RSA are reasonable for commercial use.

Speed of Encryption

Some encryption algorithms perform a constant amount of work per character encrypted. For example, the substitution ciphers, all of which are essentially table lookup processes, possess this property. The DES, Skipjack, RSA, Merkle–Hellman, and El Gamal algorithms, although much more complicated, also use only a constant amount of work per block. All these algorithms operate in time proportional to the size of the plaintext message; only the constant of proportionality is different.

Speed is important because it ensures that if an encryption algorithm can handle one block before the second one is received, the algorithm will not degrade the speed of the application. There are hardware (chip) implementations of most common algorithms that work at reasonable speeds.

Public key algorithms are *significantly* slower than symmetric ones. Symmetric algorithms are based on efficient operations, such as table lookup, shift, transposition, and logical operations (and, or, exclusive or, and complement), all of which are standard hardware functions. Asymmetric algorithms are based on inherently difficult problems, but to keep the encryption suitably daunting for the opponent, each instance of one of these problems is chosen to be large. Longer key lengths (corresponding to larger problem instances) increase the mathematical complexity at least exponentially. It can be difficult to gather fair and precise data for comparing running speeds, but relative performance data are usually consistent. The data in Table 4-1 come from [LAM92], and show that symmetric encryption performs 1000 to 5000 times faster than public key cryptography.

Propagation of Errors

Errors in transmission are prevalent and serious. As we learn in later chapters, local and remote networks are prone to errors of transmission. These errors may not indicate an interceptor. Ideally encryption algorithms should be immune to the network's errors. Often the network is responsible for detecting faulty communications and retransmitting faulty messages, so that the user will not know there had been a difficulty.

A true error (the result of an interceptor's attempted change) should be apparent in the ciphertext, so that any modification is readily noticed. None of the common algorithms has any tamper-protection mechanism. With these, the encryption algorithm is so contorted that changing even a single output bit would lead to a severely garbled decrypted message. If the plaintext is prose, a change will be evident. If the plaintext is binary data with little or no pattern, a change may not be detected.

Table 4-1   Relative Performance of Cryptography

	Hardware (bits/sec.)	Software: (bits/sec./MIPS)
RSA encrypt	220K	0.5K
RSA decrypt	—	32K
MD4	—	1300K
DES	1.2G ($1.2 * 10^9$)	400K

Size of Ciphertext

The size of the resulting ciphertext is also important. In some instances, the encrypted ciphertext is expected to fit back in the space previously occupied by the plaintext. If this is true, then even a slight increase in text size is intolerable. Note that block ciphers must encrypt a full block at a time. Although it is easy to pad a short last block to bring it up to size, this padding increases the size of the output text. DES and Skipjack produce an output that is either exactly the same size as the input or a few bits longer. (An initialization vector or the padding to fill a final incomplete block can account for a minor increase, at most one or two blocks.) In the public key algorithms, the output is related to, but not necessarily proportional to, the size of the input.

4.4   Enhancing Cryptographic Security

The DES and RSA are believed to be secure encryption algorithms, and have justified this confidence by withstanding many years of study by cryptanalysts. The Skipjack and El Gamal algorithms are also believed to be secure, although they do not yet have such a long track record. Thus, an intruder is unlikely to discover the content of a message encrypted under one of them. However, the description of possible attacks on a secure system (described in Chapter 1) included many more potential security weaknesses than just breaking the secrecy of a message. In this section we consider some of these attacks.

Error Prevention and Detection

In the DES each block is an entity. An interceptor who understood the format of a sender's messages could modify messages without needing to break the encryption.

Block Replay

For example, consider the following situation. Two banks agree to electronic exchange of information about transfers of money between the two banks, using encrypted data for security. They agree to transmit records having a certain fixed format:

name of depositor	account number	transfer amount
24 bytes	8 bytes	8 bytes

These records consist of 40 bytes = 320 bits = five 64-bit blocks, as shown in Figure 4-21. Suppose John is able to tap the data channel between these banks. The first day, John has his bank transfer $100 on his behalf from the one bank to the other. The next day he does the same thing. On both days he taps, intercepts, and records the transmission from the one bank to the other. Assume that both transmissions were sent under the same encryption key and that both transmissions begin at the start of a record. John knows that both transmissions will contain three blocks representing his name, one representing his account number, and one representing the amount, and that these five blocks in a row will be the same on both days. Identifying the data in these fields is merely a process of looking for duplicates, a tedious task that can be performed easily by computer.

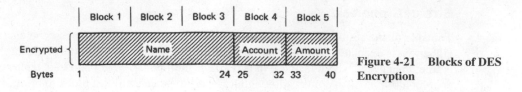

Figure 4-21   **Blocks of DES Encryption**

The next day, John verifies his supposition by sending through another transaction for a different amount, again looking for four blocks identical to before, but with a different fifth block. If only one set of blocks fits this pattern, John has the encrypted form of his name, account number, and two amounts.

By *inserting* data onto the transmission line, instead of simply reading messages from it, John can now replace any person and account number with his own name and account number, leaving the amount alone. John does not need to know who should be getting the money or how much is being obtained; John simply changes names and account numbers to his own and watches the balance in his account grow. This technique is known as **block replay**, in which encrypted blocks from one transmission are sent in a second transmission. To use block replay, the interceptor does not necessarily have to break the encryption, as shown in this example.

At the end of each transmission, the banks probably send the total of all transfers in the transmission, but John leaves that alone, so the total will balance. If John is lucky, at least one of the altered transmissions will net John a substantial sum. Customers may not notice the lack of a transfer (which John has diverted to his own account) until a month after John begins his transmission interference. John carries on this game for slightly less than a month, withdraws all the money from his account in cash, and heads for another country.

John is probably an "insider," meaning that he knows the format of the transmissions, the frequency with which encryption keys are changed, how often these transmissions occur, and so forth. John also probably has ways to guarantee a good return in one tampering incident. The technique used here has been simplified somewhat, both to make the explanation easier and to avoid a detailed guide to larceny.

Because they treat each block of plaintext independently, the DES and other block ciphers are prone to this type of attack. Fortunately, there is an easy solution, called **block chaining**.

Block Chaining

Recall that if you exclusive-or any binary string with itself, the result is 0, and the exclusive-or operation is commutative. Therefore, for any strings a and b, letting $\oplus$ represent exclusive or,

$$(a \oplus b) \oplus a = (a \oplus a) \oplus b$$
$$= 0 \oplus b$$
$$= b$$

With block chaining, each block to be transmitted is combined with the exclusive or of all blocks up to that block. If the blocks are B_1, B_2, B_3, and the encryption function is $E(\ )$, the following blocks are transmitted:

$$C_1 = E(B_1)$$
$$C_2 = E(E(B_1) \oplus B_2) = E(C_1 \oplus B_2)$$
$$C_3 = E(E(E(B_1) \oplus B_2) \oplus B_3) = E(C_2 \oplus B_3)$$

This process is shown in Figure 4-22.

The receiver decrypts the first block received, C_1, as normal. The receiver decrypts the second received block (which is $C_2 = E(C_1 \oplus B_2)$), obtaining $C_1 \oplus B_2$. From the previously obtained C_1, the receiver then computes $(C_1 \oplus B_2) \oplus C_1$. Thus this expression simplifies to

$$(C_1 \oplus B_2) \oplus C_1 = (C_1 \oplus C_1) \oplus B_2 = 0 \oplus B_2 = B_2$$

or the plaintext value of block 2. The receiver proceeds this way with all subsequent blocks.

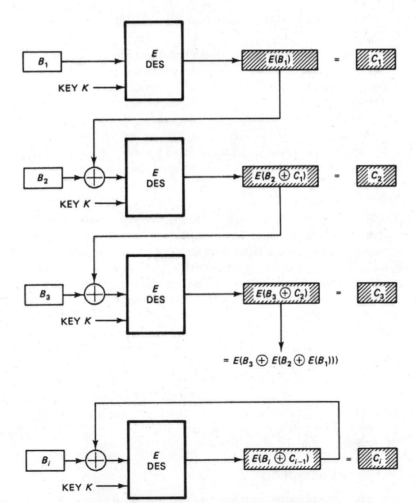

Figure 4-22   Example of Block Chaining

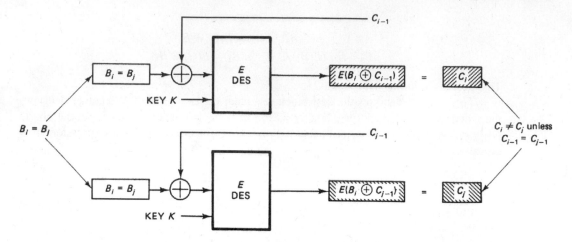

Figure 4-23   Encryption of Identical Plaintext Blocks

As shown in Figure 4-23, identical plaintext blocks transmitted separately or within the same transmission do not necessarily produce the same ciphertext. The difference occurs because each block depends on all the blocks that precede it. Thus, it will be impossible for an interceptor to repeat certain blocks from one transmission in another or even to find blocks that come from identical plaintext.

For the DES, one block does not disclose another because $E(C_1 \oplus B_2) \neq E(C_1) \oplus E(B_2)$. Even if the interceptor knows that $C_2 = E(C_1 \oplus B_2)$ and the interceptor has just obtained C_1, that information does not reveal B_2, or even $E(B_2)$.

Initial Chaining Value

Block chaining conceals identical blocks, as long as each is preceded by something unique. For some messages, however, the first few blocks may follow a set format (for example, memoranda that begin with the stock pattern "MEMORANDUM FROM: JANE BELL. TO: ALL EMPLOYEES. SUBJECT:"). With the same encryption key all such memoranda would produce the same ciphertext output.

If this exposure is unacceptable, added security is obtained by using an **initial chaining value**. This value is any random string used as the initial block. Any string can be used, such as the current time and date, or even a random number. The string must be different for every message encrypted. Both the sender and receiver know to decrypt this block but use it only in the exclusive or of subsequent blocks; it carries no data of importance.

With the use of an initial chaining vector, the message $B_1B_2B_3 \ldots$ essentially becomes $IB_1B_2B_3 \ldots$. The first block sent is $E(I)$, where I is the initial chaining value. The next block sent is $E(E(I) \oplus B_1)$. Even if two identical blocks appear in different messages, for example B_1, they will not result in identical ciphertext. Because I is different for each message, $E(E(I) \oplus B_1)$ will be different, too.

One-Way Encryption

Some encryptions depend on a function that is difficult to compute. For a simple example, consider the cube function $y = x^3$. It is relatively easy to compute x^3 by hand, with pencil and paper, or with a calculator. The inverse function, $\sqrt[3]{y}$, is much more difficult to compute. And the function $y = x^2$ has no inverse function because there are two possibilities for $\sqrt[2]{y}$; $+x$ and $-x$. Functions such as these, which are much easier to compute than their inverses, are called **one-way functions**.

Uses of One-Way Encryption

One-way functions are especially useful in authentication. Passwords are often used to check that a particular user is the person trying to log in as that user. A public table of user passwords is risky in a computing system, so many systems use a one-way function to encrypt the password table. The system stores $f(pw)$ when a user obtains a new password, pw, where f is a one-way function. When the user later tries to log on, the system asks for the password. The user types t, and the system computes $f(t)$. Finally, the system compares $f(t)$ to $f(pw)$ to authenticate the user. For example, the system could store $E(pw, pw)$, that is, the password encrypted with itself as a key.

The password system is secure because it is computationally infeasible or impossible to compute f^{-1}. An intruder might find the password table and detect that the encrypted form of a user's password is $f(pw)$. However, this information does not allow the intruder to infer pw. Furthermore, the intruder could try different passwords with a brute force attack until finding a word w for which $f(w) = f(pw)$. With long passwords chosen from a large alphabet, this attack is effectively rendered infeasible.[2]

Cryptographic Sealing

Another useful property of encryption is its ability to protect data from tampering. For example, in an ordinary data file, a value, a line, a record, or a whole file can be changed without detection. In this discussion we refer to files, although the same considerations apply to a record, field, or single byte.

Encryption is most commonly used for secrecy. In some cases, however, integrity is a more important concern than secrecy. For example, in a document retrieval system it may be important to know that the copy retrieved is exactly what was stored. Likewise, in a secure communications system, need for the correct transmission of messages may override secrecy concerns. Encryption can ensure integrity as well as secrecy.

In most files there is no force that binds the elements together. That is, each byte or bit or character is independent from every other one in the file. Changing one value affects the integrity of the file, but that one change can easily go undetected.

Cryptography can be used to **seal** a file, essentially encasing it in plastic, so that any change becomes apparent. One technique is to compute a cryptographic function, sometimes called a **hash** or **checksum**, of the file. In Chapter 3 we studied the Secure Hash Algorithm (SHA), and the MD4 and MD5 hash algorithms. The function must depend on all bits of the file being sealed, so that any change to even a single bit alters the checksum result.

The checksum value is stored with the file. Then each time the file is accessed or used, the checksum is recomputed. If the computed checksum matches the stored value, it is likely that the file has not been changed.

---

[2] Note: See Chapter 5 for a description of how this attack was used successfully by the Internet worm. Even though the intruder could not invert f, he was able to enter many systems because people had used common English words as passwords. The encryption was flawless; it was human procedures that failed.

A cryptographic function, such as the DES, is especially appropriate for sealing values because an outsider will not know how to modify the stored value to match with data being modified. As described earlier, chaining applied to DES produces a result where each block depends on the value of previous blocks. A file cryptographic checksum could be the last block of the chained DES encryption of a file because that block depends on all other blocks.

Authentication

Remember the folk legends in which two people would cut a coin in half, and one would take a half and then leave, saying "if a messenger brings something with this half of the coin, you'll know it is from me"? With encryption we can do something similar. With personal communication, when dealing with people we know, we have ways of being sure the person to whom we speak is who we think it is. We recognize voices, mannerisms, patterns of behavior. With computer communication, we do not have as many clues to assure us of identity.

The primary means of authentication is a password: a word or string that only one person knows. The computer system presumes that anyone knowing the password is the person to whom the password belongs. As we will discover later, passwords can be secure, although if misused they offer little protection.

Another form of authentication is encryption. If you receive an encrypted message that can be decrypted with a key known only to you and one other person, the message is authentic. Unless the encryption scheme has been broken or the key has been compromised (both of which are unlikely), the message could have been created only by the one other person having the key.

This certainty extends to the entire message. With a strong encryption algorithm, it is impossible for someone else to substitute a desired phrase for part of the message, or to "paste together" pieces from two or more old messages. For example, cipher block chaining described earlier prevents substituting one block in a message. The message received was sent by the known person with no tampering before its receipt.

Time Stamps

Another security problem is the possibility that a message in its entirety might have been intercepted by someone else and is now being replayed. (This is the electronic equivalent of trying to negotiate a photocopy of a check, where the person cashing the copy does not detect it is a copy.) If this is a potential problem, the sender and receiver can identify each message with a message number or a time stamp.

A message number is a number embedded within the message. The interceptor has no way to know where the message number bits appear within the message, or how to change the bits to produce the enciphered version of the next number, or how to change these bits without corrupting the decryption of the rest of the message. Being embedded, message numbers cannot be substituted, modified, or forged.

The receiver keeps count of message numbers received. If two people use one set of numbers, the receiver can tell immediately if a message before the current one has been lost or delayed, because the number encrypted with the current message will be more than one higher than the number of the previous message.

A sender with many messages can run into the problem of extremely long message numbers. For this reason, it is usual to reset the message number counter when it gets too high, say after its length exceeds 30 bits. In this case all recipients must be informed (by a message) that the next message number sent will be reset to a small number such as 0. Another problem is that a separate counter is maintained for each pair of sender and receiver. A popular sender or receiver must maintain many different counters for many different correspondents.

Alternatively, a sender will have a single message number generator for messages to all recipients. If the sender sends messages to two people, A and B, message 1 might go to A, 2 to B, 3 and 4 to A, 5 to B, and so on. Neither recipient can tell whether a particular message was lost, because the message numbers are only an ascending sequence, not necessarily all numbers in the range. However, a recipient can instantly spot a replay of a previous message. The message number should be encrypted or otherwise protected to inhibit modification.

Time and date stamps are somewhat more flexible. They are markings of the time and date the message was sent, with enough precision that no two messages will have the same marking. They need not be reset.

The receiver must match the sender's time closely. In a fast transmission, if the sender's and receiver's clocks are not synchronized, the sender's time stamp could be later than the recipient's current time. It is typical to allow a small tolerance for unsynchronized times, or recognition that one sender's time stamps are all slightly fast.

We have now studied various aspects of DES encryption in specific applications, such as ensuring integrity, preventing replay, and ensuring secrecy. These can be achieved with any encryption system because they depend only on general properties of encryption.

4.5 Modes of Encryption

Now we investigate different ways that encryption can be used. However, the general principles here apply to most common encryption algorithms, both symmetric and asymmetric.

The version of DES presented in Chapter 3 is called the electronic code book (ECB) use of DES. Essentially a message is translated one independent 64-bit block at a time, as if one had a huge code book of all 64-bit quantities and their DES encryption (for a particular key). However, we discussed the limitation of that mode of encryption with identical plaintext. In the following sections, we present other modes of use of the DES.

Cipher Block Chain

As described earlier, the cipher block chain (CBC) mode of operation starts with a random initialization vector (IV), which is encrypted and sent as block 1. Then the initialization vector is combined by exclusive or with the first plaintext block ($E(p_1 \oplus IV, k)$); this result is encrypted as block 2. Then the second ciphertext block is combined by exclusive or with the next plaintext block, and that result is encrypted. Each ciphertext block is chained to the next plaintext block of the message, so that it is impossible to substitute one ciphertext block for another without being discovered. Cipher block chaining is shown in Figure 4-24.

CBC mode also has the property of being self-healing, so that a change in block c_i affects the decryption of blocks p_i and p_{i+1}. However, blocks p_{i+2} and beyond are unaffected. After two blocks, the exclusive-or function cancels any error. (Recall that for any string x, $x \oplus x = 0$.) The self-healing property is convenient because an error in transmission or encryption will not damage a large amount of ciphertext.

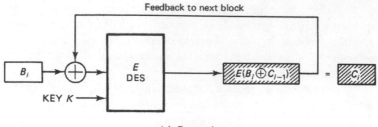

(a) Encryption

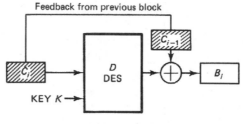

(b) Decryption

Figure 4-24   Cipher Block Chaining

Cipher Feedback

The block-oriented nature of DES is inconvenient for two reasons noted earlier. First, a partial final block must be padded. Thus, the size of the resulting ciphertext can be slightly larger than the size of the corresponding plaintext. Second, encryption cannot begin until all 64 bits of a block have been received. Therefore, the speed of encryption of one character can depend on how fast several later characters are received. Some applications require immediate encryption of each character. For example, in a secure network environment, a user must transmit each character as it is entered at the terminal.

The cipher feedback (CFB) mode of operation works on one character at a time. Therefore, the ciphertext is not expanded in order to fill the last block, and no delay is imposed because of needing 64 bits to encrypt.

The CFB algorithm operates on a 64-bit queue. Initially, the queue is filled with an initialization vector, like the *IV* of cipher block chaining mode. The queue is enciphered, and the leftmost eight bits of the result are combined by exclusive or with the first character to be encrypted. These encrypted eight bits are transmitted. The eight bits also move into the rightmost eight bit positions of the queue, all other bits move eight bits left, and the leftmost eight bits are discarded. A similar process occurs at the receiving end. This procedure is shown in Figure 4-25.

The advantage of CFB mode is the ability to encipher one character at a time. As with CBC mode, each character affects all succeeding characters, so that a change to any character during transmission affects subsequent characters. An error during encryption affects the character being transformed, as well as the next eight characters because it will be in the queue for eight more character encryptions until the erroneous character is pushed off the left end of the queue.

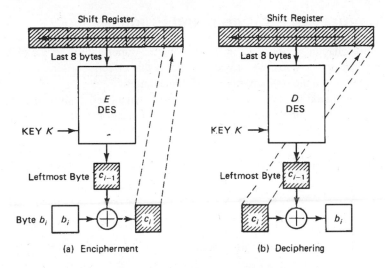

Figure 4-25   **Cipher Feedback**

These two modes extend the usefulness of the DES substantially. They overcome two major limitations on DES: the flaw of duplicate encryption of repeated plaintext and the delay from waiting to encrypt a block of text at once. Without these limitations, the DES has similar qualities to stream encryption algorithms.

Two Keys Give the Effect of a 112-Bit Key

Although the DES key length is *believed* by most analysts to be long enough, some people are still unsure about its 56-bit length. There is a method for increasing the effective length of the key. The method requires no change to the algorithm itself, which is convenient in case the algorithm is to be implemented by a hardware device or in an unmodifiable piece of software.

Because there is considerable concern for the security available with only one 56-bit key, a reasonable approach may involve using two keys. If somehow an exhaustive search defeats one key, the second lock should double the time required to break in (or so the analogies to the physical world would imply.) Unfortunately, this is not quite so. Merkle ([MER81]) argues that two 56-bit keys in series can be broken with a chosen plaintext attack in 2^{57} tries, instead of the 2^{112} that would be expected. Therefore, the second encryption adds almost no security.

Tuchman ([TUC79]) counters that two keys used in a special way enhances security. Tuchman uses a technique, called **triple DES**, invented by Matyas and Meyer for use by IBM in encrypting master keys in some of their encryption systems. With two keys, K_1 and K_2, the sender encrypts with K_1, decrypts with K_2, and encrypts with K_1 again. The receiver decrypts with K_1, encrypts with K_2, and decrypts with K_1 again.

This approach is desirable for use with an automatic encrypting device (which might be either hardware or software). If the device expects two keys and the user wants to use only one, the user supplies K_1 all three times. The device encrypts with K_1, decrypts with K_1 (which returns the original plaintext), and finally encrypts with K_1. In that way one device can produce both single and double encryptions.

4.6   Summary of Protocols and Practices

In this chapter we looked at several problems important in the use of computers and communications systems. We studied protocols that effectively separate design of a problem's solution from the implementation of that solution.

We identified tasks for which protocols have been designed. These tasks have application in electronic commerce, private communication, and other day-to-day activities that we might want to automate. These tasks are

- digital signing
- mental poker (key distribution)
- key escrow
- voting
- oblivious transfer (coin flipping)
- contract signing
- certified mail

The protocols solved problems that ordinarily require face-to-face interaction between humans. However, by careful design, we have been able to ensure properties of secrecy and authenticity while maintaining absolute fairness.

As noted earlier, separating design from implementation is desirable. Protocols, which can be analyzed and verified, are a good design medium because the correctness of the protocol can be determined exclusive of any specific use of the protocol.

For each protocol, we first explored the *problem* to be solved. Then we identified the *security requirements* we wished to satisfy with the protocol. Next, we designed a *protocol* that met the security requirements. Finally, we performed an *analysis* of the protocol to confirm that it met the requirements.

We also looked at appropriate practices in the use of encryption. Just using encryption does not guarantee secrecy, privacy, or authenticity; it is the *correct* use of encryption that brings about these results. We evaluated DES and RSA encryption systems against the classic Shannon criteria and other standards of security. Finally, we investigated cryptographic techniques to limit undetected errors, such as replay, through techniques such as time stamps and chaining.

4.7   Bibliographic Notes

Two important surveys of computer protocols are by DeMillo and Merritt [DEM83] and Akl [AKL83]. Fundamental papers presenting protocols are by Merkle [MER80], Needham and Schroeder [NEE78], Popek and Kline [POP78], Rabin [RAB78], Rivest, Shamir, and Adelman [RIV78], and Bellovin and Merritt [BEL92b]. Analysis of problems in protocol design is covered well by Abadi and Needham [ABA94], Simmons [SIM94], Anderson [AND94], Fagin [FAG96], and Moore [MOO88].

Additional uses of DES are described in [NBS80], and by Voydock and Kent in [VOY83].

4.8   Terms and Concepts

4.9   Exercises

1. Why is an arbiter not desirable in a protocol for exchange of secrets?

2. Give an example of a self-enforcing protocol in real life.

3. The first cryptographic sealing function suggested (the sum of the numeric values of all bytes of a message) has a serious flaw: exchanging the places of two bytes of the message will not be detected by the sealing function. Suggest an alternative function that does not have that weakness.

4. The Merkle–Hellman knapsack encryption is not an "onto" function; that is, some binary number is *not* the result of applying the knapsack encryption to a piece of plaintext. With which protocols would this characteristic cause a problem? Explain the problem.

5. There is a flaw in the cryptographic sealing mechanism presented: if R can compute f_S to verify that document M has been received as it was transmitted, then R can also compute f_S to forge a digital signature. Suggest a solution to this flaw.

6. Describe a protocol for fair exchange of secrets (in a human setting, that is, a non-computer setting). Two people each wish to exchange secret information; neither wants to give up a secret without getting one in return.
   (a) What are the security requirements of this situation?
   (b) What is a protocol for fair exchange of secrets?

7. List the requirements for a secret key digital signature scheme. Can any of these requirements be met with an adjudicated protocol? Why or why not? Can any of these requirements be met with a self-enforcing protocol? Why or why not?

8. Present a digital signature protocol using conventional key encryption so that the sender and receiver do not have to expose the contents of their message to the arbiter.

9. Explain why the digital signature protocol using public key encryption prevents a receiver from forging a message from the sender, using the sender's public key.

10. Show that RSA encryption has both commutative and onto properties. Why are these two properties necessary for the public key digital signature protocol.

11. A hash function reduces a (large) block of data to a (smaller) digest. That usually implies that not all possible modifications to the original data would be detected by the hash function. However, a text compression algorithm also reduces large data to a smaller compressed form. Would a text compression algorithm be able to detect all changes in the original text? Why or why not? Would a text compression algorithm be useful as a hash function? Why or why not?

12. In the Clipper protocol, the message key K is communicated separately to the receiver. Why is the same key included in the message?

13. Why does the Clipper protocol encrypt the message key K under both the unit key U and the family key F?

14. What are the security properties necessary in the card distribution protocol? Explain how the protocol meets each of these properties.

15. As initially described, the mental poker protocol has a flaw. If there are only ten cards, as soon as Ann sees her hand, she knows from set difference what cards Bill must have. Suggest an alternative protocol that does not have this flaw.

16. A similar problem is faced in centralized key generation: if the key generation center produces a reasonable number of key pairs (for example, 1 million) and it is known that a user obtained one of those keys, the key space to search for that user is only 1 million, not the full number of possible keys of the appropriate size. There are two vulnerabilities: someone watching the output of the key generation center and someone inside the key generation center keeping copies of the keys proposed. Suggest a means by which a key generation center can securely deliver keys to users so that neither the key generation center nor an outside observer has an advantage in trying to guess which key a user has.

17. In the card distribution protocol, what prevents Ann from cheating by putting five cards in one box and none in four boxes?

18. Describe a protocol to distribute ID numbers from an instructor to students so that each student can submit a piece of work to be graded anonymously, but the instructor can be assured that each piece of work comes from a legitimate person in the class.

19. In the voting protocol, explain how each user can be assured that his or her vote is still in the set to be counted.

20. In the voting protocol, if Jan knew there was at least one 1 vote and one 0 vote, could she remove a vote at random and replace it by $E_J(E_K(E_L(1)))$? Why or why not?

21. In the voting protocol, what prevents Lee (or anyone) from finding out the answers early by computing $E_J(E_K(E_L(1)))$ and $E_J(E_K(E_L(0)))$ and counting the images of these encrypted votes?

22. In the voting protocol, how can Keith work backward from $E_K(E_L(v))$ to $E_J(E_K(E_L(v)))$ to convince himself that Jan did not cheat?

23. In step 5 of the oblivious transfer, if length of the message is significant, Pete could tell whether he guessed correctly (by noticing that the decryption produced a result of exactly 64 bits, for example, if the object being transferred was a 64-bit encryption key). Propose a solution for this problem.

24. Design an oblivious transfer protocol that uses only conventional key encryptions.

25. Asymmetric encryption keys are hard to select. At the end of the oblivious transfer, to show fairness, Pete reveals his two pairs of encryption keys to Nancy. Having revealed all of both pairs, Pete can no longer use them if Nancy might be able to affect the use. Design an oblivious transfer protocol in which it is not necessary to reveal the key pairs at the end.

26. Suppose one party, say Diane, decides to terminate the contract signing protocol early. She has one more bit of each c_i than Charles does of the d_j. Thus she has less work to do to break the c_i. What condition on the use of this protocol would nullify this advantage?

27. Design a protocol to allow a remote host on a network to identify itself and be authenticated by the other hosts on the network. What are the security requirements of this situation?

28. Design a protocol so that three different users can access certain secret information. There are four pieces of information, called W, X, Y, and Z; the three users are called A, B, and C. A should have access only to W and Z; B only to X and Z, and C only to Y and Z.

29. Suppose in the previous exercise, A was to have access to W and X, B to X and Y, and C to Y and Z. Would your protocol still work? If not, design a new one.

30. When used in cipher block chaining mode, the DES is said to be self-healing: an error in transmission of one block does not cause faulty decryption of all the rest of the transmission. Explain how this is so.

5
Program Security

In this chapter:
- *Malicious code: viruses, worms, Trojan horses*
- *Program development controls against malicious code and program flaws: software engineering principles, process models*

In this chapter we begin to study the applications of security in computing, both *why* we need it and *how* we can achieve it. We examine programs that do not behave as their designers intended or users expected, calling all unexpected behavior **program flaws**. We also study ways of preventing harm from flaws.

Computing is just programs running on processors, including instructions integrated into chips, firmware in read-only memory, the basic hardware-to-software interface (often called the BIOS), device drivers, operating systems, network implementations, data base management systems, utilities, applications, and user programs. Thus, in one form or another, protection of programs is at the heart of security in computing. This chapter introduces that basic issue: how to keep programs free from flaws and how to protect computing from programs that do contain flaws. In later chapters we examine specific types of programs—operating systems, data base management systems, and networks—but the general themes from this chapter carry forward to them as well. Thus, this chapter is groundwork for future topics, as well as a significant topic on its own.

Program flaws include everything from a misunderstanding of program requirements to a one-character error in coding or even typing, from failure of two program pieces to interact compatibly through a shared interface to code intended to do harm. Logically it makes sense to divide program flaws into inadvertent human errors and malicious, intentionally induced flaws. But, in the words of Don Quixote in *Man of La Mancha*, "it doesn't matter whether the stone hits the pitcher or the pitcher hits the stone, it's going to be bad for the pitcher." An inadvertent error can cause just as much harm to the users of computation as can an intentionally induced flaw. Furthermore, a system attack often exploits an unintentional program flaw to perform intentional damage. From reading the popular press, you might conclude that viruses are the biggest security threat today. In fact, unintentional human errors cause much more damage.

We start this chapter by studying intentional malicious code because it is a definite threat, but then we expand the study to all kinds of program flaws because they all can have bad consequences. Viruses are the prime example of nonspecific malicious code: they are not directed specifically at any one system or user. A second class of flaw is created by programmers who want to harm a single specific installation. Finally, there are unintentional flaws. You can protect against program flaws by keeping programs containing them off your system or by ensuring programs are free of them. This chapter looks at both ways because they are useful in different cases.

Regrettably, we do not have techniques to stop all program flaws, for two reasons:

- Program controls still apply at the level of the individual program and programmer. It is almost impossible to ensure that a program does precisely what its designer or user intended, and nothing more. Ignoring malicious intent for the moment, in a large and complex system, the number of pieces that have to fit together properly interact in an unmanageably large number of ways, so sheer size and complexity preclude total flaw prevention. Now assume that a programmer intends to implant malicious code. With the techniques described in this chapter, we can detect some intentional flaws (as well as some nonmalicious flaws) but, in general, a dedicated programmer can still hide flaws successfully.

- Programming and software engineering techniques change and evolve far more rapidly than do techniques in computer security. While software developers are rapidly adopting today's new technology, computer security experts are still trying to secure the technology of last week, or last year.

Do not be discouraged by this rather bleak introduction. Computer security *does* have much to offer in the area of program security. We begin this chapter with a study of malicious code (viruses, Trojan horses, and the other forms that are very widely publicized); we then look into available forms of protection. You need to understand what can go wrong and how to protect against it, because these elements form the building blocks for many of the topics in the following chapters, and they are at the heart of most computer security applications. Study this chapter for the guidance it can give you for all your future activity as a computer user or programmer.

5.1 Viruses and Other Malicious Code

Programs operate on data. By themselves, programs are seldom security threats. However, because computer data is usually not directly seen by users, malicious people can make programs serve as vehicles to access data and other programs. We begin by studying the possible effects of malicious code and then examine in detail several kinds of programs that can be used for interception or modification of data.

Why Worry About Malicious Code?

As already noted, malicious code behaves in a way unexpected by its designer or user, through the intention of a programmer. Malicious code can be a program or part of a program; a program part can even attach itself to another (good) program so that the malicious effect occurs whenever the good program runs.

When you last installed a major software package, such as a word processor, you ran one command, typically INSTALL or SETUP, and the installation program took control, creating files, writing in others, deleting some, perhaps renaming a few that it would change; a few minutes and quite a few disk accesses later, you had plenty of new code and data, all installed for you. Other than the general descriptions on the box (and, if you were lucky, in a printed manual), you had absolutely no idea exactly what gifts you had received. You hoped all you received was good; probably it was. But think of the millions of bytes of programs and data that were transferred, and the hundreds of modifications to your existing files, that occurred without your consent or knowledge.

Malicious Code Can Do Much (Harm)

Malicious code can do anything any other program can, such as writing a message on a computer screen, stopping a running program, generating a sound, or erasing a stored file; malicious code can even do nothing at all. It can be planted to lie dormant, undetected, until some event triggers the code to act. The trigger can be a time or date, an interval (for example, after 30 minutes), an event (for example, when a particular program is executed), a condition (for example, when communication occurs on a modem), a count (for example, the fifth time something happens), some combination of these, or a random situation. Malicious code can do different things each time, or it can do nothing most of the time and something dramatic on occasion. In general, malicious code can act with all the predictability of a two-year-old child: we know in general what two-year-olds do, we may even know what a specific two-year-old often does in certain situations, but two-year-olds have an amazing capacity to do the unexpected.

Malicious code runs under the authority of the user. Thus, everything the user can touch, the malicious code can touch, and in the same ways. Users typically have complete control over their own program code and data files: they can read, write, modify, append, and even delete them. Of course, they should. But malicious code can do the same, without the user's permission or even knowledge.

Malicious Code Has Been Around Long

It often seems from the popular literature as if malicious code is a relatively recent phenomenon; it is not. Cohen [COH84] is sometimes credited with the discovery of viruses, but really a virus is just a special form of malicious code known well before Cohen. For example, Thompson, in his 1984 Turing award lecture "Reflections on Trusting Trust" [THO84], describes code that can be passed by a compiler, referring to an earlier Air Force document of which he could not remember the citation. Thompson was probably referring to Schell's paper [SCH79]. But in fact, references go back at least to 1970 in Ware's 1970 study (publicly released in 1979 [WAR79]) and Anderson's planning study for the U.S. Air Force [AND72] (to which Schell also refers), both of which *still* accurately describe threats and vulnerabilities from program flaws, especially intentional ones. What *is* new about malicious code is how many distinct instances there are and how many copies of each have appeared.

What is malicious code? What does it look like? How can it take control of a system? How can it lodge in a system? How does malicious code spread? How can it be recognized? How can it be detected? How can it be stopped? How can it be prevented? We try to answer these questions in the following sections.

Kinds of Malicious Code

Malicious code or **rogue program** is the general name for unanticipated or undesired effects in programs or program parts, caused by an agent intent on damage. This definition eliminates unintentional errors, although they can also have a serious negative effect. This definition also excludes coincidence, in which two benign programs combine for a negative effect. The agent is the writer of the program, or the person who causes its distribution. By this definition, a bug or error does not qualify as malicious code, because we think of these flaws or errors as unintentional. However, you should keep unintentional errors in mind throughout this chapter, because all of the effects of malicious code here can also result from unintentional errors.

Because viruses appear in much of the popular literature of computer security, they are a good starting point. A **virus** is a program that can pass on malicious code to other nonmalicious programs by modifying them. The term *virus* arises because the affected program acts like a biological virus: modification of good programs is like a virus that infects other healthy subjects. A virus "infects" a program by attaching itself to the program and either destroying the program or co-existing with it. A good program can be modified to include a copy of the virus program, so the infected good program begins to act as a virus, infecting other programs itself. The infection spreads at a geometric rate. The viruses can eventually overtake an entire computing system and spread to all other connected systems. (This section sounds like a low-grade science fiction plot, but the exposure identified here is real.)

A virus can be either transient or resident. A **transient** virus runs when its attached program executes and terminates when its attached program ends. (Note, however, that during its execution, the transient virus may have spread its infection to other programs.) A **resident** virus locates itself in memory so that it can remain active, or be activated, even after its attached program ends.

A **Trojan horse** is a piece of malicious code that, in addition to its primary effect, has a second, nonobvious malicious effect.[1] An example of a computer Trojan horse is a login script that solicits a user's identification and password, passes the identification information on to the rest of the system for login processing, but also retains a copy of the information for later, malicious use. In this example, the user sees only the login occurring as expected, so he or she has no evident reason to suspect anything else.

A **logic bomb** is a class of malicious code that "detonates" or goes off when a specified condition occurs. A **time bomb** is a logic bomb whose trigger is a time or date.

A **trapdoor** or **backdoor** is a feature in a program by which someone can access the program other than by the obvious, direct call, perhaps with special privileges. An example is an automated bank teller program that allows anyone entering the number 990099 on the keypad to process the log of everyone's transactions at that machine. In this example, the trapdoor could be intentional, for maintenance purposes, or it could be an illicit way for the implementer to wipe out records of a crime.

A **worm** is a program that spreads copies of itself through a network. The primary difference between a worm and a virus is that a worm operates through networks and a virus can spread through any medium, but usually copied program or data files. Additionally, the

---

[1] The name is a reference to the story in Homer's *Iliad* in which the Greeks presented an enormous wooden horse to the citizens of Troy, but it secretly contained Greek soldiers who emerged from the horse at night and attacked the city.

worm spreads copies of itself as a stand-alone program, whereas the virus spreads copies of itself as a program that attaches to other programs.

White et al. [WHI89] define a **rabbit** as a virus or worm that self-replicates without bound, with the intention of exhausting some computing resource. A rabbit might create copies of itself and store them on disk in an effort to completely fill the disk, for example.

These definitions match current careful usage. The distinctions between these terms are small, and often the terms are confused, especially in the popular press. The term *virus* is often used for any piece of malicious code. Furthermore, two or more forms of malicious code can be combined to produce, for example, a virus that is triggered at a particular time (the combination of a virus and a time bomb). The kinds of malicious code are summarized in Table 5-1.

In the next few sections, we focus on viruses, because there is significant popular interest in them and because many characteristics of viruses extend to other forms of malicious code.

How Viruses Attach

A printed copy of a virus does nothing. Even a copy of the executable code of a virus sitting on a disk does nothing. In order for a virus to do its malicious work and spread itself, it has to be activated by being executed. Fortunately for virus writers, but unfortunately for the rest of us, programs are executed all the time on a running computer.

In the example of the setup program described in the last section, the setup program may have called dozens or hundreds of other programs, some on the distribution medium, some already residing on the computer, some in memory. If any one of those programs contained a virus, the virus code would be activated. For example, if the virus code was in a program on the distribution medium, when it was executed, it could install itself on the permanent storage medium (typically hard disk) of the computer, and the virus could also install itself in any executing programs in memory. In the beginning, a human being had to put the virus on the distribution medium, then a human had to execute the program to which the virus was attached. After that point the virus could spread by itself.

Appended Viruses

A program virus attaches itself to a program; then, whenever the program is run, the virus is activated. This kind of attachment is usually easy.

Table 5-1   Types of Malicious Code

Code Type	Characteristics
Virus	Attaches itself to program and propagates copies of itself to other programs
Trojan horse	Contains unexpected, additional functionality
Logic bomb	Triggers action when condition occurs
Time bomb	Triggers action when specified time occurs
Trapdoor	Allows unauthorized access to functionality
Worm	Propagates copies of itself through a network
Rabbit	Replicates itself without limit to exhaust resource

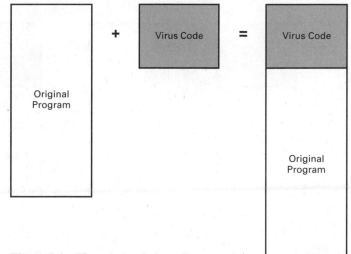

Figure 5-1   Virus Appended to a Program

In the simplest case, a virus simply inserts a copy of itself into the executable program file before the first executable instruction, so that all the virus instructions execute first, and after the last virus instruction, control flows naturally to what used to be the first program instruction. Such a situation is shown in Figure 5-1.

This kind of attachment is simple and usually effective. The virus writer does not need to know anything about the program to which the virus will attach and, often, the attached program simply serves as a carrier for the virus. The virus does its task and then transfers to the original program. Typically, the user is unaware of the effect of the virus if the original program still does all that it used to. Most viruses attach in this manner.

Viruses That Surround a Program

An alternative to the attachment is a virus that runs the original program but has control before and after its execution. For example, a virus might want to avoid being detected. If the virus is stored on disk, it will show as a file, or its size will affect the amount of space used on the disk. The virus might want to attach itself to the program that constructs the listing of files on the disk. If it regains control after the listing program has generated the listing but before the listing is displayed or printed, the virus could eliminate its entry from the listing and falsify space counts so that it appears not to exist. A surrounding virus is shown in Figure 5-2.

Integrated Viruses and Replacements

A virus might replace some of its target, integrating itself into the original code of the target. Such a situation is shown in Figure 5-3. Clearly the virus writer had to know the exact structure of the original program to know where to insert which pieces of the virus.

Finally, the virus can replace the entire target, either mimicking the effect of the target or ignoring the expected effect of the target and performing only the virus effect. In this case, the user is most likely to perceive the loss of the original program.

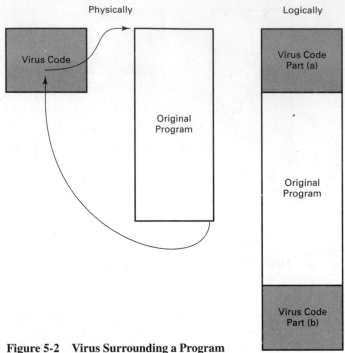

Figure 5-2   Virus Surrounding a Program

How Viruses Gain Control

The virus (V) has to be invoked instead of the target (T). Essentially the virus either has to seem to be T, saying effectively "I am T," or the virus has to push T out of the way and become a substitute for T, saying effectively "Call me instead of T."

The virus can assume T's name by replacing (or joining to) T's code in a file structure; this invocation technique is most appropriate for ordinary programs. The virus can overwrite T in storage (simply replacing the copy of T on disk, for example). Alternatively, the

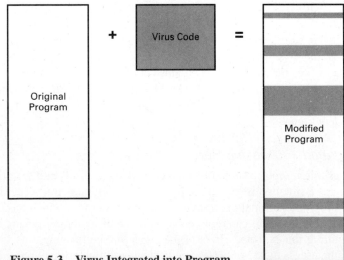

Figure 5-3   Virus Integrated into Program

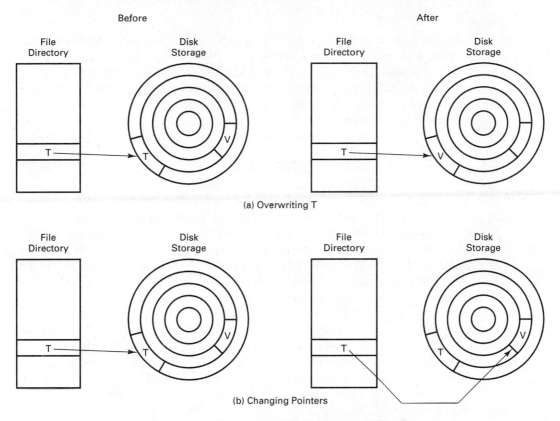

Figure 5-4   Virus Completely Replacing a Program

virus can change the pointers in the file table so that V is located instead of T whenever T is accessed through the file system. These two cases are shown in Figure 5-4.

The virus can supplant T by altering the sequence that would have invoked T to now invoke V; this invocation can be used to replace parts of the resident operating system by modifying pointers to those resident parts, such as the table of handlers for different kinds of interrupts.

Homes for Viruses

The virus writer may want a virus with these qualities:

- hard to detect
- hard to destroy or deactivate
- spreads infection widely
- can reinfect
- easy to create
- machine independent (and operating system independent)

Choices among these objectives affect what kind of virus a writer creates and where the writer decides to place the virus. Next we look at places where a virus writer would want to cause a virus to attach.

Boot Sector Viruses

A special case of virus attachment, but a fairly popular one, is the so-called **boot sector virus**. When a computer is started, control starts with firmware that determines which hardware components are present, tests them, and transfers control to an operating system. A given hardware platform can run many different operating systems, so the operating system is not coded in firmware but is instead invoked dynamically, perhaps even by a user's choice, after the hardware test.

The operating system is software stored on disk. The operating system has to start with code that copies it from disk to memory and transfers control to it; this copying is called the **bootstrap** (often **boot**) load because the operating system pulls itself into memory by its bootstraps. The firmware does its control transfer by reading a fixed number of bytes from a fixed location on the disk (called the **boot sector**) to a fixed address in memory and then jumping to that address (which contains the first instruction of the bootstrap loader). The bootstrap loader then reads into memory the rest of the operating system from the disk. To run a different operating system, the user just inserts a disk with the new operating system and a bootstrap loader. When the user reboots from this new disk, the loader there brings in and runs another operating system. This same scheme is used for personal computers, workstations, and large mainframes.

To allow for change, expansion, and uncertainty, hardware designers reserve a large amount of space for the bootstrap load. The boot sector on a PC is slightly less than 512 bytes, but because the loader is larger than that, the hardware designers support "chaining," in which each block of the bootstrap is chained to (contains the disk location of) the next block. This chaining allows big bootstraps but also simplifies the installation of a virus. The virus writer simply breaks the chain at any point, inserts a pointer to the virus code to be executed, and reconnects the chain after the virus has been installed. This situation is shown in Figure 5-5.

The boot sector is an especially appealing place to house a virus because the virus gains control very early in the boot process, before most detection tools are active, so that it can avoid, or at least complicate, detection. Also, because the files in the boot area are crucial parts of the operating system, in order to keep users from accidentally modifying or deleting them with disastrous results, the operating system makes them "invisible" by not showing them as part of a normal listing of stored files, thus preventing their deletion. Thus, the virus code is not readily noticed by users.

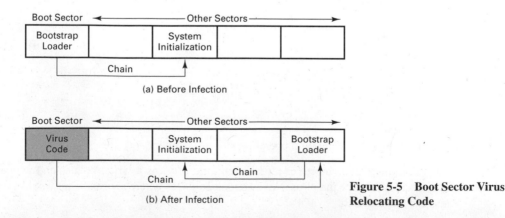

Figure 5-5   Boot Sector Virus Relocating Code

The next steps in the boot process are loading and invoking standard parts of the operating system, reading files that personalize this installation, and loading and invoking files called for in the personalization. For an MS-DOS/PC, for example, the standard parts of the operating system are files named IO.SYS and MSDOS.SYS, the personalization files are called CONFIG.SYS and AUTOEXEC.BAT. A virus can

- attach itself to either of the system files, IO.SYS or MSDOS.SYS
- attach itself to any other program loaded because of an entry in CONFIG.SYS or AUTOEXEC.BAT or
- add an entry to CONFIG.SYS or AUTOEXEC.BAT to cause it to be loaded

These options are listed in decreasing order of stealth; that is, a virus is less likely to be noticed if it is attached to a system part, more likely if it is attached to a dynamically loaded file, and even more likely if it is loaded dynamically by name. Similar situations apply for Macintoshes, Unix workstations, and mainframes.

Memory-Resident Viruses

Some parts of the operating system and most user programs execute, terminate, and disappear, with their space in memory being available for anything executed later. For very frequently used parts of the operating system, and a few specialized user programs, it would take too long to reload the program each time it was needed. Such code remains in memory and is called resident code. Examples of resident code are the routine that interprets keys pressed on the keyboard, the code that handles error conditions that arise during a program's execution, and a program that acts like an alarm clock, sounding a signal at a time the user determines. Resident routines are sometimes called TSRs, or terminate and stay resident routines.

Virus writers also like to attach viruses to resident code because the resident code is activated many times while the machine is running. Each time the resident code runs, the virus does too. Once activated, the virus can look for and infect uninfected carriers. For example, after activation, a boot sector virus might attach itself to a piece of resident code. Then, each time the virus is activated it might check whether any removable disk in a disk drive was infected and, if not, infect it. In this way the virus could spread its infection to all removable disks used during the computing session.

Other Homes for Viruses

A virus that does not take up residence in one of these cozy establishments has to fend for itself. But that is not to say that the virus will go homeless.

One popular home for a virus is an application program. Many applications, such as word processors and spreadsheets, have a macro feature, by which a user can record a series of commands and repeat those commands with one invocation. Such programs also provide a startup macro that is executed every time the application is executed. A virus writer can create a virus macro that adds itself to the startup directives for the application. It also embeds a copy of itself in data files so that the infection spreads to anyone receiving one of those files.

Libraries are also excellent places for malicious code to reside. Libraries are used by many programs, and thus the code in them has broad effects. Additionally, libraries are often shared between users and transmitted from one user to another, which spreads the infection. Finally, the executing code of a library can pass on the infection of a virus to other transmission media. Compilers, loaders, linkers, runtime monitors, runtime debuggers, and even virus control programs are good candidates for hosting viruses because they are widely shared.

Virus Signatures

A virus cannot be completely invisible. Code must be stored somewhere and code must be in memory to execute. The virus executes in a particular way. And viruses use certain methods to spread. Each of these characteristics is a telltale pattern, called a **signature**, that can be found. The signature of a virus is important for creating a program called a **virus scanner** that can automatically detect and, in some cases, remove viruses. The scanner searches memory and long-term storage and monitors execution, watching for the telltale signatures of viruses. The scanner can then block the virus, inform the user, and deactivate or remove the virus.

Storage Patterns

Most viruses attach to programs that are stored on disks. The attached virus piece is invariant, so that the start of the virus code becomes a detectable signature. The attached piece is always located at the same relative position to its attached file (for example, at the beginning, 400 bytes from the top, or at the bottom). Usually, the virus is at the beginning of the file because the virus writer wants to obtain control of execution before the infected program. In the simple case, the virus code is sitting at the top of the program. In other cases, the virus infection is only a handful of instructions, such as condition testing and a jump or call to the virus module, but then the code to which the virus transferred also has a recognizable pattern. Both of these situations are shown in Figure 5-6.

A virus may attach itself to a file, in which case the file's size grows, or the virus may obliterate all or part of the underlying program, in which case the program's size does not change, but the program's functioning is impaired. The virus writer has to choose one of these detectable effects.

The virus scanner can use a code or checksum to detect changes to a file. Virus scanners can also look for suspicious patterns, such as a JUMP instruction as the first instruction of a system program (in case the virus has positioned itself at the bottom of the file but wants to be executed first, as in Figure 5-6).

Execution Patterns

A virus writer may want a virus to do several things—most commonly, to spread infection, avoid detection, and cause harm. A virus can do any or all of these. These goals are shown in Table 5-2. Unfortunately, many of these kinds of behavior are perfectly normal, such as modifying the file directory: many normal programs create files, delete files, and write to disks. Thus, there are no key signals that point to the presence of a virus.

Most viruses seek to avoid detection. Because a disk's boot sector is not visible to normal operations (for example, the contents of the boot sector do not show on a directory listing), many virus writers hide their code there. A resident virus can monitor disk accesses and fake the result of a disk operation that would show the virus hidden in a boot sector, by showing the data that *should* be in the boot sector (which the virus has moved elsewhere).

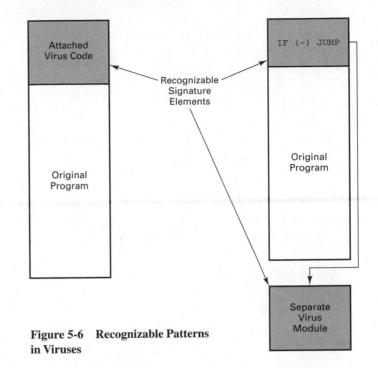

**Figure 5-6   Recognizable Patterns
in Viruses**

Table 5-2   Virus Effects and Causes

Virus Effect	How It Is Caused
Attach to executable program	• Modify file directory • Write to executable program file
Attach to data or control file	• Modify directory • Rewrite data • Append to data • Append data to self
Remain in memory	• Intercept interrupt by modifying interrupt handler address table • Load self in nontransient memory area
Infect disks	• Intercept interrupt • Intercept operating system call (to format disk, for example) • Modify system file • Modify ordinary executable program
Conceal self	• Intercept system calls that would reveal self and falsify result • Classify self as "hidden" file
Spread infection	• Infect boot sector • Infect system program • Infect ordinary program • Infect data ordinary program reads to control its execution
Prevent deactivation	• Activate before deactivating program and block deactivation • Store copy to reinfect after deactivation

The harm that a virus can cause is unlimited. On the modest end, the virus might do nothing. Some writers have created viruses just to show they can do it. Or they display a message on the screen, sound the buzzer, or play music. From there the problems escalate. One virus erases files, another erases an entire disk, another prevents a computer from booting, and another prevents writing to disk.

Transmission Patterns

A virus also has to have some means of transmission from one disk to another. As already seen, viruses can travel during the boot process, with an executable file, or in data files. Viruses travel during execution of an infected program. Because a virus can execute any instructions a program can, virus travel is not confined to any single medium or execution pattern. For example, a virus can arrive on a diskette or from a network connection, travel during its host's execution to a hard disk boot sector, reemerge next time the host computer is booted, and remain in memory to infect other diskettes as they are accessed.

Polymorphic Viruses

The virus signature may be the most reliable way to identify a virus. If a particular virus always begins with the string 47F0F00E08 (in hex) and has string 00113FFF located at word 12, it is unlikely that other programs or data files will have these characteristics. For longer signatures, the probability of a correct match increases.

If the virus scanner always looks for those strings, then the clever virus writer will put something other than those strings in those positions. For example, the virus could have two alternative but equivalent beginning words; after being installed the virus will choose one of the two words for its initial word. Then a virus scanner would have to look for both patterns. A virus that can change its appearance is called a **polymorphic** virus (*poly-* means "many" and *morph* means "form").

A two-form polymorphic virus can be handled easily as two independent viruses. Therefore, the virus writer intent on preventing detection of the virus will want either a large or an unlimited number of forms, so that the number of possible forms is too large for a virus scanner to search for. Simply embedding a random number or string at a fixed place in the executable version of a virus is not sufficient, because the signature of the virus is just the constant code excluding the random part. A polymorphic virus must randomly reposition all parts of itself, and randomly change all fixed data. Thus, instead of containing the fixed (and therefore searchable) string "HA! INFECTED BY A VIRUS," a polymorphic virus has to change even that pattern sometimes.

A simple variety of polymorphic virus uses encryption under various keys to make the stored form of the virus different. However, this virus really contains three parts: a decryption key, the (encrypted) object code of the virus, and the (unencrypted) object code of the decryption routine. The decryption routine thus can be used as a signature.

A more sophisticated polymorphic virus randomly intersperses harmless instructions throughout its code. Examples of harmless instructions are *add zero to a number, move a data value to its own location,* or *jump to the next instruction.* These "extra" instructions make it more difficult to locate an invariant signature.

To avoid detection, not every copy of a polymorphic virus has to differ from every other copy. If the virus changes occasionally, not every copy will match a signature of every other copy.

The Source of Viruses

Because a virus can be rather small, its code can be "hidden" inside other larger and more complicated programs. Two hundred lines of a virus could be separated into one hundred packets of two lines of code and a jump each; these one hundred packets could be easily hidden inside a compiler, a data base manager, a file manager, or some other large utility.

Discovering a virus could be aided by a procedure to determine whether two programs are equivalent. However, theoretical results in computing are very discouraging on the complexity of the equivalence problem. The question is undecidable in general, meaning that it may be extremely difficult to determine whether an infected compiler and an uninfected one produce the same results. Therefore, we are unlikely to develop a screening program that can separate infected modules from uninfected ones.

You can detect certain known viruses; that is, if you know that a particular virus may infect a computing system, you can check for and detect that virus. Having found the virus, however, you are left with the task of cleansing the system of it. Removing the virus in a running system requires being able to detect and eliminate its instances faster than it can spread.

Preventing Virus Infection

The only way to prevent infection by a virus is to not share executable code with an infected source. Because you cannot always know which sources are infected, you should assume that any outside source is infected. Fortunately, you know when you are receiving code from an outside source; unfortunately, it is not feasible to cut off all contact with the outside world.

In their interesting paper comparing computer virus transmission with human disease transmission, Kephart et al. [KEP93] observe that individuals' efforts to keep their computers free from viruses lead to communities that are generally free from viruses because members of the community have little (electronic) contact with the outside world. In this case, transmission is contained not because of limited contact but because of limited contact outside the community. The trick seems to be in choosing one's community prudently.

Techniques for building a reasonably safe community for electronic contact include these:

- *Use only commercial software acquired from reliable, well-established vendors.* Although you may receive a virus from even a large manufacturer with a name everyone would recognize, these organizations have significant reputations that could be seriously damaged by even one bad incident. Similarly, software distribution companies are careful about products they handle.

- *Test all new software on an isolated computer.* If you must use software from a questionable source, test the software first on a computer with no hard disk, not connected to a network, and with the boot disk removed. Run the software and look for unexpected behavior, even simple behavior such as unexplained figures on the screen. Test the computer with a copy of a virus scanner, created before running the suspect program. Only if the program passes these tests should it be installed on a less isolated machine.

- *Make a bootable diskette and store it safely.* Revise the startup files on the diskette so that system files (drivers, memory management software) are loaded from the diskette. If your system does become infected, this clean diskette will let you reboot securely. Keep the diskette write-protected during reboot. Prepare this diskette now, before infection; after infection it is too late. For safety, prepare an extra copy of the safe boot diskette

- *Make and retain backup copies of executable system files.* This way, in the event of a virus infection, you can remove infected files and reinstall from the clean backup copies.

- *Use virus detectors (often called virus scanners) regularly.* Many of the virus detectors available can both detect and eliminate viruses. Several scanners are better than one, because one may detect viruses others miss. Scanners search for virus signatures. They are constantly being revised as new viruses are discovered. New virus signature files, or new versions of scanners, are distributed frequently.

Truths and Misconceptions About Viruses

There is much misinformation in circulation about viruses. Here we debunk some popular misconceptions.

- *Viruses* can *infect systems other than PCs/MS-DOS/Windows.* PCs are the most popular computers, so there are more people writing software (and viruses) for them than for any other. Also, there is more active exchange of PC software, which contributes to virus distribution. Thus the PC is the most common target. However, the principles of virus attachment and infection can occur on Macintosh computers, Unix workstations, and mainframe computers. No writable stored-program computer is immune to possible virus attack.

- *Viruses* can *modify "hidden" or read-only files.* Each of these protections is applied by software, and software (the virus) can override protection software has put in place. Software protection is layered, with the operating system providing the most elementary protection. If a secure operating system obtains control *before* a virus contaminator has executed, the operating system *can* prevent contamination as long as it blocks the attacks the virus will make.

- *Viruses* can *appear in data files.* What is data and what is an executable file? The distinction between these is not always clear, because a data file can control how a program executes and even cause execution of a program. Some data files, such as the MS-DOS CONFIG.SYS file, list steps to be taken by the program that reads the data, and these steps can include executing a program. Similarly, word processing document files may contain startup commands to execute when the document is opened, and these startup commands can contain malicious code. Strictly speaking, a virus can activate and spread only when a program executes. In fact, however, data files are acted on by programs, and clever virus writers have been able to make data control files cause programs to do things, including pass along copies of the virus to other data files.

- *Viruses spread by ways other than just diskettes.* Sharing of files through diskettes is the most common way by which viruses are spread. However, any means of transferring files electronically will work, such as networks or bulletin boards. Any form of sharing—of programs, data, documents, and so forth—can be used to transfer a virus.

- *Viruses* cannot *remain in memory after a complete power off/power on reboot.* Computer memory (RAM) is volatile, meaning that all contents are deleted when power is lost.[2] Of course, viruses written to disk or diskette certainly can remain on disk through a reboot cycle and reappear after the reboot. Note that some viruses *can* persist through a software reboot (CTRL+ALT+DELETE on an IBM PC). Also note that boot sector viruses gain control when a machine reboots (hardware or software reboot), so it can seem as if a boot sector virus has remained through a reboot cycle because it is active immediately when a reboot has completed.

- *Viruses* cannot *infect hardware.* Viruses can infect only things they can modify: memory, executable files, and data are the primary targets. If hardware contains writable storage that can be accessed under program control, that storage *is* subject to virus attack. Because a virus can control hardware that is subject to program control, it may seem as if a hardware device has been infected by a virus, but really the software driving the hardware has been infected. Viruses can also exercise hardware in any way a program can; for example, a virus could cause a disk to loop incessantly, moving to the innermost track, then the outermost, and back again to the innermost track.

- *Viruses can be malevolent, benign, or benevolent.* Not all viruses are bad. For example, a virus might locate uninfected programs, compress them so that they occupy less memory, and insert a copy of a routine that decompresses the program when its execution begins, as well as spreading the compression function to other programs. This virus could substantially reduce the amount of storage required for stored programs, possibly by up to 50%. However, the compression would be done at the request of the virus, not at the request, or even knowledge, of the program owner.

Two examples of malicious code complete this section. These examples detail the effects just described.

Virus Example: Brain Virus

One of the most heavily studied viruses, in part because it was a very early virus, is the Brain virus, so named because it labels any diskette it attacks BRAIN. It affects IBM PC/MS-DOS computers. It is believed to have originated in Pakistan. Numerous variants have been produced; because of the number of variants, people believe that the source code of the virus was released to the underground virus community.

What It Does

The Brain virus, like all viruses, seeks to pass on its infection. This virus first locates itself in upper memory and then executes a system call to reset the upper memory bound below itself, so that it is not disturbed. It traps interrupt number 19 (disk read) by resetting the interrupt address table to point to it and then sets the address for interrupt number 6 (unused) to the former address of the interrupt 19. In this way, the virus screens disk read calls, handling any that would read the boot sector (passing back the original boot contents

---

[2] Some very-low-level hardware settings (such as the size of disk installed) are retained in memory called non-volatile RAM, but these locations are not directly accessible by programs, and are written only by programs run from read-only memory (ROM) during hardware initialization. Thus, they are immune to virus attack.

that were moved to one of the bad sectors); it then redirects other disk calls to the normal disk read handler, through interrupt 6.

The Brain virus appears to have no effect other than passing its infection, as if it were an experiment or a proof of concept. However, variants of the virus erase diskettes, erase the hard disk, or destroy the file allocation table (the table that shows which files are where on a disk).

How It Spreads

The Brain virus positions itself in the boot sector and in six other sectors of the diskette. One of the six sectors contains the original boot code, moved there from the original boot sector, and two others contain the remaining code of the virus. The remaining three sectors contain a duplicate of the others. The virus marks these six sectors "faulty" so that the operating system does not try to use them. (With low-level calls you can force the disk drive to read from what the operating system has marked as bad sectors.) The virus allows the boot process to continue.

Once established in memory, the virus intercepts disk read requests for the diskette drive. With each read the virus reads the disk boot sector and inspects the fifth and sixth bytes for the hexadecimal value 1234 (its signature). If it finds that value, it concludes that the disk is infected; if not, it infects the disk.

What Was Learned

This virus uses some of the standard tricks of viruses, such as hiding in the boot sector and intercepting and screening interrupts. The virus is almost a prototype for later efforts. In fact, many other virus writers seem to have patterned their work on this basic virus. Thus, one could say it was a useful learning tool for the virus-writer community.

Sadly, however, its infection did not raise public consciousness of viruses, other than a certain amount of fear and misunderstanding. Subsequent viruses, such as the Lehigh virus that swept through the computers of Lehigh University, the nVIR viruses that sprang from prototype code posted on bulletin boards, and the Scores virus that was first found at NASA in Washington, D.C., circulated more widely and with greater effect. Fortunately, most viruses have a modest effect, such as displaying a message or emitting a sound. However, that is a matter of luck because the writers who could put together the simpler viruses obviously had all the talent and knowledge to make much more malevolent viruses.

There is no general cure for viruses. Virus checkers are effective against today's known viruses and general patterns of infection, but they cannot counter tomorrow's variant. The only sure prevention is complete isolation from outside contamination, which is not feasible; in fact, networking is increasing, thereby increasing the risk of virus exchange. Now we turn to a network virus/worm (there is disagreement about what to call it) that is a good exemplar of its type.

Other Malicious Code Example: Internet Worm

On the evening of 2 November 1988 a worm was released onto the common computer network the Internet.[3] This worm caused serious damage to the network, leading to many

---

[3] Note: This incident is normally called a worm, although it shares most of the characteristics of viruses.

infected systems; many more uninfected systems severed their connections to the network. The worm was extensively studied by Gene Spafford and his team at Purdue University [SPA89] and by Mark Eichen and Jon Rochlis at MIT [EIC89].

Robert T. Morris Jr., a graduate student at Cornell University, created and released the worm. Morris was convicted in 1990 of violating the 1986 Computer Fraud and Abuse Act, section 1030 of U.S. Code Title 18. He received a $10,000 fine, a three-year suspended jail sentence, and 400 hours of community service.

What It Did

Judging from its code, Morris programmed the Internet worm to accomplish three main objectives:

- determine where it could spread
- spread its infection
- remain undiscovered and undiscoverable

What Effect It Had

The primary effect was exhaustion of resources. The source code of the worm indicated that it was supposed to check whether a target host was already infected and, if so, negotiate so that either the existing infection or the new infector would terminate. However, because of a supposed flaw in the code, many new copies did not terminate. Therefore, an infected machine soon became burdened with many copies of the worm, all busily attempting to spread the infection. The primary observable effect was serious degradation in performance of affected machines.

The ensuing effect was for system administrators to sever their connection with the Internet, either to stop the processes looking for sites to which to spread, or to avoid being infected.

The third-order effect was that disconnected systems could not communicate with other systems to carry on the normal research, collaboration, business, or information exchange users expected. System administrators on disconnected systems could not use the network to exchange information with their counterparts at other installations, so status and containment or recovery information was unavailable.

The worm caused an estimated 6,000 installations to shut down or disconnect from the Internet. In total, several thousand systems were disconnected for several days and several hundred of these systems were closed to users for a day or more while they were being disconnected. Estimates of the cost of the damage range from $100,000 to $97 million.

How It Worked

The main goals of the worm, as listed earlier, were determining where to spread, spreading itself, and remaining undetected. The worm exploited several known flaws and configuration failures of Berkeley version 4 of the Unix operating system. It accomplished—or had code that appeared to try to accomplish—these three objectives as follows.

Where To Spread   The worm had three techniques for locating potential victim machines. It first tried to find user accounts on the target machine that it could invade. In parallel it tried to exploit a bug in the *finger* program and then to use a trapdoor in the *send-mail* mail handler. *All three of these flaws were well-known in the general Unix community.*

The first flaw was a joint user and system error, in which the worm tried guessing passwords and succeeded when it found one. The Unix password file is stored in encrypted form, but readable (the ciphertext, that is) by anyone. (This is the system error.) The worm encrypted various popular passwords and compared the ciphertext against the ciphertext of the stored password file. The worm tried the account name and owner's name and a short list of 432 common passwords (e.g., "guest," "password," "help," "coffee," "coke," "aaa"). If none of these succeeded, the worm finally tried the dictionary file stored on the system for use by spelling checkers. (Choosing a recognizable password is the user error.) When it got a match, the worm could login to the corresponding account by presenting the plaintext password. As a user, the worm could look for other machines to which the user could obtain access. (See the article by Robert T. Morris Sr. and Ken Thompson [MOR79] on selection of good passwords, published a decade before the worm. Morris Sr. is a computer security professional now employed by the National Security Agency, and Thompson is still with AT&T Laboratories, where they were when they wrote this paper.)

The second flaw concerned *fingerd*, the program that runs continuously to respond to other computers' requests for information about system users. The flaw was to cause the input buffer to overflow, spilling into the return address stack. Thus, when the finger call terminated, the routine executed instructions that had been pushed there as another part of the buffer overflow, causing the worm to be connected to a remote shell.

The third flaw was a trapdoor in the *sendmail* program. Ordinarily this program runs in the background, awaiting signals from others wanting to send mail to the system. When it receives such a signal, the program receives a destination address, which it verifies, and then begins a dialog to receive the message. However, when running in DEBUG mode, the program received and executed a command string instead of the destination address.

Spread Infection   Having found a suitable target machine, the worm used one of these three methods to send to the target machine a bootstrap loader. This loader consisted of 99 lines of C code that were compiled and executed on the target machine. The bootstrap loader then fetched the rest of the worm from the sending host machine. There was an element of good computer security—or stealth—built into the exchange between the host and the target. When the target's bootstrap requested the rest of the worm, it supplied a one-time password back to the host. Without this password, the host would immediately break the connection to the target, presumably in an effort to guard against "rogue" bootstraps (ones that a real administrator might develop to try to obtain a copy of the rest of the worm for subsequent analysis).

The bootstrap used techniques to avoid detection; for example if a transmission error occurred while fetching the rest of the worm, the loader zeroed and then deleted all code already transferred, and exited.

Remain Undiscovered and Undiscoverable   The worm went to considerable lengths to prevent its discovery once established on a host. As soon as the worm received its full code, it brought the code into memory, encrypted it, and deleted the original copies from disk. Thus, no traces were left on disk, and even a memory dump would not readily expose the code of the worm. The worm periodically changed its name and process identifier so that no single name would run up a large amount of computing time.

What Was Learned

The Internet worm sent a shock wave through the Internet community, which was largely populated at the time by academics and researchers. The affected sites closed some of the loopholes exploited by the worm, and generally tightened security. Some users changed passwords. An automated security-checking program called COPS was developed to check for known flaws including ones the worm exploited. However, as time has passed and as many new installations have joined the Internet, security analysts checking for site vulnerabilities still find many of the same problems. A new attack on the Internet would not succeed to as great a scale as did the Internet worm, but it would still cause significant inconvenience to many. The Internet worm was also benign in that it only spread to other systems: it collected sensitive data, such as account passwords, but it did not retain them. While acting as users, the worm could have deleted or overwritten files, distributed them elsewhere, or encrypted them and held them for ransom. The next worm may not be so benign.

A very positive outcome from this worm was development in the United States of an infrastructure for reports and corrections for malicious and nonmalicious code flaws. Both this incident and Cliff Stoll's later experience [STO89] of tracking an electronic intruder (and subsequent difficulty finding anyone to deal with the case) showed the computer community the need to organize. The Computer Emergency Response Team (CERT) at Carnegie Mellon University has done an excellent job of collecting and disseminating information on malicious code attacks and their countermeasures. System administrators now interchange information on problems and solutions. Security comes from informed protection, not from ignorance.

5.2   Targeted Malicious Code

So far the discussion in this chapter has concerned anonymous code written to affect indiscriminately. Another class of malicious code is written for a particular system, for a particular application, and for a particular purpose. Many of the techniques of virus writers apply, but there are also some new techniques.

Trapdoors

A **trapdoor** is a secret, undocumented entry point into a module. The trapdoor is inserted during code development, perhaps to test the module, perhaps to provide "hooks" by which to connect future modifications or enhancements, and perhaps to allow access in the event of future errors. In addition to these legitimate uses, trapdoors can allow a programmer access into a program once it is placed into production.

Examples of Trapdoors

Because computing systems are complex structures, programmers usually develop and test systems in a modular manner. Each small component of the system is tested. Then components are grouped into logical clusters of a few components, and each cluster is tested individually.

Each component is initially tested without all surrounding routines that prepare input or work with output. To test a single module it may be necessary to write **stubs** and **drivers**, simple routines to inject data into and extract results from the routine being tested. As testing continues, these stubs and drivers are discarded because they are replaced by the actual routines whose functions they mimic. The two modules MODA and MODB in Figure 5-7 are being tested by stubs and drivers.

During program testing, flaws may be discovered in modules. Sometimes, when the source of the flaw is not obvious, debugging code is inserted into suspicious modules, causing these modules to display intermediate results of a computation or to perform extra computations to check the validity of previous modules.

To control stubs or invoke debugging code, special control sequences are embedded in the design of the module to be tested. For example, a module in a text formatting system

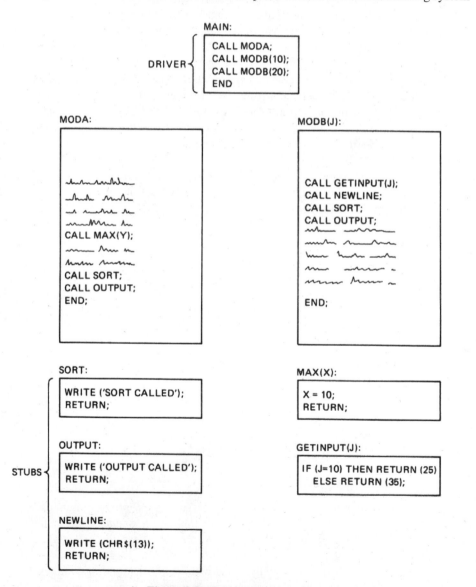

Figure 5-7   Stubs and Drivers

might be designed to recognize commands such as .PAGE, .TITLE, and .SKIP. During program testing, the programmer may have inserted a command .DEBUG that has a series of parameters of the form *var = value*. This command allows the programmer to modify the values of internal program variables during execution, either to test corrections to this module or to supply values passed to modules this one calls.

Command insertion is a recognized testing practice. If left in place after testing, the extra commands can become a problem. They are undocumented control sequences that produce side effects and can be used as trapdoors. In fact, a debugging trapdoor in an electronic mail program was one way the Internet worm spread its infection.

Poor **error checking** is another source of trapdoors. In some poorly designed systems, unacceptable input may not be caught and may be accepted. For example, a routine may look only for one of three expected sequences; finding none of the three it should recognize an error. If the three possibilities are tested in a CASE statement, a failure may simply fall through the CASE. The *fingerd* flaw exploited by the Morris worm occurs because a C library I/O routine fails to check whether there are characters left in the input buffer before returning a pointer to a supposed next character.

Another common example of this kind of flaw can be found in hardware processor design, where not all possible binary opcode values have matching machine instructions. The **undefined opcodes** sometimes implement peculiar instructions, either for testing the design of the processor or due to an oversight by the designer of the processor. This is the hardware counterpart of the software flaw described.

Trapdoors are not always bad. They can be very useful in finding security flaws. Auditors sometimes request trapdoors in production programs so that they can insert fictitious but identifiable transactions into the system, and trace the flow of these transactions through the system. However, trapdoors must be documented, access to them must be strongly controlled, and they should be used only with full understanding of the potential consequences.

Causes of Trapdoors

The programmer usually removes trapdoors during program development. However, trapdoors can persist in production programs because the programmer

- *forgets* to remove them
- intentionally leaves them in the program for *testing*
- intentionally leaves them in the program for *maintenance* of the finished program
- intentionally leaves them in the program as a *covert means of access* to the routine after it becomes an accepted production program

The first of these cases is an unintentional security blunder; the next two are serious exposures of the security of a system, and the fourth is the first step in an outright attack. The fault is not the trapdoor; these are very useful techniques for program testing, correction, and maintenance. The fault is the program development environment. The trapdoor becomes a vulnerability if no one notices it or acts to prevent or control its use in vulnerable situations.

Trapdoors are a vulnerability because they expose the system to modification during execution. The trapdoor can be exploited by the original programmer; it can also be used by anyone who discovers the trapdoor by accident or through exhaustive trials. Security is not built by someone's belief that no one else would find the hole.

Salami Attack

Another kind of program attack is called a **salami attack**. This attack gets its name from the way odd bits of meat are formed together in a salami. Programs that compute amounts of money may be subject to a salami attack. In this attack, a small amount of money is shaved from each computation. The amount shaved is so small that an individual case is unlikely to be noticed. However, accumulated amounts can add up.

Examples of Salami Attacks

The classic, perhaps apocryphal, story of a salami attack involves computations of interest. The computation of 6.5% interest on $102.87 for 31 days is $31/365*0.065*102.87 =$ $0.5495726. Because banks deal only in full cents, a typical practice is to round down if a residue is less than half a cent, and round up if a residue is half a cent or more. However, few people check their interest computation closely, and fewer still would complain about having the amount $0.5495 rounded down to $0.54, instead of up to $0.55. Most programs that perform computations on currency recognize that because of rounding, a sum of individual computations may be a few cents different from the computation applied to the sum of the balances.

What happens to these fractional cents? The computer security folk legend is told of a programmer who collected the fractional cents and credited them to a single account: hers! The interest program merely had to balance total interest paid to interest due on the total of the balances of the individual accounts. Auditors will probably not notice one specific account. In a situation with many accounts, the roundoff error can be substantial, and the programmer's account pockets this roundoff.

Salami attacks that net more are more interesting. For example, instead of shaving fractional cents, the programmer may take a few cents from each account, again assuming that no individual has the desire or understanding to recompute the amount the bank reports. Most people finding a result a few cents different from that of the bank would accept the bank's figure, attributing the difference to an error in arithmetic or a misunderstanding of the conditions under which interest is credited. Or a program might record a $20 fee for a particular service, while the company standard is $15. If unchecked, the extra $5 could go to an account of the programmer's choice.

Why Salami Attacks Persist

Computer computations are notoriously subject to small errors involving rounding and truncation, especially when large numbers are to be combined with small numbers. Rather than document the exact errors, it is easier for programmers and users to accept a small amount of error as natural and unavoidable. To reconcile accounts, an error correction is included in computations. Inadequate auditing of these corrections is one reason why the salami attack may be overlooked.

Usually the source code of a system is too large or complex to be audited for salami attacks, unless there is reason to suspect one. Size is definitely on the side of the programmer.

Covert Channels: Programs That Leak Information

Next we consider programs that communicate their information to people who should not receive that information. The communication travels unnoticed with other, perfectly proper communications. A general name for these extraordinary paths of communication is **covert channels**. The concept of a covert channel comes from a paper by Lampson [LAM73]; Millen [MIL88] presents a very good taxonomy of covert channels.

In this section we describe how a programmer can create covert channels. Actually the attack is a bit more complex than one programmer and a data source: a programmer who wants to obtain data can usually just read the data and write it to another file or print it out. However, if the programmer is one step removed—for example, outside the organization owning the data—the programmer has to figure a way to get at the data. One way is to provide a program with a built-in Trojan horse that will get the data. It would be too bold to generate a report labeled "Send this report to Jane Smith in Camden, Maine," so the programmer has to extract the data more surreptitiously. Covert channels are a means of extracting data clandestinely.

Figure 5-8 shows a "service program" that contains a Trojan horse that tries to copy information from a legitimate user (who is allowed access to the information) to a "spy" (who ought not be allowed to access the information). The user may not know that a Trojan horse is running and may not be in collusion to leak information to the spy.

Figure 5-8   Covert Channel Leaking Information

Covert Channel Overview

A programmer should not have access to sensitive data that a program processes after the program has been put into operation. For example, a programmer for a bank has no need to access the names or balances in depositors' accounts. Programmers for a securities firm have no need to know what buy and sell orders exist for the clients. During program testing, access to the real data may be justifiable, but not after the program has been accepted for regular use.

Still, a programmer might be able to profit from knowledge that a customer is about to sell a large amount of a particular stock, or that a large new account has just been opened. In many cases a programmer may want to develop a program that secretly communicates some of the data on which it operates. In this case, the programmer is the "spy," and the "user" is whoever ultimately runs the program written by the programmer.

How to Create Covert Channels

A programmer can always find ways to communicate data values covertly. Running a program that produces a specific output report or displays a value may be too obvious. For example, in some installations, a printed report might occasionally be scanned by a security person before it is delivered to its intended recipient.

If printing the data values themselves is too obvious, the programmer can encode the data values in another innocuous report by varying the format of the output, changing the lengths of lines, or printing or not printing certain values. For example, changing the word *TOTAL* to *TOTALS* in a heading would not be noticed, but this creates a 1-bit covert channel. The absence or presence of the *S* conveys one bit of information. Numeric values can be inserted in insignificant positions of output fields, and the number of lines per page can be changed. These subtle channels are shown in Figure 5-9.

Storage Channels

Some covert channels are called **storage channels** because they pass information by the presence or absence of objects in storage.

A simple example of a covert channel is the **file lock** channel. In multiuser systems, in order to prevent two people from writing to the same file at the same time (which could corrupt the file, if one person writes over some of what the other wrote), files are "locked": the operating system allows only one program to write to a file at a time, by blocking, delaying, or rejecting write requests from other programs. A covert channel can signal one bit of information by whether or not a file is locked.

Remember that the service program contains a Trojan horse written by the spy, but it is run by the unsuspecting user. As shown in Figure 5-10, the service program reads confidential data (to which the spy should not have access) and signals the data one bit at a time by locking or not locking some file (any file, the contents of which are arbitrary and not even modified). The service program and the spy need a common timing source, broken into intervals. To signal a 1 the service program locks the file for the interval; for a 0 it does not lock. Later in the interval the spy tries to lock the file itself. If the spy program cannot lock the file, it knows the service program must have, and thus it concludes the service program is signaling a 1; if the spy program can lock the file, it knows the service program is signaling a 0.

```
                                          UT COMPUTING CENTER
                                              AUDIT TRAIL
                                               03/04/87                  PAGE:   5

   ACCOUNT CODE:      040095    DEPT. NO: 741        CONSULTANT: LORETTA HAACK

                                      *** JOB SUMMARY MODEL/3081 ***

                        (HRS)   (KB*HRS)         ---(EXCP)---
   DATE   JOB#  JOB-NAME CPU# PGMER#  CPU  CCRE-CPU 3330- DISR -3380   TAPE   READER     (STD)    (TOTAL)
   TIME   CLASS PROGRAMMER-NAME    PLOTTER  CCRE-EXCP 3350-       TP   3480 LOCATION    PAGES   PRINTER   PAGES   MACHINE
                                                                                       CARDS    PUNCH    6670     COST
   2/15/87 8217 PROJECTI MVS1 007549  0.0000   0.00      0      0      0      29         2       29       2      0.0231
   13.29.56 (P) GREEN              0.0000   0.00      0      0      0 L31.SR1             0       0        0
            2/15/87 13.29.48 FCB-6  UCS-GN  FORM-0316 UNIT-COST-0.0110 UNITS-   2 COST-  0.022            33 RM1.PR1

   2/15/87 8227 PROJECTI MVS1 007549  0.0000   0.00      0      0      0      29         2       29       2      0.0231
   13.32.52 (P) GREEN              0.0000   0.00      0      0      0 L31.SR1             0       0        0
            2/15/87 13.32.45 FCB-6  UCS-GN  FORM-0316 UNIT-COST-0.0110 UNITS-   2 COST-  0.022            33 RM1.PR1

   2/21/87 5676 DAVID    MS1 007549  0.0000   0.00      0      0      0      52         3       52       3      0.0345
   11.00.03 (P) GREEN              0.0000   0.00      0      0      0 L31.SR1             0       0        0
            2/21/87 11.00.06 FCB-6  UCS-GN  FORM-0316 UNIT-COST-0.0110 UNITS-   3 COST-  0.033            55 RM1.PR1

   2/21/87 6297 PROJECTI MVS1 007549  0.0000   0.00      0      0      0      13         4       13       4      0.0196
   13.30.14 (P) GREEN              0.0000   0.00      0      0      0 L31.SR1             0       0        0
            2/21/87 13.30.16 FCB-6  UCS-GN  FORM-0316 UNIT-COST-0.0110 UNITS-   2 COST-  0.022            14 RM1.PR1
            2/21/87 13.30.26 FCB-6  UCS-GN  FORM-0316 UNIT-COST-0.0110 UNITS-   2 COST-  0.022            14 RM1.PR1
   21 JOBS                        0.0000   0.00      0      0      0     925        54      925      54      0.6951
                                  0.0000   0.00      0      0      0       0         0        0       0

   2/16/87 6125 MYTIME   MVS1 007569  0.0000   0.00      0      0      0      25         2       25       2      0.0189
   15.33.20 (P) SENG               0.0000   0.00      0      0      0 L31.SR1             0       0        0
            2/16/87 15.36.40 FCB-6  UCS-GN  FORM-0316 UNIT-COST-0.0110 UNITS-   2 COST-  0.022            27 RM2.PR1
   1 JOBS                         0.0000   0.00      0      0      0      25         2       25       2      0.0189
                                  0.0000   0.00      0      0      0      25         2       25       2

   2/05/87 2591 MAIL     MVS1 007579  0.0000   0.00      0      0      0      68         2       68       2      0.0490
   10.43.33 (P) MCCARTER           0.0000   0.00      0      0      0 L31.SR1             0       0        0
            2/05/87 10.42.40 FCB-6  UCS-GN  FORM-0316 UNIT-COST-0.0110 UNITS-   2 COST-  0.022            70 RM1.PR1

   2/05/87 2625 MAIL$999 MVS1 007579  0.0000   0.00      0      0      0      46         2       46       2      0.0329
   10.48.35 (P) MCCARTER           0.0000   0.00      0      0      0 L31.SR1             0       0        0
            2/05/87 10.47.43 FCB-6  UCS-GN  FORM-0316 UNIT-COST-0.0110 UNITS-   2 COST-  0.022            47 RM1.PR1

   2/05/87 2635 MAIL$000 MVS1 007579  0.0000   0.00      0      0      0      40         2       40       2      0.0294
   10.49.44 (P) MCCARTER           0.0000   0.00      0      0      0 L31.SR1             0       0        0
            2/05/87 10.48.51 FCB-6  UCS-GN  FORM-0316 UNIT-COST-0.0110 UNITS-   2 COST-  0.022            42 RM1.PR1

   2/05/87 2651 MAIL$000 MVS1 007579  0.0000   0.00      0      0      0      65         2       65       2      0.0476
   10.51.24 (P) MCCARTER           0.0000   0.00      0      0      0 L31.SR1             0       0        0
            2/05/87 10.50.34 FCB-6  UCS-GN  FORM-0316 UNIT-COST-0.0110 UNITS-   2 COST-  0.022            68 RM1.PR1

   2/05/87 2656 MAIL$000 MVS1 007579  0.0000   0.00      0      0      0      71         2       71       2      0.0525
   10.52.22 (P) MCCARTER           0.0000   0.00      0      0      0 L31.SR1             0       0        0
            2/05/87 10.51.30 FCB-6  UCS-GN  FORM-0316 UNIT-COST-0.0110 UNITS-   2 COST-  0.022            75 RM1.PR1

   2/05/87 2733 MAIL$000 MVS1 007579  0.0000   0.00      0      0      0      69         2       69       2      0.0504
   11.01.42 (P) MCCARTER           0.0000   0.00      0      0      0 L31.SR1             0       0        0
            2/05/87 11.00.52 FCB-6  UCS-GN  FORM-0316 UNIT-COST-0.0110 UNITS-   2 COST-  0.022            72 RM1.PR1

   2/05/87 2745 MAIL$000 MVS1 007579  0.0000   0.00      0      0      0      40         2       40       2      0.0287
   11.02.20 (P) MCCARTER           0.0000   0.00      0      0      0 L31.SR1             0       0        0
            2/05/87 11.01.28 FCB-6  UCS-GN  FORM-0316 UNIT-COST-0.0110 UNITS-   2 COST-  0.022            41 RM1.PR1

   2/05/87 2753 MAIL$000 MVS1 007579  0.0000   0.00      0      0      0      42         2       42       2      0.0308
   11.03.26 (P) MCCARTER           0.0000   0.00      0      0      0 L31.SR1             0       0        0
            2/05/87 11.02.36 FCB-6  UCS-GN  FORM-0316 UNIT-COST-0.0110 UNITS-   2 COST-  0.022            44 RM1.PR1

   2/05/87 2759 MAIL$000 MVS1 007579  0.0000   0.00      0      0      0      46         2       46       2      0.0335
   11.04.02 (P) MCCARTER           0.0000   0.00      0      0      0 L31.SR1             0       0        0
            2/05/87 11.06.50 FCB-6  UCS-GN  FORM-0316 UNIT-COST-0.0110 UNITS-  -2 COST-  0.022            48 RM1.PR1

   2/05/87 2764 MAIL$000 MVS1 007579  0.0000   0.00      0      0      0     169         2      169       2      0.1197
   11.04.51 (P) MCCARTER           0.0000   0.00      0      0      0 L31.SR1             0       0        0
            2/05/87 11.07.03 FCB-6  UCS-GN  FORM-0316 UNIT-COST-0.0110 UNITS-   2 COST-  0.022           171 RM1.PR1

   2/05/87 2770 MAIL$000 MVS1 007579  0.0000   0.00      0      0      0      46         2       46       2      0.0329
   11.05.08 (P) MCCARTER           0.0000   0.00      0      0      0 L31.SR1             0       0        0
```

(1) Number of spaces after :

(2) Last digit in field that would not be checked

(3) Presence or absence of word (TOTAL) in header line

(4) No space after last line of subtotal

(5) Last digit in insignificant field

(6) Number of lines per page

(7) Use of . instead of :

Figure 5-9   Covert Channels

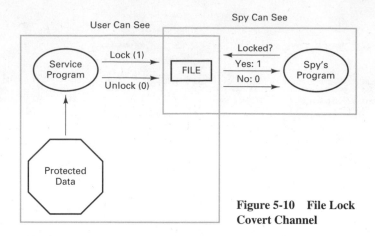

Figure 5-10   File Lock
Covert Channel

This same approach can be used with disk storage quotas or other resources. With disk storage, the service program signals a 1 by creating an enormous file, so large that it consumes most of the available disk space. The spy program later tries to create a large file. If it succeeds, the spy program infers that the service program did not create a large file, and so the service program is signaling a 0; otherwise the spy program infers a 1. Similarly, the existence of a file or other resource of a particular name can be used to signal. Notice that the spy does not need access to a file itself; the mere existence of the file is adequate to signal. The spy can determine the existence of a file it cannot read by trying to create a file of the same name; if the request to create is rejected, the spy determines that the service program has such a file.

To signal more than one bit, the service program and the spy program signal one bit in each time interval. Figure 5-11 shows a service program signaling the string 100 by toggling the existence of a file.

A final example of a storage channel uses a server of unique identifiers. Some bakeries have a machine that distributes numbered tickets so that customers can be served in the order in which they arrived. Some computing systems provide a similar server of unique identifiers, usually numbers, for use to name temporary files, to tag and track messages, or to record auditable events. Different processes can request the next unique identifier from the server. But two cooperating processes can use the server to signal by the spy process observing whether the numbers it receives are sequential or a number is missing. A missing number implies that the service program also requested a number, thereby signaling 1.

In all of these examples, the service program and the spy need access to a shared resource (such as a file, or even knowledge of the existence of a file) and a shared sense of time. As shown, shared resources are common in multiuser environments, where the resource may be as seemingly innocuous as whether a file exists, a device is free, or space remains on disk. A source of shared time is also typically available, because many programs need access to the current system time to set timers, to record the time at which events occur, or to synchronize activities.

Transferring data one bit at a time must seem awfully slow. But computers operate at such speeds that even a rate of 1 bit per millisecond (1/1000 sec.) is minuscule, would

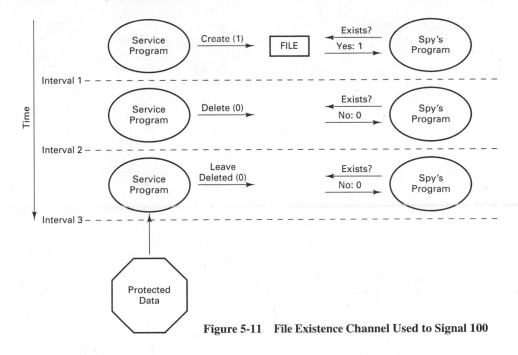

Figure 5-11   File Existence Channel Used to Signal 100

never be noticed, but could easily be handled by two processes. At that rate of 1000 bits per second (which is unrealistically conservative), this entire book could be leaked in about two days. Increasing the rate by an order of magnitude or two, which is still quite conservative, reduces the transfer time to minutes.

Timing Channels

Other covert channels, called **timing channels**, pass information by the speed at which things happen. Actually, timing channels are shared resource channels in which the shared resource is time.

A service program uses a timing channel to communicate by using or not using an assigned amount of computing time. In the simple case, a multiprogrammed system with two user processes divides time into blocks and allocates blocks of processing alternately to one process and the other. A process is offered processing time, but if the process is waiting for another event to occur and has no processing to do, it rejects the offer. The service process either uses its block (to signal a 1) or rejects its block (to signal a 0). Such a situation is shown in Figure 5-12, first with the service process and the spy's process alternating, and then with the service process communicating the string 101 to the spy's process. In the second part of the example, the service program wants to signal 0 in the third time block. It will do this by using just enough time to determine that it wants to send a 0 and then pause. The spy process then receives control for the remainder of the time block.

So far all examples have involved just the service process and the spy's process; multiuser computing systems typically have more than just two active processes. The only complications added by more processes are that the two cooperating processes must adjust their timings and deal with the possible interference from others. For example, with the

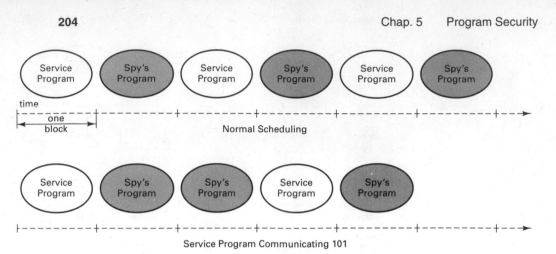

Figure 5-12   Covert Timing Channel

unique identifier channel, other processes will also request identifiers. If on average *n* other processes will request *m* identifiers each, then the service program will request more than $n * m$ identifiers for a 1 and no identifiers for a 0. The gap dominates the effect of all other processes. Also, the service process and the spy's process can use sophisticated coding techniques to compress their communication and detect and correct transmission errors caused by the effects of other unrelated processes.

Identifying Potential Covert Channels

In this description of covert channels, ordinary things, such as the existence of a file or time used for a computation, have been the medium through which a covert channel communicates. Covert channels are not easy to find because these media are so numerous and frequently used. Two relatively old techniques remain the standards for locating potential covert channels. One works by analyzing the resources of a system, while the other works at the source code level.

Shared Resource Matrix   Because the basis of a covert channel is a shared resource, the search for potential covert channels involves finding all shared resources and determining which processes can write to and read from the resources. The technique was introduced by Kemmerer [KEM83]. Although laborious, the technique can be automated.

With this technique, you construct a matrix of resources (rows) and processes that can access them (columns). The entries in the matrix are R for "can read (or observe) the resource" and M for "can set (or modify, create, delete) the resource." For example, the file lock channel has the matrix shown in Table 5-3.

Table 5-3   Shared Resource Matrix

	Service Process	Spy's Process
Locked	R,M	R,M
Confidential data	R	

You then look for two columns and two rows having the following pattern.

	M		R	
	R			

This pattern identifies two resources and two processes such that the second process is not allowed to read from the second resource. However, the first process can pass the information to the second by reading from the second resource and signaling the data through the first resource. Thus, this pattern implies the potential information flow as shown here.

	M		R	
	R		R	

You then complete the shared resource matrix by adding these implied information flows, and analyze it for undesirable flows. Thus, you can tell that the spy's process can read the confidential data by using a covert channel through the file lock, as shown in Table 5-4.

Table 5-4   Complete Shared Resource Matrix

	Service Process	Spy's Process
Locked	R, M	R, M
Confidential data	R	R

Information Flow Method   Denning [DEN76a] derived a technique for flow analysis from the syntax of a program. Conveniently, this analysis can be automated within a compiler, so that information flow potentials can be detected as a program is under development.

Using this method, one recognizes there are nonobvious flows of information between statements in a program. For example, we know that the statement B:=A, which assigns the value of A to the variable B, obviously supports an information flow from A to B. This type of flow is called an explicit flow. Similarly, the pair of statements B:=A; C:=B indicates an information flow from A to C (by way of B). The conditional statement IF D=1 THEN B:=A has two flows: from A to B because of the assignment, but also from D to B, because the value of B can change if and only if the value of D is 1. This second flow is called an implicit flow.

The statement B:=*fcn(args)* supports an information flow from the function *fcn* to B. At a superficial level, we can say that there is a potential flow from the arguments *args* to B. However, we could analyze the function more closely to determine whether the function's value depended on all of its arguments and whether any global values, not part of the argument list, affected the function's value. These information flows can be traced from the bottom up: at the bottom there must be functions that call no other functions, and we can use their analysis to analyze the functions that call them. By analyzing the elementary functions first, we could say definitively whether there is a potential information flow from each argument to the function's result and whether there are any flows from global variables. In Table 5-5 are some examples of syntactic information flows.

Finally, we put all the pieces together to show which outputs are affected by which inputs. Although this analysis sounds frightfully complicated, it can be automated during the syntax analysis portion of compilation. This analysis can also be performed on the higher level design specification.

Covert Channel Conclusions

Covert channels represent a real threat to secrecy in information systems. A covert channel attack is fairly sophisticated, but the basic concept is not beyond the capabilities of even an average programmer. Because the subverted program can be practically any user service, such as a printer utility, planting the compromise can be as easy as planting a virus or any other kind of Trojan horse. And recent experience has shown how readily viruses can be planted.

Capacity and speed are not problems; our estimate of 1000 bits per second is unrealistically low, but even at that rate much information leaks swiftly. On modern hardware architectures, certain covert channels inherent in the hardware design have capacities in millions of bits per second. The attack does not require significant finance. Thus, the attack could be very effective in certain situations of highly sensitive data.

For these reasons, security researchers have worked diligently to develop techniques for closing covert channels. The closure results have been bothersome, because in ordinarily open environments, there is essentially no control over the subversion of a service program, nor is there an effective way of screening such programs for covert channels. And other than in a few very high security systems, operating systems cannot control the flow of information from a covert channel. The hardware-based channels cannot be closed, given the underlying hardware architecture.

For variety (or sobriety), Kurak and McHugh [KUR92] present a very interesting analysis of covert signaling through graphic images. In their work they demonstrate that two different images can be combined by some rather simple arithmetic on the bit patterns of digitized pictures. The second image in a printed copy is undetectable to the human eye,

Table 5-5 Syntactic Information Flows

Statement	Flow
B:=A	from A to B
IF C=1 THEN B:=A	from A to B; from C to B
FOR K:=1 to N DO *stmts* END	from K to *stmts*
WHILE K>0 DO stmts END	from K to *stmts*
CASE *(exp) val1: stmts*	from *exp* to *stmts*
B:=*fcn(args)*	from *fcn* to B
OPEN FILE *f*	none
READ (*f*, X)	from file *f* to X
WRITE (*f*, X)	from X to file *f*

but it can easily be separated and reconstructed by the spy receiving the digital version of the image.

Although covert channel demonstrations are highly speculative—reports of actual covert channel attacks just do not exist—the analysis is sound. The mere possibility of their existence calls for more rigorous attention to other aspects of security, such as program development analysis, system architecture analysis, and review of output.

5.3   Controls Against Program Threats

The picture just described is not very pretty: there are many ways a program can be made to fail. In this section we begin by considering controls used during software development—the design, writing, and testing of the program—to cover those sorts of exposures. We follow with descriptions of other controls, from operating systems to administrative procedures. All of these controls are complete subjects by themselves, and so in this section we only skim the surface of these capabilities; the bibliography points to more complete sources.

Programming Controls

We begin by discussing the controls that can be applied during program development to help to ensure the quality and trustworthiness of code to be produced.

Description of the Programming Task

In the original model of programming, a programmer received a description of a task to be performed, went away independently to derive a program to perform the task, and returned with the program in hand. The programmer worked alone on this task. Arguments in favor of working alone were these:

- Programming is an individual task, requiring independent thought. Communicating these ideas to another takes more time, to no gain.
- Programs, as creative expressions on the part of programmers, are very individualistic. Two individual programmers cannot work together on one project.
- Programmers are basically solitary people who prefer to work alone. Disrupting that preferred work style could have a negative influence on either the program or the programmer.
- Programming is an art understood only by programmers. Management is incapable of understanding programs (or management would prefer not to have to try to understand programs).

None of those arguments holds. The basic case against programming by the individual is size. The expected output of a good programmer in a single year is at most a few thousand lines of code (perhaps modified by a factor of two or three depending on programming language, complexity of programming task, and environment). Some good programmers of complex tasks produce on the average only two or three lines of code per day! That level of output is insufficient to produce current major systems involving hundreds of thousands or even millions of lines of code.

The field of **software engineering** addresses the problem of "programming in the large," that is, writing code for enormous systems. The basic principles of software engineering are division of labor, reuse of code, use of standard preconstructed software tools, and organized activity.

Peer Reviews

When a system is large enough that several people are programming it concurrently, all must have a precise design document that shows what each piece does and how each piece interacts with other pieces. Because the design document is somewhat subject to the individual interpretation of each programmer, the team needs to identify inconsistencies in understanding early. The team must also locate programmers' flaws of logic.

Correct code is the responsibility of all programmers on the team. For this reason, members of a team participate in **peer design reviews** and **peer code reviews**. When a designer or a programmer has completed a particular section of code, several other designers or programmers are invited to participate in a **walk-through** of the design or code. The original developer presents the material in an orderly manner, pausing for the comments, questions, and suggestions of others. These questions are designed to identify misunderstandings or errors.

This style of programming is called **egoless programming** [WEI71]. All group members recognize that the product belongs to the *group*, not to the *individual* who produced it. The purpose of the review is not to chastise the programmer for making errors, but to identify errors for the good of the product. The group succeeds only if its products are right; therefore, all members of the group have a vested interest in the correctness of the product.

Because all reviewers are designers or programmers themselves, they understand programming. They can distinguish between an error and a section that is correct but is not what they would have used. They know what things are suspicious in a program, or do not belong, or have a nonobvious side effect.

A rigorous design or code review can locate trapdoors, Trojan horses, salami attacks, worms, viruses, and other program flaws. A crafty programmer can conceal some of these flaws, but the chance of discovery rises when competent programmers review the code, especially at the level of a module of 30 to 60 lines. Management should use demanding code reviews throughout code development as a way of ensuring security of the programs produced.

Modularity, Encapsulation, and Information Hiding

The principles of software engineering recommend writing code in small, self-contained units called **modules**. Modularity offers advantages for program development, as well as security advantages. A module can be isolated from the negative effects of other modules with which it interacts. This isolation occurs due to a design principle called **encapsulation**. **Information hiding** is another benefit of modularization. With information hiding, other modules know that a module performs a certain task, but not *how* it performs that task. In this section we describe these three principles and their role in computer security.

Modularity   **Modularization** is the process of dividing a task into subtasks. This division is done on a logical or functional basis. Each module performs a separate, independent part

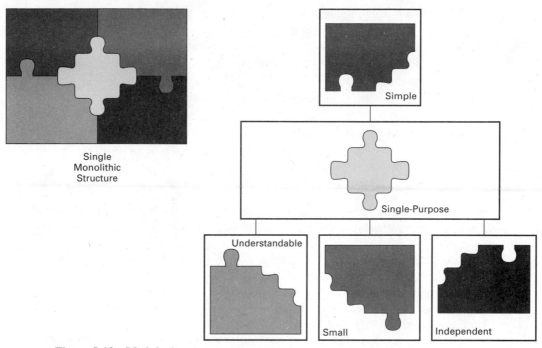

Single
Monolithic
Structure

Single-Purpose

Simple

Understandable

Small

Independent

Figure 5-13   Modularity

Hierarchical Modularity

of the task. **Modularity** is depicted in Figure 5-13. Although modularity seems to be in the eye of the beholder, people often cite the following characteristics of a module:

- *Unity:* performs one purpose
- *Smallness:* consists of an amount of information of which a person can readily grasp both structure and content
- *Simplicity:* is of a low degree of complexity so that a person can readily understand the purpose and structure of the module
- *Independence:* performs a task isolated from other modules

Other qualities, such as single input/single output or use of a limited set of programming constructs, have been proposed. From a security standpoint, modularity should improve the likelihood that an implementation is correct.

Program units should be only as large as needed to perform their required duties. There are several advantages to writing a program as a series of small, self-contained modules.

- *Maintenance.* If a function is implemented as a single module, the module can be replaced with a revised one, if necessary. The new module may be needed due to a change in requirements, hardware, or the environment. Sometimes the replacement is just an enhancement, by use of a smaller, faster, more correct, or otherwise better module. The interfaces between this module and the remainder of the program are few and well-described, so the effects of the replacement are evident.

- *Understandability.* A program composed of many small modules is easier to comprehend than one large, unstructured program.
- *Reuse.* Modules developed for one purpose can often be reused in other programs. Reuse of correct, existing program modules can significantly reduce the difficulty of programming and testing.
- *Correctness.* An error can be quickly traced to its cause if the modules perform only one task each.
- *Testing.* A single module with well-defined inputs, output, and function can be tested exhaustively by itself, without concern for its effects on other modules (other than the expected function and output, of course).

From a standpoint of security, programmers and analysts must be able to understand each module as an independent unit and be assured of its limited effect on other modules. Proper modularity leads to modules that have minimal interaction with other modules.

Encapsulation   Modularity enables each module to function as an independent object. A well-designed module has little **coupling** to other routines of the same program. The other routines are free of interference from other modules. This characteristic is called **encapsulation**, in which a module essentially operates as if it were surrounded by a shield that prevents unwanted access from the outside.

With encapsulation, modules interact only through certain well-defined interfaces. A module is entered only at specified entry points, and a module interacts with the fewest other modules possible. Encapsulation is shown in Figure 5-14.

Encapsulation does not mean complete isolation. Modules need certain inputs and must exchange information with other modules. However, this sharing is carefully documented, so that a module is affected only in known ways by other modules in the system. Sharing is also minimized, so that the fewest interfaces possible are used. Limited interfaces reduce the number of covert channels that can be constructed.

Information Hiding   A modular design leads to modules with limited effects on other modules. Conversely, programmers who work where modularization is stressed can be sure that other modules will have limited effect on ones they write. In this sense, a module can be seen as a black box, with certain well-defined inputs and outputs and a well-defined function. Other modules and other designers do not need to know *how* the module completes its function; it is enough to be assured that the module does its task in some correct manner.

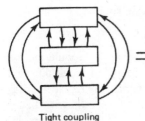

Tight coupling

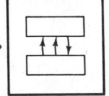 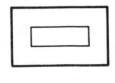

Independent, loosely coupled modules

Figure 5-14   Encapsulation

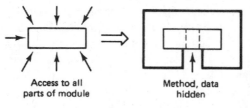

Figure 5-15   Information Hiding

Concealing the way a module does its task is called **information hiding**. Information hiding is depicted in Figure 5-15. Information hiding is desirable, because programmers cannot maliciously alter the modules of others if they do not know how the modules work.

The three characteristics of modularity, encapsulation, and information hiding are fundamental principles of software engineering. They are good practices for security because they lead to modules that can be understood, analyzed, and trusted.

Independent Testing

The purpose of testing is to certify the *correctness* of a program, not necessarily to assign blame for errors. A test that finds errors is more useful than one that finds none: with demonstrated errors, you know that the test was rigorous. When no errors are found, however, either the routine being tested was correct, or the test procedures were ineffective.

Programmers are too close to their code to test it effectively. For this reason, independent test teams improve the quality of testing. This team begins to develop test data as soon as the program design is complete. Test data can be constructed without reference to the source code of the program itself. The test cases designed by the test team check whether the program does what its design says it *should*, not necessarily what the programmer *interpreted* the design to require. The test team and the programmer may differ in their interpretation of the design, but they need to identify that ambiguity and resolve it.

From a security standpoint, independent testing is highly desirable because a programmer attempting to hide something in a routine does not develop the tests that will be applied to the routine. Independent testing increases the likelihood that a test will expose the effect of a hidden feature.

Configuration Management

Configuration management is another aspect of software engineering that offers advantages in security. When configuration management is practiced, a person or system controls and records all changes to a program or documentation. A group of professionals, called a **change control board**, judges the desirability and correctness of all proposed changes.

The Major Need for Configuration Management

The goal of configuration management is to guarantee availability and use of the correct version of all system components: software, design documents, documentation, control files, and so forth. Configuration management is simply strongly enforced organization and bookkeeping.

Virtually every programmer has "lost" a version of a program. After making one change, the programmer makes another change, then another, then another, and finally decides to abandon that approach. By this time, the original version may be deleted, confused with other versions, or merged with unrelated changes.

The situation is even worse if there are several parallel versions of a program. For example, suppose a company has a computer program for sale. After the first version is released, users report small errors, which the company fixes. So as not to distribute errors, the company updates its distribution version, so that known errors are fixed in it. Meanwhile, the company works on an enhanced version of the product, which will eventually be marketed. In this scenario, there are at least three separate versions of the product: the original, the one with some errors corrected, and the expanded one under development. Further error fixes or enhancements can create even more versions.

As another example, consider a company that has developed a software product. The product runs in three different environments, Apple Macintosh, PC/DOS, and UNIX. Although these implementations are similar, there are differences among them. Every time a module is changed, the change must be installed in all three versions, which must then be tested. Changing one version may require changing other parts of that version. Therefore, for each version there is one copy in form for distribution and one copy being changed. These separate versions and the changes being applied to them must be documented and controlled.

If the program is large enough to consist of several modules produced by several programmers, all programmers must recognize when someone has changed a module, because that module might affect other modules. The person who wrote a program cannot be free to change that code at will, even if those changes correct known errors. Commonly programmers keep **shadow copies** of corrected or revised routines, waiting for an update cycle when all programmers will combine new versions of their code and retest the entire system. Thus, there are stable versions of modules and working versions belonging to programmers. As system development progresses, there may be several different stable versions, in various stages of testing or integration with other modules.

These situations have identified three purposes for configuration management:

- to guard against inadvertent loss (deletion) of a version of a program
- to manage the parallel development of several similar versions of one program
- to provide facilities for controlled sharing of modules that combine to form one system

These goals can all be achieved by a systematic method of managing source code, object code, and documentation. The system must provide careful records so that someone knows where a copy of each version is located and what characteristics distinguish that version from all others. Companies commonly designate one or more configuration management specialists to do this job.

Typically a programmer "freezes" a module at some point in time and gives control of that copy to configuration management. The programmer no longer has the right or ability to modify that version. All changes from that point on are carefully monitored by a configuration management panel. The panel scrutinizes all change requests for correctness and for potential effect on other modules.

Security Advantages of Configuration Management   There are two security advantages to using configuration management. The first advantage protects against unintentional threats; the second guards against malicious ones.

Protecting the integrity of programs and documentation is the main security motivation for using configuration management. Because changes occur only after explicit approval from a configuration management authority, all changes are also carefully evaluated for side effects. With configuration management, previous versions of programs are archived, so that a programmer can retract a faulty change.

The other security advantage of configuration management is protecting a program from malicious modification. Once a reviewed program is accepted for a system, the programmer cannot sneak in and make changes, such as inserting trapdoors. The programmer has access to the running production program only through the configuration management panel, and these people are alert to such security breaches.

In order to have intelligible, auditable control over changes, the configuration management team often accepts program changes only at the source code level. Even though the programmer has compiled and tested the program and could provide object code, the configuration management team accepts only source code changes: statement insertions, deletions, and replacements. The configuration management team keeps the original source code plus the individual changes to produce each version. When a new version is to be produced, the configuration management team creates a temporary source program to be compiled. In this way, there is a precise record of all changes, when they were made, and by whom.

Proofs of Program Correctness

A security specialist wants to be certain that a given program computes a particular result, computes it correctly, and does nothing more. Unfortunately, results in computer science theory indicate that security specialists can never be certain about every possible program. There can be no general decision procedure that, given any two programs, determines whether the two are equivalent. This is a result of the "halting problem," which states that there is no general technique to determine whether an arbitrary program will halt when processing an arbitrary input.

Despite this disappointing general result, a technique called **program verification** can demonstrate formally the "correctness" of certain specific programs. Program verification involves making initial assertions about the inputs. Each program statement is translated into a logical statement about the contribution of that statement to the logical flow of the program. Finally, the terminal statement of the program is associated with the desired results of the program. Then, by applying a logic analyzer, it is possible to prove that the initial assumptions, through the implications of the program statements, produce the terminal conclusion. In this way, it is shown that the program achieves its goal. An example of program verification is given in Chapter 7.

Program correctness proofs are hindered by several factors.

- Correctness proofs depend on the programmer or the logician to translate a program's statements into logical implications. Just as programming is prone to errors, so is this translation.
- Deriving the correctness proof from the initial assertions and the implications of statements is difficult. The logical engine used to generate proofs runs slowly. The speed of the engine degrades as the size of the program increases, so that proofs of correctness are even less appropriate for large programs.
- The current state of program verification is less well-developed than code production. Proofs of correctness have not been consistently and successfully applied to large production systems.

Program verification systems are being improved constantly. Larger programs are being verified in less time than before. As program verification continues to mature, it will become a more important control to ensure the security of programs.

Process Improvement

We have looked at specific ways to improve quality of developed software, using ways by which the individual programmer or designer can better organize and implement. Curtis et al. [CUR87] examined very large programming projects and found that too often high-quality software depends on a few key individuals, whom Curtis called the *super-conceptualizers*. These people served both as the bridges between the customer or end user and the implementation team and as the high-level project designers. The super-conceptualizers passed on to every project team member not just what to do, but *how* to do it, in terms of quality. The success of the project depended very much on these people and their vision. A project without a vision or a visionary was less likely to succeed. But the organization cannot rely on the chance that a person with the right technical, managerial, and communication skills will be in the right place to assume the visionary role for a project. Curtis argues that software development must focus on the organization in order to reduce the variability in quality between projects within an organization.

Good programs result from each of the program development methodologies described here, as well as from practically every other one in the literature. If there is no one right way to program, we should make sure that however we program, it is logical. Process modeling does not try to make an organization adopt any particular software development methodology. Four approaches to quality in the programming process are represented by the DOD-STD-2167A, SEI CMM, ISO 9000, and SSE CMM standards. Measurement is intricately intertwined with the process improvement approach, as can be seen in this definition of **process assessment** by an international standards committee:

> The disciplined examination of the processes used by an organization against a set of criteria to determine the capability of those processes to perform within quality, cost and schedule goals. The aim is to characterise current practice, identifying strengths and weaknesses and the ability of the process to control or avoid significant causes of poor quality, cost and schedule performance. [ISO94]

Standard 2167A

In 1988, the U.S. Department of Defense established standard 2167A [DOD88] to present uniform requirements applicable throughout the development life cycle of a system. The requirements of 2167A largely result in documentation that gives external visibility to the software development, testing, maintenance, and evaluation activities.

Development is expected to follow a typical top-to-bottom-to-top progression of system requirements, high-level design, detailed design, coding, unit testing, component integration, component testing, system integration, and system testing. Each major development stage concludes with a phase report (for example, the preliminary design document) and a review of the status and results of the phase (for example, the preliminary design review). No particular development methods or environment are required, but the standard requires "systematic and well-documented software development methods."

Development consists of eight stages:

- system requirements design
- software requirements analysis
- preliminary design
- detailed design
- coding and unit testing
- component integration and testing
- subsystem (configuration item) integration and testing
- system integration and testing

Each of these eight phases has five areas of requirements:

- *software development management:* planning, organization, reviews
- *software engineering:* software development, decomposition, tracing through code to functioning in actual system, adherence to standards for coding and language
- *formal qualification testing:* planning testing for this and subsequent phases
- *software product evaluation:* conducting testing for this phase and providing data for testing in subsequent phases
- *configuration management:* maintaining a controlled library of documentation and code

Standard 2167A is useful both for producers (developers and managers) and consumers (users or purchasers). Standard 2167A is most useful when thought of as an organizing tool, like the matrix in Table 5-6. It describes what to think about (and document) as the framework for a development.

In this way, a producer responsible for testing, for example, would recognize that testing must be planned for each of the eight phases of the *Testing* column, and would construct a plan that addresses those eight points. Similarly, someone doing a smaller

Table 5-6   Standard 2167A Considerations

	Development Management	Software Engineering	Testing	Quality Assurance	Configuration Management
System requirements design					
Software requirements analysis					
Preliminary design					
Detailed design					
Coding and unit testing					
Component integration and testing					
Subsystem (configuration item) integration and testing					
System integration and testing					

part, such as a developer of a single software unit, would recognize how that part had to fit into a larger framework. The smaller part might be complex enough to entail its own development plan, which would then be incorporated into the development plan of the whole system. Alternatively, the piece might be small enough that it represented only the *Coding and unit testing* row; still, the developer would learn that this unit had requirements and implementations in the areas of management, software engineering testing, quality assurance, and configuration management. Finally, the consumer could use the structure of 2167A to determine that all significant categories of the project, from development through delivery, and all aspects of those categories, had been considered. Standard 2167A is often used in formal contracts to ensure that documentation is produced for all parts of the development process.

However, standard 2167A does not cause quality by itself. Its primary value is to provide *visibility* of the development process used on a particular project, and to provide a structure for documenting and reviewing that visibility. Any assessment of quality comes from examining through the visibility provided.

Capability Maturity Model

The *Capability Maturity Model* (CMM) was developed by the U.S. Software Engineering Institute (SEI) to assist the Department of Defense in assessing the quality of its contractors. The CMM had its beginning as the Process Maturity Model, where an organization was rated from 1 to 5, based on the answers to 110 questions about its development process. There were many problems with this approach, and the CMM was developed to address them and replace the process maturity model. Version 1.1 of the CMM was published in February 1993 [PAU93].

The CMM describes principles and practices that are assumed to lead to better software products. These principles and practices relate more to the organization (company or agency) than to the specific software development project within that organization. Saiedian and Kuzara [SAI95] point out that "the CMM is based on the premise that major software development problems and, hence, causes for software project failures are managerial rather than technical." The model groups organizations in five levels, with the higher levels exhibiting more visibility and control of the software development process. The model is used by potential customers to identify the strengths and weaknesses of their suppliers, and by software developers themselves to assess their capabilities and set a path toward process improvement.

Each capability level is characterized by *key process areas* on which an organization should focus in order to improve. Table 5-7 shows the primary process requirements for each level.

In the first level of the maturity model, *initial*, the software development process is ad hoc or even chaotic. The success of development depends on the quality of individuals, not on team accomplishments or organization. Good outcomes are thus more a matter of luck than of planning.

The next level is *repeatable*, where some degree of management and planning occurs. There is some discipline among team members, so that successes on earlier projects can be repeated with similar, new ones. Here, the key process areas include requirements management, software project planning, software configuration management, and other project management activities by which the actions and outcomes of the process become more predictable.

Table 5-7   Key Process Areas in the Capability Maturity Model

CMM Level	Key Process Areas	Characteristics of Level
Initial	None	Chaotic Quality depends on luck
Repeatable	Requirements management Software project planning Software project tracking and oversight Software subcontract management Software quality assurance Software configuration management	Discipline Learn from experience
Defined	Organization process focus Organization process definition Training program Integrated software management Software product engineering Intergroup coordination Peer reviews	Standardization Documentation Stress similarity of projects
Managed	Quantitative process management Software quality management	Measurement Analysis Early problem identification
Optimizing	Defect prevention Technology change management Process change management	Feedback

Improving the repeatable process leads to the third level, a *defined* process. The key to this level is standardization. Management and engineering activities are documented, standardized, and integrated, resulting in a standard process for everyone in the organization. Projects are regarded as more similar than different, and the standards emphasize the similarity. Where differences must exist between projects, deviation from standard must be reviewed and approved. At this level of maturity, the key process areas are organization and training, so that new group members understand the process in place. There are peer reviews, intergroup coordination, and a process definition for the entire organization.

A *managed* process directs its efforts at measurement as a means to achieve product quality. The organization focuses on using measurement and analysis to identify problems early and to assess the effect of possible actions. At this level, for example, a variation from the standard process, seen in level three, would be measured, so that the standard process could be modified, if appropriate, or so that future specialization would profit from the lessons learned on this project. Thus, the key process areas address quantitative as well as qualitative software management.

The highest, and arguably most desirable, level of capability maturity is *optimizing*, where feedback from early projects is incorporated in the process to improve subsequent projects. This feedback process occurs continuously. In particular, new tools, techniques, and approaches are tested and monitored to understand how they affect the process and products. Key process areas include defect prevention, technology change management, and process change management.

The Capability Maturity Model has another set of attributes not shown in the table: each process area comprises a set of *key practices* whose presence indicates that the organization

Table 5-8   Key CMM Process Areas

Key Practice	Determiner	Indicators
Commitment to perform	Actions the organization must take to ensure its process is established and will endure	Policy Leadership
Ability to perform	Preconditions that must exist in the organization to implement software practice competently	Resources Training Orientation Organizational structure Tools
Activities performed	Roles and procedures necessary to implement a key process area	Plans Procedures Work performed Tracking Corrective action
Measurement and analysis	Procedures needed to measure the process and analyze the results	Process measurement Analysis
Verifying implementation	Steps needed to ensure activities comply with established practices	Management reviews Audits

has implemented the process area. The key practices are supposed to allow one to determine that the process area is effective, repeatable, and long-lasting. The key practices are organized by their common features in Table 5-8.

An organization is rated against the Capability Maturity Model by authorized CMM appraisers. Two well-publicized examples of use of the SEI model are from Hughes Corp., which reported an annual savings of $2 million from process improvements recommended from the model [HUM91b], and Raytheon, which estimated it saved about $9.2 million of its annual $115 million software costs [DIO92].

There have been difficulties with the appraisals, however: different appraisers sometimes rate the same organization differently, and the same appraiser sometimes rates the same organization differently over time. The difficulties include different evaluation methods, uneven evaluator background and training, unclear compliance criteria, and a difference between two views of the same data. These inconsistencies occur in part because an appraiser can obtain only a limited amount of information in a small period of time before making a rating. Still, the SEI recognizes the need for higher reliability in its ratings.

A more fundamental objection to the CMM is that there is no unique right way to improve software quality. And improvement of process must be organic: developed within and accepted throughout the organization, not imposed from outside. The process maturity model on which the CMM is based is yet unproven; only a few anecdotes of its benefits have been published. A final concern is that the CMM is not closely integrated with other quality improvement methodologies, such as Total Quality Management (TQM) and the ISO-9000 quality standards more popular outside the United States.

SSE CMM

After some experience with the SEI CMM, scientists at the U.S. National Security Agency (NSA) decided to extend the SEI model to the more specific field of developing software that had to enforce security requirements, as well as perform some computing task. The

SSE CMM, the System Security Engineering Capability Maturity Model [NSA95a], is the result of that extension. This capability maturity model, like the SEI CMM, is to be used to evaluate the quality of security engineering practices, define improvements, and justify confidence in products from the evaluated organizations.

In the SSE CMM there are three areas: engineering (development process), project (management), and organizational. Engineering includes such processes as deriving requirements, analyzing candidate solutions, developing a physical architecture, and analyzing security vulnerabilities. The project category includes such factors as ensuring quality and implementing an assurance strategy. Finally, the organizational category includes improving the organization's system engineering process or managing system engineering training.

The SSE CMM is still being defined. The SEI CMM is intentionally descriptive and not prescriptive: it describes qualities of organizations at a particular level but does not prescribe how to achieve those qualities. The SSE CMM will probably be more prescriptive than the SEI CMM, in that it lists specific accomplishments.

ISO 9000

ISO, the International Standards Organization, has produced a series of quality standards collectively known as **ISO 9000**. The standards specify actions to be taken when any system (that is, not necessarily a software system) has quality goals and constraints. Thus, ISO 9000 quality standards are applicable to organizations of all types, not just those in computing. There is growing pressure for organizations to become ISO 9000–certified, particularly when selling to government agencies. In particular, ISO 9000 applies when a buyer requires a supplier to demonstrate a given level of expertise in designing and building a product. The buyer and supplier need not belong to separate companies; buyer and seller can even be part of the same organization.

In the ISO 9000 standards suite, standard 9001 [ISO94] applies to design and developing activities. It explains what a buyer must do to ensure that the supplier conforms to design, development, production, installation, and maintenance requirements. Table 5-9 lists the clauses of ISO 9001. Because ISO 9001 is quite general, there is a separate document, ISO 9000-3, that provides guidelines for interpreting ISO 9001 for software development [ISO90].

The ISO 9000 standards are used to regulate internal quality and to ensure the quality of suppliers. These standards are often used to document a quality control process. An organization must be certified by an ISO 9000 auditor as compliant to the standard. ISO 9000 identifies minimal quality requirements, like the SSE CMM, whereas the SEI CMM focuses on continuous improvement of an unspecified process.

The Reliability of Measuring Maturity

The maturity models and their assessment methods are becoming de facto standards in many organizations. For example, the CMM scores have a significant effect on some U.S. Defense Department contract award decisions, and the number of affected decisions is expected to increase. Also, to even be allowed to bid for many European government projects, a supplier must be ISO 9000–certified. But ever since the introduction of the Software Engineering Institute's original process maturity model, there have been objections to its application and use. Bollinger and McGowan [BOL91] noted that because the SEI CMM asked relatively few questions, their results could reflect only a small number of the characteristics of good software practice, and their yes/no answers made partial compliance

Table 5-9   Major ISO 9001 Clauses

Clause Number	Subject Matter
4.1	Management responsibility
4.2	Quality system
4.3	Contract review
4.4	Design control
4.5	Document and data control
4.6	Purchasing
4.7	Control of customer-supplied product
4.8	Product identification and traceability
4.9	Process control
4.10	Inspection and testing
4.11	Control of inspection, measuring, and test equipment
4.12	Inspection and test status
4.13	Control of nonconforming product
4.14	Corrective and preventive action
4.15	Handling, storage, packaging, preservation, and delivery
4.16	Control of quality records
4.17	Internal quality audits
4.18	Training
4.19	Servicing
4.20	Statistical techniques

impossible to measure. Whereas an original goal of the SEI CMM had been descriptiveness, not prescriptiveness, the questionnaires led ultimately to prescriptions.

The CMM and other models try to address these issues, and their popularity continues to grow. As the models help to identify strengths and weaknesses, organizations make major business and technical decisions based on the assessment results. However, if the models and measurements are incorrect or misguided, the result can be misallocation of resources, loss of business, and more. As pointed out earlier, there is an almost inevitable difficulty in consistency of ratings done by different people or by the same people at different times or done on different samples within a large, complex organization.

El Emam and Madhavji [ELE95] have further investigated reliability, asking

- How reliable are such assessments?
- What are the implications of reliability for interpreting assessment scores?

They looked specifically at how requirements are derived, as compared to organizational maturity such as the SEI CMM model reflects. They looked at four specific components of maturity: standardization, project management, tools, and organization. Their study shows clear evidence of *lack* of reliability, when measured along these four dimensions. Moreover, when they investigated the relationship between organizational maturity and other attributes of process and product, they found a small, significant relationship between maturity and quality of service, but "no relationship was found with quality of products" and "a small negative correlation between the standardization and project management dimensions and the quality of projects." The authors conclude that "given the rise in the use of maturity assessment methods in industry, and given the implications of decisions made based on the results of such assessments, it would be prudent to increase the reliability of these methods and their application."

Programming Practice Conclusions

Thus, there are serious questions to be addressed in considering the use of these process and organizational frameworks. Although the El Emam and Madhavji study addressed reliability, that is, repeatability and consistency, there is also clear need to demonstrate the validity of these measures: do highly rated organizations really produce better software? Consistently?

As Brooks observed in his paper "No Silver Bullet" [BRO87], the software development community seeks, but is not likely to find, a "silver bullet," a tool or technique or method that will dramatically improve the quality of software developed. "There is no single development, in either technology or management technique that by itself promises even one order-of-magnitude improvement in productivity, in reliability, in simplicity." He bases this conjecture on the fact that software is complex, that it must conform to the infinite variety of human requirements, and that it is abstract or invisible, leading to its being hard to draw or envision. Although all these software development technologies—design tools, process improvement models, and development methodologies—help the process, software development is inherently complicated, and therefore prone to errors. This does not mean that we should not seek ways to improve; we should. However, we should be realistic and accept that no technique prevents erroneous software. We should also be skeptical and make each new technique prove that it is valid and reliable.

Operating System Controls on Use of Programs

Programmer controls like those just described are applied to large development projects in some software production environments. However, not every program is produced that way, and computer users cannot always be assured that all other users of the system have followed the proper standards of program development. Therefore, a more common standard of software security is enforcement by the operating system.

In the next two chapters we examine operating systems in some detail in order to determine what security features they provide for their users. This section outlines the kinds of protection that an operating system can provide against the program flaws identified at the beginning of this chapter.

Trusted Software

By **trusted software** we mean code that has been rigorously developed and analyzed, so there is reason to trust that it does what it is expected to do, and nothing more. Typically, trusted code is a foundation on which other, untrusted code runs. The system's results depend on the trusted code. An operating system may be a piece of trusted software. There is a basis for trusting that the operating system correctly controls the accesses of modules run from that operating system. For example, the operating system might be expected to limit the accesses of the users to certain files.

This trust is based on rigorous analysis and testing. Trusted software has several characteristics that justify its trust.

- *Functional correctness:* The program does what it is supposed to, and it works correctly.
- *Enforcement of integrity:* Even if presented erroneous commands or commands from unauthorized users, it maintains the correctness of the data with which it has contact.

- *Limited privilege:* The program is allowed to access secure data, but the access is minimized, and neither the access rights nor the data are passed along to other untrusted programs or back to an untrusted caller.
- *Appropriate security level:* The program has been examined and rated at a degree of trust appropriate for the kind of data and environment in which it is to be used.

Essentially, trusted software becomes a safe way for general users to access sensitive data. Trusted programs are used to perform sensitive operations for users without allowing the users direct access to sensitive data.

Mutual Suspicion

Programs are not always trustworthy. Even with an operating system to enforce access limitations, it may be impossible or infeasible to bound the access privileges of an untested program effectively. In this case, user U is legitimately suspicious of new program P. However, program P may be invoked by another program, Q. There is no way for Q to know that P is correct or proper, any more than U knows that of P.

Therefore, the concept of **mutual suspicion** was developed to describe the relationship between two programs. Mutually suspicious programs operate as if other routines in the system were flawed. A calling program cannot trust its called subprocedures to be correct, and a called subprocedure cannot trust its calling program to be correct. Each protects its interface data so that the other has only limited access. For example, a procedure to sort the entries in a list cannot be trusted not to modify those elements, and that procedure cannot trust its caller to provide any list at all, or to supply the number of elements predicted.

Confinement

Confinement is a technique used by an operating system on a suspected program. A **confined program** is strictly limited in what system resources it can access. If a program is not trusted, the data it can access is strictly limited. Strong confinement is helpful in limiting the spread of viruses. Because a virus spreads by means of transitivity and shared data, all the data and programs within a single compartment can affect only the data and programs in the same compartment. Therefore, the virus can spread only to things in that compartment; it cannot get outside the compartment.

Access Log

An **access** or **audit log** is a listing of who accessed which computer objects, when, and for what amount of time. Commonly applied to files and programs, this is less a means of protection than an after-the-fact means of tracking down what has been done.

Typically an access log is a file or a dedicated output device (such as a printer) to which a log of activities is written. The logged activities may be such things as logins and logouts, accesses or attempted accesses to files or directories, execution of programs, and uses of other devices.

Failures are also logged. It may be less important to record that a particular user listed the contents of a permitted directory than that the same programmer tried to but was prevented from listing the contents of a protected directory. One failed login may result from a typing error, but a series of failures in a short time from the same device may result from the attempt of an intruder to break into the system.

Unusual events in the audit log should be scrutinized. For example, a new program might be tested in a dedicated, controlled environment. After the program has been tested, an audit log of all files accessed should be scanned to determine whether there are any unexpected file accesses, which could point to a Trojan horse in the new program.

Each of these aspects of operating system control is expanded in the next two chapters. These aspects are important.

Administrative Controls

Not all controls can be imposed automatically by the computing system. In this section we mention controls that can be applied by administrative procedures. Administrative controls are studied more fully in Chapter 10.

Standards of Program Development

Major computing departments do not allow programmers to produce code at any time in any manner. In addition to correctness, there are concerns about maintainability and compatibility with other routines. Following are typical examples of administrative control over software development.

- Standards of *design,* including use of specified design tools, languages, or methodologies.
- Standards of *documentation, language,* and *coding style* (layout of code on the page, choices of names of variables, and use of recognized program structures).
- Standards of *programming,* including mandatory programmer peer reviews and periodic code audits for correctness and compliance with standards.
- Standards of *testing,* such as use of program verification techniques, independent testing, and archiving of test results for future reference.
- Standards of *configuration management,* to control access to and changes of stable or completed program units.

Standardization of this kind is intended to improve the situation for all programmers by establishing a common framework within which all programmers work, so that anyone can assist or take over for another programmer. Standards also assist in maintenance because the maintenance team can find required information in a well-organized source program.

Enforcing Program Development Standards

Standards must be enforced to be effective. Trivial though this idea sounds, management sometimes does not recognize it. When a project falls behind schedule, or when key people leave a project team, the common reaction is to emphasize completing the project rather than following established standards.

Firms committed to following software development standards often perform **security audits**. In a security audit an independent security evaluation team checks each project on an unannounced basis. The team reviews designs, documentation, and code to verify that standards are being followed. Knowing that programs are routinely scrutinized, a programmer is unlikely to put suspicious code in a module in the first place.

Separation of Duties

Banks often break tasks into two or more pieces to be performed by separate employees. Employees are less tempted to do wrong if they need the cooperation of another employee to do so. In programming, the same practice can be used. Modular programming and design forces programmers to cooperate in order to achieve illicit results with programs. Independent test teams, not the programmers who wrote a piece of code, will test a module more rigorously. All of these forms of separation lead to a higher degree of security in programs.

5.4   Summary of Program Threats and Controls

This chapter has covered the programming issues of computer security: the kinds and effects of flaws and malicious code and the techniques that can help to control program threats. Malicious code gets a lot of attention in the popular media; the terminology certainly draws people, but we must hope that the seriousness of the threat and the degree of vulnerability would also cause people to pay attention. The amount of damage is not known, and it may even be that many successful attacks go undetected—for now, at least. With the explosive growth in connectivity to massive public networks, such as the Internet, the exposure to threats is increasing dramatically, yet there seems to be little public concern about the obvious danger.

In this chapter we have considered two general classes of program flaws: programs that compromise or change data, and those that affect computer service. There are essentially three controls on such activities. Programmer controls limit the programming activity to make it harder for a programmer to create malicious programs. These same controls are effective against inadvertent mistakes by programmers. The operating system provides some degree of control by limiting access to objects of the computing system. Finally, administrative controls limit the kinds of actions people can take.

You shouldn't consider these controls only for their negative aspects, that is, for actions they *prohibit*. All of these controls have positive effects that are, in fact, more important and more commonly used than their constraining features. Program controls in software engineering have as their primary purpose improving the quality of software produced. Operating systems limit access as a way of promoting the safe sharing of information between programs. And administrative controls and standards improve the usability and maintainability of code produced. For all of these controls, the security features are a secondary aspect.

Program controls are part of the more general problem of limiting the effect of one user on another. In the next chapter we consider the role of the operating system in regulating the interaction between users.

5.5   Bibliographic Notes

Programs that compromise data are some of the earliest examples of computer security vulnerabilities. Start with the reports of Anderson [AND72] and Ware [WAR79], both of which are still valid. Then read the papers of Thompson [THO84] and Schell [SCH79] and ask yourself why people act as if malicious code is a new phenomenon.

Various examples of program flaws are described by Parker [PAR83] and Denning [DEN82]. The volumes edited by Hoffman [HOF90] and Denning [DEN90a] are excellent collections on malicious code.

Worth reading both for their lighthearted tone and for the serious situation they describe are Stoll's accounts of dealing with intrusions [STO88, STO89].

Software engineering principles of program development are described by numerous authors. The book by Pfleeger [PFL91] is good for readers unfamiliar with the field, whereas the book by Sommerville [SOM96] contains more advanced material. The books by DeMarco and Lister [DEM87] and DeMarco [DEM95] are filled with sensible, creative ways to address software development. Special issues of *IEEE Software* in July 1994 and January 1996 focused on process improvement and quality. These are good starting points to explore that area.

5.6   Terms and Concepts

5.7   Exercises

1. Suppose you are a customs inspector. You are responsible for checking suitcases for secret compartments in which bulky items such as jewelry might be hidden. Describe the procedure you would follow to check for these compartments.

2. Your boss hands you a microprocessor and its technical reference manual. You are asked to check for undocumented features of the processor. Because of the number of possibilities, you cannot test every operation code with every combination of operands. Outline the strategy you would use to identify and characterize unpublicized operations.

3. Your boss hands you a computer program and its technical reference manual. You are asked to check for undocumented features of the program. How is this activity similar to the task of the previous exercise? How does it differ? Which is the more feasible? Why?

4. Could a computer program be used to automate testing for trapdoors? That is, could you design a computer program that would be given the source or object version of another program and a suitable description of that other program, and the first program would reply *Yes* or *No* to show whether the second program had any trapdoors? Explain your answer.

5. A program is written to compute the sum of the integers from 1 to 10. The programmer, well-trained in reusability and maintainability, writes the program so that it computes the sum of the numbers from k to n. However, a team of security specialists scrutinizes the code. The team certifies that this program properly sets k to 1 and n to 10; therefore, the program is certified as being properly restricted in that it always operates on precisely the range 1 to 10. List different ways that this program can be sabotaged so that during execution it computes a different sum, such as 3 to 20.

6. One means of limiting the effect of an untrusted program is confinement: controlling what processes have access to the untrusted program and what access the program has to other processes and data. Explain how confinement would apply to the earlier example of the program that computes the sum of the integers 1 to 10.

7. List three controls that could be applied to detect or prevent salami attacks.

8. The distinction between a covert *storage* channel and a covert *timing* channel is not clear-cut. Every timing channel can be transformed into an equivalent storage channel. Explain how this transformation could be done.

9. List the limitations on the amount of information leaked per second through a covert channel in a multiaccess computing system.

10. An electronic mail system could be used to leak information. First, explain how the leakage could occur. Then, identify controls that could be applied to detect or prevent the leakage.

11. Modularity can have a negative effect as well as a positive one. A program that is overmodularized performs its operations in very small modules, so that a reader has trouble acquiring a perspective. Although it may be easy to determine what many individual modules do, it is not easy to understand what they do together. Suggest an approach that can be used during program development to maintain this perspective.

12. You are given a program that purportedly manages a list of items through hash coding. The program is supposed to return the location of an item if the item is present, or return the location where the item should be inserted if the item is not in the list. Accompanying the program is a manual describing parameters such as the expected format of items in the table, the table size, and the specific calling sequence. You have only the object code of this program, not the source code. List the cases you would apply to test the correctness of the program's function.

13. You are writing a procedure to add a node to a doubly linked list. The system on which this procedure is to be run is subject to periodic hardware failures. The list your program is to maintain is very important. Your program must ensure the integrity of the list, even if the machine fails in the middle of executing your procedure. List the individual statements to update the list. (Your list should be about a half dozen statements long.) Tell the effect of a machine failure after each instruction. Describe a procedure to run that will restore the integrity of the basic list after a machine failure.

14. Explain how information in an access log could be used to identify the true identity of an impostor who has acquired unauthorized access to a computing system. Describe several different pieces of information in the log that combine to identify the impostor.

15. Several proposals have been made for a processor that could decrypt encrypted machine instructions and data and then execute the instructions on the data. The processor would then encrypt the results. How would such a processor be useful? What are the design requirements for such a processor?

6

Protection in General-Purpose Operating Systems

> *In this chapter:*
> - *Protection features provided by general-purpose operating systems: protecting memory, files, and the execution environment*
> - *User authentication*

In this chapter and the next we study operating systems and their role in computer security. We begin by studying the contributions that operating systems have made to user security. Operating systems support multiprogramming, the concurrent use of a system by more than one user, so they have developed ways to protect the computation of one user from inadvertent or malicious interference from another. Among the facilities operating system security provides are memory protection, file protection, general control of access to objects, and user authentication. This chapter contains a survey of controls that provide those four features. This chapter is oriented to the user: how do those controls protect users, and how do users apply those controls? In the next chapter we see how operating system design is affected by security considerations.

6.1 Protected Objects and Methods of Protection

We begin by considering the history of protection in operating systems. From the history we determine what kinds of things operating systems can protect, and what methods are available for protection.

A Bit of History

Originally in computing there were no operating systems: users entered their programs in binary through switches. Each user had exclusive use of the computing system, so that users scheduled blocks of time to use the machine. Users loaded their own libraries of support routines—assemblers, compilers, shared subprograms—and "cleaned up" after use by removing any sensitive data.

228

The first operating systems were simple utilities, called **executives**, to assist individual programmers and to smooth the transition as a new user started to use the machine. The early executives provided linkers and loaders for relocation, easy access to compilers and assemblers, and automatic loading of subprograms from libraries. The executives handled the tedious aspects of support for programmers. The major function of these programs was support for a single programmer during execution.

With the development of multiprogramming, operating systems assumed an entirely different role, and a different name. When it was realized that two users could interleave access to the resources of a computing system, the concepts of scheduling, sharing, and parallel use developed. Multiprogrammed operating systems, also known as **monitors**, oversaw the execution of programs. Whereas an executive stayed passively in the background, waiting to be called into service by a requesting user, a monitor actively asserted control of the computing system and gave resources to the user only when it was consistent with general good use of the system. Whereas the executive provided service on demand, the monitor oversaw all computing and lent resources to users.

Multiprogramming brought another important change in computing. In the single-user case, the only force to be protected against was oneself. The user felt foolish after making an error, but one user could not adversely affect the computation of any other user. With multiple users, however, a user would rightfully be angry if another user caused a negative effect on a program's execution. Therefore, protection of one user from another became an important issue in multiprogrammed operating systems.

Protected Objects

With the rise of multiprogramming, several objects of a computing system required protection:

- memory
- sharable I/O devices, such as disks
- serially reusable I/O devices, such as printers and tape drives
- sharable programs and subprocedures
- sharable data

The operating system had to protect these objects when it assumed responsibility for controlled sharing. In the following sections we consider mechanisms by which operating systems have enforced protection for these objects.

Security Methods of Operating Systems

The basis of protection is **separation,** keeping one user's objects separate from other users'. Rushby and Randell [RUS83] note that separation in an operating system can occur in several ways:

- *Physical separation,* in which processes use different physical objects, such as separate printers for output requiring different levels of security
- *Temporal separation,* in which processes having different security requirements are executed at different times

- *Logical separation,* in which users operate under the illusion that no other processes exist, as when an operating system constrains a program's accesses so that it cannot access objects outside its permitted domain
- *Cryptographic separation,* in which processes conceal their data and computations in such a way that they are unintelligible to outside processes

Of course, combinations of two or more of these forms of separation are also possible.

The categories of separation are listed roughly in increasing order of complexity to implement, and, for the first three, in decreasing order of the security provided. However, the first two approaches are very stringent and can lead to poor resource utilization. Therefore, we would like to shift the burden of protection to the operating system to allow concurrent execution of processes having different security needs.

But separation is only half the answer. We want to separate users and their objects, but we also want to be able to provide sharing for some of those objects. An operating system may offer protection at any of several levels.

- *No protection.* These systems are appropriate when sensitive procedures are being run at separate times.
- *Isolation.* When an operating system provides isolation, different processes running concurrently are unaware of the presence of each other. Each process has its own address space, files, and other objects. The operating system must confine each process to completely conceal the objects of the other processes.
- *Share all or share nothing.* With this form of protection the owner of an object declares it to be public or private. A public object is available to all users, whereas a private object is available only to its owner.
- *Share via access limitation.* With protection by access limitation, the operating system checks the allowability of each potential access. Access control is implemented for a specific user and a specific object. By means of lists, the operating system determines whether a particular user should have access to a particular object. The operating system acts as a guard between users and objects, ensuring that only authorized accesses occur.
- *Share by capabilities.* An extension of limited access sharing, this form of protection allows dynamic creation of sharing rights for objects. The degree of sharing can depend on the owner or the subject, on the context of the computation, or on the object itself.
- *Limit use of an object.* This form of protection limits not just the access to an object, but the use made of that object after it has been accessed. For example, a user may be allowed to view a sensitive document, but not to print a copy of it. More powerfully, a user may be allowed access to data in a data base in order to derive statistical summaries (such as average salary at a particular grade level), but not to determine specific data values (salaries of individuals).

Again, these modes of sharing are arranged in increasing order of difficulty to implement, but also in increasing order of fineness of protection they provide. A given operating system may provide different levels of protection for different objects, users, or situations.

Granularity of control is also a concern. For data, access can be controlled at the level of the bit, the byte, the element or word, the field, the record, the file, or the volume.

The larger the level of object controlled the easier it is to implement access control. However, with large objects a user needing access to only part of an object (such as a single record in a file) must be allowed access to the entire object (the whole file).

We now look at several different kinds of objects and their specific kinds of protection.

6.2   Protecting Memory and Addressing

The most obvious problem of multiprogramming is preventing one program from affecting the memory of other programs. Fortunately, protection can be built into the hardware mechanisms that provide for efficient use of memory, so that solid protection can be provided at essentially no additional cost.

Fence

The simplest form of memory protection was introduced in single-user systems, in order to prevent a faulty user program from destroying part of the resident portion of the operating system. As its name implies, a **fence** is a method to confine users to one side of a boundary.

In one implementation, the fence was a predefined memory address, so that the operating system resided on one side and the user on the other. This situation is shown in Figure 6-1. Unfortunately, that implementation was very restrictive because a predefined amount of space was reserved for the operating system. If less than that amount of space was required, the excess space was wasted and the operating system could not grow beyond the fence boundary.

Another implementation used a hardware register, often called a **fence register**, that contained the address of the end of the operating system. In contrast to a fixed fence, the location of this fence could be changed. Each time a user program generated an address for data modification, the address was automatically compared against the fence address. If the address was greater than the fence address (that is, in the user area), the instruction was

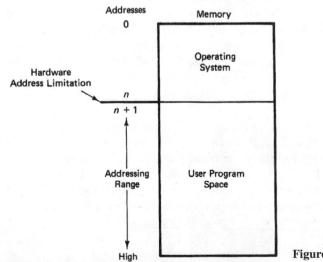

Figure 6-1   Fixed Fence

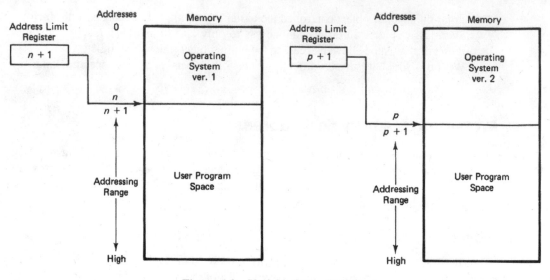

Figure 6-2   Variable Fence Register

executed; if it was less than the fence address (that is, in the operating system area), an error condition was raised. The use of fence registers is shown in Figure 6-2.

A fence register protects only in one direction. An operating system can be protected from a single user, but the fence cannot protect one user from another. Similarly, a user cannot identify certain areas of the program as inviolable (such as the code of the program itself, or a read-only data area).

Relocation

If the operating system can be assumed to be of a fixed size, programmers can write their code assuming that the program begins at a constant address. This makes it easy to determine the address of any object in the program, but it also makes it essentially impossible to change the starting address if, for example, a new version of the operating system is larger or smaller than the old. If the size of the operating system is allowed to change, then programs must be written in a way that does not depend on placement at a specific location in memory.

Relocation is the process of taking a program written as if it began at address 0 and changing all addresses to reflect the actual address at which the program is located in memory. In many instances, this entails merely adding a constant **relocation factor** to each address of the program. The relocation factor is the starting address of the memory assigned for the program.

Conveniently, the fence register can be used in this situation to provide an important extra benefit. The fence register can be a hardware relocation device. To each program address, the contents of the fence register are added. This both relocates the address and guarantees that no one can access a location lower than the fence address. (Addresses are treated as unsigned integers, so adding the value in the fence register to any number is guaranteed to produce a result at or above the fence address.) Special instructions can be added for the few times when a program legitimately intends to access a location of the operating system.

Base/Bounds Registers

The advantage of fence registers is the ability to relocate, which is even more important in a multiuser environment. With two or more users, neither can know in advance where a program will be loaded for execution. The relocation register solves the problem by providing a base or starting address. All addresses inside a program are offsets from that base address. A variable fence register is generally known as a **base register**.

Fence registers provide a lower bound (a starting address), but not an upper one. To overcome the difficulty, a second register is often added, as shown in Figure 6-3. The second register, called a **bounds register**, is an upper address limit, in the same way that a base or fence register is a lower address limit. Each program address is forced to be above the base address because the contents of the base register are added to the address; each address is also checked to ensure that it is below the bounds address. In this way, a program's addresses are neatly confined to the space between the base and the bounds registers.

This technique protects a program's addresses from modification by another user. When execution changes from one user's program to another's, the operating system must change the contents of the base and bounds registers to reflect the true address space for that user. This change is part of the general preparation, called a **context switch**, that the operating system must perform when transferring control from one user to another.

With a pair of base/bounds registers, a user is perfectly protected from outside users or, more correctly, outside users are protected from errors in any other user's program. Erroneous addresses *inside* a user's address space can still affect that program because the base/bounds checking guarantees only that each address is inside the user's address space. A possible user error would be a subscript out of range or an undefined variable that generates an address reference within the user's space but, unfortunately, inside the executable instructions of the user's program. Therefore, a user can inadvertently store data on top of instructions. Such an error can let a user inadvertently destroy a program, but only the user's own program.

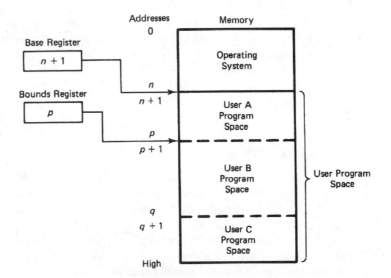

Figure 6-3   Pair of Base/Bounds Registers

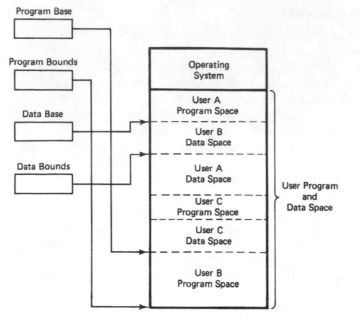

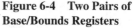

Figure 6-4   Two Pairs of
Base/Bounds Registers

A solution is to use another pair of base/bounds registers, one for the instructions (code) of the program and a second for the data space. Then, only instruction fetches (instructions to be executed) are relocated and checked with the first register pair, and only data accesses (operands of instructions) are relocated and checked with the second register pair. The use of two pairs of base/bounds registers is shown in Figure 6-4. Although two pairs of registers do not prevent all program errors, they do limit the effect of data-manipulating instructions to the data space. They offer another more important advantage: being able to split a program into two pieces that can be relocated separately.

These two advantages seem to call for the use of three or more pairs of registers, one for code, one for read-only data, and one for modifiable data values. Although in theory this concept can be extended, two pairs of registers is the limit for practical computer design. For each additional pair of registers added, something in the machine code of each instruction must indicate which relocation pair is to be used to address the operands of the instruction. With two pairs, the decision can be automatic: instructions with one pair, data with the other. With more than two pairs, each instruction specifies one of two or more data spaces.

Tagged Architecture

Another problem with base/bounds registers for protection or relocation is their contiguous nature. Each pair of registers confines accesses to a consecutive range of addresses. A compiler or loader can easily rearrange a program so that all code sections are adjacent and all data sections are adjacent, too.

However, in some cases you may want to protect *some* data values but not *all*. A programmer may want to ensure the integrity of certain data values by allowing them to be written when the program is initialized, but prohibiting the program from modifying them later. This protects against errors in the programmer's own code. A programmer may also want to invoke a shared subprogram from a common library. In Chapter 5 we studied information hiding and modularity in program design, good design characteristics. These characteristics dictate that one program module share with another module only the *minimum* amount of data necessary for both of them to do their work.

Base/bounds registers create an all-or-nothing situation for sharing: either a program makes all its data available to be accessed and modified, or it prohibits access to all. Even if there were a third set of registers for shared data, all data would need to be located together. A procedure could not effectively share data items *A, B,* and *C* with one module, *A, C,* and *D* with a second, and *A, B,* and *D* with a third. The only way to do this would be by moving each appropriate set of data values to some contiguous space, a solution that would not be acceptable if the data items were large records, arrays, or structures.

An alternative is **tagged architecture**, in which every word of machine memory has one or more extra bits to identify the access rights to that word. These access bits can be set only by privileged (operating system) instructions. The bits are tested every time an instruction accesses that location.

For example, as shown in Figure 6-5, one memory location may be protected as execute-only (object code of instructions), while another is protected for fetch-only (read) data access, and another accessible for modification (write). Two adjacent locations can have different access rights. Furthermore, with a few extra tag bits, different classes of data (numeric, character, address or pointer, and undefined) can be separated, and data fields can be protected for privileged (operating system) access only.

This protection technique has been used on a few systems, although the number of tag bits has been rather small. The Burroughs B6500-7500 system uses three tag bits to separate data words (three types), descriptors (pointers), and control words (stack pointers and

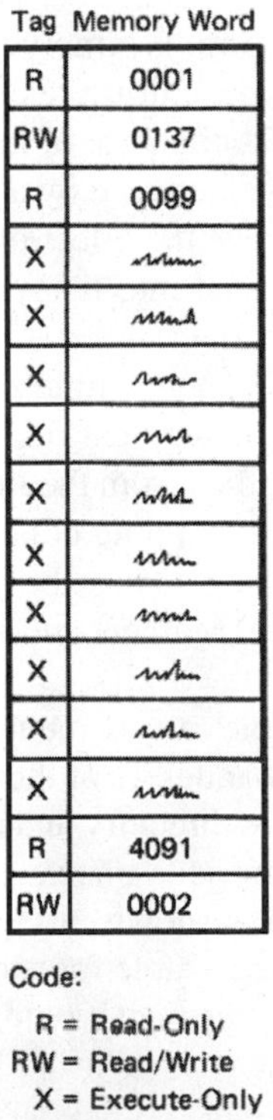

Tag Memory Word

Tag	Memory Word
R	0001
RW	0137
R	0099
X	∿∿∿
X	∿∿∿
X	∿∿∿
X	∿∿∿
X	∿∿∿
X	∿∿∿
X	∿∿∿
X	∿∿∿
X	∿∿∿
X	∿∿∿
R	4091
RW	0002

Code:

    R = Read-Only
    RW = Read/Write
    X = Execute-Only

Figure 6-5   Example of Tagged Architecture

addressing control words). The IBM System/38 uses a tag to control both integrity and access.

A variation that has also been used is one tag that applies to a group of consecutive locations, such as 128 or 256 bytes. With one tag for a block of addresses, the added cost for implementing tags is not as high as with one tag per location. The Intel I960 extended architecture processor uses a tagged architecture with a bit on each memory word that marks the word as a capability, not an ordinary location for data or instructions. This large number of possible tag values supports memory segments that can range in size between 64 and 4 billion bytes, with a potential 2^{256} different protection domains.

A problem with the acceptance of a tagged architecture is compatibility of code. Major computer vendors are still working with operating systems that were designed and implemented 10 or 20 years ago for architectures of that era. The price of memory has fallen so much recently that implementation of a tagged architecture is more feasible now than before. However, most manufacturers are locked into a more conventional memory architecture because of wide availability of components and desire to maintain compatibility among operating systems and machine families. A tagged architecture would require fundamental changes to substantially all of the operating system code, which is prohibitive.

Segmentation

The last two approaches for protection we present can be implemented on top of a conventional machine structure, so that they have a better chance of acceptance. These approaches were designed between 1965 and 1975 and have been implemented on many machines since then. Furthermore, they offer important advantages in addressing, with memory protection being a delightful bonus.

The first of these two approaches, **segmentation**, is simply the notion of dividing a program into separate pieces. Each piece has a logical unity, a relationship among all of its code or data values. For example, a segment may be the code of a single procedure, or the data of an array, or the collection of all local data values used by a particular module. Segmentation was developed as a feasible means to have the effect of an unbounded number of base/bounds registers: a program could be divided into many pieces having different access rights.

Each segment has a unique name. A code or data item within a segment is addressed as the pair ⟨*name, offset*⟩, where *name* is the name of the segment containing the data item and *offset* is its location within the segment, that is, its offset from the start of the segment.

Logically, the programmer pictures a program as a long collection of segments. Segments can be separately relocated, allowing any segment to be placed in any available memory location. The relationship between a logical segment and its true memory position is shown in Figure 6-6.

The operating system must maintain a table of segment names and their true addresses in memory. When a program generates an address of the form ⟨*name, offset*⟩, the operating system must look up *name* in the segment directory and determine its real memory address. To that address the operating system adds *offset*, giving the true memory address of the code or data item. This translation is shown in Figure 6-7. For efficiency there is usually one operating system segment address table for each process in execution. Two processes that want to share access to a single segment would have the same segment name and address in their segment tables.

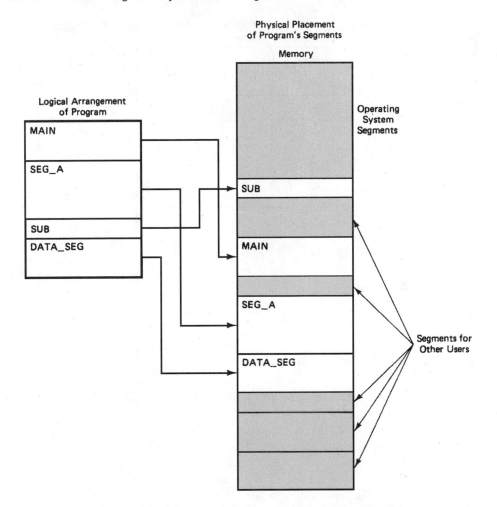

Figure 6-6   Logical and Physical Representation of Segments

Thus, a user's program does not know what true memory addresses it uses. It has no way—and no need—to determine the actual address associated with a particular ⟨*name*, *offset*⟩. The ⟨*name*, *offset*⟩ pair is adequate to access any data or instruction to which a program should have access.

This hiding of addresses has three advantages for the operating system.

- The operating system can place any segment at any location or move any segment to any location, even after the program begins to execute. Because all address references are translated by the operating system using a segment address table, the operating system need only update the address in that one table when a segment is moved.

- A segment can be removed from main memory (and stored on an auxiliary device) if it is not being used currently.

- Every address reference passes through the operating system, so that there is an opportunity to check each for protection.

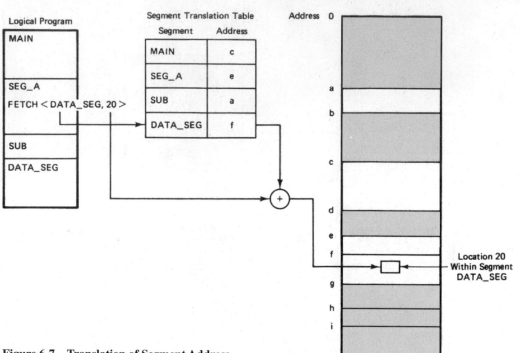

Figure 6-7   Translation of Segment Address

Because of the third characteristic, a process whose segment translation table does not list a particular segment is denied all access to that segment. The operating system controls which programs have entries for a particular segment in their segment address tables. This provides strong protection of segments from access by unpermitted processes. For example, program *A* might have access to segments *BLUE* and *GREEN* of another user, but not to other segments of that user or of any other user.

A user can assign different protection classes to segments of a program. The process of segmentation is handled by a combination of hardware and software. Therefore, it is feasible to associate certain levels of protection with certain segments, and to have the operating system/hardware check that protection on each access to the segment. For example, one segment might be read-only data, a second might be execute-only code, and a third might be writable data. This situation means that segmentation can approximate the goal of separate protection of different pieces of a program, as outlined in the previous section on tagged architecture.

Relative to protection, segmentation offers these benefits:

- Each address reference is checked for protection.
- Many different classes of data items can be assigned different levels of protection.
- Two or more users can share access to a segment, with potentially different access rights.
- A user cannot generate an address or access to an unpermitted segment.

One protection difficulty inherent in segmentation concerns segment size. A segment has a particular size, but a program can generate a reference to a valid segment *name*, but with an *offset* beyond the end of the segment. For example, reference ⟨*A*,9999⟩ looks perfectly valid, although in reality segment *A* may be only 200 bytes long. If left unplugged, this security hole could allow a program to access any memory address beyond the end of a segment, just by using large values of *offset* in an address.

This problem cannot be stopped during compilation, or even when a program is loaded, because effective use of segments requires that they be allowed to grow in size during execution. For example, a segment might contain a dynamic data structure such as a stack. Therefore, secure implementation of segmentation requires checking an address generated to verify that it is not beyond the current end of the segment referenced. Although it is an extra expense, segmentation systems maintain the current segment length in the translation table, and compare every address generated.

Efficient implementation of segmentation has two problems. First, segment names are inconvenient to encode in instructions, and the operating system's lookup of the name in a table can be slow. To overcome this difficulty, segment names are often converted to numbers by the compiler when a program is translated; the compiler also appends a linkage table matching numbers to true segment names. This presents an implementation difficulty when two procedures wish to share the same segment because the assigned segment numbers of data accessed by that segment must be the same.

Segments can lead to fragmentation of main memory because they are of varying sizes. After time, unused fragments of space can lead to poor memory utilization. A solution to fragmentation is periodic compaction of memory, but compaction and updating of appropriate tables takes time.

Paging

An alternative to segmentation is **paging**. As with segmentation, each address is a two-part object, this time consisting of ⟨*page, offset*⟩. The program is divided into equal-sized pieces called **pages**, and memory is divided into the same sized units, called **page frames**. (For implementation reasons, the page size is usually chosen to be a power of two between 512 and 4096 bytes.)

Each address is again translated by a process similar to that of segmentation: the operating system maintains a table of user page numbers and their true addresses in memory. The *page* portion of every ⟨*page, offset*⟩ reference is converted to a page frame address by a table lookup; the *offset* portion is added to the page frame address to produce the real memory address of the object referred to as ⟨*page, offset*⟩. This process is shown in Figure 6-8.

Unlike segmentation, all pages are of the same fixed size, so fragmentation is not a problem: each page can fit in any available page in memory. There is no problem of addressing beyond the end of a page. The binary form of a ⟨*page, offset*⟩ address is designed so that the *offset* values fill a range of bits in the address. Therefore, an *offset* beyond the end of a particular page results in a carry into the *page* portion of the address, which changes the address.

For example, with a page size of 1024 bytes ($1024 = 2^{10}$), 10 bits are allocated for the *offset* portion of each address. A program cannot generate a *offset* value larger than 1023 in 10 bits. Moving to the next location after ⟨*x*,1023⟩ causes a carry into the *page* portion, thereby moving translation to the next page. During the translation, there is a check to verify that a ⟨*page, offset*⟩ reference does not exceed the maximum number of pages the process has defined.

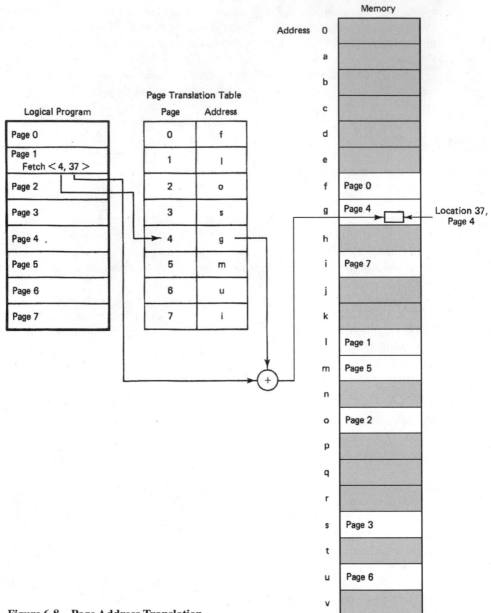

Figure 6-8   Page Address Translation

A programmer has to be conscious of segments, but a programmer is oblivious to page boundaries. There is no logical unity to a page: a page is just the next 2^n bytes of the program. A change to a program, such as the addition of one instruction, will push all subsequent instructions to lower addresses and move a few bytes from the end of each page to the start of the next. This is not something about which the programmer need be concerned because the entire mechanism of paging and address translation is hidden from the programmer.

However, from the standpoint of protection, this is a serious loss. Because segments are logical units we can associate different segments with individual protection rights, such as read-only or execute-only. This problem could be handled efficiently during address translation. With paging, because there is no necessary unity to the items on a page, there is no way to establish all values on a page as read-only or execute-only.

Combined Paging with Segmentation

Because of the efficiency of implementation of paging, and the desirable logical protection characteristics of segmentation, these two approaches have been combined.

The IBM 370 systems use a form of paged segmentation. The Multics operating system (implemented on a GE-645 machine) applied paging on top of segmentation. In both cases, the programmer can divide a program into logical segments. Then each segment is broken into fixed-sized pages. In Multics, the segment *name* portion of an address is an 18-bit number, with a 16-bit *offset*. The addresses are then broken into 1024-byte pages. The translation process is shown in Figure 6-9. This approach retains the logical unity of a segment and permits differentiated protection for the segments, but it adds an additional

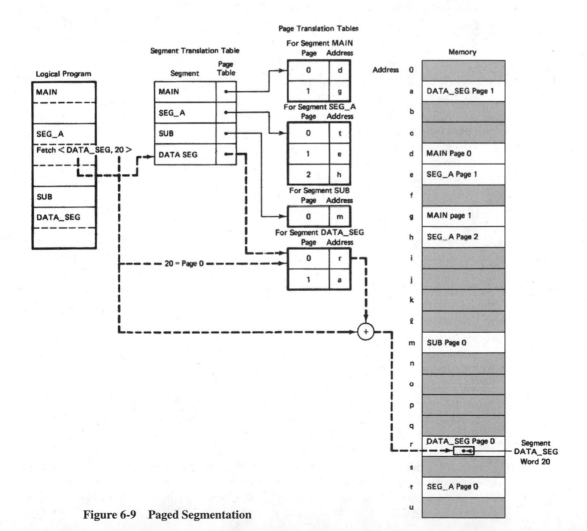

Figure 6-9   Paged Segmentation

layer of translation for each address. Additional hardware improves the efficiency of the implementation.

6.3   Protecting Access to General Objects

Protection of memory is a specific case of the more general problem of protection of *objects*. As multiprogramming has developed, the number and kind of objects shared have also increased. Here are some examples of the kinds of objects for which protection is desirable.

- memory
- a file or data set on an auxiliary storage device
- an executing program in memory
- a directory of files
- a hardware device
- a data structure, such as a stack
- a table of the operating system
- instructions, especially privileged instructions
- passwords and the user authentication mechanism
- the protection mechanism itself

The memory protection mechanism can be fairly simple because every memory access is guaranteed to go through certain points in the hardware. With more general objects, the number of points of access may be larger, there may be no central authority through which all accesses pass, and the kind of access is not simply limited to read, write, or execute.

Furthermore, all accesses to memory occur through a program, so we can refer to the program or the programmer as the accessing agent. We will use terms such as *the user* and *the subject* in describing an access to a general object. This user or subject could be a person who uses a computing system, a programmer, a program, another object, or something else that seeks to use an object.

There are several complementary goals in protecting objects.

- *Check every access.* We may want to revoke a user's privilege to access an object. If we have previously authorized the user to access the object, we do not necessarily mean the user should retain indefinite access to the object. In fact, in some situations, we may want to prevent further access immediately after we revoke authorization. For this reason, every access by a user to an object should be checked.
- *Allow least privilege.* The principle of least privilege states that a subject should have access to the smallest number of objects necessary to perform some task. Even if extra information would be useless to the subject, the subject should not have additional access. For example, a program should not have access to the absolute memory address to which a page number reference translates, even though the program could not use that address in any effective way. Not allowing access to unnecessary objects guards against security weaknesses if a part of the protection mechanism should fail.

- *Verify acceptable usage.* Ability to access is a yes–no decision. Of more interest is checking that the activity to be performed on an object is appropriate. For example, a data structure such as a stack has certain acceptable operations, including *push, pop, clear,* and so on. We may want not only to control who has access to a stack but to be assured that the accesses performed are legitimate stack accesses.

In the next section we consider protection mechanisms appropriate for general objects of unspecified types, such as the kinds of objects listed. To make the explanations easier to understand, we sometimes use an example of a specific object, such as a file. Note, however, that a general mechanism can be used to protect any of the types of objects listed.

Directory

One simple protection mechanism works like a file directory. Imagine the set of objects to be files and the set of subjects to be users of a computing system. Every file has a unique owner who possesses "control" access rights, including the rights to declare who has what access and to revoke access to any person at any time. Each user has a file directory, which lists all the files to which that user has access.

Clearly no user can be allowed to write in the file directory because that would be a way to forge access to a file. Therefore, the operating system must maintain all file directories, under commands from the owners of files. The obvious rights to files are the common *read*, *write*, and *execute* familiar on many time sharing systems. Furthermore, another right, *owner*, is possessed by the owner, permitting that user to grant and revoke access rights. Figure 6-10 shows an example of a file directory.

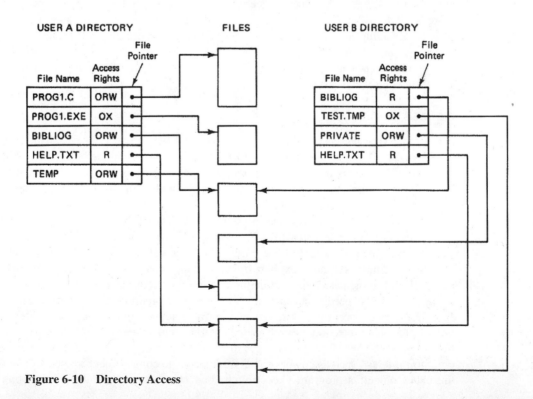

Figure 6-10   Directory Access

This approach is easy to implement because it uses one list per user, naming all the objects that user is allowed to access. However, the list becomes too large if there are many shared objects accessible to all users, such as libraries of subprograms or a common table of users. Then the directory of each user must have one entry for each such shared object, even if the user has no intention of accessing the object.

A second difficulty is revocation of access. If owner A has passed to user B right to read file F, an entry for F is made in the directory for B. This implies a level of *trust* between A and B. If A later questions that trust, A may want to revoke the access right of B. The operating system can respond easily to the single request to delete the right of B to access F because that involves deleting one entry from a specific directory. If A wants to remove the access rights of *everyone* to F, the operating system must search each individual directory for the entry F, which can be time-consuming on a large system. For example, large timesharing systems have 5,000 to 10,000 active accounts. But if B passed the access right for F to another user, A may not know that access exists and should be revoked. This problem is worse in a network.

A third difficulty is pseudonyms. Owners A and B may have two different files named F, and they may both want to allow access by S. Clearly the directory for S cannot contain two entries for the same file name. Therefore, S has to be able to uniquely identify the F from A (or B). One approach is to include the original owner's designation as if it were part of the file name, with a notation like $A{:}F$ (or $B{:}F$).

Suppose, however, that S has trouble remembering file contents from the name F. Another approach is to allow S to name F with any name unique to the directory of S. Then, F from A could be called Q to S. As shown in Figure 6-11, S may have forgotten that Q is F from A, and so S requests access again from A for F. By now however, A trusts S more, so A transfers F with greater rights than before. This leaves the possibility of one subject, S, having two distinct sets of access rights to F, once under the name Q and once under the name F. Allowing pseudonyms leads to the possibility of multiple permissions, which are not necessarily consistent. The directory approach, therefore, is too simple for most object protection situations.

Access Control List

An alternative representation is the **access control list**. There is one such list for each object, and the list shows all subjects who should have access to the object and what their access is. This differs from the directory list because there is one access control list per *object*, while a directory is created for each *subject*. Although this difference seems small, there are some significant advantages.

For example, if subjects A and S both have access to object F, the operating system will maintain just one access list for F showing the access rights for A and S, as shown in Figure 6-12. The access control list can have general default entries for any users. In this way, specific users can have explicit rights, and all other users can have a default set of rights. With this organization, a public file or program can be shared by all possible users of the system without needing an entry for the object in the individual directory of each user.

The Multics operating system uses a form of access control list in which each user belongs to three protection classes: a *user*, a *group*, and a *compartment*. The user designation identifies a specific subject; the group designation brings together subjects who have a common interest, such as coworkers on a project. The compartment is used to confine an untrusted object: a program executing in one compartment cannot access objects in

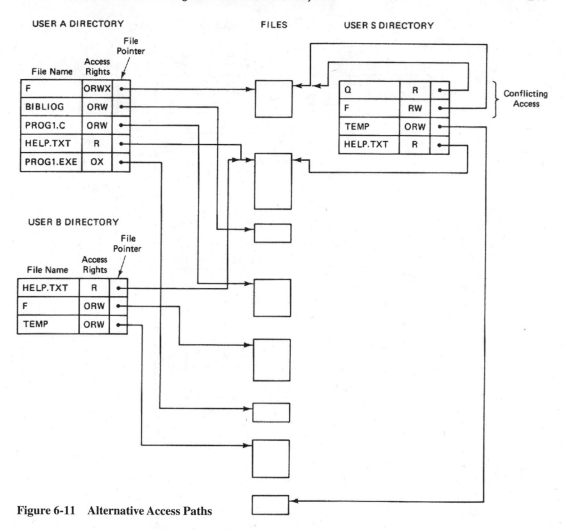

Figure 6-11   Alternative Access Paths

another compartment without specific permission. The compartment is also a way to collect objects that are related, such as all files for a single project.

Suppose every user who initiates access to the system identifies a group and a compartment with which to work. If Adams logs on as user Adams in group Decl and compartment Art2, only objects having Adams-Decl-Art2 in the access control list are accessible in the session.

By itself that mechanism would be too restrictive to be usable. Adams cannot create general files to be used in any session. Worse yet, shared objects would not only have to list Adams as a legitimate subject, they would have to list Adams under all acceptable groups and all acceptable compartments for each group.

The solution is the use of **wild cards**, placeholders meaning "any user" (or "any group" or "any compartment"). An access control list might specify access by Adams-Decl-Art1, giving specific rights to Adams if working in group Decl on compartment Art1. The list might also specify Adams-*-Art1, meaning that Adams can access the object from any group in compartment Art1. A notation of *-Decl-* would mean "any user in group

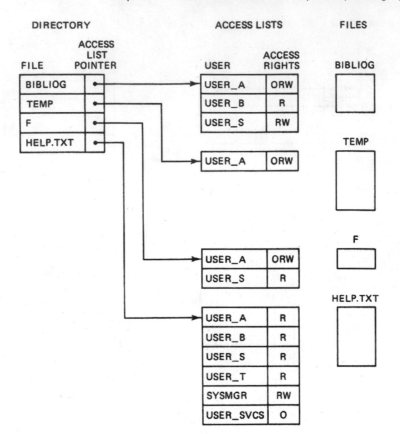

Figure 6-12   Access Control List

Decl in any compartment." Different placements of the wildcard * have the obvious interpretations.

The access control list can be maintained in sorted order, with * sorted as coming after all specific names. Adams-Decl-* would come after all specific compartment designations for Adams. The search for access permission continues just until the first match. All explicit designations will be checked before wild cards in any position, so a specific access right would take precedence over a wild card right. The last entry on an access list could be *-*-*, specifying rights allowable to any user not explicitly on the access list. This device means that a shared public object can have a very short access list, explicitly naming the few subjects who should have access rights different from the default.

Access Control Matrix

Think of the directory as listing objects accessible by a single subject, and the access list as identifying subjects who can access a single object. The total data in these two representations is equivalent; the distinction is the ease of use in given situations.

An alternative is the **access control matrix**, which is a table in which each row represents a subject, each column represents an object, and each entry is the set of access rights for that subject to that object. A representation of an access control matrix is shown

	BIBLIOG	TEMP	F	HELP.TXT	C_COMP	LINKER	SYS_CLOCK	PRINTER
USER A	ORW	ORW	ORW	R	X	X	R	W
USER B	R	—	—	R	X	X	R	W
USER S	RW	—	R	R	X	X	R	W
USER T	—	—	—	R	X	X	R	W
SYS_MGR	—	—	—	RW	OX	OX	ORW	O
USER_SVCS	—	—	—	O	X	X	R	W

Figure 6-13   Access Control Matrix

in Figure 6-13. In general, the access control matrix is sparse: most subjects do not have access rights to most objects. The access matrix can be represented as a list of triples, having the form ⟨*subject, object, rights*⟩. Searching a large number of these triples is inefficient enough that this implementation is seldom used.

Capability

A **capability** is an unforgeable token giving the possessor certain rights to an object. A capability is analogous to a ticket to a movie or an ID card that cannot be duplicated. The Multics system [SAL74] and later CAL [LAM76] and Hydra [WUL74] systems used capabilities for access control. These fundamental research efforts laid the groundwork for subsequent production use in systems such as Kerberos [STE88] (which is studied in greater detail in Chapter 9). In theory, a subject can create new objects and can specify the operations allowable on those objects. Certainly users can create new objects such as files, data segments, or subprocesses; and the user should also be able to specify the kinds of operations acceptable, such as *read, write,* and *execute.* But a user can also create completely new objects, such as new data structures, and define types of accesses previously unknown to the system.

A capability is a ticket giving permission to a subject to perform a certain type of access on an object. The ticket must be unforgeable. One way to make an unforgeable ticket is to not give the ticket directly to the user. Instead, the operating system holds all tickets on behalf of the users. The operating system returns to the user a pointer to an operating system data structure, which also links to the user. A capability can be created only by specific request from a user to the operating system. Each capability also identifies the allowable accesses.

One possible access right to an object is *transfer* or *propagate.* A subject having this right can pass copies of capabilities to other subjects. Each of these capabilities also has a list of permitted types of accesses, one of which might also be *transfer.* In this instance, process *A* can pass a copy of a capability to *B,* who can then pass a copy to *C. B* can prevent further distribution of the capability (and therefore prevent further dissemination of the access right) by omitting the *transfer* right from the rights passed in the capability to *C. B* might still pass certain access rights to *C,* but not the right to propagate access rights to other subjects.

DOMAIN FOR MAIN

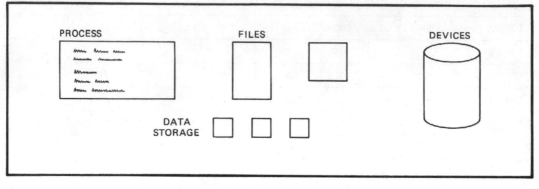

Figure 6-14   Process Execution Domain

As a process executes, it operates in a **domain** or **local name space**. This is the collection of objects to which the process has access. A domain for a user at a given time might include some programs, files, data segments, and I/O devices such as a printer and a terminal. Such a domain is shown in Figure 6-14.

As execution continues, the process may call a subprocedure, passing some of the objects to which it has access as arguments to the subprocedure. The domain of the subprocedure is not necessarily the same as that of its calling procedure; in fact, a calling procedure may pass only some of its objects to the subprocedure, and the subprocedure may have access rights to other objects not accessible to the calling procedure. The caller may also pass only some of its access rights for the objects it passes to the subprocedure. For example, a procedure might pass to a subprocedure the right to read but not modify a particular data value.

Because each capability identifies a single object in a domain, the collection of capabilities defines the domain. When a process calls a subprocedure and passes certain objects to the subprocedure, the operating system forms a stack of all the capabilities of the current procedure. The operating system then creates new capabilities for the subprocedure, as shown in Figure 6-15.

Operationally, capabilities are a straightforward way to keep track of the access rights of subjects to objects during execution. The capabilities will be backed up by a more comprehensive table, such as an access control matrix or an access control list. Each time a process seeks to use a new object, the operating system examines the master list of objects and subjects to determine whether the object is accessible. If so, the operating system creates a capability for that object.

Capabilities must be stored in memory inaccessible to normal users. One way of accomplishing this is to store capabilities in segments not pointed at by the user's segment table, or by enclosing them in protected memory as from a pair of base/bounds registers. Another approach is to use a tagged architecture machine to identify capabilities as structures requiring protection.

During execution only the capabilities of objects that have been accessed by the current process are kept readily available. This restriction improves the speed with which access to an object can be checked. This approach is essentially the one used in Multics, as described in [FAB74].

DOMAIN FOR MAIN

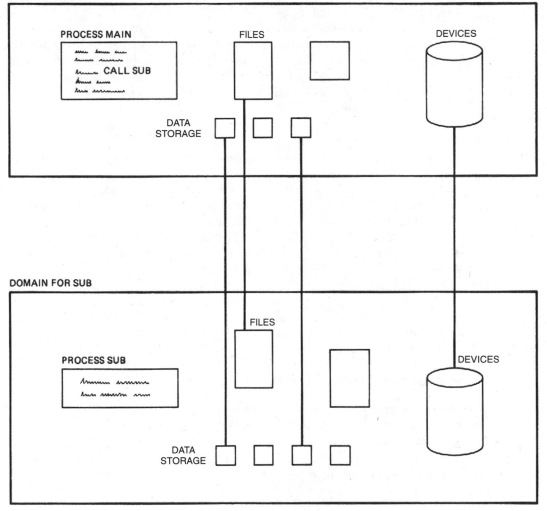

Figure 6-15   Passing Objects to a Subject

Capabilities can be revoked. When an issuing subject revokes a capability, no further access under the revoked capability should be permitted. A capability table can contain pointers to the active capabilities spawned under it, so that the operating system can trace what access rights should be deleted if a capability is revoked. A similar problem is deleting capabilities for users who are no longer active.

Procedure-Oriented Access Control

A goal in access control is to restrict not just what subjects have access to an object, but also what they can *do* to that object. Read versus write access can be controlled rather readily by most operating systems, but more complex control is not so easy to achieve.

By **procedure-oriented** protection, we imply the existence of a procedure that controls access to objects (for example, by performing its own user authentication to strengthen that provided by the basic operating system). Essentially the procedure forms a capsule around the object, permitting only certain specified accesses.

Procedures can enforce that accesses to an object be done through a trusted interface. For example, neither users nor general operating system routines might be allowed direct access to the table of valid users. The only accesses might be through three procedures, one to add a user, one to delete a user, and one to check whether a particular name corresponds to a valid user. These procedures, especially add and delete, could use their own checks to make sure that calls to them are legitimate.

Procedure-oriented protection implements the principle of information hiding, because the means of implementing an object is known only to the control procedure of the object. Of course, this degree of protection carries a penalty of efficiency. There can be no simple, fast access, even if the object is frequently used.

This survey of mechanisms for access control has intentionally progressed from simple to complex. As the mechanisms have provided greater flexibility, they have done so at the price of increased overhead. For example, implementing capabilities that must be checked on each access is far more difficult than implementing a simple directory structure that is checked only on a subject's first access to an object. This complexity is apparent both to the user and to the implementer. The user is aware of additional protection features, but the naive user may be frustrated or intimidated at having to select protection options with little understanding of their usefulness. The implementation complexity becomes apparent in slow response to users. The balance between simplicity and functionality is a continuing battle in security.

6.4   File Protection Mechanisms

Several existing programs or techniques for file protection are studied in this section. These examples are only representative; they do not cover all possible means of file protection on the market.

Basic Forms of Protection

As described earlier, all multiuser operating systems must provide some minimal protection to keep one user from maliciously or inadvertently accessing or modifying the files of another. As the number of users has grown, so has the complexity of these protection schemes.

All–None Protection

In the original IBM OS operating systems, files were by default public. Any user could read, modify, or delete a file belonging to any other user. The principal protection was trust, combined with ignorance. The first supposition was that users could be trusted not to read or modify others' files because the users would expect the same respect from others. Ignorance helped this situation, because a user could access a file only by name, and presumably users knew the names of only the files to which they had legitimate access.

Certain system files were considered sensitive, and the system administrator could protect them with a password. A normal user could use this feature, but it was clearly most valuable for protecting files of the operating system. The password could control all accesses (read, write, or delete), or it could control only write and delete accesses because only these had an effect on other users. The password mechanism required intervention by the system operator each time access to the file began.

This type of protection is unacceptable for several reasons.

- *Lack of trust.* The assumption about trustworthy users is not necessarily justified. For systems with few users who knew each other, mutual respect might suffice, but in large systems where not every user knows every other user, there is no basis for trust.

- *All or nothing.* Even if a user identifies a set of trustworthy users, there is no convenient way to allow access only to them.

- *Rise of timesharing.* This protection scheme is more appropriate for a batch environment, where users have little chance to interact with other users, and where users do their thinking and exploring off the system. On timesharing systems, users interact with other users. Because users choose when to execute programs, they are more likely to arrange computing tasks to be able to pass results from one program or one user to another.

- *Complexity.* Because (human) operator intervention is required, its use degrades the performance of the operating system. Its use is, therefore, discouraged by computing centers for all but the most sensitive data sets.

- *File listings.* For accounting purposes and to help users remember for what files they are responsible, various system utilities can produce a list of all files. Users are not ignorant of what files are on the system. Interactive users may try to browse through any unprotected files.

Group Protection

For reasons such as these, the next major development was the identification of *groups* of users who had some common relationship. In a typical implementation, the world is divided into three classes: the user, a trusted working group associated with the user, and the rest of the users. For simplicity these can be called *user, group,* and *world.* This form of protection is used on Digital Equipment Corp. DEC-10 computers, the Unix system, and VAX VMS systems.

All authorized users are separated into groups. A group may be several members working on a common project, a department, a class, or a single user. The basis for selection of the group is *need to share.* The members of a group have some common interest and therefore are assumed to have files to share with the other members of the group. No user belongs to more than one group.

When creating a file, a user defines access rights to the file for the user, for other members of the same group, and for all other users in general. Typically the choices for access rights are a limited set, such as {read, write, execute, delete}. For a particular file, a user might declare read-only access to the general world, read and write access to the group, and all rights to the user. This would be appropriate for a paper being developed by a group, where the different members of the group might modify sections being written within the group, and the paper itself should be available for people outside the group to review but not change.

The implementation is easy. A user is recognized by two identifiers (usually numbers), a user ID and a group ID. These identifiers are stored in the file directory entry for each file, and are obtained by the operating system when a user logs in. Therefore, we can easily check whether a proposed access to a file is from someone whose group ID matched the group ID for the file to be accessed.

This protection scheme overcomes some of the shortcomings of the all-or-nothing scheme described previously, and it has the advantage of being easy to implement. However, the scheme introduces some new difficulties of its own.

- *Group affiliation.* A single user cannot belong to two groups. Suppose Tom belongs to one group with Ann and a second group with Bill. If Tom indicates that a file is to be readable by the group, to which group(s) does this permission refer? Suppose a file of Ann's is readable by the group; does Bill have access to it? These ambiguities are most simply resolved by declaring that every user belongs to exactly one group. (This does not mean that all users belong to *the same* group.)

- *Multiple personalities.* To overcome the one-person one-group restriction, certain people could obtain multiple accounts, permitting them, in effect, to be multiple users. This introduces new problems as a person can be only one user at a time. Suppose Tom obtains two accounts, thereby becoming Tom1 in a group with Ann and Tom2 in a group with Bill. Tom1 is not in the same group as Tom2, so any files, programs, or aids developed under the Tom1 account can be available to Tom2 only if they are available to the entire world. This solution leads to proliferation of accounts, redundant files, limited protection for files of general interest, and inconvenience to users.

- *All groups.* To overcome this problem, we may decide that Tom should have access to all his files any time he is active. This solution puts the responsibility on Tom to control with whom he share what things. For example, he may be in Group1 with Ann and Group2 with Bill. He creates a Group1 file to share with Ann. But if he is active in Group2 next time, he still sees the Group1 file and may not realize that it is not accessible to Bill, too.

- *Limited sharing.* Files can be shared only within groups or with the world. Users want to be able to identify sharing partners for a file on a per-file basis, for example, sharing one file with 10 people and another file with 20 others.

Single Permissions

The simplicity of implementing these schemes spawned other easy-to-manage methods that provided finer degrees of security. The next protection design allowed a user to associate permission with a single file.

Password or Other Token

A simplified form of password protection is applicable for file protection. A user can assign a password to a file. User accesses are limited to those who can supply the correct password at the time the file is opened. The password can be required for any access or for modifications (write access) only.

Password access gives a user the effect of a different "group" for every file. However, file passwords suffer from difficulties similar to those of authentication passwords, as listed below.

- *Loss.* Depending on the implementation, no one may be able to replace a lost (forgotten) password. The operator or system administrator can certainly intervene and unprotect or assign a particular password, but often they cannot determine what password a user has assigned; if the user loses the password, a new one must be assigned.

- *Disclosure.* If a password is disclosed to an unauthorized individual, the file becomes immediately accessible. If the user then changes the password to reprotect the file, all the other legitimate users must be informed of the new password because their old password will fail.

- *Revocation.* To revoke one user's access right to a file, the password must be changed, which causes the same problems as disclosure.

Temporary Acquired Permission

An interesting permission scheme is provided by the Unix operating system. As described previously, the basic protection is a three-level user–group–world hierarchy. One important addition is called the **set userid (suid)** permission. If this protection is set for a file to be executed, the protection level is that of the file's *owner*, not the *executor*. That is, if Tom owns a file and allows Ann to execute it, while Ann executes it she has the protection rights of Tom, not of herself.

This peculiar-sounding permission does have a useful application. It permits a user to establish data files to which access is allowed only through specified procedures.

For example, you might want to set up a computerized dating service that manipulates a data base of people available on particular nights. Suc might be interested in a date for Saturday, but she might have already refused a request from Jeff, saying she had other plans. Sue instructs the service not to reveal to Jeff that she is available. In order to use the service, Sue and Jeff and others must be able to read and write (at least indirectly) to the file to determine who is available or to post their availability. But if Jeff can read the file directly, he would find that Sue has lied. Therefore, your dating service must force Sue and Jeff (and all others) to access this file only through an access program that would screen the data Jeff obtains. But if the file access is limited to read and write by you, its owner, Sue and Jeff will never be able to enter data into it.

The solution is the Unix SUID protection. You create the data base file, giving only you access permission. You also write the program that is to access the data base, and save it with the SUID protection. Then when Jeff executes your program, he temporarily acquires your access permission, only during execution of the program. Jeff never has direct access to the file because your program will do the actual file access. When Jeff exits from your program, he regains his own access rights and loses yours. Thus, your program can access the file, but the program obtains only the data Jeff is allowed to see.

This mechanism is convenient for system functions that general users should be able to perform only in a prescribed way. For example, only the system should be able to modify the file of users' passwords, but individual users should be able to change their own passwords any time they wish. With the SUID feature, a password change program can be owned by the system, which will therefore have full access to the system password table. The program to change passwords also has SUID protection, so that when a normal user executes it, the program can modify the password file in a carefully constrained way on behalf of the user.

Per-Object and Per-User Protection

The primary limitation of these protection schemes is the ability to create meaningful groups of related users who should have similar access to one or more data sets. The access control lists or access control matrices described earlier provide very flexible protection. Their disadvantage is for the user who wants to allow access to many users to many different data sets; such a user must still specify each data set to be accessed by each user. As a new user is added, that user's special access rights must be specified by all appropriate users.

VAX SE-VMS

Digital Equipment Corporation's VAX SE-VMS operating system provides access control lists (ACLs). A user can create an ACL for any file, specifying who has access to the file, and what type of access each person has.

Each user belongs to one group, as described earlier. Additionally, the system administrator can create effective groups by defining what are called "general identifiers." For example, a software project team might include Tom from group 1, Ann from group 2, and Bill and Sally from group 3; the system administrator can define a new general identifier, SOFTPROJ, which includes only those four people. A user can allow access to a file to people in the general identifier SOFTPROJ, without allowing access to any other users from groups 1, 2, or 3. The ACL lists specific users, groups, or general identifiers.

In VMS an ACL can also be applied to a specific device or device type, allowing users access only to certain printers, or restricting which users can enter the system through dialup (telephone) lines. Furthermore, network access and batch access to resources can also be limited through ACLs.

IBM RACF, ACF2

An IBM enhancement for the MVS operating system, RACF (Resource Access Control Facility) provides similar protection for its data sets. Two competitors are ACF2 and Top Secret. All of these systems allow the owner of a file to assign a default protection for a file (access allowed to any user), and then to refine that access for specific listed users.

The files can be identified individually or with a general file name. Once access has been given, it can also be revoked.

6.5 User Authentication

An operating system bases much of its protection on knowing who a user of the system is. In real-life situations, people commonly ask for identification of people they don't know: a bank employee may ask for a driver's license before cashing a check, and library employees may require some identification before charging out books. Some universities do not give out grades over the telephone because the office workers do not necessarily know the students calling. However, a professor who recognizes the voice of a certain student can give out that student's grades. People have developed systems of authentication using documents, voice recognition, and other trusted means of identification.

In computing, obviously, the situation is less secure. Anyone can attempt to login to a computing system. Unlike the professor who recognizes a student's voice, the computer cannot recognize electrical signals from one person as being any different from those of anyone else. Thus, most authentication systems must be based on some knowledge shared only by the computing system and the user.

The most common authentication mechanism is a **password**, a "word" known to computer and user. Although this would seem a relatively secure system, human practice sometimes degrades its quality. In this section we consider passwords, selection criteria, and authentication mechanisms. We conclude with the study of problems in the authentication process, notably Trojan horses masquerading as the computer authentication process, and other techniques of authentication.

Use of Passwords

Passwords are mutually agreed-upon code words, assumed to be known only to the user and the system. In some cases a user chooses passwords; in other cases they are assigned by the system. The length and format of the password also vary from one system to another.

The use of passwords is fairly straightforward. A user enters some piece of identification, such as a name or an assigned user ID; this identification can be available to the public or easy to guess, because it does not provide the real security of the system. The system then requests a password from the user. If the password matches that on file for the user, the user is authenticated to the system. If the password match fails, the user may have mistyped, in which case the system requests the password again.

Loose-Lipped Systems

So far the process seems secure. Let us consider the actions of a would-be intruder. Authentication is based on knowing the ⟨*name, password*⟩ pair. A complete outsider is presumed to know nothing of the system. Suppose the intruder attempts to access a system in the following manner. (In the following examples, the system messages are in uppercase, and the user's responses are in lowercase.)

```
WELCOME TO THE XYZ COMPUTING SYSTEMS
ENTER USER NAME: adams
INVALID USER NAME—UNKNOWN USER
ENTER USER NAME:
```

We assumed that the intruder knew nothing of the system, but without having to do much, the intruder found out that *adams* is not the name of an authorized user. The intruder could try other common names, first names, and likely generic names such as *system* or *operator* to build a list of authorized users.

An alternate arrangement of the login sequence is shown below.

```
WELCOME TO THE XYZ COMPUTING SYSTEMS
ENTER USER NAME: adams
ENTER PASSWORD: john
INVALID ACCESS
ENTER USER NAME:
```

This system notifies a user of a failure only after accepting both the user name and the password. The failure message should not indicate whether it is the user name or password that is unacceptable. In this way, the intruder does not know which failed.

These examples also gave a clue as to which computing system is being accessed. The true outsider has no right to know that, and legitimate insiders already know what system they have accessed. In the example below, the user is given no information until the system is assured of the identity of the user.

```
ENTER USER NAME: adams
ENTER PASSWORD: john
INVALID ACCESS
ENTER USER NAME: adams
ENTER PASSWORD: johnq
WELCOME TO THE XYZ COMPUTING SYSTEMS
```

Additional Authentication Information

There is more information available to authenticate users. Suppose Adams works the shift between 8:00 a.m. and 5:00 p.m., Monday through Friday, and works in the accounting department. Any legitimate attempt by Adams should be during those times, through a terminal in the accounting department offices. By limiting Adams to logging in under those conditions, the system protects against two problems:

- Someone from outside might try to impersonate Adams. This attempt would be thwarted by either the time of access or the port through which the access was attempted.

- Adams might attempt to access the system from home or on a weekend, to use resources not allowed, or to do something that would be too risky with other people around.

Limiting users to certain terminals or to certain times of access can cause complications (as when a user legitimately needs to work overtime, or a person has to access the system while out of town on a business trip). However, some companies use those authentication techniques because the added security they provide outweighs these inconveniences.

Attacks on Passwords

How secure are passwords themselves? Passwords are somewhat limited as protection devices because of the relatively small number of bits of information they contain.

Here are some ways you might be able to determine a user's password.

- Try all possible passwords
- Try many probable passwords
- Try passwords likely for the user
- Search for the system list of passwords
- Ask the user

Of course, these are arranged in decreasing order of difficulty, although the later ones are, or at least should be, less likely to succeed.

Exhaustive Attack

In an **exhaustive** or **brute force attack**, the attacker tries all possible passwords. The number of possible passwords depends on the implementation of the particular computing system.

If passwords are words, consisting of the 26 characters A–Z, and passwords can be of any length from 1 to 8 characters, there are 26^1 passwords of 1 character, 26^2 passwords of 2 characters, and 26^8 passwords of 8 characters. The system as a whole has $26^1 + 26^2 + \cdots + 26^8 = 26^9 - 1 \approx 5 * 10^{12}$ possible passwords. That number seems intractable enough. At a rate of one password per millisecond, it would take on the order of 150 years to test all passwords. But if we can speed up the search to one password per microsecond, the work factor drops to about two months.

Searching for a single particular password, however, does not necessarily require all those passwords to be tried. If the passwords were evenly distributed, half of the password space would be the expected number of searches to find any particular password. However, passwords are not evenly distributed. Because a password has to be remembered, people tend to pick simple passwords.

Probable Passwords

Think of a word.

Is the word you thought of long? Is it uncommon? Is it hard to spell or to pronounce? The answer to all three of these questions is probably "no."

A penetrator searching for passwords realizes these characteristics of humans. Therefore, penetrators try techniques that are likely to lead to rapid success. If people prefer short passwords to long ones, the penetrator will try all passwords, but try them in order by length. There are only $26^1 + 26^2 + 26^3 = 18{,}278$ passwords of length 3 or less. At the assumed rate of one password per millisecond, all of these passwords can be checked in 18.278 seconds, hardly a challenge with a computer. Even going to 4 or 5 characters raises the count to only 475 seconds (about 8 minutes) and 12,356 seconds (about 3.5 hours), respectively.

This analysis assumes that people choose passwords such as *vxlag* and *msms* as often as they pick *enter* and *beer*. However, people tend to choose names or words they can remember. Many computing systems have spelling checkers that can be used to check for spelling errors and typographic mistakes in documents. These spelling checkers sometimes carry on-line dictionaries of the most common English words. One contains a dictionary of 80,000 words. Trying all of these words takes only 80 seconds.

Passwords Likely for a User

If Sandy is picking a password, she is probably not choosing a word completely at random. Most likely Sandy's password is something meaningful to her. People typically choose personal passwords, such as the name of a spouse, a child, a brother or sister, a pet, a street name, or something similar. Selecting just names of people (first names), streets, projects, and so forth, produces a list of only a few hundred possibilities, at most. These can all be tried in under a second! Even a person working by hand could try 10 likely candidates in a minute or two.

The likelihood of success in this approach is frightening. Morris and Thompson [MOR79] report on the results of having gathered passwords from many users over a long

Table 6-1   Distribution of Actual Passwords

15	(0.5%)	were a single(!) ASCII character
72	(2%)	were two ASCII characters
464	(14%)	were three ASCII characters
477	(14%)	were four alphabetic letters
706	(21%)	were five alphabetic letters, all of the same case
605	(18%)	were six lowercase alphabetic letters
492	(15%)	were words in dictionaries or lists of names
2831	(86%)	total of all above categories

period of time shown in Table 6-1. Figure 6-16 (based on data from that study) shows the characteristics of the 3289 passwords gathered. The results from that study are distressing, at the least. Of those passwords, 86% could be uncovered in about one week's worth of 24-hour a day testing, using the very generous estimate of 1 millisecond per password check.

Lest you dismiss these results as dated (they do come from 1979), Klein repeated the experiment in 1990 [KLE90] and Spafford in 1992 [SPA92]. Each collected approximately 15,000 passwords. Klein reported that 2.7% of the passwords were guessed in only 15 minutes of machine time and 21% were guessed within a week! Spafford found the average password length was 6.8 characters and 28.9% consisted of only lowercase alphabetic characters. Notice that both these studies were done *after* the Internet worm succeeded, in part, by breaking weak passwords.

Several network sites post dictionaries of phrases, science fiction characters, places, mythological names, Chinese words, Yiddish words, and other specialized lists. All of these are posted to help site administrators identify users who have chosen weak passwords, but the same dictionaries can also be used by attackers of sites that do not have such attentive administrators.

Finding a Plaintext System Password List

In order to validate passwords, the system must have a way of comparing entries with actual passwords. Rather than trying to guess a user's password, an attacker may instead target the system password file. Why guess when with one table you can determine passwords with total accuracy?

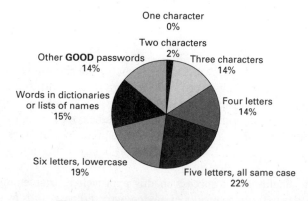

Figure 6-16   Users' Password Choices

On some systems, the password list is a file, organized essentially as a two-column table of user IDs and corresponding passwords. Certainly that is too obvious to leave out in the open. Various security approaches are used to conceal this table from those who should not see it.

You might protect the table with strong access controls, limiting its access to the operating system. This is even looser than it should be, because not every module of the operating system needs or deserves access to this table. For example, the operating system scheduler, accounting routines, or storage manager have no need to know the contents of that table. Unfortunately, in some systems, there are $n + 1$ known users: n regular users and the operating system. The operating system is not divided, so that all its modules have access to all privileged information. This implies that a user who exploits a flaw in one section of the operating system has access to all the deepest secrets of the system. A better approach, then, is to limit the access to this table to the modules that need access: the user authentication module and the parts associated with installing new users, for example.

Dumping memory at a convenient time is another way to get access to a password table if the table is stored in plain sight. A user who can time things carefully may be able to dump the contents of all of memory and, by exhaustive search, find values that look like the password table.

System backups can also be used to obtain the password table. In order to be able to recover from system errors, periodically the file space is backed up onto some auxiliary medium, often magnetic tape, for safe storage. In the unlikely event of a problem, the file system can be reloaded from a backup, with a loss of only the changes made since the last backup. Backup tapes often contain only file contents; usually there is no protection mechanism to control access to the files on a backup tape. (Physical security and access controls to the tapes themselves are depended upon to provide security for the contents of backup tapes.) If a regular user can access these tapes, even ones from several weeks, months, or years ago, the password table stored in them may still contain some valid entries.

Encrypted Password File

It is safer to encrypt the password list so that reading it will not help the penetrator. Two commonly used ways to encrypt the password list are conventional encryption and one-way ciphers. These methods of protection are described in this section.

With conventional encryption, the entire password table is encrypted, or perhaps just the password column. When a user's password is received, the stored password is decrypted, and the two are compared.

There is still a slight exposure with this method. For an instant the user's password is available in plaintext in main memory. It is available to anyone who could obtain access to all of memory.

A safer approach uses one-way encryption, defined in Chapter 4. Entries in the password table are encrypted by a one-way encryption and then stored. When the user enters a password, it is encrypted to be compared with the table. If the two values are equal, the authentication succeeds. Of course, the encryption has to be such that it is unlikely that two passwords would encrypt to the same ciphertext, but this characteristic is true for most secure encryption algorithms.

With one-way encryption the password file can be stored in plain view; in fact, the password table for the Unix operating system can be read by any user, unless special access controls have been installed. Backup copies of the password table are also not a problem.

Two people might choose the same password, which would create two identical entries in the password file. Even though these entries are encrypted, each user will know the plaintext equivalent. If Bill and Kathy both choose their passwords on April 1, they might choose APRILFOOL as a password. Bill might read the password file and notice that the encrypted version of his password is the same as Kathy's.

Unix circumvents this vulnerability by using a password extension, called the salt. The **salt** is a 12-bit number formed from the system time and the process identifier. Thus, the salt is likely to be unique for each user. The salt is concatenated to Bill's password (pw) when he chooses it; $E(pw + salt_B)$ is stored for Bill; his salt value is also stored. When Kathy chooses her password, the salt is different because the time or the process number is different. Call this new one $salt_K$. For her, $E(pw + salt_K)$ and $salt_K$ are stored. When either tries to login, the system fetches the appropriate salt from the password table and combines that with the password before performing the encryption. The encrypted versions of ($pw + salt$) are very different for these two users. When Bill looks down the password list, the encrypted version of his password will not look at all like Kathy's.

Storing the password file in a disguised form relieves much of the pressure to secure it. Better still is to limit access to processes that have a legitimate need for access. In this way, the password file is protected to a level commensurate with the protection provided by the password itself. Someone who has broken the controls of the file system has access to data, not just passwords, and that is a serious threat. But if an attacker successfully penetrates the outer security layer, the attacker still has to get past the encryption of the password file to have access to the useful information in the password file.

Asking the User

But there is a much easier way to obtain passwords. The easiest way to obtain unauthorized access may be simply to obtain the password directly from the user. People often tape a password to the side of a terminal, or write it on a card just inside the top desk drawer. Users are afraid they will forget their passwords, or cannot be bothered trying to remember them. Users with several accounts are especially tempted to write the passwords down.

Users sharing work or data may also be tempted to share passwords. If someone needs a file, it is easier to say "my password is x; get the file yourself" than to arrange to share the file. This situation is certainly a result of user weakness, but it may be brought about by a system that makes sharing inconvenient.

Password Selection Criteria

The preceding discussion leads to some conclusions regarding appropriate passwords. Passwords should be hard to guess and hard to determine exhaustively. The security needs of the situation also affect password selection. Here are some suggestions regarding password selection.

- *Use characters other than just A–Z.* If passwords are chosen from the letters A–Z, there are only 26 possibilities. Adding digits expands the number of possibilities to 36. Using both uppercase and lowercase letters plus digits expands the number of possibilities to 62. Although this change seems small, the effect is large when testing a full space of all possible combinations of characters. It takes about 100 hours to test all 6-letter words from letters of one case only, but it takes about 2 years to test all 6-symbol passwords from upper- and lowercase letters and digits. Although 100 hours is reasonable, 2 years is oppressive enough to make this attack far less attractive.

- *Choose long passwords.* The combinatorial explosion of passwords begins at length 4 or 5. Choosing 6-character or longer passwords makes it less likely that a password will be uncovered. Remember that a brute force penetration can stop as soon as the password is found. Some penetrators will try the easy cases—known words and short passwords—and move on to another target if those attacks fail.
- *Avoid actual names or words.* Theoretically there are 26^6 or about 300 million "words" of length 6, but there are only about 150,000 words in a good collegiate dictionary, ignoring length. By picking one of the 99.95% nonwords, you force the attacker to use a longer brute force search, instead of the abbreviated dictionary search.
- *Choose an unlikely password.* Password choice is a double bind. In order to remember the password easily, you want one that has special meaning to you. However, you don't want someone else to be able to guess this special meaning. One easy-to-remember password is 2Brn2B. That unlikely-looking jumble is a simple transformation of "to be or not to be." The first letters of a line from a song, a few letters from different words of a private phrase, or a memorable football score are examples of reasonable passwords.
- *Change the password regularly.* Even if there is no reason to suspect that the password has been compromised, change is advised. A penetrator may break a password system by obtaining an old list or working exhaustively on an encrypted list.
- *Don't write it down.* (Note: This time-honored advice is relevant only if physical security is a serious risk. People who have accounts on many different machines and servers, not to mention bank and charge card PINs, may have trouble remembering all the access codes. Setting all codes the same or using insecure but easy to remember passwords may be more risky than writing passwords on a reasonably well-protected list.)
- *Don't tell anyone else.*

To help users select good passwords, some systems provide meaningless but pronounceable passwords. For example, the VAX VMS system randomly generates five passwords from which the user chooses one. They are pronounceable, so that the user should be able to repeat and memorize them. However, the user may interchange syllables or letters of a meaningless string.

Other systems encourage users to change their passwords regularly. The regularity of password change is usually a system parameter, which can be changed for the characteristics of a given installation. Suppose the frequency is set at 30 days. Some systems begin to warn the user after 25 days that the password is about to expire. Others wait until 30 days and inform the user that the password has expired. Some systems nag without end, while other systems cut off a user's access if a password has expired. Other systems force the user immediately into the password change utility on the first login after 30 days.

Grampp and Morris [GRA84a] argue that this process is not necessarily good. Choosing passwords is not difficult, but under pressure a user may adopt any password, just to satisfy the system's demand for a new password. Furthermore, if this is the only time when a password can be changed, a user who selects a bad password and realizes it cannot change until the next scheduled time.

Some systems force users to change passwords periodically. Users with favorite passwords alternate between two passwords each time a change is required. To prevent password reuse, IBM MVS systems refuse to accept any of the most recently used passwords. One user of such a system went through 24 password changes each month, just to cycle back to the favorite password.

One-Time Passwords

A **one-time password** is one that changes every time it is used. Instead of assigning a static phrase to a user, the system assigns a static mathematical function. The system provides an argument to the function, and the user computes and returns the function value. Such systems are also called **challenge–response systems** because the system presents a challenge to the user and judges the authenticity of the user by the user's response. Here are some simple examples of one-time password functions; these functions are overly simplified just to make the explanation easier. Very complex functions can be used in place of these simple ones for host authentication in a network.

- $f(x) = x + 1$. With this function, the system prompts with a value for x, and the user enters the value $x + 1$. The kinds of mathematical functions used are limited only by the ability of the user to compute the response quickly and easily. Other similar possibilities are $f(x) = 3x^2 - 9x + 2$, $f(x) = p_x$ where p_x is the xth prime number, or $f(x) = d * h$ where d is the date and h is the hour of the current time.

- $f(x) = r(x)$. For this function, the receiver uses the argument as the seed for a random number generator (available to both the receiver and host). The user replies with the value of the first random number generated. A variant of this scheme uses x as a number of random numbers to generate. The receiver generates x random numbers and sends the xth of these to the host.

- $f(a_1a_2a_3a_4a_5a_6) = a_3a_1a_1a_4$. With this function, the system provides a character string, which the user must transform in some manner. Again many different character operations can be used.

- $f(E(x)) = E(D(E(x)) + 1)$. In this function, the computer sends an encrypted value, $E(x)$. The user must decrypt the value, perform some mathematical function, and encrypt the result to return it to the system. Clearly for human use, the encryption function must be something that can be done easily by hand, unlike DES. For machine-to-machine authentication, however, an encryption algorithm such as DES is appropriate.

One-time passwords are very secure for authentication because an intercepted password is useless. However, their usefulness is limited by the complexity of algorithms people can be expected to remember. A password generating device, similar to a pocket calculator, can implement more complex functions. Several models are readily available at reasonable prices. They are very effective at countering the threat of transmitting passwords in plaintext across a network.

The Authentication Process

Authentication usually operates as described previously. However, users occasionally mistype their passwords. A user who receives a message of INCORRECT LOGIN will carefully retype the login and gain access to the system. Even a user who is a terrible typist should be able to login successfully in three to five tries.

Some authentication procedures are intentionally slow. A legitimate user will not complain if the login process takes 5 or 10 seconds. To a penetrator who is trying an exhaustive search or a dictionary search, however, 5 or 10 seconds per trial makes this class of attack generally infeasible.

Someone who continually fails to login may not be an authorized user. Systems commonly disconnect a user after three to five failed logins, forcing the user to reestablish a connection with the system. (This action will slow down a penetrator who is trying to penetrate the system by telephone. After a small number of failures, the penetrator must redial, which takes a few seconds.)

In more secure installations, stopping penetrators is more important than tolerating users' mistakes. For example, the developers of one system assume that all legitimate users can type their passwords correctly within three tries. After three successive password failures, the account for that user is disabled, and only the security administrator can reenable it. This action identifies accounts that may be the target of attacks by penetrators.

Flaws in the Authentication Process

Password authentication assumes that anyone who knows a password is the user to whom the password belongs. As we have seen, passwords can be guessed, deduced, or inferred. Some people give out their passwords for the asking. Other passwords have been obtained just by watching a user typing in the password. The password, then, is a piece of evidence, but skeptics will want more convincing proof.

Challenge–Response Systems

The login is usually time-invariant. Except for password changes, each login looks like every other. A more sophisticated login requires a user id and password, followed by a **challenge–response interchange.** The system prompts the user for a reply that is different each time the user logs in. For example, the system might display a four-digit number, and the user would have to correctly enter a function such as the sum or product of the digits. Each user is assigned a different challenge function to compute. Because there are many possible challenge functions, a penetrator who captures the user ID and password cannot necessarily infer the proper function. A physical device similar to a calculator can be used to implement a more complicated response function. The user enters the challenge number, and the device computes and displays the response for the user to type in order to log in.

Impersonation of Login

In the systems we have described, the proof is one-sided. The system demands certain identification of the user, but the user is supposed to trust the system. A programmer can easily write a program that displays the standard prompts for user ID and password, captures the pair entered, stores the pair in a file, displays SYSTEM ERROR; DISCONNECTED, and exits. This attack is a type of Trojan horse. The perpetrator sets it up, leaves the terminal unattended, and waits for an innocent victim to attempt a login. The naive victim may not even suspect that a security breach has occurred.

To foil this type of attack, the user should be sure the path to the system is reinitialized each time. On some systems, turning the terminal off and on again or pressing the BREAK key generates a clear signal to the computer to halt any running process for the terminal. Not every computer recognizes power off or BREAK as an interruption of the current process, however.

Alternatively, the user can be suspicious of the computing system, just as the system is suspicious of the user. The user will not enter confidential data (such as a password) until convinced that the computer is legitimate. Of course, the computer acknowledges the user only after passing the authentication process. A computing system can display some information known only by the user and the system. For example, the system might read the user's name and reply "YOUR LAST LOGIN WAS 10 APRIL AT 09:47." The user can verify that the date and time are correct before entering a secret password. If higher security is desired, the system can send an encrypted time stamp. The user decrypts this and discovers that the time is current. The user then replies with an encrypted time stamp and password, in order to convince the system that a malicious intruder has not intercepted a password from some prior login.

Authentication Other Than Passwords

Some very sophisticated authentication devices are now available. These devices include handprint detectors, voice recognizers, and identifiers of patterns in the retina. Authentication with such devices uses unforgeable physical characteristics to authenticate users. The cost is coming down because these devices are now selling to major markets; these devices are useful in very-high-security situations.

More normal security needs can be handled by a combination of login and characteristics. As described earlier, a user may be restricted to terminals in certain physical locations or during certain hours. Another characteristic might be pattern of access. A user who sought access to files for which there was no justifiable reason might not be authentic. After a system detects such an access violation attempt, the system might disconnect the user and suspend access until a security administrator cleared the matter. Therefore, a penetrator who gets into the system as Jones has to continue to act like Jones in order to remain on the system.

Authentication is a very important matter for an operating system, because accurate identification of users is the key to individual access rights. Most operating systems and computing system administrators have applied reasonable but stringent security measures to lock out illegal users before they can access system resources.

6.6 Summary of Security for Users

This chapter has addressed four topics: memory protection, file protection, general object access control, and user authentication. Memory protection in a multiuser setting has evolved with advances in hardware and system design. Fences, base/bounds registers, tagged architecture, paging, and segmentation are all mechanisms designed both for addressing and for protection.

File protection schemes on general-purpose operating systems are often based on a three- or four-level format (for example, user–group–all). This format is reasonably straightforward to implement, but it restricts the granularity of access control to few levels.

Access control in general is addressed by the access control matrix, or access control lists organized on a per-object or per-user basis. Although very flexible, these mechanisms can be difficult to implement efficiently.

User authentication is a serious issue that becomes even more serious when unacquainted users seek to share facilities by means of computer networks. The traditional authentication device is the password. A plaintext password file presents a serious vulnerability for a computing system. These files are usually either heavily protected or encrypted. The more serious problem, however, is establishing administrative procedures that make users' passwords adequately secure. Additional protocols are needed to perform mutual authentication in an atmosphere of distrust.

This chapter concentrated on the user's side of protection: it presented protection mechanisms visible to and invoked by users of operating systems. Chapter 7 addresses security from the perspective of the operating system designer. It includes material on how the security features of an operating system are implemented, and why security considerations should be a part of the initial design of the operating system.

6.7   Bibliographic Notes

The survey article by Denning and Denning [DEN77] gives a good background on access control in operating systems, and the paper by Linden [LIN76] describes operating systems components that affect protection. Lampson [LAM71], Graham and Denning [GRA72], Popek [POP74a], and Saltzer [SAL74] and [SAL75] are good treatments of protection in operating systems.

Capability-based protection is described in Fabry [FAB74] and Wulf [WUL74]. Lampson and Sturgis [LAM76] and Karger [KAR84] discuss the subject in general.

Several other papers on different aspects of operating system design are noted in the bibliographic notes for Chapter 7.

6.8   Terms and Concepts

6.9   Exercises

1. Give an example of the use of physical separation for security in a computing environment.

2. Give an example of the use of temporal separation for security in a computing environment.

3. Give an example of an object whose security level may change during execution.

4. Respond to the allegation, "An operating system requires no protection for its executable code (in memory) because that code is a duplicate of code maintained on disk."

5. Explain how a fence register is used for relocation of a user's program.

6. Can any number of concurrent processes be protected from each other by just one pair of base/bounds registers?

7. The discussion of base/bounds registers implies that program code is execute-only, and data areas are read–write-only. Is this ever not the case? Explain your answer.

8. A design using tag bits presupposes that adjacent memory locations hold dissimilar things: a line of code, a piece of data, a line of code, two pieces of data, and so forth. Most programs do not look like that. How can tag bits be appropriate in a situation where programs have the more conventional arrangement of code and data?

9. What are some other levels of protection that users might want to apply to code or data, in addition to the common *read, write,* and *execute* permission?

10. If two users share access to a segment, they must do so by the same name. Must their protection rights to it be the same? Why or why not?

11. A problem with segmented and with paged address translation is I/O. Suppose a user wishes to read some data from an input device into memory. For efficiency during data transfer, often the actual memory address where the data is to be placed is provided to the I/O device. The real address is passed so that time-consuming address translation does not have to be performed during a very fast data transfer. What security problems does this approach bring?

12. A directory is also an object to which access should be controlled. Why is it *not* appropriate to allow a user to modify his or her own directory directly?

13. Why should the directory of one user not be generally accessible (for read-only access) to other users?

14. Describe each of the following four kinds of access control mechanisms in terms of (a) ease of determining authorized access during execution, (b) ease of adding access for a new subject, (c) ease of deleting access by a subject, and (d) ease of creating a new object to which all subjects by default have access.
    - per-subject access control list (that is, one list for each subject tells all the objects to which that subject has access)
    - per-object access control list (that is, one list for each object tells all the subjects who have access to that object)
    - access control matrix
    - capability

15. Suppose a per-subject access control list is used. Deleting an object in such a system is very inconvenient because all changes must be made to the control lists of all subjects who did have access to the object. Suggest an alternative, less costly means of handling deletion.

16. File access control relates largely to the secrecy dimension of security. What is the relationship between an access control matrix and the integrity of the objects to which access is being controlled?

17. One feature of a capability-based protection system is the ability of one process to transfer a copy of a capability to another process. Describe a situation in which one process should be able to transfer a capability to another.

18. Describe a mechanism by which an operating system can enforce *limited* transfer of capabilities. That is, process A might transfer a capability to process B, but A wants to prevent B from transferring the capability to any other processes.

    Your design should include description of the activities to be performed by A and B, as well as the activities performed by and the information maintained by the operating system.

19. List two disadvantages to using physical separation in a computing system. List two disadvantages to using temporal separation in a computing system.

20. Explain why asynchronous I/O activity is a problem with many memory protection schemes, including base/bounds and paging. Suggest a solution to the problem.

21. Suggest an efficient scheme for maintaining a per-user protection scheme. That is, the system maintains one directory per user, and that directory lists all the objects to which the user is allowed access. Your design should address the needs of a system with 1000 users, of whom no more than 20 are active at any time. Each user has an average of 200 permitted objects; there are 50,000 total objects in the system.

22. (a) If passwords are three uppercase alphabetic characters long, how long would it take to determine a particular password, assuming that testing an individual password requires 5 seconds.
    (b) Argue for a particular amount of time as the starting point for "secure." That is, argue that an attacker would use a brute force attack to determine a password if the attack took less than x amount of time.
    (c) If the cutoff between "insecure" and "secure" was x amount of time, how long would a secure password have to be? State and justify your assumptions regarding

the character set from which the password is selected and the amount of time required to test a single password.

23. Design a protocol by which two mutually suspicious parties can authenticate each other. Your protocol should be usable the first time these two parties try to authenticate each other.

24. A flaw in the protection system of many operating systems is argument passing. Often a common shared stack is used by all nested routines for arguments as well as the remainder of the context of each calling process.
    (a) Explain what vulnerabilities this flaw presents.
    (b) Explain how the flaw can be controlled. The shared stack is still to be used for passing arguments and storing context.

25. Outline the design of an authentication scheme that "learns." The authentication scheme would start with certain primitive information about a user, such as name and password. As the use of the computing system continued, the authentication system would gather such information as commonly used programming languages; dates, times, and lengths of computing sessions; and use of distinctive resources. The authentication challenges would become more individualized as the system learned more information about the user.

    Your design should include a list of many pieces of information about a user that the system could collect. It is permissible for the system to ask an authenticated user for certain additional information, such as favorite book, to use in subsequent challenges. Your design should also consider the problem of presenting and validating these challenges: does the would-be user answer a true-false or a multiple-choice question? Does the system interpret natural language prose?

7

Designing Trusted Operating Systems

In this chapter:

- *What makes an operating system secure? Or trusted?*
- *How are trusted systems designed, and which of those design principles carry over naturally to other program development tasks?*
- *How do we develop assurance of the correctness of a trusted operating system?*

Operating systems are the prime providers of security in computing systems. They support many programming capabilities, permit multiprogramming and sharing of resources, and enforce restrictions on program behavior. Because they have such power, operating systems are also targets for attack because breaking through the defenses of an operating system gives access to the secrets of computing systems.

In Chapter 6 we considered operating systems from the perspective of users: what primitive security services do general operating systems provide? We studied these four services:

- memory protection
- file protection
- general object protection
- access authentication

In this chapter we take the position of a designer of a trusted operating system: what components of a trusted operating system provide security services, and how are these components designed? The first four sections of this chapter address four major underpinnings of a trusted operating system:

- *Policy.* The security requirements are a set of well-defined, consistent, and implementable rules that have been clearly and unambiguously expressed. In this way, the produced system meets the user's expectations. We begin this chapter by studying some security policies for trusted operating systems.

- *Model.* Before beginning to create a trusted operating system, the designer must have confidence that the proposed system will meet its requirements. The designer constructs a model of the environment to be secured and studies different ways of enforcing that security. In the second part of this chapter we consider several different models for operating system security. The model is actually a representation of the policy that the operating system will enforce.

- *Design.* After having selected a model of security, the designer must choose a means to implement that model. The design covers both what the trusted operating system is and how it is to be constructed. The third major section of this chapter addresses choices that can be made during development of a trusted operating system.

- *Trust.* Because the operating system bears such a central role in enforcing security, we want some basis for believing that it will meet our expectations. Trust is based on two aspects: *features* (the operating system has all the necessary functionality needed to enforce the expected security policy) and *assurance* (the operating system has been implemented in such a way that we have confidence it will enforce the security policy). In the fourth part of this chapter we explore what makes a particular design or implementation worthy of trust.

Finally, we look at some examples. Several trusted operating systems have been written, and more are under development. Some secure systems were originally designed for security; in others, security features were added to existing operating systems. The fifth part of this chapter presents examples of both of these ways to produce a secure operating system.

7.1   What Is a Trusted System?

Before we begin to examine these parts in detail, however, we should develop a common understanding of important terms. What would it take to consider something secure? The word *secure* is binary: something either is or is not secure. If it is secure, it should withstand all attacks, today, tomorrow, and a century from now. And if I sell you a secure lock, for example, it is my assertion that it is secure; you either accept my assertion (and buy the lock) or reject it (and not buy). Let's move from *secure* to another, similar adjective: *good*. If I am selling a "good" used car, you are less interested in my thinking it good ("I really did enjoy driving that car; it was a good one") than you are in a fair appraisal of its condition and being able to judge for yourself that it meets your needs.

For reasons such as the ones in the previous paragraph, security professionals speak of *trusted* rather than *secure* operating systems, connoting ones that meet their intended security requirements, are of high enough quality, and justify confidence in their quality. Trust is a quality of the receiver, not of the giver. I would not say my used car is trusted; you trust my description, your evaluation, or the opinion of a friend or a mechanic. But in the end, the responsibility is yours to develop the level of trust you require.

Also there can be degrees of trust: you trust certain friends with deep secrets, but others you trust only to give you the correct time of day. You develop trust based on evidence and experience: banks increase their trust in borrowers as the borrowers repay loans as expected, so that borrowers with good trust (credit) records can borrow larger amounts. Finally, trust is earned, not claimed or conferred. The comparison in Table 7-1 highlights some of these distinctions.

Table 7-1   Qualities of Security and Trustedness

Secure	Trusted
• *Either–or:* Something either is or is not secure	• *Graded:* There are degrees of "trustedness"
• Property of *presenter*	• Property of *receiver*
• *Asserted:* based on product characteristics	• *Judged:* based on evidence and analysis
• *Absolute:* not qualified as to how, where, when, or by whom used	• *Relative:* viewed in context of use
• A *goal*	• A *characteristic*

You will see the adjective *trusted* many times in this chapter, as in *trusted process* (a process that can affect system security; a process whose incorrect or malicious execution is capable of violating system security policy), *trusted product* (an evaluated and approved product), *trusted software* (the software portion of a system that can be relied on to enforce security policy), *trusted computing base* (the set of all protection mechanisms in a computing system, including hardware, firmware, and software, that together enforce a unified security policy over a product or system), or *trusted system* (a system that employs sufficient hardware and software integrity measures to allow its use for processing sensitive information). These definitions are paraphrased from [NIS91b]. Common to these definitions you can see the concepts of

- enforcement of security policy
- sufficient measures and mechanisms
- evaluation

In this chapter we study trusted operating systems, and examine closely what makes them trustworthy.

7.2   Security Policies

In order to know that an operating system maintains the security we expect, we have to be able to state what that security is. A **policy** is a statement of the security we expect the system to enforce. An operating system (or any other piece of a trusted system) can be trusted only in relation to a security policy, that is, to the security needs the system is expected to satisfy.

We begin by studying the military security policy because it has been the basis of much of the work in development of trusted operating systems, and because it is fairly easy to state precisely. Then we move to security policies that commercial establishments might adopt.

Military Security Policy

The military security policy is based on protecting classified information. Each piece of information is ranked at a particular sensitivity level, such as *unclassified*, *restricted*, *confidential*, *secret*, or *top secret*. We can denote the sensitivity of an object O by $rank_O$. In the rest of this chapter we assume these five sensitivity levels. The ranks are shown in increasing order of sensitivity, as in Figure 7-1.

Information access is limited by the **need-to-know** rule: access to sensitive data is allowed only to subjects who need to know that data to perform their jobs. Each piece of

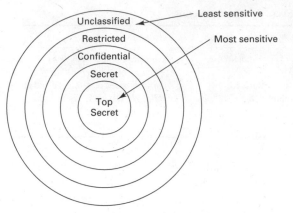

Figure 7-1   Hierarchy of Sensitivities

classified information may be associated with one or more projects, called **compartments**, describing the subject matter of the information. Compartments help to enforce need-to-know restrictions so that people can obtain access only to information that is relevant to their jobs. A compartment may cover information at only one sensitivity level, or it may include information of more than one sensitivity level. The relationship between compartments and sensitivity levels is shown in Figure 7-2.

Examples of compartment names might be *snowshoe*, *crypto*, and *Sweden*. A single piece of information is coded with zero, one, two, or more compartments, depending on the categories to which it relates. The association of information and compartments is shown in Figure 7-3. For example, one piece of information may be a list of publications on cryptography, while another may describe development of snowshoes in Sweden. The compartment of this first piece of information is {*crypto*}; the second is {*snowshoe, Sweden*}.

The combination ⟨*rank*; *compartments*⟩ is called the **class** or **classification** of a piece of information.

A person seeking access to sensitive information must be cleared. A **clearance** is an indication that a person is trusted to access information up to a certain level of sensitivity, and that the person needs to know certain categories of sensitive information. The clearance of a subject is a combination ⟨*rank*; *compartments*⟩. This combination has the same form as the classification of a piece of information.

Now we introduce a relation ≤, called **dominance**, on sensitive objects and subjects. For a subject *s* and an object *o*,

$$s \leq o \quad \text{if and only if}$$
$$rank_s \leq rank_o \quad \text{and}$$
$$compartments_s \subseteq compartments_o$$

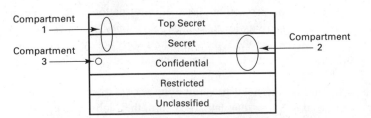

Figure 7-2   **Compartments and Sensitivity Levels**

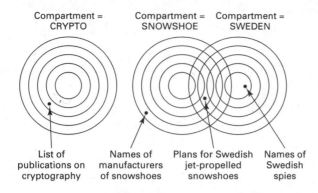

Figure 7-3   **Association of Information and Compartments**

We say that *o* **dominates** *s* (or *s* **is dominated by** *o*) if *s* ≤ *o*; the relation ≥ is defined correspondingly. Dominance is used to limit the sensitivity and content of information a subject can access. A subject can read an object only if (a) the clearance level of the subject is *at least as high* as that of the information, and (b) the subject has a need to know about *all* compartments for which the information is classified; these conditions are equivalent to saying that the subject dominates the object.

Information classified ⟨*secret*; {*Sweden*}⟩ could be read by someone cleared for access to ⟨*top secret*; {*Sweden*}⟩ or ⟨*secret*; {*Sweden, crypto*}⟩, but not by someone with a ⟨*top secret*; {*crypto*}⟩ clearance or someone cleared for ⟨*confidential*; {*Sweden*}⟩.

Military security enforces both sensitivity requirements and need-to-know requirements. Sensitivity requirements are known as **hierarchical** requirements; need to know restrictions are **nonhierarchical**. This model is appropriate for a setting in which access is rigidly controlled by a central authority. Someone, often called a security officer, controls clearances and classifications, which are not generally up to individuals to alter.

Commercial Security Policies

The commercial world is less rigidly and less hierarchically structured. Still, we find many of the same concepts.

A large organization, such as a corporation or a university, may be broken into divisions or departments, with each of those responsible for a number of disjoint projects. There are also some corporate-level responsibilities, such as accounting and personnel files. Data items may have different degrees of sensitivity, such as *public*, *proprietary*, or *internal*; the names vary between organizations, and so there is no universal hierarchy of degrees. Let us assume that *public* is less sensitive than *proprietary*, which is less sensitive than *internal*. Projects and departments tend to be fairly well-separated, with some overlap as people work on two or more projects. Corporate-level responsibilities tend to overlay projects and departments, as people throughout the corporation may have need for accounting or personnel data. However, even corporate data may have degrees of sensitivity. There also tends to be more sensitivity due to projects: people on project *old-standby* have no need to know about project *new-product*, although people on *new-product* may have access to all data on *old-standby*. Thus, a commercial layout of data might look like Figure 7-4.

Two significant differences exist between commercial and military information security. First, outside the military, there is no formalized notion of clearances: a person is not

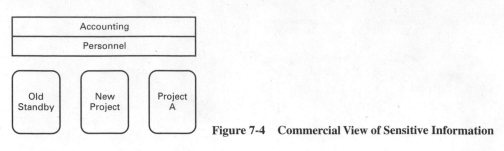

Figure 7-4   Commercial View of Sensitive Information

approved for project MARS access by a central security officer nor, typically, is an employee conferred a different degree of trust by being allowed access to *internal* data. Second, because there is no formal concept of a clearance, the rules for allowing access are less regularized: if a senior manager decides that a person needs access to a piece of MARS *internal* data, the manager will instruct someone to allow the access, either one-time or continuing. Thus, there is no *dominance* function for most commercial information access because there is no formal concept of a commercial clearance.

So far, we have considered only read access, which addresses *confidentiality* in security, and this is true for much of the existing work in computer security. Obviously, however, integrity and availability are at least as important as confidentiality in many instances. Policies for integrity and availability are significantly less well-formulated than those for confidentiality, for both military and commercial needs. We will see some instances of integrity in the next two examples of policies.

Clark–Wilson Commercial Security Policy

In many commercial applications, integrity is at least as important as confidentiality. The correctness of accounting records, the accuracy of legal work, and the proper timing of medical treatments are the essence of these fields. Clark and Wilson [CLA87] proposed a policy for what they call *well-formed transactions,* which they assert are as important in their field as is confidentiality in a military realm.

Consider a company that orders and pays for materials. A representation of this process might be

1. A purchasing clerk creates an order for a supply, sending copies of the order to both the supplier and the receiving department.
2. The supplier ships the goods, which arrive at the receiving department. A receiving clerk checks the delivery, ensures that the correct quantity of the right item has been received, and signs a delivery form. The delivery form and the original order go to the accounting department.
3. The supplier sends an invoice to the accounting department. An accounting clerk compares the invoice with the original order (as to price and other terms) and the delivery form (as to quantity and item) and issues a check to the supplier.

The sequencing of these activities is important: a receiving clerk will not sign a delivery form without already having received a matching order (because suppliers should not be allowed to ship any quantities of any items they want and be paid), and an accounting clerk will not issue a check without already having received a matching order and delivery form (because suppliers should not be paid for goods not ordered or received). Furthermore, in most cases, both the order and the delivery form must be signed by an authorized individual. Performing the steps in order, performing exactly the steps listed, and authenticating the individuals who perform the steps constitute a **well-formed transaction**. The goal of the Clark–Wilson policy is to maintain consistency between the internal data and its external (users') expectations of that data.

Clark and Wilson present their policy in terms of **constrained data items**, which are processed by **transformation procedures**. A transformation procedure is like a monitor in that it performs only particular operations on specific kinds of data items, and these data items are manipulated only by transformation procedures. The transformation procedures maintain the integrity of the data items by validating the processing to be performed. Clark and Wilson propose defining the policy in terms of **access triples**: $\langle userID, TP_i, \{CDI_j, CDI_k, \ldots\}\rangle$, combining a transformation procedure, one or more constrained data items, and the identification of a user who is authorized to operate on those data items by means of the transaction procedure.

Separation of Duty

A second commercial security policy that has been studied involves separation of responsibility. Clark and Wilson [CLA87] raised this issue in their analysis of commercial security requirements, and Lee [LEE89] and Nash and Poland [NAS90] added to the concept.

In the previous example in a small company, several people might be authorized to issue orders, receive goods, and write checks. However, you would not want the same person issuing the order, receiving the goods, and writing the check, because there is the potential for abuse. Therefore, you might want a policy that specifies that three separate people issue the order, receive the goods, and write the check, even though any of the three might be authorized to do any of these tasks. This required division of responsibilities is called **separation of duty**.

Separation of duty is commonly accomplished manually with dual signatures. Clark and Wilson triples are "stateless," meaning that a triple does not have a context of prior operations; triples are incapable of passing control information to other triples. Thus if one person is authorized to perform operations TP_1 and TP_2, the Clark and Wilson triples cannot prevent the same person from performing both TP_1 and TP_2 on a given data item. However, it is quite easy to implement distinctness if it is stated as a policy requirement.

Chinese Wall Security Policy

Brewer and Nash [BRE89] defined a security policy that reflects certain commercial needs for information access protection. Their base is people in legal, medical, investment, or accounting firms who might be subject to conflict of interest. Basically, a conflict of interest exists when one person can obtain sensitive information on competing companies.

Their policy starts by building three levels of abstraction.

- *Objects.* At the lowest level are elementary objects, such as files. Each file contains information concerning only one company.
- *Company groups.* At the next level, all objects concerning each company are grouped together.
- *Conflict classes.* At the highest level, all groups of objects for competing companies are clustered.

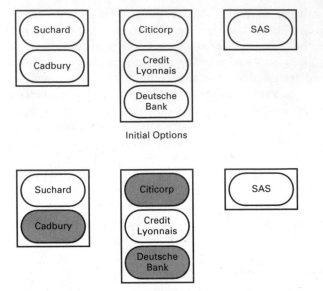

Figure 7-5   Chinese Wall Security Policy

Each object thus belongs to a unique company group, and each company group is contained in a unique conflict class. A conflict class may contain one or more company groups. As an example, one might have data on chocolate companies Suchard and Cadbury; on banks Citicorp, DeutscheBank, and Credit Lyonnais; and on airline SAS. There would be six company groups (one for each company) and three conflict classes: {Suchard, Cadbury}, {Citicorp, DeutscheBank, Credit Lyonnais}, and {SAS}.

The access control policy is rather simple. A person can access any information as long as the person has never accessed information from a different company in the same conflict class. That is, access is allowed if either the object requested is in the same company group as an object that has previously been accessed, or the object requested belongs to a conflict class that has never before been accessed. In the previous example, initially you can access any objects. Suppose you read from a file on Suchard. A subsequent request for access to any bank or to SAS would be granted, but a request to access Cadbury files would be denied. If you next access SAS, this does not affect future accesses. But if you then access a file on Credit Lyonnais, you will then be blocked from future accesses to DeutscheBank or Citicorp. From that point on, as shown in Figure 7-5, you can access objects only on Suchard, SAS, Credit Lyonnais, or for a new conflict class.

The Chinese Wall policy is a commercially inspired confidentiality policy, whereas most commercial policies focus on integrity. It is also interesting because access permissions change dynamically: as a subject accesses some objects, other objects that would previously have been accessible are now denied.

7.3 Models of Security

Models are often used, both in security and in other areas, to describe, study, or analyze a particular case. In security, models are used to

- test a particular policy for completeness and consistency
- document a policy
- help conceptualize and design an implementation
- check whether an implementation meets its requirements

We assume that some access control policy dictates whether a given user can access a particular object. We also assume that this policy is established outside of any model. That is, a policy decision determines whether a specific user should have access to a specific object; the model is only a mechanism that shows that policy. We begin the study of models by considering simple ways to control access by one user.

Multilevel Security

We want to build a model that represents a range of sensitivities and that can reflect the need to separate subjects rigorously from objects to which they should not have access. As an example of a range of sensitive data, consider an election. The names of the candidates are probably not sensitive. If the results have not yet been released, the name of the winner is somewhat sensitive. If one candidate received an embarrassingly low number of votes, the vote count may be more sensitive. Finally, the way any individual voted is extremely sensitive. Users, too, are ranked by the degree of sensitivity of information to which they can have access.

For obvious reasons, the military has developed extensive procedures for securing information. A generalization of the military model of information security has also been adopted as a model of data security within an operating system. Bell and La Padula [BEL73] were first to describe the properties of the military model in mathematical notation, and Denning [DEN76a] first formalized the structure of this model. The generalized model is called the **lattice model** of security because its elements form a mathematical structure called a lattice. In this section we describe the military example and then use it to explain the lattice model.

Lattice Model of Access Security

The military security model is a representative of a more general scheme, called a lattice. A **lattice** is a mathematical structure of elements under a relational operator. The elements of a lattice are ordered under a partial ordering $\leq$. (We also use the notation $\geq$ to denote this same relation: $b \geq a$ means the same thing as $a \leq b$.) A partial ordering is a relation $\leq$ that is transitive and antisymmetric, meaning that for every three elements a, b, and c,

$$\text{transitive: if } a \leq b \text{ and } b \leq c \text{ then } a \leq c$$

and

$$\text{antisymmetric: if } a \leq b \text{ and } b \leq a \text{ then } a = b$$

In a lattice, not every pair of elements needs to be comparable; that is, there may be elements a and b for which neither $a \leq b$ nor $b \leq a$. However, every pair of elements possesses an **upper bound**, an element at least as large as ($\geq$) both a and b. Even though a and b may be incomparable under $\leq$, in a lattice there is an upper bound element u such that

$a \leq u$ and $b \leq u$. Furthermore, in a lattice, every pair of elements possesses a **lower bound**, an element l dominated by both a and b; that is, $l \leq a$ and $l \leq b$.

For example, in the lattice in Figure 7-6, G dominates all other elements; F dominates B, C, D, H, and J; and C and D dominate H and J. But B and H are noncomparable.

Notice that the military security model is a lattice. The relation $\leq$ defined in the military model is the relation for the lattice. The relation $\leq$ is transitive and antisymmetric. The largest element of the lattice is the classification ⟨*top secret*; *all compartments*⟩ and the smallest element is ⟨*unclassified*; *no compartments*⟩; these two elements respectively dominate and are dominated by all elements. Therefore, the military model is a lattice.

However, many other structures are lattices. For example, a commercial security policy may contain data sensitivities such as *public*, *proprietary*, and *internal*, with the natural ordering that *public* data is less sensitive than *proprietary*, which is less sensitive than *internal*. These three levels also form a lattice. A lattice is a fairly general structure; lattices appear in most common interpretations of the relation "less than," such as "subset of," "reports to [for employees]," or "descendant of."

Because a lattice is a natural representation of increasing degrees, security specialists have chosen to base security systems on lattices. A security system designed to implement lattice models of security can be used in a military environment. However, it can also be used in commercial environments with other labels for the security degrees. Thus, the lattice representation of sensitivity levels is applicable to many different kinds of computing situations.

Bell–La Padula Confidentiality Model

The Bell and La Padula model [BEL73] is a formal description of the allowable paths of information flow in a secure system. The goal of the model is to identify allowable communication where it is important to maintain secrecy. The model has been used to define the security requirements for systems concurrently handling data at different sensitivity levels. This model is a formalization of the military security policy.

We are interested in secure information flows because they describe acceptable connections between subjects and objects of different levels of sensitivity. One purpose of analysis of security levels is to construct systems that can perform concurrent computation on data of two sensitivity levels. For example, one machine might be used for top secret and confidential data at the same time. The programs processing top secret data would be prevented from leaking top secret data to the confidential data, and the confidential users would be prevented from accessing the top secret data. The Bell–La Padula model is used as the basis for the design of systems that handle data of multiple sensitivities.

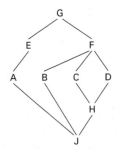

Figure 7-6   Sample Lattice

Consider a security system with the following properties. The system covers a set of subjects S and a set of objects O. Each subject s in S and each object o in O has a fixed security class $C(s)$ and $C(o)$ (denoting clearance and classification level). The security classes are ordered by a relation $\leq$. (Note: The classes may form a lattice, although the Bell–La Padula model can apply to even less restricted cases.)

Two properties characterize the secure flow of information.

> **Simple Security Property.** A subject s may have *read* access to an object o only if $C(o) \leq C(s)$.

In the military model, this property says that the security class (clearance) of a someone receiving a piece of information must be at least as high as the class (classification) of the information.

> **∗-Property.** A subject s who has *read* access to an object o may have *write* access to an object p only if $C(o) \leq C(p)$.

In the military model, this property says that the contents of a sensitive object can be written only to objects at least as high.

In the military model, one interpretation of the *∗-property* is that a person obtaining information at one level may pass that information along only to people at levels no lower than the level of the information. The ∗-property is used to prevent **write-down**, which occurs when a subject with access to high-level data transfers that data by writing it to a low-level object.

Literally, the ∗-property requires that a person receiving information at one level not talk with people cleared at levels lower than the level of the information—not even about the weather! This example points out that this property is stronger than necessary to ensure security; the same is also true in computing systems.

The implications of these two properties are shown in Figure 7-7. The classifications of subjects (represented by squares) and objects (represented by circles) are indicated by

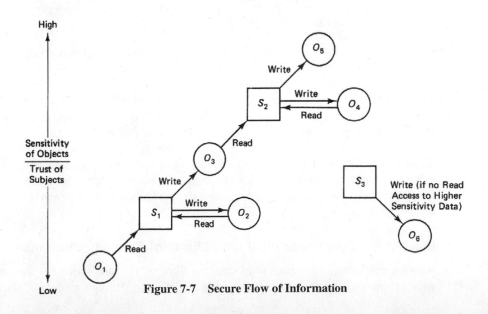

Figure 7-7   Secure Flow of Information

their positions: as the classification of an item increases, it is shown higher in the figure. The flow of information is generally horizontal (to and from the same level) and upward (from lower levels to higher). A downward flow is acceptable only if the highly cleared subject does not pass any high-sensitivity data to the lower-sensitivity object.

Downward flow of information is difficult in the case of computers because a computer program cannot readily distinguish between having read a piece of information and having read a piece of information that influenced what was later written. (McLean [MCL90b], in work related to Goguen and Meseguer [GOG82], presents an interesting counter to the ∗-property of Bell and La Padula with noninterference, which can be loosely described as tracing the *effects* of inputs on outputs. If we can trace all output effects, we can determine conclusively whether a particular low-level output was "contaminated" with high-level input.)

The models described so far have been successfully used in the design of secure operating systems. The Bell–La Padula model is central to the U.S. Department of Defense evaluation criteria, which will be described later in this chapter.

Biba Integrity Model

The Bell–La Padula model applies only to secrecy of information: the model identifies paths that could lead to inappropriate *disclosure* of information. However, the integrity of data is important, too. Biba [BIB77] constructed a model for preventing inappropriate modification of data.

The Biba model is the counterpart (dual) of the Bell–La Padula model. Biba defines integrity levels, which are analogous to the sensitivity levels of the Bell–La Padula model. Subjects and objects are ordered by an integrity classification scheme, denoted $I(s)$ and $I(o)$. The properties are

> **Simple Integrity Property.** Subject s can modify (have *write* access to) object o only if $I(s) \geq I(o)$

> **Integrity ∗-Property.** If subject s has *read* access to object o with integrity level $I(o)$, s can have write access to object p only if $I(o) \geq I(p)$

These two rules cover untrustworthy information in a natural way. Suppose someone is known to be untruthful. If that person can create or modify a document, people should distrust the truth of the statements in the document. Thus, an untrusted subject who has write access to an object reduces the integrity of that object. Similarly, people are rightfully skeptical of a report based on unsound evidence. The low integrity of a source object implies low integrity for any object based on the source object.

This model addresses the integrity issue that the Bell–La Padula model ignores, but in doing so, the Biba model ignores secrecy. Secrecy-based security systems have been much more fully studied than integrity-based systems. The current trend is to join secrecy and integrity concerns in security systems, although no widely accepted formal models achieve this compromise.

Models Proving Theoretical Limitations of Security Systems

Now we consider another class of models that allow us to address formally the question of what properties a security system can achieve. This new class of models is based on the general theory of computability. The results from these models show the limitations of abstract security systems.

Graham–Denning Model

Lampson [LAM71] and Graham and Denning [GRA72] introduced the concept of a formal system of protection rules. Graham and Denning constructed a model having generic protection properties. This model forms the basis for two later models of security systems.

The Graham–Denning model operates on a set of subjects S, a set of objects O, a set of rights R, and an access control matrix A. The matrix has one row for each subject and one column for each subject and each object. The rights of a subject on another subject or an object are shown by the contents of an element of the matrix. For each object, one subject designated the "owner" has special rights; for each subject, another subject designated the "controller" has special rights.

In the Graham–Denning model, there are eight primitive protection rights. These rights are phrased as commands that can be issued by subjects, with effects on other subjects or objects.

- *Create object* allows the commanding subject to introduce a new object into the system.
- *Create subject, delete object,* and *delete subject* have the similar effect of creating or destroying a subject or object.
- *Read access right* allows a subject to determine the current access rights of a subject to an object.
- *Grant access right* allows the *owner* of an object to convey any access rights for an object to another subject.
- *Delete access right* allows a subject to delete a right of another subject for an object, provided that the deleting subject either is the owner of the object or controls the subject from which access should be deleted.
- *Transfer access right* allows a subject to transfer one of its rights for an object to another subject. Each right can be transferable or nontransferable. If a subject receives a transferable right, the subject can then transfer that right (either transferable or not) to other subjects. If a subject receives a nontransferable right, it can use the right, but cannot transfer that right to other subjects.

These rules are shown in Table 7-2 (taken from [GRA72]), which shows prerequisite conditions for the execution of each command and its effect. The access control matrix is $A[s,o]$, where s is a subject and o is an object. The subject executing each command is denoted x. A transferable right is denoted $r*$; a nontransferable right is written r.

This set of rules provides the properties necessary to model access control mechanisms of a protection system. For example, this mechanism can represent a reference monitor, or a system of sharing between two untrustworthy, mutually suspicious subsystems.

Harrison–Ruzzo–Ullman Result

Harrison, Ruzzo, and Ullman [HAR76] proposed a variation on the Graham–Denning model. This revised model answered several questions concerning what protection systems can determine.

Table 7-2   Protection System Commands

Command	Pre-Condition	Effect
Create object o	—	Add column for o in A; place *owner* in A[x,o]
Create subject s	—	Add row for s in A; place *control* in A[x,o]
Delete object o	*Owner* in A[x,o]	Delete column o
Delete subject s	*Control* in A[x,s]	Delete row s
Read access right of s on o	*Control* in A[x,s] or *owner* in A[x,o]	Copy A[s,o] to x
Delete access right r of s on o	*Control* in A[x,s] or *owner* in A[x,o]	Remove r from A[s,o]
Grant access right r to s on o	*Owner* in A[x,o]	Add r to A[s,o]
Transfer access right r or $r*$ to s on o	$r*$ in A[x,o]	Add r or $r*$ to A[s,o]

The Harrison–Ruzzo–Ullman model (called the HRU model) is very similar to the Graham–Denning model. The model is based on **commands**, where each command involves **conditions** and **primitive operations**.

The structure of a command is as follows.

$$
\begin{aligned}
&\textbf{command } name(o_1, o_2, \ldots, o_k) \\
&\quad\textbf{if} \qquad r_1 \text{ in A}[s_1, o_1] \text{ and} \\
&\qquad\qquad r_2 \text{ in A}[s_2, o_2] \text{ and} \\
&\qquad\qquad \ldots \\
&\qquad\qquad r_m \text{ in A}[s_m, o_m] \\
&\quad\textbf{then} \\
&\qquad\qquad op_1 \\
&\qquad\qquad op_2 \\
&\qquad\qquad \ldots \\
&\qquad\qquad op_n \\
&\textbf{end}
\end{aligned}
$$

This command has a structure like a procedure, with parameters o_1 through o_k. The notation of the HRU model is slightly different from the Graham–Denning model: in HRU every subject is an object, too. Thus, the columns of the access control matrix are all the subjects *and* all the objects that are not subjects. For this reason, all the parameters of a command are labeled o, although they could be either subjects or nonsubject objects. Each r is a generic right, as in the Graham–Denning model. Each op is a primitive operation, defined in the following list. The access matrix is shown in Figure 7-8.

The primitive operations op, which are similar to those of the Graham–Denning model, are

- create subject s
- create object o
- destroy subject s
- destroy object o
- enter right r into A[s,o]
- delete right r from A[s,o]

Objects

Subjects	S_1	S_2	S_3	O_1	O_2	O_3
S_1	Control	Own Suspend Resume		Own	Own	Read Propagate
S_2		Control			Extend	Own
S_3			Control	Read, Write	Write	Read
. . .						

Figure 7-8   Access Matrix in HRU Model

The interpretations of these operations are what their names imply. A **protection system** is a set of subjects, objects, rights, and commands.

Harrison et al. demonstrate that these operations are adequate to model several examples of protection systems, including the Unix protection mechanism, and an *indirect* access mode introduced by Graham and Denning [GRA72]. Thus, like the Graham–Denning model, the HRU model can represent "reasonable" interpretations of protection.

Two important results derived by Harrison et al. have major implications for designers of protection systems. The proofs of these results are omitted, although the methods of proof are outlined here.

The first result applies when commands are restricted to contain just one operation each. In this case, it is possible to decide whether a given protection system, started with a given initial configuration of the access control matrix, can allow a given user a given access right to a given object. In other words, suppose one wants to know whether a particular protection system can allow a subject s to obtain access right r to object o. (Harrison et al. say that such a system **leaks** the access right.)

As long as each command consists of only a single operation, there is an algorithm that can answer this question. The proof involves analysis of the minimum number of commands by which a right can be conferred. Certain operations, such as *delete* and *destroy,* have no effect on expanding access rights, so they can be ignored. The shortest sequence of commands by which such a right can be conferred contains at most $m = |r| * (|s| + 1) * (|o| + 1) + 1$ commands, where $|r|$ is the number of rights, $|s|$ is the number of subjects, and $|o|$ is the number of objects in the protection system. The decision is made by testing all sequences of commands of length up to m. (There are 2^{km} such sequences, for some constant k.)

Thus, the first result from HRU indicates that

> In the modeled system, where commands are restricted to a single operation each, it *is* possible to decide whether a given subject can ever obtain a particular right to an object.

Therefore, it is decidable whether a low-level subject can ever obtain *read* access to a high-level object, for example. The second result is less encouraging.

As a second result, Harrison et al. show that

> If commands are *not* restricted to one operation each, it is *not* always decidable whether a given protection system can confer a given right.

This result indicates that one cannot determine in general whether a subject can obtain a particular right to an object.

The proof uses commands of an HRU protection system to represent operations of a formal system called a Turing machine. Turing machines are general models of computing devices; any conventional computing system can be modeled with a Turing machine. Several decidable results about Turing machines are well-known, including one that shows it is impossible to develop a general procedure to determine whether a given Turing machine will halt when performing a given computation. The proof of the second HRU result follows by showing that a decision procedure for protection systems would also solve the halting problem for Turing machines, which is known to be unsolvable.

As an example, consider protection in Unix. The Unix protection scheme is relatively simple: protection systems for other systems are more complex. Because the Unix protection scheme requires more than one operation per command in the HRU model, there can be no general procedure to determine whether a certain access right can be given to a subject.

The HRU result is bleak. In fact, the HRU result can be extended: there may be an algorithm to decide the access right question for a particular collection of protection systems, but even an infinite number of algorithms *cannot* decide the access right question for all protection systems. However, the negative results do not say that no decision process exists for any protection system. In fact, for certain specific protection systems, it is decidable whether a given access right can be conferred. Therefore, the HRU results are negative for general procedures, but do not rule out the possibility of making decisions about given protection systems.

Take–Grant Systems

One final model of a protection system is the **take–grant** system, introduced by Jones [JON78a] and expanded by Lipton and Snyder [LIP77], [SNY81].

In this model, there are only four primitive operations: create, revoke, take, and grant. Create and revoke are similar to operations from the Graham–Denning and HRU models; take and grant are new types of operations. These operations are presented most naturally through the use of graphs.

As in other systems, let S be a set of subjects and O be a set of objects; objects can be either active (subjects) or passive (nonsubject objects). Let R be a set of rights. Each subject or object is denoted by a node of a graph; the rights of a particular subject to a particular object are denoted by a labeled directed edge from the subject to the object. Figure 7-9 shows examples of subjects, objects, and rights.

Let s be the subject performing each of the operations. The four operations are defined as follows. The effects of these operations are shown in Figure 7-10.

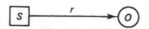

Figure 7-9   Subjects, Objects, and Rights

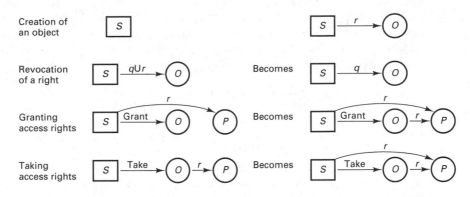

Figure 7-10   Creating an Object; Revoking, Granting, and Taking Access Rights

- *Create(o,r)*. A new node with label *o* is added to the graph. From *s* to *o* there is a directed edge with label *r*, denoting the rights of *s* on *o*.

- *Revoke(o,r)*. The rights *r* are revoked from *s* on *o*. The edge from *s* to *o* was labeled *q* ∪ *r*; the label is replaced by *q*. Informally, *s* can revoke its rights to do *r* on *o*.

- *Grant(o,p,r)*. Subject *s* grants to *o* access rights *r* on *p*. A specific right is *grant*. Subject *s* can grant to *o* access rights *r* on *p* only if *s* has *grant* right on *o*, and *s* has *r* rights on *p*. Informally, *s* can grant (share) any of its rights with *o*, as long as *s* has the right to grant privileges to *o*. An edge from *o* to *p* is added, with label *r*.

- *Take(o,p,r)*. Subject *s* takes from *o* access rights *r* on *p*. A specific right is *take*. Subject *s* can take from *o* access rights *r* on *p* only if *s* has *take* right on *o*, and *o* has *r* rights on *p*. Informally, *s* can take any rights *o* has, as long as *s* has the right to take privileges from *o*. An edge from *s* to *p* is added with label *r*.

This set of operations is even shorter than the operations of either of the two previous models. However, *take* and *grant* are more complex rights.

Snyder shows that in this system certain protection questions are decidable; furthermore, they are decidable in reasonable (less than exponential) time. In [SNY81], Snyder considers two questions: first, can we decide whether a given subject can share an object with another subject, and second, can we decide whether a given subject can steal access to an object from another subject? Clearly these are important questions to answer about a protection system, for they show whether the access control mechanisms are secure against unauthorized disclosure.

The answer to Synder's first question is "yes": sharing can occur only if several other subjects together have the desired access to the object, and the first subject is connected to each of the group of other subjects by a path of edges having a particular form. There is an algorithm to detect sharability that runs in time proportional to the size of the graph of the particular case.

Snyder also answers the second question affirmatively, in a situation heavily dependent on the ability to share. Thus, an algorithm can decide whether access can be stolen by direct appeal to the algorithm to decide sharability.

Landwehr [LAN81] points out that the take–grant model assumes the worst about users: if a user *can* grant access rights, the model assumes that the user will. Suppose a user can create a file and grant access to it to everyone. In that situation, every user could allow access to every object by every other user. This worst-case assumption limits the applicability of the model to situations of controlled sharing of information. In general, however, the take–grant model is useful because it identifies conditions under which a user can obtain access to an object.

Summary of Models of Protection Systems

There are two purposes to studying models of computer security. First, models are important in determining the policies a secure system should enforce. For example, the Bell–La Padula and Biba models identify specific conditions to enforce in order to ensure secrecy or integrity. Second, the study of abstract models can lead to an understanding of the properties of protection systems. For example, the HRU model states certain characteristics that can or cannot be decided by an arbitrary protection system. These characteristics are important for designers of protection systems to know.

In the next section we study the design of secure operating systems. These designs follow from the policies established after analyzing models of protection systems.

7.4   Design of Trusted Operating Systems

Operating systems by themselves are very difficult to design. They handle many duties, are subject to interruptions and context switches, and must minimize overhead so as not to slow user computations. Adding the responsibility for security enforcement to the operating system substantially increases the difficulty of designing an operating system.

In this section we study the design of operating systems for a high degree of security. First we examine the basic design of a standard multipurpose operating system. Then we consider isolation, through which one operating system supports both sharing and separation of user domains. We look at the kernel design of an operating system, an effective way to provide security. There are actually two different interpretations of the kernel, both of which are studied. Finally, we consider layered or ring structured designs.

Trusted System Design Elements

Security considerations pervade the design and structure of operating systems, which implies two things about the design of secure operating systems. First, security must be considered in every aspect of the design of operating systems. When a section has been designed, it must be checked for the degree of security it enforces or provides. Second, because security appears throughout an operating system, it is hard to retrofit security features to an operating system designed with no or inadequate security. Security must be part of the initial design of a trusted operating system and carried throughout the design and implementation.

Saltzer [SAL74] and Saltzer and Schroeder [SAL75] list the following principles of the design of secure protection systems:

- *Least privilege.* Each user and each program should operate using the fewest privileges possible. In this way, the damage from an inadvertent or malicious attack is minimized.
- *Economy of mechanism.* The design of the protection system should be small, simple, and straightforward. Such a protection system can be carefully analyzed, exhaustively tested, perhaps verified, and relied upon.

- *Open design.* The protection mechanism must not depend on the ignorance of potential attackers; the mechanism should be public, depending on secrecy of relatively few key items, such as a password table. An open design is also available for extensive public scrutiny, thereby providing independent confirmation of the design security.

- *Complete mediation.* Every access attempt must be checked. Both direct access attempts (requests) and attempts to circumvent the access checking mechanism should be considered, and the mechanism should be positioned so that it cannot be circumvented.

- *Permission-based.* The default condition should be denial of access. A conservative designer identifies the items that should be accessible, rather than those that should not.

- *Separation of privilege.* Ideally, access to objects should depend on more than one condition, such as user authentication plus a cryptographic key. In this way, someone who defeats one protection system will not have complete access.

- *Least common mechanism.* Shared objects provide potential channels for information flow. Systems employing physical or logical separation reduce the risk from sharing.

- *Easy to use.* If a mechanism is easy to use, it is unlikely to be avoided.

These design principles are as accurate now as they were when written. They have been used in the design and implementation of numerous trusted systems.

Security Features of Ordinary Operating Systems

As described in Chapter 6, a multiprogramming operating system performs several functions that relate to security. These are listed as follows:

- *Authentication of users.* The operating system must identify each user who requests access and ascertain that the user is actually who he or she purports to be. The most common authentication mechanism is password comparison.

- *Protection of memory.* Each user's program must run in a portion of memory protected against unauthorized accesses. The protection will certainly prevent outsiders' accesses, and it may also control a user's own access to restricted parts of the program space. Differential security, such as read, write, and execute, may be applied to parts of a user's memory space. Memory protection is usually performed by hardware mechanisms, such as paging or segmentation.

- *File and I/O device access control.* The operating system must protect user and system files from access by unauthorized users. Similarly, I/O device use must be protected. Data protection is usually achieved by table lookup, as with an access control matrix.

- *Allocation and access control to general objects.* General objects, such as constructs to permit concurrency and allow synchronization, must be provided to users. However, use of these objects must be controlled so that one user does not have a negative effect on other users. Again, table lookup is the common means by which this protection is provided.

- *Enforcement of sharing.* Resources should be made available to users as appropriate. Sharing brings about the need to guarantee integrity and consistency. Table lookup, combined with integrity controls such as monitors or transaction processors, is often used to support controlled sharing.

- *Guarantee of fair service.* All users expect CPU usage and other service to be provided so that no user is indefinitely starved from receiving service. Hardware clocks combine with scheduling disciplines to provide this fairness. Hardware facilities and data tables combine to provide this control.

- *Interprocess communication and synchronization.* Executing processes sometimes need to communicate with other processes or to synchronize their accesses to shared resources. Operating systems provide these services by acting as a bridge between processes, responding to process requests for asynchronous communication with other processes or synchronization. Interprocess communication is mediated by access control tables.

- *Protection of operating system protection data.* The operating system must maintain data by which it can enforce security. Obviously if this data is not protected against unauthorized access (read, modify, and delete), the operating system cannot provide enforcement. Various techniques, including encryption, hardware control, and isolation, support isolation of operating system protection data.

Figure 7-11 relates these security concerns to the more traditional functions of an operating system.

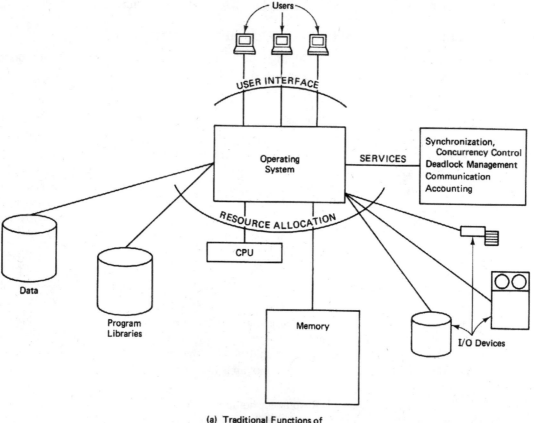

(a) Traditional Functions of Operating Systems

Figure 7-11a   Security Properties in Operating Systems

Security Features of Trusted Operating Systems

Trusted systems technology covers both **features** and **assurance**. The design of a trusted system is delicate, involving selection of an appropriate and consistent set of features together with an appropriate degree of assurance that the features have been assembled and implemented correctly. Next we consider prominent features of a trusted system.

The features of trusted operating systems include

- user identification and authentication
- mandatory access control
- discretionary access control
- object reuse protection
- complete mediation
- audit
- audit log reduction
- trusted path
- intrusion detection

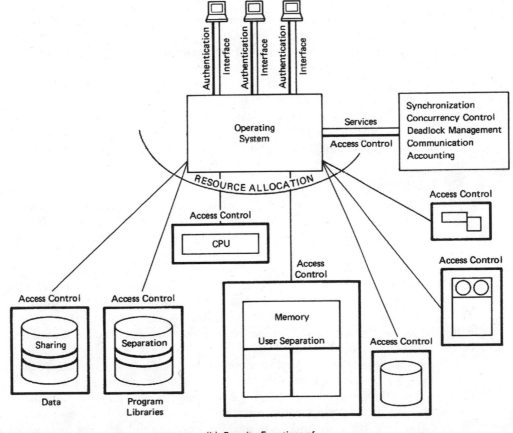

(b) Security Functions of
Operating Systems

Figure 7-11b

Identification

If access is to be controlled based on individuals' identities (most access controls, including mandatory and discretionary access control described next, are fundamentally based on the identity of a potential accessor), those identities must be accurate. Thus, identification also carries a requirement to authenticate or verify an identity. Trusted operating systems require secure identification of individuals, and each individual must be uniquely identified.

Mandatory and Discretionary Access Control

Mandatory access control (**MAC**) means that access control policy decisions are made beyond the control of the individual owner of an object. A central authority determines what information is to be accessible by whom, and the user cannot change access rights. An example of MAC occurs in military security, where an individual data owner does not decide who has a top secret clearance, nor can the owner change the classification of an object from top secret to secret.

By contrast, **discretionary access control** (**DAC**), as its name implies, leaves a certain amount of access control to the discretion of the object's owner, or anyone else who is authorized to control the object's access. The owner can determine who should have access rights to an object and what those rights should be. Commercial environments typically use DAC to allow anyone in the accounting group, and also Sarah and Tad, to access a particular file. Typically DAC access rights can change dynamically. The owner of the accounting file may add Ralph and remove Tad from the list of allowed accessors.

MAC and DAC can both be applied to an object. In that case, MAC has precedence; DAC then means that of all those who are approved for MAC access, only those who also pass DAC will actually be allowed to access the object. So, for example, a file may be classified secret, meaning that only people cleared for secret access can potentially access the file. But out of those millions of people, only people on project "deer-park," or in the "environmental" group, or at location "Fort Hampton" are actually allowed access.

Object Reuse Protection

One flaw that often exists even in current operating systems is failure to control reusable objects. As an example, when a new file is created, space for the file comes from a pool of freed previously used space on a disk or other storage device. Released space is returned to the pool "dirty," that is, still containing the data from the previous user. Because most users would write to a file before trying to read from it, the new user's data obliterates the previous owner's, and so there is no inappropriate disclosure of information. However, a malicious user may claim a large amount of disk space and then scavenge for sensitive data. This kind of attack is called **object reuse**. The problem is not limited to disks; it can occur with main memory, processor registers and storage, other magnetic media (such as tapes), or any other reusable storage medium.

To prevent object reuse leakage, operating systems clear (overwrite) all space to be reassigned. (A sophisticated threat involves reading data previously recorded on a magnetic medium. Very precise and expensive equipment can sometimes separate the most recent data from the data previously recorded, from the data before that, and so forth. This threat, called **magnetic remnance**, is beyond the scope of this book. For more information, see [NCS91a].)

Complete Mediation

Clearly, for mandatory or discretionary access control to be effective, *all* accesses must be controlled. It is insufficient to control access only to files if the attack will acquire access through memory or an outside port or a network or a covert channel. The design and implementation difficulty of a trusted operating system rises significantly as more paths for access must be controlled. Highly trusted operating systems perform **complete mediation**, meaning that all accesses are checked.

Trusted Path

An attack involves "spoofing" users into thinking they are communicating directly with the security enforcement portion of the operating system when, in fact, their keystrokes and commands are being intercepted by an attacker. For critical operations, such as setting a password or changing access permissions, users want an unmistakable communication, called a **trusted path**. On some trusted systems the user invokes a trusted path by pressing a unique key sequence that, by design, is intercepted directly by the security enforcement software; on other trusted systems, security-relevant changes can be made only at system startup, before any processes other than the security enforcement code runs.

Accountability and Audit

A security-relevant action may be as simple as an individual access to an object, such as a file, or it may be as major as a change to the central access control data base affecting all subsequent accesses. Accountability usually entails maintaining a log of security-relevant events that have occurred, listing each event and the person responsible. This audit log must obviously be protected from outsiders and every security-relevant event must be recorded.

Audit Log Reduction

The central problems with audit are volume and analysis. At an extreme, one can argue that every modification or even each character read from a file is potentially security relevant because the modification could affect the integrity of data, or the single character could divulge the only really sensitive part of an entire file. And because the path of control through a program is affected by the data the program processes, the sequence of individual instructions is also potentially security relevant. If an audit record is to be created for every access to a single character from a file and for every instruction executed, the audit log will be enormous. (In fact, for instructions, it would be impossible to audit every instruction, because then the audit commands themselves would have to be audited, but these commands would be implemented by instructions that would have to be audited, and so on forever.)

A simplification in most trusted systems is to audit only the opening (first access to) and closing of (last access to) files or similar objects. Similarly, objects such as individual memory locations, hardware registers, and instructions are not audited. Even with these restrictions audit logs tend to be very large. Even a simple word processor may open fifty or more support modules (separate files) when it begins, it may create and delete a dozen or more temporary files during execution, and it may open many more drivers to handle specific tasks such as complex formatting or printing. Thus, one simple program can easily cause a hundred files to be opened and closed, and complex systems can cause thousands of files to be accessed in relatively short time. On the other hand, some systems continuously read from or update a single file. A bank teller may process transactions against the general customer accounts file throughout the entire day; what is significant is not that the teller accessed the accounts file, but *which entries* in the file. Thus, audit at the level of file opening and closing is in some cases too much data and in other cases too nonspecific.

A final difficulty is the needle-in-a-haystack phenomenon. Even if the audit data could be limited to the right amount, there will typically be many legitimate accesses and perhaps one attack. Finding the one attack access out of a thousand legitimate accesses can be difficult.

Some trusted systems perform **audit reduction**, using separate tools to reduce the volume of the audit data. In this way, if there is an event, all the data has been recorded and can be consulted directly. However, for most analysis, the reduced audit log is enough to review.

Intrusion Detection

Closely related to audit reduction is being able to detect security lapses, ideally while they occur. There may well be too much information in the audit log for a person to analyze, but the computer can help correlate independent data. **Intrusion detection** software builds usage patterns of the normal system and triggers an alarm any time the usage is abnormal. Although there have been some promising results in intrusion detection (see [LUN93], [DEN87b], [SMA88], and [KUM95]), the field is still rather young. Some trusted systems include a primitive degree of intrusion detection software.

In the remaining parts of this section, we examine successful implementations of security in the design of operating systems. We consider three properties: kernelized design (a result of least privilege and economy of mechanism), isolation (the logical extension of least common mechanism), and ring structuring (an example of open design and complete mediation).

Kernelized Design

A **kernel** is the part of an operating system that performs the lowest-level functions. In standard operating system design, the kernel implements operations such as synchronization, interprocess communication, message-passing, and interrupt-handling. The kernel is also called a **nucleus** or **core**. The notion of designing an operating system around a kernel is described by Lampson [LAM76] and by Popek and Kline [POP78].

A **security kernel** is responsible for enforcing the security mechanisms of the entire operating system. The security kernel provides the security interfaces among the hardware, the operating system, and the other parts of the computing system. Typically the security kernel is contained within the operating system kernel. Security kernels are discussed by Ames [AME83].

Security functions may be isolated in a security kernel for several reasons.

- *Coverage.* Every access to a protected object must pass through the security kernel. This makes it possible to ensure that every access is checked.
- *Separation.* By isolating security mechanisms from the rest of the operating system and from the user space, it is easier to protect them from penetration by the operating system or the users.

- *Unity.* All security functions are performed by a single set of code.
- *Modifiability.* Changes to the security mechanism are easier to make and easier to test.
- *Compactness.* Because it performs only security functions, the kernel is likely to be relatively small.
- *Verifiability.* Being relatively small, the security kernel may be analyzed rigorously.

Notice the similarity between these advantages and the design goals of operating systems from Saltzer and Schroeder described earlier. Also note the similarity of these characteristics to modularity, as described in Chapter 5.

On the negative side, implementation of a security kernel may degrade system performance because the kernel adds yet another layer of interface between user programs and operating system resources. Presence of a kernel does not guarantee that it contains *all* security functions, or that it has been implemented correctly. And, in some cases, a security kernel can be quite large.

The design and usefulness of a security kernel depend somewhat on the design approach. The kernel can be designed as an addition to the operating system or it can be the basis of the entire operating system. These two design approaches are described in the next two sections.

Reference Monitor

The most important part of a security kernel is the **reference monitor**, the portion that controls accesses to objects [AND72, LAM71]. The reference monitor is an abstraction that controls all accesses. A reference monitor is not necessarily a single piece of code that controls all accesses; rather, it is the collection of access controls for devices, files, memory, interprocess communication, and other kinds of objects. As shown in Figure 7-12, a reference monitor must be:

- tamperproof
- always invoked
- small enough to be subjected to analysis and testing, the completeness of which can be ensured

A reference monitor can control access effectively only if it cannot be modified or circumvented by a rogue process, and it is the single point through which all access requests must pass. Furthermore, the crucial role of the reference monitor in enforcing security means that it must function correctly. Because the likelihood of correct behavior decreases as the complexity and size of a program increase, the best assurance of correct policy enforcement is a small, simple, understandable reference monitor.

The reference monitor is not all the security mechanisms of a trusted operating system. Other parts of the security suite include audit, identification and authentication processing, and setting enforcement parameters, such as who the allowable subjects are and what objects they are allowed to access. These other parts interact with the reference monitor, providing it the data it needs to operate or receiving data from the reference monitor.

The reference monitor concept has been used for many trusted operating systems and for smaller pieces of trusted software. The validity of this concept is well-supported both in research and in practice.

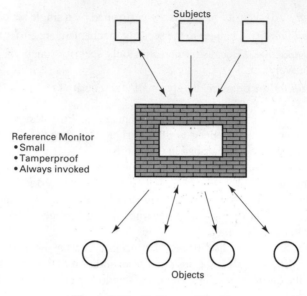

Figure 7-12   Reference Monitor

Trusted Computing Base (TCB)

The **trusted computing base** (**TCB**) is everything in the trusted operating system necessary to enforce the security policy. Alternatively, we can say that the TCB is the parts of the trusted operating system on which we depend for correct enforcement of policy. Some people say that if you divide a trusted operating system into the parts that are in the TCB and those that are not, and you allow the most skillful malicious programmers to write all the *non*-TCB parts, there is nothing the malicious non-TCB parts can do to impair the correct security policy enforcement of the TCB. This definition clarifies the meaning of *trusted* in *trusted operating system:* the TCB is the part of the operating system on which our trust in the security of the whole system depends.

Typically we focus on the division between the TCB and non-TCB elements of the operating system and spend our effort on ensuring the correctness of the TCB.

TCB Functions   What is in the TCB? We can answer this by listing things on which security enforcement could depend:

- *hardware,* including processors, memory, registers, and I/O devices
- some notion of *processes,* so that we can separate and protect security-critical processes
- primitive *files,* such as the security access control data base and identification and authentication data
- *protected memory,* so that the reference monitor can be protected against tampering
- some *interprocess communication,* so that different parts of the TCB can pass data to and activate other parts, for example, the reference monitor invoking and passing data securely to the audit routine

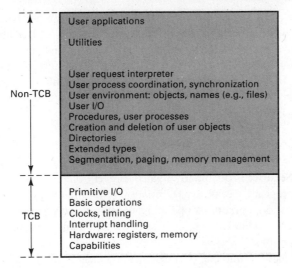

Figure 7-13   TCB and Non-TCB Code

It may seem as if this list encompasses most of the operating system, but this need not be true. For example, although the TCB requires access to files of enforcement data, it does not need an entire file structure of tree-structured directories, virtual devices, indexed files, and multidevice files. Thus, the TCB might contain a primitive file manager that handles only the small, simple files needed for the TCB, and the more complex file manager to provide externally-visible files could be outside the TCB. A typical division into TCB and non-TCB sections is shown in Figure 7-13.

The TCB, which must maintain the secrecy and integrity of each domain, monitors four basic interactions.

- *Process activation.* In a multiprogramming environment, activation and deactivation of processes occur frequently. Changing from one process to another requires a complete change of registers, relocation maps, file access lists, process status information, and other pointers, much of which is security-sensitive information.

- *Execution domain switching.* Processes running in one domain often invoke processes in other domains to obtain more sensitive data or services.

- *Memory protection.* Because each domain includes code and data stored in memory, the TCB must monitor memory references to ensure secrecy and integrity for each domain.

- *I/O operation.* In some systems, software is involved with each character transferred in an I/O operation. This software connects a user program, in the outermost domain, to an I/O device, in the innermost (hardware) domain. Thus, I/O operations can cross all domains.

TCB Design   This division of the operating system into TCB and non-TCB is convenient for designers and developers because it means that all security-relevant code is located in one (logical) part. The distinction is more than just logical, however. In order to ensure that the security enforcement cannot be affected by non-TCB code, TCB code must run in some protected state that distinguishes it. Thus, the structuring into TCB and non-TCB must be done very consciously. However, once this structuring has been done, code outside the TCB can be changed at will, without affecting the TCB's ability to enforce security. This ability to change helps developers because it means that major sections of the operating system—utilities, compilers, applications, user interface managers, and the like—can be revised or replaced any time; only the TCB code must be controlled more carefully. Finally, for anyone evaluating the security of a trusted operating system, a division into TCB and non-TCB simplifies evaluation considerably, because non-TCB code need not be considered.

Retrofitting a TCB   Security-related activities are likely to be performed in a very large number of different places. Security is potentially related to every memory access, every I/O operation, every file or program access, every initiation or termination of a user, and every interprocess communication. In modular operating systems, these separate activities can be handled in independent modules. Each of these separate modules, then, has both security-related and other functions.

Collecting all security functions into the TCB may destroy the modularity of an existing operating system. A unified TCB may also be too large to be analyzed easily. Nevertheless, a designer may decide to separate the security functions of an existing operating system, creating a security kernel. This form of kernel is depicted in Figure 7-14.

Figure 7-14   Combined Security Kernel/Operating System

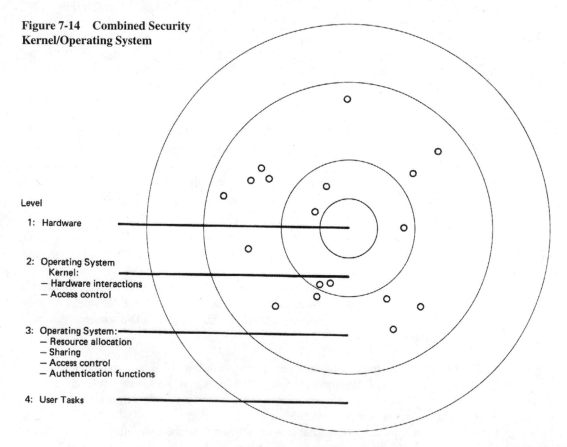

Level

1: Hardware

2: Operating System
    Kernel:
    — Hardware interactions
    — Access control

3: Operating System:
    — Resource allocation
    — Sharing
    — Access control
    — Authentication functions

4: User Tasks

O = Security activities

Starting with the TCB   A more sensible approach is to design the security kernel first, and then design the operating system around it. This technique was used by Honeywell in the design of a prototype for its secure operating system Scomp [FRA83]. That system contained only twenty modules to perform the primitive security functions, and consisted of fewer than 1,000 lines of higher level language source code. The actual security kernel of Scomp contains approximately 10,000 lines.

In a security-based design, a security kernel is an interface layer, just on top of the system hardware. The security kernel monitors all operating system hardware accesses and performs all protection functions. The security kernel, which relies on support from hardware, allows the operating system to handle most functions not related to security. In this way, the security kernel can be small and efficient. As a byproduct of this partitioning there are at least three execution domains of a computing system, as shown in Figure 7-15. These domains are security kernel, operating system, and user.

Separation/Isolation

Recall from Chapter 6 that there are four ways to separate one process from others: physical separation, temporal separation, cryptographic separation, and logical separation (from Rushby and Randell [RUS83]). With **physical separation**, processes use different hardware facilities. For example, sensitive computation may be performed on a reserved computing system; nonsensitive tasks are run on a public system. Recommended hardware separation features are support for multiple independent threads of execution, memory protection, mediation of I/O, and at least three different degrees of execution privilege. **Temporal separation** occurs when processes are run at different times. Some military systems run nonsensitive jobs between 8:00 a.m. and noon, with sensitive computation only from noon to 5:00 p.m. Encryption is used for **cryptographic separation**, so that unauthorized users cannot access sensitive data in a readable form. **Logical separation**, also called **isolation**, is provided when a process such as a reference monitor separates the objects of one user from those of another. Secure computing systems use all of these forms of separation.

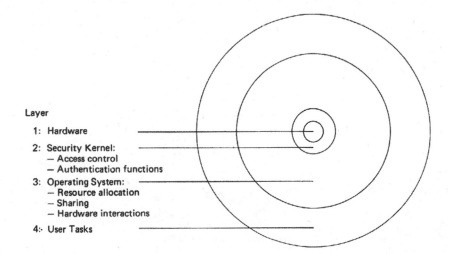

Layer

1: Hardware

2: Security Kernel:
   — Access control
   — Authentication functions

3: Operating System:
   — Resource allocation
   — Sharing
   — Hardware interactions

4: User Tasks

O = Security activities

Figure 7-15   Separate Security Kernel

Multiprogramming operating systems should isolate each user from all others, allowing only carefully controlled interactions between the users. Most operating systems provide a single environment with one copy of the operating system for many users, as shown in Figure 7-16. There are often two pieces of the operating system, located at the highest and lowest addresses of memory.

Virtualization

Virtualization is a powerful tool for trusted system designers because it allows users to access complex objects in a carefully controlled manner. By **virtualization** we mean an emulation or simulation of a collection of resources of a computer system. A **virtual machine** is a collection of real or simulated hardware facilities: a (central) processor that runs an instruction set, an amount of directly addressable storage, and some I/O devices. These facilities support the execution of programs.

Obviously, virtual resources must be supported by real hardware or software, but the real resources do not have to be the same as the simulated ones: printers are often simulated on direct access devices for sharing in multiuser environments, several small disks can be simulated with one large one, with demand paging some noncontiguous memory can support a much larger contiguous virtual memory space, and it is common even on PCs to sim-

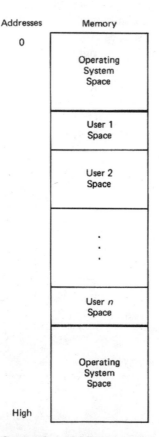

Figure 7-16   Conventional Multiuser Operating System Memory

ulate space on slower disks with faster memory. The operating system provides the virtual resource to the user, and hence the security kernel can control user accesses precisely.

Multiple Virtual Memory Spaces

The IBM MVS/ESA operating system uses virtualization to provide logical separation that gives the user the impression of physical separation. IBM MVS/ESA is a paging system, so that each user's logical address space is separated from that of other users by the page mapping mechanism. Additionally, MVS/ESA includes the operating system in each user's logical address space, so that a user runs on what seems to be a complete, separate machine.

Most paging systems present to a user only the user's virtual address space; the operating system is outside the user's virtual addressing space. However, the operating system is part of the logical space of each MVS/ESA user. Therefore, to the user MVS/ESA seems like a single-user system, as shown in Figure 7-17.

A primary advantage of MVS/ESA is memory management: each user's virtual memory space can be as large as total addressable memory, in excess of 16 million bytes. However, a second advantage of this representation of memory is protection. Because each user's logical address space includes the operating system, the user has the illusion of running on a separate machine, which could even be true.

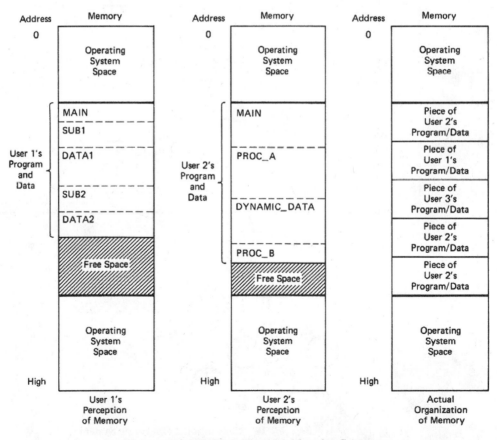

Figure 7-17   Multiple Virtual Addressing Spaces

Virtual Machines

The IBM Processor Resources/System Manager (PR/SM) operating system provides a level of protection that is stronger still. A conventional operating system has hardware facilities and devices that are under the direct control of the operating system, as shown in Figure 7-18. The PR/SM operating system provides an entire virtual machine to each user, so that each user has not only logical memory, but logical I/O devices, logical files, and other logical resources, too. PR/SM does this by strict separation of resources.

The PR/SM system is a natural extension of the concept of virtual memory. Virtual *memory* gives the user a memory space that is logically separated from real memory; a virtual memory space is usually larger than real memory, as well. A virtual *machine* gives the user a full set of hardware features, that is, a complete machine that may be substantially different from the real machine. These virtual hardware resources are also logically separated from those of other users. The relationship of virtual machines to real is shown in Figure 7-19.

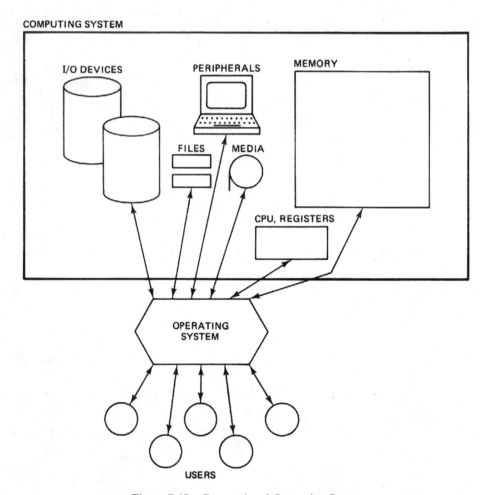

Figure 7-18   Conventional Operating System

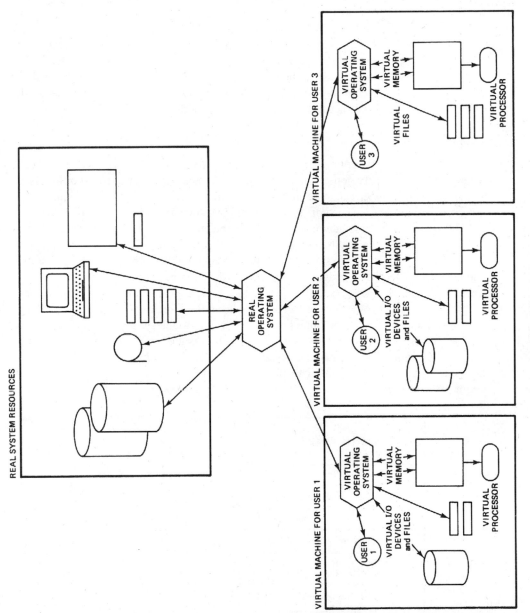

Figure 7-19   Virtual Machine

REAL SYSTEM RESOURCES

REAL OPERATING SYSTEM

VIRTUAL MACHINE FOR USER 3

VIRTUAL OPERATING SYSTEM

VIRTUAL MEMORY

VIRTUAL FILES

VIRTUAL PROCESSOR

USER 3

VIRTUAL MACHINE FOR USER 2

VIRTUAL OPERATING SYSTEM

VIRTUAL MEMORY

VIRTUAL I/O DEVICES and FILES

VIRTUAL PROCESSOR

USER 2

VIRTUAL MACHINE FOR USER 1

VIRTUAL OPERATING SYSTEM

VIRTUAL MEMORY

VIRTUAL I/O DEVICES and FILES

VIRTUAL PROCESSOR

USER 1

Both MVS/ESA and PR/SM improve the isolation of each user from other users and from the hardware of the system. Of course, this added complexity increases the overhead incurred with these levels of translation and protection. In the next section we study alternative designs that reduce the complexity of providing security in an operating system.

Layered Design

As described previously, a kernelized operating system consists of at least four levels: hardware, kernel, operating system, and user. Each of these layers may itself include sublayers. For example, in [SCH83b], the kernel has five distinct layers. At the user level, it is not uncommon to have quasi-system programs, such as data base managers or user interface shells, that constitute separate layers of security themselves.

Layered Trust

This view of a secure operating system can be depicted as a series of concentric circles, where the most sensitive operations are in the innermost layers. The trustworthiness and access rights of a process can be judged by its proximity to the center: the more trusted processes are closer to the center. Such a system is shown as a stack in Figure 7-20.

In this design, some activities related to protection functions are performed outside the security kernel. For example, user authentication may include accessing a password table, challenging the user to supply a password, verifying the correctness of the password, and so forth. The disadvantage of performing all of these operations inside the security kernel is that some of them (such as formatting the user–terminal interaction and searching for the user in a table of known users) do not warrant high security.

A single logical function implemented in several modules is an example of a **layered design**. In the examples just described, trustworthiness and access rights are the basis of layering. A single function may be performed by a set of modules operating in different layers, as shown in Figure 7-21. The modules of each layer perform operations of a certain degree of sensitivity.

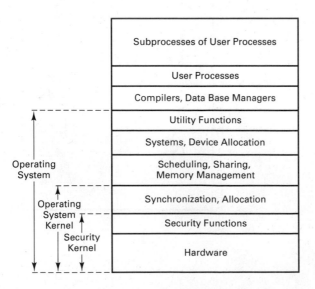

Figure 7-20   Layered Operating System

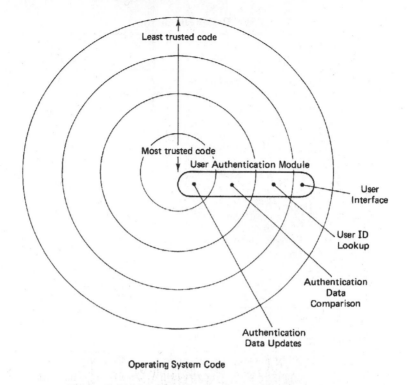

Figure 7-21   Modules Operating in Different Layers

Neumann [NEU83] describes the layered structure used for the Provably Secure Operating System (PSOS). As shown in Table 7-3 some lower level layers present some or all of their functionality to higher levels, but each layer properly encapsulates those things below itself.

A layered approach is recognized as a good operating system design. Each layer uses the more central layers as services, and each layer provides a certain level of functionality to the layers farther out. In this way, we can "peel off" each layer and still have a logically complete system with less functionality.

Another justification for layering is damage control. Neumann [NEU86] gives two parallel examples of risk, shown in Table 7-4 and Table 7-5. In a conventional, nonhierarchically designed system, any problem—hardware failure, software flaw, or unexpected condition, even in a supposedly non–security-relevant portion—can cause disaster because the effect of the problem is unbounded, and because the lack of structure to the system means that one cannot be confident that any given function has no (indirect) security effect. By contrast, as shown in Table 7-5, hierarchical structuring has two benefits:

- Hierarchical structuring permits identification of the most critical parts, which can then be analyzed intensely for correctness, so that the number of problems should be smaller.
- Isolation limits effects of problems or flaws to the hierarchical levels at and above the point of the problem, so that the effects of many problems should be confined.

Table 7-3   PSOS Design Hierarchy

Level	Function	Hidden by Level	Visible to User
16	User request interpreter		Y
15	User environments and name spaces		Y
14	User I/O		Y
13	Procedure records		Y
12	User processes and visible I/O		Y
11	Creation and deletion of user objects		Y
10	Directories	11	P
9	Extended types	11	P
8	Segments	11	P
7	Paging	8	
6	System processes and I/O	12	
5	Primitive I/O	6	
4	Arithmetic and other basic operations		Y
3	Clocks	6	
2	Interrupts	6	
1	Registers and addressable memory	7	P
0	Capabilities		Y

Ring Structure

The Multics operating system carries a layered design one step further. Protection during execution is implemented by a **ring structure**, specifying what access rights a process has. (Schroeder [SCH72] explains the ring structure in detail.) In Multics, a ring is a domain in which a process executes. The rings are numbered, from 0 up, with the kernel being ring 0. Rings are implemented as if they were concentric bands around the hardware of a computing system.

Each executing process runs at a particular ring level. More trusted processes operate at lower-numbered rings. The rings are overlapping, so that running at ring i includes privileges of all rings j where $j > i$. The lower the ring number, the more access a process has but, correspondingly, the lower the ring number the less protection covers its operation.

Each data area or procedure is called a **segment**. A segment is protected by means of three numbers, b_1, b_2, and b_3, where $b_1 \leq b_2 < b_3$. The three numbers $\langle b_1, b_2, b_3 \rangle$ are called the **ring bracket**, (b_1, b_2) is called the **access bracket**, and (b_2, b_3) is called the **call bracket** or **gate extension**. The range from b_1 to b_2 is the set of rings of processes that can access this segment freely. The rings beyond b_2 up to b_3 constitute the rings of processes that can call this segment only at certain distinguished entry points. The representation of a ring bracket is shown in Figure 7-22.

For example, a kernel segment might have an access bracket of (0,4), meaning that processes at levels 0 through 4 could execute it freely. A user segment might have an

Table 7-4   Conventionally (Nonhierarchically) Designed System

Level	Functions	Risk
2	Noncritical functions	Disaster possible
1	Less-critical functions	Disaster possible
0	Most critical functions	Disaster possible

Table 7-5   Hierarchically Designed System

Level	Functions	Risk
2	Noncritical functions	Few disasters likely from noncritical software
1	Less-critical functions	Some failures possible from less-critical functions, but because of separation, effect limited
0	Most critical functions	Disasters possible but unlikely if system simple enough to be analyzed extensively

access bracket of (4,6), indicating that it is normally accessed by user processes only. The ring bracket indicates the degree of trust in a segment. Segments that are highly trusted to be correct have access brackets that start at low numbers. Segments that are less highly trusted are seldom called by highly trusted kernel processes; therefore, less-reliable segments have access brackets that start at higher numbers.

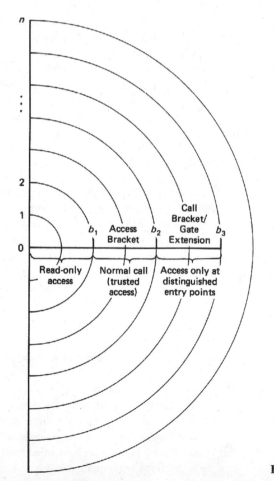

Figure 7-22   Ring Bracket

This chapter started with a study of different models of protection systems. In this section we have examined three design principles—isolation, security kernel, and layered structure—that are used in the design of secure operating systems. This presentation concludes the study of how operating systems are designed for security. In the next section we consider **assurance**, ways of convincing others that a model, design, and implementation are correct. We begin by examining how operating systems are tested, both before and after they are delivered. The first issue of testing involves users' attempts to defeat the controls of the system.

7.5   Assurance in Trusted Operating Systems

In previous sections we looked at security features that operating systems must provide, and different mechanisms for providing that security. We studied models of protection systems and ways to design operating systems for security.

Now we consider what it means to have confidence in the security features of an operating system: what justifies confidence and how confidence levels of operating systems have been rated. Because operating systems are used in different environments, in some applications less secure operating systems may be acceptable. We need ways of determining whether a particular operating system is appropriate for a certain set of needs. In Chapter 5 and in the previous section, we looked at design and process techniques. Adherence to a structured design methodology or progress in business process improvement are two ways to inspire confidence in the quality and correctness of a system.

In this section we explore ways to demonstrate the security of an operating system: testing, formal verification, and informal validation. These methods have been applied separately and in combination to assess the security of operating systems. All of these methods are used in independent evaluation schemes.

Typical Operating System Flaws

Periodically throughout this analysis of security features of operating systems, the phrase *exploit a flaw* has been used. Throughout the years many flaws have been uncovered in many operating systems. Gradually the flaws have been corrected and the knowledge of likely weak spots has grown.

In this section we discuss typical flaws that have been uncovered in operating systems. The goal is not to provide a how-to guide for potential penetrators of operating systems. We study these flaws to understand the careful analysis necessary in the design and testing of operating systems.

Known Flaws

The largest single source of flaws is *I/O processing*. There are probably several reasons why I/O is a weak spot.

- I/O is performed by independent, intelligent hardware subsystems. (A so-called intelligent device can take some independent action of its own, such as reordering disk requests in order to optimize head movement or executing a series of I/O operations asynchronously from the central processor.) These independent units often fall outside the security kernel or the security restrictions implemented by an operating system.

- The code to perform I/O is often much more complex, and much more dependent on the specific device hardware than code for any other component of the computing system. For this reason, it is harder to review I/O device drivers, access code, and service routines for correctness, let alone verify them formally.
- I/O activity sometimes bypasses other operating system functions, such as page or segment address translation, in the interest of fast data transfer. It may also thus bypass the protection features associated with those functions.
- I/O operations are often character-oriented. Again, in the interest of fast data transfer, the operating systems designers may have tried to take shortcuts by limiting the number of instructions executed by the operating system during actual data transfer. Sometimes the instructions eliminated are those that enforce security policies as each character is transferred.

A second prominent weakness in operating system security reflects an *ambiguity in access policy.* On one hand, we want to separate users and protection of their individual resources. On the other hand, users depend on shared access to libraries, utility programs, common data, and system tables. The distinction between isolation and sharing is not always clear at the policy level, so the distinction cannot be sharply drawn at implementation.

A third potential flaw area is *incomplete mediation.* Recall that Saltzer recommended an operating system design in which every requested access was checked for proper authorization. However, some systems check access only once per I/O operation, per process execution, or per machine interval. The mechanism is available to implement full protection, but the policy decision on when to invoke the mechanism is not complete. Therefore, in the absence of any explicit requirement, system designers adopt the "most efficient" enforcement, that is, the one that will lead to the least use of machine resources.

A fourth protection weakness is *generality,* especially among commercial operating systems for large computing systems. Operating system implementors try to provide a means for users to customize their installation of an operating system, and to allow installation of software packages written by other companies. Some of these packages, which operate as part of the operating system themselves, must execute with the same access privileges as the operating system. Examples are programs that provide stricter access control than the standard control available from the operating system. The "hooks" by which these packages are installed are also trapdoors for any user to penetrate the operating system.

Thus, there are several well-known points of security weakness common to many commercial operating systems. Now we consider several example of actual flaws that have been exploited in order to penetrate operating systems.

Examples of Exploitations

As noted earlier, I/O is a weak point in many major operating systems. The first example of an exploited weakness involves I/O. On some systems, after access has been checked to initiate an I/O operation, the operation continues without subsequent checking. Checking access permission with each character transferred is a substantial overhead for the protection system. The I/O command often resides in the user's memory space. Any user can alter the source or destination address of the command after the I/O operation has commenced. Because access has been checked once, it is not checked each time a piece of data is transferred, but the new address will be used. By using this flaw, users have been able to transfer data to or from any memory address they desire. Similarly, in demand paging systems, when I/O begins, a memory page frame may be occupied by one user's data, for whom I/O is performed; however, while the I/O is in progress, that page frame may be reassigned to another user, but the I/O subsystem is not necessarily notified. Complete mediation would have prevented these attacks.

I/O is also involved in another example of illegal access. One operating system uses a common system buffer to retain data scheduled for delivery to all users. Any user can search this buffer and extract data that would be more carefully protected if it had been transferred to the user. In a particular attack, the data was the user authentication data, showing user IDs and passwords waiting to be read and validated by the operating system. Again, complete mediation would have eliminated this vulnerability.

Another example of exploitation involves a procedural flaw. In one system a special supervisor function was reserved for the installation of other security packages. When executed, this supervisor call returned control to the user in privileged mode. The operations allowable in that mode were not monitored closely, so that the supervisor call could be used for access control or for any other high-security system access. The particular supervisor call required some effort to execute, but it was fully available on the system. Additional checking should have been used to authenticate the program executing the supervisor request. As an alternative, the access rights for any subject entering under that supervisor request could have been limited to the objects necessary to perform the function of the added program.

Another flaw is the *time-of-check to time-of-use* mismatch. In this attack, access permission is checked for a particular user to access an object, such as a buffer. But between the time when the access is approved and the access actually occurs, the user changes the designation of the object, so that instead of accessing the approved object, the user now accesses another, unacceptable one.

Other penetrations have occurred by exploiting more complex combinations of flaws. In general, however, security flaws have resulted from a faulty analysis of a complex situation, such as I/O, or from an ambiguity or omission in the security policy. When simple security mechanisms are used to implement clear and complete security policies, the number of penetrations falls dramatically.

Assurance Methods

In this section we consider three approaches to deriving confidence in the correctness of a system: testing, verification, and validation. None of these is complete or foolproof, and each has advantages and disadvantages. Used with understanding, however, each can play an important role in deriving overall assurance of the security of a system.

Testing

Testing is the most widely accepted assurance technique. As Boebert [BOE92] observes, conclusions from testing are based on the actual product being evaluated, not on some abstraction or precursor of the product. This realism is a security advantage. However, those conclusions are limited because

- Testing can demonstrate the *existence* of a flaw, but passing tests does not demonstrate the absence of flaws.

- It is hard to achieve adequate test coverage within reasonable time or effort because the combinatorial explosion of inputs and internal states makes testing very complex.
- Testing based only on the observable effects, not on the internal structure of a product (so-called closed- or black-box testing) does not ensure any degree of completeness.
- Testing based on the internal structure of a product (so-called open-, crystal-, clear-, glass-, or white-box testing) involves modifying the product by adding code to extract and display internal states, and that extra functionality affects the behavior of the product and can be a later source of vulnerabilities.

Functional testing, unit testing, integration testing, system testing, regression testing, and test coverage are all well-covered in various books on software engineering.

Another testing strategy sometimes used in computer security is called **penetration** or **tiger team** analysis. In this approach, a team of experts in the use and design of operating systems tries to crack the system being tested. The tiger team knows typical flaws in operating systems and computing systems, as described in previous sections and chapters. With this knowledge, the team attempts to identify and exploit flaws in the system.

This approach is much like asking a mechanic to look over a used car on a sales lot. The mechanic knows potential weak spots and checks as many of them as possible. If the mechanic checks the fuel system, the cooling system, and the brakes, there is no guarantee that the muffler is good. Similarly, an operating system that *fails* a penetration test is known to have errors, but a system that does *not* fail is *not* guaranteed to be error-free. Penetration testing is more useful to determine the presence of errors than their absence.

Formal Verification

The most rigorous method of analyzing security is through formal verification. In formal verification the operating system is reduced to a theorem, which is then proven. The theorem asserts that the operating system is correct; that is, it provides the security features it should and nothing else.

Proving correctness of an entire operating system is a formidable task, often requiring months or even years of effort by several people. Computer programs that apply rules of logic, called **theorem provers,** can assist in this effort, although there is still much human activity needed. The amount of work required and the methods used are well beyond the scope of this book. However, we present an example of the use of proofs of correctness, as applied to a smaller program. (More extensive coverage of this topic is provided in [GRI81], [HAN76], and [CHE81].)

Consider the flow diagram of Figure 7-23, which determines the smallest of a set of n values, $A[1]$ through $A[n]$. The flow chart has a single identified beginning point, a single identified ending point, and five internal blocks, including an if–then structure and a loop.

In program verification, we begin with an initial assertion, a statement of conditions on entry to the module. We identify a series of intermediate assertions, associated with the work of the module. We also determine an ending assertion, a statement of the expected result of the flowchart. We then show that the initial assertion leads logically to the intermediate assertions, in order, which lead logically to the ending assertion.

Formally, we can do this with four assertions. The first assertion, P, is a statement of initial conditions, assumed to be true on entry to the procedure.

$$P: \quad n > 0$$

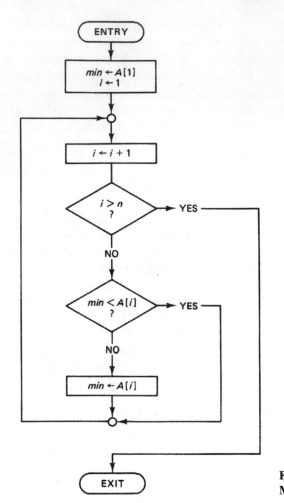

Figure 7-23   **Flow Diagram for Finding the Minimum Value**

The second assertion, Q, is the result of applying the initialization code in the first box.

$$Q: \quad n > 0 \quad \text{and}$$
$$1 \le i \le n \quad \text{and}$$
$$min \le A[1]$$

The third assertion, R, is the loop assertion. It asserts what is true at the start of each iteration of the loop.

$$R: \quad n > 0 \quad \text{and}$$
$$1 \le i \le n \quad \text{and}$$
$$\text{for all } j, \ 1 \le j \le i - 1 \ min \le A[j]$$

The final assertion, S, is the concluding assertion, the statement of conditions true at the time the loop exit occurs.

$$S: \quad n > 0 \quad \text{and}$$
$$i = n + 1 \quad \text{and}$$
$$\text{for all } j, \; 1 \le j \le n \; min \le A[\,j\,]$$

These four assertions, which are shown overlaid on the flowchart in Figure 7-24, capture the essence of the work of the flowchart shown. Next in the verification process we must show the logical progression of these four assertions. That is, we must show that, assuming P is true on entry to this procedure, Q is true after completion of the initialization section, R is true the first time the loop is entered, R is true each time through the loop, and the truth of R implies that S is true at the termination of the loop.

Clearly Q follows from P and the semantics of the two statements in the second box. The first time into the loop, $i = 2$, so $i - 1 = 1$. Thus, the assertion about min applies only for $j = 1$, which follows from Q. To prove that R remains true with each execution of the loop, we can use the principle of mathematical induction. The statement was true the first time

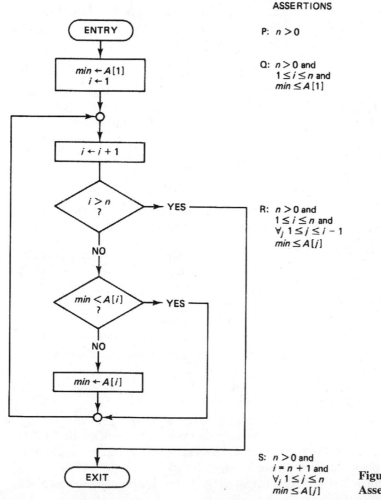

ASSERTIONS

P: $n > 0$

Q: $n > 0$ and
   $1 \le i \le n$ and
   $min \le A[1]$

R: $n > 0$ and
   $1 \le i \le n$ and
   $\forall_j \; 1 \le j \le i - 1$
   $min \le A[j]$

S: $n > 0$ and
   $i = n + 1$ and
   $\forall_j \; 1 \le j \le n$
   $min \le A[j]$

Figure 7-24   Verification Assertions

through the loop, which forms a basis. With each iteration of the loop the value of i increases by 1, so it is necessary only to show that $min \leq A[i]$ for this new value of i . That proof follows from the meaning of the comparison and replacement statements. Therefore, R is true with each iteration of the loop. Finally, S follows from the final iteration value of R. This step completes the formal verification that this flowchart exits with the smallest value of $A[1]$ through $A[n]$ in min.

The algorithm (*not* the verification) shown here is often used as an example in the first few weeks of introductory programming classes. It is quite simple; in fact after studying the algorithm for a short time, most students convince themselves that the algorithm is correct. The verification itself takes much longer to explain; it also takes far longer to write than the algorithm itself. There are two principal difficulties with formal verification methods:

- *Time.* The methods of formal verification are time-consuming to perform. Stating the assertions at each step and verifying the logical flow of the assertions are both slow processes.
- *Complexity.* Formal verification is a complex process. For some large systems it is hopeless to try to state and verify the assertions. This is especially true for systems that have not been designed with formal verification in mind.

These two difficulties reduce the number of situations in which formal verification is used successfully. Gerhart [GER89] succinctly describes the advantages and disadvantages of use of formal methods. As Schaefer [SCH89a] points out, too often people focus so much on the formalism and on deriving a formal proof that they ignore the underlying security properties to be ensured.

Validation

Validation is a more general term than *verification*. It includes verification, but it also includes other less rigorous methods of convincing people of the correctness of a program. There are several different ways to perform validation of an operating system.

- *Requirement checking.* One validation technique is to cross check each requirement of the operating system with the source code or execution-time behavior of the system. The goal here is to demonstrate that the system does each thing listed in the functional requirements. This process tends to demonstrate only that the system does everything it should do, in at least one situation. The process seldom produces any result guaranteeing that the system does *not* do a host of things it should not.
- *Design and code reviews.* In this approach, the designers and programmers scrutinize the design or the code of the system as it is being written to identify errors, incorrect assumptions, inconsistent behavior, or faulty logic. The success of this process depends on the rigor of the review.
- *Module and system testing.* During development of a program, the programmers or an independent test team select data to check the correctness of the system. This test data can be organized so as to examine each execution path, each conditional statement, each type of output report produced, each variable change, and so forth. The important point here is to make sure that all objects are checked in a methodical manner.

Evaluation

Most "consumers" (users, system purchasers) are not security experts, and·thus they are incapable of verifying the accuracy or adequacy of test coverage, checking the validity of a proof of correctness, or determining in any other way that a system correctly implements a security policy. An independent third-party evaluation is very desirable: independent experts can review the requirements, design, implementation, and assurance evidence of a system. For the nonexpert, an evaluation by independent experts is most appropriate. Several evaluation schemes exist for structuring an independent review of a system. In this section we examine three different approaches from the United States, from Europe, and an emerging scheme that combines all known approaches.

U.S. Orange Book Evaluation

In the late 1970s, the U.S. Department of Defense became aware that system acquisition personnel (users and buyers) were not in the best position to specify or evaluate trusted systems. The department generated a set of standards for computing systems having different levels of security requirements. These were published in a document [DOD85], which has become known informally as the Orange Book because of the color of its cover. The actual name of the document is *Trusted Computer System Evaluation Criteria,* often abbreviated TCSEC.

There are four basic divisions, A, B, C, and D, where A is the division with the most comprehensive degree of security. Within divisions there are additional distinctions, denoted with numbers, where the higher numbers indicate tighter security requirements. The complete set of ratings from lowest to highest assurance is D, C1, C2, B1, B2, B3, and A1. Table 7-6 (from Appendix D of [DOD85]) shows the security requirements for each of the seven evaluated levels of NCSC certification. (Level D has no requirements because it denotes minimal protection.)

The pattern of this table reveals that there are really four clusters: class D, with no requirements; classes C1/C2/B1, which require security features common to many commercial operating systems; class B2, requiring a precise proof of security of the underlying model and a narrative specification of the trusted computing base; and classes B3/A1, which require more precisely proven descriptive and formal designs of the trusted computing base. This is not to imply that classes C1, C2, and B1 are equivalent. However, there are substantial increases of stringency between B1 and B2, and between B2 and B3. An operating system developer might be able to add security measures to an existing operating system in order to qualify for a C1 or C2 or B1 rating. However, security must be included in the *design* of the operating system for a B2 rating. Furthermore, the design of a B3 or A1 system must begin with construction and proof of a formal *model* of security. Thus, the distinctions between B1 and B2 and between B2 and B3 are significant.

The descriptions of these levels, and the qualities required for each rating, are listed. Within these descriptions, terms in quotation marks have been taken directly from the orange book, in order to convey the spirit of the evaluation criteria.

Class D: Minimal Protection   This class is applied to systems that have been evaluated for a higher category but have failed that evaluation. No security characteristics are needed for a D rating.

Table 7-6   Trusted Computer System Evaluation Criteria

Criteria	D	C1	C2	B1	B2	B3	A1
Security Policy							
Discretionary access control	—	⊗	⊗	⇒	⇒	⊗	⇒
Object reuse	—	—	⊗	⇒	⇒	⇒	⇒
Labels	—	—	—	⊗	⊗	⇒	⇒
Label integrity	—	—	—	⊗	⇒	⇒	⇒
Exportation of labeled information	—	—	—	⊗	⇒	⇒	⇒
Labeling human-readable output	—	—	—	⊗	⇒	⇒	⇒
Mandatory access control	—	—	—	⊗	⊗	⇒	⇒
Subject sensitivity labels	—	—	—	—	⊗	⇒	⇒
Device labels	—	—	—	—	⊗	⇒	⇒
Accountability							
Identification and authentication	—	⊗	⊗	⊗	⇒	⇒	⇒
Audit	—	—	⊗	⊗	⊗	⊗	⇒
Trusted path	—	—	—	—	⊗	⊗	⇒
Assurance							
System architecture	—	⊗	⊗	⊗	⊗	⊗	⇒
System integrity	—	⊗	⇒	⇒	⇒	⇒	⇒
Security testing	—	⊗	⊗	⊗	⊗	⊗	⊗
Design specification and verification	—	—	—	⊗	⊗	⊗	⊗
Covert channel analysis	—	—	—	—	⊗	⊗	⊗
Trusted facility management	—	—	—	—	⊗	⊗	⇒
Configuration management	—	—	—	—	⊗	⇒	⊗
Trusted recovery	—	—	—	—	—	⊗	⇒
Trusted distribution	—	—	—	—	—	—	⊗
Documentation							
Security features user's guide	—	⊗	⇒	⇒	⇒	⇒	⇒
Trusted facility manual	—	⊗	⊗	⊗	⊗	⊗	⇒
Test documentation	—	⊗	⇒	⇒	⊗	⇒	⊗
Design documentation	—	⊗	⇒	⊗	⊗	⊗	⊗

Legend: —: no requirement; ⇒: same requirement as previous class; ⊗: additional requirement

Class C1: Discretionary Security Protection   Class C1 is intended for an environment of cooperating users processing data at the same level of sensitivity. A system evaluated as class C1 provides a separation of users from data. There must be controls that appear sufficient to implement access limitation, in order to allow users to protect their own data. The controls of a C1 system may not have been stringently evaluated; the evaluation may be based more on the presence of certain features. In order to qualify for a C1 rating, a system must have a domain including security functions, which is protected against tampering. A key word in the classification is "discretionary." A user is "allowed" to decide when the controls apply, when they do not, and which named individuals or groups are allowed access.

Class C2: Controlled Access Protection   A class C2 system still implements discretionary control, although the granularity of control is finer: protection must be implementable to the degree of a single user. The audit trail must be capable of tracking each individual's access (or attempted access) to each object.

Class B1: Labeled Security Protection   All B-level certifications include *non*-discretionary access control. At the B1 level, each controlled subject and object must be assigned a security level. (For class B1, the protection system does not need to control every object.)

Each controlled object must be individually labeled for security level, and these labels must be used as the basis for access control decisions. The access control must be based on a model employing both hierarchical levels and nonhierarchical categories. (The military model is an example of a system with hierarchical levels—unclassified, classified, secret, top secret—and nonhierarchical categories—need-to-know category sets.) The mandatory access policy is the Bell–La Padula model. Thus, a B1 system must implement Bell–La Padula controls for all accesses, and then user discretionary access controls to further limit access.

Class B2: Structured Protection   The major enhancement for B2 level is a design requirement: the design and implementation of a B2 system must enable a more thorough testing and review. A verifiable top-level design must be presented, and testing must confirm that the system implements this design. The system must be internally structured into "well-defined largely independent modules." The principle of least privilege is to be enforced in the design. Access control policies must be enforced on all objects and subjects, including devices. Analysis of covert channels is required.

Class B3: Security Domains   The security functions of a class B3 system must be small enough for extensive testing. A high-level design must be complete and conceptually simple, and a "convincing argument" must exist that the system implements this design. The implementation of the design shall "incorporate significant use of layering, abstraction, and information hiding."

The security functions must be tamperproof. The system must furthermore be "highly resistant to penetration." There is also a requirement that the system audit facility be able to identify when a violation of security is imminent.

Class A1: Verified Design   Class A1 requires a formally verified system design. The capabilities of the system are the same as for class B3. There are five important criteria for class A1 certification: a formal model of the protection system and a proof of its consistency and adequacy, a formal top-level specification of the protection system, a demonstration that the top-level specification corresponds to the model, an implementation "informally" shown to be consistent with the specification, and formal analysis of covert channels.

European ITSEC Evaluation

The TCSEC was exclusively a U.S. development. Although the United States used it in evaluations, representatives from several European countries also recognized the need for a criterion and methodology for evaluations of security-enforcing products. The European efforts have culminated in the ITSEC, the *Information Technology Security Evaluation Criteria* [ITS91b].

Origins of the ITSEC   England, Germany, and France independently began work on evaluation criteria at approximately the same time. England and Germany both published their first drafts in 1989; France had its criteria in limited review when these three nations, joined by the Netherlands, decided to work together to develop a common criteria document. We will examine Britain and Germany's efforts separately, followed by their combined output.

German Green Book   The (then West) German Information Security Agency (GISA) produced a catalog of criteria [GIS88] five years after the first use of the U.S. TCSEC. It bore a green cover and, keeping with tradition, the security community began to call the document the German Green Book. The German criteria identified eight basic security functions, which were deemed sufficient to enforce a broad spectrum of security policies:

- *identification and authentication:* unique and certain association of an identity with a subject or object
- *administration of rights:* the ability to control the assignment and revocation of access rights between subjects and objects
- *verification of rights:* mediation of the attempt of a subject to exercise rights with respect to an object
- *audit:* a record of information on the successful or attempted unsuccessful exercise of rights
- *object reuse:* resetting reusable resources in such a way that no information flow occurs in contradiction to the security policy
- *error recovery:* identification of situations from which recovery is necessary, and invocation of an appropriate action
- *continuity of service:* identification of functionality that must be available in the system and what degree of delay or loss (if any) can be tolerated
- *data communication security:* peer entity authentication, control of access to communications resources, data confidentiality, data integrity, data origin authentication, and nonrepudiation

Note that the first five of these eight functions closely resemble the U.S. TCSEC, but the last three move into entirely new areas: integrity of data, availability, and a range of communications concerns.

Like the U.S. DoD, GISA did not expect ordinary users (that is, those who were not security experts) to select appropriate sets of security functions, so 10 functional classes were defined. Classes F1 through F5 corresponded closely to the functionality requirements of U.S. classes C1 through B3 (recall that the *functionality* requirements of class A1 are identical to those of B3). Class F6 was for high data and program integrity requirements, class F7 was appropriate for high availability, and classes F8 through F10 relate to data communications situations. Then, the German method addressed assurance by defining eight quality levels, Q0 through Q7, corresponding roughly to the assurance requirements of U.S. TCSEC levels D through A1, respectively. For example,

- The evaluation of a Q1 system is intended merely to ensure that the implementation more or less enforces the security policy and that no major errors exist.
- The goal of a Q3 evaluation is to show that the system is largely resistant to simple penetration attempts.

- In order to achieve assurance level Q6, it must be formally proven that the highest specification level meets all the requirements of the formal security policy model. In addition, the source code is analyzed very precisely.

These functionality classes and assurance levels can be combined in any way, producing, potentially, 80 different evaluation results, as shown in Table 7-7. The region in the upper right portion of the table represents requirements in excess of U.S. TCSEC requirements, showing higher assurance requirements for a given functionality class. Even though assurance and functionality can be combined in any way, there may be limited applicability for a low-assurance multilevel system (such as F5, Q1) in usage. The Germans did not assert that all possibilities would necessarily be useful, however.

The other significant contribution of the German approach was to support evaluations by independent, commercial evaluation facilities.

British Criteria   The British criteria development was a joint activity between the U.K. Department of Trade and Industry (DTI) and Ministry of Defence (MoD). The first public version, published in 1989 [DTI89a] was issued in several volumes.

The original U.K. criteria were based on what was called the claims language, a metalanguage by which a vendor could make claims about functionality in a product. The claims language consisted of lists of action phrases and target phrases with parameters. A typical action phrase is

> This *product* can [not] determine . . . [using the mechanism described in paragraph *n* of this document].

The parameters *product* and *n* are, obviously, replaced with specific references to the product to be evaluated. An example of a target phrase is

> . . . the *access-type* granted to a [*user, process*] in respect to a(n) *object*.

These two phrases can be combined, and parameters replaced, to produce a claim about a product.

> This **access control subsystem** can determine the **read access** granted to **all subjects** in respect to **system files.**

Table 7-7   Relationship of German and U.S. Evaluation Criteria

	Q0	Q1	Q2	Q3	Q4	Q5	Q6	Q7
F1		= U.S. C1						Beyond U.S. A1
F2			= U.S. C2					Beyond U.S. A1
F3				= U.S. B1				Beyond U.S. A1
F4					= U.S. B2			Beyond U.S. A1
F5						= U.S. B3	=U.S. A1	Beyond U.S. A1
F6				New functional class				
F7				New functional class				
F8				New functional class				
F9				New functional class				
F10				New functional class				

The claims language was intended to provide an open-ended structure by which a vendor could assert qualities of a product and independent evaluators could verify the truth of those claims. Because of the generality of the claims language, there was no direct correlation of U.K. and U.S. evaluation levels.

In addition to the claims language, there were six levels of assurance evaluation, numbered L1 through L6, corresponding roughly to U.S. assurance C1 through A1 or German Q1 through Q6.

The claims language was intentionally open-ended because the British felt it was impossible to predict which functionality manufacturers would choose to put in their products. In this regard, the British differed from Germany and the United States, who thought manufacturers needed to be guided to include specific functions with precise functionality requirements. The British envisioned certain popular groups of claims being combined into bundles that could be reused by many manufacturers.

The British defined and documented a scheme for Commercial Licensed Evaluation Facilities (CLEFs) [DTI89b], with precise requirements for the conduct and process of evaluation by independent commercial organizations.

Other Activities   As if these two efforts were not enough, Canada, Australia, and France were also working on evaluation criteria. The similarities between these efforts were far greater than their differences. It was as if each profited by building on the successes of predecessors.

Three difficulties, which were really different aspects of the same problem, became immediately apparent.

- *Comparability.* It was not clear how the different evaluation criteria related. Whereas a German F2/E2 evaluation was structurally quite similar to a U.S. C2 evaluation, and an F4/E7 or F6/E3 evaluation had no direct U.S. counterpart, it was not obvious what U.K. claims would correspond to a particular U.S. evaluation level.
- *Transferability.* Would a vendor get credit for a German F2/E2 evaluation in a context requiring a U.S. C2? Would the stronger F2/E3 or F3/E2 be accepted?
- *Marketability.* Could a vendor be expected to have a product evaluated independently in the United States, Germany, Britain, Canada, and Australia? How many evaluations would a vendor support? (Many suggested that a vendor would be interested in at most one.)

For reasons including these problems, Britain, Germany, and France, together with the Netherlands, decided to pool their knowledge and produce a synthesis of their work.

ITSEC: Information Technology Security Evaluation Criteria   In 1991 the Commission of the European Communities sponsored the work of these four nations to produce a harmonized version for use by all European Union member nations. The result was a good amalgamation.

The ITSEC preserved the German functionality classes F1–F10, while at the same time allowing the flexibility of the British claims language. There is similarly an **effectiveness** component to the evaluation, corresponding roughly to the U.S. notion of assurance and to the German E0–E7 effectiveness levels.

A vendor (or other "sponsor" of an evaluation) has to define a **target of evaluation** (TOE), the focus of the evaluation. The TOE is considered in the context of an operational environment (that is, an expected set of threats) and security enforcement requirements. An evaluation can be made of either a *product* (in general distribution, for use in a variety of environments) or a *system* (designed and built for use in a specified setting). The sponsor or vendor states

- *system security policy* or *rationale:* why this product (or system) was built
- specification of *security-enforcing functions:* security properties of the product (or system)
- definition of the *mechanisms* of the product (or system) by which security is enforced
- a claim as to the *strength* of the mechanisms
- the target *evaluation level,* in terms of functionality and effectiveness

The evaluation proceeds to determine

- *suitability of functionality:* whether the chosen functions implement the desired security features
- *binding of functionality:* whether the chosen functions work together synergistically
- *vulnerabilities:* whether vulnerabilities exist either in the construction of the TOE or in how it will work in its intended environment
- *ease of use*
- *strength of mechanism:* the ability of the TOE to withstand direct attack

The results of these subjective evaluations determine whether the evaluators agree that the product or system deserves its proposed functionality and effectiveness rating.

Significant Departures from the Orange Book   The European ITSEC offers the following significant changes over the orange book. These variations have both advantages and disadvantages, as listed in Table 7-8.

U.S. Combined Federal Criteria

Partly in response to these criteria efforts occurring largely in Europe, in 1992 the United States embarked on a plan to update the TCSEC, which had been written over a decade earlier. This effort produced a single draft of the *Combined Federal Criteria* [NSA92], produced jointly by the National Institute for Standards and Technology (NIST) (formerly the National Bureau of Standards, NBS) and the National Security Agency (NSA) (which formerly handled criteria and evaluations through its National Computer Security Center, or NCSC).

The team that produced the *Combined Federal Criteria* was strongly influenced by the criteria from Canada [CSS93], released in draft status just before the combined criteria effort began. The combined criteria draft resembled the European model, with some separation between features and assurance. The United States was faced with a compatibility issue with which the Europeans were not: the United States needed to be fair to vendors who had already passed evaluations at a particular level and, more importantly, to those who were planning for or in the middle of evaluations. Within that context, the United States moved very far in its criteria development.

The main contribution of the U.S. *Combined Federal Criteria* was the notion of security target (not to be confused with a target of evaluation or TOE) and protection profile.

Table 7-8   Advantages and Disadvantages of ITSEC Approach Versus TCSEC

Quality	Advantages	Disadvantages
New functionality requirement classes	• Surpasses traditional confidentiality focus of TCSEC • Shows additional areas in which products are needed	• Complicates user's choice
Decoupling of features and assurance	• Allows low-assurance or high-assurance product	• Requires user sophistication to decide when high assurance is needed • Some functionality may inherently require high assurance, but not guarantee receiving It
Permitting new feature definitions; independence from specific security policy	• Allows evaluation of any kind of security-enforcing product • Allows vendor to decide what products the market requires	• Complicates comparing evaluations of differently described but similar products • Requires vendor to formulate requirements to define product's features best • Preset feature bundles not necessarily hierarchical
Commercial evaluation facilities	• Subject to market forces for time, schedule, price	• Government does not have direct control of evaluation • Evaluation cost paid by vendor

A user would generate a **protection profile** to detail the protection needs, both functional and assurance, for a specific situation or a generic scenario. This user might be a government sponsor, a commercial user, an organization representing many similar users, a product vendor's marketing representative, or a product inventor. The protection profile would be an abstract specification of the security aspects needed in an information technology (IT) product. The protection profile would contain the elements listed in Table 7-9.

In response to a protection profile, a vendor might produce a product that, the vendor would assert, met the requirements of the profile. The vendor would then map the requirements of the protection profile in the context of the specific product, onto a statement called a **security target**. As shown in Table 7-10, the security target matches the elements of the protection profile.

The security target then becomes the basis for the evaluation. The target details which threats are countered, by which features and to what degree of assurance, using what mechanisms. The security target outlines the convincing argument that the product satisfies the requirements of the protection profile. Whereas the protection profile is an abstract description of requirements, the security target is a detailed specification of *how* each of those requirements is met in the specific product.

The criteria document also included long lists of potential requirements (a subset of which could be selected for a particular protection profile), covering topics from object reuse to accountability, and from covert channel analysis to fault tolerance. Much of the work of specification of precise requirement statements came from the Canadian criteria, then in draft form.

Table 7-9 Protection Profile	**Table 7-10 Security Target**
Rationale	**Rationale**
• Protection policy and regulations • Information protection philosophy • Expected threats • Environmental assumptions • Intended use	• Implementation fundamentals • Information protection philosophy • Countered threats • Environmental assumptions • Intended use
Functionality	**Functionality**
• Security features • Security services • Available security mechanisms (optional)	• Security features • Security services • Security mechanisms selected
Assurance	**Assurance**
• Profile-specific assurances • Profile-independent assurances	• Target-specific assurances • Target-independent assurances
Dependencies	**Dependencies**
• Internal dependencies • External dependencies	• Internal dependencies • External dependencies

The U.S. *Combined Federal Criteria* was issued only once, in initial draft form. After receiving a round of comments, the editorial team announced that they had decided to join forces with the Canadians and the editorial board from the ITSEC to produce a *Common Criteria* for the entire world.

Common Criteria

The Common Criteria [CCE94] approach closely resembles the U.S. *Federal Criteria* (which, of course, was heavily influenced by the ITSEC and Canadian efforts). It preserves the concepts of security targets and protections profiles. The U.S. *Federal Criteria* was intended to have packages of protection requirements that were complete and consistent for a particular type of application, such as a network communications switch, a local area network, or a stand-alone operating system. The example packages received special attention in the *Common Criteria*.

The *Common Criteria* defined topics of interest to security, which are shown in Table 7-11.

Table 7-11   Classes in *Common Criteria*

Functionality	**Assurance**
Identification and authentication	Development
Trusted path	Testing
Security audit	Vulnerability assessment
Invocation of security functions	Configuration management
User data protection	Life-cycle support
Resource utilization	Guidance documents
Protection of the trusted security functions	Delivery and operation
Privacy	
Communication	

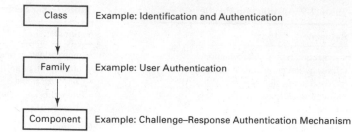

Figure 7-25   Classes, Families, and Components in *Common Criteria*

Under each of these classes, they defined families of functions or assurance needs, and from the families they defined individual components, as shown in Figure 7-25.

Individual components were then combined into packages of components that met some comprehensive requirement (for functionality) or some level of trust (for assurance), as shown in Figure 7-26.

Finally, the packages were combined into requirements sets or assertions for specific applications or products, as shown in Figure 7-27.

Summary of Evaluation Criteria

Have the criteria development efforts been successful? For some, it is too soon to tell. For others, the answer lies in the number and kinds of products that have passed evaluation, and how well the products have been accepted in the marketplace.

Desirable qualities of evaluations are listed in Table 7-12. The applicability and extensibility of the TCSEC are somewhat limited. Compatibility is being addressed by combining criteria, although the experience with the ITSEC has shown that simply combining the words of criteria documents does not necessarily produce a consistent understanding of those words. The British criteria documents—and this carried through to the ITSEC and its companion evaluation methodology, the ITSEM—stressed consistency of evaluation results. It was unacceptable for a vendor to receive different results after bringing the same product to two different evaluation facilities, or to one facility at two different times. Speed, thoroughness, and objectivity are three qualities that many people acknowledge as important, but evaluations still take a long time, relative to a commercial computer product delivery cycle of 6 to 18 months. You should review new criteria developments against these objectives as new documents emerge.

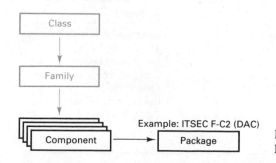

Figure 7-26   Functionality or Assurance Packages in *Common Criteria*

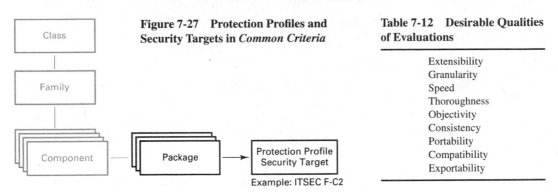

Figure 7-27   Protection Profiles and Security Targets in *Common Criteria*

Example: ITSEC F-C2

Table 7-12   Desirable Qualities of Evaluations

Extensibility
Granularity
Speed
Thoroughness
Objectivity
Consistency
Portability
Compatibility
Exportability

As a guide to progress in computer security evaluation, look at the times when different criteria documents were published to see which had effects on which others. Figure 7-28 shows the timing of the different criteria publications; the writing preceded the publication by one or more years. The figure starts with the original Anderson *Security Technology Planning Study* [AND72], which was the initial call for methodical, independent evaluation.

The criteria development activities have made enormous progress since 1983. The U.S. TCSEC was based on the state of best practice known at the time it was originally debated (approximately 1980). (A workshop was held in 1979 to discuss a tentative draft for what later became the TCSEC.) It draws heavily from the structured programming paradigm that was popular throughout the 1970s. Its major difficulty was that it was used in a very prescriptive manner to force that model on all developments and all types of products. The TCSEC applied most naturally to monolithic, stand-alone, multiuser operating systems, not to the heterogeneous, distributed, networked environment based largely on individual intelligent workstations that followed in the next decade.

To date, criteria efforts have not led to much commercial acceptance of trusted products. The computer security research community is heavily dominated by defense needs

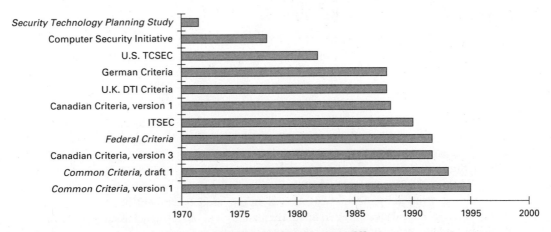

Figure 7-28   Criteria Development Efforts

because much of the funding for security research is derived from defense departments. Ware [WAR95] points out that the initial TCSEC was

- driven by the defense department
- focused on threat as perceived by the defense department
- based on a defense department concept of operations, including cleared personnel, strong respect for authority/management, and generally secure physical environments
- of little relevance to networks, LANs, WANs, Internets, client–server distributed architectures, and other more recent modes of computing

There is one other fatal flaw of criteria activities: when the TCSEC was introduced, there was an implicit contract between the government and vendors, saying that if vendors built products and had them evaluated, the government would buy them. Anderson [AND82] warned how important it was for the government to keep its end of the bargain. The vendors did their part by numerous developments now of only historical interest: KSOS, PSOS, Scomp, KVM, and Multics. The government did not follow through and create the market that would encourage these vendors to continue and other vendors to join. If there were many evaluated products on the market, support and usability would be more adequately addressed, and there would be a good chance for commercial adoption. As it is, there has been almost no commercial acceptance of any of these products, even though they have been developed to some of the highest quality standards.

Some major vendors are actively embracing low assurance evaluations. Some have announced corporate commitments to evaluation, noting that independent evaluation is a mark of quality that will always be a stronger selling point than so-called emphatic assertion (when a vendor makes loud claims about the strength of a product with no independent evidence to substantiate those claims). The current trends in criteria writing support objectives such as integrity and availability as strongly as confidentiality, and allow a vendor to identify a market niche and build a product for it, rather than building a product for a paper need that is not matched by purchases. There is reason for optimism regarding criteria and evaluations. But realism requires everyone to accept that the market—not a criteria document—will dictate what is truly desired and delivered.

What *Doesn't* Lead to Assurance?

The principles presented here have been derived over time and have shown that they can produce high-quality, reliable products, deserving of confidence. In this section we consider some small points that do *not* lead to confidence in the implementation.

Emphatic Assertion

When you buy a used car, you expect the sales agent to tell you the car is wonderful, was carefully treated, and would be a bargain at twice the price. You expect the agent to stress, perhaps even exaggerate, the best points.

Some marketers for secure systems similarly assert that their product is very trustworthy. Phrases like "designed to be B2" or "contains some B3 features" have little meaning. The point of an independent evaluation is an unbiased assessment of features and assurance, *and* of the balance between them. B2 features without adequate assurance are of questionable value. And why include only some B3 features? The marketing representative must stress the best qualities; consider carefully what those best qualities are.

Security Through Obscurity

A phrase frequently used in the security community is **security through obscurity,** as something to be avoided. The phrase means that there is little security obtained by hiding functionality or data, hoping no one will find it. Like a trapdoor, someone may stumble upon the hidden item, and some attackers will search diligently for things supposedly well hidden.

Better than obscurity is an open design, one that can be analyzed and debated publicly.

I Couldn't Find Flaws

One vendor introduced a product by saying, essentially, "This product cannot have any flaws because I looked for them carefully, and I couldn't find any." The vendor was strangely silent when, not surprisingly, a flaw in the use of the product was discovered by a user who did something the vendor had never expected.

Challenges

Another manufacturer has introduced a product by offering a challenge and a modest prize to anyone who defeats the security in the product. As Spafford [SPA95] points out, the successful attacker may profit more from knowing of a flaw, and being able to exploit it quietly at will, than from publicizing the flaw and winning the modest prize. And if the flaw were reported, would the vendor publicize it? What if fixing the fault would require a substantial redesign and redevelopment effort, taking many months? And would experienced professionals voluntarily spend a significant amount of uncompensated time and effort trying to make a vendor's product look good?

Careful design work, serious and organized testing, and professional independent assessment will demonstrate the quality of a product.

7.6   Implementation Examples

In the preceding sections we studied the design of the security portions of operating systems. You need to understand the features and assurance qualities of operating systems that can contribute to the overall security of a computing system. However, not every application requires A1 or F-A1/E6 quality security, which is fortunate because few operating systems have the features needed to make them A1 and fewer still are built with the care and discipline necessary to be judged E6.

In this section we consider actual operating systems, looking at features such as access control, security kernel, and design. We will see two examples from the general commercial world, and then two other examples from the more restricted world of TCSEC-inspired systems. In order to keep the descriptions short, we cover only features relevant to security, and then only some of those features.

General Purpose Operating Systems

First we look at two examples of general purpose operating systems that are in wide use. The first of these is Unix, which we have already seen in numerous examples throughout this book. We explore some of the design and development characteristics of Unix that have had an impact on its security. The second operating system is IBM's PR/SM, which is also in widespread use on mainframe computers, and whose origin and development have influenced its security.

Unix

The Unix operating system was never intended to have a high degree of security. It was designed in 1969 by two programmers, primarily for their own use to develop, test, and maintain programs. The system was intended for use in "nonhostile" environments, places such as research laboratories and universities, where the advantages of easy sharing of objects far outweighed the possibility of unfriendly access.

As a result, sharing of files, data, devices, and storage volumes is relatively simple, unencumbered by a strong protection mechanism. The Unix system administrator is assumed to be a programmer, too, who administers only part of the time and who does not, cannot, or should not perform many security functions.

Unix grew essentially without plan. The Unix designers, Ken Thompson, Dennis Ritchie, Doug McIlroy, and J.F. Ossanna, were programmers at Bell Laboratories when a decision was made to withdraw from the Multics project. Having grown used to the luxury of interactive use of a computing utility, they searched until they found an available machine on which to write their system. The design of Unix was largely the product of Thompson, who designed the initial version and was heavily involved in the development of the system for over a decade.

Thompson's goal was to provide a simple toolbox, in which a user could store and access a variety of tools that could be combined for individual uses. Generality and compactness were two qualities prominent in the design of the elementary Unix functions, and that is still a hallmark of the operating system. Unix was intended to be extensible. However, this freedom brought security problems. If each user could add to the functionality of Unix, so could a malicious user. Simplicity and economy of design are virtues for the users of the system, but they are a nightmare to the designer of a secure system. Security decisions permeate the Unix commands.

There is one identified user, called the superuser, who can perform essentially any operation in the system. Because the superuser is all-powerful, most system attacks are aimed at obtaining rights of the superuser. After having obtained this right once, even for only a few seconds, a penetrator can establish a trapdoor that permits superuser access at any time in the future.

A user sharing access to a system program can obtain high security rights if the system program runs in *setuid* mode; when a user executes such a program, the file access rights during execution of the program are the rights of the program's owner, not the program's user. The intended purpose of this feature is so that a user can use a utility program, such as *mail*, and through the program, access files at the level of *mail*. However, most sensitive utility programs are "owned" by the superuser, so that a security flaw exploited in one utility program gives very wide access.

To Unix all objects—directories, I/O devices, even parts of memory—are files and are accessed with the same structure. Again, this simplicity is good for the user, but it makes security difficult. File access permission is checked only once, when the file is opened. By changing the characteristics of the file or device after it has been opened, a user can obtain unchecked access permission.

Unix is distributed in modular form: an individual installation decides which features or modules it wants to use. Administrators can acquire modules from a wide range of external providers or even write their own and link them into the Unix operating system. A user can also build an individual environment of commands and functions. Of course, in order for Unix to support additions and replacements, all Unix interfaces must be clearly and completely documented, which they are. This ability to change is an advantage to attackers, who can replace practically any functions, including login, password management, object-level access control, and auditing, often without the knowledge of administrators or users.

Unix provides reasonable security for the environment for which it was designed: essentially a friendly environment. However, the inherent lack of security in the basic Unix system is evident from the fact that Unix-based secure operating systems have actually been implemented by substantial rewrites of the Unix kernel, to provide a system that has the outward functionality of Unix with a different internal structure. Sibert et al. [SIB87] describe the difficulties that would occur if Unix were to be evaluated for B2 certification.

PR/SM

The IBM Processor Resources/System Manager (PR/SM) is not really an operating system. It is a resource manager that provides strong separation and strictly controlled sharing of virtual machines. PR/SM does not support ordinary user tasks; instead, its "users" are other operating systems. PR/SM follows a long line of IBM mainframe virtual machine operating systems, including VM/370 and MVS.

PR/SM implements a very simple security policy: strict separation. All resources are partitioned into separate domains, so that resources and processes running in one domain are unaware of and perceive no effect from resources and processes in other domains. PR/SM manages all hardware resources, which are shared only serially; that is, when each resource (such as memory or processor registers) is to be reallocated to another operating system, the resource is completely purged of data before being reallocated. Other resources, such as direct access storage devices, are allocated to just one domain.

The PR/SM operating system was designed to run other operating systems. The PR/SM operating system consists of a **logical partition manager (LPAR)** that maps physical devices and hardware interactions to signals passed between LPAR and each subject operating system.

PR/SM was intended as a way to support two or more different operating systems on a single computing system. Two systems might be desirable during a gradual changeover from one operating system to another, so that both systems could be available at the same time. Another reason for two systems is to be able to change and test one operating system in an environment where a system error in one (virtual) machine would not affect other users.

Virtualization was originally designed to provide flexibility in addressing and memory management; security was achieved as a bonus. The PR/SM operating system turned out to have a security advantage as well. Because LPAR performs all actual interaction with hardware, it acts as a second security layer between the operating system and the hardware.

Suppose a user identifies and exploits a flaw in the operating system (that is, in the operating system running in the user's virtual machine, such as MVS/ESA). Under PR/SM, the user might get outside the user domain and reach the operating system domain (where MVS/ESA is run). The user still does not have access to the actual machine hardware, nor to users or domains running on other operating systems on other virtual machines. To penetrate another user or operating system, the user would have to find and exploit yet another flaw, this one in the security mechanism of PR/SM itself.

The separation of PR/SM is not just for security purposes. Strictly separate domains permit an installation to run a testing environment without risking interfering with a domain supporting commercial needs. Separate domains can also serve as redundant backup capabilities, ready to take over instantly in the event of a hardware or software failure. Finally, separate domains can run different operating systems for separate communities of users.

PR/SM security capabilities include extensive hardware and software support for domain separation, strong role-based security management for such things as configuring the partitioning of resources to domains, audit of actions of security administrators, and a secure communications path to PR/SM from security administrators and from the domains.

Operating Systems Designed for Security

The examples just described are commercial operating systems. These systems meet well-defined security needs, such as an environment of trustworthy collaborators for Unix or a situation requiring protection against either inadvertent or, less likely, malicious attempts of a process in one domain to interfere with one in another domain. In the case of Unix, the degree of security is moderate; in the case of PR/SM, the degree of security is high, but is implemented largely by hardware, to avoid a major performance penalty. The security requirements for these systems are commensurate with the degree of threat expected.

Following are operating systems designed for environments having far greater security needs. In the design, security was the foremost requirement, with such factors as usability and efficiency having lower importance. Such systems might be used for government security applications, diplomatic communication, or projects where the value of the assets of the system is high.

VAX Security Kernel

VAX Security Kernel was a project from Digital Equipment Corp. targeted at the A1 level of the TCSEC. It would have led to a very high assurance (A1) security kernel supporting the widely used commercial operating systems VMS and Ultrix. Standard VMS utilities and other software would run on the security kernel, so that it would have a large number of widely used, well-supported applications. This kernel would have been the bridge between high assurance and mainstream commercial operating systems.

The security kernel faithfully emulated the underlying VAX hardware, including exporting all privilege states (virtualized versions), virtualized I/O (through monitoring of specific memory locations that reflect I/O data and status registers), and virtualized memory. The security kernel concurrently enforced Bell–La Padula mandatory confidentiality *and* Biba mandatory integrity.

The design of the security kernel was carefully constructed in 16 layers, each of which exported a capability to the layers above but depended on only layers below. This layered structure simplifies debugging and imposes an order on the data and control flows of the system. The layers protect themselves from above.

The A1 requirements dictate a development philosophy and methodology, starting with a formal model of security policy, a formal presentation of the highest level design, and an argument that the formal design carries through to the implementation. The VAX security kernel was developed using rigid configuration control. The system was, in fact, built twice, once as a research and learning vehicle and once for real. Performance was significantly better in the second version.

The project began as a proposal for a research prototype in 1981, which was implemented between 1982 and 1984. This first version was redone at production quality by 1988. Tuning, additional development, and final documentation and preparation for the evaluation took place between 1988 and 1990. In 1990 the project was terminated. The two reasons people have cited for the termination were corporate unwillingness to support multiple versions of the VAX family of operating systems (one for the security kernel and the other for general—not A1— distribution) and export control restrictions.

The VAX virtual machine monitor project remains an outstanding example of high-quality development of trusted systems. Excellent descriptions of this project, especially the security design issues, are in [KAR90, KAR91a].

TMach

Trusted Mach (**TMach**) is a research and product development activity initially sponsored by the U.S. Defense Advanced Research Projects Agency (DARPA). TMach, from Trusted Information Systems, Inc., is a trusted version of the Mach operating system, originally from Carnegie Mellon University and now part of the Open Software Foundation (OSF) microkernel project.

Mach is a kernel-based, multithreaded (supporting multiple concurrent points of execution, called threads, for each task), server-oriented (structured so that each operating system service is provided by an identifiable server, in response to a service request from a client) operating system. Trusted Mach retains these qualities, at the B3 or E5 level of assurance. TMach will be easily portable to a wide range of hardware platforms, easily extensible, able to support multiple operating system interfaces (called personalities) including Unix, and easily extensible.

TMach is implemented as multiple independent servers, each performing a specific function, as shown in Figure 7-29. The servers are hierarchically ordered.

Figure 7-30 shows how TMach supports multiple operating system personalities. All operating system servers could be instances of the same or different systems. Because the operating systems run as untrusted code, they have no impact on the security of the system, and thus they are not a part of the evaluation. Although at first that might seem negative, it actually is very positive. First, as with virtual machines, each operating system personality is completely confined within its own TMach-imposed domain. Thus, no one operating system, which might be malicious, can affect user processes in another operating system server. From the standpoint of evaluation and use, a user is free to change operating systems, adopt a new release, or reconfigure the operating system at will, without affecting the security of the system. This flexibility solves the problem of long evaluation times relative to the short interval between new versions.

7.7   Summary of Security in Operating Systems

Operating systems are at the heart of security systems for modern computers. Operating systems must provide the mechanisms for both separation and sharing; these mechanisms must be robust yet easy to use.

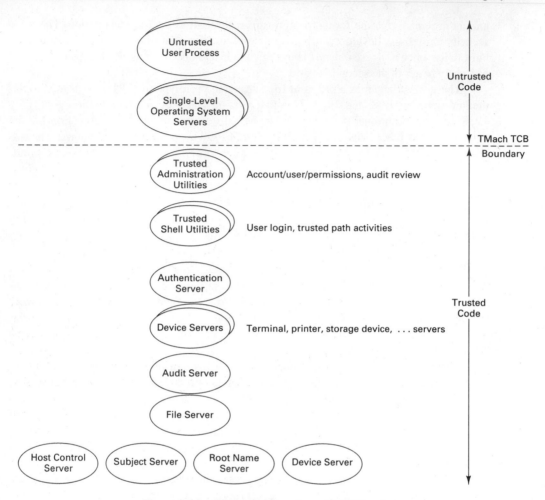

Figure 7-29   TMach TCB and non-TCB Structure

Development of secure operating systems involves four activities. First, the environment to be protected must be well-understood. Through policy statements and models, the essential components of systems are identified and the interactions between these components can be studied. This chapter presented a variety of policies and models of security. Whereas the policies covered confidentiality and integrity, the models ranged from reference monitors and information flow filters to multilevel security and integrity models. Models such as the one by Bell and La Padula describe permissible access in a multilevel environment, and the HRU model demonstrates the limits of computer security.

After an environment is understood, a system must be designed to provide the desired protection. Certain design principles for secure operating systems were presented. Not surprisingly, features such as least privilege, openness of design, and economy of mechanism are quite similar to the software engineering design principles described in Chapter 5. Characteristics that lead to good design of an operating system apply to the design of other

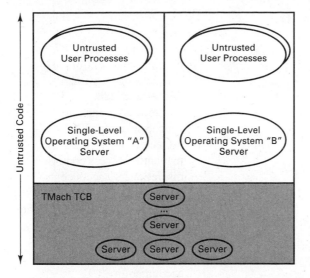

Figure 7-30   **TMach Supporting Multiple Operating System Personalities**

programs as well. Isolation or separation, layered design, and security kernel were studied in some detail.

After having an operating system design, one wants assurance that the design (and its implementation) are correct. This chapter considered three methods to demonstrate correctness: formal verification, validation, and penetration testing. Several evaluation criteria were examined in detail because they represent the current standard for certification of trusted computing systems.

Finally, several examples of the implementations of secure operating systems were studied. These examples included both widely available commercial systems and systems designed specifically for their security features.

In Chapter 8, secure data base management systems are studied. Data base systems have many of the same requirements as operating systems: access control, availability, and multilevel security. Data base management systems are implemented on top of operating systems, and thus they use some of the services provided by operating systems. Integrity and granularity are substantially different in those systems, however.

7.8   Bibliographic Notes

The topic of secure computing systems includes fundamental papers such as Lampson [LAM71], Popek [POP74a], Hoare [HOA74], Graham [GRA68], Saltzer and Schroeder [SAL75], and Jones [JON78a]. Landwehr [LAN81] provides a good overview of models of protection systems. Additional information on policy and models of security is provided by Bell [BEL83], Harrison [HAR85], Goguen and Meseguer [GOG82], Clark and Wilson [CLA87], Badger [BAD89], Karger [KAR88], Brewer and Nash [BRE89].

The design of secure systems is discussed by Gasser [GAS88], Ames [AME83] and Landwehr [LAN83]. Certification of security-enforcing systems is discussed by Neumann [NEU78] and Neugent [NEU82]. Criteria documents are the easiest to locate, in [CCE94], [NSA92], [ITS91a, ITS91b], [CSS93], [DTI89a, DTI89b, DTI89c], and [GIS88]. Also read commentary by Neumann [NEU90a, NEU90b] and Ware [WAR95].

7.9 Terms and Concepts

7.10 Exercises

1. There is another principle of the Bell–La Padula model that was not mentioned in this chapter. This principle, called the **tranquility principle,** states that the classification of a subject or object does not change while it is being referenced. Explain the purpose of the tranquility principle. What are the implications of a model in which the tranquility principle is *not* true?

2. A subject can access another subject. Describe how a reference monitor would control access in the case of a subject acting on another subject. Describe how a reference monitor would control access in the case of two subjects interacting.

3. List the source and end of all information flows in each of the following statements.
   ```
   a. sum := a+b+c;
   b. if a+b < c+d then q:=0 else q:=1;
   c. write (a,b,c);
   d. read (a,b,c);
   e. case (k) of
        0: d:= 10;
        1,2: d:= 20;
        other: d:= 30;
      end; /* case */
   ```

```
   f. for i:=min to max do k:= 2*k+1;
   g. repeat
          a[i]:=0;
          i:=i-1;
          until i ≤ 0;
```

4. Does the system of all subsets of a finite set, under the operation "subset of" (⊆) form a lattice? Why or why not?

5. Can a user cleared for ⟨*secret*; {dog, cat, pig}⟩ have access to documents classified in each of the following ways under the military security model?
   a. ⟨*top secret*;dog⟩
   b. ⟨*secret*; {dog}⟩
   c. ⟨*secret*; {dog,cow}⟩
   d. ⟨*secret*; {moose}⟩
   e. ⟨*confidential*; {dog,pig,cat}⟩
   f. ⟨*confidential*; {moose}⟩

6. According to the Bell–La Padula model, what restrictions are placed on two active subjects (for example, two processes) that wished to send and receive signals to each other? Justify your answer.

7. Write a set of rules combining the secrecy controls of the Bell–La Padula model with the integrity controls of the Biba model.

8. Demonstrate a method for limited transfer of rights in the Graham–Denning model. A limit of one is adequate. That is, give a method by which A can transfer to B right R, with the provision that B can transfer that right to any one other subject. The subject to which B transfers the right cannot transfer the right, nor can B transfer it again.

9. Explain what is necessary to provide temporal separation. That is, what conditions must be met in order for two processes to be adequately separated?

10. Does the standard Unix operating system use a nondiscretionary access control? Explain your answer.

11. Why is labeling of objects a security requirement? That is, why cannot the trusted computing base just maintain an access control table with entries for each object and each subject?

12. Label integrity is a technique that ensures that the label on each object is changed only by the trusted computing base. Suggest a method to implement label integrity for a data file. Suggest a method to implement label integrity for a callable procedure.

13. Describe a situation in which you might want to allow the security kernel to violate one of the security properties of the Bell–La Padula model.

14. Explain the meaning of the term *granularity* in reference to access control. Discuss the tradeoff between granularity and efficiency.

15. Explain how a semaphore could be used to implement a covert channel in concurrent processing. Explain how concurrent processing primitives, such as *fork* and *join*, could be used to implement a covert channel in concurrent processing.

16. The Unix operating system structures files by use of a tree. Each file is at a leaf of the tree, and the file is identified by the (unique) path from the root to the leaf. Each interior node is a subdirectory, which specifies the names of the paths leading from that

node. A user can block access through a node by restricting access to the subdirectory. Devise a method that uses this structure to implement a discretionary access policy.

17. In the Unix file system described in this chapter, could a nondiscretionary access policy be defined so that a user has access to a file only if the user has access to all subdirectories higher (closer to the root) in the file structure? What would be the effect of this policy?

18. I/O appears as the source of several successful methods of penetration. Discuss why I/O is hard to secure in a computing system.

8

Data Base Security

In this chapter:
- *Integrity for data bases: record integrity, data correctness, update integrity*
- *Security for data bases: access control, inference, aggregation*
- *Multilevel secure data bases: partitioned, cryptographically sealed, filtered*

In this chapter we consider the security of data base management systems. This is an area of substantial interest in computing security because data bases are newer than programming and operating systems, data bases are becoming very important in business and government, and, most importantly, data bases contain information that is of far greater general interest than a piece of software. The value of information is just now being recognized as a major corporate asset.

The protection provided by data base systems has had mixed results. Recently we have come closer to understanding the problems of data base security, and several good controls have been developed. However, there are still more security concerns than there are available controls.

We begin this chapter with a brief summary of data base terminology. We then consider the security requirements for data base management systems. Two major security problems—integrity and secrecy—are explained in a data base context. The chapter concludes with a study of two major data base security problems, the inference problem and the multilevel problem, which are really related problems. Both of these problems are complex, and there are no immediate solutions. However, by understanding the problems we become more sensitive to ways of reducing the potential threat to the data.

8.1 Introduction to Data Bases

We begin by describing a data base and defining the terminology of data base use. We focus on what is called the relational data base because it is the most widely used. We define the basic concepts first and then discuss security concerns.

Concept of a Data Base

A **data base** is a collection of *data* and a set of *rules* that organize the data by specifying certain relationships among the data. Through these rules, the user describes a *logical* format for the data. The data items are stored in a file, but the precise *physical* format of the file is of no concern to the user. A **data base administrator** is a person who defines the rules that organize the data and controls who should have access to what parts of the data. The user interacts with the data base through a program called a **data base manager** or a **data base management system (DBMS),** informally known as a **front end**.

Components of Data Bases

The data base file consists of **records**, each of which contains one related group of data. As shown in Figure 8-1, a record in a name and address file would consist of one name and address. Each record consists of **fields** or **elements**, the elementary data items themselves. The fields in the name and address record are NAME, ADDRESS, CITY, STATE, and ZIP. This data base may be viewed as a two-dimensional table, where a record is a row and each field of a record is an element of the table.

Not every data base is easily represented as a single, compact table. The data base in Figure 8-2 logically consists of three files with possibly different uses. These three files could be represented as one large table, but that may not improve the utility of or access to the data.

The logical structure of a data base is called a **schema**. A particular user may have access to part of the data base, called a **subschema**. The overall schema of the data base in Figure 8-2 is pictured in Figure 8-3. The three separate blocks are examples of subschemas, although other subschemas of this data base can be defined.

ADAMS	212 Market St.	Columbus	OH	43210
BENCHLY	501 Union St.	Chicago	IL	60603
CARTER	411 Elm St.	Columbus	OH	43210

Figure 8-1   Example of a Data Base

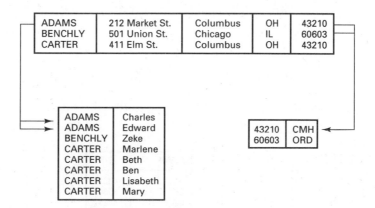

Figure 8-2   Related Parts of a Data Base

NAME	FIRST	ADDRESS	CITY	STATE	ZIP	AIRPORT
ADAMS	Charles	212 Market St.	Columbus	OH	43210	CMH
ADAMS	Edward	212 Market St.	Columbus	OH	43210	CMH
BENCHLY	Zeke	501 Union St.	Chicago	IL	60603	ORD
CARTER	Marlene	411 Elm St.	Columbus	OH	43210	CMH
CARTER	Beth	411 Elm St.	Columbus	OH	43210	CMH
CARTER	Ben	411 Elm St.	Columbus	OH	43210	CMH
CARTER	Lisabeth	411 Elm St.	Columbus	OH	43210	CMH
CARTER	Mary	411 Elm St.	Columbus	OH	43210	CMH

Figure 8-3   Schema of Previous Data Base

The rules of a data base identify the columns with names. The name of each column is called an **attribute** of the data base. A **relation** is a set of columns. For example, using the data base in Figure 8-3, NAME–ZIP is a relation formed by taking the NAME and ZIP columns, as shown in Figure 8-4. The relation specifies clusters of related data values, in much the same way that the relation "mother of" specifies a relationship among pairs of humans. In this example, each cluster contains a pair of elements, a NAME and a ZIP. Other relations have more columns, so that each cluster may be a triple, a 4-tuple, or an *n*-tuple (for some value *n*) of elements.

Queries

Users interact with data base managers through commands that retrieve, modify, add, or delete fields and records of the data base. A command is called a **query**. Data base management systems have precise rules of syntax for queries. Most query languages use an English-like notation. The example queries in this chapter resemble English sentences so that they are easy to understand. For example, the query

```
SELECT NAME = 'ADAMS'
```

retrieves all records having the value *ADAMS* in the NAME field.

The result of executing a query is a subschema. One way to form a subschema of a data base is by selecting records meeting certain conditions. For example, we might select records in which ZIP = 43210, producing the result shown in Figure 8-5.

Other more complex selection criteria are possible, using logical operators such as *and* ($\wedge$) and *or* ($\vee$), and comparisons such as *less than* ($<$). An example of a select query is

```
SELECT (ZIP = '43210') ∧ (NAME = 'ADAMS')
```

After having selected records, we may **project** these records onto one or more attributes. The select operation extracts certain rows from the data base, whereas a project

NAME	ZIP
ADAMS	43210
BENCHLY	60603
CARTER	43210

Figure 8-4   Relation in a Data Base

NAME	FIRST	ADDRESS	CITY	STATE	ZIP	AIRPORT
ADAMS	Charles	212 Market St.	Columbus	OH	43210	CMH
ADAMS	Edward	212 Market St.	Columbus	OH	43210	CMH
CARTER	Marlene	411 Elm St.	Columbus	OH	43210	CMH
CARTER	Beth	411 Elm St.	Columbus	OH	43210	CMH
CARTER	Ben	411 Elm St.	Columbus	OH	43210	CMH
CARTER	Lisabeth	411 Elm St.	Columbus	OH	43210	CMH
CARTER	Mary	411 Elm St.	Columbus	OH	43210	CMH

Figure 8-5   Result of Select Query

operation extracts the values from certain fields (columns) of those records. The result of a select–project operation is the set of values of specified attributes for the selected records. For example, we might select records meeting the condition ZIP = 43210 and project the results onto the attributes NAME and FIRST, as in Figure 8-6. The result is the list of first and last names of people whose addresses have zip code 43210.

Notice that you do not have to project onto the same attribute(s) on which the selection is done. An example of a project query is

```
SHOW FIRST WHERE (ZIP = '43210') ∧ (NAME = 'ADAMS')
```

Finally, two subschema can be merged on a common element by a **join** query. The result of this operation is a subschema whose records have the same value for the common element. The example in Figure 8-7 shows that the subschema NAME–ZIP and the subschema ZIP–AIRPORT can be joined on the common field ZIP to produce the subschema NAME–AIRPORT.

Advantages of Using Data Bases

A data base is one collection of data, stored and maintained at one central location, to which many people have access as needed. (This is the logical principle of a data base; the actual implementation may involve some other physical storage arrangement or access, so long as the user's perception is as above.) The advantages of using a data base are

- *shared access,* so that many users can use one common, centralized set of data
- *minimal redundancy,* so that individual users do not have to collect and maintain their own sets of data

ADAMS	Charles
ADAMS	Edward
CARTER	Marlene
CARTER	Beth
CARTER	Ben
CARTER	Lisabeth
CARTER	Mary

Figure 8-6   Results of Select–Project Query

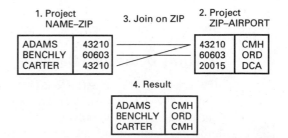

Figure 8-7   Results of Select–Project–Join Query

- *data consistency,* so that a change to a data value affects all users of the data value
- *data integrity,* so that data values are protected against accidental or malicious incorrect changes
- *controlled access,* so that only authorized users are allowed to view or to modify data values

A DBMS is designed to provide these advantages efficiently. However, as often happens, the objectives can conflict with each other. In particular, as we shall see, security interests can conflict with performance. This is not surprising because measures to enforce security often increase the size or complexity of a computing system. What is surprising, however, is that security interests may also reduce the ability of the system to provide data to users, by limiting certain queries that seem innocuous by themselves.

8.2   Security Requirements

The basic security requirements of data base systems are not unlike the security requirements of other computing systems we have studied. The basic problems—access control, exclusion of spurious data, authentication of users, and reliability—have appeared in many contexts so far in this book. Following is a list of requirements for security of data base systems.

- *Physical data base integrity,* so that the data of a data base is immune to physical problems such as power failures and so that someone can reconstruct the data base if it is destroyed through a catastrophe.
- *Logical data base integrity,* so that the structure of the data base is preserved. With logical integrity of a data base, a modification to the value of one field does not affect other fields, for example.
- *Element integrity,* so that the data contained in each element is accurate.
- *Auditability,* to be able to track who has accessed (or modified) the elements in the data base.
- *Access control,* so that a user is allowed to access only authorized data and so that different users can be restricted to different modes of access (such as read or write).
- *User authentication,* to ensure that every user is positively identified, both for the audit trail and for permission to access certain data.
- *Availability,* meaning that users can access the data base in general and all the data for which they are authorized.

We examine each of these requirements briefly.

Integrity of the Data Base

If a data base is to serve as a central repository of data, users must be able to trust the accuracy of the data values. This implies that the data base manager must be assured that updates are performed only by authorized individuals. It also implies that the data must be protected from corruption, either by an outside illegal program action or by an outside force such as a fire or power failure. Two situations can affect the integrity of a data base: when the whole data base is damaged (as happens, for example, if a disk pack is damaged) or when individual data items are unreadable.

Integrity of the data base as a whole is the responsibility of the DBMS, the operating system, and the computing system manager. From the perspective of the operating system and the computing system manager, data bases and DBMSs are files and programs, respectively. Therefore, one form of protection for the data base as a whole is regular backup copies of all files on the system. Periodic backups of a data base can be adequate controls against catastrophic failure.

If it is important to be able to reconstruct the data base at the point of an error, the DBMS must maintain a log of transactions. For example, a bank account data base manager might generate a printed message each time a transaction is processed. In the event of a system failure, accurate account balances can be obtained by starting with a backup copy of the data base and reprocessing all later transactions from the log.

Element Integrity

The **integrity** of elements of a data base is their correctness or accuracy. Ultimately, authorized users are responsible for putting correct data into data bases. However, users make mistakes collecting data, computing results, and entering values. Therefore, DBMSs sometimes help a user catch errors as they are entered and correct errors after they are inserted.

The DBMS maintains the integrity of each item in the data base in three ways. First, it can apply **field checks**, which are tests for appropriate values in a position. A field might be required to be numeric, or an uppercase letter, or one of a set of acceptable characters. The check ensures that a value falls within specified bounds or is not greater than the sum of the values in two other fields. These checks prevent simple errors as the data is entered.

Integrity is also maintained by **access control**. A data base may contain data from several sources. Before the development of a data base, redundant data might have been stored in many places. For example, a student's address may be stored in many different campus files, some of which the student would not know. When the student moves, each separate file requires correction. Data bases have led to the collection and control of this data at one central source. This makes it easy for the student and users to be sure of having the correct address.

However, ownership of a shared central file is a question. Who has authorization to update which elements? What if two people apply conflicting modifications? What if modifications are applied out of sequence? How are duplicate records detected? What action is taken when duplicates are found? These are policy questions that must be resolved by the data base administrator.

The third means of maintaining the integrity of a data base is to maintain a **change log** for the data base. A change log is a list of every change made to the data base; the log contains both original and modified values. With this log a data base administrator can undo any changes that were in error. For example, a library fine might erroneously be posted against Charles W. Robertson, instead of Charles M. Robertson, flagging Charles W. Robertson as ineligible to participate in varsity athletics. Upon discovering this error, the data base administrator obtains Charles W.'s original eligibility value from the log and corrects the data base.

Auditability

In some applications it may be desirable to generate an audit record of all access (read or write) to a data base. Such a record can help to maintain the integrity of a data base or, at least, to discover after the fact who affected what values and when. A second advantage, as discussed later, is that users can build up access to protected data incrementally: no single access reveals protected data, but a set of accesses taken together reveals the data like the clues to a mystery. In this case, an audit trail would be useful to identify which clues a user has already been given, as a guide to whether to tell the user more.

Granularity becomes an impediment in auditing. Audited events in operating systems are things like *open file* or *call procedure*; they are seldom as specific as *write record* or *execute instruction*. To be useful for the purposes just described, audit trails for data bases must include accesses at the record, field, and element levels. This level of detail is prohibitive for most data base applications.

Furthermore, a record may be accessed but not reported to a user, as when the user performs a select operation. (Accessing a record or an element without transferring the data received to the user is called the pass-through problem.) Also, you can determine the values of some elements without accessing them directly. Thus, a log of all records accessed directly may both overstate and understate what a user actually knows.

Access Control

Data bases are often logically separated by user access privileges. For example, all users can be granted access to general data, but only the personnel department can obtain salary data and only the marketing department can obtain sales data. Data bases are very useful because they centralize the storage and maintenance of data. Limited access is both a responsibility and a benefit of this centralization.

The data base administrator specifies who should be allowed access to which data, at the field, or record, or even element level. The DBMS must enforce this policy, granting access to all specified data or no access where prohibited. Furthermore, the number of modes of access can be many. A user or program may have the right to read, change, delete, or append to a value, add or delete entire fields or records, or reorganize the entire data base.

Superficially, access control for a data base seems like access control for operating systems or any other component of a computing system. However, the data base problem is more complicated, as we will see throughout this chapter. Operating system objects, such as files, are unrelated items, whereas records, fields, and elements are related. Although a user cannot determine the contents of one file by reading others, a user might be able to determine one data element just by reading others. The problem of obtaining data values from others is called inference; that problem is considered later in this chapter.

You can access data by inference, without needing to have direct access to the secure object itself. Restricting inference may mean prohibiting certain paths in order to prevent possible inferences. However, restricting access to control inference also limits queries from users who did not intend to access values not authorized. Access to the data base may also be degraded by attempts to check requested accesses for possible unacceptable inferences.

Finally, size or granularity is different between operating system objects and data base objects. An access control list of several hundred files is much easier to implement than an access control list for a data base with several hundred files of perhaps a hundred fields each. Size affects efficiency of processing.

User Authentication

The DBMS can require rigorous user authentication. For example, a DBMS might require a user to pass both specific password and time-of-day checks. This authentication is in addition to authentication performed by the operating system. Typically, the DBMS runs as an application program on top of the operating system. This means that it has no trusted path to the operating system, and it must be suspicious of any data it receives, including user authentication. Thus the DBMS must do its own authentication.

Availability

A DBMS has aspects of both a program and a system. It is a program that uses other hardware and software resources, yet to many users it is the only application run. The availability requirements of a DBMS are high. One availability problem stems from arbitrating two users' requests for the same record. A second problem comes from needing to withhold some unprotected data in order to avoid revealing protected data. Both of these problems are described later.

Integrity/Secrecy/Availability

In this section we have outlined the three aspects of computer security—integrity, secrecy, and availability—as they relate to data base management systems. As we have described, integrity applies to the individual elements of a data base as well as to the data base as a whole. Thus, integrity is a major concern in the design of data base management systems. Integrity issues are covered in the next section.

Secrecy becomes a large issue with data bases because of inference. A user can access sensitive data indirectly. Inference and access control are covered in later sections of this chapter.

Finally, availability is important because of the shared access motivation underlying the development of data bases. However, availability can conflict with secrecy. The last sections of the chapter address availability in an environment where secrecy is also important.

8.3   Reliability and Integrity

Data bases are an amalgamation of data from many sources. Users entrust their data to a DBMS and rightfully expect protection of the data from loss or damage. Concern for reliability and integrity are general security issues, but they are more apparent with data bases.

Data bases really have three dimensions of reliability or integrity concerns:

- *Data base integrity:* concern that the data base as a whole is protected against damage, as from the failure of a disk drive or the corruption of the master data base index. These concerns are addressed by operating system integrity controls and recovery procedures.

- *Element integrity:* concern that the value of a specific data element is written or changed only by authorized users. Proper access controls protect a data base from corruption by unauthorized users.

- *Element accuracy:* concern that only correct values are written into the elements of a data base. Checks on the values of elements can help to prevent insertion of improper values. Also, constraint conditions can detect incorrect values.

There are several ways that a DBMS guards against the loss or damage of data. In this section we study methods to ensure data base integrity, element integrity, and element accuracy. However, these controls are not absolute: no control can prevent an authorized user from inadvertently entering an acceptable but incorrect value. Therefore, the ability to correct erroneous data in a data base is an important mechanism for ensuring accuracy.

Protection Features from the Operating System

In Chapter 6 we discussed the protection an operating system provides for its users. The files of a data base are backed up periodically, as are other user files. The files are protected during normal execution against outside access by standard access control facilities of the operating system. Finally, the operating system performs certain integrity checks for all data as a part of normal read and write operations for I/O devices. These controls provide basic security for data bases, but the data base manager must enhance these controls.

Two-Phase Update

A serious problem for a data base manager is the failure of the computing system in the middle of modifying data. If the data to be modified was a long field, half of the field might show the new value, while the other half would contain the old. Even if errors of this type were spotted easily (which they are not), a more subtle problem occurs when updating several fields, where no single field appears in obvious error. The solution to this problem, proposed first by Lampson and Sturgis [LAM76] and adopted by most DBMSs, uses a two-phase update.

Update Technique

During the first phase, called the **intent phase**, the DBMS gathers the information and other resources it needs to perform the update. It may gather data, create dummy records, open files, lock out other users, and calculate final answers; in short, it does everything to prepare for the update, but it makes no changes to the data base. The first phase is repeatable an unlimited number of times because it takes no permanent action. If the system fails during execution of the first phase, there is no harm because all of these steps can be restarted and repeated after the system resumes processing.

The last event of the first phase, called **committing**, involves writing a **commit flag** to the data base. The commit flag means that the DBMS has passed the point of no return: after committing, the DBMS begins making permanent changes.

The second phase is making the permanent changes. During the second phase, no actions from before the commit can be repeated, but the update activities of phase two can also be repeated as often as needed. If the system fails during the second phase, the data base may contain incomplete data, but this data can be repaired by performing all activities of the second phase. After the second phase has been completed, the data base is again complete.

Two-Phase Update Example

Suppose a data base contains an inventory of office supplies for a company. A central stockroom for the company stocks paper, pens, paper clips, and the like, and the different departments of the company requisition these items as they need them. The company buys in bulk to obtain the best prices. Each department has a budget for office supplies, so there is a charging mechanism by which the cost of supplies is recovered from the department. Also, the central stockroom monitors quantities of supplies on hand so as to be able to order new supplies when the stock becomes low.

The process begins with a requisition, for example, from the accounting department, for 50 boxes of paper clips. Assume that there are 107 boxes in stock and a new order is placed if the quantity in stock ever falls below 100. Here are the steps followed after the stockroom has received the requisition.

1. The stockroom checks the data base to determine that 50 boxes of paper clips are on hand. If not, the requisition is rejected and the transaction is finished.
2. If there are enough paper clips in stock, the stockroom deducts 50 from the inventory figure in the data base. $(107 - 50 = 57)$.
3. The stockroom charges accounting's supplies budget (also in the data base) for 50 boxes of paper clips.
4. The stockroom checks its remaining quantity on hand (57) to determine whether the remaining quantity is below the reorder point. Because it is, a notice to order more paper clips is generated, and the item is flagged as "on order" in the data base.
5. A delivery order is prepared to cause 50 boxes of paper clips to be sent to accounting.

All five of these steps must be completed in the order listed for the data base to be accurate and for the transaction to be processed correctly.

Suppose a failure occurs while these steps are being processed. If the failure occurs before step 1 is complete, there is no harm because the entire transaction can be restarted. However, during steps 2, 3, and 4, changes are made to elements in the data base. If a failure occurs then, the values in the data base are inconsistent. Worse, the transaction cannot be reprocessed because a requisition would be deducted twice, or a department would be charged twice, or two delivery orders would be prepared.

Using a two-phase commit, **shadow values** are maintained for key data points. A shadow data value is computed and stored locally during the intent phase, and it is copied to the actual data base during the commit phase. The operations on the data base would be performed as follows for a two-phase commit.

Intent:

1. Check the value of COMMIT-FLAG in the data base. If it is set, this phase cannot be performed. Compare number of boxes of paper clips on hand to number requisitioned; if more are requisitioned than on hand, halt.
2. Compute TCLIPS = ONHAND – REQUISITION.

3. Obtain BUDGET, the current supplies budget remaining for accounting department. Compute TBUDGET = BUDGET − COST, where COST is the cost of 50 boxes of clips.

4. Check whether TCLIPS is below reorder point; if so, set TREORDER = TRUE; else set TREORDER = FALSE.

Commit:

1. Set COMMIT-FLAG in data base.
2. Copy TCLIPS to CLIPS in data base.
3. Copy TBUDGET to BUDGET in data base.
4. Copy TREORDER to REORDER in data base.
5. Prepare notice to deliver paper clips to accounting department. Indicate transaction completed in log. Unset COMMIT-FLAG.

With this example, each step of the intent phase depends only on unmodified values from the data base and previous results of the intent phase. Each variable beginning with T is a shadow variable used only in this transaction. The steps of the intent phase can be repeated an unlimited number of times without affecting the integrity of the data base.

Once the DBMS begins the commit phase, it writes a COMMIT flag. When this flag is set, the DBMS will not perform any steps of the intent phase. Intent steps cannot be performed after committing because data base values are modified in the commit phase. Notice, however, that the steps of the commit phase can be repeated an unlimited number of times, again with no negative effect on the correctness of the values in the data base.

The one remaining flaw in this logic occurs if the system fails after writing the "transaction complete" message in the log but before clearing the commit flag in the data base. It is a simple matter to work backward through the transaction log to find completed transactions for which the commit flag is still set and clear those flags.

Redundancy/Internal Consistency

Many data base managers maintain additional information to detect internal inconsistencies in data. The additional information ranges from a few check bits to duplicate or shadow fields, depending on the importance of the data.

Error Detection and Correction Codes

One form of redundancy is error detection and correction codes, such as parity, Hamming codes, and cyclic redundancy checks. These codes can be applied to single fields, records, or the entire data base. Each time data is placed in the data base, the appropriate check codes are computed and stored; each time data is retrieved, a similar check code is computed and compared to the stored value. If the values are unequal, they identify that an error has occurred in the data base. Some of these codes point out the place of the error; others show precisely what the correct value should be. The more information provided, the more space required to store the codes.

Shadow Fields

Entire attributes or entire records can be duplicated in a data base. If the data is irreproducible, this second copy can provide an immediate replacement if an error is detected. Obviously, redundant fields require substantial storage space.

Recovery

In addition to the processes just described for error correction, a DBMS can maintain a log of accesses, particularly changes, by the users. Therefore, in the event of a failure, the data base is reloaded from a backup copy and all later changes are applied from the audit log.

Concurrency/Consistency

Data base systems are often multiuser systems. Accesses by two users sharing the same data base must be constrained so that neither interferes with the other. Simple locking is done by the DBMS. If two users attempt to read the same data item, there is no conflict because both obtain the same value.

If both users try to modify the same data items, there is no conflict because presumably each knows what to write; the value to be written does not depend on the previous value of the data item. However, this supposition is not quite accurate.

Suppose that the data base consists of seat reservations for a particular airline flight. Agent A, booking a seat for passenger Mock, submits a query to find what seats are still available. The agent knows that Mock prefers a right aisle seat, and the agent finds that seats 5D, 11D, and 14D are open. At the same time, Agent B is trying to book seats for a family of three traveling together. In response to a query, the data base indicates that 8A–B–C and 11D–E–F are the two remaining groups of three adjacent unassigned seats. Agent A submits the update command

```
SELECT (SEAT-NO = `11D')
ASSIGN `MOCK,E' TO PASSENGER-NAME
```

while agent B submits the update sequence

```
SELECT (SEAT-NO = `11D')
ASSIGN `LAWRENCE,S' TO PASSENGER-NAME
```

as well as commands for seats 11E and 11F. Then two passengers have been booked into the same seat (which would be uncomfortable at least).

Both agents have acted properly: each sought a list of empty seats, chose one seat from the list, and updated the data base to show to whom the seat was assigned. The difficulty in this situation is the time delay between reading a value from the data base and writing a modification of that value. During the delay time, another user has accessed the same data.

To resolve this problem, a DBMS treats the entire query–update cycle as a single atomic operation. The command from the agent must now resemble "read the current value of seat PASSENGER-NAME for seat 11D, if it is 'UNASSIGNED', modify it to

'MOCK,E' (or 'LAWRENCE,S')." The read–modify cycle must be completed as an uninterrupted item without allowing any other users access to the PASSENGER-NAME field for seat 11D. The second agent's request to book would not be considered until after the first agent's had been completed; at that time, the value of PASSENGER-NAME would no longer be 'UNASSIGNED'.

A final problem in concurrent access is read–write. Suppose one user is updating a value when a second user wishes to read. If the read is taken while the write is in progress, the reader may receive data that is only partly updated. The DBMS locks any read requests until a write has been completed.

Monitors

A **monitor** is a unit of a DBMS that is responsible for the structural integrity of the data base. A monitor can check values being entered to ensure their consistency with the rest of the data base, or with characteristics of the particular field. For example, a monitor might reject alphabetic characters for a numeric field. We discuss several forms of monitors.

Range Comparisons

A range comparison monitor tests each new value to ensure that the value is within an acceptable range. If the data value is outside the range, it is rejected and not entered into the data base. For example, the range of dates might be 1–31, '/,' 1–12, '/,' 0–99. An even more sophisticated range check might limit the day portion to 1–30 for months with 30 days, or might take into account leap year for February.

Range comparisons are also convenient for numeric quantities. For example, a salary field might be limited to $200,000, or the size of a house might be constrained to be between 500 and 5,000 square feet. Range constraints can also apply to other data having a predictable form.

Range comparisons can be used to ensure internal consistency of a data base. When used in this manner, the comparisons are between two elements of the data base. For example, a grade level from K to 8 would be acceptable if the record described a student at an elementary school, while only 9–12 would be acceptable for a record of a student in high school. A person could be assigned a job qualification score of 75–100 only if the person had completed college or had had at least 10 years work experience.

Checks of these types can control the data allowed in the data base. They can also be used to test existing values for reasonableness. If you suspect that the data in a data base has been corrupted, a range check of all records could identify ones having suspicious values.

State Constraints

State constraints describe the condition of the entire data base. At no time should the data base values violate these constraints. Phrased differently, if these constraints are not met, some value of the data base is in error.

In the section on two-phase updates, we saw the use of a commit flag, which is set at the start of the commit phase and cleared at the completion of the commit phase. Therefore, a state constraint for a data base would be: at the end of every transaction the commit flag is not set. We described a process to reset the commit flags in the event of a failure after a commit phase. Therefore, the status of the commit flag is an integrity constraint on the data base.

Another example of a state constraint is in a data base of employees' classifications. At any time, at most one employee is classified as "president." Furthermore, each employee has an employee number different from that of every other employee. If a mechanical or software error causes portions of the data base file to be repeated, one of these constraints might be violated. Testing the state of the data base would identify records with duplicate employee numbers or two records classified as "president."

Transition Constraints

State constraints describe the state of a correct data base. **Transition constraints** describe conditions necessary before changes can be applied to a data base. For example, before a new employee can be added to the data base, there must be a position number in the data base with status "vacant." (That is, an empty slot must exist.) Furthermore, after the employee is added, exactly one slot must be changed from "vacant" to the number of the new employee.

Simple range checks can be implemented within most data base management systems. However, the more sophisticated state and transition constraints can require special procedures for testing. Such user-written procedures are invoked by the DBMS each time an action must be checked.

Summary of Data Reliability

Reliability, correctness, and integrity are three closely related concepts in data bases. Users trust the DBMS to maintain their data correctly, so integrity issues are very important in the security of data bases.

8.4   Sensitive Data

Some data bases contain what is called sensitive data. As a working definition let us say that **sensitive data** is data that should not be made public. Determining which data items are sensitive depends on the individual data base and the underlying meaning of the data. Obviously, some data bases, such as a public library catalog, contain no sensitive data; other data bases, such as defense data bases, are totally sensitive. These two cases—nothing sensitive and everything sensitive—are the easiest to handle because they can be covered by access controls to the data base itself. Someone either is or is not an authorized user. These controls are provided by the operating system.

The more difficult problem, which is also more interesting, is the case in which *some but not all* of the elements in the data base are sensitive. There may be varying degrees of sensitivity. For example, a university data base might contain student data consisting of name, financial aid, dorm, drug use, sex, parking fines, and race. Name and dorm are probably the least sensitive; financial aid, parking fines, and drug use the most; and sex and race somewhere in between. That is, many people may have legitimate access to name, some to sex and race, and relatively few to financial aid, parking fines, or drug use. An example of this data base is shown in Table 8-1.

Table 8-1   Sample Data Base

Name	Sex	Race	Aid	Fines	Drugs	Dorm
Adams	M	C	5000	45.	1	Holmes
Bailey	M	B	0	0.	0	Grey
Chin	F	A	3000	20.	0	West
Dewitt	M	B	1000	35.	3	Grey
Earhart	F	C	2000	95.	1	Holmes
Fein	F	C	1000	15.	0	West
Groff	M	C	4000	0.	3	West
Hill	F	B	5000	10.	2	Holmes
Koch	F	C	0	0.	1	West
Liu	F	A	0	10.	2	Grey
Majors	M	C	2000	0.	2	Grey

Furthermore, although they are all highly sensitive, the financial aid, parking fines, and drug use fields may not have the same access restrictions: few people may be authorized to see each field, but nobody is authorized to see all three. The access control problem is to limit users' access so that they can obtain only the data to which they have legitimate access. Alternatively, the access control problem is a challenge to ensure that sensitive data is not to be released to unauthorized people.

Several factors can make data sensitive.

- *Inherently sensitive.* The value itself may be so revealing that it is sensitive. Examples are the locations of defensive missiles, or the median income of barbers in a town with only one barber.

- *From a sensitive source.* The source of the data may indicate a need for confidentiality. An example is information from an informer whose identity would be compromised if the information were disclosed.

- *Declared sensitive.* The data base administrator or the owner of the data may have declared it to be sensitive. Examples are classified military data or the name of the anonymous donor of a piece of art.

- Of a sensitive *attribute* or a sensitive *record.* In a data base, an entire attribute or record may be classified as sensitive. Examples are the salary attribute of a personnel data base, or a record describing a secret space mission.

- Sensitive *in relation to previously disclosed information.* Some data becomes sensitive in the presence of other data. For example, the longitude coordinate of a secret gold mine reveals little, but the longitude coordinate in conjunction with the latitude coordinate pinpoints the mine.

All of these factors must be considered to determine the sensitivity of the data.

Access Decisions

Remember that a data base administrator is a *person* who decides *what* data should be in the data base and *who* should have access to it. The data base administrator considers the need for different users to know certain information and decides who should have what access. Decisions of the data base administrator are based on an access *policy*.

The data base manager or DBMS is a *program* that operates on the data base and auxiliary control information to implement the decisions of the access policy. We say that the data base manager "decides" to permit user x to access data y. Clearly, a program or machine cannot decide anything; it is more precise to say that the program performs the instructions by which x accesses y as a way of implementing the policy established by the data base administrator. (Now you see why we use the simpler wording.) To keep explanations concise, we occasionally describe programs as if they can carry out human thought processes.

The DBMS may consider several factors when deciding whether to permit an access. These factors include availability of the data, acceptability of the access, and authenticity of the user. We expand on these three factors below.

Availability of Data

First, one or more required elements may be inaccessible. For example, if a user is updating several fields, other users' accesses to those fields must be blocked temporarily. This blocking ensures that users do not receive inaccurate information, such as a new street address with an old city and state. This blocking should be temporary. When performing an update, a user may have to block access to several fields or several records in order to ensure the consistency of data for others.

Notice, however, that if the updating user aborts while the update is in progress, the other users may be permanently blocked from accessing the record. This indefinite postponement is also a security problem, resulting in denial of service.

Acceptability of Access

The second point to be considered in making an access decision is that one or more values of the record may be sensitive and not accessible by the user. A DBMS should not release sensitive data to unauthorized individuals.

Deciding what is sensitive, however, is not as simple as it sounds, because the fields may not be directly requested. A user may have requested certain records that contain sensitive data, but the user's purpose may have been only to project the values from particular fields that are not sensitive. For example, a user of the data base shown in Table 8-1 may request the NAME and DORM of any student for whom FINES is not 0. The exact value of the sensitive field FINES is not disclosed, although "not 0" is a partial disclosure. Even when a sensitive value is not explicitly given, the data base manager may deny access on the grounds that it reveals information the user is not authorized to have.

Alternatively, the user may want to derive a nonsensitive statistic from the sensitive data; for example, if the average financial aid value does not reveal any individual's financial aid value, the data base manager can safely return the average. However, the average of one data value discloses that value.

Assurance of Authenticity

Third, certain characteristics of the user, external to the data base, may also be considered. To enhance security, the data base administrator may permit someone to access the data base only at certain times, such as during working hours. Another characteristic to be considered is previous requests of the user. As we shall see, sensitive data can sometimes be revealed by combining results from several less sensitive queries.

Types of Disclosures

Data can be sensitive, but so can characteristics of the data. In this section, we see that even information about data (such as its existence or whether it is zero) is a form of disclosure.

Exact Data

The most serious disclosure is the *exact value of the sensitive data* itself. The user may know that sensitive data is being requested, or the user may request general data without knowing that some of it is sensitive. A faulty data base manager may even deliver sensitive data by accident, without the user's having requested it. In all of these cases the result is the same: the security of the sensitive data has been breached.

Bounds

Another exposure is disclosing bounds on a sensitive value, that is, indicating that a sensitive value, y, is between two values L and H. Sometimes, by using a narrowing technique not unlike the binary search, the user may first determine that $L \leq y \leq H$ and then see whether $L \leq y \leq H/2$, and so forth, thereby permitting the user to determine y to any desired precision. In another case, merely revealing that a value such as the athletic scholarship budget or the number of CIA agents exceeds a certain amount may be a serious breach of security.

Sometimes, however, bounds are a useful way to present sensitive data. It is not uncommon to release upper and lower bounds without identifying their specific records. For example, a company may announce that its salaries for programmers range from $30,000 to $42,000. If you are a programmer earning $39,700, you can presume that you are fairly well off, so you have the information you want; however, the announcement does not disclose who are the highest- and lowest-paid programmers.

Negative Result

Sometimes one can word a query to determine a negative result, that is, that z is *not* the value of y. For example, knowing that 0 is not the total number of felony convictions for a person reveals that the person was convicted of a felony. The distinction between 1 and 2 or 46 and 47 felonies is not as sensitive as the distinction between 0 and 1. Therefore, disclosing that a value is not 0 is a significant disclosure. If a student does not appear on the honors list, you can infer that the person's grade point average is below 3.50. This information is not too revealing, however, because the range of grade point averages from 0.0 to 3.49 is rather wide.

Existence

In some cases, the existence of data is itself a sensitive piece of data, regardless of the actual value. For example, an employer may not want employees to know that their use of long distance telephone lines is being monitored. In this case, discovering a LONG DISTANCE field in a personnel file would reveal sensitive data.

Probable Value

Finally, it may be possible to determine the probability that a certain element has a certain value. Suppose you want to find out if the president is a registered Tory. Knowing that the president is in the data base, you submit two queries to the data base:

How many people have 1600 Pennsylvania Avenue as their official residence? (Response: 4)

How many people have 1600 Pennsylvania Avenue as their official residence and have YES as the value of TORY? (Response: 1)

From these queries you conclude there is a 25 percent likelihood that the president is a registered Tory.

Summary of Partial Disclosure

In summary, a security problem may result if characteristics of sensitive data are revealed. Notice that some of the techniques discussed used information *about* the data, not direct access to the data, to infer sensitive results. A successful security strategy must protect from both direct and indirect disclosure.

Security Versus Precision

Through examples we have seen how hard it is to determine what data is sensitive and to protect the sensitive data. The situation is complicated by a desire to share nonsensitive data. For reasons of **secrecy** we want to disclose only data that is not sensitive. Such an outlook encourages a conservative philosophy in determining what data to disclose.

Now consider the users of the data. The conservative philosophy says to reject any query that mentions a sensitive field. We may thereby reject many reasonable and nondisclosing queries. For example, a researcher may want a list of grades for all students using drugs, or a statistician may request lists of salaries for all men and for all women. These queries probably do not compromise the identity of any individual. We want to disclose as much data as possible so that users of the data base have access to the data they need. This goal, called **precision**, aims to protect all sensitive data while revealing as much nonsensitive data as possible.

We can depict the relationship between security and precision with concentric circles. As Figure 8-8 shows, the sensitive data in the middle should be carefully concealed. We willingly disclose data at the outside in response to queries. We know that the user may put together pieces of disclosed data and infer other, more deeply hidden data. Beneath the outer layer may be yet more nonsensitive data that the user cannot infer. Finally, on the inside is the sensitive data we intend to keep secret.

The ideal combination of secrecy and precision allows us to maintain perfect secrecy with maximum precision, in other words, to disclose all and only the nonsensitive data. This is not as easy as it might seem, as shown in the next section. In fact, we often must sacrifice precision in order to maintain secrecy. In the next section we consider ways that sensitive data can be obtained from queries that appear harmless.

8.5   Inference Problem

In this section we study the **inference problem**, which is a way to infer or derive sensitive data from nonsensitive data. The inference problem is a subtle vulnerability in data base security.

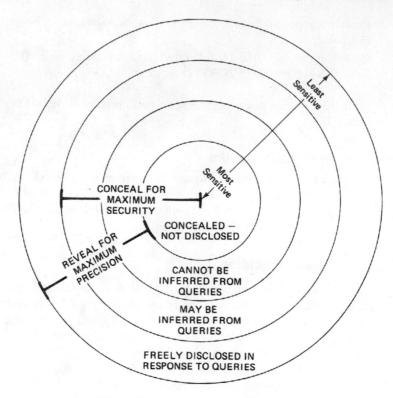

Figure 8-8   Security Versus Precision

The data base in Table 8-2 can help to illustrate the inference problem. Recall that AID is the amount of financial aid a student is receiving. FINES is the amount of parking fines still owed. DRUGS is the result of a drug-use survey: 0 means never used and 3 means frequent user. Obviously this information should be kept confidential. We assume that AID, FINES, and DRUGS are sensitive fields, although only when the values are related to a specific individual. In this section we see how to determine sensitive data from the data base.

Table 8-2   Sample Data Base (repeated)

Name	Sex	Race	Aid	Fines	Drugs	Dorm
Adams	M	C	5000	45.	1	Holmes
Bailey	M	B	0	0.	0	Grey
Chin	F	A	3000	20.	0	West
Dewitt	M	B	1000	35.	3	Grey
Earhart	F	C	2000	95.	1	Holmes
Fein	F	C	1000	15.	0	West
Groff	M	C	4000	0.	3	West
Hill	F	B	5000	10.	2	Holmes
Koch	F	C	0	0.	1	West
Liu	F	A	0	10.	2	Grey
Majors	M	C	2000	0.	2	Grey

Direct Attack

In a direct attack one tries to determine values of sensitive fields by seeking them directly with queries that yield few records. The most successful technique is to form a query so specific that it matches exactly one data item.

In the table above, a sensitive query might be

```
List NAME where
        SEX=M ∧ DRUGS=1
```

This query discloses that for record ADAMS, DRUGS = 1. However, it is an obvious attack because any name listed is one for whom DRUGS = 1.

A less obvious query is

```
List NAME where
        (SEX = M ∧ DRUGS=1) ∨
        (SEX≠M ∧ SEX≠F) ∨
        (DORM=AYRES)
```

On the surface, this query looks as if it should conceal drug usage by selecting other non–drug-related records as well. However, this query still retrieves only one record, revealing a name that corresponds to the sensitive DRUG value. The DBMS needs to know that SEX has only two possible values, so that the second clause will select no records. Even if that were possible, the DBMS would also need to know that no records exist with DORM = AYRES, even though AYRES might be an acceptable value for DORM.

Organizations that publish personal statistics, such as the U.S. Census Bureau, do not reveal results where a small number of people make up a large proportion of the category. The rule of "n items over k percent" means that data should be withheld if n items represent over k percent of the result reported. In the previous case, the one person selected represents 100 percent of the data reported, so that there is no ambiguity about which person matches the query.

Indirect Attack

Another procedure used by the U.S. Census Bureau and other people who gather sensitive data is to release only statistics. They suppress individual names, addresses, or other characteristics by which a single individual can be recognized. Only neutral statistics, such as count, sum, and mean, are released.

The indirect attack seeks to infer a result based on one or more statistical results. It requires work outside the data base itself. A statistical attack seeks to use some apparently anonymous statistical measure to infer individual data. Following are several examples of indirect attacks based on data bases that report statistics.

Sum

An attack by sum tries to infer a value from a reported sum. For example, with our sample data base, it might seem safe to report student aid by sex and dorm. Such a report is shown in Table 8-3. This seemingly innocent report reveals that no female living in Grey is

Table 8-3   Sums of Financial Aid by Dorm and Sex

	Holmes	Grey	West	Total
M	5000	3000	4000	12000
F	7000	0	4000	11000
Total	12000	3000	8000	23000

receiving financial aid. Thus, any female living in Grey (such as Liu) is certainly not receiving financial aid. This is another example of disclosure of a negative result.

Count

The count can be combined with the sum to produce some even more revealing results. Often these two statistics are released for a data base to allow users to determine average values. (Conversely, if count and mean are released, sum can be deduced.)

Table 8-4 shows the count of records for students by dorm and sex. This table is innocuous by itself. Combined with the sum table, however, this table demonstrates that the two males in Holmes and West are receiving financial aid in the amount of $5000 and $4000, respectively. The names can be obtained by selecting the subschema of NAME, DORM, which is not sensitive because it delivers only low-security data on the entire data base.

Median

By a slightly more complicated process, you can determine an individual value from medians. The attack requires finding selections having one point of intersection, which happens to be exactly in the middle, as shown in Figure 8-9.

For example, in our sample data base, there are five males and three people whose drug use value is 2. Arranged in order of aid, these two lists are shown in Table 8-5. Notice that Majors is the only name common to both lists and conveniently that name is in the middle of each list. Someone working at the Health Clinic might be able to find out that

Table 8-4   Count of Students by Dorm and Sex

	Holmes	Grey	West	Total
M	1	3	1	5
F	2	1	3	6
Total	3	4	4	11

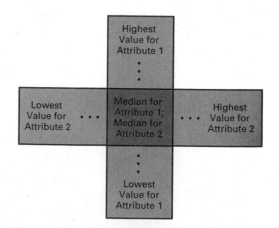

Figure 8-9   Intersecting Medians

Table 8-5   Inference from Median of Two Lists

Name	Sex	Drugs	Aid
Bailey	M	0	0
Dewitt	M	3	1000
Majors	M	2	2000
Groff	M	3	4000
Adams	M	1	5000
Liu	F	2	0
Majors	M	2	2000
Hill	F	2	5000

Majors is a white male whose drug use score is 2. That identifies Majors as the intersection of these two lists, and pinpoints Majors' financial aid as $2000. In this example, the queries

```
q = median (AID where SEX = M)
p = median(AID where DRUGS = 2)
```

reveal the exact financial aid amount for Majors.

Tracker Attacks

As already explained, data base managers may conceal data where a small number of entries makes up a large proportion of the data revealed. A **tracker attack** can fool the data base manager into locating the desired data by using additional queries that produce small results. The tracker adds additional records to be retrieved for two different queries; the two sets of records cancel each other out, leaving only the statistic desired. Instead of trying to identify a unique value, you request $n - 1$ other values (where there are n values in the data base). Given n and $n - 1$, you can easily compute the desired single element.

For instance, suppose we wish to know how many female Caucasians live in Holmes Hall. A query posed might be

```
count ((SEX = F) ∧ (RACE = C) ∧ (DORM = Holmes))
```

The data base manager will consult the data base, find that the answer is 1, and refuse to answer that query because one record dominates the result of the query. However, further analysis of the query allows us to track sensitive data through nonsensitive queries.

The query

```
q = count((SEX=F) ∧ (RACE=C) ∧ (DORM=Holmes))
```

is of the form

```
q = count(a ∧ b ∧ c)
```

By algebra, this transforms to

```
q = count(a ∧ b ∧ c) = count(a) - count(a ∧ ¬ (b ∧ c))
```

Thus, the original query is equivalent to

```
count (SEX=F)
```

minus

```
count ((SEX=F) ∧ (RACE≠C) ∧ (DORM≠Holmes))
```

Because count(a) = 6 and count($a \land \neg (b \land c)$) = 5, you can determine the suppressed value easily, $6 - 5 = 1$. Furthermore, neither 6 nor 5 is a sensitive count.

Linear System Vulnerability

A tracker is a specific case of a more general vulnerability. With a little algebra and a little more luck in the distribution of the data base contents, it may be possible to determine a series of queries that returns results relating to several different sets. For example, the following system of five queries does not overtly reveal any single c value from the data base. However, the queries (equations) can be solved for each of the unknown c values, revealing them all.

$$q_1 = c_1 + c_2 + c_3 + c_4 + c_5$$
$$q_2 = c_1 + c_2 \qquad + c_4$$
$$q_3 = \qquad\qquad c_3 + c_4$$
$$q_4 = \qquad\qquad\qquad c_4 + c_5$$
$$q_5 = \qquad c_2 \qquad\qquad + c_5$$

By algebra $q_1 - q_2 = c_3 + c_5$, and $q_3 - q_4 = c_3 - c_5$. Thus, subtracting these two equations, we obtain $c_5 = ((q_1 - q_2) - (q_3 - q_4))/2$. From c_5 the others can be obtained.

In fact, this attack can also be used to obtain results in cases *other than* statistical attacks. Notice that the same algebraic properties occur with *and* ($\land$) and *or* ($\lor$), which are typical operators for data base queries. For example, each query might ask for precise data, instead of counts, with a request of the form

$$q_1 = s_1 \lor s_2 \lor s_3 \lor s_4 \lor s_5$$

The result is a set of records satisfying that query. By set algebra, individual results can be obtained by solving the system of linear set equations analogous to the numerical queries posed earlier.

Controls for Statistical Inference Attacks

The controls for all statistical attacks are similar. Denning and Schlörer [DEN83a] present a very good survey of techniques for maintaining security in data bases. Essentially there are two ways to protect against inference attacks. Either controls are applied to the queries or controls are applied to individual items within the data base. As we have seen, it is difficult to determine whether a given query discloses sensitive data. Thus, query controls are effective primarily against direct attacks.

Two controls applied to data items are suppression and concealing. With **suppression**, sensitive data values are not provided; the query is rejected without response. With **concealing**, the answer provided is *close to* but not exactly the actual value.

These two controls reflect the contrast between security and precision. With suppression, any results provided are correct, yet many responses must be withheld in order to maintain security. With concealing, more results can be provided, although the accuracy of the results is lower. The choice between suppression and concealing depends on the context of the data base. Examples of suppression and concealing follow.

Limited Response Suppression

The n item, k percent rule eliminates certain low-frequency elements from being displayed. It is not sufficient to delete them, however, if their values can also be inferred. Consider Table 8-6, which shows counts of students by dorm and sex.

With this table, the cells with counts of 1 should be suppressed because their counts are too revealing. But it does no good to suppress the Male–Holmes cell when the value 1 can be determined by subtracting Female–Holmes (2) from the total (3) to determine 1, as shown in Table 8-7.

When one cell is suppressed in a table with totals for rows and columns, it is necessary to suppress at least one additional cell on the row and one on the column to provide some confusion. By that logic, all cells (except totals) would have to be suppressed in this small sample table. When totals are not provided, single cells in a row or column can be suppressed.

Combining Results

Another control combines rows or columns to protect sensitive values. For example, Table 8-8 shows several sensitive results that identify single individuals. (Even though these counts may not seem sensitive, they may be used to infer sensitive data such as NAME; therefore, we consider them to be sensitive.)

These counts, combined with other results such as sum, permit one to infer individual drug use values for the three males, as well as to infer that no female was rated 3 for drug use. To suppress such sensitive information, it is possible to combine the attribute values for 0 and 1, and also for 2 and 3, producing the less sensitive results shown in Table 8-9. In this instance, it is impossible to identify any single value.

Another way of combining results is to present values in ranges. Instead of releasing exact financial aid figures, results may be released for the ranges $0–1999, $2000–3999, and $4000 and above. Even if there is only one record represented by a single result, the exact value of that record is not known. Similarly, the highest and lowest financial aid values are concealed.

Yet another method of combining is by rounding. This is actually a fairly well-known example of combining by range. If numbers are rounded to the nearest 10, the effective ranges are 0–5, 6–15, 16–25, and so on. Actual values are rounded up or down to the nearest multiple of some base.

Table 8-6   Students by Dorm and Sex

	Holmes	Grey	West	Total
M	1	3	1	5
F	2	1	3	6
Total	3	4	4	11

Table 8-7   Students by Dorm and Sex, with Low Count Suppression

	Holmes	Grey	West	Total
M	—	3	—	5
F	2	—	3	6
Total	3	4	4	11

Table 8-8   **Students by Sex and Drug Use**

Sex	Drug Use			
	0	1	2	3
M	1	1	1	2
F	2	2	2	0

Table 8-9   **Suppression by Combining Revealing Values**

Sex	Drug Use	
	0 or 1	2 or 3
M	2	3
F	4	2

Random Sample

With random sample control, a result is not derived from the whole data base; instead the result is computed on a random sample of the data base. The sample chosen is large enough to be valid. Because the sample is not the whole data base, however, a query against this sample will not necessarily match the result for the whole data base. Thus a result of 5 percent for a particular query means that 5 percent of the records chosen for the sample for this query had the desired property. You would expect that approximately 5 percent of the entire data base will have the property in question, but the actual percentage may not be 5 percent.

To prevent averaging attacks from repeated, equivalent queries, the same sample set should be chosen for equivalent queries. In this way, all equivalent queries will produce the same result, although that result will be only an approximation for the entire data base.

Random Data Perturbation

Another statistical control is to perturb the values of the data base by a small error. If x_i is the true value of data item i in the data base, ε_i is a small random error term added to x_i for statistical results. The ε values are both positive and negative, so that some reported values will be higher than their true values, and other reported values will be lower. Statistical measures such as sum and mean will be close, but not necessarily exact. Data perturbation is easier to use than random sample selection because it is easier to keep all of the ε values in order to produce the same result for equivalent queries.

Query Analysis

A more complex form of security uses query analysis. Here, a query and its implications are analyzed to determine whether a result should be provided. As noted earlier, query analysis can be quite difficult. One approach involves maintaining a query history for each user and judging a query in the context of what inferences are possible given previous results.

Conclusion on the Inference Problem

There are no perfect solutions to the inference problem. The approaches to controlling it follow three paths. The first two methods can be used either to limit queries accepted or to limit data provided in response to a query. The last method applies only to data released.

- *Suppress obviously sensitive information.* This can be done fairly easily. There is a tendency to err on the side of suppression, which restricts the usefulness of the data base.

- *Track what the user knows.* Although possibly leading to the greatest safe disclosure, this approach is extremely costly. Information must be maintained on all users, even though most are not trying to obtain sensitive data. This approach seldom takes into account what any two people may know together.
- *Disguise the data.* Random perturbation and rounding can inhibit statistical attacks that depend on exact values for algebraic manipulation. The users of the data base receive slightly incorrect or, worse, inconsistent results.

It is unlikely that research will reveal a simple, easy-to-apply measure that determines exactly which data can be revealed without compromising sensitive data.

A very effective control for the inference problem is just knowing that it exists. As with other problems in security, recognition of the problem leads to understanding of the purposes of controls and to sensitivity to the potential difficulties caused by the problem.

8.6   Multilevel Data Bases

So far, we have considered data of only two categories: sensitive or nonsensitive. We have alluded to some data being more sensitive than others, but we have allowed only yes-or-no access. The presentation may have implied that sensitivity was a function of the *attribute,* the column in which the data appeared, although nothing we have done depended on this interpretation of sensitivity. Such a model appears in Table 8-10. In that table two columns are identified as sensitive. However, sensitivity is not determined just by attribute.

The Case for Differentiated Security

Consider a data base containing data on U.S. government expenditures. Some of the expenditures are for paper clips, which is not sensitive information. Some salary expenditures are subject to privacy requirements. Individual salaries are sensitive, but the aggregate (for example, the total Agriculture Department payroll, which is a matter of public record) is not sensitive. Expenses of certain military operations are more sensitive, such as the total amount the U.S. spends for ballistic missiles, which is not public. There are even operations known only to a few people, and so the amount spent on these operations, or even the fact that anything was spent on such an operation, is highly sensitive.

For example, consider the data of Table 8-10, in which sensitive data items are shaded.

Perhaps Davis is a temporary employee hired for a special project, and her whole record is of a different sensitivity. Perhaps the phone shown for Garland is his private line,

Table 8-10   Attribute-Level Sensitivity (sensitive attributes are shaded)

NAME	DEPARTMENT	SALARY	PHONE	PERFORMANCE
Rogers	training	43,800	4-5067	A2
Jenkins	research	62,900	6-4281	D4
Poling	training	38,200	4-4501	B1
Garland	user svcs	54,600	6-6600	A4
Hilten	user svcs	44,500	4-5351	B1
Davis	admin	51,400	4-9505	A3

Table 8-11   Data and Attribute Sensitivity

NAME	DEPARTMENT	SALARY	PHONE	PERFORMANCE
Rogers	training	43,800	4-5067	A2
Jenkins	research	62,900	6-4281	D4
Poling	training	38,200	4-4501	B1
Garland	user svcs	54,600	6-6600	A4
Hilten	user svcs	44,500	4-5351	B1
Davis	admin	51,400	4-9505	A3

which is not available to the public. These refinements to the sensitivity of the data are shown in Table 8-11.

From this description, three characteristics of data base security emerge:

- The security of a single element may be different from the security of other elements of the same record or from other values of the same attribute. That is, the security of one element may be different from that of other elements of the same row or column. This situation implies that security should be implemented for each individual element.

- Two levels—sensitive and nonsensitive—are inadequate to represent some security situations. Several grades of security may be needed. These grades may represent ranges of allowable knowledge, which may overlap. Typically, the security grades form a lattice.

- The security of an aggregate—a sum, a count, or a group of values in a data base— may be different from the security of the individual elements. The security of the aggregate may be higher or lower than that of the individual elements.

These three principles lead to a model of security not unlike the military model of security encountered in Chapter 7, in which the sensitivity of an object is defined as one of *n* levels and is further separated into compartments by category.

Granularity

Recall that the military classification model applied originally to paper documents and was adapted to computers. It is fairly easy to classify and track a single sheet of paper or, for that matter, a paper file, a computer file, or a single program or process. It is entirely different to classify individual data items.

For obvious reasons an entire sheet of paper is classified at one level, even though certain words, such as *and*, *the*, and *of* would be innocuous in any context, and other words, such as codewords like *Manhattan project*, might be sensitive in any context. But defining the sensitivity of each value in a data base is similar to applying a sensitivity level to each individual word of a document.

In fact, the problem is even more complicated. The word *Manhattan* by itself is not sensitive, nor is *project*. However, the combination of these words produces the sensitive codeword *Manhattan project*. A similar situation occurs in data bases. Therefore, not only can every *element* of a data base have a distinct sensitivity, every *combination of elements* may also have a distinct sensitivity. Furthermore, the combination can be more or less sensitive than any of its elements.

What is needed in order to associate a sensitivity level with each value of a data base? First, an access control policy must dictate which users may have access to what data. To implement this policy typically each data item is marked to show its access limitations. Second, a means is needed to guarantee that the value has not been changed by an unauthorized person. These two needs demonstrate the requirements for both confidentiality and integrity.

Security Issues

In Chapter 1 we introduced three general security concerns in computing: secrecy or confidentiality, integrity, and availability. In this section, we extend these concepts to include their special roles for multilevel data bases.

Integrity

Even in a single-level data base where all elements have the same degree of sensitivity, integrity is a tricky problem. In the case of multilevel data bases, integrity becomes both more important and more difficult to achieve. Because of the *-property for access control, a process that reads high-level data is not allowed to write a file at a lower level. Applied to data bases, however, this principle says that a high-level user should not be able to write a lower-level data element.

The problem with this interpretation arises when the DBMS must be able to read all records in the data base and write new records for any of the following purposes: to do backups, to scan the data base to answer queries, to reorganize the data base according to a user's processing needs, or to update all records of the data base.

With people this deficiency is handled by trust and common sense. People who have access to sensitive information are careful not to convey that information to uncleared individuals. In a computing system there are two choices: either the process cleared at a high level cannot write to a lower level, or the process must be a "trusted process," the computer equivalent of a person with a clearance.

Confidentiality

Users trust that a data base will provide correct information, which means that it is consistent and accurate. As indicated earlier, some means of protecting confidentiality result in small changes to the data. Although these perturbations should not affect statistical analyses, they may produce two different answers representing the same underlying data value in response to two differently formed queries. In the multilevel case, two different users operating at two different levels of security might get two different answers to the same query. In order to preserve secrecy, accuracy is sacrificed.

Another result of this secrecy is unknowing redundancy. Suppose a personnel specialist works at one level of access permission. The specialist knows that Bob Hill works for the company. However, Bob's record does not appear on the retirement payment roster. The specialist assumes this is an error and creates a record for Bob.

The reason that no record for Bob appears is that Bob is a secret agent, and his employment with the company is not supposed to be public knowledge. There actually is a record on Bob in the file but, because of his special position, his record is not accessible to the personnel specialist. The creation of the new record means that there are now two records for Bob Hill: one sensitive and one not, as shown in Figure 8-10. This situation is

Name	Sensitivity	Assignment	Location
. . .			
Hill, Bob	C	Program Mgr	London
Hill, Bob	TS	Secret Agent	South Bend
. . .			

Figure 8-10   Polyinstantiated Records

called **polyinstantiation**, meaning that one record can appear (be instantiated) many times, with a different level of secrecy each time.

This problem is exacerbated because *Bob Hill* is a common enough name that there might be two different people in the data base with that name. Thus, merely scanning the data base (from a high sensitivity level) for duplicates is not a satisfactory way to find records entered unknowingly by people with only low clearances.

8.7   Proposals for Multilevel Security

As you can already tell, implementing multilevel security for data bases is difficult, probably more so than in operating systems, because of the small granularity of the items being controlled. In the remainder of this chapter we study some approaches to multilevel security for data bases.

Partitioning

The obvious control for multilevel data bases is partitioning. The data base is divided into separate data bases, each at its own level of sensitivity. This approach is similar to maintaining separate files in separate file cabinets.

This control destroys a basic advantage of data bases: elimination of redundancy and improved accuracy through having only one field to update. Furthermore, it does not address the problem of a high-level user who needs to access some low-level data to be combined with high-level data.

Nevertheless, because of the difficulty of establishing, maintaining, and using multilevel data bases, many users with data of mixed sensitivities handle their data using separate, isolated data bases.

Encryption

If sensitive data is encrypted, a user who accidentally receives sensitive data cannot interpret the data. Thus each level of sensitive data can be stored in a table encrypted under a key unique to the level of sensitivity. Encryption has certain disadvantages, however.

First, a user can mount a chosen plaintext attack. Suppose party affiliation of REP or DEM is stored in encrypted form in each record. A user who achieves access to these encrypted fields can easily decrypt them by creating a new record with party = DEM and comparing the resulting encrypted version to that element in all other records. Worse, if authentication data is encrypted, the malicious user can substitute the encrypted form of his or her own data for that of any other user. Not only does this provide access for the malicious user, but it also excludes the legitimate user whose authentication data has been changed to that of the malicious user. These possibilities are shown in Figure 8-11.

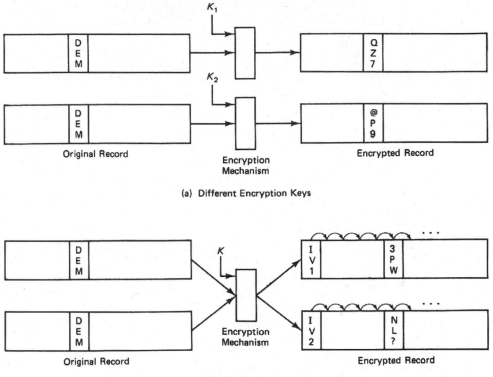

(a) Different Encryption Keys

(b) Block Chaining

Figure 8-11   Cryptographic Separation

Using a different encryption key for each record overcomes these defects. Each record's fields can be encrypted with a different key, or all fields of a record can be cryptographically linked, as with cipher block chaining.

The disadvantage, then, is that each field must be decrypted in order to perform standard data base operations such as "select all records with SALARY > 10,000." Decrypting the SALARY field, even on rejected records, increases the time to process a query. (Consider the query that selects just one record but that must decrypt and compare one field of each record to find the one that satisfies the query.) Thus, encryption is not often used to implement separation in data bases.

Integrity Lock

The **integrity lock** was first proposed at the Air Force Summer Study on Data Base Security [AFS83]. The lock is a way to provide both integrity and limited access for a data base. The operation was nicknamed "spray paint" because each element is painted with a color that denotes its sensitivity. The coloring is maintained with the element, not in a master data base table.

A model of the basic integrity lock is shown in Figure 8-12. As shown in that figure, each data item consists of three pieces: the data itself, a sensitivity label, and a checksum. The sensitivity label defines the sensitivity of the data, and the checksum is computed across both data and sensitivity label to prevent unauthorized modification of the data or its

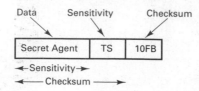

Figure 8-12   Integrity Lock

label. The data is stored in plaintext for efficiency because the DBMS may need to examine many fields when selecting records to match a query.

The sensitivity label should be

- *unforgeable* so that a malicious subject cannot create a new sensitivity level for an element
- *unique* so that a malicious subject cannot copy a sensitivity level from another element
- *concealed* so that a malicious subject cannot even determine the sensitivity level of an arbitrary element

The third piece of the integrity lock for a field is an error-detecting code, called a cryptographic checksum. In order to guarantee that a data value or its sensitivity classification has not been changed, this checksum must be unique for a given element, and must contain both the element's data and something to tie that data to a particular position in the data base. As shown in Figure 8-13, an appropriate cryptographic checksum includes something unique to the record (the record number), something unique to this data field within the record (the field attribute name), the data of this element, and the sensitivity classification of the element. These four components guard against changing, copying, or moving the data. The checksum can be computed using a strong encryption algorithm such as the Data Encryption Standard (DES).

Sensitivity Lock

The sensitivity lock shown in Figure 8-14 was designed by Graubert and Kramer [GRA84b] to meet these principles. A **sensitivity lock** is a combination of a unique identifier (such as the record number) and the sensitivity level. Because the identifier is unique, each integrity lock relates to one particular record. Many different elements will have the same sensitivity level. A malicious subject should not be able to identify two elements having identical sensitivity levels or identical data values just by looking at the sensitivity level portion of the integrity lock. Because of the encryption, the lock's contents, especially the sensitivity level, are concealed from plain view. Thus, the lock is associated with one specific record, and it protects the secrecy of the sensitivity level of that record.

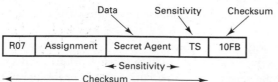

Figure 8-13   Cryptographic Checksum

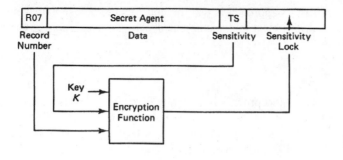

Figure 8-14   Sensitivity Lock

Integrity Lock DBMS

The integrity lock was invented as a short-term solution to the problem of security for multilevel data bases. The intention was to be able to use any (untrusted) data base manager with a trusted procedure that handles access control. The approach was informally called spray painting because the sensitive data was obliterated or concealed with encryption that protected both a data item and its sensitivity. In this way, only the access procedure would need to be trusted because only it would be able to achieve or grant access to sensitive data. The structure of such a system is shown in Figure 8-15.

The efficiency of integrity locks is a serious drawback. The space to store an element must be expanded to cover the sensitivity label. Because there are several pieces to this label and there is one label for every element, the space required is not insignificant.

The processing time efficiency of an integrity lock is also problematic. The sensitivity label must be decoded every time the data is passed to the user in order to verify that the user's access is allowable. Also, each time a value is written or modified, the label must be recomputed. Thus, substantial processing time is consumed. If the data base file can be sufficiently protected, the data values of the individual elements can be left in plaintext. Doing so benefits select and project queries across sensitive fields because an element need not be decrypted just to determine whether it should be selected.

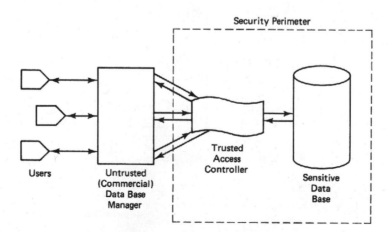

Figure 8-15   Trusted Data Base Manager

A final difficulty with this approach is that the untrusted data base manager sees all data of the data base, so it is subject to Trojan horse attacks by which data can be leaked through covert channels.

Trusted Front-End

The model of a **trusted front-end** process is shown in Figure 8-16. A trusted front-end is also known as a **guard**; it operates much like the reference monitor of Chapter 7. The motivation for this approach is the recognition that many DBMSs have been built and put into use without consideration of multilevel security. The front-end concept enhances the security of these existing systems with minimal change to the system. This concept originated with Hinke and Schaefer [HIN75]. The interaction between a user, a trusted front-end, and a DBMS involves the following steps:

1. User identifies self to front-end; front-end authenticates user's identity.
2. User issues query to front-end.
3. Front-end verifies user's authorization to data.
4. Front-end issues query to data base manager.
5. Data base manager performs I/O access, interacting with low-level access control to achieve access to actual data.
6. Data base manager returns result of query to trusted front-end.
7. Front-end verifies validity of data via checksum and checks classification of data against security level of user.
8. Front-end transmits data to untrusted front-end for formatting.
9. Untrusted front-end transmits formatted data to user.

The trusted front-end concept was implemented under the Sea Views project [LUN90a]. Sea Views used front-end filters to control data access.

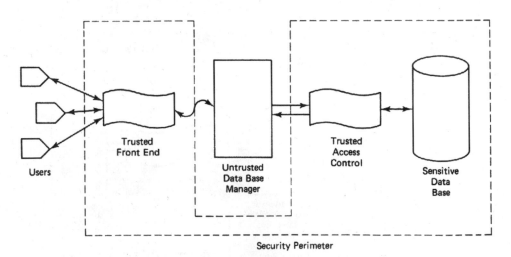

Figure 8-16   Trusted Front-End

Commutative Filters

The notion of a commutative filter was proposed by Denning [DEN85] as a simplification of the trusted interface to the data base manager. Essentially, the filter screens the user's request, reformatting it if necessary, so that only data of an appropriate sensitivity level is returned to the user.

A **commutative filter** is a process that interfaces to both the user and a data base manager. However, unlike the trusted front-end process of Graubert's integrity lock DBMS, the filter tries to capitalize on the efficiency of most DBMSs. The filter reformats the query so that the data base manager does as much of the work as possible, screening out many unacceptable records. The filter then provides a second screening to select only data to which the user has access.

Filters can be used for security at the record, attribute, or element level.

- When used at the record level, the filter requests desired data plus cryptographic checksum information; it then verifies the accuracy and accessibility of data to be passed to the user.
- At the attribute level, the filter checks whether all attributes in the user's query are accessible to the user and, if so, passes the query to the data base manager. On return, it deletes all fields to which the user has no access rights.
- At the element level, the system requests desired data plus cryptographic checksum information. When this is returned it checks the classification level of every element of every record retrieved against the user's level.

A simple example is the query

```
retrieve NAME where ((OCCUP = PHYSICIST) ∧
                     (CITY = WASHDC))
```

Suppose some physicists in Washington work on very sensitive projects, so that the current user should not be allowed to access the physicists' names. Suppose also that the current user is prohibited from knowing anything about any people in Moscow. A conventional data base manager would have access to all records and would then pass the results of its query on to the user. However, as we have seen, the user might be able to infer things about Moscow employees or Washington physicists working on secret projects without even accessing those fields directly.

The commutative filter reforms the original query in a trustable way so that sensitive information is never extracted from the data base. Our sample query would become

```
retrieve NAME where ((OCCUP = PHYSICIST) ∧ (CITY = WASHDC))
from all records R where
      (NAME-SECRECY-LEVEL (R) ≤ USER-SECRECY-LEVEL) ∧
      (OCCUP-SECRECY-LEVEL (R) ≤ USER-SECRECY-LEVEL) ∧
      (CITY-SECRECY-LEVEL (R) ≤ USER-SECRECY-LEVEL))
```

The filter works by restricting the query to the data base manager and then restricting the results before they are returned to the user. In this instance, the filter would request

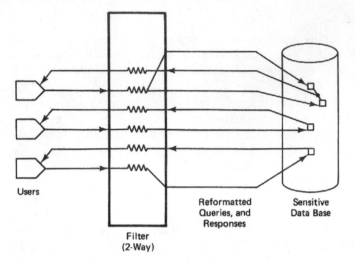

Figure 8-17   Commutative Filters

NAME, NAME-SECRECY-LEVEL, OCCUP, OCCUP-SECRECY-LEVEL, CITY, and CITY-SECRECY-LEVEL values, and would then filter and return to the user only those that are of a secrecy level acceptable for the user. Although even this simple query becomes complicated because of the added terms, these terms are all added by the front-end filter, invisibly to the user.

An example of this query filtering in operation is shown in Figure 8-17. The advantage of the commutative filter is that it allows query selection, some optimization, and some subquery handling to be done by the data base manager. This keeps the size of the security filter small, it reduces redundancy between it and the data base manager, and it improves the overall efficiency of the system.

Distributed Data Bases

A third design for a secure multilevel data base is what has been called the **distributed** or **federated data base**. In this case, a trusted front-end controls access to two unmodified commercial data base managers: one for all low-sensitivity data and one for all high-sensitivity data.

The front-end takes a user's query and formulates single-level queries to the data bases as appropriate. If the result is obtained from either back-end data base alone, the front-end passes the result back to the user. If the result comes from both data bases, the front-end has to combine the results appropriately. Notice, for example, that if the query is a join query having some high-sensitivity terms and some low, the front end has to perform the equivalent of a data base join itself.

The distributed data base design is not popular because the front-end, which must be trusted, is complex, potentially including most of the functionality of a full data base manager itself, and because the design does not scale well to many degrees of sensitivity, as each sensitivity level of data must be maintained in its own separate data base.

Window/View

An organizing principle for multilevel data base access is that of a **window** or a **view**. Denning et al. [DEN87a] survey the development of views for multilevel data base security. A window is a subset of a data base, containing exactly the information that a user is entitled to access.

A view can represent a single user's subset data base, so that all of a user's queries access only that data base. This subset guarantees that the user does not access values outside the permitted amount because nonpermitted values are not even in the user's data base. The view is specified as a set of relations in the data base, so that the data in the view subset changes as data in the data base changes.

For example, a travel agent might have access to part of an airline's flight information data base. Records for cargo flights would be excluded, as would the pilot's name and the serial number of the plane for every flight. Suppose the data base contained an attribute TYPE whose value was either CARGO or PASS (for passenger). Other attributes might be flight number, origin, destination, departure time, arrival time, capacity, pilot, and tail number.

Now suppose the airline created passenger flights that could be booked only directly through the airline. These flights might be represented as more sensitive information, unavailable to travel agents, by assigning their flight numbers a more sensitive rating. The whole data base, and the agent's view, would have the logical structure shown in Figure 8-18.

The travel agent's view of the data base is expressed as

```
view AGENT-INFO
     FLTNO:=MASTER.FLTNO
     ORIG:=MASTER.ORIG
     DEST:=MASTER.DEST
     DEP:=MASTER.DEP
     ARR:=MASTER.ARR
     CAP:=MASTER.CAP
          where MASTER.TYPE='PASS'
     class AGENT
     auth retrieve
```

(a)

FLT#	ORIG	DEST	DEP	ARR	CAP	TYPE	PILOT	TAIL
362	JFK	BWI	0830	0950	114	PASS	Dosser	2463
397	JFK	ORD	0830	1020	114	PASS	Bottoms	3621
202	LGA	LGW	1530	0710	183	PASS	Jevins	2007
749	LGA	ATL	0947	1120	0	CARGO	Witt	3116
286	STA	SFO	1020	1150	117	PASS	Gross	4026
...								
...								

(b)

FLT#	ORIG	DEST	DEP	ARR	CAP
362	JFK	BWI	0830	0950	114
397	JFK	ORD	0830	1020	114
202	LGA	LGW	1530	0710	183
286	STA	SFO	1020	1150	117
...					
...					

Figure 8-18   Airline Data Base. (a) Airline's View; (b) Travel Agent's View

Because the access class of this view is AGENT, more sensitive flight numbers (flights booked only through the airline) do not appear in this view. An alternative that would have eliminated the entire records for those flights would be to restrict the record selection with a *where* clause. A view may involve computation or complex selection criteria to specify subset data.

The data presented to a user is obtained by **filtering** the contents of the original data base. Attributes, records, and elements are stripped away so that the user sees only acceptable items. Any attribute (column) is withheld unless the user is authorized to access at least one element. Any record (row) is withheld unless the user is authorized to access at least one element. Then for all elements that still remain, if the user is not authorized to access the element, it is replaced by UNDEFINED. This last step does not compromise any data because the user knows the existence of the attribute (there is at least one element for the attribute that the user can access) and the user knows the existence of the record (again at least one accessible element exists in the record).

In addition to elements, a view consists of relations of attributes. Furthermore, a user can create new relations from new and existing attributes and elements. These new relations are accessible to other users, subject to the standard access rights. A user can operate on the subset data base defined in a view only as allowed by the operations authorized in the view. As an example, a user might be allowed to retrieve records specified in one view or to retrieve and update records as specified in another view. Thus the airline example restricts travel agents to retrieving data.

The Sea Views project described in [DEN87a, LUN89] is the basis for a system that will integrate with a trusted operating system to form a trusted data base manager. The layered implementation as described is shown in Figure 8-19. The lowest layer, the reference monitor, performs file interaction, enforcing the Bell–LaPadula access controls, and does user authentication. Part of its function is to filter data passed to higher levels. The second level performs basic indexing and computation functions of the data base. The third level translates views into the base relations of the data base. These three layers make up the trusted computing base (TCB) of the system. The remaining layers implement normal DBMS functions and user interface.

This layered approach makes views both a logical division of a data base and a functional one. The approach is an important step toward the design and implementation of a trustable data base management system.

Concluding Remarks

At the beginning of the section it was noted that the work in this section is still very fresh. The multilevel security problem for data bases has been studied for only a few years, and the solutions are still evolving. In the next decade, other approaches will probably augment or replace the approaches described here.

8.8   Summary of Data Base Security

This chapter has covered three aspects of security for data base management systems: secrecy and integrity problems specific to data base applications, the inference problem for statistical data bases, and problems of including users and data of different sensitivity levels in one data base.

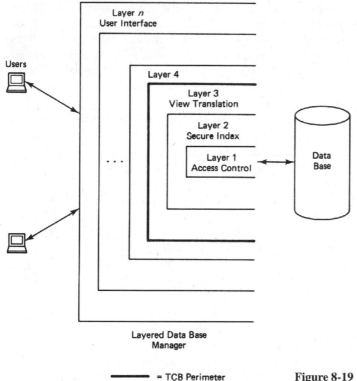

Figure 8-19   Secure Data Base Decomposition

Both secrecy and integrity are important to users of data bases. Secrecy can be broken by indirect disclosure of a negative result or the bounds of a value. Integrity of the entire data base is a responsibility of the DBMS software; this problem is handled by most major commercial systems through backups, redundancy, change logs, and two-step updates. Integrity of an individual element of the data base is the responsibility of the data base administrator, who defines the access policy.

The inference problem of a statistical data base arises from the mathematical relationships between data elements and query results. Controls studied to prevent statistical inference include limited response suppression, perturbation of results, and query analysis. One very complex control is monitoring all data provided to a user in order to prevent inference from independent queries.

Multilevel secure data bases must provide both secrecy and integrity. Integrity and access control can be implemented by use of an integrity lock. Three approaches for secrecy in multilevel secure data bases are views, trusted front-end with query modification, and commutative filters. Each of these solutions is just emerging from the prototype stage.

8.9 Bibliographic Notes

Date [DAT94] addresses general topics of data base management and the second volume [DAT88] covers recovery, integrity, concurrency, and security (secrecy). Fernandez and Wood [FER81] also cover basic security issues for data bases. The state of the art is presented by Lunt and Fernandez [LUN90] and Schaefer [SCH90a].

The inference problem dates back at least to [HOF70]. Denning and Schlörer [DEN83a] and Smith [SMI88b] survey the problems and controls for inference in data bases. Burns [BUR90] raises an issue of the secrecy/integrity trade-off. Lunt [LUN89] clarifies several issues regarding aggregation and inference. Adam and Wortmann [ADA89] covers statistical databases. Denning, Denning, and Schwartz [DEN79b] describes tracker attacks. Access control is first proposed by Stonebraker and Wong [STO74].

The best description of the multilevel security problem for data bases is [AFS83], the "Wood's Hole" report of the Air Force Studies Board of the National Academy of Sciences. Multilevel security issues for data bases have been explored by Denning [DEN85, DEN86, and DEN87a], Lunt [LUN90a], and Graubert [GRA84b, GRA85].

8.10   Terms and Concepts

8.11 Exercises

1. In an environment where several users are sharing access to a single data base, how can indefinite postponement occur? Describe a scenario in which two users could cause the indefinite postponement of each other. Describe a scenario in which a single user could cause the indefinite postponement of all other users.

2. Using the two-step commit presented in the beginning of this chapter, describe how to avoid assigning one seat to two people, as in the airline example. That is, list precisely which steps the data base manager should follow in assigning passengers to seats.

3. UNDO is a recovery operation for data bases. It is a command that obtains information from a transaction log and resets the elements of a data base to their values *before* a particular transaction is performed. Describe a situation in which an UNDO command would be useful.

4. The UNDO operation described in the previous exercise must be repeatable. That is, if x is the original value of a data base and x' is an incorrectly modified version, we want

$$\text{UNDO}(x') = x,$$

but also

$$\text{UNDO}(x) = x$$

and

$$\text{UNDO}(\text{UNDO}(x')) = x$$

   (a) Why must $\text{UNDO}(x) = x$?
   (b) Why must $\text{UNDO}(\text{UNDO}(x')) = x$?

5. Suppose a data base manager were to allow nesting of one transaction inside another. That is, after having updated part of one record, the DBMS would allow you to select another record, update it, and then perform further updates on the first record. What effect would nesting have on the integrity of a data base? Suggest a mechanism by which nesting could be allowed.

6. May a data base contain two identical records without a negative effect on the integrity of the data base? Why or why not?

7. Some operating systems perform buffered I/O. In this scheme, an output request is accepted from a user, and the user is informed of the normal I/O completion. However, the actual physical write operation is performed later, at a time convenient to the operating system. Discuss the effect of buffered I/O on integrity in a DBMS.

8. A data base transaction implements the command set STATUS to CURRENT in all records where BALANCE-OWED = 0.
   (a) Describe how that transaction would be performed using the two-step commit described in this chapter.
   (b) Suppose the relations from which that command was formed are (CUSTOMER-ID, STATUS) and (CUSTOMER-ID, BALANCE-OWED). How would the transaction be performed?
   (c) Suppose the relations from which that command was formed are (CUSTOMER-ID, STATUS), (CREDIT-ID, CUSTOMER-ID), (CREDIT-ID, BALANCE-OWED). How would the transaction be performed?

9. Show that if longitudinal parity is used as an error detection code, values in a data base can still be modified without detection. (Longitudinal parity is computed for the nth bit of each byte; that is, one parity bit is computed and retained for all bits in the 0th position, another parity bit for all bits in the 1st position, etc.)

10. Suppose query Q_1 obtains the median m_1 of a set S_1 of values. Suppose query Q_2 obtains the median m_2 of a subset S_2 of S_1. If $m_1 < m_2$, what can be inferred about S_1, S_2, and the elements of S_1 not in S_2?

11. Disclosure of the sum of all financial aid for students in Smith dorm is not sensitive because no individual student is associated with an amount. Similarly, a list of names of students receiving financial aid is not sensitive because no amounts are specified. However, the combination of these two lists reveals the amount for an individual student if only one student in Smith dorm receives aid. What computation would a data base management system have to perform in order to determine that the list of names might reveal sensitive data? What records would the data base management system have to maintain on what different users know in order to determine that the list of names might reveal sensitive data?

12. The response "sensitive value; response suppressed" is itself a disclosure. Suggest a manner in which a data base management system could suppress responses that reveal sensitive information without disclosing that the responses to certain queries are sensitive.

13. Cite a situation in which the sensitivity of an aggregate is greater than that of its constituent values. Cite a situation in which the sensitivity of an aggregate is less than that of its constituent values.

14. Explain the disadvantages of partitioning as a means of implementing multilevel security for data bases.

15. A data base management system is implemented under an operating system trusted to provide multilevel separation of users.
    (a) What security features of the operating system can be used to simplify the design of the data base management system?
    (b) Suppose the operating system has rating r, where r is C2 or B1 or B3, and so on. State and defend a policy for the degree of trust in the data base management system, based on the trust of the operating system.

16. What is the purpose of encryption in a multilevel secure data base management system?

9

Security in Networks
and Distributed Systems

In this chapter:
- *Network threats: wiretapping, impersonation, message confidentiality/integrity, denial of service*
- *Network controls: encryption, authentication, distributed authentication, integrity, traffic control*
- *Privacy-enhanced electronic mail*
- *Firewalls*
- *Multilevel networks*

This chapter covers security in networks of computers. Although networks raise new issues in security, familiar topics appear in the list of solutions to network security problems. The problems are the familiar loss of confidentiality, integrity, and availability. The solution technologies include encryption, the reference monitor concept, access controls, strong authentication, and protocols. We see an example that brings together cryptography, protocols, and operating system controls from earlier chapters into a concept called privacy enhanced electronic mail, known by the acronyms PEM, MOSS, and PGP. Also, we revisit the reference monitor concept in a new context: a network access protector called a firewall. In fact, networks can be viewed as more complex examples of computing systems, so that many of the program development and operating systems security concepts and controls apply to networks as well.

This chapter considers the broadest context of networking, from the media or devices through which network communications occur to the information being communicated. Although separating policy from mechanism is a very important principle in security, in this chapter we have to relate policy and threats to specific technology because, as we will discover, network threats arise at different points based on different technologies, and the controls must also relate to specific technologies.

This chapter begins with background to cover communications, networks, and distributed systems. We build new things from familiar concepts. Second, the chapter turns to security problems of networks. The threats are the familiar attacks on confidentiality, integrity, and availability, but in networks these can have numerous manifestations. We then progress to the controls available in networks, building from some familiar technologies such as encryption to unfamiliar ones. Finally, we look closely at two examples of very effective network security controls—firewalls and PEM—as combinations of some of these building blocks.

9.1   Network Concepts

We begin this chapter with some basic concepts from networking, to define the field and introduce some necessary terminology.

In its simplest form, shown in Figure 9-1, a network is two devices connected across some medium by hardware and software that complete the communications. In some cases, one device is a computer (sometimes called a server) and the other is a simple I/O device (sometimes called a client), minimally a keyboard for input and a screen for output.

Although this model fits the definition of a network, the actual situation is often significantly more complicated.

- The simple I/O device (for user-to-computer communication) is often a PC or a workstation, so that the client end has considerable storage and processing capability.
- A network is normally not just a single client to a single server; typically, many clients interact with many servers.
- The services of a network are often provided by many computers, with a single user's communication merely passing through some computers but pausing at others for interactions.
- The end user is quite often unaware of many of the communications and computations taking place on the user's behalf.

Thus, while a basic network resembles Figure 9-1, most real-world situations are more like Figure 9-2. In the second view, the user may communicate directly with System *C*, unaware that communication is actually passing through the active entities System *A* and *B*, and maybe unaware that sometimes System *C* passes work to System *D*.

A single computing system in a network is often called a **node**, and its processor (computer) is called a **host**. A connection between two hosts is known as a **link**. Network

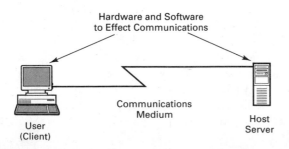

Hardware and Software
to Effect Communications

Communications
Medium

User
(Client)

Host
Server

Figure 9-1   Simple View of Network

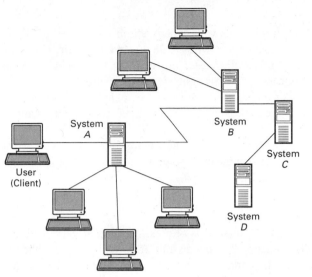

**Figure 9-2   More Complex but More
Typical View of Networks**

computing consists of users, communications media, visible hosts, and systems not generally visible to end users.

Users communicate to networked systems by direct interaction with terminals, workstations, and computers. A **terminal** is a simple device that transmits and receives strings of character data. Although a terminal may do small amounts of work, such as displaying data at specified positions on the screen, the terminal does not do any complex data manipulation. A **workstation** has more processing power at the user's end, so that it can do more sophisticated data manipulation, such as converting coded data to a graphical format and displaying the picture. A workstation usually has storage to hold data. A system is a collection of processors, perhaps a mixture of workstations and independent processors, with typically more processing power and more storage capacity than a workstation.

Communications

All data communications are either in **digital** format (in which data items are expressed as discrete binary values) or **analog** (in which data items are expressed as points in a continuous range, such as a sound or an electrical voltage). Computers typically store and process digital data, but many telephone and similar cable communications are in analog form. Thus, digital signals must be converted to analog for transmission, and back to digital for computation at the receiving end. These conversions are performed by a **modem** (standing for *mo*dulator–*dem*odulator), which converts a digital data stream to tones and back again.

Media

Communications use several kinds of media. Communications must be sent either through a physical medium, such as a wire, or through the air, using a radiation technology such as radio waves.

Cable

The most common communication medium is **wire**. The medium most often used inside homes and offices is a pair of insulated copper wires, called a **twisted pair**. Copper has good transmission properties at a relatively low cost. Unfortunately, the bandwidth of such a system is rather limited, so engineers cannot transmit a large number of communications simultaneously on a single line. For this reason, single twisted pair service is most often used locally, within a building or up to a local exchange office. A **coaxial (coax) cable** has greater capacity.

The signal quality of both twisted pairs and coax cable tends to degrade over distance. **Repeaters** can be spaced periodically along the cable to pick up the signal, amplify it, and retransmit it.

Optical Fiber

A newer form of cable is made of very thin strands of glass. Instead of carrying electrical energy, these fibers carry light energy. The bandwidth of optical fiber is higher than for copper wire, and there is also less interference, less crossover between adjacent media, lower cost, and less weight. Optical fiber is a much better transmission medium than copper; as it ages, copper is being replaced by optical fiber in most communications systems.

Microwave

Microwave is a form of radio transmission especially well-suited for outdoor communications. Microwave has a channel capacity similar to that of coax cable. The principal advantage of microwave is that the signal is strong from its point of transmission to its point of receipt. Therefore, microwave signals do not need to be regenerated with repeaters, as do signals on cable.

However, a microwave signal travels in a straight line, whereas the earth curves. Microwave signals travel by line of sight: the transmitter and receiver must be in a straight line with one another, and there must be no intervening obstacles, such as mountains. As shown in Figure 9-3, a straight microwave signal transmitted between towers of reasonable height can travel a distance of only about 30 miles because of the curvature of the

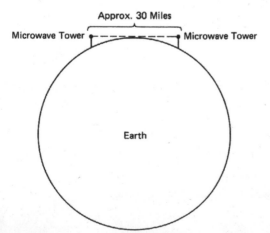

Figure 9-3   Microwave Transmission

earth. Thus, microwave signals are "bounced" from receiver to receiver, spaced less than 30 miles apart, to cover a longer distance.

Satellite

Communications companies use satellites in orbit synchronized with the rotation of the earth, called geosynchronous orbit. Although the medium is expensive to launch, once in space it is essentially maintenance-free. Furthermore, the quality of a satellite communication link is often better than that of an earth-bound wire cable.

Satellites act as naive transponders: whatever they receive they broadcast out again. These satellites receive and repeat signals; essentially the signal "bounces" off the satellite. In this way, a signal from North America travels 22,300 miles into the sky and the same distance back to a point in Europe.

We can project a signal to a satellite with reasonable accuracy, but the satellite is not expected to be able to repeat this accuracy with its repeat of the signal. Thus, to reduce complexity and eliminate beam focusing, satellites typically spread their transmissions over a very wide area. A rather narrow angle of dispersion from the satellite's transmitter produces a fairly broad pattern on the surface of the earth, because of the 22,300-mile distance from the satellite to earth. A typical satellite transmission can be received over a path several hundred miles wide; some early ones could cover the width of the entire continental U.S. in a single transmission.

Protocols

Most of us do not know whether our communication is carried over copper wire, optical fiber, satellite, microwave, or some combination of these. In many instances, our communication one day may be carried differently from a similar communication the next. This ambiguity is actually a positive feature of independence: the communication is separated from the actual medium of communication. The reason independence is possible is protocols that allow a user to think at the high (data) level of a communication, with the details of *how* the communication is accomplished hidden within software and hardware on both ends of a communication. The software and hardware create a **protocol stack**, which is a layered architecture for communications.

Two popular protocol stacks are the Open Systems Interconnection (OSI) and the Transmission Control Protocol and Internet Protocol (TCP/IP) architecture.

ISO Reference Model

The International Standards Organization (ISO) Open Systems Interconnection (OSI) model consists of layers by which a network communication occurs. The OSI reference model consists of seven layers, listed in Figure 9-4.

Communications through the different layers are shown in Figure 9-5. The layers represent different activities performed in the actual transmission of a message. Each layer serves a separate function; equivalent layers perform similar functions for the sender and receiver. For example, layer 4 of the sender affixes a header to a message, showing the sender, the receiver, and sequence information. On the receiving end, layer 4 verifies that it is the intended recipient, and removes this header. Each layer passes data in three directions: *above* with a layer communicating more abstractly, *parallel* or *across* to the same layer in another host, and *below* with a layer handling less abstract (that is, more fundamental) data

Layer	Name	Activity
7	Application	User program: initiate and process messages
6	Presentation	System utilities: standardize data appearance, text compression
5	Session	Operating system: establish user-level session and manage sessions between applications; message sequencing, recovery
4	Transport	Network manager: flow control, end-to-end error detection and correction, priority service
3	Network	Network manager: manage connection, routing, message blocking into packets
2	Data link	Hardware: reliable data delivery over physical medium; transmission error recovery, separating packets into frames
1	Physical	Hardware: actual communication across physical medium; individual bit communication

Figure 9-4   OSI Protocol Layer Levels

items. The communications above and below are actual communications, whereas the parallel one is a virtual communications path. Parallel layers are called peers.

Each layer reformats the transmissions and exchanges information with its peer layer. Figure 9-6 shows a typical message that has been acted upon by the seven layers to prepare it for transmission. Layer 6 breaks the original message data into blocks. At the session layer (5), a session header is added to show the sender, the receiver, and some sequencing information. Layer 4 adds information concerning the logical connection between the sender and receiver. At the network layer (3) routing information is added; it also divides the message into units called packets, which are the standard units of communication in a network. The data link layer (2) adds both a header and a trailer to ensure correct sequencing of the message blocks, and to detect and correct transmission errors. The individual

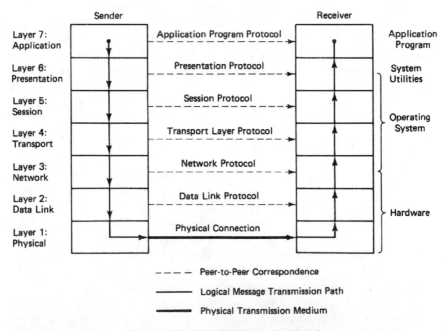

Figure 9-5   ISO OSI Network Model

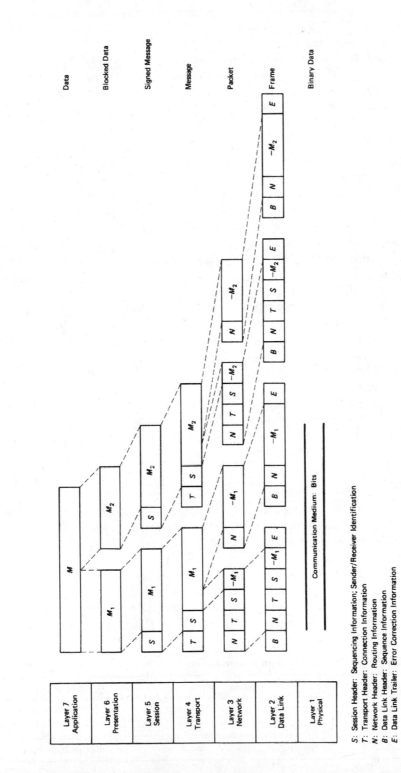

S: Session Header: Sequencing Information; Sender/Receiver Identification
T: Transport Header: Connection Information
N: Network Header: Routing Information
B: Data Link Header: Sequence Information
E: Data Link Trailer: Error Correction Information

Figure 9-6   Message Prepared for Transmission

bits of the message and the control information are transmitted on the physical medium by level 1. All of the additions to the message are checked and removed by the corresponding layer on the receiving side.

The OSI model is one of several models. Different network designers implement network activities in slightly different combinations, although there is always a clear delineation of responsibility. Some designers argue that the OSI model is overly complex—it has too many levels—so other models are typically shorter.

TCP/IP

The ISO model is a conceptual model: it shows the different activities that have to be performed to send a communication. In fact, however, full implementation of a 7-course transmission carries too much overhead for megabit-per-second communications. Instead, TCP/IP (Transmission Control Protocol/Internet Protocol) is the protocol stack used for most wide area network communications. TCP/IP is actually defined by protocols, not layers. You may want to think of it as four layers: application, host-to-host (end-to-end) transport, Internet, and physical. An application deals in abstract data items meaningful to the application user.

The transport layer deals in variable-length messages from the application layer, which the transport layer breaks down into manageable-sized units transferred in **packets**. The Internet layer transmits application layer packets in **datagrams**, which this layer passes to different physical connections based on the data's destination, provided in an address accompanying the data. The physical layer consists of device drivers to perform the actual bit-by-bit data communication. Table 9-1 shows how each layer contributes to a TCP/IP interaction.

Whatever the model, a layer will typically subdivide data it receives from a higher layer and then add a header and/or trailer to the data, which it passes to a lower layer. Each layer encapsulates the higher layer, so that higher layer headers and trailers are seen just as part of the data to be transmitted.

Addressing

All network models implement an addressing scheme. An address is a unique identification of a single point in the network. For obvious reasons, addressing in shared, wide area networks follows established rules, whereas addressing in local area networks is less constrained.

Starting at the local area network, each node has a unique address, defined in hardware on the network connector device (such as an Ethernet card in a PC) or its software driver. A network administrator may choose network addresses to be easy to work with: 1001, 1002, 1003 for nodes on one LAN, 2001, 2002, and so forth on another.

Table 9-1   TCP/IP Communication Layers

Layer	Action	Responsibilities
Application	Prepare messages from user interactions	User interaction, addressing
Transport	Convert messages to packets	Sequencing, reliability (integrity)
Internet	Convert packets to datagrams	Flow control, routing
Physical	Transmit datagrams as individual bits	Data communication

A host on a TCP/IP wide area network has a 32-bit address,[1] called an **IP address**. An IP address is expressed as four 8-bit groups in decimal notation, separated by periods, such as 100.24.48.6. People prefer speaking in words or pseudo-words, so network addresses are also known by names, such as ATT.COM or CAM.AC.UK. Addressing tables convert these acronyms to numeric format.

In addition to addresses for nodes, there are addresses for applications running within a node. If you and I begin a communication, we establish a unique channel number by which our computers can route our packets to us. The channel number is called a port or socket. A **port** is a number designating a particular application running on a computer, and a **socket** is a network address plus a port at that address. Essentially, then, a socket is the network address of an application.

Types of Networks

To classify networks, people often speak of local area networks, wide area networks, and inter-networks. Although the distinctions among these three are not always clear-cut, the following general descriptions apply.

Local Area Networks

As the name implies, a **local area network (LAN)** covers a small distance, typically within a single building. Usually a LAN connects several small computers, such as personal computers, as well as some printers and perhaps some dedicated file storage devices. Figure 9-7 shows the arrangement of a typical LAN. The primary advantage of a LAN is the opportunity for its users to share data and programs and to share access to devices such as printers.

Most LANs have these characteristics, although this list is not definitive:

- *Locally controlled.* The equipment is owned and managed by, and the users all are affiliated with, a single organization, such as a company, department, workgroup, or physical proximity.
- *Small.* Typically fewer than 100 users share a single LAN.
- *Physically protected.* Because it is located on the premises of a company or other organization, malicious outsiders cannot readily get at the LAN equipment.
- *Isolated.* Many LANs are separate from other LANs and from other network connections (although this condition is changing as the benefits of wider network connectivity become apparent).

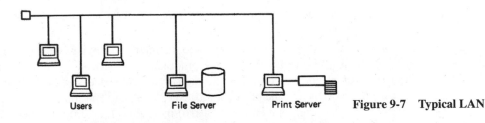

Users   File Server   Print Server   **Figure 9-7   Typical LAN**

---

[1] *Note:* The world's networks are running out of unique addresses. This 32-bit standard address is being increased in 1996.

Wide Area Networks

A **wide area network** (**WAN**) differs from a local area network in terms of both size or distance (as its name implies, it covers a wider geographic area than a LAN) and control or ownership (it is more likely *not* to be owned or controlled by a single body). Still, there tends to be some unity to a WAN: the hosts on a WAN may all belong to a company with many offices, perhaps even in different cities or countries, or they may be a cluster of independent organizations within a few miles of each other that share the cost of networking hardware. These examples also show how WANs themselves differ. Some are under close control and maintain a high degree of logical and physical isolation (typically these are WANs controlled by one organization), whereas others are only marriages of convenience. Typical characteristics of WANs are these:

- *Single control.* Typically a single organization is responsible for and controls a wide area network. Even if a network is shared by several unrelated subscribers, one organization typically determines who may join the network.

- *Covers a significant distance.* A WAN generally exists for a distance greater than a LAN can cover, typically from a few miles to the entire globe.

- *Physically exposed* (often, but not always). Most wide area networks use publicly available communications media, which are relatively exposed. However, the fact that many subscribers share those media helps to protect the privacy of any one subscriber.

Because WANs cover a wide range of possibilities, we look at the two ends of the network spectrum—LANs and Internets—and understand that WANs represent much of the area between the ends.

Inter-Networks (Internets)

Finally, there are networks of networks, or inter-network networks, sometimes called **internets**. An internet is a connection of two or more separate (separately managed and controlled) networks. The most significant inter-network is known as **the Internet**, because it connects so many of the other public networks.

The Internet is really a federation of networks, loosely controlled by the Internet Society. The Internet Society enforces certain minimal rules of fair play to ensure that all users are treated equitably, and it supports standard protocols so that users can communicate. These are the characteristics of the Internet:

- *Federation.* Almost no general statements can be made about Internet users, or even network service providers. Some may access the network through businesses or government organizations that are very restrictive, but others may obtain access simply by paying a small monthly fee.

- *Enormous.* Nobody really knows how large the Internet is, in part because new hosts are added daily, in part because one Internet access point can support hundreds or thousands of machines connected through that single access point, and in part because nobody has laid the basis for an accurate census. The Internet connects over 30,000 networks. There are currently (1996) more than 1,000,000 Internet addresses (host nodes) and well over 25,000,000 human users. The size of the Internet is said to double approximately yearly.

- *Heterogeneous.* Given the size of the Internet, probably one of every kind of commercially available hardware and software is connected to the Internet. Unix is very popular as the operating system at the Internet connection point, although most other multiuser operating systems could support access.

- *Physically and logically exposed.* Because there is no global access control, practically any attacker can access the net and, because of its complex connectivity, reach practically any resource on the net.

Topologies

The topology of a network can affect its security. Three basic patterns come from LANs, but the structures describe wider networks, or parts of wider networks, as well. These three patterns are depicted in Figure 9-8.

Common Bus

Conceptually, a **common bus** is a single wire to which each node of a LAN is connected. Timing signals on the bus help the nodes communicate. This medium is especially convenient for LANs because the configuration of offices changes often when new users are hired or old users change locations or duties.

Nodes must continually monitor the bus to retrieve communications addressed for them. In that respect, every communication is accessible to every node, not just the designated addressee. Each host acts cooperatively but autonomously.

Star or Hub

In a **star** or **hub** network, each node is connected to a central traffic controller node. All transmissions flow from the source node to the traffic controller and then from the traffic controller to the destination node. Such a central node is able to monitor and control traffic to defeat covert channels.

Each message is read only by the traffic controller (presumably for address only) and by the intended recipient. There is a unique path between any two nodes, and this path is inaccessible to any others.

Ring

In a **ring topology**, each node receives many messages, scans each, removes ones designated for it, adds any more it wants to transmit, and sends the pack of messages to the next node.

As with the bus, there is no central control. In this topology, however, each node has greater responsibility to the others, as a single node's failure to pass along all the messages it has received would deny other nodes their data.

Distributed Systems

In a **distributed system** the computation involves two or more computers. Of most interest here is the type of distributed system in which one computer invokes a process on another computer without the direct participation of, or necessarily even the knowledge of, the user. In one example of a distributed system, a user task on one machine requires data or

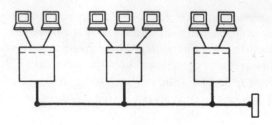

(a) Bus Topology

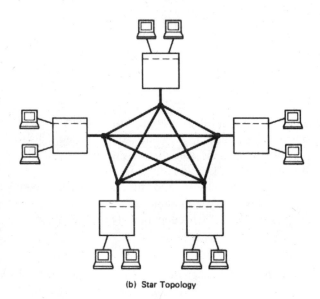

(b) Star Topology

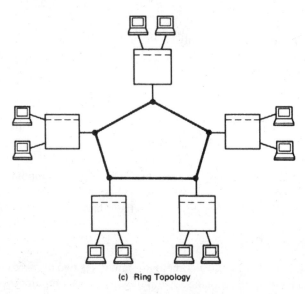

(c) Ring Topology

Figure 9–8   Network Topologies

specialized processing from another machine, such as a central machine on which a data base is maintained. In another example of a distributed system, several machines may share tasks depending on the current workload to optimize performance for all users.

For our purposes, the significant characteristic of distributed systems is multiple, independent, and physically separated computers. The computers may be directly connected, nodes on a LAN, or connected to a wider network.

Advantages of Computing Networks

Computer networks offer several advantages over single-processor systems.

- *Resource sharing.* Users of a network can access a variety of resources through the network. Sharing data bases, data and program files, and other resources reduces maintenance and storage costs while providing each user with improved access. Usage may be too low for a single individual to justify buying a specialized or expensive device. However, being able to share the device with many network users may justify its purchase.
- *Distributing the workload.* The use of a single system varies as users join and leave a system. The degree of fluctuation of workload for a single system can be moderated in a network, so the workload can be shifted from a heavily loaded system to an underused one.
- *Increased reliability.* Because a computing network consists of more than one computing system, the failure of one system or of just one component need not necessarily block users from continuing to compute. If similar systems exist, users can move their computing tasks to other systems when one system fails.
- *Expandability.* Network systems can be expanded easily by adding new nodes. This expansion of the user base can occur without the manager of any single system having to take special action.

The computing systems we have considered up to now have been self-contained entities. A single set of security policies has been associated with each computing system. Thus, each system is concerned with integrity of data, secrecy of data, and availability of service. A single operating system enforces the security policies, hardware controls assist the operating system, and some users augment the controls from the operating system with security features in individual application programs. Users trust the operating system to provide a certain level of protection. The operating system can protect resources because it exercises complete control over those resources.

Computing networks have similar characteristics. The network must ensure integrity of data, secrecy of data, and availability of service. Each user accesses the network through a single operating system, which also includes network interface responsibilities. Users still expect the operating systems to enforce the security policies of the network. However, in a network the operating systems at the two ends of the communication, as well as the operating systems of all computers in between, must cooperate to enforce security.

We cannot protect the whole network because its distant points are not under our control. However, we can think of our relationship to the rest of the network and focus on local users' accesses to the network, data received from and sent to the network, and possible accesses by other more distant users. In the next section we analyze the security ramifications of these pieces.

9.2 Threats in Networks

We have developed a basic understanding of networks and their terminology, without mentioning many security implications. Perhaps you have thought of some security issues as you read. In this section we look at networks using analytic skills developed from the previous chapters. Our analysis identifies some of the threats and vulnerabilities of networks.

Network Security Issues

Networks have security problems for the following reasons:

- *Sharing.* Because of the resource and workload sharing of networks, more users have the potential to access networked systems than single computers. Perhaps worse, access is afforded to *more systems,* so that access controls for single systems may be inadequate in networks.

- *Complexity of system.* In Chapter 7 we saw that an operating system is a complicated piece of software. Reliable security is difficult if not impossible on a large operating system, especially one not designed specifically for security. A network combines two or more possibly dissimilar operating systems. Therefore, a network operating/control system is likely to be more complex than an operating system for a single computing system. This complexity limits confidence in the security of a network.

- *Unknown perimeter.* The expandability of a network also implies uncertainty about the network boundary. One host may be a node on two different networks, so that resources on one network are accessible to the users of the other network as well. Although wide accessibility is an advantage, this unknown or uncontrolled group of possibly malicious users is a security disadvantage. A similar problem occurs when new hosts can be added to the network. Every network node must be able to react to the possible presence of new, untrustable hosts. Figure 9-9 points out the problems in defining the boundaries of a network. Notice, for example, that a user on a host in network *D* may be unaware of the potential connections from users of networks *A* and *B*.

- *Many points of attack.* A simple computing system is a self-contained unit. Access controls on one machine preserve the secrecy of data on that processor. However, when a file is stored in a network host remote from the user, the file may pass through many hosts to get to the user. Although the administrator of one host may enforce rigorous security policies, that administrator has no control over other hosts in the network. The user has to depend on the access control mechanisms of all of these systems.

- *Anonymity.* An attacker can mount an attack from thousands of miles away and thus never have to touch the system attacked or come into contact with any of its administrators or users. The attack can be passed through many other hosts, in an effort to disguise from where the attack originated. Finally, computer-to-computer authentication is not the same as for humans to computers; secure distributed authentication requires thought and attention to detail.

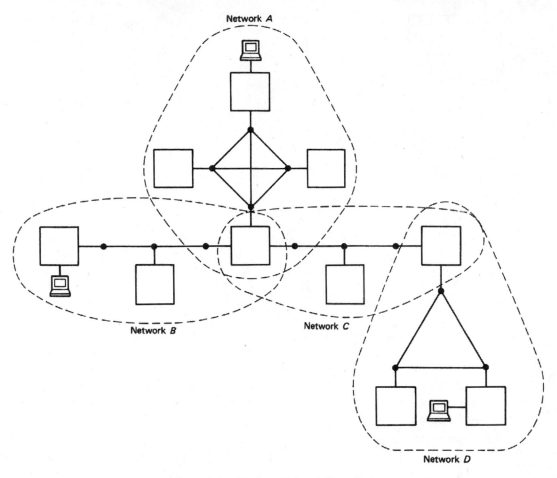

Figure 9-9   Unclear Network Boundaries

- *Unknown path.* As shown in Figure 9-10, there may be many paths from one host to another. Suppose that a user on host A_1 wants to send a message to a user on host B_3. That message might be routed through hosts A_2 and B_2 before arriving at host B_3. Host A_3 may provide acceptable security, but not A_2 or B_2. Network users seldom have control over the routing of their messages.

Security Threat Analysis

Let us recall how we performed security threat analysis in other situations. We looked at all the parts of a system; considered damage to confidentiality, integrity, and availability; and hypothesized the kinds of attacks that could cause this damage. So, in a network, we have

- *local nodes* connected via
- *local communications links* to a
- *local area network,* which also has
- *local data storage,*

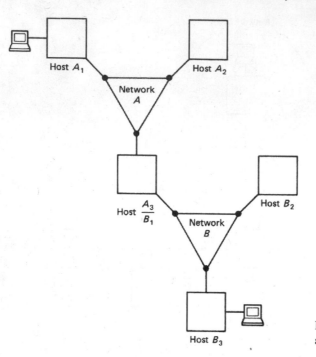

Figure 9-10   Message Routing in a Network

- *local processes,* and
- *local devices.* The local area network is also connected to a
- *network gateway,* which gives access via
- *network communications links* to
- *network control resources,*
- *network routers,* and
- *network resources,* such as data bases.

For example, in Figure 9-11, user Andy at workstation *A* wants to communicate with user Bo at workstation *B,* to use resources on the LAN to which Bo is attached, or use resources from LAN *C* elsewhere in the network.

All of those functional needs are typical for users of networks. But let us now add a malicious outsider, Marv at workstation *M,* as in Figure 9-12, and consider the negative effects Marv can cause.

- *Read communications* from Andy to Bo. These are exposed inside Andy's machine, at all places through the network, and inside Bo's machine. Thus a confidentiality attack can be mounted from practically any place in the network.
- *Modify communications* from Andy to Bo. Again, these are exposed at all places through the network.
- *Forge communications* allegedly from Andy to Bo. This is even easier than modifying a communication, because a forgery can be inserted any place in the network and does not require catching a communication in transit to modify. Because Andy does

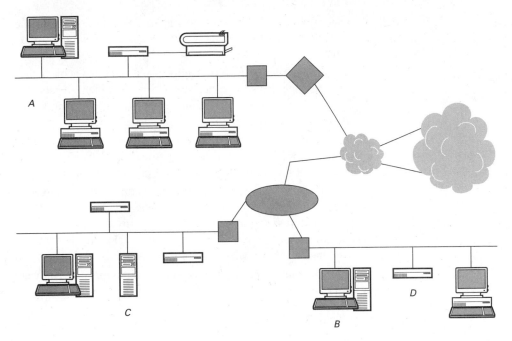

Figure 9-11   Typical Network

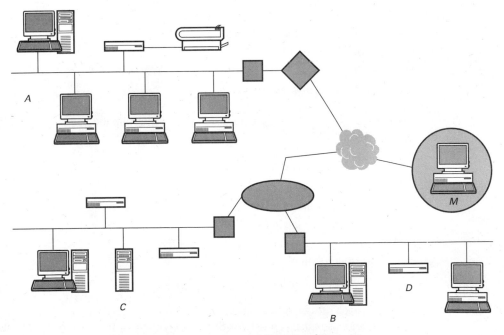

Figure 9-12   Vulnerabilities in a Network

not deliver his communications personally, and because Bo might even never have met Andy, Bo has little basis for judging whether a communication purportedly from Andy is authentic.

- *Inhibit communications* from Andy to Bo. Here again, Marv can achieve this result by invading Andy's machine, Bo's machine, routers between them, or communications links. Marv can also disrupt communications in general by flooding the network or any unique path on the network.

- *Inhibit all communications* passing through a point. If the point represents a unique path to or from a node, all traffic to or from that node is blocked. If the point is not unique, blocking it will shift traffic to other nodes, perhaps overburdening them.

- *Read data* at *C* or *D*. Marv can impersonate Andy (who is authorized to access data at *C* or *D*). Bo might question a message out of character for Andy, but machines *C* and *D* will just apply the access controls for Andy. Alternatively, Marv can invade (run a program at) machines *C* or *D* to override access controls. Finally, Marv can search the network for machines that have weak or improperly administered access controls.

- *Modify* or *destroy data* at *C* or *D*. Here again Marv can impersonate Andy and do anything Andy could, or Marv can try to circumvent controls.

Thus, in summary, the threats are

- interception of data in transit
- access to programs or data at remote hosts
- modification of programs or data at remote hosts
- modification of data in transit
- insertion of communications impersonating a user
- insertion of a repeat of a previous communication
- blocking of selected traffic
- blocking of all traffic
- running a program at a remote host

How are all of these threats accomplished? We can group the potential threats into the following categories:

- wiretapping
- impersonation
- message confidentiality violations
- message integrity violations
- hacking
- code integrity violations
- denial of service

We investigate each of these threat classes in the following sections.

Why are all these attacks possible? Size, anonymity, ignorance or misunderstanding, complexity, dedication, and programming all contribute. In this section we look at specific threats and their countermeasures. Then later in this chapter we can see how these counter-measures fit together into specific tools.

Wiretapping

The general term **wiretap** means to intercept communications. Although the term has a physical connotation, no actual contact is necessary. Also, a wiretap can be done covertly so that neither the sender nor the receiver of a communication knows that the contents have been intercepted.

Passive wiretapping is just "listening," that is, intercepting the communication. But in the analysis from the previous section, we found that Marv could replace Andy's com-munications with his own or create communications purported to be from Andy. **Active wiretapping** means injecting something into the communication.

Cable

At the most local level, in an Ethernet or other LAN all signals are available on the cable for anyone to intercept. Each LAN connector (such as a computer board) has a unique address; each board and its drivers are programmed to label all packets from the board's host with its unique address (as a sender's "return" address) and to take from the net only packets addressed to its host.

However, a board called a **packet sniffer** can retrieve all packets on the net. And one board can be reprogrammed to have the supposedly unique address of another existing board on the LAN, so that two different boards both fetch packets for one address. (To avoid detection, the rogue board must put back on the net copies of the packets it has intercepted.) Usually LANs are used only in environments that are fairly friendly, so these kinds of attacks occur infrequently. However you should keep them in mind as possibilities.

Additionally, ordinary wire (and many other electronic components) emits radiation. By a process called **inductance** an intruder can tap a wire without making physical contact with the cable. Signals from cable travel only short distances, and they are blocked by other conductive materials. However, the equipment needed to pick up signals is inexpen-sive and easy to obtain, so inductance threats are a concern. They do require the intruder to be fairly close to the cable, so this form of attack is not too popular.

Moving out from the local environment more hostile agents appear. Signals on a net-work are **multiplexed**, meaning that more than one signal is transmitted at a given time. For example, two analog (sound) signals can be combined, like two tones in a musical chord, and two digital signals can be combined by sending them interleaved, like playing cards being shuffled. A LAN carries distinct packets, but data on a WAN may be heavily multiplexed as it leaves its sending host. Thus a wiretapper on a WAN needs to be able not just to intercept the desired communication but also to extract that one communication from the others with which it is multiplexed. Although this can be done, the effort involved means it is not very common.

Microwave

Because microwave signals are not carried along a wire, there is some problem with preci-sion in aim. Typically a signal from a transmitter is focused at its corresponding receiver, but the signal path must be fairly wide to compensate for errors in aim, as shown in Figure

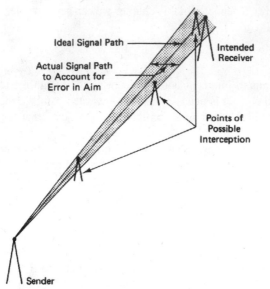

Figure 9-13   **Path of Microwave Signals**

9-13. From a security standpoint, that situation is very undesirable. Not only can someone intercept a microwave transmission by interfering with the line of sight between sender and receiver, but someone can also pick up an entire transmission from an antenna somewhere along the path but somewhat off the direct focus point.

Microwave signals are sent through the air, available to anyone who wants to pick them up. A signal is not shielded or isolated to prevent interception. Microwave is therefore a very insecure medium. However, because of the large volume of traffic carried by microwave links, it is unlikely—although not impossible—that someone could separate an individual transmission. A privately owned microwave link, carrying only communications for one organization, is not so well-protected by volume.

Satellite Communication

As shown in Figure 9-14, a satellite communication can be intercepted in an area several hundred miles wide and about a thousand miles long. Therefore, the potential for interception is even greater. However, because satellite communications are generally heavily multiplexed, the risk is small that any one communication will be intercepted.

Optical Fiber

Optical fiber offers two significant security advantages. First, the entire optical network must be tuned carefully each time a new connection is made. Therefore, no one can tap an optical system without detection. Clipping just one fiber in a bundle will destroy the balance in the network.

Secondly, optical fiber carries light energy, not electricity. Light does not emanate a magnetic field as electricity does. Therefore, an inductive tap is impossible on an optical fiber cable.

Just using fiber, however, does not guarantee security, any more than does using encryption. The repeaters, splices, and taps along a cable are places where data may be

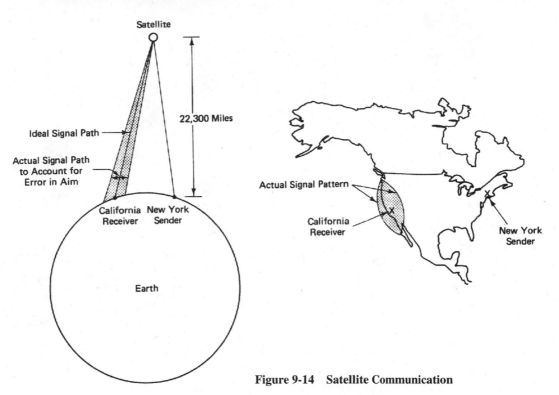

Figure 9-14   Satellite Communication

available more easily than in the fiber cable itself. The connections from computing equipment to the fiber may also be points for penetration. By itself, fiber is much more secure than cable, but it has vulnerabilities also.

Summary of Wiretapping

So far we have identified many points where all network traffic is available to an interceptor. As shown in Figure 9-15, communications are exposed from their origin to their destination.

From a security standpoint, you should assume that *all* communication links between network nodes can be broken. For this reason, commercial network users apply encryption to protect the confidentiality of their communications. We see how encryption is used later in this chapter.

Impersonation

Wiretapping is a threat, but in many instances there is an easier way to obtain at least as much information: impersonation of another person or process. Why risk tapping a line, and why bother extracting one communication out of many, if you can obtain the same data directly?

Usually impersonation is a more significant threat in a wide area network than in a local one. Local individuals often have better ways to obtain access as another user, such as sitting at an unattended workstation. Still, these kinds of attacks should not be ignored even on local area networks because local area networks are sometimes attached to wider area networks without anyone's thinking through the security implications first.

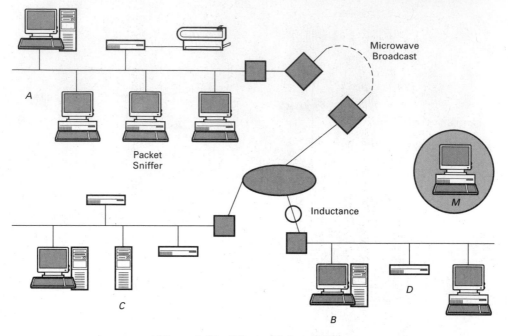

Figure 9-15   Wiretap Vulnerabilities

In an impersonation, the attacker has several choices:

- guess the identity and authentication details of the target
- pick up the identity and authentication details of the target from a previous communication
- circumvent or disable the authentication mechanism at the target computer
- use a target that will not be authenticated
- use a target whose authentication data is known

These choices are explained in the following sections.

Authentication Foiled by Guessing

In Chapter 6 we saw the results of several studies that showed how many users chose easy-to-guess passwords. In Chapter 5 we saw that the Internet worm of 1988 capitalized on exactly that flaw: Morris's worm tried to impersonate each use of an attacked machine by trying, in order, a handful of variations of the user name, a list of about 250 common words as passwords and, finally, the words in a dictionary. Sadly, many people's accounts are still open to these easy attacks.

In a trustworthy environment, such as an office LAN, a password may simply be a signal that the user does not want others to use the workstation or account. Users may not think they have any reason to protect against attacks. However, if that trustworthy environment is connected to an untrustworthy wider area network, all users with simple passwords become easy targets. And some systems were not originally connected to a wider network, so their users began in a less exposed situation.

Authentication Foiled by Eavesdropping

Because of the rise in distributed and client–server computing, some users have access privileges on several connected machines. But in order to protect against arbitrary outsiders using these accesses, authentication is required between hosts. This access can directly involve the user, or it can be done automatically on behalf of the user, through a host-to-host authentication protocol. In either case, the account and authentication details of the subject are passed to the destination host. When these details are passed on the network, they are exposed to anyone observing the communication on the network. These same authentication details can be reused by an impersonator until they are changed.

Authentication Foiled by Avoidance

Authentication is obviously effective only when it works. A weak or flawed authentication allows access to any who can circumvent the authentication.

In a classic operating system flaw, the buffer for typed characters in a password was of fixed size, counting all characters typed, including backspaces for correction. If a user typed more characters than the buffer would hold, the overflow caused the operating system to bypass password comparison and act as if a correct authentication had been supplied. Any such flaws or weaknesses can be exploited by anyone seeking access.

Many network hosts, especially hosts that connect to wide area networks, run variants of Unix System V or BSD Unix. In a local environment, many users are not aware of which networked operating system is in use and still fewer would know of or be capable of (or be interested in) exploiting flaws. However, some hackers regularly scan wide area networks for hosts running weak or flawed operating systems. Thus, connection to a wide area network, especially the Internet, exposes these flaws to a wide audience intent on exploiting them.

Nonexistent Authentication

If two computers are used by the same users to store data and run processes, and if each has authenticated its users on first access, it would seem there is no need for computer-to-computer or local user-to-remote process authentication. These two computers and their users are a trustworthy environment in which the added complexity of repeated authentication seems excessive.

In Unix, the file *.rhosts* lists trusted hosts and *.rlogin* lists trusted users who are allowed access without authentication. They are intended for computer-to-computer connection by users who have already been authenticated at their primary hosts. These trusted hosts can also be exploited by outsiders who obtain access to one system, through one of these other authentication weaknesses, and then transfer to another system that accepts the authenticity of a user who comes from a system on its trusted list.

Another way to attack a network system is to use an identity that requires no authentication. Some systems have "guest" or "anonymous" accounts for outsiders to access things the systems want to release to anyone. For example, a bank might post a current listing of foreign currency rates, or a library with an on-line catalog might make that catalog available for anyone to search, or a company might allow access to some reports it has written. A user can log in as "guest" and retrieve these things that have been made publicly available. Typically no password is required, or the user is shown a message saying to type "GUEST" (or *your name*, which really means any string that looks like a name) when asked for a password. However, each of these accounts allows unauthenticated users access.

Well-Known Authentication

Authentication should be unique and difficult to guess. One computer manufacturer planned to use the same password for its remote maintenance personnel to access any of its computers belonging to any of its customers throughout the world. Fortunately, security experts pointed out the potential danger before that idea was put in place.

Some vendors still ship computers with one system administration account installed, having a default password. Or the systems come with a demonstration or test account, with no required password. Some administrators fail to change the passwords or delete these accounts.

Trusted Authentication

Still another way to circumvent controls that authentication should stop is to make use of a "trusted" identification. As described earlier, the Unix *.rhosts* and *.rlogin* and */etc/hosts/equiv* files indicate hosts or users that are trusted on other hosts. Although these features are useful to users who have accounts on multiple machines or for network management, maintenance, and operation, they must be used very carefully. Each of these represents a potential hole through which a remote user, or a remote attacker, can achieve access.

Message Confidentiality Violations

All of the wiretapping and impersonation attacks just described can lead to violation of the confidentiality of a message. Some other vulnerabilities can also affect confidentiality.

Misdelivery

Sometimes messages are misdelivered due to some flaw in the network hardware or software. Most often, messages are lost entirely, which is an integrity or availability issue. Occasionally, however, a destination address is modified or some handler malfunctions, causing a message to be delivered to someone other than the intended recipient. All of these "random" events are quite uncommon.

More common than network flaws are human errors. It is far too easy to mistype an address such as 100064,30652 as 10064,30652 or 100065,30642, or to type *idw* or *iw* instead of *diw* for David Ian Walker, who is called Ian by his friends. There is simply no justification for a computer network administrator to identify people by meaningless long numbers or cryptic initials when *iwalker* would be far less prone to human error.

Exposure

To protect the confidentiality of a message, we need to consider it all the way from its creation to its disposal. Along the way the content of a message is exposed in temporary buffers; at switches, routers, gateways, and intermediate hosts throughout the network; and in the workspaces of processes that build, format, and present the message. In earlier chapters, we considered confidentiality exposures in programs and operating systems. All of these exposures apply to networked environments as well. Furthermore, a malicious attacker can use any of these exposures as part of a general or focused attack on message confidentiality.

Passive wiretapping is one source of message exposure. So is subversion of the routing structure by which communications are routed to their destinations. Finally, interception of the message at it source, destination, or any intermediate node can lead to its exposure.

Traffic Flow Analysis

Sometimes, not just the content of a message but the mere fact that a message *exists* is sensitive. For example, knowing that a message had been sent from the president of one company to the president of a competitor could lead to speculation about a takeover or conspiracy to fix prices. Or a message from the prime minister of a country to a country with whom diplomatic relations were suspended could lead to inferences about a rapprochement between the countries. The volume of messages can also be significant. Unusually heavy traffic from a military headquarters to a particular base could signal a pending operation from that base.

In these cases, we need to protect both the content of messages and the header information that identifies sender, origin, receiver, and destination.

Message Integrity Violations

So far we have concentrated almost exclusively on confidentiality in communications. Confidentiality is certainly important, but in many cases, the integrity or correctness of a communication is at least as important as its confidentiality.

Obviously, for some situations, such as passing authentication data, the integrity of the communication is paramount. In other cases, the need for integrity is less obvious. In the next sections we consider threats based on failures of integrity in communications.

Falsification of Messages

Increasingly people depend on electronic messages to justify and direct actions. For example, if you receive a message from a friend asking you to meet for a drink next Tuesday evening, you will probably go to meet your friend. And you will likewise comply with a message from your supervisor telling you to stop work on project A and devote your energy to project B. As long as the message is reasonable, we tend to act on an electronic message the same as we would on a signed letter, a telephone call, or a face-to-face communication.

An attacker can

- change the content of a message
- change any part of the content of a message
- replace a message entirely
- reuse an old message
- change the apparent source of a message
- redirect a message
- destroy or delete a message

Sources of these kinds of attacks are

- active wiretap
- Trojan horse
- impersonation
- preempted host
- preempted workstation

Noise

Signals sent over communications media are subject to interference from other traffic on the same media, as well as from natural sources, such as lightning, electric motors, and animals. Such unintentional interference is called **noise**. These forms of noise are inevitable.

Fortunately, or rather intentionally, communications protocols have been designed to overcome the negative effects of noise. For example, the TCP/IP protocol suite ensures detection of almost all transmission errors, and processes in the communications stack detect errors and arrange for retransmission, all invisible to the higher-level applications. Thus, noise is scarcely a consideration for users in security-critical applications.

Hacking

Hacking is mentioned briefly as a source of threat to security in computer communications. However, the kinds of attacks hackers can create involve one or more of the attacks just presented. A hacker may use impersonation to achieve access on one host, and then use a trusted relationship from that host to another to establish a session on the second host. From the second session, the hacker may send spurious messages or mount a denial-of-service attack by flooding a local area network.

We consider the hacker as a separate threat because a hacker can develop tools to search widely and quickly for particular weaknesses and move swiftly and stealthily to exploit those weaknesses. Sometimes the hacker merely stores a marker by creating an account to which to return later. In this way, the hacker has unlimited time to analyze, plan, code, simulate, and test a future attack. Thus, in reviewing the effects of possible threats, you should assume that a hacker has already carried out successfully every other possible attack. You should also project forward the effects of this attack: if it succeeds, what additional capability would that give the hacker for future attacks?

Code Integrity

A serious threat in networking is damage to executable code. This threat is usually malicious, designed to delete or replace running programs on a host. The program threats of viruses, worms, Trojan horses, and other malicious code discussed in Chapter 5 apply to networks as well. The transfer method is similar: an unsuspecting user accepts or downloads a file that changes, replaces, or deletes other program files.

The transfer of files on the World-Wide Web increases the seriousness of this threat for several reasons.

- The user typically is unaware what a downloaded file actually contains. Code from unreliable sources could be anything. Even code from reliable sources normally will have just a brief description.

- Sometimes file downloading occurs without the user's permission. Some on-line services (such as America OnLine) change their software as often as once a day. Each time the user logs onto the service, new software is downloaded to the user's system, without the user's having been asked whether to do so.

- Sometimes file downloading occurs without the user's knowledge. Sun's language system, Java, is designed to supply new code any time the user visits a web site that has objects for which the user has no processor code. As described later, the current version of Java has serious security problems.

Downloaded code has the potential to do anything to a system that programs can do, including modifying or deleting files or data, encrypting data, rebooting the system, disabling access, or degrading performance severely.

Trusted systems could limit the damage possible from downloaded code or, in some cases, block the attacks entirely. However, few people use trusted systems. The most common network access machines are DOS/Windows PCs and Unix machines. Neither offers strong protection against malicious network code.

The Java Flaw

A specific example of a network code flaw is illustrative from a security perspective, both because the method of attack is interesting and because the analysis of the flaw reinforces many classic security points.

Sun Microsystems developed the concept of an "applet," a program that runs inside a web browser. Such programs are dynamically downloaded to handle new data types appearing on web pages, making the browser potentially extensible to an unlimited range of content types. Whereas such extensibility allows a web browser to "grow" as new content types are developed, the downloading of code without the user's direct participation or knowledge has obvious security implications. Sun designed the Java subsystem in part to address security concerns. Netscape has licensed the Java technology to incorporate in its Netscape Navigator version 2.0.

Java consists of an interpreter for a virtual machine, called *Java bytecode,* which is machine independent, so that a single applet can be downloaded to any machine. Security features in the interpreter were intended to protect the interpreter, and hence the browser and user, against security attacks. However, Dean and other researchers at Princeton University [DEA96] identified attacks that can cause

- denial of service
- degradation of service
- covert communication to other processes on the Internet
- modification of the browser

When announcing Java, Sun stated that they had carefully designed the system so that its security could not be defeated. The Princeton researchers found a flaw within months of

Java's release. Furthermore, after Sun reported fixing that one, the same researchers found many others. Details of the flaws are contained in the paper.

Dean et al. point out the following design and development problems that contributed to the security flaws in the Java system:

- *Absence of a well-defined security policy.* Without a precise definition of a security policy, the security goal is not likely to be paramount to developers.
- *Lack of a security mechanism that is always invoked.* The Java security manager must be invoked by any routine that wants to verify access permission; failure to call the manager defaults to "access permitted."
- *Lack of a security mechanism that is tamperproof.* Attackers can change both the Java enforcement mechanism and the data it depends on to do its enforcement.
- *Lack of a security mechanism that is small and simple.* There were logic flaws in the security subsystem. There are at least 41 separate calls to the security enforcement mechanism, so that it is difficult to assert convincingly that those 41 are sufficient, or that if code is changed these 41 calls will be changed as needed.
- Consequently, *lack of a reference monitor.*
- *Lack of a trusted computing base.* The Java code is not well structured to highlight security-enforcing and security-relevant code, thereby hampering analysis.
- *Lack of control over the integrity of the running system.* The system was designed to download code supporting its own extension, but this feature ultimately leads to an attack in which the applet loader itself is overwritten.
- *Lack of modularity and limited scope.* Whereas the object-oriented design was intended to protect by scope, an attacker who can replace the system class loader has access to all data.
- *Lack of defense in depth.* There are not redundant and backup security mechanisms.
- *Lack of logging or auditing.* If a security violation does occur, or an attempt is blocked, there is no logging to record this fact for analysis or provide a trail of evidence up to a failure for post mortem analysis.

As a consequence of these shortcomings, Dean et al. conclude that "the Java system in its current form cannot easily be made more secure. Significant redesign of the language, the bytecode format, and the runtime system appear to be necessary steps toward building a higher assurance system."

Notice how closely these shortcomings correspond to the design principles for trusted operating systems presented in Chapter 7.

Denial of Service

A final major source of harm in computer communications is denial of service. As people become increasingly dependent on computer communications for business, education, research, and interaction, the impact of denial of service on individuals and society grows alarmingly. In this section we review some of the threats to continuity of service.

Connectivity

A network is like a large and complex web. To be useful, every point must be reachable from every other point.

Of course, hardware and software are not perfect or error-free. Links and h
stantly fail or are taken off line, and new or repaired links and hosts are constantly put back
on line. Thus, the topology of every network changes: small networks change slowly, and
large networks change very frequently.

Most nodes are connected by multiple paths, so that when one path is unavailable,
communication can be maintained using another path. However, the failure of a critical
path or node will block communication.

Flooding

An intruder can damage network communications by generating spurious messages. These
phony messages may appear authentic, or they may not even be similar to legitimate messages. Their essential purpose is to increase the traffic on the network, thereby degrading
service to the users.

Routing Problems

Every host cannot know how to route a message to every other host. For this reason, each
host knows to which hosts it is directly connected and which of them to use to route to
other addresses. Transmission of a message thus occurs by a series of hops: from the
source to a neighbor expected to be closer to the destination, and from that neighbor to one
of its neighbors, and so forth.

A classic early failure in the Arpanet, a component of the Internet, occurred when,
because of a software flaw, one node told all other nodes that it was the closest node to all
other nodes. Every node sent it all messages for forwarding. Pathways to that node became
blocked. Furthermore, if that node ever sent something to another node for further handling, the other node sent the message right back because the first node was assumed to be
closer to the destination than any other.

Although this threat (and most routing failures) was unintentional, an attacker who
wants to disable a network may think first of the routing tables. Routing table modifications can either disable all communication, disable communication to a particular node, or
route communications to the attacker, who can then selectively read, modify, destroy, or
forward.

Disruption of Service

An active host can also tamper with the flow of messages on the network. For example, a
host can flood a network with spurious messages, thereby blocking legitimate network
traffic. A host can disrupt service without even being able to determine the content of legitimate messages on the network. Both of these attacks deny service to users of the network.

9.3 Network Security Controls

We have just gone through a long list of threats and possible attacks on networks and their
communications. Fortunately, our bag of security controls contains some good things. We
now investigate what controls can protect these network exposures. The first tool, and perhaps the most powerful, is encryption. But we also discuss the use of several techniques
we have seen before, such as user authentication and access control. We also see some new
techniques, such as traffic padding.

Encryption

As we have seen in earlier chapters, encryption is a very powerful tool for providing privacy, authenticity, integrity, and limited access to data. Because of the greater risks involved, networks often secure data with encryption, perhaps in combination with other controls.

In network applications, encryption can be applied either between two hosts or between two applications. We consider these two forms of encryption below. Key distribution is always a problem with encryption. Encryption keys must be delivered to the sender and receiver in a secure manner. Techniques for safe key distribution in networks are studied here. Finally, we discuss a cryptographic facility for a network computing environment.

Link Encryption

In **link encryption**, data is encrypted just before the system places it on the physical communications link. In this case, encryption occurs at layer 1 or 2 in the OSI model. (A similar situation occurs with TCP/IP protocols.) Decryption occurs just as the communication enters the receiving computer. A model of link encryption is shown in Figure 9-16.

Encryption protects the message in transit between two computers, but the message is in plaintext inside the hosts. (A message in plaintext is said to be "in the clear.") Notice that because the encryption is added at the bottom protocol layer, the message is exposed at all other layers in the sender and receiver. Because of physical security, we may not be too concerned about this exposure: it is on the host or workstation of the sender or receiver. However, notice that the message is exposed in two layers of the intermediate host (or of all intermediate hosts through which the message may pass). This exposure occurs because routing and addressing is not read at the bottom layer, but only at higher layers.

A message may be adequately protected by the sending and receiving hosts, and encryption protects the message along the links. However, the message is in the clear in the intermediate host, and that host may not be especially trustworthy. If the intermediate node is compromised, all messages passing through *C* are exposed.

Link encryption is invisible to the user. Encryption becomes a transmission service performed by a low-level network protocol layer, just like message routing or transmission error detection. A typical link-encrypted message is shown in Figure 9-17. As the message *M* is handled at each layer, header and control information is added on the sending side and removed on the receiving side. Hardware encryption devices operate quickly and reliably; in this case, link encryption is invisible to both the operating system and the operator.

Link encryption is especially appropriate where the transmission line is the point of greatest vulnerability. If all hosts on a network are reasonably secure, but the communica-

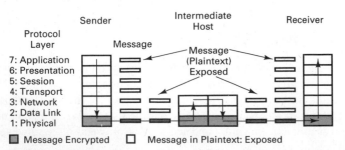

Figure 9-16   Link Encryption

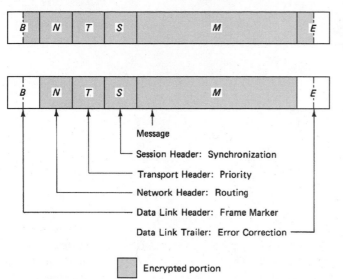

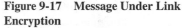

Figure 9-17   **Message Under Link Encryption**

tions medium is shared with other users or is not secure, link encryption is an easy control to use.

End-to-End Encryption

As its name implies, end-to-end encryption provides security from one end of a transmission through the other. The encryption can be applied by a hardware device between the user and the host. Alternately, the encryption can be done by software running on the host computer. In either case, the encryption is performed at the highest levels (layer 7, application, or perhaps at layer 6, presentation) of the OSI model. A model of end-to-end encryption is shown in Figure 9-18.

Because the encryption precedes all routing and transmission processing of the layer, the message is transmitted in encrypted form throughout the network. The encryption covers potential flaws in lower layers in the transfer model. If a lower layer should fail to preserve security and reveal data it has received, the secrecy of that data is not endangered. A typical message using end-to-end encryption is shown in Figure 9-19.

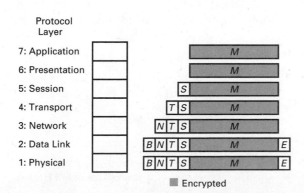

Figure 9-18   **End-to-End Encryption**

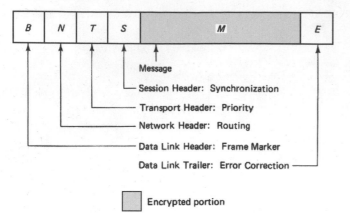

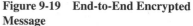

Message

Session Header: Synchronization

Transport Header: Priority

Network Header: Routing

Data Link Header: Frame Marker

Data Link Trailer: Error Correction

Encrypted portion

Figure 9-19   End-to-End Encrypted Message

Messages sent through several hosts are protected. The data content of the message is still encrypted, as shown in Figure 9-20. Therefore, even though a message must pass through insecure node *C* on the path between *A* and *B*, the message is encrypted while in *C*.

Comparison of Encryption Methods

Simply encrypting a message is not absolute assurance that the message will not be revealed during or after transmission. In many instances, however, the strength of encryption is adequate protection, considering the likelihood of the interceptor's breaking the encryption and the timeliness of the message.

With link encryption, encryption is invoked for all transmissions along a particular link. Typically a host has only one link to a network, meaning that all network traffic is encrypted by that host. This means, however, that every other host receiving these communications must also have a cryptographic facility in order to decrypt the messages. Furthermore, all hosts must share keys. Note that a message may pass through one or more intermediate hosts on the way to its final destination. Part of the advantage of encryption is lost if a message is encrypted along some links of a network but not along others. Therefore, link encryption is usually performed on all links of a network if it is performed at all.

By contrast, end-to-end encryption is applied to logical links, which are channels between two processes, at a level well above the physical path. Because the intermediate hosts along a transmission path do not need to encrypt or decrypt a message, they have no need for cryptographic facilities. Thus, encryption is used only for messages and applications where it is needed. Furthermore, the encryption can be done with software, so that

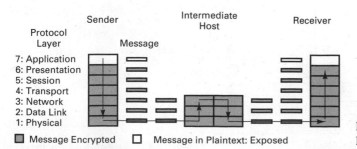

Figure 9-20   Encrypted Message Passing Through a Host

we can apply it selectively to one application, or even to one message within a given application.

This selective advantage of end-to-end encryption is also a disadvantage regarding encryption keys. Under end-to-end encryption there is a virtual cryptographic channel between each pair of users. In order to provide proper security, each pair of users should share a unique cryptographic key. The number of keys required is thus equal to the number of pairs of users, which is $n * (n - 1)/2$ for n users. This number increases rapidly as the number of users increases. This count assumes that single key encryption is used. With a public key system, only one pair of keys is needed per recipient.

As shown in Table 9-2, link encryption is faster, easier for the user, and uses fewer keys. End-to-end encryption is more flexible, can be used selectively, is done at the user level, and can be integrated with the application. Neither form is right for all situations.

Both forms of encryption can be applied. A user who doesn't trust the quality of link encryption provided in a system can apply end to end encryption as well. A system administrator who is concerned about the security of an end to end encryption scheme applied by an applications program can also install a link encryption device. If both encryptions are reasonably fast, this duplication of security will have little negative effect.

Access Control

Encryption is especially good for protecting data within a network. However, access to data, programs, and other resources of the network is also a serious concern in network security. In a single computing system, the number of authorized users may be limited because of the physical characteristics of the system. Often all users are within the same room or building, or are affiliated with the same organization. However, when a computing system is part of a network, users and even administrators may not know which other users may be connected to the same network. Thus, in a network environment, access control

Table 9-2   Comparison of Link and End-to-End Encryption

Link Encryption	End-to-End Encryption
Security Within Hosts	
Message exposed in sending host	Message encrypted in sending host
Message exposed in intermediate nodes	Message encrypted in intermediate nodes
Role of User	
Applied by sending host	Applied by sending process
Invisible to user	User applies encryption
Host maintains encryption	User must find algorithm
One facility for all users	User selects encryption
Can be done in hardware	Software implementation
All or no messages encrypted	User chooses to encrypt or not, for each message
Implementation Concerns	
Requires one key per host pair	Requires one key per user pair
Provides node authentication	Provides user authentication

must protect a single system of the network and also prevent unauthorized users from passing through one system of a network to access other systems of the network. Two aspects of network access control that we consider now are protecting access points and authenticating network nodes.

Port Protection

A serious vulnerability to a network system is dial-in port access. User authentication is difficult enough in a single computing system, but it becomes far more difficult when users can dial in from a telephone, literally anywhere in the world. Port protection is accomplished by several administrative and hardware techniques.

Automatic Call-Back   With an **automatic call-back** system, an authorized user dials a computer system. After the user identifies him- or herself, the computer breaks the communication line, effectively hanging up on the user. The computer then consults an internal table of telephone numbers and calls the user back at a predetermined number.

For example, if Cathy needed to access a computer from a terminal at her house, her home telephone number would be recorded on the list. An intruder accessing the computer and alleging to be Cathy would have to call in from Cathy's house in order to receive the return call.

This scheme works for people who expect to be at one number. If Cathy might be at, say, up to three different locations, she could list all three with the computer as legitimate locations. When she dials in, she identifies herself and gives the telephone number at which she expects to be called back. If the number she gives is one of the three registered for her, the computer calls her back there. If the number is not one of the three, the computer issues a warning to the security officer.

In a network this technique can also be used between two computers. The telephone number associated with a host computer seldom changes, so host computer *A* could have a table containing the phone number of host computer *B*. If host *B* wishes to establish a connection with *A*, it calls *A* at *A*'s regular number. *A* determines that *B* wants to communicate, so *A* terminates the communication and calls *B* at *B*'s regular number. *B* is reasonably well assured that *A* is calling if the call comes shortly after the first connection with *A* is terminated. *A* is sure to be communicating with *B* because it used the prescribed number for *B*. Clearly, the table of telephone numbers must be well-protected against modification.

Differentiated Access Rights   Sensitive data can be protected by limiting the places from which access is allowed. People can be allowed to access the most sensitive data only from secure places; even though the individuals are trusted for more sensitive access, the access path is not trusted. For example, when dialing in, people might be allowed to obtain only less sensitive information. In this way, sensitive accesses must be made at the site, where it is more difficult to compromise data, or where it would be more noticeable if one were being forced to reveal the data. On a network, users with access to sensitive objects can do so only by direct connection, not through another network host. This restriction reduces the threat of malicious hosts in a network.

Differentiated access rights can be useful for people such as sales representatives who travel to many locations. These people can telephone their offices after making sales calls to send in data and transfer nonsensitive electronic messages. Sensitive data, such as sales projections or pricing structures, could be accessed only at the office.

Silent Modem   Several movies have publicized the penetration technique of systematic dialing of telephone numbers until a carrier tone (modem) is detected. As explained in Chapter 6, a loose-lipped system gives away information without obtaining assurance that its caller is legitimate. Typically, a computer receiving an incoming call establishes the connection by sending a modem signal. However, it can also wait silently until the caller's modem sends the first tone. In this way, the computer does not reveal itself as a computer until the caller has revealed that it is a computer.

This solution does not solve the problem of mutual suspicion, however; it merely forces the intruder to take a second step. A penetrator with a modem can send a modem tone to each telephone number dialed and wait for a modem tone in response. For this reason, authenticating nodes and remote users is very important for networked computing systems. We address these two topics in the next sections.

Authentication in Distributed Systems

Applications are not always completed on the user's local computer. Several computers joined on a network can share files, applications, and other resources. In this case, a user on one host may be unaware of the fact that a computation uses resources or facilities of some other hosts. Authentication and access control can all be done at the computer-to-computer level. There are then two problems to be solved:

- How can one host be assured of the authenticity of a remote host? Before sending sensitive data to a remote site, the host should be sure of the computer at the destination.
- How can a host be assured of the authenticity of a user on a remote host? Conversely, how can the user be assured of the authenticity of the remote host?

In the following sections, we study approaches to host-to-host and user-to-host authentication.

Digital Distributed Authentication

Digital Equipment Corp. recognized the problem of needing to authenticate nonhuman entities in a computing system. For example, a process might retrieve user queries, which it then reformats, perhaps limits, and submits to a data base manager. Both the data base manager and the query processor want to be assured that a particular communication channel between the two is authentic. Neither of these servers is running under the direct control or supervision of a human (although each process was, of course, somehow initiated by a human). Human forms of access control are, thus, inappropriate.

Digital [GAS89, GAS90] created a simple architecture for this requirement. This architecture was effective against the following threats:

- *impersonation* of a server by a rogue process, for either of the two servers involved in the authentication
- *interception or modification* of data exchanged between servers
- *replay* of a previous authentication

The architecture assumes that each server has its own private key, and that the corresponding public key is available to or held by every other process that might need to establish an authenticated channel. To begin an authenticated communication between server A and server B, A sends a request to B, encrypted under B's public key. B decrypts the request and replies with a message encrypted under A's public key. To avoid replay, A and B can append a random number to the message to be encrypted, as with the protocols in Chapter 4.

A and B can establish a private channel by one of them choosing an encryption key (for a secret key algorithm) and sending it to the other in the authenticating message. Once the authentication is complete, all communication under that secret key can be assumed to be as secure as was the original dual public key exchange. To protect the privacy of the channel, Gasser recommends a separate cryptographic processor, such as a smart card, so that private keys are never exposed outside the processor.

Two implementational difficulties remain to be solved: how can a potentially large number of public keys be distributed, and how can the public keys be distributed in a way that ensures the secure binding of a process with the key? Digital recognizes that a key server (perhaps with multiple replications) is necessary to distribute keys. The second difficulty is addressed with certificates and a certification hierarchy, as described in Chapter 4.

Both of these design decisions are to a certain degree implied by the nature of the rest of the protocol. A different approach was taken by Kerberos and DCE, as we see in the following sections.

Kerberos

Kerberos is a system that supports authentication in distributed systems. Although it was originally designed to work with secret key encryption, the latest version of Kerberos uses public key technology to support key exchange. The Kerberos system was designed at Massachusetts Institute of Technology [STE88, KOH93].

Kerberos is used for authentication between intelligent processes, such as client to server tasks, or a user's workstation to other hosts. The basis of Kerberos is a central server that provides authenticated tokens, called **tickets**, to requesting applications. A ticket is an unforgeable, nonreplayable, authenticated object. It is an encrypted data structure naming a user and a service that user is allowed to obtain. It also contains a time value and some control information.

The first step in using Kerberos is to establish a session with the Kerberos server, as shown in Figure 9-21. A user's workstation sends the user's identity to the Kerberos server when the user logs on. The Kerberos server verifies that the user is authorized. The Kerberos server sends two messages.

- To the user's workstation it sends a session key S_G for use in communication with the Ticket Granting Server (G) and a ticket T_G for the Ticket Granting Server; S_G is encrypted under the user's password: $E(S_G + T_G, pw)$.[2]
- To the Ticket Granting Server, it sends a copy of the session key S_G and the identity of the user (encrypted under a key shared between the Kerberos server and the Ticket Granting Server).

If the workstation can decrypt $E(S_G + T_G, pw)$ using pw, the password typed by the user, then the user has succeeded in an authentication with the workstation.

---

[2] In Kerberos version 5, only S_G is encrypted; in Kerberos version 4, both the session key and the ticket were encrypted when returned to the user.

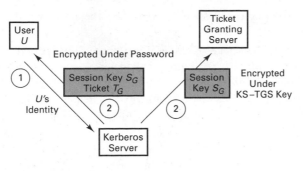

Figure 9-21   Initiating a Kerberos Session

Notice that passwords are stored at the Kerberos server, *not* at the workstation, and that the user's password did not have to be passed across the network, even in encrypted form. Holding passwords centrally but not passing them across the network is a security advantage.

Next the user will want some other services of the distributed system—for example, to access a file. Using the key S_G provided by the Kerberos server, the user requests a ticket to access file F from the ticket granting server. As shown in Figure 9-22, after the ticket granting server verifies U's access permission, it returns a ticket and a session key. The ticket contains the authenticated identity of user U (in the ticket U obtained from the Kerberos server), an identification of F (the file to be accessed), the access rights (for example, to read), a session key S_F for the file server to use while communicating this file to U, and an expiration date for the ticket. The ticket is encrypted under a key shared exclusively between the ticket granting server and the file server. This ticket cannot be read, modified, or forged by the user U (or anyone else). The ticket granting server must therefore also provide U a copy of S_F, the session key for the file server. Requests for access to other services and servers are handled similarly.

Kerberos was carefully designed to withstand attacks in distributed environments.

- *No passwords communicated on the network.* As already described, a user's password is stored only at the Kerberos server. The user's password is not sent from the user's workstation when the user initiates a session.

- *Cryptographic protection against spoofing.* Each access request is mediated by the ticket granting server, which knows the identity of the requester based on the authentication performed initially by the Kerberos server and on the fact that the user was

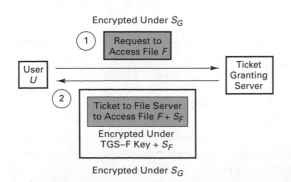

Figure 9-22   Obtaining a Ticket to Access a File

able to present a request encrypted under a key that had been encrypted under the user's password.

- *Limited period of validity.* Each ticket is issued for a limited time period; the ticket contains a time stamp with which a receiving server determines the ticket's validity. In this way, certain long-term attacks, such as brute force cryptanalysis, are usually neutralized because the attacker does not have time to complete the attack.

- *Time stamps to prevent replay attacks.* Kerberos requires reliable access to a universal clock. Each user's request to a server is stamped with the time of the request. A server receiving a request compares this time to the current time and fulfills the request only if the time is reasonably close to the current time. This time checking prevents most replay attacks because the attacker's presentation of the ticket is delayed too much.

- *Mutual authentication.* The user of a service can be assured of the authenticity of any server by requesting an authenticating response from the server. The user sends a ticket to a server and then sends a request to the server encrypted under the session key for that server's service; the ticket and the session key were provided by the ticket granting server. The server can decrypt the ticket only if it has the unique key it shares with the ticket granting service. Inside the ticket is the session key which is the only means the server has of decrypting the user's request. If the server can return to the user a message, encrypted under this same session key but containing 1 + the user's timestamp, the server must be authentic. Because of this mutual authentication, a server can provide a unique channel to a user, and the user may not need to encrypt communications on that channel to ensure continuous authenticity. Avoiding encryption saves time in the communication.

Kerberos is not a perfect answer to security problems in distributed systems.

- *Kerberos requires continuous availability of a trusted ticket granting server.* Because the ticket granting server is the basis of access control and authentication, constant access to that server is crucial. Both reliability (hardware or software failure) and performance (capacity) problems must be addressed.

- *Authenticity of servers requires a trusted relationship between the ticket granting server and every server.* The ticket granting server must share a unique encryption key with each trustworthy server. The ticket granting server (or that server's human administrator) must be convinced of the authenticity of that server. In a local environment, this degree of trust is warranted. In a widely distributed environment, an administrator at one site can seldom justify trust in the authenticity of servers at other sites.

- *Kerberos requires timely transactions.* In order to prevent replay attacks, Kerberos limits the validity of a ticket. There is still a chance for a replay attack during the period of validity, however. And setting the period fairly is hard: too long increases the exposure to replay attacks, but too short requires prompt user actions and might provide the user with a ticket that will not be honored when presented to a server. Similarly, subverting a server's clock allows reuse of an expired ticket.

- *A subverted workstation can save and later replay user passwords.* This vulnerability exists in any system in which passwords, encryption keys, or other constant, sensitive information is entered in the clear on a workstation that might be subverted.

- *Password guessing works.* A user's initial ticket is returned under the user's password. An attacker can submit an initial authentication request to the Kerberos server and then try to decrypt the response using password guessing.

- *Kerberos does not scale well.* The architectural model of Kerberos, shown in Figure 9-23, assumes one Kerberos server and one ticket granting server, plus a collection of other servers, each of which shares a unique key with the ticket granting server. Adding a second ticket granting server (for example, to enhance performance or reliability) would require duplicate keys or a second set for all servers. Duplication increases the risk of exposure and complicates key updates, and second keys more than double the work for each server to act on a ticket.

- *Kerberos is a complete solution.* All applications must use Kerberos authentication and access control. Currently few applications use Kerberos authentication, so integration of Kerberos into an existing environment requires modification of existing applications, which is not feasible.

Kerberos is a carefully designed system that covers many vulnerabilities in a distributed environment. Having been developed partly as a research activity, its design and code are readily available (in the United States and Canada). Its greatest contribution may be the thought put into its design, which influenced the later distributed authentication effort of the Distributed Computing Environment (DCE) products from the Open Software Foundation. We consider DCE next.

DCE

DCE is a project of the Open Software Foundation (OSF). Principal contributors to the DCE effort were Digital Equipment Corp., Hewlett-Packard, and IBM, although all members of OSF (over 200 companies) share in this technology. DCE is a set of software tools and services that make it easier to develop and operate distributed, heterogeneous computer applications. DCE supports these applications in a way that is not specific to any single vendor. Thus, all members of OSF benefit by being able to sell products into environments that might otherwise be the exclusive territory of a single vendor.

DCE presents a complete support environment for building distributed applications. In addition to distributed authentication, DCE manages controlled, shared access to remote and distributed resources (in particular to a distributed directory and file system). The DCE

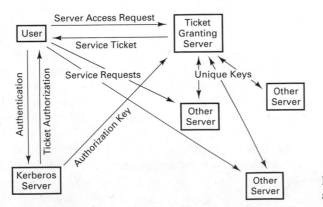

Figure 9-23   Access to Services and Servers in Kerberos

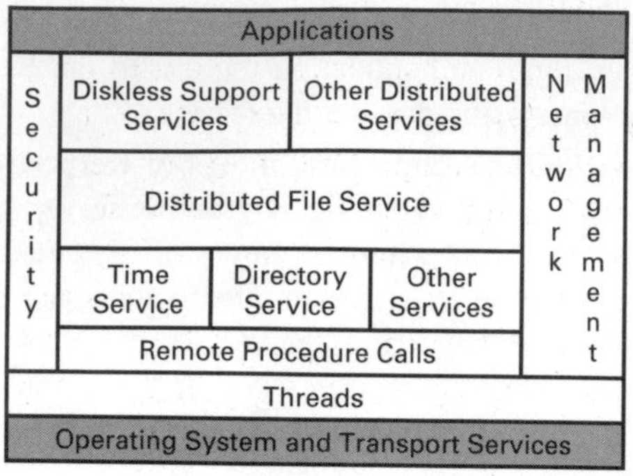

Figure 9-24   DCE Services

remote procedure call (RPC) mechanism supports running distributed applications between hosts. In this way, DCE is the foundation that manages "distributedness"; OSF members can build their applications on this foundation. The DCE foundation services are accompanied by distributed security services: authentication, authorization, and access control. (See Figure 9-24.)

The security aspects of DCE are built on Kerberos technology. Instead of a separate user authentication server and ticket granting server, DCE merges these into one **security server**. The initial exchange is the same as under standard Kerberos. Ticket granting is similar, except that the ticket the user receives contains a **privilege attribute certificate**, which lists the user's privileges; these privileges are reviewed by the server for any object for which the user has requested a ticket.

Each server implements its own access control, based on access control lists, implemented using the three-part user–group–world scheme described in Chapter 6. This scheme is extended to include the notion of local or foreign subjects and objects. A cell is the set of subjects and objects managed together; a cell is an administrative domain. Subjects and objects from the same cell can have different rights from those of remote cells, corresponding to the notion that local users may be accorded greater access rights.

DCE was originally developed from the Kerberos approach, which means that it was also based on symmetric key cryptography. However, both Kerberos and DCE are moving to support public key cryptography because of the ease of key exchange.

SESAME

SESAME is a European research and development project, supported by the European Commission. It is a cooperative activity involving primarily the computing companies Bull, ICL, and Siemens.

SESAME is quite similar to DCE, both in the services it provides and in the technology it uses to provide those services. It uses Kerberos extensively, but it preceded both Kerberos and DCE in use of public key technology for secure authentication. With public key authentication, the initial authentication ticket is encrypted by the user's public key. The authentication service stores only the public keys of users, so there is little exposure if the authentication server is compromised.

SESAME can also use public key technology for distributing privilege attributes and tickets to users, so there is no need for a key distribution center to provide keys for secure user-to-server communication.

CORBA

Another popular technology for distributed applications is CORBA, which stands for **Common Object Request Broker Architecture** [OMG92]. This technology handles a client's request of a server to perform some action on an object. An object request broker (ORB) is a traffic director that joins clients' requests to appropriate servers. Unlike DCE, which is licensed code, CORBA is a set of specifications. Thus, interoperability between vendors depends on the completeness and precision of the specification and the degree of conformity of the vendor's implementation. A specification for security was released late in 1995 [OMG95].

From a security perspective, an ORB can provide authentication, access control, audit, and message protection functionality. The CORBA philosophy is to protect objects that are not security-aware in such a way that security policy enforcement can be performed automatically by the ORB. Two "interceptors," the access control function and the secure invocation function, are the means by which the ORB can invoke security mechanisms on behalf of CORBA objects that are not security-aware. The word *can* was used deliberately in this paragraph, however. Because CORBA is a set of specifications instead of an actual implementation, the security specification describes the means by which security functionality can be linked, but there is no requirement to do so.

Because CORBA products will have to address different architectures and different assurance demands, the vendor has been left to determine and meet market demands. Each user must determine the suitability of a product for a particular use. To help the user, the security specification recommends a *conformance statement*, which is similar to the security target of recent trusted systems evaluation criteria. The conformance statement is produced by the vendor to describe the security of the ORB product, to describe which architectural and security tradeoffs were made and how they were selected, and to allow a user (that is, administrator) to make an informed choice of ORB products. The conformance statement is *not* intended to replace formal evaluation.

Three important goals of the security specification are flexibility of security policy, independence of security technology, and interoperability. These goals, and the degree to which they are realized, become security issues themselves.

1. *Flexibility of security policy.* CORBA is intended to support virtually *any* security policy, at the level of the object request broker (ORB). This implies that different ORBs within a distributed system could support different security policies.

2. *Independence of security technology.* The CORBA framework is intentionally security mechanism/technology neutral. The implementation in any environment will necessarily depend on specific technology, but, in a heterogeneous setting, it will not necessarily be possible for a client or server to depend on the existence of a particular technology at the opposite server or client.

3. *Interoperability.* There are four dimensions to interoperability in the CORBA framework: throughout a heterogeneous (multivendor) system, across systems that use different security technology, between domains of a distributed system, and between secure systems and those without security. While all of these are useful goals in the proper context, interoperation between secured and non-secured systems places additional burdens on the secured system.

Conclusions on Security in Distributed Applications

Trusted distributed systems are difficult to achieve for all of the following reasons. Distributed systems are hard to administer securely because of their size and complexity. Dynamic systems are hard to analyze. Disjoint environments can lead to problems of trustworthiness of authentication and policy administration. Disjoint policy domains may not interoperate securely.

The Kerberos, DCE, and SESAME authentication and access control systems are becoming very popular in commercial distributed applications, and the CORBA architecture is emerging as a popular approach to distributed computing. Work on these technologies continues, and the products are impressive. A major advantage is that these solutions are not vendor-specific; that is, they are techniques that can be implemented by any vendor. Consequently, there is a high degree of interoperability among vendors supporting one of these technologies. These approaches also have the advantage of providing security services in the infrastructure, where they can be invoked by or applied to user (client) applications.

Traffic Control

We now turn to controls for a fairly sophisticated threat: traffic flow analysis. Few attackers can, or want to, monitor and analyze enough traffic to obtain much information from this form of attack. Furthermore, there are fairly simple defenses against such analysis.

Because an interceptor can tap all blocks of messages passing through the network, the interceptor can determine who is communicating frequently with whom. Knowing that many messages are being transmitted between the personnel department and company management, a user might be able to infer that some substantial reorganization is about to occur. During wartime, the military has trouble planning surprise offensives because a large volume of messages to a particular place may arouse the suspicion of the enemy. In both these cases, it is not just the content, but also the mere existence of messages that is sensitive.

In both cases, the attack is called a **traffic analysis**. The standard control is introduction of many spurious messages between points of low traffic. In this way, communication between the two sensitive places will not seem outstandingly heavy. Of course, this added traffic places an extra burden on the network, and service to all users may be degraded.

An attacker can also establish a covert channel in a network by generating traffic, even spurious traffic as described. The technique is to represent a binary 1 by a message to a single node and a 0 by either no message or a message to another node. A listening interceptor observes the network traffic going to these nodes and records the data. The network tap does not require active participation from the listener. Furthermore, the traffic can appear innocuous if the spurious traffic is to a reasonable host, such as a file system. It is very difficult to detect, much less to prevent, a process from creating such a covert channel.

Such traffic can permit a surprisingly high rate of data leakage. If confinement is a goal in a network, this covert channel must be denied. We can prevent users from using the covert channel by padding traffic or controlling routing.

Pad Traffic

To deter a listener who is monitoring messages only from or to a particular host (or sitting somewhere in the middle in a position to be able to count messages accurately), the network administrator generates spurious messages for many pairs of hosts. A network administrator inserts "noise" into the system by randomly sending messages to each node in the network. These messages must follow no pattern of frequency, source, or destination.

In this control, the administrator tries to add sufficient noise to the system so that the noise distorts the flow of information in the covert channel. The intended host must be able to recognize the messages as false messages so that they do not interfere with communication of a legitimate user. However, if an intended host can recognize these as false messages, the covert listener can, too. The administrator does not need to participate in the network traffic, other than to generate noise messages periodically.

Routing Control

To control covert channels, the administrator can exercise active control of routing in the network. For example, if the covert channel were 1 for a message from A to B and 0 for a message from A to C, the administrator might try to redirect messages. The administrator might reroute messages from A to C to go from A through B, and ultimately to C. In this way, an A–C message (0) would be converted to an A–B message (1) followed by a B–C message (no value).

If the network has a protocol to detect missing messages, the administrator can periodically delete or misroute messages. In this way, B might realize much later that a message from A was not received. If so, B would ask for the message to be retransmitted. Repeating the message would not affect normal communication. It would disturb the flow of the covert channel because other messages might have been transmitted already, and this message representing one bit would be transmitted out of sequence.

A third possibility is for the administrator to periodically delay a message. By delaying, the administrator hopes to destroy the synchronization between the sender and the listener without seriously affecting legitimate network traffic. This control is effective if the channel depends on the timing of messages.

All of these controls depend on an active network administrator who can perform network actions to destroy covert channels.

Data Integrity

The integrity of the data in the network is also vulnerable. Integrity is a function of two things: correct generation of the data and correct storage and transmission. We assume that data is generated correctly initially. Our security concern now is ensuring that data is correctly stored, communicated, and modified in the network.

Protocols

Network communication operates through protocols designed for reliable communication. The protocol must be able to detect messages that are duplicates, deleted pieces, pieces out of order, or modified messages. Most transmission protocols use a numbering scheme to preserve order of datagrams or packets. However, for security this is inadequate because a malicious intruder can modify the order number to interchange message pieces. For efficient routing and handling by low-level protocol layers, the order number may be transmitted in plaintext, but for integrity a second, tamperproof copy should also accompany the message part. Link-level encryption covers sequence numbers applied at a low level. With end-to-end encryption, the application must be aware of, and manage, its own sequencing.

Checksums

A cryptographic checksum is an important network guard against message tampering and failures during message transmission. Normal message traffic on a network is subject to noise and occasional mistransmission of bits or data. Some network transmission protocols have additional check data built into a message to detect and perhaps correct failures. If a correction is impossible, the receiver will ask for the message to be retransmitted.

Parity   Error checking in network messages uses complex error detection and correction codes, but use of these codes can be demonstrated by using the simple example of parity. As a byte is transmitted, an additional bit is appended; this bit is set to 1 if the sum of the bits in the byte is even, and to 0 if the sum of the bits in the byte is odd. Parity can detect all errors involving the change of a single bit out of the byte; parity can also detect some multiple-bit errors. As shown in Figure 9-25, parity can identify the byte, but not necessarily the bit in error. Parity also cannot identify the substitution of one byte (with correct parity) for another in a message.

Parity can also be used longitudinally; that is, parity can be computed for the 0th bit of all bytes, the 1st, the 2nd, and so on. This process yields 8 more parity bits, one for each bit position in a message. With these longitudinal check bits, we can determine the bit position, but not the exact byte of an error. An erroneous bit in a message will appear at the intersection of a byte parity error with a longitudinal parity error. Figure 9-26 shows how to locate an incorrect bit.

Byte parity and longitudinal parity together will detect changes to a message text. Network data error checking is added by a low-level layer in the transfer model; it is added to all messages, and its form is visible to anyone reading actual messages on the network. Because all messages are required to have error codes to ensure their integrity, the form, placement, and computation of error codes is a public matter known to all network hosts. A spurious host that wanted to modify network traffic could do so, as long as the check bits were modified accordingly. For example, to replace the first byte

$$01101100;1$$

of the previous example with

$$10101100;1$$

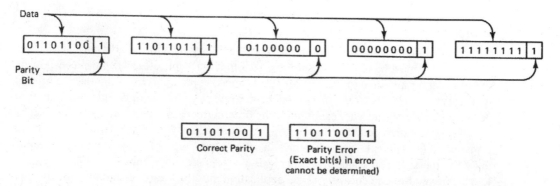

Figure 9-25   Use of Parity to Detect Errors

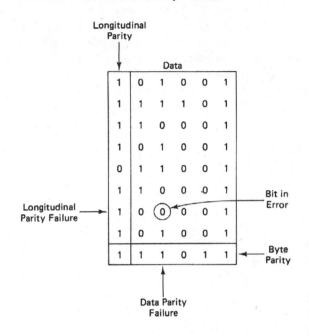

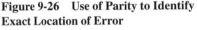

Figure 9-26   Use of Parity to Identify Exact Location of Error

the host would also change the longitudinal parity to

$$00110111;1$$

A malicious host could replace a segment or an entire communication on a network.

More Sophisticated Error Codes   Parity is a rather simple code. It can be used to detect single-bit errors, but errors in pairs cancel each other. More sophisticated error codes permit detection of errors in two or more bits; some codes even allow correction. Standard network textbooks, such as Comer [COM88], describe other error detection and correction codes used in networks. A more intricate function is needed to ensure the integrity of messages from modification by network hosts. At the application layer, a program may compute a **hash value** or **cryptographic checksum**, as described in Chapter 4.

Digital Signatures

As we have already seen, a digital signature is a means to certify the authenticity of a set of data (which might represent a document, a message, a file, or something else). The person affixing the digital signature confirms that the data is authentic.

In a network, many unknown individuals have the ability to create transactions that can affect the integrity of data. For example, in an airline reservation system, numerous travel agents can generate commands that book seats on flights, thereby affecting the data base. Therefore, the data base application program must retain signed requests so that the source of any error can be determined and incorrect data can be corrected.

Notarization

Finally, a network authority can be called upon to attest to the authenticity of a message. The use of a cryptographic checksum requires that sender and receiver share a single encryption algorithm and key. A digital signature is most easily implemented where two users share either the public key of a two-key system or a single encryption key.

Each network user cannot have a key for each other network user. Therefore, a protocol involving the services of a trusted notary is useful to ensure the integrity of messages in a network. The cryptographic checksum or digital signature can be implemented as an arbitrated protocol by using a notary to mediate the transmission between two network hosts.

Summary of Network Security Control Techniques

The security controls just studied are

- encryption
- access control
- authentication of users
- authentication of distributed systems
- traffic control
- data integrity

But these controls are only building blocks. In the next section we consider how these controls can be assembled into fuller solutions. The three solutions we will study are privacy enhanced electronic mail, firewalls, and multilevel networks.

9.4   Privacy Enhanced Electronic Mail

Privacy enhanced electronic mail addresses the specific problems of confidentiality, integrity, and authenticity in electronic mail (e-mail). It uses a combination of encryption, protocols, and data integrity controls to protect e-mail.

Requirements and Solutions

Consider threats to electronic mail:

- message interception (confidentiality)
- message interception (blocked delivery)
- message interception and subsequent replay
- message content modification
- message origin modification
- message content forgery by outsider
- message origin forgery by outsider
- message content forgery by recipient
- message origin forgery by recipient
- denial of message transmission

Confidentiality breaches and content forgery are often prevented by encryption. Encryption can also help in a defense against replay, although this requires a protocol in which each message contains something unique (such as a sequence number) that is encrypted.

Symmetric encryption cannot protect against forgery by a recipient because both sender and recipient share a common key; however, public key schemes can let a recipient decrypt but not encrypt. Because of lack of control over the middle points of a network, it is difficult for a sender or receiver to protect against blocked delivery.

Now we will study how the following protections can be afforded to electronic mail:

- *message confidentiality* (the message is not exposed en route to the receiver)
- *message integrity* (what the receiver sees is what was sent)
- *sender authenticity* (the receiver is confident who the sender was)
- *nonrepudiation* (the sender cannot deny having sent the message)

Not all of these qualities are needed for every message, but a secure e-mail package allows these capabilities to be invoked selectively. The solution goes under the generic name privacy enhanced [electronic] mail, or PEM.

PEM was developed by the Internet Society, through its architecture board (IAB) and research (IRTF) and engineering (IETF) task forces. The PEM protocols are documented as an Internet standard (called request for comments or RFC) in documents 1421, 1422, 1423, and 1424 [LIN93, KEN93, BAL93, KAL93a]. These standards are actually the third refinements.

Terminology can be a bit confusing because PEM refers to the *concept* of privacy enhancement for e-mail, the *standard* specified in the RFCs, and particular *implementations* that conform to that standard. It should be clear whether a reference in this book means the concept, the standard, or an implementation.

A design goal for PEM was that enhanced messages should travel as ordinary messages through the existing Internet e-mail system. This requirement ensures that the large existing e-mail network would not require change to accommodate PEM. Thus, all PEM protection occurs in the body of a message.

PEM

The basis of PEM is encryption. We can easily encrypt an electronic mail message; the tricky parts are getting it to travel through a network in encrypted form, doing the encryption so that the receiver can reverse the encryption, and managing keys.

In order to send a PEM message, the sender must have a **certificate** for the receiver. The certificate follows the X.509 structure presented in Chapter 4: each certificate contains a user's identity and public key and a chain of authorities who vouch for the correspondence between the identity and public key.

We will start by considering how to provide confidentiality enhancements. The sender chooses a (random) symmetric algorithm encryption key. The sender encrypts a copy of the entire message to be transmitted, including FROM:, TO:, SUBJECT:, and DATE: headers. The sender then prepends duplicate headers. For key management, the sender encrypts the message key under the recipient's public key and attaches that to the message as well. The process of creating a PEM message is shown in Figure 9-27.

Encryption can potentially yield any value. Many e-mail handlers expect that message traffic will not contain characters other than the normal printable characters. Network e-mail handlers use unprintable characters as control signals in the traffic stream. To avoid problems in transmission, PEM converts the entire ciphertext message to printable characters. An example of a PEM message is shown in Figure 9-28. Notice the three portions: an

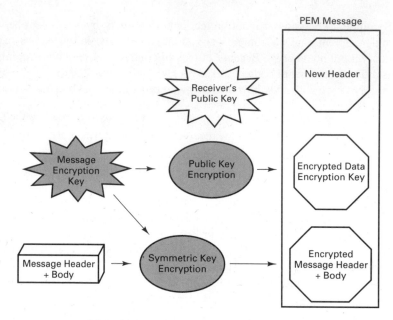

Figure 9-27   Overview of PEM Processing

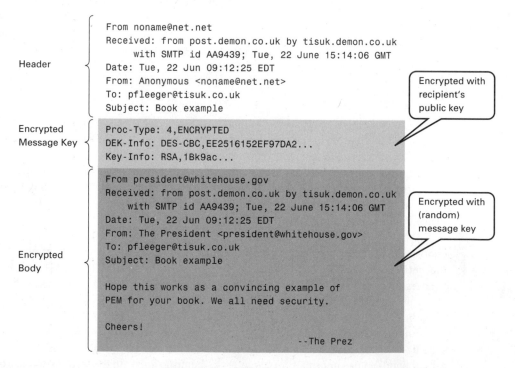

Figure 9-28   PEM-Secured Message

external (plaintext) header, a section by which the message encryption key can be transferred, and the encrypted message itself. (The encryption is shown with shading.)

The PEM standard works most easily as just described, using both symmetric and asymmetric encryption. The standard is also defined for symmetric encryption only: to use symmetric encryption, the sender and receiver must have previously established a shared secret encryption key. The processing type (Proc-Type) field tells what privacy enhancement services have been applied. In the data exchange key field (DEK-Info), the kind of key exchange (symmetric or asymmetric) is shown. The key exchange (Key-Info) field contains the message encryption key, encrypted under this shared encryption key. The field also identifies the originator (sender) so that the receiver can determine which shared symmetric key was used. If the key exchange technique used asymmetric encryption, the key exchange field contains the message encryption field, encrypted under the recipient's public key. Also included is the sender's certificate (used for determining authenticity and for generating replies).

The PEM standard is designed to support multiple encryption algorithms, although currently only DES is accepted for message encryption and either DES or RSA for key exchange. Additionally, MD2 or MD5 (introduced in Chapter 3) can be used as a message digest (hash) algorithm. In principle, there is nothing to prevent using other algorithms. By setting fields in the message a user could specify other algorithms, such as MD4, IDEA, or El Gamal.

PEM messages always carry a digital signature, so the authenticity and nonrepudiability of the sender is ensured, and the integrity is also ensured because of a hash function (called a **message integrity check**, or **MIC**) in the digital signature; optionally, PEM messages can be encrypted for confidentiality.

Notice in Figure 9-28 that the header inside the message (in the encrypted portion) differs from that outside. A sender's identity or the actual subject of a message can be concealed within the encrypted portion.

The PEM processing can integrate with ordinary e-mail packages so that a person can send both enhanced and nonenhanced messages as shown in Figure 9-29. The sender decides to add enhancements and an extra bit of PEM processing is invoked on the sender's end; the receiver must also remove the enhancements. But without enhancements, messages flow through the mail handlers as usual.

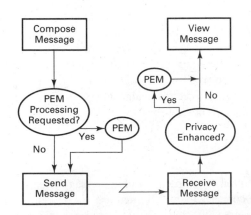

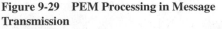

Figure 9-29   PEM Processing in Message Transmission

The Internet Society is working to accommodate exchange of other than just text messages: support for voice, graphics, video, and other kinds of complex message parts is being planned. Part of this planning will support privacy enhanced body parts, in a PEM-like format.

PEM programs are available from many sources. Several universities (including Cambridge and University of Michigan) and companies (BBN, RSA-DSI, and Trusted Information Systems) have developed either prototype or commercial versions of PEM.

PEM provides strong end-to-end security for electronic mail. The DES and RSA cryptography are quite strong, especially if RSA is used with a 1024-bit key. The vulnerabilities remaining with PEM come from the points not covered: the end points. An attacker with access could subvert a sender's or receiver's machine, modifying the code that did the privacy enhancements or arranging to leak a cryptographic key.

The major problem with PEM is key management. The certificate scheme described in Chapter 4 is excellent for exchanging keys and for associating an identity with a public encryption key. The difficulty with certificates is building the hierarchy. As described in Chapter 4, many organizations have hierarchical structures. The PEM dilemma is moving beyond the organization to an interorganizational hierarchy. Precisely because of the problem of imposing a hierarchy on a nonhierarchical world, PGP was developed as a simpler form of PEM.

PGP

Phil Zimmerman designed Pretty Good Privacy (PGP) to offer a reasonable degree of privacy for e-mail. The software for PGP is in the public domain [ZIM95a, ZIM95b], in Zimmerman's hope that many people will begin to use it, thereby raising the general level of privacy for e-mail communications. It uses a message structuring scheme similar to PEM.

The key management for PGP is ad hoc. Each user has a set of people he or she knows and trusts. The user exchanges public keys with those friends, exactly as one might swap business cards at a meeting. Some people accept not just the friends' public keys, but also all public keys their friends have. The assumption here is that any friend of yours is a friend of mine. But if a friend has taken all public keys from a friend who took all public keys from a friend, and so on, the chain of believability becomes strained. Computer clubs even host swap meets at which each user brings a disk with a public key and shares that key with everyone at the meeting.

A PGP user builds a **key ring**, which is the set of all public keys that person possesses. In that way, when an encrypted message arrives, the person can decrypt it if the key is on that person's key ring. PGP allows a user to assign a "confidence value" to key providers. Although PGP has a reasonable basis for key management among friends, once it passes the bounds of direct friends, the credibility becomes strained.

PGP also expands on the PEM suite of acceptable algorithms, to allow use of IDEA as well as DES, and RSA with a 512-, 1024-, or 1280-bit key.

9.5   Firewalls

PEM counters the threat of interception or tampering with a message stream in electronic mail. Although that is a significant concern, there is limited use of electronic mail for sensitive communication. More significant is the threat that an intruder would penetrate a system connected to the Internet. This threat is more significant for two reasons: an electronic message contains very little data, usually only hundreds or thousands of bytes, whereas a network-connected system holds millions, billions, or more bytes of data; and the user recognizes the possibility of attack when choosing to send certain information in a message, but users of systems attached to a LAN, one of whose hosts is connected to a wide area network, may be unaware of the threat to all stored data. Thus, protection of network-connected resources is very important.

The simplest form of protection of sensitive resources is not to connect them to any system accessible from outside the organization's security perimeter. Physical isolation is totally effective against outside attack, but many users need, and more want, access to the outside.

In the worst case, a user will buy an inexpensive modem and connect it to a LAN-connected workstation to link to the outside. This practice is harmful because the security staff does not even know of the modem, so they cannot control it or educate the user about how to limit the exposure or build defenses for other resources connected to the maverick user.

Ideally, we want a filter that will let through only desirable interactions. Two problems of controlling access are determining what constitutes desirable (or not desirable) interactions, and permitting desirable interactions, blocking the others, and not interfering too severely with users' operations (to keep users from buying their own modems and defeating the purpose of the filter). The model is like a defensive medieval castle: these castles had strong and solid walls with slits through which archers could shoot arrows. These slits were so narrow that it was almost impossible to shoot an arrow through it from the outside. This kind of computer defense is called a **firewall**. As shown in Figure 9-30,

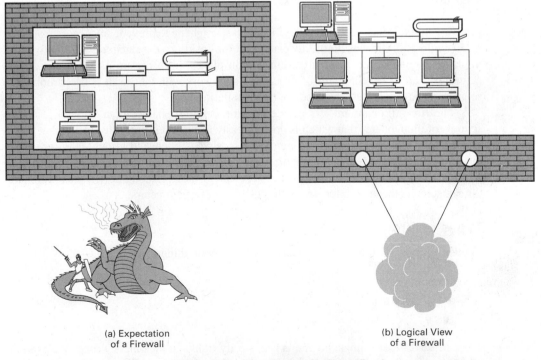

(a) Expectation
of a Firewall

(b) Logical View
of a Firewall

Figure 9-30   Two Views of a Firewall

people *expect* a firewall to be a solid brick wall protecting some computing resources. In fact, a firewall is a brick wall through which people *intentionally* break holes, with the intention of carefully controlling what goes through the holes.

Design of Firewalls

A firewall is a special form of reference monitor. Remember from Chapter 7 that the three qualities of a reference monitor were that it be

- always invoked
- tamperproof
- small and simple enough for rigorous analysis

By careful positioning of a firewall within a network, we can ensure that all network accesses that we want to control must pass through it. This meets the always-invoked condition. A firewall is typically well isolated, making it highly immune to modification. Usually a firewall is implemented on a separate computer, with direct connections generally just to the outside and inside networks. This isolation is expected to meet the tamperproof requirement. And firewall designers strongly recommend keeping the functionality of the firewall simple.

What Is a Firewall?

A firewall is a process that filters all traffic between a protected or "inside" network and a less trustworthy or "outside" network.

The purpose of a firewall is to keep "bad" things outside a protected environment. Firewalls implement a security policy. The policy might be to prevent any access from outside (while still allowing traffic to pass *from* the inside *to* the outside). Alternatively, it might be to permit accesses only from certain places, from certain users, or for certain activities. Part of the challenge of protecting a network with a firewall is determining the security policy that meets the needs of the installation.

The firewall community is divided on the default behavior of a firewall. The two schools of thought are "that which is not expressly forbidden is permitted" and "that which is not expressly permitted is forbidden." Users, always interested in new features, prefer the former. Security experts, relying on several decades of experience, strongly counsel the latter. A firewall implementation must choose one of these, although often the administrator can achieve the other effect by setting the firewall's parameters.

Types of Firewalls

The term *firewall* is used rather loosely. Three different things are known as firewalls:

- screening routers
- proxy gateways
- guards

They all do different things; no one is necessarily right and the others wrong. We examine all of these in this section to see what each is, how it works, and what its strengths and weaknesses are. In general, screening routers tend to implement rather simplistic security policies, whereas guards and proxy gateways have a richer set of choices for security policy. Simplicity in a security policy is not a bad thing; the question is what threats an installation needs to counter.

A firewall is a type of host. Often it is as programmable as a good-quality workstation. A screening router *can* be fairly primitive, but the tendency is to host even routers on complete computers with operating systems, because editors and other programmed tools assist in configuring and maintaining the router. However, firewall developers are minimalists: they try to eliminate from the firewall all that is not strictly necessary for the firewall's functionality. The reason for that is to give as little assistance as possible to a successful attacker. For this reason, firewalls tend not to have user accounts, so they do not have, for example, a password file to conceal. The most desirable firewall is one that runs contentedly in back room; except for periodic scanning of its audit logs, there is seldom reason to touch it.

Screening Router

A screening router is the simplest and, in some situations, the most effective type of firewall.

Hosts tend not to be connected directly to a wide area network; more often, hosts are connected to a **router**, which is a computer that, as its name implies, routes a communication toward its target. A router has the rather simple task of receiving each packet, consulting stored routing tables, and passing the packet to one of several physical ports that will get the packet to its destination, as shown in Figure 9-31. A router usually works in both directions, passing packets both to the left and to the right in our figure. That is, the router takes packets from the local network and dispatches them either to wide area network 1 or wide area network 2, as appropriate; it also receives packets from both wide area networks and passes ones with addresses in the local network to it.

For example, suppose an international company has three LANs, at three locations throughout the world, as shown in Figure 9-32. In this example, the router has two sides: we say that the local LAN is on the inside of the router and the two connections to distant LANs through wide area networks are on the outside. The company might want communication *only* among the three LANs of the corporate network. They could use a screening router on the LAN at 100.24.4.0 to allow *in* only communications destined to the host at 100.24.4.0, and allow *out* only communications addressed to address 144.27.5.3 or 192.19.33.0.

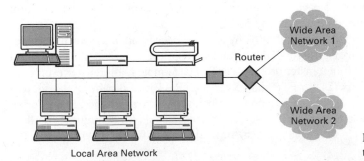

Figure 9-31   **Router Joining LAN to Two WANs**

Local Area Network

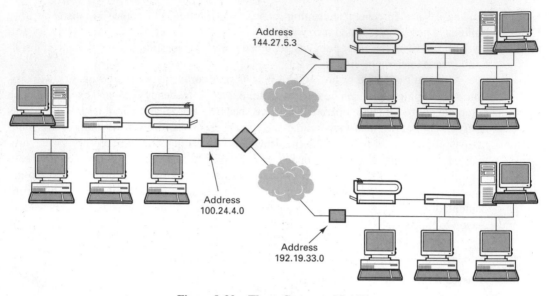

Figure 9-32   Three Connected LANs

Packet-level filtering operates at a very fine (detailed) level of granularity. A packet is a small subunit of communication, typically a few hundred bytes, and a router could pass many thousands of packets in a second. Thus, the screening rules have to be ones that the router can check and apply quickly, without significantly impeding the traffic flow. Also, a router is designed to look only at packet header information. Depending on the protocol, a header may contain source and destination addresses, protocol, source and destination ports, packet length, sequencing, priority, and error correction information, so these are the only kinds of conditions on which the router can filter.

Screening routers can perform the very important service of ensuring the validity of inside addresses. Inside hosts typically trust other inside hosts for all the reasons described as characteristics of LANs. But the only way an inside host has to distinguish another inside host is the address shown in the source field of a message. Source addresses in packets can be forged, so that an inside application might think it was communicating with another host on the inside, instead of an outside forger. A router sits between the inside network and the outside net, so it can know whether a packet from the outside is forging an inside address, as shown in Figure 9-33. A screening router might be configured to block all packets from the *outside* that claimed their source address was an *inside* address. In this example, the router blocks all packets claiming to come from any address of the form 100.50.25.*x* (but, of course, it permits in any packets with *destination* 100.50.25.*x*).

A screening router can also control traffic by application. The address seen by a router is actually the combination of a network address and the application port number. Standard applications, such as FTP (file transfer protocol) or SMTP (simple mail transfer protocol), have standard port numbers (21 for FTP and 25 for SMTP). The destination (and source) address of a packet actually identifies the port number, too, such as 100.50.25.325 for an SMTP connection on host 100.50.25.3. A screening router could be configured to allow packets from the inside only to the outside nets for mail transfer, for example.

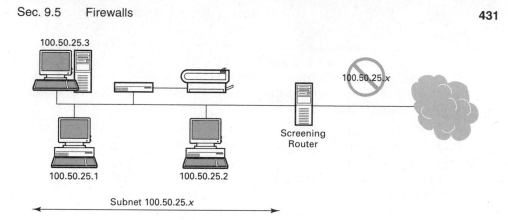

Figure 9-33   Router Screening Outside Addresses

Proxy Gateway

Screening routers look only at the headers of packets, not at the data *inside* the packets. Therefore, a screening router would pass anything to port 25, assuming its screening rules said to allow inbound connections to that port. Applications are complex and sometimes contain errors. Worse, applications (such as the e-mail delivery agent) often act on behalf of all users, so they require privileges of all users, for example, to store incoming mail messages so that inside users can read them. A flawed application, running with all users' privileges, can cause much damage.

A **proxy gateway**, also called a **bastion host**, is a firewall that simulates the (proper) effects of an application so that the application will receive only requests to act properly. A proxy gateway is a two-headed piece of software: to the inside it looks as if it is the outside (destination) connection, while to the outside it responds just as the inside would.

A proxy gateway runs pseudo-applications. When electronic mail is transferred to a location, for example, a sending process at one site and a receiving process at the destination communicate by a protocol that establishes the legitimacy of a mail transfer and then actually transfers the mail message. The protocol between sender and destination is carefully defined. A proxy gateway essentially intrudes into the middle of this protocol exchange, seeming like a destination in communications with the sender that is outside the firewall, and then seeming like the sender in communications with the real destination on the inside. The proxy in the middle has the opportunity to screen the mail transfer, ensuring that only acceptable e-mail protocol commands are sent to the destination.

To understand the real purpose of a proxy gateway, we consider some examples.

- A company wants to set up an on-line price list so that outsiders can see the products and prices offered. It wants to be sure that no outsider can change the prices or product list and that outsiders can access only the price list, not any of the more sensitive files stored inside.

- A school wants to allow its students to retrieve any information from the World-Wide Web resources on the Internet. To help provide efficient service, it wants to know what sites have been visited, and what files from those sites have been fetched; particularly popular files will be cached locally.

- A government agency pays to gather statistics for the benefit of its citizens. It wants to make this information available only to citizens. Recognizing that it cannot prevent a citizen from passing the information to a foreign citizen, the government will implement this policy by permitting the data to be delivered only to destination addresses inside the country.
- A company with multiple offices wants to encrypt the data portion of all e-mail to addresses at its other offices. (A corresponding proxy at the remote end will remove the encryption.)
- A company wants to allow dial-in access by its employees, without exposing its company resources to login attacks from remote nonemployees.

Each of these requirements can be met with a proxy. In the first case, the proxy would monitor the file transfer protocol *data* to ensure that only the price list file was accessed, and that file could only be read, not modified. The school's requirement could be met by a logging procedure as part of the web browser. The agency's need could be satisfied by a screening router; typically, however, the configuration commands of a firewall are easier to administer than those of a screening router. The requirement for limited login could be handled by a specially written proxy that required strong user authentication (such as a challenge–response system), which many operating systems do not require. These functions are shown in Figure 9-34.

A proxy firewall is typically an isolated machine with very limited capability. It does not allow user logins (on the *firewall machine*, although it may support them by proxy on internal hosts), it does not have programming tools (compilers, linkers), and it does not contain programs unnecessary to its limited purposes. By having the bare minimum of software, it has fewer places for flaws to exist, and offers little support for an attacker who might visit it.

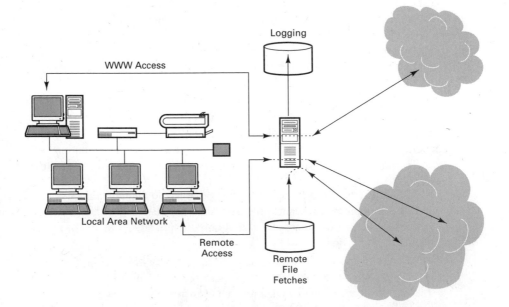

Figure 9-34   Actions of Firewall Proxies

The proxies on the firewall can be tailored to specific requirements, such as logging details about accesses. It can even present a common user interface to what may be dissimilar internal functions. Suppose the internal network has a mixture of operating system types, none of which supports strong authentication through a challenge–response token. The proxy can demand strong authentication (name, password, and challenge-response), validate the challenge–response itself, and then pass on only simple name and password authentication details in the form required by a specific internal host's operating system.

The distinction of a proxy over a screening router is that the proxy interprets the protocol stream to an application in order to control actions through the firewall on the basis of things visible *within* the protocol, not just on external header data.

Guard

A guard is a sophisticated proxy firewall. Like a proxy firewall, it receives protocol data units, interprets them, and passes through the same or different protocol data units that achieve either the same result or a modified result. The guard decides what services to perform on the user's behalf based on its available knowledge, such as whatever it can reliably know of the (outside) user's identity, previous interactions, and so forth. The degree of control a guard can provide is limited only by what is computable. There is also no clear-cut definition of when something is too sophisticated to be called a proxy firewall and is thus considered a guard.

Here are some more sophisticated examples of guard activities:

- A university wants to allow its students to use e-mail up to a limit of so many messages or so many characters of e-mail in the last so many days. Although this result could be achieved by modifying e-mail handlers, it is more easily done by monitoring the common point through which all e-mail flows, the mail transfer protocol.

- A school wants its students to be able to access the World-Wide Web but, because of the slow speed of its connection to the web, it will allow only so many characters per downloaded image (that is, allowing text mode and simple graphics, but disallowing complex graphics, animation, music, or the like).

- A library wants to make available certain documents but, in order to support fair use of copyrighted matter, it will allow a user to retrieve the first so many characters of a document but after that amount, it will require the user to pay a fee, which the library will forward to the copyright holder.

- A company wants to allow its employees to fetch files via FTP. However, in order to prevent introduction of viruses, it will pass all incoming files through a virus scanner. Even though many of these files will be nonexecutable text or graphics, the company administrator thinks that the expense of scanning those (which should pass) will be negligible.

Each of these scenarios can be implemented as a modified proxy, but because the proxy decision is based on some quality of the data of the communication, we call the proxy a **guard**. Because the security policy the guard implements is somewhat more complex than the action of a proxy, the code of a guard is also more complex and, therefore, more prone to error. Simpler firewalls have fewer possible ways to fail or be subverted.

Table 9-3   Comparison of Types of Firewalls

Screening Router	Proxy Gateway	Guard
Simplest	Somewhat complex	Most complex
Sees only addresses and service protocol type	Sees full text of communication	Sees full text of communication
Auditing difficult	Can audit activity	Can audit activity
Screens based on connection rules	Screens based on behavior of proxies	Screens based on interpretation of message content
Complex addressing rules can make configuration tricky	Simple proxies can substitute for complex addressing rules	Complex guard functionality can limit assurance

Comparison of Firewall Types

In this section we try to summarize the differences between these three types of firewalls. These comparisons are shown in Table 9-3.

Example Firewall Configurations

Now we are ready to consider uses of firewalls. The situations presented are examples, designed to show how a firewall complements a sensible security policy and architecture.

The simplest use of a firewall is shown in Figure 9-35. This environment has a screening router, positioned between the internal LAN and the outside network connection. In many cases this is an adequate installation, when only the address screening of a router is needed.

To use a proxy machine, however, this organization is not ideal. Similarly, configuration of a router for a complex set of approved or rejected addresses is difficult. If the firewall router is successfully attacked, then all traffic on the LAN to which the firewall is connected is visible. To reduce this exposure, a proxy firewall is often installed on its own LAN, as shown in Figure 9-36. In this way the only traffic visible on that LAN is the traffic going into and out of the firewall.

For even more protection we can add a screening router to this configuration, as shown in Figure 9-37. Here the screening router ensures address correctness to the proxy firewall (so that the proxy firewall cannot be fooled by an outside attacker forging an address from an inside host); the proxy firewall filters traffic based on its proxy rules. Here, also, if the screening router is subverted, only the traffic to the proxy firewall is visible, not any of the sensitive information on the internal protected LAN.

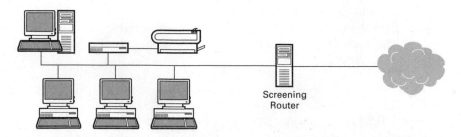

Figure 9-35   Firewall with Screening Router

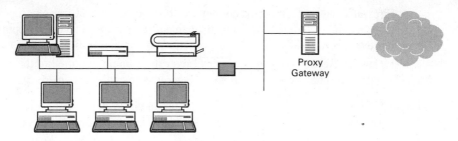

Figure 9-36   Firewall on Separate LAN

Although these examples are simplifications, they show the kinds of configurations firewalls protect. In the next section we review the kinds of attacks against which firewalls can and cannot protect.

What Firewalls Can—and Cannot—Block

Firewalls are not complete solutions to all computer security problems, as you can see. A firewall protects the perimeter of its environment against attacks from outsiders who want to execute code or access data on the machines in the protected environment. Keep in mind these points about firewalls:

- Firewalls can protect an environment only if the firewalls control the entire perimeter, that is, only if there are no connections through the perimeter that are not mediated by the firewall. If even one inside host connects to an outside address (by a modem, for example), the entire inside net is vulnerable through the modem and its host.
- Firewalls do not protect data outside the perimeter; data that has properly passed through the firewall is just as exposed as if there were no firewall.
- Firewalls are the most visible part of an installation to the outside and they are the most attractive target for attack. Several different layers of protection, called **defense in depth**, are better than relying on the strength of a single firewall.
- Firewalls are targets of penetrators. Firewalls are designed to withstand attack, but they are not impenetrable. Designers intentionally keep them small and simple, so that even if a penetrator breaks them, the firewall does not have further tools such as compilers, linkers, loaders, and the like to continue an attack.

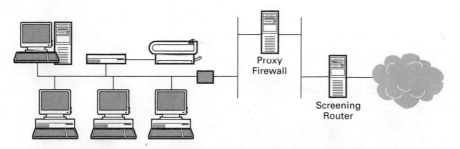

Figure 9-37   Firewall with Proxy and Screening Router

- Firewalls must be correctly configured, that configuration must be updated as the internal and external environment changes, and firewall activity reports must be reviewed periodically for evidence of attempted or successful intrusion.

- Firewalls exercise only minor control over the content admitted to the inside, meaning that inaccurate data or malicious code must be controlled inside the perimeter.

Firewalls are very important tools in protecting an environment connected to a network. However, the environment must be viewed as a whole, all possible exposures must be considered, and the firewall must fit into a larger, comprehensive security strategy. Firewalls alone cannot secure an environment.

PEM uses cryptography to address confidentiality and integrity exposures in electronic mail. Firewalls use their key positioning and resistance to penetration to protect against intrusions. One final example combines both of these approaches.

9.6   Encrypting Gateway

Go back to our example earlier in this chapter of the organization that has three offices. It has a firewall where each office connects to the Internet, to protect against intrusions. Naturally, there is a significant amount of communication among the three offices on business matters, as well as communications with other sites. The corporation would like to encrypt all e-mail among the three sites.

The solution is a firewall plus a cryptography server, using cryptographic separation to create what is called a **virtual private network**. Because all e-mail passes through the firewall on SMTP port 25, and because the Internet addresses of the two distant hosts are constant, this solution can be handled in a straightforward manner. We will look at only one site; the other two sites are equivalent.

As shown in Figure 9-38, the ordinary proxy firewall shares a LAN with another host, which provides PEM-like cryptographic services. The server provides encryption on a per-host basis instead of a per-user basis, as does standard PEM. A user's message to another of the company's nodes, say at address 144.27.5.3, would be routed first to the cryptographic server, which would encrypt the packet using a key shared with 144.27.5.3. The firewall

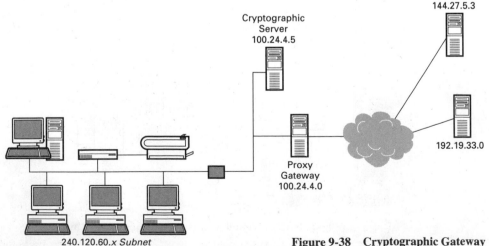

Figure 9-38   Cryptographic Gateway

would inspect the source address of each packet: addresses in the 240.120.60.*x* subnet would require encryption, so the gateway would route it to 100.24.4.5. A packet with a source address of 100.24.4.5 would have already been encrypted, and so it should be routed to its appropriate destination, 144.27.5.3. At the far end the encryption would be removed.

All this activity could be performed in the firewall, but that would increase the exposure: a successful attack of the firewall would expose the cryptographic keys and the implementation of the cryptography. It is more secure to perform the encryption on a separate encryption server (or to use a dedicated hardware cryptographic processor, such as a circuit board).

This solution combines the strength of encryption with the centralized point of control of a firewall. Management of encryption does not have to be performed by the user; in fact, the user is unaware that encryption has occurred. This approach protects against confidentiality or integrity attacks in the more exposed area of the Internet, at little cost.

9.7   Multilevel Security on Networks

In previous chapters we studied multilevel security in operating systems and data bases. Many of the same principles—such as mandatory access control, labeling, and trust—apply to network situations as well. However, a multilevel security network has its own particular security properties. We consider the security of multilevel networks in this section.

With a **multilevel secure network** two or more people want to share network access at different sensitivity levels. A multilevel security network must preserve two properties of access to data:

- The *simple security property* states that no user may read data at a level higher than that for which the person is authorized.
- The *∗-property* states that no person may write data to a level lower than the level the person has accessed.

These properties are the Bell–La Padula security properties first presented in Chapter 7.

Size and complexity make it difficult to ensure and demonstrate the security of a network. One attempt to achieve multilevel security certification of a computer network is to form a trusted network base, called the trusted network interface. This approach is described next.

Trusted Network Interface

Figure 9-39 shows graphically the structure of a trusted computing base for an operating system. Although the figure is usually presented as on the left, the right figure is more accurate in terms of user capabilities: each user is isolated from the other users, and a user's access to resources or to other users is strictly controlled by the trusted computing base. There is actually only one trusted computing base (on a single machine), even though in the figure it appears to be duplicated for each user.

The trusted interface for networks is developed naturally, in a manner similar to operating systems, as shown in Figure 9-40. Here each host has a distinct and possibly different version of the trusted network interface. Because each host is independent, each host must be cautious in case another host joins the network without having a trusted network interface. Each interface is responsible for maintaining the security of the resources it controls.

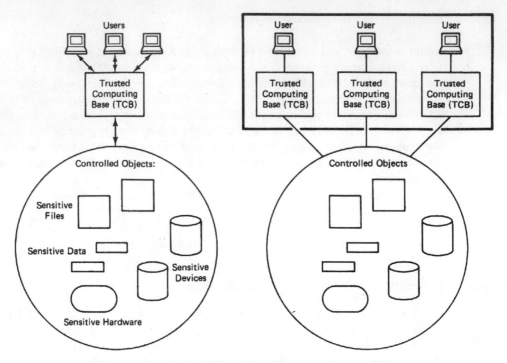

Figure 9-39   Trusted Computing Base for Operating Systems

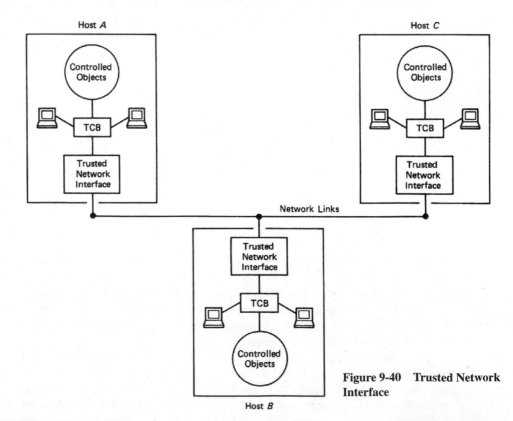

Figure 9-40   Trusted Network Interface

The network and the network interfaces must provide the following things:

- *Secure multilevel hosts.* Each network interface is responsible for preserving the security of its host.
- *Labeled output.* A network host must label its output so that other hosts can be aware of the security level of the data, even if the output is passed from one host through several others to its final destination.
- *Classification check before releasing data.* A host must be sure to release data only to an approved recipient who has been properly authenticated.
- *Integrity of data.* The network host must take some measure, such as a cryptographic checksum, to ensure that data is not accidentally or intentionally modified during transmission.
- *Confinement.* The interface must ensure that no host can leak information to another host.
- *Protection from line compromise.* The network interface must ensure that a compromise of the links of the network will not compromise data.

Rushby and Randell [RUS83] present the design of such a secure system. In their example a number of Unix systems form a local area network. The network design is shown in Figure 9-41. A basic premise for their work is that the host operating systems themselves should be unmodified; all security should be provided by the trusted network interface.

In the system proposed by Rushby and Randell, hosts encrypt all communications on the network. Each host operates at a specific security level, and all of its communications are protected under one key unique to that level. Therefore, cryptographic separation provides the separation between hosts and their data and computation.

Secure Communication

An alternative view of network security is presented by Walker [WAL85]. In this paper, Walker compares models of hosts at several security levels operating on the same network. As a simplification, assume three hosts are connected to a network as shown in Figure 9-42. Hosts X and Y are trusted, in the sense of Chapter 7, at a level of B1 or higher. This means that they correctly implement a nondiscretionary access control policy limiting access of subjects to objects based on security levels. The network also contains an untrusted host, U.

In the first representation, the network does not enter into security considerations; all hosts are responsible for verifying the security of their own communications. Therefore, when process $X1$, running as a top secret process on host X, wishes to communicate with process $Y1$, running as a top secret process on host Y, hosts X and Y determine that this is an acceptable communication. When process $X1$ wishes to communicate with process $Y2$, running at secret level on host Y, host X prevents this communication because of the no-write-down requirement of the *-property.

Unreliable communications in networks cause a security problem. Process $Y2$, at secret level, can send a message to $X1$, at top secret level, because $Y2$ is allowed to write to any process whose security level is greater than or equal to the level of $Y2$. For example, $Y2$ might write a message to a high-security process $X1$ that maintains an audit log. Process

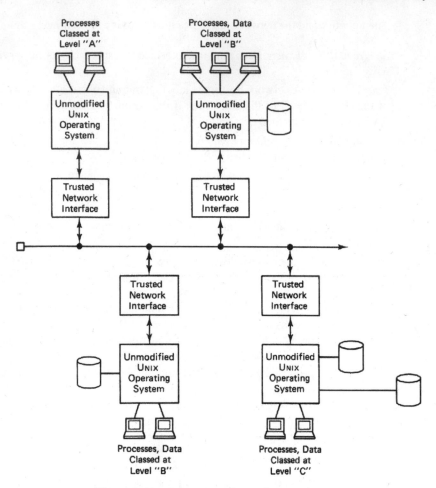

Figure 9-41   Secure Multilevel Network Design

$X1$ cannot reply to $Y2$ because that reply would constitute a write-down. Within a *single* system, hardware and software are so reliable that $Y2$ does not need a reply to be confident that the message was received properly. However, suppose $X1$ is a process on another host in a network. Because of the unreliability of network communications, $Y2$ wants an acknowledgment that the message has been received. Even this simple acknowledgment of message receipt constitutes a write-down from $X1$ to $Y2$, which strictly is not allowable because it could be used as a covert channel.

A communications server on trusted host X can transfer data reliably. Let XS be a secret level communications server on X. Because XS and $Y2$ are at the same level, they can both read and write to each other. Thus $Y2$ can send its message to XS, and XS can respond that the message was successfully received at host X. XS will forward the message to $X1$ but, because of the difference in their levels, $X1$ will not acknowledge the receipt to XS. $Y2$ will accept an acknowledgment from XS to verify that $X1$ received the message because communications within a single host are reliable.

An untrusted host cannot use this technique because the host cannot be relied upon to enforce an access policy on its processes. All processes on an untrusted host are assumed

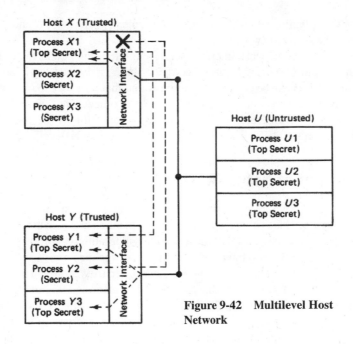

Figure 9-42   Multilevel Host Network

to operate at the same level, which becomes the level of the host. Suppose U is an untrusted host at level top secret and $Y2$ is a secret level process on trusted host Y. $Y2$ wishes to send a message to process $U1$ on U. Although $Y2$ can send the message, it cannot receive an acknowledgment that the message was received by U or $U1$.

Walker describes a multilevel trusted network. As shown in Figure 9-43, a trusted network manager intervenes in communications. Thus, when $Y2$ wishes to send a message to

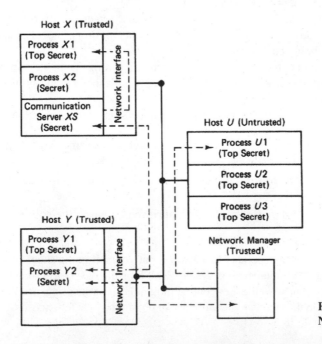

Figure 9-43   Multilevel Trusted Network Interface

$U1$ with reply, the network manager communicates with both U and Y to assure $Y2$ that the message was properly delivered.

The trusted network interface serves the same function as the trusted computing base of an operating system. A trusted computer base is allowed to violate the Bell–La Padula *-property if it can be rigorously demonstrated that none of the information it reads from a high-level source is transferred to a lower-level object. Thus, a program can communicate with sources at different levels if a rigorous inspection of the code shows that the high-level data does not affect the output it produces for lower-level objects.

9.8   Summary of Network Security

In this chapter we have considered several security characteristics of networks. The network security issues of secrecy, integrity, authenticity, and availability have been studied. Networks possess many of the security vulnerabilities of other computing systems, although networks also have their own specific weaknesses.

Encryption is a powerful tool in network security, although it is not the only tool, nor is it all-powerful. Link level encryption can be performed without the knowledge or participation of a user's process. Thus, link level encryption can be useful when users do not have the background to implement an appropriate encryption method. By contrast, with end-to-end encryption, the user is responsible for performing encryption. End-to-end encryption thus gives the user a choice of when to use encryption and which encryption algorithm to use.

The possible network vulnerabilities that have been studied include access by unauthorized users or nodes and impersonation of authorized users or nodes. Access control and authentication techniques are similar to those for operating systems. A serious problem that remains in network security is establishing trust of a remote node, because a remote node can be impersonated, subverted, or replaced.

In network security integrity is an important issue that affects all users. Therefore, much attention has been devoted to developing network transmission protocols that ensure the integrity of the data being communicated.

We examined several controls effective in a networked setting. Then we showed how those controls can fit together in solutions, such as privacy enhanced e-mail, firewalls, and multilevel networks.

Before trying to intercept a transmission, an intruder must ask three questions:

- *Is this the weakest link?* If there is an easier way to obtain the same data, the interceptor may try that first.
- *Do I have the skills to intercept?* Some links are secure enough to inhibit even very skilled interceptors.
- *Is it worth doing?* Will the value of the data retrieved be worth the cost (time, difficulty) of getting it?

To determine the most vulnerable points of a network, put yourself in the shoes of an interceptor as you analyze the communications system. Think of the easy ways to access data (wastebaskets, bribery, theft), as well as network tapping or address spoofing, and make sure that all are secure. Then make sure that the difficulty to obtain the data far exceeds its value.

9.9   **Bibliographic Notes**

Classic network technology is covered well by Martin [MAR94] and Comer [COM88]. Davies and Price [DAV89] and the book edited by Abrams and Podell [ABR87] are good overviews of the field of network security. Kerberos is presented by Steiner [STE88] and Kohl [KOH93]. As the major problem with Unix is its use in networks, Unix security is particularly relevant; the material in Garfinkel and Spafford [GAR96] is especially well presented. A good reference for DCE is [LOC94].

The book by Chapman and Zwicky [CHA95] is an outstanding presentation of firewall design and use. PEM is fully described in the RFCs [BAL93, KAL93a, KEN93, and LIN93]; the article by Kent [KEN93a] describes PEM well.

9.10   **Terms and Concepts**

server, 378
client, 378
node, 378
host, 378
link, 378
terminal, 379
workstation, 379
digital communication, 379
analog communication, 379
modem, 379
twisted pair, 380
coaxial (coax) cable, 380
repeater, 380
optical fiber, 380
microwave, 380
satellite communication, 381
protocol, 381
OSI reference model, 381
application layer, 382
presentation layer, 382
session layer, 382
transport layer, 382
network layer, 382
data link layer, 382
physical layer, 382
flow control, 382
routing, 382
TCP/IP, 384
packet, 384
datagram, 384
address, 384
port, 385

socket, 385
local area network (LAN), 385
wide area network (WAN), 386
inter-network (internet), 386
the Internet, 386
bus topology, 387
star or hub topology, 387
ring topology, 387
distributed system, 387
resource sharing, 389
distributed workload, 389
reliability, 389
expandability, 389
complexity, 390
unknown perimeter, 390
anonymity, 390
multiple paths, 391
wiretapping, 395
passive wiretapping, 395
active wiretapping, 395
packet sniffer, 395
inductance, 395
multiplexing, 395
impersonation, 397
guessing authentication, 398
eavesdropping on authentication, 399
avoiding authentication, 399
no authentication, 399
well-known authentication, 400
trusted authentication, 400
message confidentiality violation, 400
misdelivery, 400

9.11 Exercises

1. What controls prevent a malicious user from inserting or deleting a new piece of hardware into a simple (*non*network) computing system?

2. What assurance does an operating system in a simple (*non*network) environment have of the authenticity of a component? That is, could a telephone line known internally as line 1 actually be cabled to line 2 without the knowledge of the operating system?

3. Are there network security problems that depend on distance? That is, are there problems that do not exist at, for example, 10 miles but do exist at 100 miles or more? If yes, what are these problems?

4. In the ISO model, peer processes communicate without regard for precise implementation of activities at other layers. For example, the application does not know or care what specific routing has been chosen by the network layer. What is the security effect of an application program's not knowing the routing selected for a particular message, or even a particular session?

5. A user wishes to establish a covert channel by control and analysis of the total traffic on the network. At what layer would this analysis have to be performed?

6. Can a single malicious node cause a denial of service fault to another node in a network with the bus topology? The ring topology? The star topology? Tell how or explain why not for each of these.

7. Network users can perform simple encryption to shield their messages. As presented in earlier chapters, simple encryptions are sensitive to volume: if an interceptor obtains a large amount of ciphertext, the likelihood of breaking the encryption increases. With what network topologies should users be concerned about availability of much ciphertext?

8. The network advantages of increased reliability and distributed workload are disadvantages to security because more nodes have potential access to sensitive data or computations. What controls can allow distributed data or computing without sacrificing security?

9. Expandability is an advantage of network use: new nodes can be added easily to a network. What security disadvantage does this present?

10. What is the security impact of the unknown perimeter of a network? Does it matter to user A if the network is also accessible to user B, and user C through a network shared with B, and user D through a network shared with C, and so on?

11. Where (at what times during its transmission) is a message exposed if it is protected using link encryption? Where is a message exposed if end-to-end encryption is used?

12. Explain why node authentication is a continuous problem in a network. Describe a solution to this problem.

13. What are two difficulties to producing time-stamped messages in a network?

14. Suggest a control to prevent a covert channel via traffic analysis in a network without an administrator. That is, what control can an arbitrary user node provide against these kinds of covert channels?

15. Design a checking mechanism (other than parity) to ensure data integrity in a network communication.

16. In what circumstances can parity detect two-bit errors? Three-bit errors?

17. Integrity is an important network concern. Control information to ensure data integrity is a significant part of the information transmitted with messages. Are the Biba integrity properties (from Chapter 7) appropriate in a multilevel secure network? Why or why not?

18. Explain how output can be labeled on a multilevel security network. Why is it unsatisfactory to have a message saying "the following message is classified top secret"?

19. Which communications security issues are important considerations in a local area network environment? Which are important in a conventional (wide area) network? Which are important for communications strictly within a single building?

20. Is a signal transmitted by digital communication or by analog communication less susceptible to interception? Which is less susceptible to intentional modification? Which is less susceptible to unintentional modification? Why?

21. Is encryption an effective control against passive wiretapping? Against active wiretapping? Why or why not?

22. Identify all points of exposure of a signal between its transmission from New York and its reception in California, assuming satellite communication is used for the major cross-country transmission.

23. Explain how the simple security and *-properties of the Bell–La Padula security model relate to communications security.

24. Design a protocol for communication between two network hosts that guards against communications fabrication by an active wiretap. Your protocol should use encryption to ensure authenticity of each message transmitted.

25. Design a protocol for communication between two network hosts that guards against substitution of a malicious host for a legitimate one. Your protocol should not depend on encryption of each message.

26. Is it secure to transmit communications of different levels of sensitivity (in the sense of multilevel secure operating systems, data bases, or networks) simultaneously on one communications medium? Why or why not?

27. If digital communications facilities are used for a network communication, is there any need for error detection or correction codes in the messages communicated? If so, what is their purpose; if not, why not?

10

Administering Security

In this chapter:
- *Managing security for PCs, Unix systems, and networks*
- *Risk analysis*
- *Security plans and policies*
- *Disaster recovery*

In the last three chapters we have studied program flaws and protection as they relate to operating systems, data base management systems, and networks. These have given us a substantial background in security analysis, controls, and design in environments ranging from single users to local groups to remote and distributed settings. Now we follow with some information on managing and administering security.

In this chapter we consider administration from two different perspectives: the type of computing resources (PCs, multiuser Unix workstations or systems, or networks) and the human aspects (physical protection, security planning, and protection strategies).

10.1 Personal Computer Security Management

A few years ago most computing was done on mainframe computers, and data processing centers were responsible for protection. Computing centers developed expertise in security, and they carried out many protection activities in the background, without users having to be conscious of protection needs and practices. Much sensitive computing is still done that way. Many of the security concepts we have studied relate to multiuser, shared-resource environments typical of large mainframe systems. It would be an overstatement to say that security problems in that context are solved or trivial. Nevertheless, the security problems there are recognized and being dealt with effectively by the computing professionals who run computing centers.

More recently the use of personal computers has spread substantially, especially among professional, managerial, and clerical workers. We use the generic term *personal computer* to include microcomputers, office automation workstations, intelligent workstations, and even intelligent terminals. Each is a reasonably small machine, typically used by a single person at a time. A personal computer contrasts with a mainframe computer, the multiuser machine typical in major computing centers.

Personal computer users often do not recognize the risks they face, nor do they think of the simple measures that could contain those risks. A person who will carefully lock up company confidential records overnight will leave a running personal computer on a secretary's or a manager's desk, where anyone walking past can retrieve confidential memoranda and data. A box of diskettes may contain many times more data than a printed report, yet the report is an apparent, visible exposure, whereas the diskette is not obvious.

The basic security problems for personal computers are the same as for every other computer situation we have studied so far: applications require secrecy, integrity, and availability, as applied to the data, programs, and computing machinery. Security problems for personal computers are more serious than on mainframe computers for two reasons, one related to people and one related to hardware and software.

> **Lack of Sensitivity.** Users often do not appreciate the security risks associated with the use of personal computers.

In the mainframe environment, computing professionals are skilled and experienced. Computing is the principal concern for these people, who can support and assist each other in security considerations. However, personal computer users may be much less skilled and experienced in computing. Often, users are not computer professionals. Instead, they use personal computing as a support tool in some other field, such as accounting, engineering, or office communication.

> **Lack of Tools.** The security tools—hardware, software, and combinations of these—are fewer and less sophisticated than in the mainframe environment.

Many of the software and hardware facilities important in ensuring security—facilities such as access control mechanisms, operating system aids, supervisor mode, trusted computing bases, and professionally developed software—are inappropriate or unavailable in the personal computer environment.

In this chapter we consider security as it relates to personal computers. First we survey the problems of security for personal computers. Even though they have a different context, personal computer security needs and solutions often resemble solutions for mainframes. Thus, we focus on how personal computers are different from mainframes in their security capabilities. We identify some of the security facilities that are appropriate for users of personal computers. Note that the emphasis of this section is on software solutions to security problems. Later in the chapter we consider physical security measures and additional devices that can be used to enhance security.

Contributors to Security Problems

Personal computers are essentially no different from the more general forms of computers studied extensively in Chapters 5 through 9. The major problems facing personal computer users involve secrecy, integrity, and availability of programs, data, and machines, just as with mainframe computers. The standard controls, such as access control lists, protected memory, user authentication techniques, and trusted operating systems, can apply equally well to the small computer situation as the large.

Hardware Vulnerabilities

Most personal computers have no hardware-level protection or do not take full advantage of the protection available. There is limited protection of one memory space from another, even by a simple fence. Every user can execute every instruction, and can read and write every memory location. Although there may be software user authentication, a clever user can bypass the authentication code, or modify authentication data. The operating system may declare certain files as "system" files, but it cannot prevent a user from accessing them. Thus, the controls for personal computers are much less stringent than for mainframe computers. The popular Intel 386/486/+ and Pentium, as well as the Motorola 68030/40/+ microprocessors provide a protected mode of execution for the operating system, but so far operating systems designers for these processors have failed to take advantage of the hardware protection.

Other Vulnerabilities

The machine is not the source of the security problem; the problem is *users* of the machine. The way people view the machine and their responsibilities for its use affect the security of personal computers. People must think about the potential vulnerabilities inherent in processing text and data on a microcomputer. Most users do not often consider these kinds of security risks. Thus, although the controls for personal computers are less powerful, the vulnerabilities are more numerous. The following list describes some of the vulnerabilities in personal computer security.

- *Low awareness of the problem.* Former mainframe users are used to passing responsibility for computer security to the data processing department. To many new, inexperienced users, a personal computer is an office tool, analogous to a calculator or a typewriter. People who are unaware of or insensitive to the other vulnerabilities in use of personal computers are themselves a vulnerability.

- *No unique responsibility.* If a machine is shared by several users, no one acknowledges individual responsibility for maintenance, supervision, or control of the machine.

- *Few hardware controls.* Few personal computers take advantage of hardware features that simplify installation of security measures (such as a supervisor mode for sensitive instructions, hardware addressing limitation, or restricted access to I/O devices). Therefore, relatively unsophisticated attacks can overcome access control software or authentication techniques.

- *No audit trail.* If a problem arises, it is impossible to tell who has accessed a machine and when. Because unsophisticated attacks can defeat these machines, it is not possible even to determine what access occurred when trying to recover from an attack.

- *Environmental attacks.* Smoke particles, food crumbs, beverages, power surges, and static electricity can all cause failures of personal computers. These factors are well-controlled in major computer rooms but not with desktop personal computers.

- *Physical access.* Often a machine is left unattended and running in an office. The entire file structure is accessible to anyone who touches the keyboard.

- *Care of media, components.* Diskettes, containing the only copies of valuable software or data, are not consistently stored in a safe, appropriate environment.

- *No backups.* Even experienced computer users are often remiss in making backup copies of important files. New users may not even appreciate the need for periodic full and partial backups.

- *Questionable documentation.* Some software and hardware comes with complete, readable instructions for use, but some documentation is dreadful or (sometimes mercifully) nonexistent. Poor documentation leads to mistakes in use, which can be catastrophic.

- *Amateur quality software.* Personal computer software is sometimes produced by amateurs, who may not practice the same rigorous development or testing as do professional software writers for mainframe computers. Similarly, users may be unaware of possible vulnerabilities in the use of untested or untrustworthy software.

- *High portability.* A personal computer and its components, such as memory, are highly vulnerable to theft because of the same portability characteristics that make it desirable.

- *Magnetic retention.* Typed or handwritten scratch copies are usually thrown away; computer scratch copy (or initial draft) media are often reused, sometimes for other files, and sometimes by other users. On many systems, the ERASE or DELETE command merely removes a file pointer; it does not erase or overwrite the file itself. This file can be retrieved by simple techniques, and it can be accessed by other users intentionally or through a user or system error.

- *Combination of duties.* In a classic principle in financial auditing, no one person has full responsibility for performing a complete transaction. By contrast, most personal computer applications are designed for one user to perform all steps. Lack of checks and balances raises the possibility of malicious wrongdoing.

This list is long, but not complete; many other personal computer vulnerabilities can be identified. It may seem as if there is little that can be done to provide effective security. Fortunately, that is not the case: techniques affording some security for personal computers are not difficult to identify.

Security Measures

Although the list of vulnerabilities is long and varied, the issues involved fall into three major classes: improper procedures for use, hardware concerns, and software concerns. In each area some controls are reasonably effective. Combinations of controls of two or more types can be especially effective. We consider what can be done in terms of these three classes.

Issues Addressed by Procedures for Use

Some of the vulnerabilities identified here can be controlled by administrative procedures. Sensible policies for the use of machines can reduce the risk associated with unattended machines, care of media, backups, the environment, magnetic residue, and separation of duties. Users who understand the vulnerabilities of their machines will appreciate and comply with sensible procedures for their use.

Several procedures can improve the security of use of personal computers.

- *Do not leave personal computers unattended in an exposed environment if they contain sensitive information or are running sensitive computations.* Ease-of-use considerations for software have made it simple for unskilled users to learn how to use new packages. Similarly, many packages employ a similar user interface to reduce learning time, and some companies have adopted one standard data base manager or one standard spreadsheet package, for example. These factors, which make it simple for users to learn new applications, also make it simple for unauthorized users to access sensitive data on unattended machines.

- *Do not leave printers unattended if they are printing sensitive output.* This restriction is especially important if one printer is shared by two or more computers, or if the printer is located in a public place.

- *Secure media as carefully as you would the equivalent confidential reports.* Diskettes containing sensitive information should be locked up. Machines with hard disks containing sensitive information should be locked up. Turn off a personal computer after using it to clear volatile memory. Label each disk, showing its contents and its sensitivity. Remember that data persists even after being erased. Overwrite spare disks at least three times, once with 0s, once with 1s, and once with a mixture of 0s and 1s, before releasing them for others to use. When a personal computer must be sent out for repair, understand that fixed disk systems may retain data; if the data on a disk is especially sensitive, either remove the disk or have the machine repaired by a trusted repair facility. If necessary, copy the contents of the hard disk to another medium and then destroy the entire disk.

- *Perform periodic backups.* Depending on the criticality of the application, daily backups of changed files from a hard disk to a diskette or another device may be in order. In some cases, it may be better to back up a file every time it has been substantially changed. Also, make periodic (such as weekly or monthly) backups of all files so that a full system can be replaced in the event of a failure or so that backup copies are available of even supposedly insignificant files. Retain a full backup set, including system disks and software, in a building separate from the machine. This backup set will permit resumption of work on a new machine in case of fire, theft, or other catastrophe.

- *Practice separation of authority.* Design sensitive procedures so that no person alone has authority to affect sensitive data. For example, design accounting systems so that data is maintained on two systems by two people and so that total figures must balance between the two systems. In this way, fraud requires the cooperation of two people.

Issues Addressed by Hardware Controls

As noted earlier, hardware controls are not as useful for personal computers as for mainframes. Although personal computers have no privileged mode of execution or hardware memory protection, some controls depend on hardware.

- *Secure the equipment.* Portability is a special advantage of personal computers, but that portability is also a vulnerability. Simple as it sounds, bolting the computer to a desk or securing it with an adhesive or mechanical lock provides good security against theft. A computer can be unlocked to be moved and then resecured at its new location.

- *Consider using add-on security boards.* Different vendors have developed access control packages to run in the limited personal computer environment. Some of these packages offer only software controls, which are easily defeated or circumvented.

Some more sophisticated packages combine hardware (usually an added board) with software. The board receives control every time the machine is initialized (booted), and it limits access to certain operating system commands, including file I/O, file directory maintenance (ERASE, DELETE, COPY, FORMAT), and any other desired commands. Although these solutions, too, can be circumvented, they do provide security against casual attack and untrusted software.

Issues Addressed by Software Controls

Common software vulnerabilities include the lack of audit trail, the use of software from untrusted sources, poor documentation, and the lack of operating system controls, such as reuse of file space or access control. As already noted, personal computers cannot provide true access control, including limited access by subjects to objects, proper auditing of accesses, and secure identification and authentication of users.

Other than access control, protection against software vulnerabilities can include the following controls:

- *Use all software with full understanding of its potential threats.* Communications software can leak information that it transmits, programs can compute incorrect answers, and any software can damage or destroy files or other programs to which it has access.

- *Don't use software from dubious sources.* Software from large, reliable manufacturers and distributors is less likely to exhibit problems than software from small, unknown companies, user groups, or public access to bulletin boards.

- *Be suspicious of all results.* Increasingly, applications are being developed by nonprogrammers. These developers know little about software engineering practices such as design methods, data validation, and thorough testing. Data produced by such programs may not be correct and may even corrupt correct data from other sources.

- *Maintain periodic complete backups of all system resources.* In the event of an incident due to faulty software, the only way to recover may be to reinstall the entire system from backup copies. With program flaws such as worms, it may be necessary to rebuild the system from a very old version because later versions may have been infected.

Protection for Files

In Chapter 6 we studied a general approach to file access control. That approach involved access control lists, an access control matrix, capabilities, and other techniques. Although very effective, these techniques are most appropriate for multiuser operating systems in situations where high security is important. In this chapter we study the general problem of protection of personal computer files, which may contain either data or programs. In our discussion the whole file is the unit to be secured: a user either has access to the entire file or no access at all.

Essentially there are four types of protection applicable to personal computer files.

- *Access control features,* provided either as a part of the operating system or as auxiliary packages
- *Encryption* applied by the individual user
- *Copy protection* to limit someone's ability to copy a file

- *No protection,* which is really the case of having controlled the environment so that protection is not necessary

Access Control Mechanisms for Personal Computers

Most personal computer operating systems do not provide access controls to limit the access of people to files; where these controls are available, people do not always use them. This negligence results from the environment and the ease of use of a personal computer.

Large-capacity disk drives, powerful operating systems, and networks are creating situations in which several users can productively share the use of one personal computer. Even with only one user per machine, there are good reasons for access control mechanisms. Some of the motivations for access controls for personal computer files are listed here.

- *Outside interference.* Even single-user systems are vulnerable to access by outsiders, such as coworkers, service and maintenance personnel, visitors, and others who could affect the contents of a file.
- *Two users, one machine.* It is not uncommon for two coworkers to share a single machine. Although it may be reasonable to assume no malicious intent, one user can inadvertently destroy data or programs belonging to the other.
- *Network access.* Even in a trustworthy office environment, as personal computers are networked, the number of users grows, and the ability to trust all users of a network declines. Furthermore, shared devices require some form of access control mechanism to ensure equitable sharing.
- *Errors.* Access protection can limit the effect of errors by restricting the files that are accessible (that is, can be damaged) when certain applications are running.
- *Untrusted software.* Personal computer software often does not have nearly the rigor of development or testing before release as does that for mainframe computers. Therefore, until a software package is known to be safe, it is prudent to run it in an environment where it can do only minimal damage.
- *Separation of applications.* Access control mechanisms can facilitate logical separation of files by contents. Besides the protection advantages of this separation, it may be easier to keep track of files organized by category.

Features of Personal Computer Access Control Systems

Several companies have developed access control systems using a variety of hardware and software techniques. The packages all provide three basic features: user authentication, usually through password checking; file access limitation, such as read-only, execute-only, read–write, or no access; and an audit log, a report showing who has accessed which files and when.

Additional features provided on individual systems include these:

- *Transparent encryption.* The access mechanism can be useless if a user obtains access to the operating system, through programming, through an off-line backup copy of important files, by exiting from a running program (for example, by pressing control-C or control-alt-delete), or from a flaw in the security system. Some systems automatically encrypt files so that even if they become accessible, their contents will not be evident.

- *Time of day checking.* The security administrator can set up permissions for users allowing access only during certain times (for example, between 7:00 a.m. and 6:00 p.m.) and only on certain days of the week (for example, Monday through Friday). This control ensures that employees or intruders cannot sneak into an office when the office is closed to try to defeat the system or to obtain furtive access.

- *Automatic timeout.* With this control activated, the system terminates the session of a user who fails to strike any keyboard key during a specified period (for example, 15 minutes). The system blanks the screen and requires a new user authentication to restart. If a user leaves a personal computer unattended, this control reduces the threat of an interceptor who walks past and finds an unoccupied but active machine.

- *Machine identification.* One system uses an added hardware device that responds with a unique serial number that can be read by application software. Each hardware device thus identifies a unique machine. In this way a program can query the device to be sure that it is running on a particular authorized machine as a form of authentication.

Access control systems usually use a combination of hardware and software to achieve their results. The hardware is often a board that plugs into the personal computer; this board is activated each time the machine is powered up or rebooted, thereby ensuring that the security mechanism is in force any time the machine is used. The board contains memory, often a clock with which to maintain the correct time and date, and space for the program that enforces security. The code can be permanently installed at the factory on a read-only memory, or it can be loaded from a disk when the board is first installed.

User-Invoked Encryption

Encryption is a form of access control mechanism: only users who know how to decrypt can obtain access to the plaintext of encrypted data. Any user can perform encryption; no complicated or expensive mechanism is required. Users of word processing systems and personal computers would be wise to perform their own encryption. The techniques from Chapter 2 in this book can provide protection against casual observers, and the algorithms of Chapter 3 are adequate for very sensitive information.

Several of the access control systems listed earlier provide automatic file encryption (not under user control). Others provide file encryption as an option, using a hardware implementation of the DES or a proprietary encryption algorithm.

Summary of Personal Computer Security

The demands of personal computer security are the same as those for other modes of computers; the difference is in the users' attitudes and the protection controls available. User attitude affects the understanding of and sensitivity to the problem and the willingness to spend money or use certain procedures in order to achieve some controls.

10.2   Unix Security Management

Unix systems are the most prevalent multiuser systems, and they are also the most prevalent hosts on the Internet. Thus, it makes sense to consider issues in proper management and administration of Unix systems.

Unix systems are counterintuitive and mystical. Their terse commands (*grep* for Generalized Regular Expression Processor or *su* for change identity) and terse syntax deter the uninitiated and lead to errors. Some configuration files are positive lists of actions that will be taken; others are negative lists of subjects barred from actions. With this background, any Unix administrator can easily be forgiven for making an error in setting up a system or failing to notice an added character whose effect can be disastrous. Much to the detriment of security, Unix seems here to stay.

In the following sections we will see a few features that should be considered in the administration of any Unix system. This section presents some highlights, although it is not intended to be a complete guide on the care and administration of Unix systems. For more comprehensive explanations of security for Unix systems, consult [GAR96].

The three most significant steps a Unix administrator can take are

- keep the installation current
- manage accounts properly
- keep user authentication strong

We describe each of these three steps.

Current Software

Unix is under constant change. In some cases, the change is to add new features; other times it is to fix flaws in previous distributions.

The Morris Internet worm exploited Unix flaws that were well-known, for which there were well-known fixes, and that were fixed in distributions from the vendors. Unfortunately, many sites had not gotten around to installing the new versions they had received much earlier. For the busy administrator who is always fighting today's fire, the adage "If it ain't broke, don't fix it" applies well: why risk causing a problem for users with a new release as long as the old release works well (or well enough)?

As security flaws are uncovered, the Computer Emergency Response Team (CERT, which is described later in this chapter) does an excellent job of coordinating announcement of the flaw, publishing any corrective or offsetting action a site can take, and distributing new software that will address the problem. But the CERT can only reach the administrator's mailbox (postal or electronic); it is up to the administrator to fix what others report is broken.

Accounts

A second problem in administering any system is keeping accounts current. A user will always press for a new account to be set up, so there is no problem knowing when accounts need to be added. However, often the administrator does not know when to *delete* an account.

Unused Accounts

Accounts that have not been used for some time may belong to someone who is away on leave for an extended period of time, or they may correspond to users who have moved from one host to another but still possess an account on the old host. Some attackers look for infrequently-used accounts to invade, figuring that any files the attackers store there will escape user notice.

Dormant accounts should be terminated after inactivity. The files can be retained in a different but retrievable portion of the file structure.

Terminated Accounts

Users who leave an organization are a more serious problem. A user who has been suspended or made redundant may hold a grudge against the organization. Arrangements should be made to deliver to the user all code and data to which the user is entitled, but the user's account access should be terminated as soon as the user is notified of the termination. The personnel or human relations office should notify the system administrator when an employee is terminated.

Obviously, a user with privileged access, especially a system administrator, should be blocked from access on all machines. This may require changing system administration passwords.

Guest Accounts

Some systems arrive with guest or demo accounts; in other cases these are installed to allow outsiders to store or fetch files easily.

General unrestricted accounts with trivial passwords should be removed. Accounts for outside users should be created for specific individuals as required and closed when the individuals no longer require access.

Anonymous Accounts

Anonymous accounts are often used to allow outsiders to access, usually to retrieve specific public files. These should be established very cautiously. It may be best to dedicate a machine to such public information, to place only public information on the machine, and not to connect it to any other machines with more sensitive information.

Privileges

Unix recognizes user privileges. However, different parts of the operating system and utilities were developed by different people in a trusting environment of shared information. It was easiest to allow utilities and the operating system to run with significant privilege.

A more prudent approach is to limit programs to accessing just the resources they need. As we learned in Chapter 7, there is a strong security advantage to running programs with the least degree of privilege they require.

The Unix password file contains many things unrelated to user authentication. In Chapter 6 we studied the advantage of splitting the password file into a public part (users' names and other administrative data) and a more protected part (the encrypted passwords). Many programs need access to the public part, but only a few programs, those dealing with authentication and password management, require access to the encrypted password file. To further strengthen security, the authentication routine requires privilege only to access the password file, not to access other sensitive files. Thus, giving the authentication routine general read access is excessive. A better solution is to create a group that has access to the encrypted password file and to change group membership for the authentication routine to that group. In this way, an intruder who overtakes the authentication routine can access only the password file, not every sensitive file.

Audit

Administrators should use the audit facilities provided in the Unix system and develop tools of their own for automating the audit analysis. Administrators should be in the habit of reviewing a snapshot of the system's status—user names, login times, lengths of sessions, processes run—randomly throughout the day. Although this is not guaranteed to catch an attack, often an administrator will develop a sense for things that feel wrong. Similarly, the administrator should scan the audit logs for anomalies, and should use automated tools to highlight inconsistencies.

Audit logs should be sent to separate machines or written immediately to a printer (not to a file). One of the first things an attacker does is to try to disable auditing, so as to hide the traces of the attack. Attackers often delete the audit log. If it is on a separate machine or already printed, the last few entries show valuable information about what happened just before auditing was disabled or some other suspicious event occurred.

Passwords

Despite well-publicized studies of poor password choice ([MOR79], [GRA84a], [KLE90], and [FAR90]) and incidents such as the Internet worm, which succeeded in part due to poor password management, password security in Unix systems continues to be weak. The issues were introduced in Chapter 6.

Many users do not choose good passwords. As Grampp and Morris [GRA84a] observe, "left to their own ways, some people will still choose cute doggie names as passwords." There is little an administrator can do except

- educate users about proper password choice
- explain the importance of passwords as the primary means of user—and ultimately system—protection
- periodically scan the encrypted password file for encrypted versions of common words and variations of the user's name

The CRACK program, described in the next section, can help to scan for weak passwords.

10.3 Network Security Management

In this section we consider management of security in networks, with special emphasis on the Internet. We have already studied the exposures and controls available, so this section focuses on more of the *how* and less of the *what* of securing networks. This section is not intended to provide detailed guidance on proper management of networks and network sites; much more detailed references for that topic are [HOL91] and [GAR96].

Wide Area Networks and the Internet

Securing wide area networks is complicated by reasons of distance and size. Now there is a need for seemingly every host and every LAN to be connected to the Internet. Distance and size considerations explode in that arena, and considerations of ownership and responsibility also add to the difficulty. Let's explore these issues one at a time.

Distance and Size

Distance and size are not problems per se: it is perfectly possible to implement a secure network that has nodes on several continents and that has several thousand nodes. The proof of this security is by example: many military organizations have very large networks that are quite secure, and large multinational corporations, such as telecommunications service providers and manufacturing companies, have similarly secure networks.

However, distance and size can affect security if the network is not administered in a clear and consistent manner. If a change must be made to the network configuration for security reasons, the same change must be made promptly at all affected sites. Similarly, each site must implement its own version of a common master organization, so that all pieces of the network support each other cooperatively.

Insiders and Outsiders

The term **protected perimeter** is often used to describe a virtual "fence" that separates outsiders from inside resources. Presumably all harm arises from outside the fence. This conceptual model fails for at least two reasons. First, as the number of discrete hosts and the separation between them rise, it becomes harder to determine what is "inside" the fence: if the research group of a company has a strong relationship with a local university, the group may perceive its sphere of trust as including some parts of the university, or if a subsidiary in one country engages in collaborative work with a competitor, it is easy to think that a few colleagues (who happen to work for the competitor) deserve to share access to corporate resources. Before long, the virtual protection perimeter for the whole company includes the company units, all business partners, most universities, every possible competitor, several agencies of several governments, and so forth.

The second reason the model of perimeter protection fails is that not all harm arises from outside: the risk from a malicious or careless insider also becomes significant. Twenty people working in close proximity get to know and trust each other, and none of them would do something as antisocial as to harm a colleague; twenty thousand people cannot build such a level of trust.

For both of these reasons, **need-to-know** protection becomes significant in large organizations. There is no reason why everybody in the Brazilian arm of the company needs to know about customers and activities by the group in Finland. Enforcement of need-to-know can reduce the risk that rises naturally as size and distance increase.

Ownership and Responsibility

The Internet differs from even enormous organizational networks in one significant way: it is not "owned" or "managed" or "controlled" by any single authority. This situation results from the way the Internet developed. Originally the Internet (known first as the Arpanet because of its support from ARPA, the Defense Department research agency in the United States) was a vehicle for collaborative work. Qualities of the Arpa/Internet were and remain openness, experimentation, and flexibility. The positive side of this spirit was that tremendous advances in network technology were achieved in very short time.

On the negative side, the Internet is a loose federation, not a monarchy, democracy, republic, or dictatorship. Because the formalities of joining the Internet or expanding or changing one's configuration are almost nonexistent, it is essentially impossible to block access by anyone.

Security throughout the Internet is uneven. Some sites practice very solid security and depend on the strength of their installation and of their Internet connection for everyday business. Other sites are simply service providers that sell access to anyone who will pay. One must expect the lowest degree of security and the worst degree of potential harm from remote sites.

Consequently, each host connected to the Internet is separately at risk. Each host's administrator must defend against all possible outside attacks.

Network Architecture

As stated earlier, each host and each connected network is responsible for its own protection. Even that is difficult because of size, distance, and other sources of complexity.

Structure

In order to defend against the outside, the network administrator must clearly understand what is being protected against what for whom. Trivial though this sounds, some administrators do not know specifically what resources they control or how they are organized. Some administrators do not know which hosts are on their network, which physical machines correspond with which network addresses, and which machines are visible to the outside.

The administrator often is not to blame. Some administrators inherited a topology from a previous administrator. Others work in a dynamic setting in which people can add, remove, or reconfigure equipment without informing the administrator. Organizations seem to continually reorganize, leading to physical shuffling of equipment and restructuring of networks. Finally, the low price of equipment and the tendency toward easy-to-use (and easy to reconfigure) software makes it very difficult for even the best administrator to maintain a current view of the configuration. Each network administrator should have a complete, up-to-date map of all network resources.

Connectivity

Hard though it can be to track physical machines, it can be even harder to track how those machines are connected, both inside and outside the network. Outside connections are, of course, the major concern. An attack is seldom one single event, but a series built on several weaknesses. For this reason, it is important to attend to the security of all reachable machines. An ignored, poorly administered machine in a corner that is reachable from the outside can serve as a platform from which an outsider can attack other machines, either at the local site or elsewhere in the network.

A map of physical connections is essential. So is a trace showing which machines can pass processes to which other machines (to be able to trace the ultimate flow of outsiders' or insiders' capabilities).

Permissions

Once all machines and all connections are known, the next step in developing a secure environment is to check permissions between connected machines. For convenience, users on connected machines want to be able to run processes and access data on all machines to which they have access. The easiest way for users to move back and forth is to have a reciprocal account on each machine. System files such as *hosts.equiv*, *.rhosts*, and *.rsh* are designed to support seamless connectivity between machines. However, the administrator must continually monitor the permissions in these files to be sure that only necessary connections are permitted. Even if they initially were set properly, an unwitting user or malicious outsider may have changed the settings in these files.

Backups

Backups of data and applications are necessary so that they can be recovered in case of an emergency, but a system administrator should also maintain backups of all system configuration files. Preferably, these backups should be on separate media stored off line. In this way, if a system becomes damaged, the administrator can know that the off-line backup copy has not been damaged. Thus, the administrator can safely restore the system from that copy without having to rebuild or rethink the appropriate settings.

Host Security

Securing a network requires securing the connections and securing each connected host. As noted previously, even an unused, ignored machine in a corner can become a platform from which an attack can be launched.

Software Versions

Software is constantly evolving. In some cases, the evolution brings new features or functionality; in other cases it updates software to handle new situations, such as new devices. In yet other cases, a new release of software brings repairs to discovered flaws.

The Internet worm incident, described in Chapter 5, succeeded in part because many sites used old versions of the *finger* program. Despite the publicity from that incident, some installations still use outdated, and flawed, versions.

As new software versions are released, the prudent administrator tests them in isolation and then sees that they are installed on all hosts.

Accounts

No networked host should provide an easy home for an intruder. No administrator would post a sign saying "account for intruders here," yet poorly protected accounts convey just such a message.

Some systems are shipped by the manufacturer with a demo, guest, or startup account to let the new owner begin to use the system quickly and easily. These accounts either have no password or a trivial one, such as *guest* or *test*. It is intended that these accounts will be removed, yet many administrators do not know or forget to. Some systems arrive with a maintenance account for remote diagnosis and service.

Once a system is ready to become operational, and especially when it is about to be connected to an accessible network, every account should be necessary and every account should be protected by a strong password.

Incidents

In spite of the best administration of the system, sometimes incidents occur. Dealing with the incident can be as important as all other security measures. The worst time to think about handling an incident is in the middle of the incident. It is far better to plan in advance how you will handle the incident.

Each system administrator should develop an incident handling plan. The plan should have the following features:

- Users should know what is *suspicious behavior* and to whom to report it.
- The administrator should have an ordered list of *management to contact* in the event of an emergency, to inform them and to obtain support for actions to handle the situation.
- Management should have decided on the *course of action* for an attack: close down operations, disconnect from networks, monitor the situation in an attempt to determine who is the attacker, attempt to scare off the attacker, and so forth. If the course of action is not decided in advance (because, for example, the action might depend on the circumstances of the attack), a process should be established for deciding rapidly what to do.
- A *means to notify all affected users* should be planned. For example, if the action to be taken is to shut down operations, the network cannot be used to inform users of the situation or of changes in status.

Additionally, each system administrator should maintain the tools, programs, and data necessary to rebuild the system safely. Periodic backups should be made and saved. As suggested previously, the administrator should have a copy of configuration files on a separate medium so that a system known to be clean can be built from that configuration. Similarly, known copies of the operating system and application programs should be reserved in a safe place.

CERT: Computer Emergency Response Team

In addition to the direct damage, the Internet worm incident showed the network community that there was no central source of information or coordination for security incidents involving Internet hosts. To provide such a focal point, the U.S. Department of Defense established the Computer Emergency Response Team (CERT) at the Software Engineering Institute at Carnegie–Mellon University. The CERT monitors reports of incidents and security flaws, helps manufacturers develop fixes to security problems, and issues notices of problems and solutions.

Incident handling is ticklish: if a flaw is uncovered at one site, and if the same flaw could be exploited at other sites with similar systems, publicizing the flaw would alert sites to protect themselves. If no protection is known, publicizing the flaw advises attackers of possible means of attack. At the same time, the publicity advises attackers of vulnerabilities against which some sites may not have defended themselves yet.

The CERT is very effective at helping sites learn about and control vulnerabilities, while not providing too much help to attackers. The CERT can be contacted at cert@cert.org or via telephone at +1 (412) 268-7090.

Tools

Attackers have developed sophisticated tools to check an exposed host for weaknesses, such as accounts with no passwords, accounts with trivial passwords, permissions settings that would allow an intruder to overwrite important configuration files, and the like. An attacker will use these tools on any accessible host to determine whether an attack could be furthered from that host. If the attackers can develop such tools, so also can system administrators. There are several tools to help the network administrator. Most of these tools are available as part of the Purdue University Computer Operations, Audit, and Security Technology (COAST) project via FTP from coast.cs.purdue.edu/pub/tools.

CRACK is a collection of password-checking tools. It uses common word lists to identify accounts that have passwords that could be determined easily. It works on Unix systems that store passwords in standard Unix encrypted form.

Tripwire is a tool to use after a suspected penetration. In a large system, many files may be changed in a short period of time. However, some files, such as binary versions of operating system files and configuration files, should not be changed. Tripwire is a file integrity checker that compares the active versions of files against a backup to determine which files have been changed. Tripwire can report on the effect of a penetration. After an administrator has supposedly restored the system and the system has run for a while, it is also useful to run Tripwire again to determine whether a persistent program left by the attacker is capable of modifying the system to allow a repeat attack. Tripwire is a product of the COAST project.

COPS, written by Farmer [FAR90], is a set of programs that check important system files, user configurations, and permissions settings to list potential security flaws or weaknesses that could contribute to undesirable events. COPS is used by system administrators for testing systems inside their networks.

Finally, SATAN (Security Administrator Tool for Analyzing Networks) is a collection of network analysis tools. Unlike COPS, SATAN works from *outside* a network's perimeter to check for externally visible flaws. The SATAN tool is controversial, because if a network administrator can use it, so can any attacker. Its authors point out that SATAN simply collects information that is available to everyone with access to the network from the outside. With proper perimeter security, the network should provide only limited information and nothing that is security sensitive.

A Final Word

In summary, the administrator of a network should be clairvoyant, to predict what changes will occur, omniscient, to know what changes users have caused without saying anything, and ubiquitous, to be able to attend to all problems at the same time. It helps to be able to leap tall buildings at a single bound, too. Few network administrators fit these requirements, although most do an excellent job with what they have. Probably the strongest support an administrator can have is complete backing from management to do the unpopular things that are needed and to set priorities that are necessary. In the next section we begin to study the management side of administering the security of installations.

We consider two aspects of managing computed security: analyzing risks and developing a security plan. This section is appropriate both for computing professionals and managers who oversee the use of computers.

10.4   Risk Analysis

Security planning begins with **risk analysis**. Risk analysis is a process to determine the exposures and their potential harm. First, all exposures of a computing system are listed. Then, for each exposure, possible controls and their costs are listed. The last step of the analysis is a cost–benefit analysis: does it cost less to implement a control or to accept the expected cost of the loss? This chapter contains a description of the risk analysis method and its strengths and weaknesses.

Risk analysis leads to a security plan, which identifies responsibility for certain actions to improve security. The last half of this chapter describes how a security plan is written and what it should contain.

A **risk analysis**, as its name implies, is a study of the risks of doing something. Buying a lottery ticket is a form of risk, although most people think of it as a minor loss with a (very small) chance of large gain. Crossing streets, driving race cars, and eating oysters all involve some degree of risk. Each person considers the risk and chooses whether or not to do a particular thing.

Some risks are simply part of the cost of doing business: risks that must be taken as a part of normal operation. For example, there is a risk that a new technology will make gasoline-powered automobiles instantly obsolete. Every gas station owner accepts this risk. Similarly, every computer user accepts the risk that a storage device will fail, losing all the user's data.

Controls can reduce the seriousness of a threat. For example, a computer user can perform an independent backup of files as a defense against the possible failure of a file storage device. Large companies involved in extensive computing at many sites cannot easily determine the risks and controls of their computing installations. For this reason an organized approach to analyzing risks is necessary.

Reasons to Perform a Risk Analysis

Some of the benefits of careful risk analysis are listed below.

- *Improve awareness.* Discussing issues of security can raise the general level of interest and concern among employees.
- *Identify assets, vulnerabilities, and controls.* Some companies are unaware of their computing assets and the vulnerabilities associated with those assets. A systematic analysis produces a comprehensive list of assets and risks.
- *Improve basis for decisions.* Controls reduce productivity through increased overhead and inconvenience to users. Some controls cannot be justified from the perspective of protection they provide. Also, some risks are so serious that they warrant a continuing search for more effective controls. In both of these situations, the seriousness of the risk affects the desirability of controls.
- *Justify expenditures for security.* Some security mechanisms are very expensive without an obvious benefit. A risk analysis can help to identify instances that are worth the expense of a major security mechanism. It is often useful to identify the much larger risks from *not* spending for security.

Steps of a Risk Analysis

Risk analysis is an orderly process adapted from practices in management. Following are the steps to analyzing the security risks in a computing system. Examples are shown of the kinds of questions asked during a risk analysis. Because any computing system is complex and distinctive, these points must be modified and expanded in an actual risk analysis.

The basic steps of risk analysis are listed below.

1. Identify assets.
2. Determine vulnerabilities.
3. Estimate likelihood of exploitation.
4. Compute expected annual loss.
5. Survey applicable controls and their costs.
6. Project annual savings of control.

These steps are described in the following sections.

Identify Assets

The first step of a risk analysis is to identify the assets of the computing system. The assets can be collected into categories, as listed below. The first three categories are the assets identified in Chapter 1 and described throughout this book. The remaining items are not strictly a part of a computing system, but are important to its proper functioning.

- *Hardware:* central processors, boards, keyboards, monitors, terminals, microcomputers, workstations, tape drives, printers, disk drives, cables, connections, communications controllers, and communications media
- *Software:* source programs, object programs, purchased programs, in-house programs, utility programs, operating systems, systems programs (such as compilers), and maintenance diagnostic programs
- *Data:* data used during execution, stored data on magnetic media, printed data, archival data, update logs, and audit records
- *People:* needed to run the computing system or specific programs
- *Documentation:* on programs, hardware, systems, administrative procedures, and the entire system
- *Supplies:* paper, forms, laser cartridges, magnetic media, and printer fluid

A risk analysis starts with a list of all of the specific assets of a computing system. In a certain sense, this is an inventory of the system. Although in some computing systems, the inventory of hardware items may be done as an annual accounting exercise, at other places these inventories may be out of date. Furthermore, the annual inventory seldom includes intangibles such as data or human resources.

Identify Vulnerabilities of Assets

Listing the assets of a computing system is relatively easy, because many assets are tangible or easily identified. The next step of risk analysis is to determine the vulnerabilities of those assets. This step requires imagination in order to predict what damage might occur to the assets and from what sources.

The three basic goals of computer security are ensuring secrecy, integrity, and availability. A vulnerability is any situation that could cause loss of one of those three qualities. Possible vulnerabilities can be identified by considering situations that could cause loss of secrecy for a particular object, then loss of integrity, and then loss of availability.

Table 10-1   Assets and Security Properties

Asset	Secrecy	Integrity	Availability
Hardware			
Software			
Data			
People			
Documentation			
Supplies			

A table, as shown in Table 10-1, can be used to organize the consideration of threats and assets. One vulnerability can affect more than one asset or cause more than one type of loss. The table is a guide to stimulate thinking, but its format is not rigid.

Questions to consider include

- What are the effects of unintentional errors? Consider typing the wrong command, typing the wrong data, mounting the wrong data pack, discarding the wrong listing, and disposing of output insecurely.
- What are the effects of willfully malicious insiders? Consider disgruntled employees, bribery, and curious browsers.
- What are the effects of outsiders? Consider network access, dial-in access, hackers, people walking through the building, and people sifting through the trash.
- What are the effects of natural and physical disasters? Consider fires, storms, floods, power outages, and component failures.

Table 10-2 is a version of the previous table with some of the entries filled in. It shows certain general problems that can affect the assets of a computing system. In a given installation it is necessary to determine what can happen to specific hardware, software, data items, and other assets.

Predict Likelihood of Occurrence

Step 3 of a risk analysis is determining how often each exposure will be exploited. Likelihood of occurrence relates to the stringency of the existing controls and the likelihood that someone or something will evade the existing controls. It may be impossible to predict the likelihood of occurrence of some events. However, there are ways by which the likelihood of an event can be estimated.

- Probability, from observed data of the general population. It is impossible to determine when a fire will strike a particular house. Insurance companies have collected massive amounts of data from which they can predict that in a year, fires will strike n houses, with an average loss of x. Similar data are available on other natural disasters. Insurance companies also have data from which they can rate the likelihood of employee fraud, armed robbery, and so on. Manufacturers have data on the expected lifetimes of machinery. Professional organizations can also provide some guidance concerning the likelihood of occurrence of other events, such as human errors of different sorts.

Table 10-2   Assets and Attacks

Asset	Secrecy	Integrity	Availability
Hardware		Overloaded Destroyed Tampered with	Failed Stolen Destroyed Unavailable
Software	Stolen Copied Pirated	Trojan horse Modified Tampered with	Deleted Misplaced Usage expired
Data	Disclosed Accessed by outsider Inferred	Damaged • Software error • Hardware error • User error	Deleted Misplaced Destroyed
People			Quit Retired Terminated On vacation
Documentation			Lost Stolen Destroyed
Supplies			Lost Stolen Damaged

- Probability, from observed data for a specific system. Local failure rates are fairly easy to record. Operating systems can track data on hardware failures, failed login attempts, numbers of accesses, and sizes of data files.

- Estimate of number of occurrences in a given time period. The analyst is asked to approximate the number of times a described event has occurred in the last year, for example. Although the count is not exact, because the analyst will probably not have full information, the analyst may be able to select some reasonable estimates.

- Estimate of likelihood from a table. Several different risk analysis methodologies ask the analyst to estimate the likelihood of occurrence of an event, choosing one of the ranges in Table 10-3. Completing this analysis depends on the professional expertise of the rater. Instead of picking a number with no basis, however, the rater has a framework within which to consider each likelihood.

- The **Delphi approach**. This is a technique in which several raters individually estimate the probable likelihood of an event. The estimates are collected, reproduced, and distributed to all raters. All raters are then asked whether they wish to modify their ratings in light of values their colleagues have supplied. After a round of revisions, all values are collected. If the values are reasonably consistent, the final value is inferred. If the values are inconsistent, the raters meet to discuss the reason for the inconsistency and to select a final value.

Table 10-3   Ratings of Likelihood

Frequency	Rating
More than once a day	10
Once a day	9
Once every three days	8
Once a week	7
Once in two weeks	6
Once a month	5
Once every four months	4
Once a year	3
Once every three years	2
Less than once in three years	1

Compute Uncovered Cost per Year (Annual Loss Expectancy)

Determining the expected cost of each incident is the next step of performing a risk analysis. Like likelihood of occurrence, this value is difficult to determine. Some costs, such as the cost to replace a hardware item, are simple to obtain. Even the cost to replace a piece of software can be approximated reasonably well from the initial cost to acquire it (design it, write it, or buy it). However, the cost to others of not having a piece of hardware or software, or the cost of release of a piece of data, is substantially harder to measure.

Some data needs to be protected for legal reasons. Personal data, such as police records, tax information, census data, and medical information, is so sensitive that there are criminal penalties for releasing the data to unauthorized people. Other data is company confidential. Data on a new product, sales results, or certain financial information might give a competitor an advantage. Some financial data, especially adverse data, could seriously affect public confidence in a bank, an insurance company, or a stock broker. It is difficult to determine the cost of release of this data.

If a computing system, a piece of software, or a key person is unavailable, causing a particular computing task to be delayed, there are serious consequences. If a program that prints paychecks is delayed, employees' confidence in the company may be shaken, or some employees may face penalties from not being able to pay their own bills. If customers cannot make transactions because the computer is down, they may choose another company. For some time-critical services, such as life-support systems in a hospital or guidance systems for spacecraft with humans aboard, the costs of failure are infinitely high.

The following questions can lead to an analysis of the ramifications of a computer security failure. The answers to these questions will not produce precise cost figures, but they will help to identify the sources of tangible and intangible costs.

- What legal obligations are there to preserve confidentiality or integrity of this data?
- Could release of this data cause a person or an organization harm? Would there be the possibility of legal action?

- Could unauthorized access to this data cause the loss of future business opportunity? Might it give a competitor an unfair advantage? What would be the estimated loss in sales?
- What is the psychological effect of lack of computer service? Embarrassment? Loss of credibility? Loss of business? How many customers would be affected? What is their value as customers?
- What is the value of access to data or programs? Could this computation be deferred? Could this computation be performed elsewhere? How much would it cost to have a third party do the computing elsewhere?
- What is the value to someone else of access to data or programs? How much would a competitor be willing to pay for access?
- What problems would arise from loss of data? Could it be replaced? Could it be reconstructed? With what amount of work?

As just mentioned, these are not easy costs to evaluate. Nevertheless, they must be evaluated in order to perform a thorough analysis of the risks in computing. Furthermore, the vulnerabilities in computer security are often considerably higher than managers expect. Realistic estimates of potential harm can raise concern for computer security and identify places where attention is especially needed.

The cost of an incident is determined, using the guidelines stated. That cost is then multiplied by the expected number of such incidents per year, to produce an estimate of the yearly loss (called the annual loss expectancy, or ALE). For example, an event whose expected cost is $10,000 may have an expected frequency of 3 times per year, while another event whose cost is $1,000,000 may have an expected frequency of only once every 5 years (0.2 times per year). The expected annual loss from the first event is $30,000, while the expected annual loss from the second is $200,000.

Survey New Controls

These computations reflect the current situation: with the controls currently in effect, the expected loss is a particular amount. If that loss is unacceptably high, new controls must be investigated. For example, if the risk of unauthorized access is too high, access control hardware, software, and procedures can be evaluated.

One way to identify additional controls is on a per-exposure basis. For example, a risk of data loss could be covered by periodic backups, redundant data storage, access controls to prevent unauthorized deletion, physical security to keep someone from stealing a disk, or program development standards to limit the effect of programs on the data. The effectiveness of each of these controls is considered.

Another way to find additional controls is to review the material already covered in this book. We have described a number of types of controls, including

- cryptographic controls
- secure protocols
- program development controls
- program execution environment controls
- operating system protection features
- identification

- authentication
- secure operating system design and implementation
- data base access controls
- data base reliability controls
- data base inference controls
- multilevel security controls for data, data bases, and operating systems
- personal computer controls: procedural, physical, hardware, and software
- network access controls
- network integrity controls
- physical controls

To identify controls for a particular exposure, it may be helpful to think of all of these aspects of computer security and to select controls that cover the specific exposure.

Project Savings

Finally, it is possible to compute the true cost or savings from implementing a new control. The effective cost is the cost of the control minus any reduction in annual loss expectancy from using the control. Thus, the true cost can be negative if reduction in risk is greater than the cost of the control.

For example, suppose a department has had trouble with unauthorized access to (use of) the computing system. Although outsiders have succeeded only in gaining access to the system, it is feared that they might intercept or even modify sensitive data on the system. One approach is to install a more secure data access control program (software). Even though the cost of the access control program is high ($25,000), its cost is easily justified when compared to its value, as shown in Table 10-4. Because the entire cost of the package is charged in the first year, even greater benefits are expected for subsequent years.

In the next example, a company uses a common carrier to link to a network for certain computing applications. The company has identified risks of unauthorized access to data and computing facilities through the network. These risks can be eliminated by replacing network access by a machine operated on the company premises. The machine is not owned; a new one would have to be acquired. The economics of this example are not promising, as shown in Table 10-5.

Table 10-4   Justification of Access Control Software

Item	Amount
Risks: disclosure of company confidential data, computation based on incorrect data	
Cost to reconstruct correct data: $1,000,000 @ 10% likelihood per year	$100,000
Effectiveness of access control software: 60%	–$60,000
Cost of access control software	+$25,000
Expected annual costs due to loss and controls: $100,000 – $60,000 + $25,000	$65,000
Savings: $100,000 – $65,000	$35,000

Table 10-5   Cost–Benefit Analysis for Replacing Network Access

Item	Amount
Risk	
Access to unauthorized data and programs: $100,000 @ 2% likelihood per year	$2,000
Unauthorized use of computing facilities: $10,000 @ 40% likelihood per year	$4,000
Expected annual loss	$6,000
Effectiveness of network control: 100%	–$6,000
Control Cost	
Hardware ($50,000 amortized over 5 years)	+10,000
Software ($20,000 amortized over 5 years)	+4,000
Support personnel (each year)	+$40,000
Annual cost	$54,000
Expected annual loss: $6,000 – $6,000 + $54,000	$54,000
Savings: $6,000 – $54,000	–$48,000

As shown in these two examples, risk analysis can be used to evaluate the true costs of proposed controls. In this way, risk analysis can be used as a planning tool. The effectiveness of different controls can be compared on paper. Risk analysis can thus be used repeatedly, in order to select an optimum set of controls.

Arguments Against Risk Analysis

Risk analysis is a well-known planning tool used by auditors, accountants, and managers. Despite its common usage, there are arguments against its use.

Not Precise

The lack of precision of risk analysis is often cited as a deficiency. The values used in the method, the likelihood of occurrence, and the cost per occurrence are not precise. Several different techniques were suggested earlier for deriving reasonable approximations of these values.

The precision of the numbers is a red herring. Risk analysis is best used as a planning tool. One may not be able to differentiate between a loss that is expected once a year and one expected once in three years. Nevertheless, it is possible to distinguish that degree of risk from vulnerabilities expected to occur once every week. When risk analysis is used as a planning tool, it shows which security expenditures are likely to be most cost-effective. This basis is important for choosing between controls when money available for security is limited.

False Sense of Precision

Another argument is that providing numbers yields a false sense of precision or security. Again, the numbers themselves are much less important that their relative sizes. Whether an expected loss is $100,000 or $150,000 is relatively unimportant. It is much more significant that the expected loss is far above the $10,000–20,000 category. A large potential loss deserves analysis for some control. Placing too much importance on the numbers is the fault of the user, not the method.

Immutability

Risk analyses, like contingency plans and five-year plans, have a tendency to be filed and promptly forgotten. Ideally, the risk analysis should be updated annually. However, it is tempting to accept the figures of the previous year, rather than analyze and justify them annually.

An important step in the annual review is considering what conditions have changed over the past year. What has significantly changed the likelihood of occurrence or the severity of a threat? It is important not to be too dependent on the old plan, but to use each review as an opportunity to rethink and perhaps correct prior estimates based on recent experience. In this way, the values of the plan become more precise each time the analysis is done.

No Scientific Foundation

A final argument is that risk analysis does not depend on scientific theories and principles. This is not true. Risk analysis depends on principles of probability theory and statistical analysis.

Summary of Benefits of Risk Analysis

The discussion here is not intended to glorify risk analysis as a precise, all-purpose planning tool. The results of risk analysis are no more precise than the figures used in the analysis, which are often mere guesses. Still, there are several benefits of a risk analysis, as we outlined earlier. The list is repeated here for reference.

- improve awareness
- identify assets, vulnerabilities, and controls
- provide basis for decisions
- justify expenditures for security

A risk analysis forces a systematic study of the exposures in a computing system. As shown in the examples given, a justification of the amount required for security is an expected loss. Sometimes it is necessary to decide between two controls or, because of limited funds, to invest in controls for only one vulnerability. A high-quality risk assessment can provide the basis for making these decisions. A risk analysis done with computer support can also be an excellent planning tool, permitting the user to work through several what-if scenarios simulating the effects of instituting various controls. As such, it can allow the user to choose the most effective controls at the least cost. The discussion generated during risk analysis will improve general awareness of the need for security measures. A risk analysis is part of a general security plan, described in the next section.

10.5   Security Planning

A **security plan** is a document that describes how an organization will address its security needs. The plan is subject to periodic review and revision as the security needs of the organization change. In this section we study how to define and implement a security plan.

Three aspects of writing a security plan are described: what the plan should contain, who writes the plan, and how to acquire support for the plan.

Creating a Security Plan

A security plan identifies and organizes the security activities for a computing system. The plan is both a description of the current situation and a plan for change. Every security plan must address six issues:

- *policy,* indicating the goals of a computer security effort and the willingness to work to achieve those goals
- *current state,* describing the status of security at the time of the plan
- *recommendations and requirements,* which lead to meeting the security goals
- *accountability,* describing who is responsible for each security activity
- *timetable,* identifying when different security functions are to be done
- *continuing attention,* specifying a structure to update the security plan periodically

A good security plan is an official documentation of current security practices. It also identifies a plan for orderly change to improve those practices. In this way, a plan can be used later to measure the effect of the change, and to suggest further improvements. The impact of the security plan is important, too. A carefully written plan, supported by management officials, notifies employees that security is important to management (and therefore to everyone). Thus, both the content and the effect of the plan are important.

Content of a Security Plan

Every security plan contains the same basic material. The following sections describe the content of a security plan.

Policy

A security plan states a policy on security, which is one of the most difficult sections to write well. The policy statement addresses three questions:

- *who* should be allowed access?
- to *what* resources?
- *how* should access be regulated?

The policy statement should specify

- the organization's goals on security (for example, protect data from leakage to outsiders, protect against loss of data due to physical disaster, protect the integrity of data, protect against loss of business due to failure of computing resources)
- where the responsibility for security lies (for example, with a small computer security group, with each employee, with relevant managers)
- the organization's commitment to security (for example, support for staff, where security fits into the organization's structure)

Current Security Status

A risk analysis can form the basis of a description of the current status of security. The status includes a listing of the assets of the organization, the security threats to the assets, and the controls in place to protect the assets.

The plan should define the limits of responsibility: which assets are to be protected, what groups may be excluded (for example, joint ventures with other organizations), and where the boundaries are (is control of the network router a responsibility of the organization?).

The plan should present a procedure for addressing a vulnerability that has not been considered. These vulnerabilities can arise from new equipment, new data, and new situations, or they can result from the oversights of the security planners. Someone who identifies a new vulnerability should be instructed on how to integrate controls for that vulnerability into the existing security procedures.

Recommendations and Requirements

The heart of the security plan is action that will be taken. What requirements are being imposed as part of the plan, and over what period of time will they be instituted?

Most plans cannot be accomplished immediately. There must be some period to phase in the new requirements. The plan should specify the elements of each phase and their time periods for implementation.

Furthermore, the plan must be extensible. Conditions will change: new equipment will be acquired, new degrees and modes of connectivity will be requested, and new threats will be identified. The plan must include a procedure for change and growth, so that the security aspects of changes are considered as a part of preparing for the change, not after. Also, the plan should remain largely intact through change in the organization; only if the plan includes steps for accommodating change can the plan match an organization's development.

Responsibility for Implementation

A section of the report should identify specific people responsible for the implementation. In this way, people understand for what they are responsible, and people who share responsibility know with whom they must coordinate. Furthermore, this section becomes a plan of accountability so that the responsible people can later be judged on the results they have achieved.

Some examples of groups with responsibilities for computer security are listed below.

- *Personal computer users* are responsible for their own machines, or a coordinator of personal computer security may be appropriate.
- *Project leaders* are responsible for data and computations of the project.
- *Data base administrators* are responsible for the access to and integrity of data in their data bases.
- *Information officers* are responsible for overseeing the creation and use of data; these officers may be responsible for retention and proper disposal of data.
- *Personnel staff members* are responsible for security involving employees, such as screening potential employees for trustworthiness and arranging training programs for employees.

Timetable

If the controls are expensive or complicated, they may be acquired and implemented gradually. Similarly, procedural controls may require training of the staff to ensure that everyone understands and accepts the reason for the control. The plan should specify the order in which the controls are to be implemented, so that the most serious exposures are covered as soon as possible. A timetable also gives milestones by which the progress of the security program can be judged.

Continuing Attention

An important part of the timetable is establishing a date for evaluation and review of the security situation. As users, data, and equipment change, new exposures develop and old means of control become obsolete or ineffective. Periodically the inventory of objects and the list of controls should be updated, and the risk analysis should be reviewed. The security plan should set a time for this periodic review.

The preceding six sections have outlined the major issues to be addressed in a security plan. The next two sections describe who should write this plan and how support for the plan can be obtained.

To summarize, a security plan should cover

- policy
- current status
- recommendations and requirements
- responsibility
- timetable
- continuing planning

Security Planning Team Members

Who performs the security analysis and recommends a security program? Like any large function, it will probably be done by a committee. The size of the committee depends on the size and complexity of the computing organization and the degree of commitment to security. From organizational behavior studies, the optimum size for a working committee is 5 to 9 members. A larger committee may serve primarily as an oversight body to review and comment on the work of a working committee. A large committee might designate subcommittees to obtain the information for various sections of the plan.

The membership of a computer security planning team relates to the different aspects of computer security described in this book. Encryption, protocols, and security in operating systems and networks require the cooperation of the systems programming staff. Program security measures can be understood and recommended by applications programmers. Physical security controls are implemented by those responsible for general physical security against both human attacks and natural disasters. Finally, because controls will affect system users, the plan should encompass users' views of usability and desirability of controls.

A security planning team should represent each of the following groups. In some cases a group may be adequately represented by someone who is consulted at appropriate times, instead of having a committee member from each possible constituency.

- computer hardware group
- systems programmers
- applications programmers
- data entry personnel
- physical security personnel
- representative users

Securing Commitment to a Security Plan

After the plan is written, it must be accepted and its recommendations carried out. Acceptance is a function of sensibility, understanding, and management commitment.

Education and publicity can help people to understand and accept a security plan. Remember the true case of the employee who went through 24 password changes at a time to get back to a favorite password, in a system that prevented use of any of the 23 most recently used passwords. Clearly the employee either did not understand or did not agree with the reason for restrictions on passwords. If people understand the need for controls and accept the recommended controls as sensible, they will use the controls. If people think the controls are bothersome, capricious, or counterproductive they will work to avoid them.

The other key to success is management commitment. Management commitment is obtained through understanding (knowing the cause and the potential effects of lack of security), cost effectiveness, and presentation of the plan.

Some managers do not understand computing and the special risks associated with it. Education and avoiding technical jargon can help management to appreciate security in computing. Outside experts are often called in to justify to management the recommendations of a security plan.

Management is often reticent to allocate funds for controls until the value of those controls is explained. Risk analysis is an excellent tool for communicating the benefits of implementing controls. Descriptions of vulnerabilities related to ordinary business activities (such as leakage of data to a competitor or an outsider) may help managers to understand the need for controls.

Finally, a well-organized, concise report that includes a plan of implementation and justification of costs is likely to be accepted. The sections establishing accountability, time for accomplishment, and continuing reevaluation are especially important.

10.6   Organizational Security Policies

A key element of any organization's security planning is an effective security policy. The three questions a security policy must answer are *who* can access *which resources* in *what manner*. In this section we examine how to write a useful security policy.

Purpose

A security policy is written for several different groups of readers; each group has a different reason to use the security policy and, therefore, a different expectation.

Beneficiaries

Schools, universities, governments, and companies all have "customers" or beneficiaries of some sort. A business has paying customers or clients, but the general public also may benefit through employment or the existence of a service, such as a telecommunications infrastructure. Government customers are the covered citizens. And a school or university's customers include its students, faculty, and the world (enriched through an educated population or the results of research and service).

All of these customers, to varying degrees, depend on the existence of or access to computers, their data and programs, and computational power. For these people, continuity and integrity of this computing are very important.

Also, in some cases, confidentiality or correctness of data held is a consideration. Protection of sensitive data becomes significant.

Some of these beneficiaries are indirect: they do not invoke or use computer services themselves. The needs of beneficiaries should be considered and reaffirmed in a security policy.

Users

Users legitimately expect a certain degree of confidentiality, integrity, and continuous availability in the computing resources provided to them. Although the degree varies with the situation, a security policy should reaffirm a commitment to this requirement for service.

Users need to know and appreciate what is acceptable use of computers, data, and programs. For users, a security policy should define acceptable use in general.

Owners

Finally, each piece of computing equipment is owned by someone, who may not be the user. An owner, such as a business or university, provides the equipment to users for a purpose, such as to further education, support commerce, or enhance productivity. A security policy should also reflect the expectations of owners.

Balance

A security policy thus has to relate the needs of beneficiaries, users, and owners. Unfortunately, the needs of these groups may conflict. A beneficiary might want immediate access to data, but owners or users might not want to bear the expense or inconvenience of providing access at all hours of the night. Continuous availability may be a goal of users, but that goal is inconsistent with a need to perform preventive or emergency maintenance. Thus, the policy must balance the priorities of all affected communities.

Attributes

Now we consider some of the attributes of a good security policy.

Purpose

The policy should state the purpose of the computing, reflecting the requirements of beneficiaries, users, and owners. Examples of purposes are to "protect customers' confidentiality or preserve a trust relationship," "ensure continual usability," or "maintain profitability." Of course, there may be more than one purpose for computing.

A clear and succinct statement of the purpose of the computing helps to justify the protection requirements that are stated later.

Protected Resources

The policy should also state to what it applies. All computers? Networked ones only? All data? Customers' data? Management data? All programs? Products under development? All service? Service to time-critical processes? The answers to these questions help to identify classes of resources requiring more or less protection.

Protection

The portions so far have addressed *who* should have access to *what*; now the policy must state *how* that access will be ensured (and *how* unauthorized people will be denied access). All the previous chapters of this book have contributed ways to provide protection, so there is no point in repeating them here. A security policy should state, in general, what degree of protection should be provided to which kinds of resources.

Coverage

A security policy must be comprehensive: it must either apply to or explicitly exclude all possible situations. Furthermore, a security policy will not be updated as each new situation arises, so it must be general enough to apply naturally to new cases.

Durability

A security policy must grow and adapt well. In large part, it will survive growth and expansion in the environment without change. As just noted, it must be applicable to new situations. However, it must also be changeable when needed.

One important key to durability is that the policy not be tied to specific data that could change or to specific protection mechanisms that almost certainly will change. For example, a policy might require a 10-character password for anyone to access data on the workstation in room 110, but when that workstation is replaced or moved, the policy gives little guidance. Strong authentication for access to sensitive student grades or customers' proprietary data would make more sense. Better still would be a policy that recognized two bodies of sensitive data, one including data to be protected to preserve confidentiality of a personal or trusting relationship, to be protected through the use of strong authentication.

Realism

The policy must be realistic. The protection requirements stated must be realizable with existing mechanisms. There is no point in requiring absolute protection of confidentiality if there are no controls that can give absolute protection; such unrealistic requirements simply weaken readers' acceptance of the whole policy.

Usefulness

In order to be useful the policy must be read, understood, and followed by all. A brief policy, written in clear, direct language, is most likely to be effective.

Examples

In this section we study a few examples from security policies to illustrate some of the points presented.

Organizational Policy

An organization decided to classify all its resources into four levels and to base the required protection on the level of the resource. The classification, in turn, depended on severity of effect of damage to a resource. The organization then followed with a thorough analysis of threats, their possible severities, countermeasures, and their effectiveness, based on these four levels.

> Four security levels (Security Level 1 through Security Level 4) have been defined with increasing strength of protection.
>
> **Security Level 1** (SL1) is not designed to protect any specific resources or to provide any specific level of protection to the business services of the organization.
>
> **Security Level 2** (SL2) is designed to protect regular resources and to provide normal protection against threats that could lead to damage or that have temporary consequences to the business services of the organization.
>
> **Security Level 3** (SL3) is designed to protect important resources and to provide high protection against threats that could lead to serious damage or that have serious consequences to the business services of the organization.
>
> **Security Level 4** (SL4) is designed to protect critical resources and to provide very strong protection against threats that could lead to very serious damage or that have irrecoverable consequences to the business services of the organization.

Although adjectives such as *serious* damage and *very strong* protection are open to interpretation, the intent of these levels is clear: all information assets are to be classified as unaffected, short-term, critical, and essential, and protection requirements for these four types are detailed in the remainder of the document.

U.S. Department of Energy

The U.S. Department of Energy (DOE), like many government units, has established its own security policy. The following excerpt is from the policy on protecting classified material, although the form is appropriate for many unclassified uses as well.

> It is the policy of DOE that classified information and classified ADP [automatic data processing] systems shall be protected from unauthorized access (including the enforcement of need-to-know protections), alteration, disclosure, destruction, penetration, denial of service, subversion of security measures, or improper use as a result of espionage, criminal, fraudulent, negligent, abusive, or other improper actions. The DOE shall use all reasonable measures to protect ADP systems that process, store, transfer, or provide access to classified information, to include but not limited to the following: physical security, personnel security, telecommunications security, administrative security, and hardware and software security measures. This order establishes this policy and defines responsibilities for the development, implementation, and periodic evaluation of the DOE program.

The policy then continues for several more pages to list specific responsibilities for specific people.

The cited paragraph is comprehensive, covering practically every possible source (espionage, crime, fraud, etc.) of practically every possible harm (unauthorized access, alteration, destruction, etc.), and practically every possible kind of control (physical, personnel, etc.). The generality of that header paragraph is complemented by subsequent paragraphs giving specific responsibilities ("Each data owner shall determine and declare the required protection level of information . . . ," "Each security officer shall . . . perform a risk assessment to identify and document specific . . . assets, . . . threats, . . . and vulnerability . . . ," "Each manager shall . . . establish procedures to ensure that systems are continuously monitored . . . to detect security infractions . . .").

Internet

The Internet does not have a governing security policy per se, because it is a federation of users. Nevertheless, the Internet Society drafted a security policy for its members [PET91]. The policy contains the following interesting portions:

- Users are individually responsible for understanding and respecting the security policies of the systems (computers and networks) they are using. Users are individually accountable for their own behavior.
- Users have a responsibility to employ available security mechanisms and procedures for protecting their own data. They also have a responsibility for assisting in the protection of the systems they use.
- Computer and network service providers are responsible for maintaining the security of the systems they operate. They are further responsible for notifying users of their security policies and any changes to these policies.
- Vendors and system developers are responsible for providing systems which are sound and which embody adequate security controls.
- Users, service providers, and hardware and software vendors are responsible for cooperating to provide security.
- Technical improvements in Internet security protocols should be sought on a continuing basis. At the same time, personnel developing new protocols, hardware or software for the Internet are expected to include security considerations as part of the design and development process.

These statements clearly state to whom they apply and for what each party is responsible.

10.7   Disaster Recovery

In this section we consider how to cope with what goes wrong. There are two pieces to this process: preventing things that can be prevented and recovering from the things that cannot be prevented. **Physical security** is the term used to describe protection provided outside the computer system. Typical physical security facilities are guards, locks, and fences to deter direct attacks, although protection against less direct disasters is also a part of physical security. Fortunately, many physical security measures result from just good common sense. As Mark Twain observed, "common sense is a most uncommon virtue." Thus, this section describes some of the obvious aspects of physical security.

Perils

Most security vulnerabilities described in this book have been exploited by people who broke encryptions, tapped lines, circumvented access controls, and wrote malicious programs. Although people may be the biggest source of security problems for computing systems, people are not the only source. This section contains a catalog of the different physical vulnerabilities to security.

Natural Disasters

Computers are subject to the same natural disasters that can occur to homes, stores, and automobiles. They can be flooded, burned, melted, hit by falling objects, and destroyed by earthquakes, storms, and tornadoes. Additionally, computers are sensitive to their operating environment, so that excessive heat or inadequate power is also a threat. Because many of these perils cannot be prevented or predicted, controls focus on limiting possible damage and recovering from a disaster. Issues to be considered include the cost of replacing equipment, the speed with which equipment can be replaced, the need for available computing power, and the cost or difficulty of replacing data and programs.

Human Vandals

Because computers and their media are rather sensitive, a vandal can do a great amount of destruction rather easily. Human attackers can be people off the street, disgruntled employees, bored operators, saboteurs, people seeking excitement, or unwitting bumblers. Crude attacks using axes or bricks can be very effective, but more subtle attacks can also be quite serious. An unskilled vandal may try the crude attack, but people carrying large or dangerous objects are often seen and stopped. People with only slightly more sophisticated knowledge can short circuit a computer with a car key or disable a disk drive with a paper clip. These implements would not attract attention until the attack has been completed.

Unauthorized Access and Use

Movies and newspaper reports exaggerate the ease of gaining access to a computing system. Still, as distributed computing systems become more prevalent, protecting the system from outside access becomes more difficult and more important. Interception is a form of unauthorized access; in this context, interception is a *passive* attack, but *active* use is also a concern. Protection is needed both to prevent unauthorized users from obtaining access to the system and to verify the identity of accepted users.

   The following sections expand on these four vulnerabilities: natural perils, human intrusion, interception, and unauthorized access and use.

Natural Disasters

It is impossible to prevent natural disasters, but through careful planning it is possible to reduce the damage they inflict. Some measures can be taken to reduce their impact.

Flood

Water from a natural flood comes from ground level, rising gradually, and bringing with it mud and debris. There is generally time for an orderly shutdown of the computing system, losing at worst some of the processing in progress. The machinery may be destroyed or damaged by mud and water, but most computing systems are insured and replaceable by the manufacturer. Managers of unique or irreplaceable equipment who recognize the added risk sometimes obtain duplicate redundant hardware systems to insure against disruption of service.

Thus, hardware is replaceable. The real concern is the data and programs stored on magnetic media. Time works in the favor of the computing center because there is often adequate time to move critical data to higher ground. Typically even in an extensive tape library the lowest tape is several inches above the floor, and disk packs are often stored on shelves between waist and eye level.

Unfortunately, most computing centers do not have an easy way to identify the most important media. In case of a flood, personnel may be available to help with the removal of sensitive media, but these people may not be computer operators or may not have the time to locate the two hundred most important volumes from a media inventory of several thousand volumes. A simple scheme is to mark each volume with a colored label: red for most important, yellow for second, and so on. Volunteers can be told to take every volume with a red label first, then if there is time, to pick up ones with yellow labels, and so forth.

Falling Water

The opposite water problem is water from above, either from a burst water pipe, from a sprinkler system, or from flood water seeping down to a below-ground computing center. Depending on the source and the volume of the water, there may not be concern with accumulation beyond a few inches at floor level. The major problem is to protect the equipment and media from this unwanted "rainfall."

Here, again, a simple measure can be quite effective. Every computing installation should have available a box or roll of large plastic bags (such as trash bags). Volunteers can quickly wrap important media and cover much equipment to prevent damage. Several rolls of tape are also helpful to seal odd-shaped components.

These same precautions apply to users of personal computers, as well as to managers of major computing centers. A plastic bag or cover should sit next to each personal computer (or workstation or terminal). Usually, however, the machine is far easier to replace than the programs and data. All important removable media should be kept in one closed box for easy rescue.

Fire

Fire is more serious than water because often there is not as much time to react, and because human lives are more likely to be in immediate danger.

Every computing center should have a plan for shutting down the system in an orderly manner. Such a process takes only a few minutes but can make recovery much easier. This plan should include individual responsibilities for all people, some to halt the system, others to protect crucial media, others to close doors on media cabinets. Provision should be made for people not present due to illness, vacations, and so on.

Water is not a good fire protector for computer rooms. In fact, more destruction has been done by sprinkler systems trying to stop fires in computer rooms than by fires themselves. A fire sensor will activate many sprinklers, dousing an entire room for a fire in a wastebasket. Magnetic media and electronic equipment are sensitive to water and, in many cases, the fire being "doused" was under control so that it was not a threat to the computing equipment. Most computing centers use carbon dioxide extinguishers or an automatic system using a gas that smothers a fire but leaves no residue. Unfortunately, these gas systems displace the oxygen, which chokes the fire but also affects humans. When these protection devices are activated, humans must leave, which stops efforts to protect media.

A defense against fire is careful placement of a computing facility. A windowless location with fire-resistant access doors and nonflammable full-height walls can prevent some fires from spreading from adjacent areas to the computing room. With a fire- and smoke-resistant facility, personnel merely shut down the system and leave, perhaps carrying out the most important media.

Fire prevention is quite effective, especially because most computer goods are not especially flammable. Advance planning, reinforced with simulation drills, can help to make good use of the small amount of time available before evacuation is necessary.

Power Loss

Computers need their food—electricity—and they require a constant, pure supply of it. With a direct power loss, all computation ceases immediately. Because of possible damage to media by sudden loss of power, many disk drives monitor the power level and quickly retract the recording head if power fails. For certain time-critical applications, loss of service from the system is intolerable; in these cases alternative complete power supplies must be instantly available.

Uninterruptible Power Supply

One protection against power loss is called an **uninterruptible power supply**. This device stores energy during normal operation so that it can return the backup energy if power fails. One form of uninterruptible power supply uses batteries that are continually charged when the power is on, which then provide power when electricity fails. However, size, heat, flammability, and low output can be problems with batteries.

Some uninterruptible power supplies use massive wheels that are kept in continuous motion when electricity is available. When the power fails, the inertia in the wheels operates generators to produce more power. Size and limited duration of energy output are problems with this variety of power supply. Both forms of power supplies are intended to provide power for a limited time, just long enough to allow the current state of the computation to be saved so that no computation is lost.

Surge Suppressor

Still another problem with power is its "cleanness." Although most people are unaware of it, a variation of 10% from the stated voltage of a line is considered acceptable, and some power lines vary even more. A particular power line may always be 10% high or low.

In many places lights dim momentarily when a large appliance, such as an air conditioner, begins operation. When a large motor starts, it draws an exceptionally large amount of current, which reduces the flow to other devices on the line. When a motor stops, the sudden termination of draw can send a temporary surge along the line. Similarly, lightning strikes may send a momentary large pulse. Instead of being constant, the power delivered along any electric line shows many brief fluctuations, called **drops**, **spikes**, and **surges**. A drop is a momentary reduction in voltage, and a spike or surge is a rise. For computing equipment, a drop is less serious than a surge. Most electrical equipment is tolerant of rather large fluctuations of current.

These variations can be destructive to sensitive electronic equipment, however. Simple devices called surge suppressors filter spikes from an electric line, blocking fluctuations that would affect computers. These devices cost from $20 to $100, and should be installed on every personal computer, printer, or other connected component. More sensitive models are typically used on larger systems.

As mentioned previously, a lightning strike can send a surge through a power line. To increase protection, personal computer users unplug the machine when it is not in use, and during electrical storms. Another possible source of destruction is lightning striking a telephone line; the phone line should be disconnected from the modem during storms. These simple measures may save much work as well as valuable equipment.

Heat

Computing systems are very sensitive to heat, and loss of cooling is rather common due to mechanical failure or electrical disruption. Unfortunately, the only solution for loss of cooling is shutting down the system. Temperature rise is slow; a change of 10 degrees in an hour is uncommon, and 20 degrees in two hours is highly unlikely. Therefore, there is usually adequate time to react before serious consequences occur.

Computing systems warm gradually from normal temperature to too hot. The environment may exceed the manufacturer's recommended operating temperature with no obvious effect. If the temperature continues to rise, components may perform unpredictably, sometimes working correctly, sometimes working apparently well but producing faulty results, and sometimes showing their failure to cooperate. The most serious state is sometimes correct/sometimes incorrect because this uncertainty can corrupt the entire system while it seems to continue to function. For this reason, only essential computations should be done in hot conditions, and the results of these computations should be suspect.

Contingency Planning

The key to successful recovery is adequate preparation. Seldom does a crisis destroy irreplaceable equipment; most computing systems—personal computers to mainframes—are standard, off-the-shelf systems that can be easily replaced. Data and locally developed programs are more vulnerable because these cannot be quickly substituted from another source. In this section we consider continuing work after a crisis.

Backup

In many computing installations some data items change frequently, while others seldom change. For example, a data base of bank account balances changes daily, but a file of depositors' names and addresses changes much less often. Also the number of changes in a period of time is different for these two files. These variations in number and extent of change relate to the amount of data necessary to reconstruct these files in the event of a loss.

A **backup** is a copy of all or a part of a file to assist in reestablishing a lost file. In professional computing systems, periodic backups are performed. Everything on the system is copied, including system files, user files, scratch files, and directories, so that the system can be regenerated after a crisis. This type of backup is called a **complete backup**. It is done at regular times, such as every Monday morning.

Major installations may perform **revolving backups**, in which the last several backups are kept. Each time a backup is done, the oldest backup is replaced. Another form of backup is a **selective backup**, in which only files that have been changed (or created) since the last backup are saved. In this case, fewer files must be saved, so the backup can be done more quickly. A selective backup combined with an earlier complete backup gives the effect of a complete backup in the time needed for only a selective backup.

Associated with performing a backup is saving the means to move from the backup forward to the point of failure. In critical transaction systems this problem is solved by keeping a complete record of changes since the last backup. If a system handles bank teller operations, the individual tellers duplicate their processing on paper records; if the system fails, people can start with the backup version and reapply all changes from the collected paper copies.

Personal computer users often do not appreciate the need for regular backups. Even minor crises, such as a failed piece of hardware, can seriously affect personal computer users. With a backup, users can simply change to a similar machine and continue work.

Off-Site Backup

A backup copy is useless if it is destroyed in the crisis. Many major computing installations rent warehouse space some distance from the computing system, in some cases 15 or 20 miles away. As a backup is completed, it is transported to the backup site. Keeping a backup version separate from the system reduces the risk of its loss. Similarly, the paper trail is stored somewhere other than at the main computing facility.

Personal computer users concerned with integrity can take home a copy of important disks as protection, or send a copy to a friend in another city. If both secrecy and integrity are important, a bank vault, or even a secure storage place in another part of the same building, can be used. The worst place to store a backup copy is where it usually is stored: right next to the machine.

Cold Site

Depending on the nature of the computation, it may be important to be able to recover from a crisis and resume computation quickly. A bank, for example, might be able to tolerate a 4-hour loss of computing facilities during a fire, but it could not tolerate a 10-month period to rebuild a destroyed facility, acquire new equipment, and resume operation.

Most computer manufacturers have several spare machines of most models that can be delivered to any location within 24 hours in the event of a real crisis. Sometimes the machine will come straight from assembly; other times the system will have been in use at a local office. Machinery is seldom the problem. The question that arises is where to put this equipment in order to begin a temporary operation.

A **cold site** or **shell** is a facility with power and cooling available, where a computing system can be installed to begin immediate operation. Some companies maintain their own cold sites, and other cold sites can be leased from disaster recovery companies. These sites come with raised floors, fire prevention equipment, separate office space, telephone access, and other features. Typically, a computing center can have equipment installed and resume operation from a cold site within a week of a disaster.

Hot Site

If the application is more critical, or if the equipment needs are more specialized, a **hot site** may be more appropriate. A hot site is a computer facility with an installed and ready-to-run computing system. The system has peripherals, telecommunications lines, power supply, and even personnel ready to operate on short notice. Some companies maintain their own; other companies subscribe to a service that has available one or more locations with installed and running computers. To activate a hot site, it is necessary only to load software and data from offsite backup copies.

Numerous services offer hot sites equipped with every popular brand and model of system. They provide diagnostic and system technicians, connected communications lines, and an operations staff. They will also assist with relocation by arranging transportation and housing, by obtaining needed blank forms, and by acquiring office space.

Because these hot sites serve as backups for many customers, most of whom will not need the service, the annual cost to any one customer is fairly low. The cost structure is like insurance: the likelihood of an auto accident is low, so the premium is reasonable, even for a policy that covers the complete replacement cost of an expensive car. Notice, however, that the first step in being able to use a service of this type is a complete and timely backup.

Intruders

Up to this point *preventing unauthorized access* has meant preventing knowledgeable users from obtaining access to protected objects. Another class of unauthorized access is the physical presence of people who are not even users. With good reason, banks and hospitals exclude total strangers; computing installations should do the same. Unauthorized visitors can cause three problems: theft of machinery or data, destruction of machinery, and viewing sensitive data.

Theft Prevention

It is difficult to steal a large mainframe computer. Not only is carrying it away difficult, but finding a willing buyer and arranging installation and maintenance also require special assistance. However, printed reports, tapes, or disks can be carried easily. If done well, the loss may not be detected for some time, or it may initially be blamed on poor organization in the machine room.

Personal computers are designed to be small and portable. Diskettes and tape backup cartridges are easily carried; in fact, the 3.5" disk size was chosen to fit in a shirt pocket. Computers and media that are easy to carry are also often easy to conceal.

Three approaches can be taken to prevent thefts: prevent access, prevent portability, or detect exit. The next three sections survey devices that prevent access, portability, and exit.

The oldest access control is a guard. Guards are traditional, well-understood, and adequate in many situations. However, guards must be continuously on duty in order to be effective; providing breaks implies at least four guards for a 24-hour operation, with extras for vacation and illness. A guard must personally recognize someone, or recognize an access token, such as a badge. People can lose or forget badges; terminated employees and forged badges are also problems. Unless the guard makes a record of everyone who has entered a facility, there is no way to know who (employee or visitor) has had access in case a problem is discovered.

The second oldest access control is a lock. This device is even easier, cheaper, and simpler to manage than a guard. However, it too provides no record of who has had access, and there are difficulties of lost and duplicated keys. With computer facilities, there is the inconvenience of fumbling for a key when someone's hands are filled with tapes or disks, which might be ruined if dropped. There is also the possibility that one person will walk through the door that someone else has just unlocked. Still, guards and locks provide simple, effective security for access to facilities such as computer rooms.

More exotic access control devices employ cards with radio transmitters, magnetic stripe cards (similar to 24-hour bank cards), and cards with electronic circuitry that makes them difficult to duplicate. Because each of these interfaces with a computer, it is easy to produce a list of who entered and left the facility, when, and by which routes. Some of these devices operate by proximity, so that a person can carry the device in a pocket or clipped to a collar; the person obtains access even with a handful of things. Also, because these are computer controlled, it is easy to invalidate an access authority when someone quits or reports the access token lost or stolen.

Depending on the application, more or less strict methods of access control can be used. Access control can cooperate with computer authentication to provide a second level of assurance.

Preventing Theft

The simplest way to prevent theft is to lock the room containing a computer. This control is effective but reduces the ease of use for legitimate users. Also, it deters but does not prevent theft by breaking a window or a door lock.

Some degree of portability of computing devices is necessary. Permanently fixing a personal computer to a desk may not be appropriate if the machine must be moved for service or to be replaced.

One anti-theft device is a pad connected to cable, similar to those used to secure bicycles. The pad is glued to the desktop with super adhesive. The cables loop around the equipment and are locked in place. Releasing the lock permits the equipment to be moved. An alternate is to couple the base of the equipment to a secure pad, in much the same way that televisions are locked in place in hotel rooms. Yet a third possibility is a large, lockable cabinet in which the personal computer and its peripherals are kept. Some people argue that cables, pads, and cabinets are unsightly and, worse, they make the equipment inconvenient to use.

Detecting Attempts to Carry Away

For devices such as personal computers, printers, or terminals, it is adequate to prevent someone from carrying away these devices. However, chaining down a disk pack makes it unusable. The other approach to theft is to detect when someone tries to leave a protected area with the protected object. In this case, the protection mechanism should be small and unobtrusive.

One such mechanism is similar to the protection system used by many libraries. Each sensitive object (such as a diskette) is marked with a special label. Although the label looks like a normal pressure-sensitive label, it can be detected at the exit door. Similar security code tags are available for vehicles, people, machinery, and documents. Another manufacturer inserts radio transmitters in magnetic tape cartridges and mass storage media. All of these controls are sensed by a detector mounted by the exit from the room. The detector sounds an alarm, and someone must apprehend the person trying to leave with the marked object.

Controlling Human Access

The surest way to present theft is to keep the thief away from the equipment. However, thieves can be either insiders or outsiders. Therefore, access control devices both prevent access by unauthorized individuals and record access by those authorized. A record of accesses can help to identify who committed a theft.

Disposal of Sensitive Media

When disposing of a draft copy of a confidential report containing a company's sales strategies for the next five years, the company wants to be especially sure the report is not reconstructed. With computers there may be two or more copies of the report: one printed on paper and the others on magnetic media. Even the printer ribbon may disclose which characters were printed. This section considers ways to destroy data on all forms of media.

Shredders

Shredders have been in existence for a long time because banks, government agencies, and others have large amounts of confidential data to dispose of. Most data shredded is on paper. Shredders can also be used for diskettes, printer ribbons, and some tapes. Shredders convert their input into thin strips or pulp; with enough volume it becomes infeasible for most people to try to piece the appropriate strands back together again. (Some organizations burn the shreds for added protection.)

Overwriting Magnetic Data

As described earlier in this chapter, for magnetic disks the ERASE or DELETE command often just changes a directory pointer; the sensitive data is still recorded on the medium, and it can be recovered by simple analysis of the directory. A more secure way to destroy data on magnetic devices is to overwrite the data several times, using a different pattern each time. This process will remove enough magnetic residue to prevent most people from reconstructing the original file. However, a person using highly specialized equipment might be able to identify each separate message, almost like peeling off layers of wallpaper. Furthermore, cleaning a disk this way takes time.

Degaussers

Degaussers destroy magnetic fields. Passing a disk, or any other magnetic medium, through a degausser generates a magnetic flux so forceful that all magnetic charges are instantly realigned, thereby fusing all the separate layers, as described. A degausser is a fast way to cleanse a magnetic medium, although there is still question as to whether it is adequate for use in the most sensitive of applications. (Media that has had the same pattern for a long time, such as a tape that is saved for archive purposes, may retain traces of the original pattern even after it has been overwritten many times or degaussed.) For most users, however, a degausser is a fast way to neutralize a disk or tape, permitting it to be reused by others.

Emanations Protection: Tempest

As described previously, computer screens give off emissions that can be detected from a distance. In fact, any components, including printers, disk drives, and main processors, can emit information. The U.S. government has a program called **Tempest** under which computer equipment is certified as not emitting detectable signals. Basically there are two approaches to preparing a device for Tempest certification: enclosing the device and modifying the emanations.

Enclosure   The obvious solution to preventing emanations is to trap the signals before they can be picked up. Enclosing a device in a conductive case, such as copper, diffuses all the waves by conducting them throughout the case. Copper is a good conductor, and the waves travel much better through copper than through the air outside the case, so the emissions are rendered harmless.

This solution works very well with cable, which is then enclosed in a solid, emanation-proof shield. Typically the shielded cable is left exposed so that it is easy to inspect visually for any signs of tapping or other tampering. The shielding must be complete. That is, it does little good to shield a length of cable but not also shield the junction box where that cable is connected to a component. The line to the component and the component itself must be shielded, too.

The shield must enclose the device completely. If top, bottom, and three sides are shielded, emanations are prevented only in those directions. However, a solid copper shield is useless in front of a computer screen. Covering the screen with a fine copper mesh in an intricate pattern carries the emanation safely away. This approach solves the emanation problem while still maintaining the usability of the computer screen (or any other part that must be seen).

Entire computer rooms or even whole buildings can be shielded in copper, so that large computers inside do not leak sensitive emanations. The shielding must be done carefully because any puncture is a possible point of emanation. Furthermore, continuous metal pathways, such as water pipes or heating ducts, act as antennas to convey the emanations away from their source. A shielded room is inconvenient because it is impossible to expand the room easily as needs change.

Emanations Modification   Emanations can also be designed in such a way that they cannot be retrieved. This process is similar to generating noise in an attempt to jam or block a radio signal. Using this approach, the emanations of a piece of equipment must be modified by adding spurious signals. Additional processors are added to Tempest equipment specifically to generate signals that will fool any interceptor. The exact Tempest modification methods are classified.

As might be expected, Tempest-enclosed components are larger and heavier than their unprotected counterparts. Tempest testing is a very rigorous testing program of the U.S. Department of Defense. Once a product has been approved, even a minor design change, such as changing from one manufacturer's power supply to an equivalent one from another manufacturer, will invalidate the Tempest approval. Therefore, these components are costly, ranging in price from 10% to 300% more than similar non-Tempest products. They are most appropriate in situations where the data to be confined is of great value, such as top-level government data. Other groups with less dramatic needs can use less rigorous shielding.

10.8   Summary of Administering Security

This chapter has examined different aspects of administering security. Previous chapters have covered the so-called *technical controls* of security; this chapter has presented the administrative and procedural aspects.

The main task of administering security for personal computers is making users appreciate the risks to the machines and data so they will take appropriate steps to protect them. Unix systems require careful attention to permissions and accounts; fortunately, many of these settings can be checked with automated tools that highlight potential dangers. In network security, the administrator must also be concerned with permissions, remembering to be skeptical of remote systems.

Security planning includes determining assets, vulnerabilities, and appropriate protection. Many organizations establish a formal security plan.

A security policy is part of the security planning process. The security policy documents actions to be taken to secure an environment.

Physical protection is just as important as the technical and administrative controls. Physical security includes planning for contingencies; having a preplanned response for an emergency can limit the damage significantly. Finally, the obvious and least expensive controls, such as locks on doors, are often overlooked.

The next chapter deals with two more important nontechnical controls: legal and ethical protection for computing.

10.9   Bibliographic Notes

A basic work on risk analysis is the IBM-NBS report, which became FIPS PUB 65 [NBS79]. This technique is explained more fully by Parker [PAR81] and Hoffman [HOF86]. A paper that provides a variation on the approach is by Miguel [MIG84].

Unix security is covered well by Garfinkel and Spafford [GAR96]. Network security is addressed well by the Internet Network Working Group Site Security Handbook [HOL91] and by Crocker's chapter in [LYN92].

Two good resources on administering security are Fites [FIT89] and Wood [WOO87b].

10.10   Terms and Concepts

10.11   Exercises

1. In what ways is denial of service (lack of availability for authorized users) a vulnerability to users of single-user personal computers?

2. Identify the three most probable threats to a personal computing system in an office with fewer than 10 employees. That is, identify the three vulnerabilities most likely to be exploited. Estimate the number of times each vulnerability is exploited per year; justify your estimate.

3. Perform the analysis of the previous exercise for a personal computing system located in a large research laboratory.

4. Perform the analysis of Exercise 2 for a personal computing system located in the library of a major university.

5. Explain why an audit trail is insecure in a personal computer without a privileged mode of execution.

6. Consider software packages, such as data base management systems or file managers, designed to run on single-user personal computers. Is it necessary for these packages to include features to mediate multiple concurrent accesses? Why or why not?

7. *Programming problem.* Write a procedure that performs file encryption and decryption for security. Estimate the amount of time that a dedicated interceptor would need in order to break your encryption. Perform a timing analysis of your program and derive a formula for its encryption and decryption speed.

8. *Programming problem.* Investigate the architecture of a particular personal computer and write a procedure to truly "delete" files by overwriting them with 0s when a file is deleted.

9. *Programming problem.* Investigate the architecture of a particular personal computer and write a procedure that blanks the screen if no key has been struck within the last 15 minutes.

10. *Design and programming problem.* Design a procedure for a particular personal computer that prompts for a user identification when the machine is booted. Then structure the file system so access is allowed only to system files and files of a single user who has been identified.

11

Legal and Ethical Issues
in Computer Security

In this chapter:

- *Protecting programs and data by patents, copyrights, and trademarks*
- *Computer crime*
- *Privacy*
- *The Clipper controversy*
- *Ethical analysis of computer security situations*
- *Codes of professional ethics*

In this chapter we study the human controls that are applicable to computer security: the legal system and ethics. The legal system has adapted quite well to computer technology by reusing some old forms of legal protection (copyrights and patents) and by creating laws where no adequate ones existed (malicious access). Still, the courts are not a perfect form of protection for computer resources. Ethics has not had to change, because ethics is more situational and personal than the law. The purpose of this section is to round out our study of protection for computing systems.

Not always do things resolve themselves pleasantly. Some people are going to think that they have been treated unfairly, and some people do act unfairly. A current reaction to redress wrongs is to go to court. Typically people ask "Isn't it illegal for them to treat me this way? Can't I get the police to arrest them? I'll sue!" The courts are seen as the ultimate arbiters and enforcers of fairness. As most lawyers will tell you, the courts' definition of *fair* may not coincide with yours. Even if you could be sure the courts would side with you, a legal battle is slow, costly, and emotionally draining. Our purpose in this section is not only to understand how the legal system helps to protect computer security but also to know how to use the legal system wisely.

Law and computer security are related in several ways. First, both federal and state laws affect privacy and secrecy. These statutes often apply to the rights of individuals to keep personal matters private. Second, laws regulate the use, development, and ownership of data and programs. Patents, copyrights, and trade secrets are legal devices to protect the rights of developers and owners of programs and data. An aspect of computer security is controlling access to programs and data; that access control is supported by these mechanisms of the law. Third, laws affect actions that can be taken to protect the secrecy, integrity, and availability of computer information and service. These basic concerns in computer security are both strengthened and confined by applicable laws. Thus, legal means coordinate with other controls to establish computer security.

However, the law does not always provide an adequate control, either in computer affairs or in others. With computer matters, the law is slowly evolving. Computers are new, compared to houses, land, horses, or money. Because computers are new, their place in law is not yet firmly established. As statutes are written and cases are decided, computers are becoming more defined in the law. However, laws do not yet cover all improper acts committed with computers. Finally, judges, lawyers, and police officers often do not understand computing, so that they cannot determine how computing relates to other, more established parts of the law.

The laws of computer security affect programmers, designers, users, and maintainers of computing systems and computerized data banks. These laws provide protection, but they also regulate the behavior of people who use computers. Furthermore, computer professionals are among the best qualified to advocate changes of old laws and creation of new ones regarding computers. Before recommending change, however, professionals must understand the current state of computers and the law. Therefore, there are three motivations for studying the legal section of this chapter:

- to know what protection the law provides for computers and data
- to appreciate laws that protect the rights of others with respect to computers, programs, and data
- to understand existing laws as a basis for recommending new laws to protect computers, data, and people

The next few sections address the following aspects of protection of the security of computers.

- *Protection of computing systems against criminals.* Computer criminals violate the principles of secrecy, integrity, and availability for computer systems. It is better to prevent the violation than to prosecute it after the fact. However, if other controls fail, legal action is necessary. In this section we study several representative laws in order to determine what acts are punishable under the law.

- *Protection of code and data.* Copyrights, patents, and trade secrets are all forms of legal protection that can be applied to programs and, sometimes, data. However, we must understand the fundamental differences between the kind of protection these three provide, and how to obtain that protection.

- *Protection of access to programs.* The law protects both programmers and people who employ programmers. Generally, programmers have only limited legal rights to access programs they have written while employed. This section contains a survey of the rights of employees and employers regarding programs written for pay.

- *Protection of private data about individuals.* Finally, we consider the rights of privacy. The private affairs of every individual are protected by laws. Computer security systems must be adequate to prevent unauthorized disclosure of sensitive data about individuals. The section concludes with a description of sensitive data that must be protected.

The area of computer law is complex and emerging rather rapidly. The content of these sections is the analysis of the situation by someone who is not a lawyer. A lawyer who understands and specializes in computer law should be consulted in order to apply the material of this section to any specific case. And, as most lawyers will advise, it is far easier to acquire legal protection by doing things correctly from the beginning than to hire a lawyer to sort out a web of conflict after things have gone wrong.

11.1   Protecting Programs and Data

Suppose Shari wrote a computer program to play a video game. She invited some friends over to play the game and gave them copies to play at home. Chuck took a copy and rewrote parts to improve the quality of the screen display. After Chuck shared the changes with her, Shari incorporated them into her program. Shari's friends have convinced her that the program is good enough to sell, so she wants to advertise and offer the game for sale by mail.

She wants to know what legal protection she can apply to protect her software. Copyright, patent, and trade secret are all legal devices that protect computers, programs, and data. However, in some cases, precise steps must be taken to protect the work before anyone else is allowed access to it. We explain how each of these forms was originally designed to be used, and what is its current use in computing.

Copyrights

Copyrights are designed to protect the expression of ideas. Thus, a copyright applies to a creative work, such as a story, photograph, song, or pencil sketch. The right to copy an *expression* of an idea is protected by a copyright. Ideas themselves, the law alleges, are free; anyone with a bright mind can think up anything anyone else can, at least in theory. The intention of a copyright is to allow regular and free exchange of ideas.

The author of a book translates ideas into words on paper. This paper, the expression of those ideas, is the author's livelihood. That is, an author hopes to earn a living by presenting ideas in such an appealing manner that others will pay to have them. (The same protection applies to music, films, and works of art, because these are all personal expressions of ideas.) The law protects an individual's right to earn a living, while recognizing that exchange of ideas is the route to the intellectual growth of society. The copyright says that a particular *way* of expressing an idea belongs to the author.

Copyright gives the author the *exclusive* right to make copies of the expression and sell them to the public. That is, only the author can sell copies of the author's book (except, of course, for booksellers or others working as the agents of the author).

Definition of Intellectual Property

The U.S. copyright law of 1978 states that copyright can be registered for "original works of authorship fixed in any tangible medium of expression, . . . from which they can be perceived, reproduced, or otherwise communicated, either directly or with the aid of a machine or device." Again, the copyright does *not* cover the *idea* being expressed. "In no case does copyright protection for an original work of authorship extend to any idea." The copyright must apply to an *original* work, and it must be in some *tangible* medium of expression.

Only the originator of the expression is entitled to copyright; if an expression has no determinable originator, then copyright cannot be granted. Certain works are considered to be in the **public domain**, owned by the public, by no one in particular. Works of the U.S. government are considered to be in the public domain and, therefore, not subject to copyright. Works generally known, such as the phrase "have a good day," or the joke about the traveling salesman, or the song "Happy Birthday to You," or a recipe for tuna noodle casserole, are also so widely known that it would be very difficult for someone to trace originality and claim a copyright. Finally, copyright lasts for only a limited period of time, so certain very old works, such as the plays of Shakespeare, are in the public domain, their possibility of copyright having expired.

The copyrighted expression must also be in some tangible medium. A story or art work must be written, printed, recorded (on a record), stored on a magnetic medium, or made concrete in some other way. Furthermore, the purpose of the copyright is to promote distribution of the work; therefore, the work must be distributed, even if a fee is charged for a copy.

Originality of Work

The work being copyrighted must be original to the author. As noted previously, some expressions are general public knowledge and not subject to copyright. These generally-known works are in the public domain. A work can be copyrighted even if it contains some public domain material, as long as there is some originality, too. The author does not even have to identify what is public and what is original.

For example, a music historian could copyright a collection of folksongs even if some are in the public domain. In order to be subject to copyright, something *in* or *about* the collection would have to be original. The historian might argue that collecting the songs, selecting which ones to include, and putting them in order was the original part. In this case, the copyright law would not protect the folk songs (which would be in the public domain), but that specific selection and organization. Someone selling a sheet of paper on which just one of the songs was written would likely not be found to have infringed on the copyright of the historian.

Fair Use of Material

The copyright law indicates that the copyrighted object is subject to "fair use." Specifically, the law allows "fair use of a copyrighted work, including such use by reproduction in copies, . . . for purposes such as criticism, comment, news reporting, teaching (including multiple copies for classroom use), scholarship or research." The purpose of the use and the effect of the use on the potential market for or value of the work affect the decision of what constitutes fair use. The copyright law usually upholds the author's right to a fair return for the work, while encouraging others to use the underlying ideas.

Requirements for Registering a Copyright

The copyright is easy to obtain, and mistakes in securing a copyright can be corrected. The first step of registration is notice. Any potential user must be made aware that the work is copyrighted. Each copy must be marked with the copyright symbol ©, the word *Copyright*, the year, and the author's name. (This used to be followed by *All rights reserved* to preserve the copyright in certain South American countries. Adding the phrase now is unnecessary but harmless.)

The order of the elements can be changed, and either © or *Copyright* can be omitted (but not both). Each copy distributed must be so marked, although the law will forgive failure to mark copies if a reasonable attempt is made to recall and mark any ones distributed without a mark.

The copyright must also be officially filed. In the United States a form is completed and submitted to the Copyright Office, along with a nominal fee and a copy of the work. Actually, the copyright office requires only the first 25 and the last 25 pages of the work, in order to help it justify a claim in the event of a court case. The filing must be done within three months after the first distribution of the work. The law allows filing up to five years late, but no infringements before the time of filing can be prosecuted.

A copyright now lasts for 50 years beyond the death of its author or last living co-author, or a total of 75 years if it is considered a work done for hire (see below), which essentially means a work being copyrighted by a business, not a person. These times are probably long enough for adequate protection of any computer works, which decrease in usefulness after a few years.

Copyright Infringement

The holder of the copyright must go to court to prove that someone has infringed on the copyright. The infringement must be substantial, and it must be copying, not independent work. In theory, two people might write identically the same song independently, neither knowing the other. These two people would *both* be entitled to copyright protection for their work. Neither would have infringed on the other, and both would have the right to distribute their work for a fee. Again, copyright is most easily understood for written works of fiction, because it is extremely unlikely that two people would express an idea with the same or similar wording.

The independence of nonfiction works is not nearly so clear. Consider, for example, an arithmetic book. Long division can be explained only in so many ways, so two independent books could use similar wording for that explanation. The number of possible alternative examples is limited, so that two authors might independently choose the same simple example. However, it is far less likely that two arithmetic textbooks would have the same pattern of presentation and the same examples from beginning to end.

Copyrights for Computer Works

The original copyright law envisioned protection for things such as books, songs, and photographs. People can rather easily detect when these items are copied. The separation between public domain and creativity is fairly clear. And the distinction between an idea (feeling, emotion) and its expression is pretty obvious. With works of nonfiction, there is understandably less leeway for independent expression. With computer programs, because of programming language constraints and speed and size efficiency, there is much less leeway still.

Can a computer program be copyrighted? Yes. The 1976 copyright law was amended in 1980 to include an explicit definition of computer software. However, copyright protection may not be an especially desirable form of protection for computer works. To see why, consider the algorithm behind a program. The algorithm is the idea, and the statements of the programming language are the expression of the idea. Therefore, protection is allowed for the program statements themselves, but not for the design: copying the code intact is prohibited, but reimplementing the algorithm is permitted.

A second problem with copyright protection for computer works is the requirement that the work be published. A program may be published by distributing copies of its object code, for example on a disk. However, if the source code is not distributed, it has not been published. An alleged infringer cannot have violated a copyright on source code if the source code was never published.

Copyright protection does not limit the kind of use of a work, only the distribution of copies. This restriction has an important implication for computer works. Suppose a single host on a network legally acquires a copy of a piece of software. That host can then allow any network user to access the software, as long as a new copy is not created, without infringing. A copyright controls the right to copy and distribute; it is not clear that allowing "distributed access" is a form of distribution.

The area of copyright protection applied to computer works is still new and subject to much interpretation by the courts. Therefore, it is not certain what aspects of a computer work are subject to copyright. Courts have ruled that a menu design can be copyrighted, but that "look and feel" (such as the Microsoft Windows user interface) cannot.

Therefore, although copyright protection can be applied to computer works, a copyright was not designed for the electronic age, and thus the protection may be less than what we desire. Copyrights do not address all the critical elements that require protection. For example, a programmer might want to protect an algorithm, not the way that algorithm was expressed in a particular programming language. Unfortunately, it may be very difficult to obtain copyright protection for an algorithm, at least as copyright law is currently interpreted.

Patents

Patents are unlike copyrights in that they protect inventions, not works of the mind. The distinction between patents and copyrights is that patents were intended to apply to the results of science, technology, and engineering, whereas copyrights were meant to cover works in the arts, literature, and written scholarship. A patent can protect a "new and useful process, machine, manufacture, or composition of matter." The law excludes "newly discovered laws of nature . . . [and] mental processes." Thus "2 + 2 = 4" is not a proper subject for a patent because it is a law of nature. Similarly, that expression is in the public domain and would thus be unsuitable for a copyright. A patent is designed to protect the device or process for *carrying out* an idea, not the idea itself.

Requirement of Novelty

If two composers happen to compose the same song independently at different times, copyright law would allow both of them to have copyright. If two inventors devise the same invention, the patent goes to the person who invented it first, regardless of who filed the patent first. A patent can be valid only for something that is truly novel or unique, so there can be only one patent for a given invention.

An object patented must also be nonobvious. If an invention would be obvious to a person ordinarily skilled in the field it cannot be patented. The law states that a patent *cannot* be obtained "if the differences between the subject matter sought to be patented and the prior art are such that the subject matter as a whole would have been obvious at the time the invention was made to a person having ordinary skill in the art to which said subject matter pertains." For example, a piece of cardboard to be used as a bookmark would not be a likely candidate for a patent because the idea of a piece of cardboard would be obvious to almost any reader.

Procedure for Registering a Patent

A copyright is registered by filing a brief form, marking a copyright notice on the creative work, and distributing the work. The whole process takes less than an hour.

In order to obtain a patent, an inventor must convince the Patent Office that the invention deserves a patent. For a fee, a patent attorney will research the patents already issued for similar inventions. This search accomplishes two things. First, it determines that the invention to be patented has not been previously patented (and, presumably, has not been previously invented). Second, the search can help to identify similar things that have been patented. These similarities can be useful when describing the unique features of the invention that make it worthy of patent protection. The Patent Office compares an application to those of all other similar patented inventions, and decides whether the application covers something truly novel and nonobvious. If the office decides the invention is novel, a patent is granted.

Typically an inventor writes a patent application listing many claims of originality, from very general to very specific. The Patent Office may disallow some of the more general claims while upholding some of the more specific ones. The patent is valid for all the upheld claims. The patent applicant reveals what is novel about the invention in sufficient detail to allow the Patent Office and the courts to judge novelty; that degree of detail may also tell the world how the invention works, thereby opening the possibility of infringement.

The patent owner will use the patented invention, by producing products or by licensing others to produce them. Patented objects are sometimes marked with a patent number to warn others that the technology is patented. The patent holder hopes this warning will prevent others from infringing.

Patent Infringement

A patent holder *must* oppose all infringement. With a copyright, the holder can choose which cases to prosecute, ignoring small infringements and waiting for serious infractions where the infringement is great enough to ensure success in court or to justify the cost of the court case. However, failing to sue a patent infringement—even a small one or one the patent holder does not know about—can mean losing the patent rights entirely. But, unlike copyright infringement, a patent holder does not have to prove that the infringer copied the invention; a patent infringement occurs even if someone independently invents the same thing, without knowledge of the patented invention.

Every infringement must be prosecuted. Prosecution is expensive and time-consuming, but even worse, suing for patent infringement could cause the patent *holder* to lose the patent. Someone charged with infringement could argue all of the following points as a defense against the charge of infringement.

- *This isn't infringement.* The alleged infringer will claim that the two inventions are sufficiently different that no infringement occurred.

- *The patent is invalid.* If a prior infringement was not opposed, the patent rights may no longer be valid.

- *The invention is not novel.* In this case, the supposed infringer will try to persuade the judge that the Patent Office acted incorrectly in granting a patent, and the invention is nothing worthy of patent.

- *The infringer invented the object first.* If so, the accused infringer, and not the original patent holder, is entitled to the patent.

The first defense does not damage a patent, although it can limit the novelty of the invention. However, the other three defenses can destroy patent rights. Worse, all four defenses can be used every time a patent holder sues someone for infringement. Finally, obtaining and defending a patent can incur substantial legal fees. Patent protection is most appropriate for large companies with substantial research and development (and legal) staffs.

Applicability of Patents to Computer Objects

The Patent Office has not encouraged patents of computer software. For a long time, computer programs were seen as the representation of an algorithm, and an algorithm was a fact of nature, which is not subject to patent. An early software patent case, *Gottschalk v. Benson*, involved a request to patent a process for converting decimal numbers into binary. The Supreme Court rejected the claim, saying it seemed to attempt to patent an abstract idea, in short, an algorithm. But the underlying algorithm is precisely what most software developers would like to protect.

In 1981, two cases (*Diamond v. Bradley* and *Diamond v. Diehr*) won patents for a process that used computer software, a well-known algorithm, temperature sensors, and a computer to calculate the time to cure rubber seals. The court upheld the right to a patent because the claim was not for the software or the algorithm alone, but for the process that happened to use the software as one of its steps. An unfortunate inference is that using the software without using the other patented steps of the process would not be infringement.

The Patent Office has issued software patents since these cases, but there have been few court challenges to uphold the legitimacy of the patent rights. Patent protection does not seem appropriate for the underlying algorithms, which programmers really want to protect. And because of the time and expense involved in obtaining and maintaining a patent, this form of protection may be unacceptable for a small-scale software writer.

Trade Secret

A trade secret is unlike a patent or copyright in that it must be kept a *secret*. The information has value only as a secret, and an infringer is one who divulges the secret. Once divulged, the information usually cannot be made secret again.

Characteristics of Trade Secrets

A **trade secret** is information that gives one company a competitive edge over others. For example, the formula for a soft drink is a trade secret, as is a mailing list of customers, or information about a product due to be announced in a few months.

The distinguishing characteristic of a trade secret is that it must always be kept secret. Employees and outsiders who have access to the secret must be required not to divulge the secret. The owner must take precautions to protect the secret, such as storing it in a safe, encrypting it in a computer file, or making employees sign a statement that they will not disclose the secret.

If someone obtains a trade secret improperly and profits from it, the owner can recover profits, damages, lost revenues, and legal costs. The court will do whatever it can to return the holder to the same competitive position it had while the information was secret and may award damages to compensate for lost sales. However, trade secret protection evaporates in case of independent discovery. If someone else happens to discover the secret independently, there is no infringement, and trade secret rights are gone.

Reverse Engineering

Another way trade secret protection can vanish is by reverse engineering. Suppose a secret is the way to pack tissues in a cardboard box to make one pop up as another is pulled out. Anyone can cut open the box and study the process. Therefore, the trade secret is easily discovered. In **reverse engineering**, one studies a finished object to determine how it is manufactured or how it works.

Through reverse engineering someone might discover how a telephone is built; the design of the telephone is obvious from the components and how they are connected. Therefore, a patent is the appropriate way to protect an invention such as a telephone. However, something like a soft drink is not just the combination of its ingredients. Making a soft drink may involve time, temperature, presence of oxygen or other gases, and similar factors that could not be learned from a straight chemical decomposition of the product. The recipe of a soft drink is a closely guarded trade secret. Trade secret protection works best when the secret is not apparent in the product.

Applicability to Computer Objects

Trade secret protection applies very well to computer software. The underlying algorithm of a computer program is novel, but its novelty depends on nobody else's knowing it. Trade secret protection allows distribution of the *result* of a secret (the executable program) while still keeping the program design hidden. Trade secret protection does not cover copying a product (specifically a computer program), so that it cannot protect against a pirate who sells copies of someone else's program without permission. However, trade secret protection makes it illegal to steal a secret algorithm and use it in another product.

Difficulty of Enforcement

Trade secret protection is of no help when someone infers a program's design by studying its output or, worse yet, decoding the object code. Both of these are legitimate (that is, legal) activities, and both cause trade secret protection to disappear.

The confidentiality of a trade secret must be ensured with adequate safeguards. If source code is distributed loosely, or if the owner fails to impress on people (such as employees) the importance of keeping the secret, any prosecution of infringement will be weakened. Employment contracts typically include a clause stating that the employee will not divulge any trade secrets received from the company, even after leaving a job. Additional protection, such as marking copies of sensitive documents or controlling access to computer files of secret information, may be necessary to impress people with the importance of secrecy.

Protection for Computer Objects

The previous sections have described three forms of protection, the copyright, patent, and trade secret laws. Each of these provides a different form of protection to sensitive things. In this section we consider different kinds of computer objects and describe which forms of protection are most appropriate for each kind. Table 11-1 shows how these three forms of protection compare in several significant ways.

Computer artifacts are very new, and they are not yet fully appreciated by the legal system. Perhaps in a decade the issue of what protection is most appropriate for what object will be more clear-cut. Perhaps a new form of protection, or a new use of an old form, will apply specifically to computer objects. For example, the European Union has recently enacted model legislation for copyright protection of computer software. However, one of their goals was to promote software that builds on what others have done. Thus, the E.U. specifically excepted a product's interface specification from copyright and permitted others to derive the interface to allow development of new products that could connect via that interface.

Until the law provides protection that truly fits computer goods, here are some guidelines for using the law to protect computer objects.

Protecting Hardware

Hardware, such as chips, disk drives, or floppy disk media, can all be patented. The medium itself can be patented, and someone who invents a new process for manufacturing it can obtain a second patent.

Protecting Firmware

The situation is a little less clear with regard to microcode. Certainly, the physical devices on which microcode is stored can be patented. Also, a special-purpose chip that can do only one specific task (such as a floating-point arithmetic accelerator) can probably be patented. However, the data (instructions, algorithms, microcode, programs) contained in the devices are probably not patentable.

Table 11-1   Comparing Copyright, Patent, and Trade Secret Protection

	Copyright	Patent	Trade Secret
Protects	Expression of idea, not idea itself	Invention: the way something works	A secret competitive advantage
Protected object made public	Yes; intention is to promote publication	Design filed at patent office	No
Requirement to distribute	Yes	No	No
Ease of filing	Very easy, do-it-yourself	Very complicated; specialist lawyer suggested	No filing
Duration	Life of human originator or 75 years for a company	19 years	Indefinite
Legal protection	Sue if copy sold	Sue if invention copied	Sue if secret improperly obtained

Can they be copyrighted? Are these the expression of an idea in a form that promotes dissemination of the idea? Probably not. And assuming that these devices were copyrighted, what would be the definition of a copy that infringed on the copyright? Worse, would the manufacturer really want to register a copy of the internal algorithm with the Copyright Office? Copyright protection is probably inappropriate for computer firmware.

Trade secret protection seems appropriate for the code embedded in a chip. Given enough time, we can reverse engineer and infer the code from the behavior of the chip. The behavior of the chip does not reveal what algorithm is used to produce that behavior. The original algorithm may have better (or worse) performance (speed, size, fault tolerance) that would not be obvious from reverse engineering.

For example, Apple Computer is enforcing its right to copyright protection for an operating system embedded in firmware. The courts have affirmed that computer software *is* an appropriate subject for copyright protection, and that protection should be no less valid when the software is in a chip than in a conventional program.

Protecting Object Code Software

Object code is usually copied so that it can be distributed for profit. The code is a work of creativity, and most agree that object code distribution is an acceptable medium of publication. Thus copyright protection seems appropriate.

A copyright application is usually accompanied by a copy of the object being protected. With a book or piece of music (printed or recorded), it is easy to provide a copy. The Copyright Office has not yet decided what is an appropriate medium in which to accept this code. A binary listing of the object code will be taken, but the Copyright Office does so without acknowledging that to be acceptable. The Office will accept a source code listing. Some people argue that a source code listing is not equivalent to an object code listing, in the same way that a French translation of a novel is different from its original language version. It is not clear *in the courts* that registering a source code version provides copyright protection to object code. However, someone should not be able to take the object code of a system, rearrange the order of the individual routines, and say that the result is a new system. Without the original source listings, it would be very difficult to compare two binary files and determine that one was the functional equivalent of the other simply through rearrangement.

Several court cases will be needed to establish acceptable ways of filing object code for copyright protection. Furthermore, these cases will have to develop legal precedents to define the equivalence of two pieces of computer code.

Protecting Source Code Software

Software developers selling to the mass market are reticent to distribute their source code. The code can be treated as a trade secret, although some lawyers also encourage that it be copyrighted. (These two forms of protection are possibly mutually exclusive, although registering a copyright will not hurt.)

Recall that the Copyright Office requires registering at least the first 25 and the last 25 pages of a written document. These pages are filed with the Library of Congress, where they are available for public inspection. This registration is to assist the courts in determining which work was registered for copyright protection. However, because they are available for anybody to see, they are not secret, and copyright registration can expose the secrecy of an ingenious algorithm. A copyright protects the right to distribute copies of the *expression* of an idea, not the idea itself. Therefore, a copyright does not prevent someone from reimplementing an algorithm, expressed through a copyrighted computer program.

As just described, source code may be the most appropriate form in which to register a copyright for a program distributed in object form. It is difficult to register source code with the Copyright Office while still ensuring its secrecy. A long computer program can be rearranged so that the first and last 25 pages do not divulge much of the secret part of a source program. Embedding small errors or identifiable peculiarities in the source (or object) code of a program may be more useful in determining copyright infringement. Again, several court cases must be decided in order to establish procedures for protection of computer programs, in either source or object form.

Protecting Documentation

Copyright protection is effective and appropriate for documentation because these are essentially written works of nonfiction. Notice that the documentation is distinct from the program. A program and its documentation must be copyrighted separately. Furthermore, copyright protection of the documentation may win a judgment against someone who illegally copies both a program and its documentation.

In cases where a written law is unclear or is not obviously applicable to a situation, the results of court cases serve to clarify or even extend the words of the law. As more unfair acts involving computer works are perpetrated, lawyers will argue for expanded interpretations of the law. The meaning and use of the law will continue to evolve through judges' rulings. In a sense computer technology has advanced much faster than the law has been able to.

11.2   Information and the Law

Source code, object code, even the "look and feel" of a computer screen are palpable, if not tangible objects. The law deals reasonably well, although somewhat belatedly, with these things. But computing is in the process of transition to a new class of object, with new legal protection requirements. Electronic commerce, electronic publishing, electronic voting, electronic banking: these are the new challenges to the legal system. In this section we consider some of these new things with new security requirements.

Information as an Object

The shopkeeper used to stock "things": buttons, automobiles, pounds of sugar. The shopkeeper sold things to customers. When the shopkeeper sold a thing, the shopkeeper's stock of that thing was reduced by one, and the customer paid for and left with a thing. In many cases, the customer could resell the thing to someone else.

Gradually, services became measurable like "things": a haircut, a root canal, defense for a trial. Some services had a fixed price (for example, a haircut), although one provider might charge more for that service than another. A "shopkeeper" (hair stylist, dentist, lawyer) essentially sold time: the price of a haircut generally related to the cost of the stylist's time, and lawyers and accountants charged by the hour for services where there was no obvious standard item. The value of a service in a free economy was somehow related to its desirability to the buyer and the seller: the dentist is willing to sell a certain amount of time, reserving the rest of the day for other things. Like a shopkeeper, once a service provider sold some time or service, it could not be sold again to someone else.

No one would argue against the proposition that information is valuable. Students are tempted to pay others for answers during examinations, and businesses pay for credit reports, client lists, and inside information about competitors. But information does not fit other familiar commercial paradigms.

Information Is Not Depletable

Unlike tangible "things" and services, information can be sold again and again. A credit bureau can sell the same credit report on an individual to an unlimited number of requesting clients. The clients pay for the information in the report. The report may be delivered on some tangible medium, such as paper, but it is the *information*, not the medium, that has the value.

This quality separates information from other creative works, such as books, CDs, or art prints. Each of these is a tangible copy, which can be individually numbered or accounted for. A bookshop can always order more copies of this book if the stock becomes depleted, but it can only sell as many copies as it has.

Information Can Be Replicated

The value of information is what the buyer will pay the seller. But after having bought the information, the buyer can then become a seller, and can potentially deprive the original seller of further sales. Because information is not depletable, the buyer can enjoy or use the information and also sell it, perhaps even making a profit.

Information Has a Minimal Marginal Cost

The marginal cost of an item is the cost to produce another one after having produced others. If a newspaper sold only one issue on a particular day, that one issue would be prohibitively expensive because it would have to cover the pro rata share of all the writers, editors, and production staff, as well as a share of all equipment for its production. These are all fixed costs to be able to produce a first copy. Under that model, the cost of the second and subsequent copies is minuscule, representing basically just the cost of paper and ink to print that copy. Fortunately, newspapers have very large press runs and daily sales, so that the fixed costs are spread evenly across a large number of copies printed. In theory a purchaser of a copy of a newspaper could print and sell other copies of that copy; few purchasers do that, in part because the newspaper is covered by copyright law, in part because the cost of reproduction is too high for the average person to make a profit, and in part because it is not fair to reproduce the newspaper that way.

The cost of information similarly depends on fixed costs and costs to reproduce. Typically, the fixed costs are large and the cost to reproduce is small, like a newspaper. However, unlike a newspaper, it is far more feasible for a buyer to resell information. The difference is that the fixed costs for the buyer are typically much lower than those for the originator, and the means to reproduce are typically convenient. Thus, the marginal cost of a piece of information can be quite low.

The Value of Information Is Often Timely

If you knew for certain what would be the trading price of a share of Microsoft stock next week, that would be extremely valuable, because you could make an enormous profit on the stock market. Of course, that price cannot be known today. But suppose you knew that Microsoft was certain to announce something next week that would cause the price to rise or fall. That information would be almost as valuable as knowing the exact price, and it could be known in advance. However, knowing *yesterday's* price for Microsoft stock or knowing that *yesterday* Microsoft announced something that sent the stock price soaring is almost worthless because it is printed in every major financial newspaper. Thus, the value of information often depends on when you know it.

Information Is Often Transferred Intangibly

With a newspaper, there is a printed artifact. The news agent hands it to a customer, who walks away with it. The seller and the buyer realize and acknowledge that something has been acquired. Furthermore, it is evident if the newspaper is seriously damaged, and if a serious flaw appears in the middle, the defect is easy to point out.

Increasingly, information is being delivered as bits on a cable. If they are visibly flawed (that is, if the error-detecting code indicates a transmission error), it is easy to demonstrate that flaw. However, if the copy of the information is accurate but the underlying information is incorrect, useless, or not as expected, it is difficult to justify a claim that the information is flawed.

Legal Issues Relating to Information

All these characterizations of information have a serious effect on the legal treatment of information.

First, there is some legal basis for the legal protection of information, although limited. Information can be related to trade secrets, in that information is the stock in trade of the information seller. While the seller has the information, trade secret protection applies naturally to the seller's legitimate ability to profit from information. Thus, the courts recognize that information has value.

However, as shown earlier, a trade secret has value only as long as it remains a secret. The Coca Cola company cannot expect to retain trade secret protection for its formula after it sells that formula. Also, the trade secret is not secure if someone else can derive or infer it.

The only other forms of protection are copyright and patent protection. As presented earlier, neither of these applies perfectly to computer hardware or software, and they apply even less well to information. The pace of change in the legal system is slow, which helps to ensure that the changes that do occur are fair and well-considered. The deliberate pace of change in the legal system is about to be hit by the supersonic rate of change in the information technology industry.

Following are several examples of situations in which information needs are about to place significant demands on the legal system.

Information Commerce

As just discussed, information is unlike most other goods traded. Still, it is undeniable that information has value and is the basis of some commerce. The market is still young, and few problems have yet developed.

Software piracy is the first example in which the value of information can be readily copied. Several approaches have been tried to ensure that the software developer or publisher receives just compensation for use of the software: copy protection, freeware, controlled distribution. The latest approach is the Java applets, which are delivered electronically as needed; potentially each applet can be tracked and charged for, and each applet can destroy itself after use, so that nothing remains to be passed for free to someone else. None of these approaches seems ideal, so it is likely that a legal remedy will be needed instead of, or in addition to, the technological ones.

Electronic Publishing

Soon news and information will be published and distributed on the Internet or some other public network. Here again there is the problem of ensuring that the publisher receives fair compensation for the work. Again, cryptographic-based technical solutions are under development. However, these technical solutions must be supported by a legal structure.

Protecting Data in a Data Base

The courts have had difficulty interpreting protection laws for application to data bases. How does one determine that a set of data came from a particular data base (so that the data base owner can claim some compensation)? Who even owns the data in a data base if it is public data, such as names and addresses?

Electronic Commerce

Laws related to trade in goods have evolved over literally centuries. Adequate legal protections exist to cover defective goods, fraudulent payment, and failure to deliver.

If you order goods electronically, digital signatures and other cryptographic protocols can provide a technical protection for your "money." However, suppose the information you order is not suitable for use, or never arrives, or arrives damaged, or arrives too late to use. How do you prove conditions of the delivery? These legal issues must be solved as we move into an age of electronic commerce.

11.3   Rights of Employees and Employers

Employers hire employees to generate ideas and make products. Thus, the protection offered by copyrights, patents, and trade secrets applies to the ideas and products. However, considering the issue of who owns the ideas and products is much more complex. Ownership is an issue of computer security because it relates to the rights of an employer to protect the secrecy and integrity of works produced by the employees. In this section we study the rights of employers and employees to computer products.

Ownership of Products

Suppose as a part of her job, Edye, who works for a computer software company, develops a program to manage windows for a computer screen display. The program belongs to her company because they paid Edye to write it. Thus, Edye cannot market this program herself. The situation depends on the fact that Edye wrote the program as a part of a work assignment. She could not sell the program even if she worked for a television company but developed the software as part of her job. Most employees understand this aspect of their responsibilities to their employer.

However, suppose that Edye develops this program in the evenings at home; it is not a part of her job. Edye tries to market the product herself. If Edye works as a programmer, her employer will probably say that Edye profited from training and experience gained on the job; at the very least, Edye probably conceived or thought about the project while at work. Therefore, the employer has an interest in (that is, owns at least part of) the rights to her program. However, the situation changes if Edye's primary job does not involve programming. If Edye is a television newscaster, her employer may have contributed nothing that relates to her computer product. If Edye's job does not involve programming, she may be free to market any computer product she makes.

Consider the legal position of a consultant. Suppose Edye is self-employed and, for a fee, she writes the program for the television station. She then wants to take the basis of the program, generalize it somewhat, and market it to others. Edye argues that she thought up, wrote, and tested the program; therefore, it is her work, and she owns it. The television station argues that it paid Edye to develop the program, and it owns the program, just as it would own a bookcase she might be paid to build for the station.

Clearly, from the situations described here, the interpretation of laws of ownership is difficult. Each type of protection must be considered in turn.

Ownership of a Patent

The person who owns a work under patent or copyright law is the inventor; in the earlier examples described, the owner is the programmer. However, in patent law, it is important to know who files the patent application. If an employee lets an employer patent an invention, the employer is deemed to own the patent and, therefore, the rights to the invention.

The employer also has the right to patent if the employee's job functions included inventing the product. In a large company a scientist may be hired to do research and development, and the results of this inventive work become the property of the employer. Even if an employee patents something, the employer can argue for a right to use the invention if the employer contributed some resources (such as computer time or access to a library or data base) in developing the invention.

Ownership of a Copyright

Ownership of a copyright is similar to ownership of a patent. The author (programmer) is the presumed owner of the work. The owner has all rights to an object. However, a special situation known as work for hire applies to many copyrights for development of software or other products.

Work for Hire

In a work for hire situation, the employer, *not* the employee, is considered the author of a work. The relationship does not have to be that of a conventional employer to employee for work for hire to exist. Work for hire is not simple to identify. An employer may be in a work for hire relationship with an employee if the following conditions are true. No one of these conditions is decisive; however, the more of these conditions that are true, the more a situation resembles work for hire.

- The employer has a supervisory relationship overseeing the manner in which the creative work is done.
- The employer has the right to fire the employee.
- The employer arranges for the work to be done before the work was created (as opposed to the sale of an existing work).
- A written contract between the employer and employee states that the employer has hired the employee to do certain work.

In the situation in which Edye develops a program on her job, her employer will certainly claim a work for hire relationship. Then the employer owns all copyright rights and should be identified in place of the author on the copyright notice.

Licenses

An alternative to a work for hire arrangement is licensed software. In this situation, the programmer develops and retains full ownership of the software. In return for a fee, the programmer grants to a company a license to use the program. The license can be for a definite or unlimited period of time, for one copy or for an unlimited number, to use at one location or many, to use on one machine or all, at specified or unlimited times. This arrangement is highly advantageous to the programmer, just as a work for hire arrangement is highly advantageous to the employer. The choice between work for hire and license is largely what the two parties will agree to.

Trade Secret Protection

A trade secret is different from either a patent or a copyright in that there is no registered inventor or author; there is no registration office for trade secrets. In the event a trade secret is revealed, the owner can prosecute the revealer for damages suffered. But first, ownership must be established because only the owner can be harmed.

A company owns the trade secrets of its business as confidential data. As soon as a secret is developed, the company becomes the owner. For example, as soon as sales figures are accumulated, a company has trade secret right to them, even if the figures are not compiled, totaled, summarized, printed, or distributed. As with copyrights, an employer may argue about having contributed to the development of trade secrets. If your trade secret is an improved sorting algorithm, and part of your job involves investigating and testing sorting algorithms, your employer will probably claim at least partial ownership of the algorithm you try to market.

Employment Contracts

Sometimes there is no contract between the software developer and a possible employer. However, commonly an employment contract will spell out rights of ownership. Having a contract is desirable both for employees and employers so that both will understand their rights and responsibilities.

Typically an employment contract specifies that the employee is hired to work as a programmer exclusively for the benefit of the company. The company states that this is a work for hire situation. The company claims all rights to any programs developed, including all copyright rights and the right to market. The contract may further state that the employee is receiving access to certain trade secrets as a part of employment, and the employee agrees not to reveal those secrets to anyone.

More restrictive contracts (from the employee's perspective) assign to the employer rights to all inventions (patents) and all creative works (copyrights), not just those that follow directly from one's job. For example, suppose an employee is hired as an accountant for an automobile company. While on the job, the employee invents a more efficient way to burn fuel in an automobile engine. The employer would argue that the employee used company time to think about the problem, and therefore it was entitled to this product. An employment contract transferring all rights of inventions to the employer would strengthen the case even more.

An agreement not to compete is sometimes included in a contract. The employee states that simply having worked for one employer will make the employee very valuable to a competitor. The employee agrees not to compete by working in the same field for a set period of time after termination. For example, a programmer who has a very high position involving the design of operating systems would understandably be familiar with a large body of operating systems design techniques. The employee might memorize the major parts of a proprietary operating system and be able to write a similar one for a competitor in a very short time. To prevent this, the employer might require the employee not to work for a competitor (including working alone). Agreements not to compete are not always enforceable in law; in some states the employee's right to earn a living takes precedence over the employer's rights.

11.4   Computer Crime

The law related to contracts and employment is difficult, but at least employees and objects and contracts and owners are fairly standard entities for which legal precedents have been developed. The definitions in copyright and patent law are strained when applied to computing, because old forms must be made to fit new objects; for these situations, however, cases being decided now are establishing legal precedents. But crimes involving computers are an area of the law that is even less clear than the other areas. In this section we study computer crime and consider why new laws are needed to address some of its problems.

Why a Separate Category for Computer Crime?

There are certain recognized categories of crimes, including such terms as *murder, robbery*, and *littering*. We do not separate crime into categories for different objects, such as *gun crime* or *knife crime*. We separate subjects of crime into *people* and *other objects,* but driving into your neighbor's picture window is as bad as driving into his evergreen tree or pet sheep. An example will explain why we need special laws relating to computers as subjects and objects of crime.

Rules of Property

A case related by Parker [PAR84] describes a theft of a trade secret proprietary software package. The theft was across state boundaries by means of a telephone line. The California Supreme Court ruled that this software acquisition was not theft because

Implicit in the definition of "article" in Section 499c(a) is that it must be something tangible. . . . Based on the record here, the defendant did not carry any tangible thing . . . from the computer to his terminal unless the impulses which defendant allegedly caused to be transmitted over the telephone wire could be said to be tangible. *It is the opinion of the Court that such impulses are not tangible and hence do not constitute an "article."*

The legal system has explicit rules of what constitutes property. Generally, property is tangible, unlike magnetic impulses. To a computer professional, taking a copy of a software package without permission is clear-cut theft. However, the courts have not yet accepted a definition of property that is so different from its traditional meaning.

A similar problem arises with computer services. We would generally agree that unauthorized access to a computing system is a crime. Unauthorized use of a neighbor's lawn mower constitutes theft, even if the lawn mower was returned in essentially the same condition as when it was taken. However, because access is not a physical object, the courts are reticent to punish that as theft.

Rules of Evidence

Computer printouts have been used as evidence in many successful fraud prosecutions. However, the legal system has yet to accept such widely used media as magnetic tapes and disks as adequate evidence. Under the rules of evidence, courts prefer an original source document over a copy, under the assumption that the copy may be inaccurate. Magnetic media are interpreted by the courts as a repository for a copy of some paper document, rather than an original.

However, magnetic and optical media are becoming the primary means of storing data. In some instances, the magnetic copy is the *only* copy; there is no paper copy. Thus, as technology advances, devices such as smart cards, optical disks, and memory chips will have to be accepted as evidence. Courts are understandably reluctant to change their procedures because varying the rules of evidence to accommodate computer media may also create a precedent that would also accept some less-desirable medium as a side effect.

Threats to Integrity and Confidentiality

The integrity and secrecy of data are also an issue in many court cases. Parker [PAR84] describes a case in which a trespasser acquired remote access to a computing system. The computing system contained confidential records about people, and the integrity of the data was important. The prosecution of this case had to be phrased in terms of theft of computer time and valued as such, even though that was insignificant compared to loss of privacy and integrity. Why? Because the law as written recognized theft of computer time as a loss, but not loss of privacy or destruction of data.

Several federal and state laws recognize the privacy of data about individuals. For example, disclosing grades or financial information without permission is a crime. These laws prevent computing center employees from disclosing data, but the laws do not apply to someone who acquires access without permission.

Value of Data

In another computer crime, a person was found guilty of having stolen a substantial amount of data from a computer data bank. However, the court determined that the "value" of that data was the cost of the paper on which it was printed, which was only a couple of

- *Fingerprints.* Police and courts have for years depended on tangible evidence, such as fingerprints. As readers of Sherlock Holmes know, seemingly minuscule clues can lead to solutions to the most complicated crimes (or so Doyle would have you believe). But with many computer crimes there simply are no fingerprints, no physical clues.

- *Forms of assets.* We know what cash is, or diamonds, or even negotiable securities. But are 20 invisible magnetic spots really equivalent to a million dollars? Is computer time an asset? What is the value of stolen computer time if the system would have been idle during the time of the theft?

- *Juveniles.* Many computer crimes involve juveniles. Society understands immaturity and can treat even very serious crimes by juveniles as being done with less understanding than when the same crime is committed by an adult. A more serious, related problem is that many adults see juvenile computer crimes as childhood pranks, the modern equivalent of tipping over an outhouse.

Prosecutors analyze costs and benefits: a case that is unlikely to win or one that will require too much preparation may never be brought to trial. If the law does not quite fit the crime, or if an inappropriate statute has to be stretched to include a computer crime, the likelihood of conviction is narrower. Even if the law fits, there may be so little evidence that a conviction is dubious. Then there is the problem of presenting very technical evidence to a jury that is potentially not very computer literate and is perhaps even afraid of (or biased against) technology.

Conventional murder cases are easier to understand and, for the elected prosecutor, easier to justify. The public cry for "law and order" is more likely to resonate with prosecuting murders, burglaries, and other violent crimes than with prosecuting more esoteric computer crime. Computer crimes seldom involve "popular victims," with whom the public immediately sympathizes; more typically the victim of a computer crime is a large corporation, which the public thinks can probably afford to lose a large sum of money. For all these reasons, prosecutors may avoid computer crimes if the workload is heavy.

Then, too, the victim may not want to prosecute because of the possibility of a negative feeling due to the publicity. Banks, insurance companies, investment firms, the government, and health care groups think their trust by the public will be diminished if a vulnerability of their computer is exposed. Also, they may fear repetition of the same crime by others. For all these reasons computer crimes are often not prosecuted.

Examples of Statutes

Computer crime laws are rather new. Most states have enacted computer crime bills, usually since 1980. Although the state bills are similar, there is no model computer crime statute; such a statute could make prosecution of computer crime cases and interchange of computer crime data and evidence easier. There is also a federal crime statute, although it covers only federal computers.

U.S. Computer Crime Statute

The primary federal statute, 18 USC 1030, was enacted in 1984. This statute prohibits

- unauthorized access to a computer containing data protected due to national defense or foreign relations

dollars. Because of that value, this crime was classified as a misdemeanor, a minor c
Fortunately, the courts have since determined that information and other intangibles
have significant value.

Paper money is accepted as a valuable commodity, even if the paper it is printed on
worth only a few cents. Cash is easy to value: a dollar bill is worth one dollar. The assets
a credit bureau are its files. Banks and insurance companies willingly pay $20 or more for
credit report, even though the paper itself is worth less than a dollar. For a credit bureau, the
amount a willing customer will pay for a report is a fair estimate of the report's value; this
estimate is called the market value of the report. However, a confidential list of clients has
no market value that can be established. The value of confidential information relates to the
loss suffered when the secret information is revealed. Although these methods of valuation
are accepted in civil suits, they have not yet been widely accepted in criminal prosecution.

Acceptance of Computer Terminology

Another area in which law is lagging behind technology is the acceptance of definitions of
terms in computing. For example, according to a federal statute, it is unlawful to commit
arson within a federal enclave (18 USC 81). Part of that act relates to "machinery or building material or supplies" in the enclave, but court decisions have ruled that a motor vehicle
located within a federal enclave at the time of the burning was not included under this
statute. Because of that ruling, it is not clear whether computer hardware constitutes
"machinery" in this context; "supplies" almost certainly does not include software. Computers and their software, media, and data must be understood and accepted by the legal
system.

Why Computer Crime Is Hard to Define

From these examples, it is clear that the legal community has not accommodated advances
in computers as rapidly as the rest of society has. Some people in the legal process do not
understand computers and computing, so that these people cannot treat properly crimes
involving computers. Creating and changing laws are slow processes, intended to involve
substantial thought about the effects of proposed changes. This deliberate process is very
much out of pace with a technology that is progressing as fast as computing is.

Adding to the problem of a rapidly changing technology, a computer can perfo
many roles in a crime. A particular computer can be the subject, object, or medium
crime. A computer can be attacked (attempted unauthorized access), used to attack (
sonating a legitimate node on a network), and used as a means to commit crime
horse or fake login). Computer crime statutes have to include all of these evils.

Why Computer Crime Is Hard to Prosecute

Even when it is acknowledged that a computer crime has been committed, th
reasons why computer crime is hard to prosecute.

- *Understanding.* Neither courts, lawyers, police agents, nor jurors
  stand computers. Many judges began practicing law before the i
  ers, and most began before the widespread use of the personal c
  computer literacy in the courts is improving, as judges, lawy
  are becoming more computer literate.

- unauthorized access to a computer containing certain banking or financial information

uction, or disclosure of a computer or
of the U.S. government

ce the value obtained by the offense,
to 20 years, or both.

mputer terms and then prohibit certain
ute, shown below. Note that the defini-
y to include everything that would typi-
ce that two crimes have been specified:
ige to a computer system. As is typical
s are classified as misdemeanors (small
higher-valued crimes are classified as
ther delineate the crimes.

computer system, computer network, or
or executing any scheme or artifice to
es by means of false or fraudulent pre-
ing theft, commits computer crime.
ization uses, alters, damages, or destroys
twork described in section 18-5.5-101 or
on, or data contained in such computer,
s computer crime.
violation of this section is less than fifty
hor; if fifty dollars or more but less than
2 misdemeanor; if two hundred dollars or
ter crime is a class 4 felony; if ten thou-
3 felony.

ng of suspected computer crimes. If sus-
more serious instances of a crime can be
seful in tracking an unknown criminal.
ie position of trust to another, simply
because one company is happy for the criminal to leave without the negative publicity of a
crime committed by an employee. If suspected crimes were reported, these criminals
would be unable to continue their crimes undetected.

U.S. Federal Statutes Related to Computing

Several federal statutes relate to common applications of computing. These are the Freedom of Information Act, the Privacy Act of 1974, and the Fair Credit Reporting Act. These
laws control uses of data; because most of this data is gathered, stored, organized, or
processed by means of computers, the laws affect many computer applications.

Freedom of Information Act

The Freedom of Information Act provides public access to information collected by the executive branch of the federal government. The act requires disclosure of any available data, unless the data fall under one of several specific exceptions, such as national security or personal privacy. The original intention of the law was to release to individuals any information the government had collected on them. However, more corporations than individuals file requests for information as a means of obtaining information about the workings of the government. Foreign governments can even file for information. This act applies only to government agencies, although similar laws could require disclosure from private sources. The effect of this law is to require increased classification and protection for sensitive information.

Privacy Act of 1974

The Privacy Act of 1974 protects the privacy of personal data collected by the government. An individual is allowed to determine what data has been collected on him or her, for what purpose, and to whom such information has been disseminated. An additional use of the law is to prevent one government agency from accessing data collected by another agency for another purpose. This act requires diligent efforts to preserve the secrecy of private data collected.

Fair Credit Reporting Act

The Fair Credit Reporting Act applies to private industry. The law governs what types of data may be collected on individuals and to what purposes the data may be used. For example, commercial credit bureaus collect data on credit history (payment records, bankruptcy proceedings, unpaid liens, and so forth). This information can legitimately be distributed for individuals seeking credit, employment, insurance, and for other business needs. The act limits what data may be stored and how long certain forms of data may be maintained (for example, most adverse information, like arrest records, bankruptcies, and lawsuits, cannot be maintained longer than seven years). The consumer has a right to know the contents of the information collected about him or her and, if the information is incorrect, the law gives a means for having the information corrected. Thus integrity of the data is legally required. Finally, the law gives penalties for unauthorized disclosure of information by the collector.

Other Statutes

These laws have been passed partially in response to the growing use of computers to maintain information about individuals. They all support the individual's right to privacy and demand that groups collecting data maintain that privacy. Other similar laws are likely to ensure the privacy of financial, medical, and other types of personal records. All of these situations place an even greater emphasis on proper computer security measures in both the public and private sector.

What Computer Crime Does Not Address

Even with the definitions included in the statutes, the courts must interpret what is a computer. Legislators cannot define precisely what a computer is because computer technology is used in many other devices, such as robots, calculators, automobiles, watches, and medical instruments. More importantly, we cannot predict what kinds of devices may be invented 10 or 50 years from now. Therefore, the language in each of these laws indicates the kinds of devices the legislature seeks to include as computers, and leaves it up to the court to rule on a specific case. Unfortunately, it takes a while for courts to build up a pattern of cases, and different courts may rule differently in similar situations. The interpretation of each of these terms will be unsettled for some time to come.

Value presents a similar problem. As noted in some of the cases presented, the courts have trouble separating the intrinsic value of an object (such as a sheet of paper with writing on it) from its cost to reproduce. The courts now recognize that a dollar bill is worth more than the cost of the paper and printing. But the courts have not agreed on the value of printed computer output. The cost of a blank diskette is less than $1, but it may have taken thousands of hours of data gathering and machine time to produce the data encoded on the diskette. The courts are still striving to compute the fair value of computer objects.

The value of a person's privacy and secrecy of data about a person are even less settled. In a later section we will consider how ethics and individual morality take over where the law stops.

Cryptography and the Law

The law is used to regulate people for their own good and for the greater good of society. Murder, theft, and eating on the underground are circumscribed by laws. Generally, the balance between personal freedom and the good of society is fairly easy to judge; for example, one's right to fire a gun ends when the bullet hits someone. Cryptography is also a regulated activity, but the issues are a little less clear-cut, in part because there is little open discussion of the subject.

People want to be able to protect their privacy, including the secrecy of communications with others. Businesses want similar confidentiality. Criminals want secrecy so that they can communicate criminal plans in private. Governments want to track illegal activity, both to prevent crime and to apprehend and convict criminals after a crime has been committed. Finally, nations want to know the military and diplomatic plans of other nations. As shown throughout this book, cryptography can be a potent tool to protect confidentiality, but being able to break cryptography can be a potent tool for government. Phrased differently, it suits governments' interests if people cannot use cryptography that is too good (meaning, unbreakable by the government).

Some governments prohibit use of cryptography by their citizens or within their borders. France, for example, generally prohibits use of encryption by individuals, asserting that in order to control terrorism, it must have access to communications of suspected terrorists.

The United States, Britain, Canada, and Germany are freer about what can be used within their borders, but they control the *export* of cryptography. Here the use of law gets complicated. It is difficult to control the export of cryptographic algorithms because they are simply mathematical functions, ideas. Thus, descriptions of algorithms, such as DES, RSA, El Gamal, and the knapsack ciphers are widely published throughout the world in journals and books, such as this one. But what constitutes the expression of an idea? The algorithm could be expressed in words, or in pseudo-code, or in a language of controlled syntax, such as a programming language. The United States has allowed free export of public algorithms in printed form. At the same time, the United States controls export of cryptography implemented in software, seeming to disregard the fact that typists, compilers, and scanners can convert printed source code into software. Thus, software and hardware are widely available essentially all over the world to perform DES, RSA, El Gamal, MD4, MD5, and other popular forms of cryptography. It is just that the hardware and software cannot be freely traded by individuals or companies between countries.

The U.S. National Research Council (NRC) performed an 18-month study [NRC96] to recommend a cryptographic policy for the U.S. Federal government. The report carefully weighed all the factors affected by cryptographic policy, such as protection of sensitive information for U.S. companies and individuals as well as foreign ones, international commerce, law enforcement (prevention, investigation, and prosecution), and intelligence gathering. The report's recommendations for policy include the following:

- No law should bar the manufacture, sale, or use of any form of encryption within the United States.
- Export controls on cryptography should be relaxed, but not eliminated.
- Products providing confidentiality at a level that meets most general commercial requirements should be easily exportable. In 1996, that level includes products that incorporate 56-bit key DES, so these products should be easily exportable.
- Escrowed encryption should be studied further but, as it is not yet a mature technology, its use should not be mandated.
- Congress should seriously consider legislation that would impose criminal penalties on the use of encrypted communications in interstate commerce with the intent to commit a crime.
- The U.S. government should develop a mechanism to promote information security in the private sector.

These strong recommendations clearly support increasing the use of encryption to protect personal privacy and sensitive business information. The U.S. government, known to favor its own key escrow technology, gave a clear signal after release of the report that it would continue to press for escrowing as a condition for export permission.

The European Commission and the United States have both suggested that they will permit export of escrowed encryption systems. Details about who would escrow keys for whom have yet to be determined, which has civil liberties groups very concerned. The United States is the key player in the export debate because the bulk of software products in export are developed by companies based in the United States, and these companies will not integrate cryptographic protection into their products unless they can sell the same products in the United States and in other countries. Thus, U.S. export policy sets a de facto limit on widespread availability of products incorporating cryptography throughout the world.

The legal status of use and trade of cryptography is changing very rapidly throughout the world. The situation is certain to have evolved between the time this is written and the time you read it.

Summary of Legal Issues in Computer Security

This section has described three aspects of the relationship between computing and the law. First, the legal mechanisms of copyright, patent, and trade secret were presented as means to protect the secrecy of computer hardware, software, and data. These mechanisms were designed before the invention of the computer, so their applicability to computing needs is somewhat limited. However, program protection is especially desired, and software companies are pressing the courts to extend the interpretation of these means of protection to include computers.

The second topic considered in this section was the relationship between employers and employees, in the context of writers of software. Well-established laws and precedents control the acceptable access an employee has to software written for a company.

Third, this section presented some of the difficulties in prosecuting computer crime. Several examples showed how breaches of computer security are treated by the courts. In general, the courts have not yet granted computers, software, and data appropriate status considering value of assets and seriousness of crime. The legal system is moving cautiously in its acceptance of computers. Several important pieces of computer crime legislation were described.

11.5   Ethical Issues in Computer Security

This final section will help to clarify thinking about the ethical issues involved in computer security. The section offers no answers. Rather, after listing and explaining some ethical principles, it presents several case studies to which the principles can be applied. Each case is followed by a list of possible ethical issues involved, although the list is not necessarily all-inclusive or conclusive. The primary purpose of this section is to explore some of the ethical issues associated with computer security and to show how ethics functions as a control in computer security.

The Law and Ethics Are Not the Same

As explained in the last section, law is not always the appropriate way to deal with issues of human behavior. It is difficult to define a law to preclude only the events we want it to. For example, a law that prevents animals in public places must be refined to *permit* guide dogs for the blind. Lawmakers, who are not computer professionals, are hard-pressed to think of all the exceptions when they draft a law. Even when a law is well-conceived and well-written, the enforcement of the law may be difficult. The courts are overburdened, and prosecuting relatively minor infractions may be excessively time-consuming relative to the benefit.

Thus, it is impossible or impractical to develop laws to describe and enforce all forms of behavior acceptable to society. Instead, society relies on **ethics** or **morals** to prescribe generally accepted standards of proper behavior. (In this section the terms ethics and morals are used interchangeably.) An **ethic** is an objectively defined standard of right and wrong. Ethical standards are often idealistic principles because they focus on one objective. In a given situation, however, several moral objectives may be involved, so that people have to determine an action that is appropriate, considering all the objectives. Even though religious groups and professional organizations promote certain standards of ethical behavior, ultimately each person is responsible for deciding what to do in a specific situation. Therefore, through choices, each person defines a personal set of ethical practices. A set of ethical principles is called an **ethical system**.

An ethic is different from a law in several important ways. First, laws apply to everyone: one may disagree with the intent or the meaning of a law, but that is not an excuse for disobeying the law. Second, there is a regular process through the courts for determining which law supersedes which if two laws conflict. Third, the laws and the courts identify certain actions as right and others as wrong. From a legal standpoint, anything that is not illegal is right. Finally, laws can be enforced, and there are ways to rectify wrongs done by unlawful behavior.

By contrast, ethics are personal: two people may have different frameworks for making moral judgments. What one person thinks is perfectly justifiable, another would never consider doing. Second, ethical positions can and often do come into conflict. As an example, the value of a human life is very important in most ethical systems. Most people would not cause the sacrifice of one life, but in the right context some would approve of sacrificing one person to save another, or one to save many others. The value of one life cannot be readily measured against the value of others, and it is precisely this ambiguity on which many ethical decisions must be founded. Yet, there is no arbiter of ethical positions: when two ethical goals collide, each person must choose which goal is dominant. Third, two people may assess ethical values differently; there is no universal standard of right and wrong in ethical judgments. Nor can one person simply look to what another has done as guidance for choosing the right thing to do. Finally, there is no enforcement for ethical choices. These differences are summarized in Table 11-2.

Studying Ethics

The study of ethics is not easy because the issues are complex. Sometimes people confuse ethics with religion because many religions supply a framework in which to make ethical choices. Religions supply several moral frameworks, but ethics can be studied apart from any religious connection. Difficult choices would be easier to make if there were a set of universal ethical principles to which everyone agreed. However, the variety of social, cultural, and religious beliefs makes the identification of such a set of universal principles impossible. In this section we explore some of these problems with studying ethics, and then consider how an understanding of ethics can help in dealing with issues of computer security.

Ethics and Religion

Ethics is a set of principles or norms for justifying what is right or wrong in a given situation. To understand what ethics *is* we may start by trying to understand what it is *not*. Ethical principles are different from religious beliefs. Religion is based on personal notions

Table 11-2   Contrast of Law Versus Ethics

Law	Ethics
Described by formal, written documents	Described by unwritten principles
Interpreted by courts	Interpreted by each individual
Established by legislatures representing all people	Presented by philosophers, religions, professional groups
Applicable to everyone	Personal choice
Priority determined by courts if two laws conflict	Priority determined by an individual if two principles conflict
Court is final arbiter of "right"	No external arbiter
Enforceable by police and courts	Limited enforcement

about the creation of the world and the existence of controlling forces or beings. Many moral principles are embodied in the major religions, and the basis of a personal morality is a matter of belief and conviction, much the same as for religions. However, two people with different religious backgrounds may develop the same ethical philosophy, while two exponents of the same religion might reach opposite ethical conclusions in a particular situation. Finally, we can analyze a situation from an ethical perspective and reach ethical conclusions without appealing to any particular religion or religious framework. Thus, it is important to distinguish ethics from religion.

Ethics Is Not Universal

Ethical values vary by society, and from person to person within a society. For example, the concept of privacy is very important in western cultures. But in eastern cultures, privacy is not desirable because people associate privacy with having something to hide. Not only is a westerner's desire for privacy not understood, but it has a negative connotation. Therefore, the attitudes of people may be affected by culture or background.

Also, an individual's standards of behavior may be influenced by past events in life. A person who grew up in a large family may place greater emphasis on personal control and ownership of possessions than would an only child who seldom had to share. Major events or close contact with others can also shape one's ethical position. Despite these differences, the underlying principles of how to make moral judgment are the same.

Although these aspects of ethics are quite reasonable and understandable, they lead people to distrust ethics because it is not founded on basic principles all can accept. Also, people from a scientific or technical background expect precision and universality.

Ethics Does Not Provide Answers

Ethical pluralism is recognizing or admitting that more than one position may be ethically justifiable—even equally so—in a given situation. Pluralism is another way of noting that two people may legitimately disagree on issues of ethics. We expect and accept disagreement in such areas as politics and religion.

However, in the scientific and technical fields, people expect to find unique, unambiguous, and unequivocal answers. In science one answer must be correct or demonstrable in some sense. Science has provided life with fundamental explanations. Ethics is rejected or misunderstood by some scientists because it is "soft," meaning that it has no underlying framework, or it does not depend on fundamental truths.

One need only study the history of scientific discovery to see that science itself is founded largely on temporary truths. For many years the earth was believed to be the center of the solar system. Ptolemy developed a complicated framework of epicycles, orbits within orbits of the planets, to explain the inconsistency of observed periods of rotation. Eventually his theory was superseded by the Copernican model of planets that orbit the sun. Similarly, Einstein's relativity theory opposed the traditional quantum basis of physics. Science is littered with theories that have fallen from favor as we learned or observed more and new explanations were proposed. As each new theory is proposed, some people readily accept the new proposal, while others cling to the old.

But the basis of science is presumed to be "truth." A statement is expected to be provably true, provably false, or unproven, but a statement can never be both true and false. Scientists are uncomfortable with ethics because ethics does not provide these clean distinctions.

Worse, there is no higher authority of ethical truth. Two people may disagree on their opinion of the ethics of a situation, but there is no one to whom to appeal for a final determination of who is "right." Conflicting answers do not deter one from considering ethical issues in computer security. Nor do they excuse us from making and defending ethical choices.

Ethical Reasoning

Most people make ethical judgments often, perhaps daily. (Is it better to buy from a home town merchant or from nationwide chain? Should I spend time with a volunteer organization or my friends? Is it acceptable to release sensitive data to someone who might not have justification for access to that data?) Because we all engage in ethical choice, we should clarify how we do this, so that we can learn to apply the principles of ethics in professional situations, as we do in private life.

Study of ethics can yield two positive results. First, in situations where we already know what is right and what is wrong, ethics should help us justify our choice. Second, if we do not know what is the ethical action to take in a situation, ethics can help us to identify the issues involved, so that we can make reasoned judgments.

Examining a Case for Ethical Issues

How, then, can issues of ethical choice in computer security be approached? There are several steps to making and justifying an ethical choice.

1. *Understand the situation.* Learn the facts of the situation. Ask questions of interpretation or clarification. Attempt to find out whether there are any relevant forces that have not been considered.
2. *Know several theories of ethical reasoning.* To make an ethical choice, it is necessary to know how those choices can be justified.
3. *List the ethical principles involved.* What are the different philosophies that could be applied in this case? Do any of these include others?
4. *Determine which principles outweigh others.* This is a subjective evaluation. It often involves extending a principle to a logical conclusion, or determining cases in which one principle clearly supersedes another.

The most important steps are the first and third. Too often people judge a situation on incomplete information, which leads to judgments based on prejudice, suspicion, or misinformation. Considering all the different ethical issues raised forms the basis for evaluating the competing interests of step four.

Examples of Ethical Principles

In this section we present two different schools of ethical reasoning: one based on the good that results from actions, and one that is based on certain prima facie duties of people.

Consequence-Based Principles   The **teleological** theory of ethics focuses on the consequences of an action. The action to be chosen is that which results in the greatest future good and the least harm. For example, if a fellow student asks you to write a program he was assigned for a class, you might consider the good (he will owe you a favor) against the bad (you might get caught, causing embarrassment and possible discipline, plus your friend will not learn the techniques to be gained from writing the program, leaving him deficient). The negative consequences clearly outweigh the positive, so you would refuse. Teleology is the general name applied to many theories of behavior, all of which focus on the goal, outcome, or consequence of the action.

There are two important forms of teleology. **Egoism** is the form that says a moral judgment is based on the positive benefits to the person taking the action. An egoist weighs the outcomes of all possible acts and chooses that one that produces the most personal good with the least negative consequence. The effects on other people are not relevant. For example, an egoist trying to justify the ethics of writing shoddy computer code when pressed for time might argue as follows. "If I complete the project quickly, I will satisfy my manager, which will bring me a raise and other good things. The customer is unlikely to know enough about the program to complain, so there is no likelihood of my being blamed. My company's reputation may be tarnished, but that will not be tracked directly to me. Thus, I can justify writing shoddy code."

The principle of **utilitarianism** is also an assessment of good and bad results, but the reference group is the entire universe. The utilitarian chooses that action that will bring the greatest collective good for all people with the least possible negative for all. In this situation, the utilitarian would assess personal good and bad, good and bad for the company, good and bad for the customer and, perhaps, good and bad for society at large (if the software were to monitor smokestack emissions, for example, so that everyone breathing would be affected). The utilitarian might perceive greater good to everyone by taking the time to write high-quality code, despite the negative personal consequence of displeasing management.

Rule-Based Principles   Another ethical theory is **deontology**, which is founded in a sense of duty. This ethical principle states that certain things are good in and of themselves. These things that are naturally good are good rules or acts, which require no higher justification. Something just *is* good, it does not have to be judged for its effect.

Examples (from Frankena [FRA73]) of intrinsic good things are

- truth; knowledge and true opinion of various kinds, understanding, wisdom
- just distribution of good and evil; justice
- pleasure, satisfaction; happiness; life, consciousness
- peace, security, freedom
- good reputation, honor, esteem; mutual affection, love, friendship, cooperation; morally good dispositions or virtues
- beauty, aesthetic experience

Rule-deontology is the school of ethical reasoning that believes there are certain universal, self-evident, natural rules that specify our proper conduct. Certain basic moral principles are adhered to because of our responsibilities to one another; these principles are often stated as rights: the right to know, the right to privacy, the right to fair compensation for work. Sir David Ross [ROS30] lists various duties incumbent on all human beings:

- *fidelity,* or truthfulness
- *reparation,* the duty to recompense for a previous wrongful act
- *gratitude,* thankfulness for previous services or kind acts
- *justice,* distribution of happiness in accordance with merit
- *beneficence,* the obligation to help other people or to make their lives better
- *nonmaleficence,* not harming others
- *self-improvement,* to become continually better, both in a mental sense and in a moral sense (for example, by not committing a wrong a second time)

Another school of reasoning is based on rules derived by each individual. Religion, teaching, experience, and reflection lead each person to a set of personal moral principles. The answer to an ethical question is found by weighing values in terms of what a person believes to be right behavior.

Summary of Ethical Theories

We have seen two bases of ethical theories, each applied in two ways. Simply stated, the two bases are consequence-based and rule-based, and the applications were either individual or universal. These theories are depicted in Figure 11-1.

Now we will start to apply these theories in analysis of certain situations that arise in the ethics of computer security situations.

11.6   Electronic Privacy

In most nations an individual is entitled to privacy, either by law or by strong precedent. The right to privacy can be abridged only in case of a stronger interest, such as prosecution of a crime or protection of rights of others. The right of privacy is often held very strongly both in the courts and personally as an ethical issue.

Electronic communication is inherently a fairly open technology. For efficiency, an individual's signals are stored, combined, and shared with signals belonging to others. Again for efficiency, these are often stored and transmitted in a very open manner. This degree of openness largely means that communications are open to intrusion of others. Significant ethical issues arise in the degree to which others intrude in private communications.

Privacy of Electronic Data

"Gentlemen do not read other's mail," said Henry L. Stimson, U.S. Secretary of State in 1929. Perhaps true, but not everyone in the world is a gentleman. Thus, information security includes the ethical question of when it is justifiable to access data not belonging to you.

	Consequence-Based	Rule-Based
Individual	Based on consequences to individual	Based on rules acquired by the individual from religion, experience, analysis
Universal	Based on consequences to all of society	Based on universal rules, evident to everyone

Figure 11-1   Taxonomy of Ethical Theories

One argument is that protection is a responsibility of the owner: anything unprotected is open to all. This position leads to the analogy of a house: if a house is left unlocked, is it ethical to enter the house and look around or take something? Most people do not think so.

Another possible position is that some people in a supervisory capacity have a legitimate right to the data of those they supervise. In this sense, a parent has a right to monitor the data of a minor child, a teacher has the right to access a student's files, and an employer is justified in observing employees. Here many people would agree, at least up to a point. The parent-child situation is presumably to protect the child from harm or wrongdoing. At some point as the child matures, the child has to make decisions independently, and thus it can be argued that a child needs some degree of privacy. With the teacher–student and employer–employee cases, education and work mix with personal life. One can argue that a student or employee using provided computing equipment should use it only for the purpose for which it was provided, and thus all use should be open for inspection. In practice, however, in school and in work a moderate amount of personal use is tacitly tolerated, and thus it can be impossible for the supervisor to separate private from open use.

A commonly agreed position is the compelling situation: because of some situation it became important enough to access the data as to override personal rights (for example, if an employee is unavailable and someone needs a copy of a report that only the employee has, or if the teacher is looking for a copy of a virus program that has recently infected many programs at the school). In these kinds of cases, the right to access is not unlimited: it is a right to access only what is necessary to meet the needs of the situation. Looking for a specific report is not a justification for reading every word in every file.

There are thus reasonable justifications for overriding someone's right to privacy of electronic data. The opposite side of this issue is whether there is a basis for blocking access.

Use of Encryption

In a paper-based case, an employer looking for a report on tree frogs would probably not have good justification for opening a folder marked "recipes" or "financial data," and a locked drawer labeled "PERSONAL!" should be off limits in all but the most serious of searches. The electronic equivalent of a locked personal drawer would be an encrypted file. Is use of encryption justifiable?

There are several cases to consider.

- In the supervisory case, if the student or employee is allowed to use computing resources for personal purposes, can the employee encrypt personal data?
- Can an employee encrypt work-related data?
- Can an employer encrypt data to protect it from competitors?
- Can a private citizen encrypt data to protect it against its being read by anyone else, including the government?

The key question in all these situations is who benefits and to what degree. Encryption excludes access by others. Does the benefit of privacy exceed the benefit of exclusion? In the case of work-related data, if the employee is absent (at a meeting, sick, or on holiday, for example), there is a strong penalty if the employer cannot access work-related materials because they are encrypted.

Cryptographic Key Escrow

The negative side of limited access because of encryption can be overcome if a key is left with a trusted party. An employee, for example, might protect a sensitive file by encryption, but leave a copy of the key with someone who might need access to the file. Key escrow is a means of allowing access to encrypted data only after demonstration of justification.

The ethical issues associated with key escrow are whether citizens should be forced to have keys escrowed and whether the escrow agents are trustworthy.

11.7   Case Studies of Ethics

To be able to analyze how ethics affects professional actions, ethicists often study example situations. The remainder of this section consists of examples to analyze. These cases are modeled after ones developed by Parker [PAR79] as part of the AFIPS/NSF study of ethics in computing and technology. Each case study is designed to bring out certain ethical points, some of which are listed following the case. You should reflect on each case, determining for yourself what are the most influential points. These cases are suitable for use in a class discussion, where other values will certainly be mentioned. Finally, each case reaches no conclusion because each individual must assess the ethical situation alone. In a class discussion it may be appropriate to take a vote. Remember, however, that ethics is not determined by majority rule. Those siding with the majority are not right, and the rest are not wrong.

Case I: Use of Computer Services

This case concerns deciding what is appropriate use of computer time. Use of computer time is a question both of access by one person and of availability of quality service to others. The person involved is permitted to access computing facilities for a certain purpose. Many companies rely on an unwritten standard of behavior that governs what people who have legitimate access to a computing system can do. The ethical issues involved in this case can lead to an understanding of that unwritten standard.

The Case

Dave works as a programmer for a large software company. He writes and tests utility programs such as compilers. His company operates two computing shifts: during the day program development and on-line applications are run; at night batch production jobs are completed. Dave has access to workload data and learns that the evening batch runs are complementary to daytime programming tasks; that is, adding programming work during the night shift would not adversely affect performance of the computer to other users.

Dave comes back after normal hours to develop a program to manage his own stock portfolio. His drain on the system is minimal, and he uses very few expendable supplies, such as printer paper. Is Dave's behavior ethical?

Values Issues

Some of the ethical principles involved in this case are listed below.

- *Ownership of resources.* The company owns the computing resources and provides them for its own computing needs.

- *Effect on others.* Although unlikely, a flaw in Dave's program could adversely affect other users, perhaps even denying them service because of a system failure.
- *Universalism principle.* If Dave's action is acceptable, it should also be acceptable for others to do the same. However, too many employees working in the evening could reduce system effectiveness.
- *Possibility of detection, punishment.* Dave does not know whether his action would be wrong or right if discovered by his company. If his company decided it was improper use, Dave could be punished.

What other issues are involved? Which principles are more important than others?

Analysis

The utilitarian would consider the total excess of good over bad for all people. Dave receives benefit from use of computer time, although for this application the amount of time is not large. Dave has a possibility of punishment, but he may rate that as unlikely. The company is neither harmed nor helped by this. Thus, the utilitarian could argue that Dave's use is justifiable.

The universalism principle seems as if it would cause a problem because clearly if everyone did this, quality of service would degrade. A utilitarian would say that each new user has to weigh good and bad separately. Dave's use might not burden the machine, and neither might Ann's, but when Bill wants to use the machine, it is heavily enough used that Bill's use *would* affect other people.

Alternative Situations

Would it affect the ethics of the situation if

- Dave began a business managing stock portfolios for many people for profit?
- Dave's salary were below average for his background, implying that Dave was due the computer use as a fringe benefit?
- Dave's employer knew of other employees doing similar things and tacitly approved by not seeking to stop them?
- Dave worked for a government office instead of a private company and reasoned that the computer belonged "to the people"?

Case II: Privacy Rights

In this case the central issue is the individual's right to privacy. This is both a legal and an ethical issue because of the Federal Privacy Act of 1974, discussed in the previous section.

The Case

Donald works for the county health department as a computer records clerk, where he has access to files of patient records. For a scientific study, a researcher, Ethel has been granted access to the medical portion—but not the corresponding names—of some records.

Ethel finds some information that she would like to use, but she needs the names and addresses corresponding with certain medical histories. Ethel asks Donald to retrieve the names and addresses in order to contact these people for more information and for permission to do further study.

Should Donald release the names and addresses?

Some Principles Involved

Here are some of the ethical principles involved in this case. What are other ethical principles? Which principles are subordinate to which others?

- *Job responsibility.* Donald's job is to manage individual records, not to make determinations of appropriate use. Policy decisions should be made by someone of higher authority.
- *Use.* The records are used for legitimate scientific study, not for profit or to expose sensitive data. (However, Ethel's access is authorized only for the medical data, not for the private information relating medical conditions to individuals.)
- *Possible misuse.* Although he believes Ethel's motives are proper, Donald cannot guarantee that Ethel will use the data only to follow up on interesting data items.
- *Confidentiality.* Had Ethel been intended to have names and addresses, they would have been given initially.
- *Tacit permission.* Ethel has been granted permission to access parts of these records for research purposes, so she should have access to complete her research.
- *Propriety.* Because Ethel has no authority to obtain names and addresses, and because the names and addresses represent the confidential part of the data, Donald should deny Ethel's request for access.

Analysis

A rule deontologist would argue that privacy is an inherent good, and that one should not violate the privacy of another. Therefore, Donald should not release the names.

Extensions to the Basic Case

In this section we consider several possible extensions to the scenario. These extensions probe other ethical issues involved in this case.

- Suppose Donald were responsible for determining allowable access to the files. What ethical issues would be involved in his deciding whether to grant access to Ethel?
- Should Ethel be allowed to contact the individuals involved? That is, should the health department release individuals' names to a researcher? What are the ethical issues for the health department to consider?
- Suppose Ethel contacts the individuals to ask their permission, and one-third respond giving permission, one-third respond denying permission, and one-third do not respond. Ethel claims that at least one-half of the individuals are needed to make a valid study. What options are available to Ethel? What are the ethical issues involved in deciding which of these options to pursue?

Case III: Denial of Service

This case addresses issues related to the effect of one person's computation on other users. This is another situation involving people with legitimate access, so that standard access controls should not exclude these people. However, because of the actions of some, other people are denied legitimate access to the system. Thus, the focus of this case is on the rights of all users.

The Case

Charlie and Carol are students at a university in a computer science program. Each writes a program for a class assignment. Charlie's program happens to uncover a flaw in a compiler which, ultimately, causes the entire computing system to fail, causing all users to lose the results of their current computation. Charlie's program uses acceptable features of the language; the compiler is at fault. Charlie did not suspect his program would cause a system failure. He reports the program to the computing center and tries to find ways to achieve his intended result without exercising the system flaw.

The system continues to fail periodically, for a total of 10 times (beyond the first failure). When the system fails, sometimes Charlie is running a program, but sometimes Charlie is not. The director contacts Charlie, who shows all of his program versions to the computing center staff. The staff concludes that Charlie may have been inadvertently responsible for some, but not all, of the system failures, but that his latest approach to solving the assigned problem is unlikely to lead to additional system failures.

On further analysis, the computing center director notes that Carol has had programs running each of the first 8 (of 10) times the system failed. The director uses administrative privilege to inspect Carol's files and finds a file that exploits the same vulnerability as did Charlie's program. The director immediately suspends Carol's account, denying Carol access to the computing system. Because of this, Carol is unable to complete her assignment on time, she receives a D in the course, and she drops out of school.

Analysis

In this case the choices are intentionally not obvious. The situation is presented as a completed scenario, but in studying it you are being asked to suggest alternative actions the players *could have taken*. In this way, you build a repertoire of actions that you can consider in similar situations that might arise.

- What additional information is needed?
- Who has rights in this case? What rights are those? Who has a responsibility to protect those rights? (This step in ethical study is used to clarify who should be considered as the reference group for a deontological analysis.)
- Has Charlie acted responsibly? By what evidence do you conclude so? Has Carol? How? Has the computing center director? How? (In this step you look for past judgments that should be confirmed, or wrongs that should be redressed.)
- What are some alternate actions Charlie or Carol or the director could have taken that would have been more responsible?

Case IV: Ownership of Programs

In this case we consider who owns programs: the programmer, the employer, the manager, or all. From a legal standpoint, most rights belong to the employer, as presented in the previous section. However, this case expands on that position by presenting several competing arguments that might be used to support positions in this case. As described in the previous section, legal controls for secrecy of programs can be complicated, time-consuming, and expensive to apply. In this case we search for individual ethical controls that can prevent the need to appeal to the legal system.

The Case

Greg is a programmer working for a large aerospace firm, Star Computers, which works on many government contracts; Cathy is Greg's supervisor. Greg is assigned to program various kinds of simulations.

To improve his programming abilities, Greg writes some programming tools, such as a cross-reference facility and a program that automatically extracts documentation from source code. These are not assigned tasks for Greg; he writes them independently and uses them at work, but he does not tell anyone about them. Greg has written them in the evenings, at home, on his personal computer.

Greg decides to market these programming aids by himself. When Star's management hears of this, Cathy is instructed to tell Greg that he has no right to market these products because when he was employed, he signed a form stating that all inventions become the property of the company. Cathy does not agree with this position because she knows that Greg has done this work on his own. She reluctantly tells Greg that he cannot market these products. She also asks Greg for a copy of the products.

Cathy quits work for Star and takes a supervisory position with Purple Computers, a competitor of Star. She takes with her a copy of Greg's products and distributes it to the people who work with her. These products are so successful that they substantially improve the effectiveness of her employees, and Cathy is praised by her management and receives a healthy bonus. Greg hears of this, and contacts Cathy, who contends that because the product was determined to belong to Star, and since Star worked largely on government funding, the products were really in the public domain and therefore they belonged to no one in particular.

Analysis

This case certainly has major legal implications. Probably everyone could sue everyone else and, depending on the amount they are willing to spend on legal expenses, they could keep the cases in the courts for several years. Probably no judgment would satisfy all.

Let us set aside the legal aspects and look at the ethical issues. We want to determine who might have done what, and what changes might have been possible to prevent a tangle for the courts to unscramble.

First, let us explore the principles involved.

- *Rights.* What are the respective rights of Greg, Cathy, Star, and Purple?
- *Basis.* What gives Greg, Cathy, Star, and Purple those rights? What principles of fair play, business, property rights, and so forth are involved in this case?
- *Priority.* Which of these principles are inferior to which others? Which ones take precedence? (Note that it may be impossible to compare two different rights, so the outcome of this analysis may yield some rights that are important but that cannot be ranked first, second, third.)
- *Additional information.* What additional facts are needed in order to analyze this case? What assumptions are you making in performing the analysis?

Next, we want to consider what events led to the situation described and what alternative actions could have prevented the negative outcomes.

- What could Greg have done differently before starting to develop his product? After developing the product? After Cathy explained that the product belonged to Star?
- What could Cathy have done differently when she was told to tell Greg that his products belonged to Star? What could Cathy have done differently to avert this decision by her management? What could Cathy have done differently to prevent the clash with Greg after she went to work at Purple?
- What could Purple have done differently upon learning that it had products from Star (or from Greg)?
- What could Greg and Cathy have done differently after Greg spoke to Cathy at Purple?
- What could Star have done differently to prevent Greg from feeling that he owned his products? What could Star have done differently to prevent Cathy from taking the products to Purple?

Case V: Proprietary Resources

In this case, we consider the issue of access to proprietary or restricted resources. Like the previous one, this case involves access to software. The focus of this case is the rights of a software developer in contrast with the rights of users, so that this case concerns determining legitimate access rights.

The Case

Suzie owns a copy of G-Whiz, a proprietary software package she purchased legitimately. The software is copyrighted, and there is a license agreement in the documentation, which says that the software is for use by the purchaser only. Suzie invites Luis to look at the software to see if it will fit his needs. Luis goes to Suzie's computer and she demonstrates the software to him. He says he likes what he sees, but he would like to try it in a longer test.

Extensions to the Case

So far the actions have all been ethically sound. The next steps are where ethical responsibilities arise. Take each of the following steps as independent; that is, do not assume that any of the other steps has occurred in your analysis of one step.

- Suzie offers to copy the disk for Luis to use.
- Suzie copies the disk for Luis to use, and Luis uses it for some period of time.
- Suzie copies the disk for Luis to use, Luis uses it for some period of time and then buys a copy for himself.
- Suzie copies the disk for Luis to try out overnight, under the restriction that he must bring the disk back to her tomorrow and must not copy it for himself. Luis does so.
- Suzie copies the disk with the same restrictions, but Luis makes a copy for himself before returning it to Suzie.
- Suzie copies the disk with the same restrictions, and Luis makes a copy for himself, but he then purchases a copy.
- Suzie copies the disk with the same restrictions, but Luis does not return it.

For each of these extensions, describe who is affected, which ethical issues are involved, and which principles override which others.

Case VI: Fraud

In previous cases, we have dealt with people acting in situations that were legal or, at worst, debatable. In this case, we consider outright fraud, which is illegal. However, the case really concerns the actions of people who are asked to do fraudulent things.

The Case

Patty works as a programmer in a corporation. David, her supervisor, tells her to write a program to allow people to post entries directly to the company's accounting files ("the books"). Patty knows that ordinarily programs that affect the books involve several steps, all of which have to balance. Patty realizes that with the new program, it will be possible for one person to make changes to crucial amounts, and there will be no way to trace who made these changes, with what justification, or when.

Patty raises these concerns to David, who tells her not to be concerned, that her job is simply to write the programs as he specifies. He says that he is aware of the potential misuse of these programs, but he justifies his request by noting that periodically a figure is mistakenly entered in the books, and the company needs a way to correct the inaccurate figure.

Extensions

First, let us explore the options Patty has. If Patty writes this program, she might be an accomplice to fraud. If she complains to David's superior, David or the superior might reprimand or fire her as a troublemaker. If she refuses to write the program, David can clearly fire her for failing to carry out an assigned task. We do not even know that the program is desired for fraudulent purposes; David suggests an explanation that is not fraudulent.

She might write the program but insert extra code that creates a secret log of when the program was run, by whom, and what changes were made. This extra file could provide evidence of fraud, or it might cause trouble for Patty if there is no fraud but David discovers it.

At this point, here are some of the ethical issues involved.

- Is a programmer responsible for the programs he or she writes? Is a programmer responsible for the results of those programs? (In contemplating this question, suppose the program were to adjust dosage in a computer-controlled medical application, and David's request were for a way to override the program controls to cause a lethal dosage. Would Patty then be responsible for the results of the program?)
- Is a programmer merely an employee who follows orders (assigned tasks) unthinkingly?
- What degree of personal risk (such as possible firing) is an employee obliged to accept for opposing an action he or she thinks is improper?
- Would a program to manipulate the books as described here ever be justified? If so, in what circumstances would it be justified?
- What kinds of controls can be placed on such programs to make them acceptable? What are some ways that a manager could legitimately ask an employee to write a program like this?

• Would the ethical issues in this situation be changed if Patty designed and wrote this program herself?

Analysis of the Basic Case

The act-deontologist would say that truth is good. Therefore, if Patty thought the purpose of the program was to deceive, writing it would not be a good act. (If the purpose were for learning, or to be able to admire beautiful code, then writing it might be justifiable.)

A more useful analysis is from the perspective of the utilitarian. To Patty, writing the program brings possible harm for being an accomplice to fraud, with the gain of having cooperated with her manager. She has a possible item with which to blackmail David, but David might also turn on her and say the program was her idea. On balance, this option seems to have a strong negative slant.

By not writing the program her possible harm is being fired. However, she has a potential gain by being able to "blow the whistle" on David. This option does not seem to bring her much good, either. But fraudulent acts have negative consequences for the stockholders, the banks, and other innocent employees. Not writing the program brings only personal harm to Patty, which is similar to the harm described earlier. Thus, it seems as if not writing the program is the more positive option.

There is another possibility. The program may *not* be for fraudulent purposes. If so, then there is no ethical conflict. Therefore, Patty might try to determine whether David's motives are fraudulent.

Case VII: Accuracy of Information

For our final case, we consider responsibility for accuracy or integrity of information. Again, this is an issue addressed by data base management systems and other access control mechanisms. However, as in previous cases, the issue here is access by an *authorized* user, so that the controls do not prevent access.

The Case

Emma is a researcher at an institute where Paul is a statistical programmer. Emma wrote a grant request to a cereal manufacturer to show the nutritional value of a new cereal, Raw Bits. The manufacturer funded Emma's study. Emma is not a statistician. She has brought all of her data to Paul to ask him to perform appropriate analyses and to print reports for her to send to the manufacturer. Unfortunately, the data Emma has collected seem to refute the claim that Raw Bits is nutritious, and in fact, they may indicate that Raw Bits is harmful.

Paul presents his analyses to Emma, but also indicates that some other correlations could be performed that would cast Raw Bits in a more favorable light. Paul makes a facetious remark about his being able to use statistics to support either side of any issue.

Ethical Concerns

Clearly, if Paul changed data values in this study he would be acting unethically. But is it any more ethical for him to suggest analyzing correct data in a way that supports two or more different conclusions? Is Paul obligated to present both the positive and the negative analyses? Is Paul responsible for the use to which others put his program results?

If Emma does not understand statistical analysis, is she acting ethically in accepting Paul's positive conclusions? His negative conclusions? Emma suspects that if she forwards negative results to the manufacturer, they will just find another researcher to do another study. She suspects that if she forwards both sets of results to the manufacturer, they will publicize only the positive ones. What ethical principles support her sending both sets of data? What principles support her sending just the positive set? What other courses of action has she?

11.8   Codes of Ethics

Because of ethical issues such as these cases, various computer groups have sought to develop codes of ethics for their members. Most computer organizations, such as the Association for Computing Machinery (ACM), the Institute of Electrical and Electronics Engineers (IEEE), and the Data Processing Management Association (DPMA), are voluntary organizations. Being a member of one of these organizations does not certify a level of competence, responsibility, or experience in computing. For these reasons, codes of ethics in these organizations are primarily advisory. Nevertheless, these codes are very good starting points for analysis of ethical issues.

IEEE

The IEEE has produced a code of ethics for the professionals who belong to the IEEE. The IEEE is an organization of engineers, not limited to computing. Thus, their code of ethics is a little broader, but the basic principles are applicable in computing situations. The IEEE Code of Ethics is shown in Figure 11-2.

ACM

The ACM code of ethics recognizes three kinds of responsibilities of its members: general moral imperatives, professional responsibilities, and leadership responsibilities, both inside the association and in general. The code of ethics has three sections (plus a fourth commitment section), as shown in Figure 11-3.

Computer Ethics Institute

The Computer Ethics Institute is a nonprofit group that aims to encourage people to consider the ethical aspects of their computing activities. The organization has been in existence since the mid-1980s, founded as a joint activity of IBM, the Brookings Institution, and the Washington Theological Consortium. They have published their ethical guidance as ten commandments of computer ethics, listed in Figure 11-4.

11.9   Conclusion

In this study of ethics, we have tried not to decide right and wrong, or even to brand certain acts as ethical or unethical. The purpose of this section is to stimulate thinking about ethical issues concerned with secrecy, integrity, and availability of data and computations.

We, the members of the IEEE, in recognition of the importance of our technologies in affecting the quality of life throughout the world, and in accepting a personal obligation to our profession, its members, and the communities we serve, do hereby commit ourselves to conduct of the highest ethical and professional manner and agree

1. to accept responsibility in making engineering decisions consistent with the safety, health, and welfare of the public, and to disclose promptly factors that might endanger the public or the environment;

2. to avoid real or perceived conflicts of interest whenever possible, and to disclose them to affected parties when they do exist;

3. to be honest and realistic in stating claims or estimates based on available data;

4. to reject bribery in all of its forms;

5. to improve understanding of technology, its appropriate application, and potential consequences;

6. to maintain and improve our technical competence and to undertake technological tasks for others only if qualified by training or experience, or after full disclosure of pertinent limitations;

7. to seek, accept, and offer honest criticism of technical work, to acknowledge and correct errors, and to credit properly the contributions of others;

8. to treat fairly all persons regardless of such factors as race, religion, gender, disability, age, or national origin;

9. to avoid injuring others, their property, reputation, or employment by false or malicious action;

10. to assist colleagues and coworkers in their professional development and to support them in following this code of ethics.

Figure 11-2   IEEE Code of Ethics (Reprinted courtesy of the Institute of Electrical and Electronics Engineers © 1996.)

The cases presented show complex conflicting ethical situations. The important first step in determining ethics in a situation is to obtain the facts, ask about any uncertainties, and acquire any additional information needed. In other words, first one must understand the situation.

The second step is to identify the ethical principles involved. Honesty, fair play, proper compensation, and respect for privacy are all ethical principles. Sometimes these conflict, and then we have to determine which principles are more important than others. This may not lead to one principle that obviously overshadows all others. Still, a ranking to identify the major principles involved is needed.

The third step is choosing an action that meets these ethical principles. Making a decision and taking action is difficult, especially if there are evident negative consequences of the action. However, taking action based on a *personal* ranking of principles is necessary.

As an ACM member I will . . .

1.1 Contribute to society and human well-being

1.2 Avoid harm to others

1.3 Be honest and trustworthy

1.4 Be fair and take action not to discriminate

1.5 Honor property rights including copyrights and patents

1.6 Give proper credit for intellectual property

1.7 Respect the privacy of others

1.8 Honor confidentiality

As an ACM computing professional I will . . .

2.1 Strive to achieve the highest quality, effectiveness and dignity in both the process and products of professional work

2.2 Acquire and maintain professional competence

2.3 Know and respect existing laws pertaining to professional work

2.4 Accept and provide appropriate professional review

2.5 Give comprehensive and thorough evaluations of computer systems and their impacts, including analysis of possible risks

2.6 Honor contracts, agreements, and assigned responsibilities

2.7 Improve public understanding of computing and its consequences

2.8 Access computing and communication resources only when authorized to do so

As an ACM member and an organization leader, I will . . .

3.1 Articulate social responsibilities of members of an organizational unit and encourage full acceptance of those responsibilities

3.2 Manage personnel and resources

3.3 Acknowledge and support proper and authorized uses of an organization's computing and communication resources

3.4 Ensure that users and those who will be affected by a system have their needs clearly articulated during the assessment and design of requirements; later the system must be validated to meet requirements

3.5 Articulate and support policies that protect the dignity of users and others affected by a computing system

3.6 Create opportunities for members of the organization to learn the principles and limitations of computer systems

As an ACM member, I will . . .

4.1 Uphold and promote the principles of this code

4.2 Treat violations of this code as inconsistent with membership in the ACM

Figure 11-3   ACM Code of Ethics and Professional Conduct (Reprinted courtesy of the Association for Computing Machinery © 1993.)

1. Thou shalt not use a computer to harm other people.
2. Thou shalt not interfere with other people's computer work.
3. Thou shalt not snoop around in other people's computer files.
4. Thou shalt not use a computer to steal.
5. Thou shalt not use a computer to bear false witness.
6. Thou shalt not copy or use proprietary software for which you have not paid.
7. Thou shalt not use other people's computer resources without authorization or proper compensation.
8. Thou shalt not appropriate other people's intellectual output.
9. Thou shalt think about the social consequences of the program you are writing or the system you are designing.
10. Thou shalt always use a computer in ways that insure consideration and respect for your fellow humans.

Figure 11-4   The Ten Commandments of Computer Ethics (Reprinted with permission, Computer Ethics Institute, Washington, D.C.)

The fact that other equally sensible people may choose a different action does not excuse one from taking some action.

This section is not trying to force the development of rigid, inflexible principles. Decisions may vary based on fine differences between two situations, or a person's views can change over time or in response to experience. Learning to reason about ethical situations is not quite the same as learning "right" from "wrong." Terms such as right and wrong or good and bad imply a universal set of values, yet we know that even widely accepted principles are overridden by some people in some situations. For example, the principle of not killing people may be superseded in the case of war or capital punishment. Few, if any, values are held by everyone or in all cases. Therefore, the purpose of this section has been to stimulate the recognition of ethical principles involved in cases related to computer security. Only by recognizing and analyzing principles can one act consistently, thoughtfully, and responsibly.

11.10   Bibliographic Notes

Two excellent and readable works on ethical reasoning are by Frankena [FRA73] and Harris [HAR86]. Harris, especially, is written clearly and concretely.

The ACM devoted a special issue (December 1995) to ethics. The articles by Huff and Martin [HUF95], Johnson and Mulvey [JOH95], and Laudon [LAU95] are thought-provoking.

The legal and ethical aspects of cryptographic escrow have been presented by Hoffman [HOF95a].

11.11 Terms and Concepts

Bibliography

[ABA94] ABADI, M., and NEEDHAM, R. "Prudent Engineering Practice for Cryptographic Protocols." *Proc IEEE Symp Security & Privacy*, IEEE Comp Soc Press 1994, pp. 122–136.

[ABB76] ABBOTT, R., et al. "Security Analysis and Enhancements of Computer Operating Systems." *NBS Tech Report*, NBSIR-76-1041, 1976.

[ABR87] ABRAMS, M., and PODELL, H. *Computer and Network Security—Tutorial*, IEEE Comp Soc Press 1987.

[ADA89] ADAM, N., and WORTMAN, J. "Security-Control Methods for Statistical Databases: A Study." *ACM Comp Surveys*, v21 n4, Dec 1989, pp. 515–556.

[ADA92a] ADAM, J. "Threats and Countermeasures." *IEEE Spectrum*, v29 n8, Aug 1992, pp. 21–28.

[ADA92b] ADAM, J. "Cryptography = Privacy?" *IEEE Spectrum*, v29 n8, Aug 1992, pp. 29–35.

[ADA92c] ADAM, J. "Data Security." *IEEE Spectrum*, v29 n8, Aug 1992, pp. 19–20.

[ADA92d] ADAM, J., ed. "A Security Roundtable." *IEEE Spectrum*, v29 n8, Aug 1992, pp. 41–44.

[ADA95] ADAM, J. "The Privacy Problem." *IEEE Spectrum*, v32 n12, Dec 1995, pp. 46–52.

[ADL82] ADLEMAN, L. "On Breaking the Iterated Merkle–Hellman Public-Key Cryptosystem." *Advances in Cryptology/Proc Crypto 1982*, Plenum Press 1982, pp. 303–308.

[ADL83] ADLEMAN, L. "On Breaking Generalized Knapsack Public Key Cryptosystems." *Proc 15th ACM Symp Theory of Computing*, 1983, pp. 402–412.

[AFS83] AFSB (Air Force Studies Board). "Multilevel Data Management Security." *National Academy of Sciences Report*, 1983.

[AGN84] AGNEW, G. "Secrecy and Privacy in a Local Area Network Environment." *Advances in Cryptology/Proc Eurocrypt 1984*, Springer-Verlag 1985, pp. 349–357.

[AGN88] AGNEW, G., et al. "A Secure Public Key Protocol Based on Discrete Exponentiation." *Advances in Cryptology/Proc Eurocrypt 1988*, Springer-Verlag 1988.

[AKL83] AKL, S. "Digital Signatures: A Tutorial Survey." *IEEE Computer*, v16 n2, Feb 1983, pp. 15–26.

[AME83] AMES, S., et al. "Security Kernel Design and Implementation: An Introduction." *IEEE Computer*, v16 n7, Jul 1983, pp. 14–23.

[AND72] ANDERSON, J. "Computer Security Technology Planning Study." *U.S. Air Force Electronic Systems Division Technical Report*, 73-51, Oct 1972.

[AND80] ANDERSON, J. "Computer Security Threat Monitoring and Surveillance." *Technical Report*, James P. Anderson Co. 1980.

[AND82] ANDERSON, J. "Accelerating Computer Security Innovations." *Proc IEEE Symp Security & Privacy*, IEEE Comp Soc Press 1982, pp. 91–97.

[AND85] ANDERSON, J. "A Unification of Computer and Network Security Concepts." *Proc IEEE Symp Security & Privacy*, IEEE Comp Soc Press 1985, pp. 77–87.

[AND94] ANDERSON, R. "Why Cryptosystems Fail." *Comm ACM*, v37 n11, Nov 1994, pp. 32–41.

[ASL95] ASLAM, T. "A Taxonomy of Security Faults in the UNIX Operating System." Purdue Univ Dept of Comp Sci MS Thesis, Aug 1995.

[ATT76] ATTANASIO, C., et al. "A Study of VM/370 Integrity." *IBM Systems J*, v15 n1, 1976, pp. 102–116.

[BAD89] BADGER, L. "A Model for Specifying Muli-Granularity Integrity Policies." *Proc IEEE Symp Security & Privacy*, IEEE Comp Soc Press 1989, pp. 269–277.

[BAD91a] BADGER, L. "Covert Channel Analysis Planning for Large Systems." *TIS Tech Report*, Feb 1991.

[BAD91b] BADGER, L. "TMach Covert Channel Analysis Plan." *TIS Tech Report*, Jan 1991.

[BAL85] BALDWIN, R., and GRAMLICH, W. "Cryptographic Protocol for Trustable Match Making." *Proc IEEE Symp Security & Privacy*, IEEE Comp Soc Press 1985, pp. 92–100.

[BAL93] BALENSON, D. "Privacy Enhancement for Internet Electronic Mail, Part III: Algorithms, Modes, Identifiers." *Internet Report*, RFC 1423, Feb 1993.

[BAM82] BAMFORD, J. *The Puzzle Palace*, Houghton Mifflin 1982.

[BAR90] BARKER, W., and PFLEEGER, C. "Civil and Military Applications of Trusted Systems Criteria." *TIS Tech Report*, 304, Feb 1990.

[BAR92] BARLOW, J. "Decrypting the Puzzle Palace." *Comm ACM*, v35 n7, Jul 1992, pp. 25–31.

[BEA88] BEAUCHEMIN, P., et al. "The Generation of Random Numbers That Are Probably Prime." *J Cryptology*, v1 n1, 1988, pp. 53–64.

[BEC80] BECK, L. "A Security Mechanism for Statistical Data Bases." *ACM Trans Data Base Sys*, v5 n3, Sep 1980, pp. 316–338.

[BEK82] BEKER, H., and PIPER, F. *Cipher Systems*, Northwood Books 1982.

[BEL73] BELL, D., and LA PADULA, L. "Secure Computer Systems: Mathematical Foundations and Model." *MITRE Report*, MTR 2547 v2, Nov 1973.

[BEL83] BELL, D. "Secure Computer Systems: A Retrospective." *Proc IEEE Symp Security & Privacy*, IEEE Comp Soc Press 1983, pp. 161–162.

[BEL91] BELLOVIN, S., and MERRITT, M. "Limitations of the Kerberos Authentication System." *Proc Usenix Conf*, Win 1991, pp. 253–267.

[BEL92a] BELLARE, M., and MICALI, S. "How to Sign Given Any Trapdoor Permutation." *J ACM*, v39 n1, Jan 1992, pp. 214–233.

[BEL92b] BELLOVIN, S., and MERRITT, M. "Encrypted Key Exchange." *Proc IEEE Symp Security & Privacy*, IEEE Comp Soc Press 1992, pp. 72–84.

[BEL92c] BELLOVIN, S. "There Be Dragons." *Proc 3rd Usenix Unix Security Symp*, Sep 1992.

[BEL96] BELL, T., et al. "Technology 1996: Communications." *IEEE Spectrum*, v33 n1, Jan 1996, pp. 30–41.

[BEN72] BENSOUSSAN, A., et al. "The Multics Virtual Memory: Concepts and Design." *Comm ACM*, v15 n5, May 1972, pp. 308–318.

[BEN84] BENZEL, T. "Analysis of a Kernel Verification." *Proc IEEE Symp Security & Privacy*, IEEE Comp Soc Press 1984, pp. 125–131.

[BER88] BERSON, T. "Interview with Roger Schell." *Unix Review*, Feb 1988, pp. 60–69.

[BER92] BERSON, T. "Differential Cryptanalysis mod 2^{32} with Applications to MD5." *Advances in Cryptology/Proc Eurocrypt 1992*, Springer-Verlag 1992, pp. 71–80.

[BIB77] BIBA, K. "Integrity Considerations for Secure Computer Systems." *U.S. Air Force Electronic Systems Division Technical Report* 76-372, 1977.

[BIH90] BIHAM, E., and SHAMIR, A. "Differential Cryptanalysis of DES-like Cryptosystems." *Advances in Cryptology/Proc Crypto 1990*, pp. 2–21.

[BIH91] BIHAM, E., and SHAMIR, A. "Differential Cryptanalysis of FEAL and N-Hash." *Advances in Cryptology/Proc Eurocrypt 1991*, pp. 1–16.

[BIH92] BIHAM, E., and SHAMIR, A. "Differential Cryptanalysis of Snefru, Khafre." *Advances in Cryptology/Proc Crypto 1991*, pp. 156–171.

[BIH93] BIHAM, E., and SHAMIR, A. "Differential Cryptanalysis of the Full 16-Round DES." *Advances in Cryptology/Proc Crypto 1992*, pp. 487–496.

[BIS86] BISHOP, M. "Analyzing the Security of an Existing Computer System." *NASA RIACS Tech Report*, TR86.13, 1986.

[BIS89] BISKUP, J. "Protection of Privacy and Confidentiality in Medical Information Systems." *Proc IFIP Workshop on Database Security*, IFIP Workgroup 11.3, 1989.

[BLA78] BLAKLEY, R., and BLAKLEY, G. "Security of Number Theoretic Public Key Cryptosystems against Random Number Attacks, part 1." *Cryptologia*, v2 n4, Oct 1978.

[BLA79a] BLAKLEY, R., and BLAKLEY, G. "Security of Number Theoretic Public Key Cryptosystems against Random Number Attacks, part 2." *Cryptologia*, v3 n1, Jan 1979, pp. 29–42.

[BLA79b] BLAKLEY, R., and BLAKLEY, G. "Security of Number Theoretic Public Key Cryptosystems against Random Number Attacks, part 3." *Cryptologia*, v3 n2, Apr 1979, pp. 105–118.

[BLA79c] BLAKELY, G. "Safeguarding Cryptographic Keys." *Proc AFIPS Natl Comp Conf*, v48, 1979, pp. 313–317.

[BLA90] BLACK, D. "Scheduling Support for Concurrency and Parallelism in MACH." *IEEE Computer*, v23 n3, Mar 1990, pp. 35–43.

[BLA96] BLAZE, M., et al. "Minimal Key Lengths for Symmetric Ciphers to Provide Adequate Security." Unpublished report, Jan 1996.

[BLU81] BLUM, M. "Coin Flipping by Telephone." *SIGACT News*, 1981, pp. 23–27.

[BLU83] BLUM, M., et al. "Reducibility Among Protocols." *Advances in Cryptology/Proc Crypto 1983*, Plenum Press 1983, pp. 137–146.

[BOE85] BOEBERT, W., and KAIN, R. "A Practical Alternative to Hierarchical Integrity Policies." *Proc Natl Comp Sec Conf*, 1985, pp. 18–27.

[BOE92] BOEBERT, E. "Assurance Evidence." *Secure Computing Corp Tech Report*, 1 Jun 1992.

[BOE93] DEN BOER, B., and BOSSELAERS, A. "Collisions for the Compression Function of MD5." *Advances in Cryptology/Proc Eurocrypt 1993*, 1993.

[BOL91] BOLLINGER, T., and MCGOWAN, C. "A Critical Look at Software Capability Evaluations." *IEEE Software*, v8 n4, Jul 1991, pp. 25–41.

[BOO81] BOOTH, K. "Authentication of Signatures Using Public Key Encryption." *Comm ACM*, v24 n11, Nov 1981, pp. 772–774.

[BOW92] BOWLES, J., and PELAEZ, C. "Bad Code." *IEEE Spectrum*, v29 n8, Aug 1992, pp. 36–40.

[BOW95] BOWEN, J., and HINCHLEY, M. "Ten Commandments of Formal Methods." *IEEE Computer*, v28 n4, Apr 1995, pp. 56–63.

[BRA73] BRANSTAD, D. "Privacy and Protection in Operating Systems." *IEEE Computer*, v6 n1, Jan 1973, pp. 43–46.

[BRA77] BRANSTAD, D., et al. "Report of the Workshop on Cryptography in Support of Computer Security." *NBS Tech Report*, NBSIR 77-1291, Sep 1977.

[BRA78] BRANSTAD, D. "Security of Computer Communication." *IEEE Comm Soc Mag*, v16 n6, Nov 1978, pp. 33–40.

[BRA79] BRANSTAD, D. "Hellman's Data Does Not Support His Conclusion." *IEEE Spectrum*, v16 n7, Jul 1979, p. 41.

[BRA88] BRASSARD, G. *Modern Cryptology*, Springer-Verlag 1988.

[BRE89] BREWER, D., and NASH, M. "The Chinese Wall Security Policy." *Proc IEEE Symp Security & Privacy*, IEEE Comp Soc Press 1989, pp. 206–214.

[BRI72] BRINCH HANSON, P. "Structured Multiprogramming." *Comm ACM*, v15 n7, Jul 1972, pp. 574–577.

[BRI82] BRICKELL, E., et al. "A Preliminary Report on Cryptanalysis of Merkle–Hellman Knapsacks." *Advances in Cryptology/Proc Crypto 1982*, Plenum Press 1982, pp. 289–303.

[BRI83] BRIGHT, H. "Modern Computational Cryptography." *Advances in Comp Sec Mgmt*, Wiley 1983, pp. 173–201.

[BRI88] BRICKELL, E., and ODLYZKO, A. "Cryptanalysis: A Survey of Recent Results." *Proc of the IEEE*, v76 n5, May 1988, pp. 578–593.

[BRI93] BRICKELL, E., et al. "Skipjack Review: Interim Report 1 Aug 1993." Unpublished tech report, 1 Aug 1993.

[BRO83] BROWNE, P., and TROY, E. "Designing Secure Data Processing Applications." *Advances in Comp Sec Mgmt v2*, Wiley 1983.

[BRO87] BROOKS, F. "No Silver Bullet." *IEEE Computer*, v20 n4, Apr 1987, pp. 10–19.

[BRO96] BROOKS, F. "The Computer Scientist as Toolsmith." *Comm ACM*, v39 n3, Mar 1996, pp. 61–68.

[BUR89] BURNS, R. "DBMS Integrity and Security Controls." *Report on Invitational Workshop on Data Integrity*, NIST Special Pub 500–168, Sep 1989, p. A7.

[BUR90] BURNS, R. "Referential Secrecy." *Proc IEEE Symp Security & Privacy*, IEEE Comp Soc Press 1990, pp. 133–142.

[CAM93] CAMPBELL, K., and WIENER, M. "Proof that DES is Not a Group." *Advances in Cryptology/Proc Crypto 1992*, Springer-Verlag 1993, pp. 512–520.

[CCE94] CCEB (Common Criteria Editorial Board). *Common Criteria for Information Technology Security Evaluations,* version 0.6, Apr 1994.

[CHA81] CHAUM, D. "Untraceable Electronic Mail, Return Addresses, and Pseudonyms." *Comm ACM*, v24 n2, Feb 1981, pp. 84–88.

[CHA82] CHAUM, D. "Blind Signatures for Untracable Payments." *Advances in Cryptology/Proc Crypto 1982*, Plenum Press 1982, pp. 199–205.

[CHA85] CHAUM, D. "Security Without Identification: Transaction Systems." *Comm ACM*, v28 n10, Oct 1985, pp. 1030–1044.

[CHA86] CHALMERS, L. "Analysis of Differences in Computer Security Practices in the Military and Private Sectors." *Proc IEEE Symp Security & Privacy*, IEEE Comp Soc Press 1986, pp. 71–74.

[CHA94] CHAPIN, S., et al. "Security for the Common Object Request Broker Architecture (CORBA)." *Proc 1994 Aerospace Comp Security Conf,* 1994, pp. 21–30.

[CHA95] CHAPMAN, D., and ZWICKY, E. *Building Internet Firewalls*, O'Reilly & Associates 1995.

[CHE81] CHEHEYL, M., et al. "Verifying Security." *Comp Surveys*, v13 n3, Sep 1981, pp. 279–339.

[CHE89] CHESS, D. "Computer Viruses and Related Threats to Computer and Network Security." *Comp Networks and ISDN Sys*, v17, 1989, pp. 141–147.

[CHE94] CHESWICK, B., and BELLOVIN, S. *Firewalls and Internet Security*, Addison-Wesley 1994.

[CHI89] CHIOU, G., and CHEN, W. "Secure Broadcasting Using the Secure Lock." *IEEE Trans Software Engr*, vSE-15 n8, Aug 1989, pp. 929–934.

[CLA87] CLARK, D., and WILSON, D. "A Comparison of Commercial and Military Computer Security Policies." *Proc IEEE Symp Security & Privacy*, IEEE Comp Soc Press 1987, pp. 184–194.

[COH84] COHEN, F. "Computer Viruses." *Computer Security: A Global Challenge*, Elsevier Press 1984, pp. 143–158.

[COL94] COLLINS, W., et al. "How Good is Good Enough?" *Comm ACM*, v37 n1, Jan 1994, pp. 81–91.

[COM88] COMER, D. *Internetworking with TCP/IP*, Prentice-Hall 1988.

[COO71] COOK, S. "The Complexity of Theorem-Proving Procedures." *Proc ACM Symp Theory of Computing*, 1971, pp. 151–158.

[COP92] COPPERSMITH, D. "DES and Differential Cryptanalysis." Private communication, 23 Mar 1992.

[COR84] CORSINI, P., et al. "Distributing and Revoking Authorizations on Abstract Objects." *Software—Practice and Experience*, v14 n10, Oct 1984, pp. 931–943.

[CSE88] CSE (Communications Security Establishment). "Proceedings Evaluation Criteria Workshop." *Canadian Trusted Comp Product Eval Rep*, Aug 1988.

[CSE90] CSE (Communications Security Establishment). "Proceedings of 1990 CTCPEC Availability Workshop." *Canadian Trusted Comp Product Eval Rep*, Feb 1990.

[CSE94] CSE (Communications Security Establishment). *A Guide to Security Risk Management for IT Systems (Draft).* Government of Canada, May 1994.

[CSR91] CSRI (Computer Systems Research Institute). "Composability of Trusted Systems." *Fifth Report*, Univ of Toronto report, Jan 1991.

[CSS93] CSSC (Canadian System Security Centre). *Canadian Trusted Computer Product Evaluation Criteria,* ver 3.0e, Jan 1993.

[CUG95] CUGINI, J., et al. "Functional Security Criteria for Distributed Systems." *Proc Natl Info Sys Security Conf*, 1995, pp. 310–321.

[CUR87] CURTIS, B., et al. "On Building Software Process Models Under the Lamppost." *Proc 9th Intl Conf on Software Engineering*, 1987, pp. 96–103.

[CUR90] CURRY, D. "Improving the Security of Your Unix System." *SRI Technical Report*, ITSTD-721-FR-90-21, Apr 1990.

[CUT91] CUTLER, K. "Commercial International Security Requirements." *DRAFT Report*, American Express Travel Related Services, 1991.

[DAT88] DATE, C. *Introduction to Data Base Systems* vol 2, (2nd ed), Addison-Wesley 1988.

[DAT94] DATE, C. *Introduction to Data Base Systems* vol 1, (6th ed), Addison-Wesley 1994.

[DAV78] DAVIDA, G. "Data Base Security." *IEEE Trans Software Engr*, vSE-4 n6, Nov 1978, pp. 531–533.

[DAV79] DAVIDA, G. "Hellman's Scheme Breaks DES in Its Basic Form." *IEEE Spectrum*, v16 n7, Jul 1979, p. 39.

[DAV80] DAVIES, D. "Protection." *Distributed Systems, An Advanced Course*, Springer-Verlag 1980.

[DAV81] DAVIES, D. *The Security of Data in Networks*, IEEE Comp Soc Press 1981.

[DAV82] DAVIES, D. "Some Regular Properties of the Data Encryption Standard Algorithm." *Advances in Cryptology/Proc Crypto 1982*, Plenum Press 1982, pp. 89–97.

[DAV83a] DAVIES, D. "Applying the RSA Digital Signature to Electronic Mail." *IEEE Computer*, v16 n2, Feb 1983, pp. 55–62.

[DAV83b] DAVIO, M., et al. "Propagation Characteristics of the Data Encryption Standard." *Advances in Cryptology/Proc Crypto 1983*, Plenum Press 1983, pp. 171–202.

[DAV85] DAVIDA, G., and MATT, B. "Crypto-Secure Operating Systems." *Proc AFIPS Natl Comp Conf*, 1985, pp. 577–581.

[DAV89] DAVIES, D., and PRICE, W. *Security for Computer Networks* (2nd ed), John Wiley & Sons 1989.

[DAV96] DAVIS, R., et al. "A New View of Intellectual Property and Software." *Comm ACM*, v39 n3, Mar 1996, pp. 21–30.

[DEA77] DEAVOURS, C. "Unicity Points in Cryptanalysis." *Cryptologia*, v1 n1, Jan 1977, pp. 46–68.

[DEA85] DEAVOURS, C. *Machine Cryptography and Modern Cryptanalysis*, Artech House 1985.

[DEA96] DEAN, D., et al. "Java Security: From HotJava to Netscape and Beyond." *Proc IEEE Comp Soc Symp Security & Privacy,* IEEE Comput Soc Press 1996, pp. 190–200.

[DEM78a] DEMILLO, R., ed. *Foundations of Secure Computation*, Academic Press 1978.

[DEM78b] DEMILLO, R., et al. "Proprietary Software Protection." In *Foundations of Secure Computation* [DEM78a], 1978, pp. 115–132.

[DEM78c] DEMILLO, R., et al. "Combinatorial Inference." In *Foundations of Secure Computation* [DEM78a], 1978, pp. 27–38.

[DEM82] DEMILLO, R., et al. "Cryptographic Protocols." *Proc 14th ACM Symp Theory of Computing*, 1982, pp. 383–400.

[DEM83] DEMILLO, R., and MERRITT, M. "Protocols for Data Security." *IEEE Computer*, v16 n2, Feb 1983, pp. 39–54.

[DEM87] DEMARCO, T., and LISTER, T. *Peopleware: Productive Projects and Teams*, Dorsett House 1987.

[DEM95] DEMARCO, T. *Why Does Software Cost So Much*, Dorsett House 1995.

[DEN76a] DENNING, D. "A Lattice Model of Secure Information Flow." *Comm ACM*, v19 n5, May 1976, pp. 236–243.

[DEN76b] DENNING, P. "Fault Tolerant Operating Systems." *Comp Surveys,* v8 n4, Dec 1976, pp. 236–243.

[DEN77] DENNING, D., and DENNING, P. "Certification of Programs for Secure Information Flow." *Comm ACM*, v20 n7, Jul 1977, pp. 504–513.

[DEN78] DENNING, D. "A Review of Research on Statistical Data Base Security." In *Foundations of Secure Computation* [DEM78a], 1978, pp. 15–25.

[DEN79a] DENNING, D., and DENNING, P. "Data Security." *Comp Surveys*, v11 n3, Sep 1979, pp. 227–250.

[DEN79b] DENNING, D., et al. "The Trackers: A Threat to Statistical Database Security." *ACM Trans Data Base Sys*, v4 n1, Mar 1979, pp. 76–96.

[DEN81a] DENNING, D. "Restricting Queries That Might Lead to Compromise." *Proc IEEE Symp Security & Privacy*, IEEE Comp Soc Press 1981, pp. 33–40.

[DEN81b] DENNING, D., and SACCO, G. "Timestamps in Key Distribution Protocols." *Comm ACM*, v24 n8, Jun 1981, pp. 533–536.

[DEN82] DENNING, D. *Cryptography and Data Security*, Addison-Wesley 1982.

[DEN83a] DENNING, D., and SCHLÖRER, J. "Inference Controls for Statistical Data Bases." *IEEE Computer*, v16 n7, Jul 1983, pp. 69–82.

[DEN83b] DENNING, D. "Protecting Public Keys and Signature Keys." *IEEE Computer*, v16 n2, Feb 1983, pp. 17–35.

[DEN83c] DENNING, D. "Field Encryption and Authentication." *Advances in Cryptology/Proc Crypto 1983*, Plenum Press 1983, pp. 231–247.

[DEN84] DENNING, P., and TICHY, W. "Advanced Operating Systems." *IEEE Computer*, v17 n9, Oct 1984, pp. 173–190.

[DEN85] DENNING, D. "Commutative Filters for Reducing Inference Threats." *Proc IEEE Symp Security & Privacy*, IEEE Comp Soc Press 1985, pp. 134–146.

[DEN86] DENNING, D. "An Intrusion-Detection Model." *Proc IEEE Symp Security & Privacy*, IEEE Comp Soc Press 1986, pp. 102–117.

[DEN87a] DENNING, D. "Views for Multilevel Database Security." *IEEE Trans Software Engr*, vSE-13 n2, Feb 1987, pp. 129–140.

[DEN87b] DENNING, D. "An Intrusion-Detection Model." *IEEE Trans Software Engr*, vSE-13 n2, Feb 1987, pp. 222–226.

[DEN88] DENNING, P. "Computer Viruses." *American Scientist*, v76, May–Jun 1988, pp. 236–238.

[DEN89] DENNING, P. "The Internet Worm." *American Scientist*, v77, Mar–Apr 1989, pp. 126–128.

[DEN90a] DENNING, P. *Computers under Attack*, Addison-Wesley 1990.

[DEN90b] DENNING, P. "Sending a Signal." *Comm ACM*, v33 n8, Aug 1990, pp. 11–13.

[DEN91] DENNING, D. "The United States vs Craig Neidorf." *Comm ACM*, v34 n3, Mar 1991, pp. 24–43.

[DEN96] DENNING, D., and BRANSTAD, D. "A Taxonomy of Key Escrow Encryption Systems." *Comm ACM*, v39 n3, Mar 1996, pp. 34–40.

[DES84] DESMEDT, Y., et al. "Dependence of Output on Input in DES: Small Avalanche Effect." *Advances in Cryptology/Proc Crypto 1984*, Plenum Press 1984, pp. 359–376.

[DIF76] DIFFIE, W., and HELLMAN, M. "New Directions in Cryptography." *IEEE Trans Info Theory*, vIT-22 n6, Nov 1976, pp. 644–654.

[DIF77] DIFFIE, W., and HELLMAN, M. "Exhaustive Cryptanalysis of the NBS Data Encryption Standard." *IEEE Computer*, v10 n6, Jun 1977, pp. 74–84.

[DIF79] DIFFIE, W., and HELLMAN, M. "Privacy and Authentication." *Proc IEEE*, v67 n3, Mar 1979, pp. 397–429.

[DIJ68a] DIJKSTRA, E. "GO TO Statement Considered Harmful." *Comm ACM*, v11 n3, Mar 1968, p. 147.

[DIJ68b] DIJKSTRA, E. "The Structure of 'THE'-Multiprogramming System." *Proc ACM Symp Oper Sys Principles* (also in *Comm ACM* v26 n1 Jan 1983), Oct 1968.

[DIJ76] DIJKSTRA, E. *A Discipline of Programming.* Prentice-Hall 1976.

[DIO92] DION, R. "Elements of a Process Improvement Program." *IEEE Software*, v9 n4, Jul 1992, pp. 83–85.

[DIO93] DION, R. "Process Improvement and the Corporate Balance Sheet." *IEEE Software*, v10 n4, Jul 1993, pp. 28–35.

[DOD85] DOD (US Dept of Defense). *Trusted Computer System Evaluation Criteria*, DOD5200.28-STD Dec 1985.

[DOD88] DOD (US Dept of Defense). *Defense System Software Development,* DOD-STD-2167A, 29 Feb 1988.

[DOD91] DOD (US Dept of Defense). *Industrial Security Manual for Safeguarding Classified Information*, DOD 5220. 22-M Supt of Documents, Jan 1991.

[DOL82] DOLEV, D., et al. "On the Security of Ping-Pong Protocols." *Advances in Cryptology/Proc Crypto 1982*, Plenum Press 1982, pp. 177–186.

[DOW85] DOWNS, D., et al. "Issues in Discretionary Access Control." *Proc IEEE Symp Security & Privacy*, IEEE Comp Soc Press 1985, pp. 208–218.

[DTI89a] DTI (UK Dept for Trade and Industry). "Security Functionality Manual." *DRAFT Report*, v21 version 3.0, Feb 1989.

[DTI89b] DTI (UK Dept for Trade and Industry). "Evaluation and Certification Manual." *DRAFT Report*, v23 version 3.0, Feb 1989.

[DTI89c] DTI (UK Dept for Trade and Industry). "Evaluation Levels Manual." *DRAFT Report*, v22 version 3.0, Feb 1989.

[EHR78] EHRSAM, W., et al. "A Cryptographic Key Management Scheme for Implementing the DES." *IBM Systems J*, v17 n2, 1978, pp. 106–125.

[EIC89] EICHLIN, M., and ROCHLIS, J. "With Microscope and Tweezers: Analysis of Internet Virus." *Proc IEEE Symp Security & Privacy*, IEEE Comp Soc Press 1989.

[ELE95] EL EMAN, K., and MADHAVJI, N. "The Reliability of Measuring Organizational Maturity." *Software Process Improvement and Practice,* v1 n1, 1995, pp. 3–25.

[ELG84] EL GAMAL, A. "A Public Key Cryptosystem and Signature Scheme Based on Discrete Logarithms" *Advances in Cryptology/Proc Crypto 1984*, Plenum Press 1985, pp. 10–18.

[ELG85] EL GAMAL, A. "A Public Key Cryptosystem and Signature Scheme Based on Discrete Logarithms." *IEEE Trans Info Theory*, vIT-31 n4, Jul 1985, pp. 469–472.

[ELG86] EL GAMAL, A. "On Computing Logarithms over Finite Fields." *Advances in Cryptology/Proc Crypto 1986*, v25, pp. 396–402.

[ENG96] ENGLISH, E., and HAMILTON, S. "Network Security Under Siege: The Timing Attack." *IEEE Computer*, v30 n3, Mar 1996, pp. 95–97.

[EST85] ESTRIN, D. "Non-Discretionary Controls for Inter-Organization Networks." *Proc IEEE Symp Security & Privacy*, IEEE Comp Soc Press 1985, pp. 56–61.

[EVA74] EVANS, A., et al. "A User Authentication Scheme not Requiring Secrecy in the Computer." *Comm ACM*, v17 n8, Aug 1974, pp. 437–441.

[EVE85] EVEN, S., et al. "A Randomizing Protocol for Signing Contracts." *Comm ACM*, v28 n6, Jun 1985, pp. 637–647.

[FAB74] FABRY, R. "Capability-Based Addressing." *Comm ACM*, v17 n7, Jul 1974, pp. 403–412.

[FAG96] FAGIN, R., et al. "Comparing Information Without Leaking It." *Comm ACM,* v39 n5, May 1996, pp. 77–85.

[FAR90] FARMER, D., and SPAFFORD, E. "The COPS Security Checker System." *Proc Summer Usenix Conf*, 1990, pp. 165–170.

[FAR93] FARMER. D., and VENEMA, W. "Improving the Security of Your Site by Breaking Into It." Unpublished tech report, 1993.

[FEI75] FEISTEL, H., et al. "Some Cryptographic Techniques for Machine Data Communication." *Proc IEEE*, v63 n1, Nov 1975, pp. 1545–1554.

[FEI77] FEIERTAG, R., et al. "Proving Multilevel Security of a System Design." *Op Sys Review*, v11 n5, Nov 1977, pp. 57–63.

[FER81] FERNANDEZ, E., et al. *Database Security and Integrity*, Addison-Wesley 1981.

[FER89] FERNANDEZ, E., et al. "A Security Model for Object-Oriented Databases." *Proc IEEE Symp Security & Privacy*, IEEE Comp Soc Press 1989, pp. 110–115.

[FIT89] FITES, P., et al. *Control and Security of Computer Information Systems*, Computer Science Press 1989.

[FOR84] FORTUNE, S., and MERRITT, M. "Poker Protocols." *Advances in Cryptology/Proc Crypto 1984*, Plenum Press 1984, pp. 454–464.

[FOS82] FOSTER, C. *Cryptanalysis for Microcomputers*, Hayden 1982.

[FRA73] FRANKENA, W. *Ethics*, Prentice Hall 1973.

[FRA83] FRAIM, L. "Scomp: A Solution to the Multilevel Security Problem." *IEEE Computer*, v16 n7, Jul 1983, pp. 26–34.

[FRI76a] FRIEDMAN, W. *Elementary Military Cryptography*, Aegean Park Press 1976.

[FRI76b] FRIEDMAN, W. *Elements of Cryptanalysis*, Aegean Park Press 1976.

[FRI76c] FRIEDMAN, W. *Advanced Military Cryptography*, Aegean Park Press 1976.

[GAN96] GANESAN, R. "The Yaksha Security System." *Comm ACM*, v39 n3, Mar 1996, pp. 55–60.

[GAO96] GAO (US General Accounting Office). "Information Security: Computer Attacks at Department of Defense Pose Increasing Risks." *GAO Report GAO/AIMD-96-84I,* 22 May 1996.

[GAR79] GAREY, M., and JOHNSON, D. *Computers and Intractability,* W.H. Freeman 1979.

[GAR91a] GARFINKEL, S., and SPAFFORD, E. *Practical Unix Security*, O'Reilly & Associates 1991.

[GAR91b] GARVEY, T., and LUNT, T. "Model-based Intrusion Detection." *Proc 14th Natl Comp Security Conf*, 1991.

[GAR96] GARFINKEL, S., and SPAFFORD, E. *Practical Unix and Internet Security* (2nd ed.), O'Reilly & Associates 1996.

[GAS88] GASSER, M. *Building a Secure System*, Van Nostrand Reinhold 1988.

[GAS89] GASSER, M., et al. "Digital Distributed System Security Architecture." *Proc Natl Comp Security Conf*, 1989, pp. 305–319.

[GAS90] GASSER, M., and MCDERMOTT, E. "An Architecture for Practical Delegation in Distributed Systems." *Proc IEEE Symp Security & Privacy*, IEEE Comp Soc Press 1990, pp. 20–30.

[GER89] GERHART, S. "Assessment of Formal Methods for Trustworthy Computing Systems." *Proc ACM TAV Conf*, 1989, pp. 152–155.

[GIF82] GIFFORD, D. "Cryptographic Sealing for Information Secrecy/Authenticity." *Comm ACM*, v25 n4, Apr 1982, pp. 274–285.

[GIS88] GISA (German Information Security Agency). *IT-Security Criteria: Criteria for the Evaluation of Trustworthiness of IT Systems,* first version, 1988.

[GLI87] GLIGOR, V., et al. "A New Security Testing Method and Applications to the Secure Xenix Kernel." *IEEE Trans Software Engr*, vSE-13 n2, Feb 1987, pp. 169–183.

[GLI88] GLIGOR, V., and CHANDERSEKARAN, C. "Assessing the Costs." *Unix Review*, Feb 1988, pp. 53–58.

[GLI91] GLIGOR, V., et al. "Logics for Cryptographic Protocols—Virtues and Limitations." *Proc IEEE Comp Soc Foundations Wkshop*, vIV, 1991, pp. 219–226.

[GOG82] GOGUEN, J., and MESEGUER, J. "Security Policies and Security Models." *Proc IEEE Symp Security & Privacy*, IEEE Comp Soc Press 1982, pp. 11–20.

[GOG84] GOGUEN, J., and MESEGUER, J. "Unwinding and Inference Control." *Proc IEEE Symp Security & Privacy*, IEEE Comp Soc Press 1984, pp. 75–86.

[GOL77] GOLD, B., et al. "VM/370 Security Retrofit Program." *Proc ACM Annual Conf*, Assoc for Comp Machinery 1977, pp. 411–418.

[GOL84] GOLD, B., et al. "KVM/370 in Retrospect." *Proc IEEE Symp Security & Privacy*, IEEE Comp Soc Press 1984, pp. 13–23.

[GOO84] GOODMAN, R., et al. "A New Trapdoor Knapsack Public Key Cryptosystem." *Advances in Cryptology/Proc Eurocrypt 1984*, Springer-Verlag 1985, pp. 150–158.

[GOS85] GOSLER, J. "Software Protection: Myth or Reality." *Advances in Cryptology/Proc Crypto 1985*, Plenum Press 1985, pp. 140–157.

[GRA68] GRAHAM, R. "Protection in an Information Processing Utility." *Comm ACM*, v11 n5, May 1968, pp. 365–369.

[GRA72] GRAHAM, R., and DENNING, P. "Protection—Principles and Practice." *Proc AFIPS Spring Joint Comp Conf*, v40, 1972, pp. 417–429.

[GRA83] GRANT, P., and RICHE, R. "The Eagle's Own Plume." *US Naval Institute Proceedings*, Jul 1983, pp. 29–33.

[GRA84a] GRAMPP, F., and MORRIS, R. "Unix Operating System Security." *AT&T Bell Labs Tech J*, v63 n8 pt2, Oct 1984, pp. 1649–1672.

[GRA84b] GRAUBERT, R., and KRAMER, S. "The Integrity Lock Approach to Secure Database Management." *Proc IEEE Symp Security & Privacy*, IEEE Comp Soc Press 1984.

[GRA85] GRAUBERT, R., and DUFFY, K. "Design Overview for Retrofitting the Integrity Lock Architecture." *Proc IEEE Symp Security & Privacy*, IEEE Comp Soc Press 1985, pp. 147–159.

[GRA86] GRABER, G. "The Difference Between Right and Wrong." Unpublished manuscript, 1986.

[GRA91] GRAY, J. "Toward a Mathematical Foundation for Information Flow Security." *Proc IEEE Symp Security & Privacy*, IEEE Comp Soc Press 1991, pp. 21–34.

[GRI81] GRIES, D. *Science of Programming*, Springer-Verlag 1981.

[GUP91] GUPTA, S., and GLIGOR, V. "Towards a Theory of Penetration-Resistant Systems and its Applications." *Proc 4th IEEE Wkshop on Comp Sec Fndtn*, 1991.

[HAB76] HABERMANN, A., et al. "Modularization and Hierarchy in a Family of Operating Systems." *Comm ACM*, v19 n5, May 1976, pp. 266–272.

[HAN76] HANTLER, S., and KING, J. "An Introduction to Proving the Correctness of Programs." *Comput Surveys*, v8 n3, Sep 1976, pp. 331–353.

[HAR76] HARRISON, M., et al. "Protection in Operating Systems." *Comm ACM*, v19 n8, Aug 1976, pp. 461–471.

[HAR85] HARRISON, M. "Theoretical Issues Concerning Protection in Operating System." *Advances in Computers*, v24, 1985, pp. 61–100.

[HAR86] HARRIS, C. *Applying Moral Theories*, Wadsworth 1986.

[HEB91] HEBERLEIN, L., et al. "A Method to Detect Intrusion Activity in a Networked Environment." *Proc 14th Natl Comp Security Conf*, 1991.

[HEL77] HELLMAN, M. "An Extension of the Shannon Theory Approach to Cryptography." *IEEE Trans Info Theory*, vIT-23 n3, May 1977, pp. 289–294.

[HEL78] HELLMAN, M. "An Overview of Public Key Cryptography." *IEEE Comm Soc Mag*, v16 n6, Nov 1978, pp. 24–32.

[HEL79a] HELLMAN, M. "The Mathematics of Public Key Cryptography." *Scientific American*, v241 n2, Feb 1979, pp. 146–157.

[HEL79b] HELLMAN, M. "DES Will Be Totally Insecure Within Ten Years." *IEEE Spectrum*, v16 n7, Jul 1979, pp. 32–39.

[HEL80] HELLMAN, M. "A Cryptanalytic Time–Memory Trade Off." *IEEE Trans Info Theory*, vIT-26 n4, Jul 1980, pp. 401–406.

[HIG88] HIGHLAND, H. "The Brain Virus: Fact and Fantasy." *Computers & Security*, v7 n5, 1988.

[HIN75] HINKE, T., and SCHAEFER, M. "Secure Data Management System." *System Development Corp. Tech Report* RADC-TD-75-266, 1975.

[HOA74] HOARE, C. "Monitors, An Operating System Structuring Concept." *Comm ACM*, v17 n10, Oct 1974, pp. 548–557.

[HOF70] HOFFMAN, L., and MILLER, W. "Getting a Personal Dossier from a Statistical Data Bank." *Datamation*, v16 n5, May 1970, pp. 74–75.

[HOF71] HOFFMAN, L. "The Formulary Model for Flexible Privacy and Access Controls." *Proc AFIPS Fall Joint Comp Conf*, 1971, pp. 587–601.

[HOF77] HOFFMAN, L. *Modern Methods for Computer Security and Privacy*, Prentice-Hall 1977.

[HOF86] HOFFMAN, L. "Risk Analysis and Computer Security: Bridging the Cultural Gap." *Proc Natl Comp Sec Conf*, 1986.

[HOF90] HOFFMAN, L. *Rogue Programs: Viruses, Worms, Trojan Horses*, Van Nostrand Reinhold 1990.

[HOF93] HOFFMAN, L. "Clipping Clipper." *Comm ACM*, v36 n9, Sep 1993, pp. 15–17.

[HOF95a] HOFFMAN, L. *Building in Big Brother*, Springer-Verlag 1995.

[HOF95b] HOFFMAN, L. "Balanced Key Escrow." *GWU Tech Report*, GWU-ICTSP-95-04, 4 Aug 1995.

[HOL91] HOLBROOK, P., and REYNOLDS, J., eds. "Site Security Handbook." *Internet report*, RFC 1244, Jul 1991.

[HSI79] HSIAO, D., et al. *Computer Security*, Academic Press 1979.

[HSI93] HSIEH, D., et al. "The Seaview Prototype." *SRI Tech Report*, 20 Aug 1993.

[HU91] HU, W. "Reducing Timing Channels with Fuzzy Time." *Proc IEEE Symp Security & Privacy*, IEEE Comp Soc Press 1991, pp. 8–20.

[HUF95] HUFF, C., and MARTIN, C. "Computing Consequences: A Framework for Teaching Ethical Computing." *Comm ACM*, v38 n12, Dec 1995, pp. 75–84.

[HUL62] HULL, T., and DOBELL, A. "Random Number Generators." *SIAM Review*, v4 n3, Jul 1962, pp. 230–254.

[HUM88] HUMPHREY, W. "Characterizing the Software Process: A Maturity Framework." *IEEE Software*, v5 n2, Mar 1988, pp. 73–79.

[HUM91a] HUMPHREY, W., and CURTIS, B. "Comments on 'A Critical Look.'" *IEEE Software*, v8 n4, Jul 1991, pp. 42–46.

[HUM91b] HUMPHREY, W., et al. "Software Process Improvement at Hughes Aircraft." *IEEE Software*, v8 n4, Jul 1991, pp. 11–23.

[ICO95] ICOVE, D., et al. *Computer Crime: A Crimefighter's Handbook*, O'Reilly & Associates 1995.

[ING86] INGRAM, D. "Investigating and Prosecuting Computer Crime and Network Abuse." *Proc 13th Natl Comp Sec Conf*, Nov 1986.

[IRV92] IRVINE, C., et al. "Using TNI Concepts for the Near Term User of High Assurance DBMS." Unpublished manuscript, 1992.

[ISO91] ISO (International Organization for Standardization). *ISO 9000-3: Guidelines for the Application of ISO 9000 to the Development, Supply, and Maintenance of Software*, ISO 1991.

[ISO94] ISO (International Organization for Standardization). *ISO 9001: Quality Systems—Model for Quality Assurance in Design/Development, Production, Installation, and Servicing*, ISO 1994.

[ITS91a] ITSEC Working Group. *ITSEC: Information Technology Security Evaluation Criteria*, version 1.1, 10 Jan 1991.

[ITS91b] ITSEC Working Group. *ITSEC: Information Technology Security Evaluation Criteria.* version 1.2, Sep 1991.

[JAG93] JAGANNATHAN, R. "Next Generation Intrusion Detection Expert Systems: System Design Doc." *SRI Tech Report*, A007, 9 Mar 1993.

[JAJ90] JAJODIA, S., and SANDHU, R. "Database Security: Current Status and Key Issues." *SIGMOD Record*, v19 n4, Dec 1990, pp. 123–126.

[JAN82] JANARDAN, R., and LAKSHMANAN, K. "A Public-Key Cryptosystem Based on the Matrix Cover NP-Compl." *Advances in Cryptology/Proc Crypto 1982*, Plenum Press 1982, pp. 21–39.

[JAV93] JAVITZ, H., et al. "Next Generation Intrusion Detection Expert Systems." *SRI Tech Report*, A016, 8 Mar 1993.

[JOH94] JOHNSON, D. *Computer Ethics* (2nd ed.), Prentice Hall 1994.

[JOH95] JOHNSON, D., and MULVEY, J. "Accountability and Computer Decision Systems." *Comm ACM*, v38 n12, Dec 1995, pp. 58–64.

[JON75] JONES, A., and WULF, W. "Towards the Design of Secure Systems." *Software—Practice and Experience*, v5 n4, Oct–Dec 1975, pp. 321–336.

[JON78a] JONES, A. "Protection Mechanism Models: Their Usefulness." In *Foundations of Secure Computation* [DEM78a], 1978, pp. 237–252.

[JON78b] JONES, A., and LISKOV, B. "A Language Extension for Expressing Constraints on Data Access." *Comm ACM*, v21 n5, May 1978, pp. 358–367.

[JON78c] JONES, A., and LIPTON, R. "The Enforcement of Security Policies for Computation." *J Comp and Sys Sci*, v17 n1, Aug 1978, pp. 35–55.

[JUE83] JUENEMAN, R., et al. "Authentication with Manipulation Detection Code." *Proc IEEE Symp Security & Privacy*, IEEE Comp Soc Press 1983, pp. 33–54.

[JUE87] JUENEMAN, R. "Electronic Document Authentication." *IEEE Network*, v1 n2, Apr 1987, pp. 17–23.

[KAH67] KAHN, D. *The Codebreakers*, Macmillan 1967.

[KAI86] KAIN, R., and LANDWEHR, C. "On Access Checking in Capability-Based Systems." *Proc IEEE Symp Security & Privacy*, IEEE Comp Soc Press 1986, pp. 95–100.

[KAL93a] KALISKI, B. "Privacy Enhancement for Internet Electronic Mail, Part IV: Key Certificates and Services." *Internet report*, RFC 1424, Feb 1993.

[KAM78] KAM, J., and DAVIDA, G. "A Structured Design of Substitution–Permutation Encryption for Networks." In *Foundations of Secure Computation* [DEM78a], 1978, pp. 95–114.

[KAR72] KARP, R. "Reducibility Among Combinatorial Problems." *Complexity of Computer Computations*, Plenum Press 1972, pp. 85–104.

[KAR84] KARGER, P., and HERBERT, A. "An Augmented Capability Architecture to Support Lattice Security." *Proc IEEE Symp Security & Privacy*, IEEE Comp Soc Press 1984, pp. 2–12.

[KAR88] KARGER, P. "Implementing Commercial Data Integrity with Secure Capabilities." *Proc IEEE Symp Security & Privacy*, IEEE Comp Soc Press 1988, pp. 130–139.

[KAR90] KARGER, P., et al. "A VMM Security Kernel for the VAX Architecture." *Proc IEEE Symp Security & Privacy*, IEEE Comp Soc Press 1990, pp. 2–19.

[KAR91a] KARGER, P., et al. "A Retrospective on the VAX VMM Security Kernel." *IEEE Trans Software Engr*, v17 n11, Nov 1991, pp. 1147–1165.

[KAR91b] KARGER, P., and WRAY, J. "Storage Channels in Disk Arm Optimization." *Proc IEEE Symp Security & Privacy*, IEEE Comp Soc Press 1991, pp. 52–61.

[KAU95] KAUFMAN, C., et al. *Network Security: Private Communication in a Public World*, Prentice Hall 1995.

[KEE89] KEEFE, T., et al. "Secure Query-Processing Strategies." *IEEE Computer*, v22 n3, Mar 1989, pp. 63–70.

[KEM83] KEMMERER, R. "Shared Resource Matrix Methodology." *ACM Trans Comp Sys*, v1 n3, Oct 1983, pp. 256–277.

[KEM86] KEMMERER, R. "Verification Assessment Study Final Report," *NCSC Tech Report* C3-CR01-86, Mar 1986.

[KEM90] KEMMERER, R. "A Multi-level Formal Specification of a Mental Health Care Database." *Proc Secure Database Workshop*, IFIP WG 11.3, 1990, pp. 1–23.

[KEN93] KENT, S. "Privacy Enhancement for Internet Electronic Mail, Part II: Certificate-Based Key Management." *Internet report*, RFC 1422, Feb 1993.

[KEN93a] KENT, S. "Internet Privacy Enhanced Mail." *Comm ACM*, v36 n3, Aug 1993, pp. 48–59.

[KEP93] KEPHART, J., et al. "Computers and Epidemiology." *IEEE Spectrum*, v30 n5, May 1993, pp. 20–26.

[KIE78] KIEBURTZ, R., and SILBERSCHATZ, A. "Capability Managers." *IEEE Trans Software Engr*, vSE-4 n6, Nov 1978, pp. 467–477.

[KIT96] KITCHENHAM, B., and PFLEEGER, S. "Software Quality: The Elusive Target." *IEEE Software*, v13 n1, Jan 1996, pp. 12–21.

[KLE90] KLEIN, D. "Foiling the Cracker: Survey and Improvements of Password Security." *Proc Usenix Unix Security II Wkshop*, 1990, pp. 5–14.

[KNU73] KNUTH, D. *The Art of Computer Programming. Vol. 1: Fundamental Algorithms*, Addison-Wesley 1973.

[KNU81] KNUTH, D. *The Art of Computer Programming. Vol. 2: Seminumeric Algorithms*, Addison-Wesley 1981.

[KOH78] KOHNFELDER, L. "Towards a Practical Public-Key Cryptosystem." *MIT EE Bachelor's Thesis*, 1978.

[KOH92] KOHL, J., et al. *The Evolution of Kerberos Authentication*, IEEE Comp Soc Press 1992.

[KOH93] KOHL, J., and NEUMAN, C. "The Kerberos Network Authentication Service (V5)." *Internet report*, RFC 1510, Sep 1993.

[KON80] KONHEIM, A., et al. "The IPS Cryptographic Programs." *IBM Systems J*, v19 n2, 1980, pp. 253–283.

[KON81] KONHEIM, A. *Cryptography, A Primer*, Wiley 1981.

[KUL76] KULLBACK, S. *Statistical Methods in Cryptanalysis*, Aegean Park Press 1976.

[KUM95] KUMAR, S. "Classification and Detection of Computer Intrusions." *Purdue Univ PhD Dissertation*, Aug 1995.

[KUR92] KURAK, C., and MCHUGH, J. "A Cautionary Note on Image Downgrading." *Proc Comp Security Applns Conf*, 1992, pp. 153–159.

[LAG83] LAGARIAS, J. "Knapsack Public Key Cryptosystems and Diophantine Approximations." *Advances in Cryptology/Proc Crypto 1983*, Plenum Press 1983, pp. 3–23.

[LAK74] LACKEY, R. "Penetration of Computer Systems: An Overview." *Honeywell Comp J*, v8 n2, Sep 1974, pp. 81–85.

[LAM69] LAMPSON, B. "Dynamic Protection Structures." *Proc AFIPS Fall Joint Comp Conf*, v35, 1969, pp. 27–38.

[LAM71] LAMPSON, B. "Protection." Republished in *Proc 5th Princeton Symp,* in *Oper Sys Rev*, v8 n1, Jan 1974, pp. 18–24.

[LAM73] LAMPSON, B. "A Note on the Confinement Problem." *Comm ACM*, v16 n10, Oct 1973, pp. 613–615.

[LAM76] LAMPSON, B., and STURGIS, H. "Reflections on an Operating System Design." *Comm ACM*, v19 n5, May 1976, pp. 251–266.

[LAM81] LAMPORT, L. "Password Authentication with Insecure Communication." *Comm ACM*, v24 n11, Nov 1981, pp. 770–771.

[LAM92] LAMPSON, B., et al. "Authentication in Distributed Systems: Theory and Practice." *Digital Equip Corp Sys Research Center*, Report 83, Feb 1992.

[LAN81] LANDWEHR, C. "Formal Models for Computer Security." *Comp Surveys*, v13 n3, Sep 1981, pp. 247–278.

[LAN83] LANDWEHR, C., et al. "The Best Available Technologies for Computer Security." *IEEE Computer*, v16 n7, Jul 1983, pp. 86–100.

[LAN84] LANDWEHR, C., et al. "A Security Model for Military Message Systems." *ACM Trans Comp Sys*, v2 n2, Aug 1984, pp. 198–222.

[LAN93] LANDWEHR, C., et al. "Computer Program Security Flaws." *NRL Tech Report*, Nov 1993.

[LAN94] LANDAU, S., et al. "Crypto Policy Perspectives." *Comm ACM*, v37 n8, Aug 1994, pp. 115–121.

[LAU95] LAUDON, K. "Ethical Concepts and Information Technology." *Comm ACM*, v38 n12, Dec 1995, pp. 33–39.

[LEC83] LECHTER, M. "Protecting Software and Firmware Devices." *IEEE Computer*, v16 n8, Aug 1983, pp. 73–82.

[LEE88] LEE, T. "Using Mandatory Integrity to Enforce Commercial Security." *Proc IEEE Symp Security & Privacy*, IEEE Comp Soc Press 1988, pp. 140–146.

[LEM79] LEMPEL, A. "Cryptology in Transition." *Comp Surveys*, v11 n4, Dec 1979, pp. 285–303.

[LEN78] LENNON, R. "Cryptographic Architecture for Information Security." *IBM Systems J*, v17 n2, 1978, pp. 138–150.

[LEX76] LEXAN CORP. "An Evaluation of the DES." *Lexan Corp. technical report*, Sep 1976.

[LIE89] LIEPINS, G., and VACCARO, H. "Anomaly Detection: Purpose and Framework." *Proc Natl Comp Security Conf*, 1989, pp. 495–504.

[LIN75] LINDE, R. "Operating System Penetration." *Proc AFIPS Natl Comp Conf*, 1975.

[LIN76] LINDEN, T. "Operating System Structures to Support Security and Reliability." *Comp Surveys*, v8 n4, Dec 1976, pp. 409–445.

[LIN90] LINN, J. "Practical Authentication for Distributed Computing." *Proc IEEE Symp Security & Privacy*, IEEE Comp Soc Press 1990, pp. 31–40.

[LIN93] LINN, J. "Privacy Enhancement for Internet Electronic Mail, Part I: Message Encipherment and Authentication Procedures." *Internet report*, RFC 1421, Feb 1993.

[LIN93a] LINN, J. "Generic Security Service Application Programming Interface." *Internet report*, RFC 1508, Sep 1993.

[LIN93b] LINN, J. "Common Authentication Technology Overview." *Internet report*, RFC 1511, Sep 1993.

[LIP77] LIPTON, R. and SNYDER, L. "A Linear Time Algorithm for Deciding Subject Security." *J ACM*, v24 n3, Jul 1977, pp. 455–464.

[LIP82] LIPNER, S. "Non-Discretionary Controls for Commercial Applications." *Proc IEEE Symp Security & Privacy*, IEEE Comp Soc Press 1982, pp. 2–10.

[LOC94] LOCKHART, H. *OSF DCE*, McGraw Hill 1994.

[LON82] LONGPRE, L. "The Use of Public-Key Cryptology for Signing Checks." *Advances in Cryptology/Proc Crypto 1982*, Plenum Press 1982, pp. 187–197.

[LU 1989] LU, W., and SUNDARESHAN, M. "Secure Communication in Internet Environments." *IEEE Trans Comm*, vCOM37 n10, Oct 1989, pp. 1014–1023.

[LUN89] LUNT, T. "Aggregation and Inference: Facts and Fallacies." *Proc IEEE Symp Security & Privacy*, IEEE Comp Soc Press 1989, pp. 102–109.

[LUN90] LUNT, T., and FERNANDEZ, E. "Database Security." *SIGMOD Record*, v19 n4, Dec 1990, pp. 90–97.

[LUN90a] LUNT, T., et al. "The SeaView Security Model." *IEEE Trans Software Engr*, vSE-16 n6, Jun 1990, pp. 593–607.

[LUN92] LUNT, T., et al. "A Real-Time Intrusion Detection Expert System (IDES)." *SRI Tech Report*, Final Report, Feb 1992.

[LUN93] LUNT, T. "A Survey of Intrusion Detection Techniques." *Computers & Security*, v12 n4, Jun 1993, pp. 405–418.

[LYN92] LYNCH, D. *Internet Systems Handbook*, Addison-Wesley 1992.

[LYO89] DE LYONS, G. "Ko Vaht Chan Ellz." Private communication, 1989.

[MAH96] MAHER, D. "Crypto Backup and Key Escrow." *Comm ACM*, v39 n3, Mar 1996, pp. 48–53.

[MAR94] MARTIN, J. *TCP/IP Networking: Architecture, Administration, and Programming*, Prentice Hall 1994.

[MAS95] MASON, R. "Ethics to Information Technology Issues." *Comm ACM*, v38 n12, Dec 1995, pp. 55–57.

[MAT78] MATYAS, S., and MEYER, C. "Generation, Distribution and Installation of Cryptographic Keys." *IBM Systems J*, v17 n2, 1978, pp. 126–137.

[MAT85] MATLEY, B. "Computer Privacy in America: Conflicting Practices—Policy Choices." *Proc IEEE Symp Security & Privacy*, IEEE Comp Soc Press 1985, pp. 219–223.

[MAT86] MATLOFF, N. "Another Look at Use of Noise Addition for Database Security." *Proc IEEE Symp Security & Privacy*, IEEE Comp Soc Press 1986, pp. 173–180.

[MAY90] MAYER, F., and PADILLA, S. "What is a B3 Architecture." Unpublished manuscript, Jan 1990.

[MAY91] MAYFIELD, T., et al. "Integrity in Automated Information Systems." *NCSC C Technical Report* 79–91, Sep 1991.

[MCA89] MCAFEE, J. "The Virus Cure." *Datamation*, v35 n4, 15 Feb 1989, pp. 29–35.

[MCC79] MCCAULEY, E., and DRONGOWSKI, P. "KSOS—The Design of a Secure Operating System." *Proc AFIPS Natl Comp Conf*, 1979, pp. 345–353.

[MCC90] MCCULLOUGH, D. "A Hookup Theorem for Multilevel Security." *IEEE Trans Software Engr*, vSE-16 n6, Jun 1990.

[MCD77] MCDONALD, N., and IPPOLITO, P. "Study of Computer Safeguards." *PRC Info Sci Co Tech report* R–2, 1977.

[MCI92] MCILROY, M., and REEDS, J. "Multilevel Security in the UNIX Tradition." *Software—Practice and Experience*, v22 n8, Aug 1992, pp. 673–694.

[MCL90a] MCLEAN, J. "The Specification and Modeling of Computer Security." *IEEE Computer*, v23 n1, Jan 1990, pp. 9–16.

[MCL90b] MCLEAN, J. "Security Models and Information Flow." *Proc IEEE Symp Security & Privacy*, IEEE Comp Soc Press 1990, pp. 180–187.

[MEA86] MEADOWS, C. "A More Efficient Cryptographic Matchmaking Protocol." *Proc IEEE Symp Security & Privacy*, IEEE Comp Soc Press 1986, pp. 134–137.

[MEA87] MEADOWS, C., and MUTCHLER, D. "Matching Secrets in Absence of Continuously Available Trusted Authentication." *IEEE Trans Software Engr*, vSE-13 n2, Feb 1987, pp. 289–290.

[MER78a] MERKLE, R. "Secure Communication over Insecure Channels." *Comm ACM*, v21 n4, Apr 1978, pp. 294–299.

[MER78b] MERKLE, R., and HELLMAN, M. "Hiding Information and Signatures in Trapdoor Knapsacks." *IEEE Trans Info Theory*, vIT-24 n5, Sep 1978, pp. 525–530.

[MER80] MERKLE, R. "Protocols for Public Key Cryptosystems." *Proc IEEE Symp Security & Privacy*, IEEE Comp Soc Press 1980, pp. 122–133.

[MER81] MERKLE, R., and HELLMAN, M. "On the Security of Multiple Encryption." *Comm ACM*, v24 n7, Jul 1981, p. 465.

[MEY82] MEYER, C., and MATYAS, S. *Cryptography: A New Dimension in Computer Security*, Wiley 1982.

[MIG84] MIGUEL, J. "A Composite Cost/Benefit/Risk Methodology." *Computer Security: A Global Challenge, Proc IFIP Conf*, 1984, pp. 307–312.

[MIL76] MILLEN, J. "Security Kernel Validation in Practice." *Comm ACM*, v19 n5, May 1976, pp. 243–250.

[MIL87a] MILLEN, J. "Covert Channel Capacity." *Proc IEEE Symp Security & Privacy*, IEEE Comp Soc Press 1987, pp. 60–66.

[MIL87b] MILLEN, J. et al. "The Interrogator: Protocol Security Analysis." *IEEE Trans Software Engr*, vSE-13 n2, Feb 1987, pp. 274–288.

[MIL88] MILLEN, J. "Covert Channel Analysis." Unpublished notes, 1988.

[MIL92] MILLEN, J. "A Resource Allocation Model for Denial of Service." *Proc IEEE Symp Security & Privacy*, IEEE Comp Soc Press 1992, pp. 137–147.

[MIL95] MILBERG, S., et al. "Values, Personal Information, Privacy, and Regulatory Approaches." *Comm ACM*, v38 n12, Dec 1995, pp. 65–74.

[MOF88] MOFFETT, J., and SLOMAN, M. "The Source of Authority for Commercial Access Control." *IEEE Computer*, v21 n2, Feb 1988, pp. 59–69.

[MOO88] MOORE, J. "Protocol Failures in Cryptosystems." *Proc IEEE*, v76 n5, May 1988, pp. 594–602.

[MOR77] MORRIS, R., et al. "Assessment of the NBS Proposed Data Encryption Standard." *Cryptologia*, v1 n3, Jul 1977, pp. 281–291.

[MOR79] MORRIS, R., and THOMPSON, K. "Password Security: A Case History." *Comm ACM*, v22 n11, Nov 1979.

[MUL90] MULLENDER, S., et al. "Amoeba—A Distributed Operating System for the 1990s." *IEEE Computer*, v23 n5, May 1990, pp. 44–53.

[NAS90] NASH, M., and POLAND, K. "Some Conundrums Concerning Separation of Duty." *Proc IEEE Symp Security & Privacy*, IEEE Comp Soc Press 1990, pp. 201–207.

[NAV86] NAVATHE, S. "Integrating User Views in Database Design." *IEEE Computer*, v19 n1, Jan 1986, pp. 50–61.

[NBS77] NBS (National Bureau of Standards). "Data Encryption Standard." *FIPS Publ* 46, Jan 1977.

[NBS79] NBS (National Bureau of Standards). *Guidelines for Automatic Data Processing,* US GPO 1979.

[NBS80] NBS (National Bureau of Standards). "DES Modes of Operation." *FIPS Publ* 81, US GPO 1980.

[NCS85] NCSC (National Computer Security Center). *Orange Book*, same as [DOD85].

[NCS85a] NCSC (National Computer Security Center). *Personal Computer Security Consideration*, NCSC Pub WA-002-85 1985.

[NCS87] NCSC (National Computer Security Center). *Trusted Network Interpretation*, NCSC-TG-005-ver1, 1987.

[NCS91a] NCSC (National Computer Security Center). *A Guide to Understanding Data Remanence*, NCSC-TG-025 ver2, Sep 1991.

[NCS91b] NCSC (National Computer Security Center). "Integrity-Oriented Control Objectives." *C Technical Report*, 111–91, Oct 1991.

[NCS92] NCSC (National Computer Security Center). "Trusted Computer System Architecture: Assessing Modularity." Internal working paper, unpublished, 18 Dec 1992.

[NEE78] NEEDHAM, R., and SCHROEDER, M. "Using Encryption for Authentication in Large Networks of Computers." *Comm ACM*, v21 n12, Dec 1978, pp. 993–999.

[NEE94] NEEDHAM, R. "Denial of Service: An Example." *Comm ACM*, v37 n11, Nov 1994, pp. 42–47.

[NES86] NESSETT, D. "Factors Affecting Distributed System Security." *Proc IEEE Symp Security & Privacy*, IEEE Comp Soc Press 1986, pp. 204–222.

[NES87] NESSETT, D. "Factors Affecting Distributed System Security." *IEEE Trans Software Engr*, vSE-13, n2, Feb 1987.

[NEU78] NEUMANN, P. "Computer System Security Evaluation." *Proc AFIPS Natl Comp Conf*, v47, 1978, pp. 1087–1095.

[NEU82] NEUGENT, W. "Acceptance Criteria for Computer Security." *Proc AFIPS Natl Comp Conf*, v51, 1982, pp. 443–448.

[NEU83] NEUMANN, P. "Experience with Formality in Software Development." In *Theory and Practice of Software Technology*, North-Holland Publishing Co. 1983, pp. 203–219.

[NEU86] NEUMANN, P. "On the Hierarchical Design of Computer Systems for Critical Applications." *IEEE Trans Software Engr*, vSE-12 n9, Sep 1986, pp. 905–920.

[NEU90a] NEUMANN, P. "Toward Standards and Criteria for Critical Computer Systems." *Proc COMPASS Conf*, 1990.

[NEU90b] NEUMANN, P. "Rainbows and Arrows: How Security Criteria Address Misuse." *Proc Natl Comp Security Conf*, 1990, pp. 414–422.

[NIS91a] NIST (National Institute of Standards and Technology). "A Proposed Digital Signature Standard." *FIPS Pub*, xx, Aug 1991.

[NIS91b] NIST (National Institute of Standards and Technology). "Glossary of Computer Security Terminology." *NIST Tech Report*, NISTIR 4659, Sep 1991.

[NIS92a] NIST (National Institute of Standards and Technology). "Secure Hash Standard (SHS)." *FIPS Pub*, yy, Jan 1992.

[NIS92b] NIST (National Institute of Standards and Technology). "The Digital Signature Standard, Proposal and Discussion." *Comm ACM*, v35 n7, Jul 1992, pp. 36–54.

[NIS93] NIST (National Institute of Standards and Technology). "Secure Hash Standard." *NIST FIPS Pub*, 180, May 1993.

[NIS94] NIST (National Institute of Standards and Technology). "Digital Signature Standard." *NIST FIPS Pub*, 186, May 1994.

[NIS95] NIST (National Institute of Standards and Technology). "Secure Hash Standard." *FIPS Pub*, 180-1, 17 Apr 1995.

[NRC91] NRC (National Research Council). *Computers at Risk: Safe Computing in the Electronic Age*, National Academy Press 1991.

[NRC96] NRC (National Research Council). *Cyptography's Role in Securing the Information Society,* National Academy Press 30 May 1996.

[NSA92] NSA (National Security Agency). *Federal Criteria for Information Technology Security,* version 1.0, Dec 1992.

[NSA95a] NSA (National Security Agency). "SSE CMM: Systems Security Engineering Capability Maturity Md." *SSE-CMM Model and Application Report*, 2 Oct 1995.

[NSA95b] NSA (National Security Agency). *Security Service API Cryptographic API Recommendations,* Jun 1995.

[NTI87] NTISS (National Telecommunications and Information Systems Security Committee). *Advisory Memo Office Automation Security Guide*, NTISS COMPUSEC/1–87, 1987.

[OLO93] OLOVSSON, T., et al. "Data Collection for Security Fault Forecasting." *PDCS Tech Rep*, ESPRIT BRA 6362 PDCS 2, Aug 1993.

[OMG92] OMG (Object Management Group). *The Common Object Request Broker: Architecture and Specification,* Wiley 1992.

[OMG95] OMG (Object Management Group). "CORBA Security." *OMG Document* 95-12-1, Dec 1995.

[PAD79] PADLIPSKY, M., et al. "KSOS—Computer Network Applications." *Proc AFIPS Natl Comp Conf*, 1979, pp. 373–381.

[PAR72] PARNAS, D. "On the Criteria to Be Used in Decomposing Systems into Modules." *Comm ACM*, v15 n12, Dec 1972, pp. 1053–1058.

[PAR75] PARNAS, D., and SIEWIOREK, D. "Use of Concept of Transparency in Design of Hierarchically Structured Operating Systems." *Comm ACM*, v18 n7, Jul 1975, pp. 401–408.

[PAR79] PARKER, D. *Ethical Conflicts in Computer Science and Technology*, AFIPS Press 1979.

[PAR81] PARKER, D. *Computer Security Management,* Reston 1981.

[PAR83] PARKER, D. *Fighting Computer Crime*, Scribners 1983.

[PAR84] PARKER, D., and NYCUM, S. "Computer Crime." *Comm ACM*, v27 n4, Apr 1984, pp. 313–321.

[PAU93] PAULK, M. et al. "Capability Maturity Model." Version 1.1, *IEEE Software*, v10 n4, Jul 1993, pp. 18–27.

[PAU95] PAULK, M. "How ISO 9001 Compares with the CMM." *IEEE Software*, v12 n1, Jan 1995, pp. 74–82.

[PCS81] PCSG (Public Cryptography Study Group). "Report of the Public Cryptography Study Group." *Comm ACM*, v24 n7, Jul 1981, pp. 434–450.

[PER95] PERSSON, S. "Security Policy for Swedish Post." *TIS tech report*, Aug 1995.

[PET90] PETHIA, R., and CROCKER, S. "Internet Security Policy Recommendations." *Internet Engineering Task Force draft report*, 28 Nov 1990.

[PET91] PETHIA, R., et al. "Guidelines for the Secure Operation of the Internet." *Internet report*, RFC 1281, Nov 1991.

[PFL88] PFLEEGER, C., and PFLEEGER, S. "A Transaction Flow Approach to Software Security Certification." *Computers & Security*, v7 n3, 1988, pp. 495–502.

[PFL89] PFLEEGER, C., et al. "A Methodology for Penetration Testing." *Computers & Security*, v8, 1989, pp. 613–620.

[PFL91] PFLEEGER, S. *Software Engineering*, Macmillan 1991.

[PFL92] PFLEEGER, C., and MAYFIELD, T. "NCSC Availability Study." Unpublished manuscript, Institute for Defense Analyses, 1992.

[PFL93] PFLEEGER, C. "How Can IT be Safe If It's Not Secure?" Presented at Safety Critical Sys Conf, Apr 1993.

[PFL94] PFLEEGER, C. "Uses and Misuses of Formal Methods in Computer Security." *Proc IMA Conf on Math of Dependable Sys*, Clarendon Press 1995.

[PFL96] PFLEEGER, C. "Software Development Issues in Computer Security." *American Programmer,* v9 n5, May 1996, pp. 14–19.

[PLE77] PLESS, V. "Encryption Schemes for Computational Confidentiality." *IEEE Trans Comp*, vC-26 n11, Nov 1977, pp. 1133–1136.

[POP74a] POPEK, G. "Protection Structures." *IEEE Computer*, v7 n6, Jun 1974, pp. 22–23.

[POP74b] POPEK, G., and GOLDBERG, R. "Formal Requirements for Virtualizable 3rd Generation Architectures." *Comm ACM*, v17 n7, Jul 1974, pp. 412–421.

[POP78] POPEK, G., and KLINE, C. "Encryption Protocols, Public Key Algorithms, and Digital Signatures." In *Foundations of Secure Computation* [DEM78a], 1978, pp. 133–155.

[POP78a] POPEK, G., and KLINE, C. "Issues in Kernel Design." *Proc AFIPS Natl Comp Conf*, 1978, pp. 1079–1086.

[POP79] POPEK, G., et al. "UCLA Secure Unix." *Proc AFIPS Natl Comp Conf*, 1979, pp. 355–364.

[PUR74] PURDY, G. "A High Security Log-In Procedure." *Comm ACM*, v17 n8, Aug 1974, pp. 442–445.

[PUR82] PURDY, G., et al. "A Software Protection Scheme." *Proc IEEE Symp Security & Privacy*, IEEE Comp Soc Press 1982, pp. 99–103.

[QIA94] QIAN, X. "Inference Channel-Free Integrity Constraints for Multilevel Databases." *Proc IEEE Symp Security & Privacy*, IEEE Comp Soc Press 1994, pp. 158–167.

[RAB78] RABIN, M. "Digitalized Signatures." In *Foundations of Secure Computation* [DEM78a], 1978, pp. 155–166.

[RAN95a] RANUM, M. "Marcus J Ranum Certified Apparently OK: On the Topic of Firewall Testing." Unpublished manuscript, 1995.

[RAN95b] RANUM, M. "Internet Firewalls Frequently Asked Questions (FAQ)." *Internet posting*, http://www.tis.com, 1995 reg. updates.

[REE77] REEDS, J. "'Cracking' a Random Number Generator." *Cryptologia*, v1 n1, Jan 1977, pp. 20–26.

[REE84] REEDS, J., and WEINBERGER, P. "File Security and the Unix Operating System 'crypt' Command." *AT&T Bell Labs Tech J*, v63 n8 pt2, Oct 1984, pp. 1673–1684.

[REI87] REID, B. "Reflections on Some Recent Widespread Computer Breakins." *Comm ACM*, v30 n2, Feb 1987, pp. 103–105.

[RIT79] RITCHIE, D. "On the Security of UNIX." *Unix Programmer's Manual, secn. 2*, AT&T Bell Labs 1979.

[RIV78] RIVEST, R., et al. "A Method for Obtaining Digital Signatures and Public-Key Cryptosystems." *Comm ACM*, v21 n2, Feb 1978, pp. 120–126.

[RIV91] RIVEST, R. "The MD4 Message Digest Algorithm." *Advances in Cryptology/Proc Crypto 1990*, Springer-Verlag 1991, pp. 303–311.

[RIV92] RIVEST, R. "The MD4 Message Digest Algorithm." *Internet report*, RFC 1186, Oct 1992.

[RIV92a] RIVEST, R. "The MD4 Message-Digest Algorithm." *Internet report*, RFC 1320, Apr 1992.

[RIV92b] RIVEST, R. "The MD5 Message-Digest Algorithm." *Internet report*, RFC 1321, Apr 1992.

[RIV92c] RIVEST, R. "Response to NIST's Proposal." *Comm ACM*, v35 n7, Jul 1992, pp. 41–47.

[ROC89] ROCHLIS, J., and EICHLIN, M. "With Microscope and Tweezers: The Worm from MIT's Perspective." *Comm ACM*, v30 n6, Jun 1989, pp. 689–698.

[ROS30] ROSS, W. *The Right and the Good,* Clarendon Press 1930.

[ROS91] ROSEN, K. "Network Security: Just Say 'Know' at Layer 7." *Data Communications*, Mar 1991, pp. 103–105.

[RUS83] RUSHBY, J., and RANDELL, B. "A Distributed Secure System." *IEEE Computer*, v16 n7, Jul 1983, pp. 55–67.

[RUS85] RUSHBY, J. "Networks are Systems." *Proc DOD Comp Sec Ctr Wksp Network Secur*, 1985, pp. 7-24–7-38.

[RUS91] RUSSELL, D., and GANGEMI, G. *Computer Security Basics*, O'Reilly and Associates 1991.

[SAI95] SAIEDIAN, H., and KUZARA, R. "SEI Capability Maturity Model's Impact on Contractors." *IEEE Computer*, v28 n1, Jan 1995, pp. 16–26.

[SAL74] SALTZER, J. "Protection and the Control of Information Sharing in MULTICS." *Comm ACM*, v17 n7, Jul 1974, pp. 388–402.

[SAL75] SALTZER, J., AND SCHROEDER, M. "The Protection of Information in Computing Systems." *Proc IEEE*, v63 n9, Sep 1975, pp. 1278–1308.

[SAL90] SALOMAA, A. *Public Key Cryptography*, Springer-Verlag 1990.

[SAN93] SANDHU, R. "Lattice-Based Access Control Models." *IEEE Computer*, v26 n11, Nov 1993, pp. 9–19.

[SCH72] SCHROEDER, M., and SALTZER, J. "A Hardware Architecture for Implementing Protection Rings." *Comm ACM*, v15 n3, Mar 1972, pp. 157–170.

[SCH77] SCHAEFER, M., et al. "Program Confinement in KVM/370." *Proc ACM Annual Conf*, Assoc for Comp Machinery 1977, pp. 404–410.

[SCH79] SCHELL, R. "Computer Security." *Air Univ Review*, Jan–Feb 1979, pp. 16–33.

[SCH83] SCHELL, R. "A Security Kernel for a Multiprocessor Microcomputer." *IEEE Computer*, v16 n7, Jul 1983, pp. 47–53.

[SCH84a] SCHAEFER, M., and SCHELL, R. "Toward an Understanding of Extensible Architectures." *Proc IEEE Symp Security & Privacy*, IEEE Comp Soc Press 1984, pp. 41–49.

[SCH84b] SCHAUMUELLER-BICHL, I., and PILLER, E. "A Method of Software Protection Based on the Use of Smart Cards." *Advances in Cryptology/Proc Eurocrypt 1984*, Springer-Verlag 1985, pp. 446–454.

[SCH86] SCHELL, R., and DENNING, D. "Integrity in Trusted Database Systems." *Proc Natl Comp Sec Conf*, 1986, pp. 30–36.

[SCH89a] SCHAEFER, M. "Symbol Security Condition Considered Harmful." *Proc IEEE Symp Security & Privacy*, IEEE Comp Soc Press 1989, pp. 20–46.

[SCH89b] SCHAEFER, M., et al. "Tea and I: An Allergy." *Proc IEEE Symp Security & Privacy*, IEEE Comp Soc Press 1989, pp. 178–182.

[SCH90a] SCHAEFER, M. "State of the Art and Trends in Trusted DBMS." *Proc Deutsche Konferenz uber Computersicherheit*, 1990, pp. 1–19.

[SCH90b] SCHELL, R., and IRVINE, C. "Performance Implications for Multilevel Database Systems." Unpublished report, 1990.

[SCH90c] SCHAEFER, M. "Reflections on Current Issues in Trusted DBMS." In *Database Security IV: Status and Prospects*, North-Holland 1991.

[SCH96] SCHNEIER, B. *Applied Cryptography* (2nd ed.), Wiley 1996.

[SEI90] SEIDEN, K., and MELANSON, J. "The Auditing Facility for a VMM Security Kernel." *Proc IEEE Symp Security & Privacy*, IEEE Comp Soc Press 1990, pp. 262–277.

[SHA49] SHANNON, C. "Communication Theory of Secrecy Systems." *Bell Systems Technical Journal*, v28, Oct 1949, pp. 659–715.

[SHA78] SHAMIR, A., et al. "Mental Poker." *MIT Lab for Comp Sci*, Report TM-125, Nov 1978.

[SHA79] SHAMIR, A. "How to Share a Secret." *Comm ACM*, v22 n11, Nov 1979, pp. 612–613.

[SHA80] SHAMIR, A., and ZIPPEL, R. "On the Security of the Merkle–Hellman Cryptographic Scheme." *IEEE Trans Info Theory*, vIT-26 n3, May 1980, pp. 339–340.

[SHA82] SHAMIR, A. "A Polynomial Time Algorithm for Breaking the Basic Merkle–Hellman Cryptosystem." *Advances in Cryptology/Proc Crypto 1982*, Plenum Press 1982, pp. 279–288.

[SHA83] SHAMIR, A. "On Generation of Cryptographically Strong Pseudorandom Sequences." *ACM Trans Comp Sys*, v1 n1, Feb 1983, pp. 38–44.

[SHO82] SHOCK, J., and HUPP, J. "The 'Worm' Programs—Early Experience with a Distributed Computing System." *Comm ACM*, v25 n3, Mar 1982, pp. 172–180.

[SIB87] SIBERT, W., et al. "Unix and B2: Are They Compatible?" *Proc NBS/NCSC Comp Sec Conf*, 1987, pp. 142–149.

[SIM77] SIMMONS, G., and NORRIS, M. "Preliminary Comments on the M.I.T. Public-Key Cryptosystem." *Cryptologia*, v1 n4, Oct 1977, pp. 406–414.

[SIM79] SIMMONS, G. "Symmetric and Asymmetric Encryption." *Comp Surveys*, v11 n4, Dec 1979, pp. 305–330.

[SIM88a] SIMMONS, G. "A Survey of Information Authentication." *Proc IEEE*, v76 n5, May 1988, pp. 603–620.

[SIM88b] SIMMONS, G. "How to Insure that Data Acquired to Verify Treaty Compliance Are Trustworthy." *Proc IEEE*, v76 n5, May 1988, pp. 621–627.

[SIM92] SIMMONS, G. *Contemporary Cryptology*, IEEE Press 1992.

[SIM94] SIMMONS, G. "Cryptanalysis and Protocol Failures." *Comm ACM*, v37 n11, Nov 1994, pp. 56–64.

[SIN66] SINKOV, A. *Elementary Cryptanalysis: A Mathematical Approach*, Math Association of America 1966.

[SIP95] SIPIOR, J., and WARD, B. "The Ethical and Legal Quandary of Email Privacy." *Comm ACM*, v38 n12, Dec 1995, pp. 48–54.

[SMA88] SMAHA, S. "Haystack: An Intrusion Detection System." *Proc 4th Aerospace Comp Security Conf*, Dec 1988, pp. 37–44.

[SMI88a] SMID, M., and BRANSTAD, D. "The Data Encryption Standard: Past Present and Future." *Proc IEEE*, v76 n5, May 1988, pp. 550–559.

[SMI88b] SMITH, G. "Inference and Aggregation Security Attack Analysis." *George Mason University Technical Paper*, Sep 1988.

[SMI91] SMITH, G. "Modeling Security-Relevant Data Semantics." *IEEE Trans Software Engr*, vSE17 n11, Nov 1991, pp. 1195–1203.

[SMI93a] SMID, M., and BRANSTAD, D. "Response to Comments on the NIST Proposed Digital Signature Standard." *Advances in Cryptology/Proc Crypto 1992*, Springer-Verlag 1993.

[SMI93b] SMITH, H. "Privacy Policies and Practices: Inside the Organizational Maze." *Comm ACM*, v36 n12, Dec 1993, pp. 105–122.

[SNA91] SNAPP, S., et al. "DIDS (Distributed Intrusion Detection System)—Motivation, Architecture." *Proc 14th Natl Comp Security Conf*, 1991.

[SNY81] SNYDER, L. "Formal Models of Capability-Based Protection Systems." *IEEE Trans Comp*, vC-30 n3, May 1981, pp. 172–181.

[SOL77] SOLOVAY, R., and STRASSEN, V. "A Fast Monte-Carlo Test for Primality." *SIAM J Comp*, v6, Mar 1977, pp. 84–85.

[SOL81] SOLOMON, D. "Processing Multilevel Secure Objects." *Proc IEEE Symp Security & Privacy*, IEEE Comp Soc Press 1981, pp. 56–61.

[SOM96] SOMMERVILLE, I. *Software Engineering* (5th ed.), Addison-Wesley 1996.

[SPA89] SPAFFORD, E. "The Internet Worm Incident." *Proc European Software Engr Conf*, 1989, pp. 203–227. In [HOF90] .

[SPA92] SPAFFORD, E. "Observing Reusable Password Choices." *Proc 1992 Usenix Unix Security III Workshop,* 1992, pp. 299–312.

[SPA95] SPAFFORD, E. Unpublished note, 26 Nov 1995.

[SPA96] SPAFFORD, E. "Kerberos 4 Keys Not So Random?" CERT Advisory CA-96.03, 2 Feb 1996.

[SPO90] SPOONER, D., and LANDWEHR, C., eds. *Database Security III: Status and Prospects*, North-Holland 1990.

[STA94] STALLINGS, W. *Data and Computer Communications* (4th ed.), Macmillan 1994.

[STE74] STEVENS, W., et al. "Structured Design." *IBM Sys J*, v13 n2, 1974, pp. 115–139.

[STE88] STEINER, J., et al. "Kerberos: An Authentication Service for Open Network Systems." *Proc Usenix Conf*, Feb 1988, pp. 191–202.

[STI94] STICKEL, M. "Elimination of Inference Channels by Optimal Upgrading." *Proc IEEE Symp Security & Privacy*, IEEE Comp Soc Press 1994, pp. 168–175.

[STO74] STONEBRAKER, M., and WONG, E. "Access Control in a Relational Data Base Management System by Query Modification." *Proc ACM Annual Conf*, Assoc for Comp Machinery 1974, pp. 180–186.

[STO81b] STONEBRAKER, M. "Operating System Support for Database Management." *Comm ACM*, v24 n7, Jul 1981, pp. 412–418.

[STO88] STOLL, C. "Stalking the Wily Hacker." *Comm ACM*, v31 n5, May 1988, pp. 484–497.

[STO89] STOLL, C. *The Cuckoo's Egg*, Doubleday 1989.

[STU89a] STUBBS, B., and HOFFMAN, L. "Mapping the Virus Battlefield." *GWU Tech Report*, GWU-IIST-89-23, Aug 1989. In [HOF90].

[STU90] STUMM, M., and ZHOU, S. "Algorithms Implementing Distributed Shared Memory." *IEEE Computer*, v23 n5, May 1990, pp. 54–64.

[SUG79] SUGARMAN, R. "On Foiling Computer Crime." *IEEE Spectrum*, v16 n7, Jul 1979, pp. 31–32.

[THO84] THOMPSON, K. "Reflections on Trusting Trust." *Comm ACM*, v27 n8, Aug 1984, pp. 761–763.

[TIC89] TICH, A. "On a Hypothesis by D. D. Downs." Private communication, 1989.

[TIS92] TIS (Trusted Information Systems, Inc). "A Proposed Interpretation of the TCSEC for Virtual Machine Monitor Architectures." TIS tech report, 10 Aug 1992.

[TOM84] TOMPKINS, J. *Report on Computer Crime*, American Bar Association 1984.

[TSA90] TSAI, J., et al. "A Noninvasive Architecture to Monitor Real-Time Distributed Systems." *IEEE Comp*, v23 n3, Mar 1990, pp. 11–23.

[TUC79] TUCHMAN, W. "Hellman Presents No Shortcut Solutions to the DES." *IEEE Spectrum*, v16 n7, Jul 1979, p. 40.

[TUR82] TURN, R. "Private Sector Needs for Trusted/Secure Computer Systems." *Proc AFIPS Natl Comp Conf*, v51, 1982, pp. 449–460.

[VAH82] VAHLE, M., and TOLENDINO, L. "Breaking a Pseudo-Random-Number-Based Cryptographic Algorithm." *Cryptologia*, v6 n4, Oct 1982, pp. 319–328.

[VOY83] VOYDOCK, V., and KENT, S. "Security Mechanisms in High-Level Network Protocols." *Comp Surveys*, v15 n2, Jun 1983, pp. 135–171.

[WAG83] WAGSTAFF, S. "How to Crack an RSA Cryptosystem." *Advances in Cryptology/Proc Crypto 1983*, Plenum Press 1983.

[WAL80] WALKER, B., et al. "Specification and Verification of the UCLA Unix Security Kernel." *Comm ACM*, v23 n2, Feb 1980, pp. 118–131.

[WAL85] WALKER, S. "Network Security Overview." *Proc IEEE Symp Security & Privacy*, IEEE Comp Soc Press 1985, pp. 62–76.

[WAL96] WALKER, S., et al. "Commercial Key Recovery." *Comm ACM*, v39 n3, Mar 1996, pp. 41–47.

[WAR79] WARE, W. "Security Controls for Computer Systems." *Rand Corp Tech Report* R-609-1, Oct 1979.

[WAR84] WARE, W. "Information System Security and Privacy." *Comm ACM*, v27 n4, Apr 1984, pp. 316–321.

[WAR95] WARE, W. "A Retrospective on the Criteria Movement." *Proc Natl Info Sys Security Conf*, 1995, pp. 582–588.

[WEI71] WEINBERG, G. *The Psychology of Computer Programming*, Van Nostrand Reinhold 1971.

[WEI73] WEISSMAN, C. "System Security Analysis/Certification." *SDC Tech Report*, SP-3728, Oct 1973.

[WEI95] WEISBAND, S., and REINIG, B. "Managing User Perceptions of Email Privacy." *Comm ACM*, v38 n12, Dec 1995, pp. 40–47.

[WEL90] WELKE, S., et al. "A Taxonomy of Integrity Models, Implementations, Mechanisms." *Proc Natl Comp Security Conf*, 1990, pp. 541–551.

[WHI89] WHITE, S., et al. "Coping with Computer Viruses and Related Problems." *IBM Corp*, 1989, pp. 7–28. In [HOF90].

[WIN90] WING, J. "A Specifier's Introduction to Formal Methods." *IEEE Computer*, v23 n9, Sep 1990, pp. 8–24.

[WIS86] WISEMAN, S. "A Secure Capability Computer System." *Proc IEEE Symp Security & Privacy*, IEEE Comp Soc Press 1986, pp. 86–94.

[WOO77] WOOD, H. "The Use of Passwords for Controlling Access to Remote Computers." *Proc AFIPS Natl Comp Conf*, 1977, pp. 27–32.

[WOO80] WOOD, C., et al. "Data Base Security: Requirements, Policies, Models." *IBM Systems J*, v19 n2, 1980, pp. 229–252.

[WOO85] WOOD, P., and KOCHAN, S. *Unix System Security*, Hayden 1985.

[WOO87a] WOODWARD, J. "Exploiting the Dual Nature of Sensitivity Labels." *Proc IEEE Symp Security & Privacy*, IEEE Comp Soc Press 1987, pp. 23–31.

[WOO87b] WOOD, C., et al. *Computer Security: A Comprehensive Controls Checklist*, Wiley 1987.

[WOO96] WOOD, A., et al. "The Ethical Systems Analyst." *Comm ACM*, v39 n3, Mar 1996, pp. 69–77.

[WUL74] WULF, W., et al. "Hydra: The Kernel of a Multiprocessor Operating System." *Comm ACM*, v17 n6, Jun 1974, pp. 337–345.

[YAC86] YACOBY, Y. "On Proving Privacy in Multiuser Systems." *Technion Comp Sci Dept Tech Report*, 398, Feb 1986.

[YAR31] YARDLEY, H. *The American Black Chamber*, Bobbs-Merrill 1931.

[ZEL78] ZELKOWITZ, M. "Implementation of a Capability-Based Data Abstraction." *IEEE Trans Software Engr*, vSE-4 n1, Jan 1978, pp. 56–64.

[ZIM86] ZIMMERMAN, P. "A Proposed Standard Format for RSA Cryptosystems." *IEEE Computer*, v19 n9, Sep 1986, pp. 21–34.

[ZIM95a] ZIMMERMAN, P. *The Official PGP User's Guide*, MIT Press 1995.

[ZIM95b] ZIMMERMAN, P. *PGP Source Code and Internals*, MIT Press 1995.

Index